D0946460

The Faculty Factor

The Faculty Factor

Reassessing the American Academy in a Turbulent Era

MARTIN J. FINKELSTEIN, VALERIE MARTIN CONLEY, JACK H. SCHUSTER

With the assistance of
Ryan P. Hudes and Wendiann R. Sethi

Johns Hopkins University Press
BALTIMORE

Printed in the United States of America on
acid-free paper
9 8 7 6 5 4 3 2 1

Johns Hopkins University Press
2715 North Charles Street
Baltimore, Maryland 21218-4363
www.press.jhu.edu

Library of Congress Cataloging-in-Publication Data

Names: Finkelstein, Martin J., 1949- author. | Conley, Valerie M., author. | Schuster, Jack H., author.
Title: The faculty factor : reassessing the American academy in a turbulent era / Martin J. Finkelstein, Valerie Martin Conley, Jack H. Schuster.
Description: Baltimore, Maryland : Johns Hopkins University Press, 2016. | Includes bibliographical references and index.
Identifiers: LCCN 2016005162| ISBN 9781421420929 (hardcover : alk. paper) | ISBN 9781421420936 (electronic) | ISBN 1421420929 (hardcover : alk. paper) | ISBN 1421420937 (electronic)
Subjects: LCSH: Universities and colleges—United States—Faculty. | College teachers—United States. | College teaching—United States. | Educational change—United States. | Education, Higher—Aims and objectives—United States.
Classification: LCC LB2331.72 .F563 2016 | DDC 378.1/2—dc23
LC record available at https://lccn.loc.gov/2016005162

A catalog record for this book is available from the British Library.

Special discounts are available for bulk purchases of this book. For more information, please contact Special Sales at 410-516-6936 or specialsales@press.jhu.edu.

Johns Hopkins University Press uses environmentally friendly book materials, including recycled text paper that is composed of at least 30 percent post-consumer waste, whenever possible.

Contents

Tables and Figures

TABLES

FIGURES

Preface

Soon after reissuing *The American Faculty* in softcover, Johns Hopkins University Press inquired whether coauthors Schuster and Finkelstein would be interested in producing an updated version of the book. This invitation was highly tempting, and so we set about the exercise of determining what more recent data were available to draw upon to inform such an update. After some months of exploration, we arrived at two unavoidable conclusions. First, in the span of approximately a decade, American higher education—and its core resource, the faculty—had transformed to such an extent that the earlier objective of "updating" could not adequately capture the magnitude and significance of what had transpired. Second, we realized that just as the world was changing, the data infrastructure to allow us to document those transformations and their probable consequences was drying up—for example, the discontinuance of the National Study of Postsecondary Faculty, about which more later; this development was greatly complicating the task of identifying appropriate new data to analyze.

We therefore counterproposed a fresh analysis of a plethora of new and sometimes fugitive sources on what was affecting American higher education and, as viewed through a more focused lens, just what was becoming of, and the outlook for, the academic profession itself. And we had the foresight to invite Valerie Martin Conley, with whom we each had collaborated in previous years, to join us in this increasingly challenging undertaking. Happily, she agreed and, too, the Press expressed enthusiasm for this, our more ambitious effort.

The result, namely, this book, explores a multitude of highly consequential issues centered on the faculty in American institutions of higher education. At base are two large questions: What have been the most significant changes in academic work and in the characteristics of academic careers? And what are likely to be the consequences of those changes—for the higher education enterprise and for those pursuing, or contemplating pursuing, careers in academic work?

The authors explore these ongoing trends and their implications, extending our earlier analyses. (Several such examples in which one or more authors had a hand: Finkelstein's *The American Academic Profession* (Ohio State, 1984); Bowen and Schuster's, *American Professors* (Oxford, 1986); Finkelstein, Seal, and Schuster, *The New Academic Generation* (Johns Hopkins, 1998); and Schuster and Finkelstein, *The American Faculty* (Johns Hopkins, 2006.) These analyses had identified incipient trends and, particularly in *The American Faculty*, we postulated whether they constituted only temporary aberrations or whether they foretold more enduring realignments. We concluded that, on balance, there seemed to be little that was merely temporary about these changes. Indeed, during the past decade or so, much evidence has surfaced, spurred by a national economic downturn that has adversely affected funding at all levels.

Allowing for the uncertainties that attend projecting even a near-term economic-political future, we believe we are in a much stronger position, bolstered by mounting evidence, to extend the description of the sweeping trends in academic work and careers. This enables us to begin to assess with greater confidence the longer-term consequences for the American higher education system and its faculty.

We now hypothesize that a new model, representing a paradigmatic shift, has taken shape as higher education and its faculty are being reconstituted and repurposed. Our (re)conceptualization—Paradigm Three, as we label this phenomenon—continues to explore the vibrant, volatile characteristics of this vast, highly decentralized system, with particular focus on its core resource: the faculty.

It is imperative to better understand this vital resource. While we authors constitute three individual and distinctive voices in our respective professional pursuits, we join together here in our belief, one that constitutes the basic foundation of this volume, that the faculty are at the core of the effectiveness of higher education. If we fail to grasp the properties and dynamics of this reformulated postsecondary system, then educators and policy makers alike will be at a serious disadvantage in preserving those ingredients that are the heart of the distinctive and globally acknowledged success of the American system and that we know will be the keys to the future performance of our colleges and universities. The stakes are enormous.

Acknowledgments

In the course of preparing this book, numerous individuals and organizations came to our assistance. Without their help, there would be no book.

Primary among those whose assistance was indispensable were two extramural benefactors: TIAA-CREF Institute and the Andrew W. Mellon Foundation. Each awarded this project both an initial grant and, when funds ran short, a follow-on grant. The financial support of these two organizations, long respected for their legendary dedication to higher learning, enabled the far-spread authors to converge numerous times over several years. At the TIAA-CREF Institute, special thanks are owed to Senior Managing Director and Head Stephanie Bell-Rose and to Marilyn Grande, Anne Ollen, Paul Yakoboski, David P. Richardson, and Lisa Calandra. At the Mellon Foundation, facilitators extraordinary included two former vice presidents: Philip E. Lewis and Harriet A. Zuckerman.

Our particular gratitude goes to a remarkable group of unselfish scholars who read with care and commented on draft chapters, several of them, in fact, reviewing two chapters: Philip G. Altbach (Boston College), Ann E. Austin (Michigan State University), John W. Curtis (American Sociological Association), Michael Middaugh (University of Delaware), Daryl G. Smith (Claremont Graduate University), John R. Thelin (University of Kentucky), and Paul Yakaboski (TIAA-CREF Institute). They undoubtedly saved us from grievous errors of commission and omission. A further word of thanks is due to Harold S. Wechsler (New York University).

At the authors' respective institutions, some individuals merit special mention. At Seton Hall University, over a two-year period, a remarkable team of doctoral students provided the infrastructure for data file management and analysis, construction of tables and figures, and scrupulous editorial oversight of the manuscript. Team members included Katherine C. Aquino, Michael Aryee, Caitlin Giordano, Ryan Hudes, Wendiann Sethi and Jonathan Stoessel. The research team was initially anchored by Kevin Iglesias. Their meticulous attention to detail, imaginative approaches to file manipulation and data analysis, their initiative, professionalism, and commitment were a godsend. When Iglesias was called to a full-time employment commitment in another state a year into the project, Wendiann Sethi and then Ryan Hudes stepped into key leadership roles on the research team. Their unique contributions are reflected on the title page of this volume. In addition to members of the research team, two doctoral students—Michael Dooney and Daria Cimih—undertook special focused reviews of the literature on distance and digital learning as well as on the distinctive characteristics of demographic generations. Seton Hall provided a year-long sabbatical leave to one of the authors in 2012–13 that helped get the project off the ground, and Grace May, dean of the College of Education and Human Services, provided strategic support for indexing the volume and supplementary travel funds.

At Ohio University, Dean Renée A. Middleton provided mentorship, encouragement, and support to one of the authors seeking to maintain an active research agenda while progressing in an academic administrative career. Her understanding and advice along the way proved indispensable to the completion of our collective work. Samantha Catania served as a graduate research assistant for one year at Ohio University and helped to prepare tables for several chapters. At the University of Colorado at Colorado Springs, Mary Coussons-Read, provost and vice chancellor, offered encouragement and support to complete the project. Beckie Blake, Shelley McClain, and Peggie Laney provided administrative support. Students in several advanced or doctoral-level courses at our respective institutions received early drafts of chapters (works in progress) and engaged in discussion with us about the content. These included Seton Hall students in ELMP 9994 Faculty Personnel Policies in spring 2013, students in ED 458 at Claremont Graduate University in fall 2013, and students in Cycle XII of the Executive PhD program and EDHE 7800, The Professoriate and Academic Administration in Higher Education, in fall 2013–14. Our thinking was stimulated by these sometimes provocative conversations.

Among individuals at Claremont Graduate University deserving our appreciation, Dean Scott Thomas for his general support, Gloria Page, a student in ED458, and (now) alumni Ngoc-Dung Firpo and Tabatha Jones Joliet were especially helpful. Elizabeth Mott is due particular appreciation for her clerical and editorial assistance. Also John Rodriguez (program administrator, School of Educational Studies), as well as former financial administrator Rebecca Lerback, have been particularly important to the administration of this project.

Gregory M. Britton, the ever-patient editorial director at Johns Hopkins University Press, has earned our deep appreciation, as has the unknown (to the coauthors) manuscript reviewers.

Finally, an undertaking of this size and scope requires a commitment from our respective spouses to indulge our need for time away and manuscript obsessiveness on the home front: Elaine M. Walker, Tom Conley, and Diane Tickton Schuster.

PART I / The American Faculty

An Overview

Part I consists of three chapters with very different objectives.

Chapter 1, "Establishing the Framework: The Emergence of a New Paradigm," provides the premises underlying this volume. These include establishing the specific reasons for concluding that a new era now exists for assessing the faculty condition and identifying the principal faculty-related issues that are raised in this "third paradigm." The chapter also previews the organization of the book.

Chapter 2, "The American Faculty in Historical Perspective: The Importance of Context," is a succinct account of how the faculty in American colleges and universities have evolved over a span of four centuries. The emphasis is on the faculty's relative influence over academic matters, particularly during the post–World War II era.

Chapter 3, entitled "The Faculty in Profile," is just that: it presents and discusses a series of tables and figures that describe key characteristics of the American faculty over time, highlighting in particular salient changes during the most recent several decades.

1

Establishing the Framework

The Emergence of a New Paradigm

This is a story about the faculty swept up in tumultuous times. It is an exploration of how the faculty have been abruptly restructured and repurposed in recent years and about ways in which the faculty are continuing to transform. It is also a projection of the academic profession into the proximate and intermediate future—and the likely consequences for higher education and the national interest.

In one sense, this is but the most recent manifestation of a timeless narrative: the academic profession ever evolving, adapting to new realities ever since the faculty began to coalesce centuries ago—or, in America itself, from the mid-seventeenth century. The faculty are, after all, constantly in flux, ever morphing (if unevenly) as a consequence chiefly of relentless changes in the roles, priorities, and resources in American higher education itself. Similar prefaces might appropriately have been recorded at many points in time along higher education's winding journey. After all, consider that Clark Kerr (1982, iv) observed a half century ago that such declarations of crisis were (even then) plentiful, citing numerous such examples recorded circa the early 1970s. (This perspective receives more attention in our succinct historical overview that follows in chapter 2.)

Over the past several decades, numerous observers, especially among the faculty, have addressed the faculty's ongoing transformation and commonly reached grim conclusions. Indeed, over the past decade much has been written about the gloomy outlook for American higher education. A veritable torrent of books, articles, essays, and the like has tumbled forth appraising the condition of postsecondary education—a near-consensus finding significant deterioration—and forecasting a future riddled with formidable obstacles (e.g., Burgan 2009; Woodhouse 2009; Schrecker 2010; Ginsberg 2011). These contributions have been important in drawing attention to ongoing changes and in underscoring what is at stake. However, these critiques stop short of substantiating the depth and breadth of the current transformation and, in particular, in proposing actionable ideas that could lead to positive change. So with this backdrop—and with dire proclamations commonplace—we ask, what is different now?

We begin by describing the aggregate changes that in recent years have pervaded all of higher education and its faculty in particular, especially since about the year 2000. We demonstrate that these changes have occurred remarkably swiftly, relative, that is, to other periods of academic transition, and we argue that these developments have generated cumulative effects that have propelled the postsecondary system into an unprecedented, new systemic model. Furthermore, we propose that the longer-term implications of this new paradigm—for higher education and the nation, as well as for the academic profession itself—are profound.

These contentions now oblige us to demonstrate that the quantitative and qualitative indicators of change, incomplete measures as they must be, mark a higher education sector that is readily distinguishable from the earlier system of postsecondary education as recently as two decades ago. So, too, we contend, are the stark implications of this current transformation.

Thus the alarm has been sounded again and again by observers of higher education's innumerable transitions, and with ample cause: the postsecondary sector and its faculty are incessantly being subjected to mounting pressures, both internally and externally driven, setting for the faculty a newish mix of tasks, holding faculty more accountable for their performance, and on and on. These system changes churn away, necessitating an array of creative adaptations, as well as deep, often painful, concessions made to the insistent demands of the new political, economic, and technological environment. Or, as D. Bruce Johnstone (2003) has observed, the US system of higher education is notable for the extent to which it has been responsive to the pressures emanating from the environment, both for good and for ill. And, as the system itself responds to and is reshaped by these forces, the effects on most constituent parts that make up that system are emphatic.

This volume focuses on one vital, pivotal component—the faculty—and how the faculty have been affected, especially in recent years. In short, the authors have set about to track "the faculty factor" in higher education, as the faculty gradually rose in importance during the first half of the twentieth century, gained momentum after World War II, and arguably reached a peak in influence circa 1960–80 (Jencks and Riesman 1968; Kerr 1982, 169). But since then, faculty influence has sharply declined, a trend that, we contend in the following chapters, is currently continuing, apparently accelerating.

Two Basic Premises

Before proceeding to describe the distinctive characteristics of the emerging paradigm, two basic premises must be established. The first of these is a conventional but essential caveat: sweeping generalizations about such radically decentralized organizational "nonsystems" as American higher education are, as always, perilous, for higher education embodies a great many contrasting realities.

The point of departure for this elemental premise is the basic reality that the contemporary postsecondary enterprise spans strikingly varied institutional types and encompasses a seemingly endless array of academic fields of study. Thus academic conditions for faculty within each subsector of higher education differ pointedly by institutional type and, to an arguably somewhat lesser degree, by academic discipline. Accordingly, despite these sharply contrasting situations "on the ground," the authors attempt herein to characterize the current dramatic transformation of higher education writ large. And so we have undertaken to postulate a general conceptual model, which we elaborate on shortly—Paradigm Three, we call it—that cuts across American higher education. This approach better enables us to capture the larger (and, we find, mostly disturbing) picture that we describe and analyze in detail. Even so, we remain keenly aware of what Burton R. Clark (1987) famously depicted as a "matrix," underscoring that innumerable subsectors exist within which higher education is conducted. Within these cells of the sprawling matrix, faculty realities—work patterns and careers—vary from one matrix cell to another. Thus broad generalizations, as we have observed, are risky, for they obscure the highly variegated circumstances in which academic life is lived and for which comprehending the matrix framework is indispensable. Indeed, if anything, academic heterogeneity has become more pronounced as external pressures and within-campus responses more crisply demarcate the haves from the have-nots and, still further, as entrepreneurial ventures multiply. So we must proceed with caution. Even so, broad generalizations are essential to enable us to describe the thrust and import of what we see unfolding.

A second basic premise is the centrality of the faculty role in the modern historical period. Whatever the varied venues and contrasting orders of priorities within types of postsecondary education institutions, the faculty are (or should be) situated conceptually at the very core of the enterprise (Metzger 1973; Bowen and Schuster 1986; Clark 1987; Schuster and Finkelstein 2006).[1] They constitute and generate the intellectual capital. They comprise higher education's principal resource.

This premise about the faculty's centrality is perhaps obvious—in principle, at least. But the salience of this proposition bears underscoring in an era in which higher learning is delivered via so many different modes, giving rise to faculty roles that are being rearranged, redefined, redistributed, repurposed. This accelerating and destabilizing trend, in turn, translates into diminishing institutional reliance on traditional faculty members for meeting an institution's teaching mission, as well as its other responsibilities. Furthermore, this expanding array of delivery options and staffing strategies will undoubtedly continue to gain momentum. One powerful reason: technological advances related to instruction continue at breathtaking rates, giving rise to the further displacement of traditional faculty. (The role of technology on campuses is addressed in chapter 7.) For another, the institutional capacity available to hire or retain (expensive) traditional faculty members is constrained by diminishing financial resources and reinforced by bleak financial and political prospects. In sum, the prospect for maintaining a vital regular—that is, traditional—faculty is shaky at best. Put another way,

> the role of the faculty may be perceived by some as less pivotal in the multifaceted "new era." Technology, obviously, plays a more prominent part in creating options for delivering educational content, including "outsourcing" to expert providers; the use of such providers—for packaged lectures and the like—is almost certain to expand, perhaps exponentially for many campuses. Accordingly, familiar, traditional faculty work roles and careers become less dominant, displaced in part, or augmented—depending on one's view—by these resources. Further, as ever-larger numbers of contingent faculty become more loosely linked to their respective institutions, many faculty members may be reckoned as less crucial, more interchangeable, more disposable temporary staff. Thus, the [once-upon-a-time] truism of the faculty's centrality is now being subjected

> to intensifying pressures. Notwithstanding these challenges, the extent to which higher education is effective (or not) in accomplishing its missions turns [especially] on the quality of the faculty. (Schuster 2011, 4–5)

We recognize that numerous critics of contemporary higher education, both from within and without, would challenge the view that the faculty are (or should be) so pivotal; these critics contend, instead, that such presumed faculty centrality is a significant distortion of priorities, a detraction from a preferable student-centric enterprise.[2] In contrast, in this era of "The New U," we underscore that the starting point of institutional effectiveness is a qualified and dedicated faculty and that should be maintained and nurtured as its most indispensable asset (Schuster and Finkelstein 2006). The bottom line: higher education's core resource, its "regular" faculty, is now confronting challenges to their traditional roles that pose existential threats. It is this nexus of activity—various dimensions of "the faculty factor"—that we scrutinize in subsequent chapters.

Establishing the Societal Context

Before we turn to identifying the distinctive characteristics that comprise the third paradigm, we should describe the broader societal context within which higher education seeks—struggles, really—to adapt. Many society-wide trends could be identified here, but at the outset of our examination we choose to underscore three especially potent megatrends that affect almost every aspect of the larger society. These forces, while they pervade society, have, as we show, particularized effects on higher education and the faculty. But before we identify their immediate impact on the academy, we highlight, if only in passing, these three enormously influential vectors that are remolding the overall societal and cultural context. First are the unceasing (even startling) successive waves of technological advances. Second are the sweeping effects of globalization (think of Thomas Friedman's [2005] "flat world" metaphor). And third are the harsh financial constraints attributable to a tight economy that has obtained for the past near-decade. Current economic conditions—unlike the relentless, irreversible progression of both technology and globalization—tend to be cyclical, so currently prevailing limitations may well soften, even reverse, in time. Nonetheless, the consequences of economic pressures currently affect virtually all elements of society and its organizations.

Additional societal megatrends with immense reach could be mentioned at this juncture, but the three pervasive trends just identified powerfully impact the work and careers of postsecondary faculty; these are elaborated on below among the principal characteristics that shape Paradigm Three and distinguish its characteristics from earlier post–World War II phases.

And so, having established these foundational points of departure—the reality of great variety among venues of higher education as practiced on the ground, the crucial importance of faculty as a variable demanding further analyses, and the several omnipotent societal megatrends—we turn now to the characteristics of this purported new paradigm.

Prologue to a Third Paradigm

Our contention, as noted, is that higher education has been thrust into a new era. So much has changed in recent years that a new conception or paradigm is appropriate, arguably indispensable, for understanding what combination of forces is now driving the higher education sector and transfiguring the academic profession. We outline in the following pages the reasons that this paradigm can be reckoned as a third such paradigm (or predominant model of higher education) since the middle of the twentieth century. Consider these transformative developments:

Soon following post–World War II's unprecedented influx into higher education of a great many students—occasioned mainly by the Servicemen's Readjustment Act of 1944 (the so-called GI Bill)—not only did higher education balloon in numbers (of enrolled students, faculty, and institutions), but also the sector became ever more differentiated in its modes of operation and in the complexity of its interactions with its social and cultural environment. This phenomenon of expansion has been enduringly described by Martin Trow (1974) (among others) as part of the conceptual progression from a previous "elite" stage of higher education (serving, and accessible to, relatively few clients), through a vibrant period of "mass" higher education (characterized by soaring numbers of students attending many more postsecondary institutions), en route to becoming a higher education enterprise that, relative to its long-evolving massification, was approaching "universal" in terms of accessibility (although that progression has largely stalled over the past two decades).[3] Our more focused concern in this volume is how the forces giving rise to a new era for postsecondary education have reshaped faculty work and careers.

In our view, two iconic 1960s reinterpretations of higher education's grander metamorphosis, taken together, can be considered as defining a first postwar model, or paradigm 1 in our terminology. One such source speaks more to the wider role of higher education, the second concentrates on the academic profession within.

In the first of these, Clark Kerr in *The Uses of the University* (1963) invoked the term "multiversity." By this he meant to describe "the really modern university" (6) featuring the wider functions then being served by the extended university: less insular, more interactive; less arcane, more pragmatic; less remote, more integrated. In a word, the "modern" university had become more intertwined with its environment; it had acquired, that is to say, more uses. Although higher education had exhibited pronounced pragmatic leanings from earliest times, Kerr's 1963 landmark dictum proclaimed that a new phase had coalesced: higher education, always a product of society, had more manifestly become society's agent. (Examples include being recipients of and contractors for an immense array of federal research grants and the emergence of policy research and policy sciences.) We think of this more multifaceted institution as integral to the first postwar paradigm.

But there is another crucial aspect. Parallel and interwoven with the transformation of the university into its more wide-ranging raison d'être is the rise of the faculty itself. This account and its significance was the bold thesis of Christopher Jencks and David Riesman in *The Academic Revolution* (1968). Though "revolution" was in the air circa mid-1960s, featuring political confrontations then dotting university campuses, the revolution they spoke to was the surge in the stature and influence of the academic profession. In their portrayal of the academy in the post–World War II era, Jencks and Riesman concluded that the faculty had acquired substantially more expertise and autonomy, amounting to the reinforcement of professionalization of the academic profession (201–02, 236–50). And although this empowerment had developed gradually (not as swiftly as their choice of "revolution" terminology might signify), the result, they proclaimed, constituted "the rise to power of the academic profession" (xiii).[4]

As the functions of the institution multiplied and the influence exercised by the faculty blossomed synergistically, a distinctly new model emerged: the university and its faculty within had acquired greater status, more respect. Each exerted more influence: the university within society itself and the faculty within the university. A new era, featuring a robust, influential faculty, had been attained.

The second defining phase—a second paradigm in our semantic—has been described by countless observers. It revolves around the pressures generated by "the marketplace." This, too, is nothing new. Despite its religious origins, no pure academic cloister ever existed. Making allowances for the many meanings that commentators employ to convey the notion of market influences (see, e.g., Brint et al. 2012), the market has always influenced the functions and priorities of higher education, albeit in recent decades these pressures (some would say utilitarian needs and opportunities) have escalated to even higher levels. This burgeoning phenomenon was perhaps most cogently—and graphically—captured by Sheila Slaughter and Larry L. Leslie in *Academic Capitalism: Politics, Policies, and the Entrepreneurial University* (1997) and then updated and elaborated on by Slaughter and Gary Rhoades in their *Academic Capitalism and the New Economy: Markets, State, and Higher Education* (2004). Their portrayal of the sector's transformation, along with Derek C. Bok's insightful *Universities in the Marketplace: The Commercialization of Higher Education*, illustrated how pervasively and forcefully market-driven pressures were reordering higher education's priorities and the innumerable ways in which the academy and its faculty were, and are, responding (some critics would insist that "capitulating" is a more apt descriptor) to those pressures. (See other commentaries in this vein, e.g., Gould 2003; Kirp 2003; Zemsky, Wegner, and Massy 2005; Woodhouse 2009; Musselin 2010; and Gerber 2014.) These pervasive adaptations, labeled in various ways as commodification, commercialization, and marketization, of course are ongoing, continuing to reshape institutional priorities and to transpose faculty work and careers.

A Third Paradigm Emerges

Our effort in this volume is to describe what we perceive to be a yet more recently emergent era in American higher education. Its characteristics, we argue, are sufficiently distinctive from the previously prevailing conditions to prompt us to label this era a third paradigm: an era of reconstitution, an era in which the faculty are being more narrowly repurposed and, as a consequence, their influence significantly diminished. Indeed, the faculty's role is being shrunk, set askew from the pivotal place they arguably had claimed in academic affairs (as celebrated, if prematurely, by Jencks and Riesman [1968]). We do not mean to suggest that this third paradigm has displaced its immediate predecessors. No, the broadened reach and pragmatism of the "more useful" university still exists, and so, too, does the rampant influence of market forces on so many dimensions of higher education and the work of the faculty.

We do not contend that any one of the successor third paradigm's defining elements is brand new; all of the features we identify below were plainly discernible, to one degree or another, over the preceding decades—with initial sightings, however attenuated, detectable across decades, even centuries. But it is the volatile, reinforcing mix of these concurrent factors that emphatically sculpts the successor paradigm, that demarcates terra nova.

Our effort, in other words, now seeks to describe the numerous ways in which this third paradigm departs markedly from its predecessor phases, yielding thereby a quite new modus operandi for institutions of higher education. At the dynamic crux of this transformation is the repurposed, rechanneled role of the contemporary faculty, in effect, a demotion of the faculty from their high perch. In sum, we find that the faculty factor has lost potency in its capacity to affect—indeed, shape—postsecondary education.

Ten Distinguishing Characteristics

To claim as we have that the higher education faculty have been shunted by myriad forces into a distinctive new era—one that is, we argue, so threatening to core academic values—places a burden on us to establish convincingly that such a transition has occurred. This is perhaps especially the case when no one to our knowledge has proposed that a singular act or pivotal development or two has triggered the transition. Rather, in our view, this transition has been just that: a process or, perhaps more accurately, a series of intertwined processes that, cumulatively, have spawned this new model. So, just what are the characteristics that we claim delineate the new paradigm in this perceptibly distinguishable era? And just why is such a reconceptualization now important to specify?

While no single variable is without precedent, it is, as we have asserted, the increasingly evident presence—the weight—of each factor that creates the starkly new landscape. The result of these profoundly transformed net conditions—the reconstitution and repurposing of which we speak—compels institutions of higher education and their faculty to scramble to adapt. We identify below ten such attributes.

These ten elements, for the sake of order, can be appropriated to one of three clusters. The first three are characteristics of the larger environment, alluded to earlier, that profoundly affect how postsecondary institutions and their faculty—and, for that matter, essentially the totality of society—must adapt and function. These macro elements can be thought of as exogenous to higher education but exerting, nonetheless, sweeping effects on higher education. The next five characteristics describe more specifically how postsecondary institutions and their faculty are adapting to looming new realities. The final two elements are clearly categorized neither as features predominantly associated with the all-encompassing environment nor, more narrowly, as examples of specific institutional responses; these two can be described as more hybrid in nature.

First and foremost among dimensions of change that are creating big differences in the way in which higher education is practiced, as transforming the work of faculty, is technology. Like the other elements of change, technological transition in higher education has a long history. Doomsayers have forewarned of the upcoming onslaught for decades (consider, e.g., Noam 1995). And yet the unprecedented rate and reach of technological change have accelerated sharply. The phenomenon of rapid technological advances—and concomitant dislocations—penetrates essentially every aspect of society, and so, in that sense, education is hardly an exceptional case. Nonetheless, academic work is being profoundly reconfigured, and the embrace of advancing technologies, spanning nearly every aspect of teaching and learning and research, is starkly manifest. Although hard boundaries do not crisply separate teaching from research activities, in the teaching realm the profusion of online courses and "blended" variations, across all kinds of institutions, continues to reshape faculty activity. (Note, for example, our subsequent explication of "MOOCs"—and their relatives—in chapter 7.) The effects are more pronounced in some academic fields than in others, naturally. And the extent of change appears to be more evident in those types of higher education institutions most affected by massification. Nonetheless, technology is transforming higher education and its faculty (as society itself is transforming). Like the burgeoning influence of the many-faceted marketplace (referred to below), technology has expanded its reach so swiftly in just recent years as to have dramatically changed the campus function and perhaps especially the modes of faculty work. (Moreover, looking ahead, whatever effects are already evident, these current changes are elemental compared with the technology-induced transformations lying just ahead.)

A second dimension, earlier alluded to, is the higher education sector's increasing responsiveness to marketplace forces. Since its inception, higher education, as noted, has never been divorced from the realities of the marketplace nor buffered from the broad effects of the environing economy. Higher education, and, especially, public higher education, struggles as governments, at all levels, along with individual donors and philanthropic foundations, grapple with priorities among so many worthy claimants (health care, infrastructure, and so on). The net result: funding for higher education is squeezed all the harder. More to the point, contemporary higher education appears to be driven more relentlessly by these market-driven pressures. This is evidenced throughout the sector: in curricular offerings (see, e.g., Brint et al. 2012), in the teaching-learning process, in the overall allocation of resources within institutions of higher education, in the competition among institutions to attract students (given the perception of intensifying student consumerism), and, perhaps most boldly and controversially, in the expansion of proprietary postsecondary institutions (Tierney and Hentschke 2007; Hentschke et al. 2010). Current conditions, exacerbated by the scarcity of resources and acutely competitive dynamics, promote increasingly entrepreneurial institutional behavior designed to exploit revenue-producing opportunities. In this process, the faculty are subjected to the often-conflicting needs of protecting traditional academic values while being more responsive to "real-world," economy-driven realities. Meanwhile, these market-driven pressures have not abated but rather continue, in our perception, to exert ever more influence in this current era.

The third distinguishing characteristic is the extent to which faculty work is increasingly molded by multinational, global considerations. There is nothing entirely new about the phenomenon itself (except its scale); the numerous transnational aspects of higher education, permeating all institutional types and fields, affect expanding proportions of faculty and students. One consequence of this development is the extent to which international collaboration enables more-accurate tracking of activities, from the movement of students across national boundaries to collaboration among investigators (Huang, Finkelstein, and Rostand 2013. These activities are examined in much more detail in part 4 (chapters 10 and 11) of this volume. Suffice it to say for now that several key activities are becoming more robust: a more-global faculty employment marketplace, research and publishing that is more commonly cross-national, and contemporary faculty who are more obliged to prepare their students as global citizens. Considered together, these global dimensions modify academic life significantly for numerous faculty members and, as well, enable readers to understand faculty work and careers in global perspective.

Now narrowing the focus to campus responses to the fluid environment, the fourth dimension is that faculty appointments are being ever more radically redistributed away from traditional tenure and tenure-track appointments. This centrifugal effect has resulted in a further profusion of academic appointment holders off the tenure track. (Kerr uses the blunt term "unfaculty" [1982, 65–66].)[5] This phenomenon of nontraditional appointments lay at the heart of *The American Faculty* (Schuster and Finkelstein 2006), as the authors detailed at the time. But that redeployment, having evolved over a long period of time, has now both accelerated and proliferated across diverse types of off-track appointments (Conley 2008; Curtis and Thornton 2013). Arguably, a kind of tipping point has now been reached, and no evidence of abating—much less any signs of a reversal in these trends—has surfaced. Thus whereas in 1993 a bare majority of newly hired full-time faculty—51.3%—had been appointed off the tenure track, by 2011 that proportion had increased to almost three of five (58.4%) appointments. Viewed through a different lens, the overall proportion of "regular" faculty (i.e., full-time tenured or tenure track) was 43.6% as late as 1993; currently (2013), that proportion has shrunk to 29.7%.[6] (These data are spelled out in more detail in chapter 3.) The effects of redistributed appointment types have indelibly imprinted virtually every aspect of the nature and content of academic work and the way academic careers are lived, thereby altering substantially the faculty factor.

A fifth (and related) dimension: Faculty roles have become increasingly more specialized. That is to say, the continuing redistribution of types of faculty appointments is closely interconnected with more specialized roles for faculty members. Whereas there previously had been more commonality across traditional faculty roles, functional specialization has been clearly ascendant. Whereas, prototypically, traditional faculty members would play all three academic positions concurrently—that is, teaching, research and scholarly writing, and service roles[7]—in the contemporary faculty makeover, a significantly larger proportion of faculty appointees more recently have been employed exclusively for teaching (with little or no expectation of scholarly productivity). Concomitantly, larger proportions of faculty appear to be dedicated predominately to research activity, with only incidental or no formalized instructional (typically, seminar or classroom settings) responsibilities. Relatively fewer faculty cut across these boundaries. Still further, there appear to be ever larger numbers of faculty members, presumably tallied by institutions as regular faculty, who hold significant administrative responsibilities that dilute their traditional academic time-on-task, for instance, having a reduced course load or mentoring obligations. At the crux of this phenomenon of specialization—often referred to as "unbundling"—are situated numerous faculty members, often part-time, pay-per-course hires or full-time but off-track appointments. As with the redistribution of types of appointments, the presence of single-role faculty members is not new, but it is the sharply escalating proportion of these role specialists that, in our view, has contributed in a pronounced way toward a new academic dynamic, indeed, a new campus culture. Put in other terms, as academic work becomes increasingly specialized, a previously more integrated, more blended faculty model is transitioning toward a more *dis*-integrated (and characteristically underfunded) faculty cohort. (See chapters 5 and 7 for more detail.)

Sixth, we now see ever more plainly a kind of polarization or restratification in the hierarchy of faculty appointment types. As the proportion of faculty with traditional faculty appointments (i.e., full-time, tenured/ tenure eligible) is shrinking, the remaining full-time, tenured faculty appear to be acquiring proportionately more status, more leverage, among all instructional staff. This in a sense constitutes a reversion, a regression, back to a previous era. Before the twentieth century's movement toward the democratization of the American faculty, a small core of professors had occupied a top stratum beneath which were arrayed tiers of underlings (tutors and other instructors in the late-nineteenth-century fashion of the classical German research university). Now, however, as the twenty-first century unfolds, an inegalitarian retrogression toward a restratified academic labor force is evident, reaching back toward a culture smacking of a more castelike hierarchy (Baldwin and Chronister 2001; Cross and Goldenberg 2009; Kezar and Sam 2010,).

A seventh aspect of the refashioned faculty is their diminishing influence. This feature defies adequate measurement, for the changes are subtle, though widely acknowledged. (See our discussion in chapter 8.) It is often characterized as the weakening of the faculty role in "shared governance." Perhaps perennially more an ideal (at least as perceived in faculty circles) than an actuality, the extent of meaningful participation of "the faculty," via its governance mechanisms (typically, a faculty senate of some sort), was often prominent in post–World War II campus decision making (Schuster et al. 1994; Kaplan 2003; Tierney and Minor 2003; Archibald 2010; Archibald and Conley 2011). This participation certainly has not disappeared; however, we contend, its impact has weakened under current conditions. In a more economically streamlined, more "efficient," more market-responsive setting, the often cumbersome shared-governance process, commonly attacked by outside critics for undue emphasis on "outdated" traditional academic values, appears frequently to be compromised. Campus decision making—slower and more deliberative than real-time business decision making is commonly perceived to be—is often excoriated for being out of sync with market-driven demands for swifter, more efficient, innovative strategies (see, e.g., Christensen and Eyring 2011).

This perception has occasionally erupted in a shocker (measuring, so to speak, eight or nine on a hypothetical ten-point governance Richter scale). Perhaps the most blatant, albeit short lived, recent illustration was the June 2012 episode at the University of Virginia in which the governing board terminated the university president, Teresa A. Sullivan—amounting to a veritable "campus coup" (Rice 2012)—on the apparent grounds that she had not adequately anticipated higher education's future direction and requirements. This governing board action, though soon reversed following a torrent of adverse publicity, had been effected with virtually no consultation with the faculty. Before the board's revoking of its decision, "shared governance" was nowhere to be found in the lead-up to the president's abrupt dismissal. Ironically, this astounding development had taken place at "Mr. Jefferson's University," at which the faculty's significant participation in governance was the long-standing norm. This incident symbolizes, in extreme form, the extent to which a more traditional governance process had given way to the dictates of managerial decision making predicated on sharply different assumptions about the purposes and priorities of higher education. As we describe in more detail in chapter 8, the evidence is mounting that the faculty's influence—judged in part by its participation in campus governance—is declining markedly (Ginsberg 2011).

An eighth characteristic distinguishing the contemporary faculty is the demographic dimension. Once more, it is not so much a dramatic "new look" in this instance (at least in comparison to the past decade or so) as it is the continuing prominent trends that add up cumulatively to make a significant difference: an older faculty (a function of somewhat later ages for both career entry and egress, as explained later, along with a more elongated "postdoc" phase), a somewhat more ethnically diverse faculty, and a clearly more female faculty. In addition, a sizable curricular shift, over the past several decades, contributes to further demographic changes. As professional and semiprofessional curriculums thrive (prototypically business- and health-related programs, as distinguished from more traditional curricular areas), a greater proportion of faculty have had significant nonacademic career experience before embarking on faculty work. In the prevailing tight academic labor market, there has been relatively little flow activity—either out of or into "regular" faculty ranks. But, on the whole, the composition of faculty has shifted further away from the outdated prototype: a predominantly white male faculty occupying tenured or tenure-eligible positions and retiring from their academic careers in a predictable "on-time" manner. Yes, faculty demographics have changed markedly.

As noted, the following two characteristics do not fit neatly into either the exogenous or internal clusters. The ninth difference is the extent to which efforts aimed at accountability and quality assurance of faculty work have changed, most palpably through an accreditation process that presses faculty to produce student-related measurable results. In recent years the dynamics of the accreditation and quality assurance processes have mutated significantly—often, however, under the radar—with potent consequences for all of higher education and its faculty. It is arbitrary just where to mark the beginnings of this transposing trend, but a case can be made for the issuance in 2006 of the report of the Commission on the Future of Higher Education (often referred to as the Spellings Commission report) (Zemsky 2011). As described in more detail subsequently (see chapter 13), Margaret Spellings, in 2005 in her role as secretary of the US Department of Education, appointed a Commission on the Future of Higher Education to develop "a comprehensive national strategy for postsecondary education that will meet [the] nation's needs . . . for an educated and competitive workforce" (Zemsky 2011, A-10). This report was one of a series of actions, before and since 2006, that featured expanding federal involvement in accreditation, marking a fundamentally changed government-accreditation relationship.

There are many facets of the retreat from accreditation of institutions and programs as a largely peer-based process and toward government oversight and accountability demands (Eaton 2012; Eaton and Neal 2015; Gaston 2013). One basic consequence of shifting responsibility away from faculty peers is a dilution of the academic profession's responsibility for defining and implementing academic standards. This development constitutes a continuing movement away from the faculty themselves and their own "productivity" as crucial "input" measures of institutional preparedness (for example, academic degrees earned) and achievement (for instance, number of publications) and toward gauging institutional effectiveness increasingly by measures of student gains—as reflected in efforts to measure "value added"—within a much more student-centric enterprise. In these senses, this highly proactive engagement by government, both at federal and state levels, can assuredly be counted as another measure of the faculty's waning influence.

A tenth characteristic or consequence of this reconfigured system has to do with faculty identity in the sense that smaller proportions of contemporary faculty members are attached to and identified with a single "home base," that is, with one particular college or university. In years past, to be sure, academic careers were often lived out sequentially in more than one institutional setting. Sometimes, of course, this was by choice as when an academic employee opted to change venues, perhaps for convenience of locale, or perhaps to "trade up," or for innumerable other reasons. At other times, a transition to another institution was an unsought result, say in those instances in which a faculty member on tenure track was denied the award of tenure (or had anticipated such an outcome) and, in order to continue an academic career, was obliged to obtain employment at another academic institution. And with the profusion of full-time but off-track appointments, as well as part-time faculty positions—often bestowing scant security—the likelihood of teaching either simultaneously or serially at two (or more) institutions has escalated. Quite often, it should be added, such relatively transitory teaching arrangements worked to the mutual benefit of employer and employee—a proverbial win-win situation.

Viewed on the whole, there appear to be fewer instances in which a faculty member and his or her institution are connected over an extended, near-symbiotic period, perhaps even throughout an entire working career. This observation is not intended as a judgment; it is a description comparing (though difficult to measure) the current and still-evolving period with times past. The result is a declining proportion of careers characterized by enduring, anchored faculty-institutional relationships that in earlier times more often featured, presumably, *mutual* loyalties, that more recently entail a multiplicity of career tracks. (Chapter 5 elaborates on changing career patterns.) This academic trend is perhaps one expression of the larger societal phenomenon that some contemporary behavioral scientists refer to as the ascending importance of some individuals striving for self-determination in order to realize the "sovereign self."[8] Accordingly, it is but one more prism through which important elements of academic work and careers are played out.

The Third Paradigm Revisited

These ten developments are all related to one another, all a part of the new contours of higher education: who its faculty members are, what they do, why they do what they do, what is asked of them, and how they are responding. No single vector of change is independent from the others; all are ongoing simultaneously (some commentators refer to this as "patch dynamics").[9] Furthermore, no one or two aspects are sufficiently weighty (as noted earlier) to redefine the academic enterprise, to tilt the sector conceptually and irrevocably into a manifest new status. Nor, to underscore the point, are any of the ten elements new to appear. All, in one form or another, as previously noted, have existed for a long time, some even for a very long time, but each strikes us as increasing in force and prominence in reconstructing higher education and in remaking its faculty.

Taken together, these convergent elements define and depict a paradigm shift, a new array of realities characterizing academic life and a distinctive (if usually unarticulated) underlying philosophical basis. These new realities or conditions have extended far beyond an earlier era of institutional muscularity and professorial ascendancy (what we label as a first postwar paradigm). That golden era (relatively speaking) was gradually undercut by emergent societal realities as different priorities, newly insistent stakeholders, and powerfully influential sociopolitical and economic realities produced a new era (our second paradigm), one more persistently and pervasively shaped by market forces. But each of the ten described elements is gathering momentum (at varying velocities) that, taken together, have redefined—and are continuing to redefine—the nature of academic work and the distribution, among endless possibilities, of how academic careers are lived. Succinctly put, it is this volatile intertwining of faculty-*un*friendly developments that has emboldened us to posit that a new model—by our reckoning, a third post-mid-twentieth-century paradigm—has taken palpable form.

In short, higher education and its faculty have been reconstituted, the sector's mission compressed and refocused. The very purposes and priorities of higher education and its faculty have been challenged and rearranged by this tectonic shift. Indeed, the new paradigm's essence is that it calls into question the centrality of the faculty. The focus has shifted perceptibly to student learning, but, with that realignment, the faculty, as this volume seeks to document, have been relegated to a much more peripheral role. Some rebalancing is urgently needed, lest the costs to higher learning—many of them subtle but nonetheless highly consequential—become irrevocable.

As noted earlier, the faculty factor—that is, the extent to which the faculty are central to the postsecondary enterprise—has been significantly diminished in recent years by circumstances both within and outside the academy. In sum, the faculty's once lofty status, as proclaimed by Jencks and Riesman (1968), is no more. The future of academic life is opaque and, at best, fragile; the indicators are seriously troubling (Finkelstein and Schuster 2011). It is no exaggeration to propose that the fate of the academic profession—and, inextricably, the role and priorities of higher education itself—hangs precariously in the balance.

Lines of Inquiry

We intend in this volume to provide the grounds to better answer five overarching questions that bear on the faculty factor.

One, what is the current condition of the contemporary American faculty (including faculty demographics, their work patterns, and the nature of their academic careers)? And, crucially, to what extent have basic dimensions of academic life changed in recent years?

Two, to what extent, and in what ways, does the contemporary American faculty exert influence over higher education? How has the role and scope of responsibility—the faculty factor—shrunk that degree of influence in recent years?

Three, what are the implications of these changes, and anticipated further changes, for academic work and careers and for higher education in general?

Four, how does the condition of the US academic profession compare with its counterparts in other advanced economies?

Five, what are the most appropriate interventions that should be undertaken by higher education leaders (including faculty leadership) and by public policy makers?

Previewing the Contents

The following pages document recent developments at greater length. And this explication culminates in describing the numerous implications for how higher education is practiced and how faculty work and careers are being rechanneled. Following the framework we have outlined in this first chapter, we provide in chapter 2 a concise historical overview of developments leading up to this new era. Then, in chapter 3, we establish an up-to-date profile of the American faculty, identifying ways in which some key characteristics have transitioned during the past decade or so. This chapter particularly describes the continuing redistribution of types of academic appointments (highlighting the declining proportion among all faculty holding traditional full-time on-track appointments). These three chapters comprise part 1 of the volume.

Part 2 consists of three pivotal chapters that reassess the trajectories of academic careers. Chapter 4 examines the shifting circumstances of entry into academic careers. This portion extends beyond an earlier examination of the pathways of talented young-adult populations into academic careers (see Schuster and Finkelstein 2006) and now focuses instead on the increasingly diverse and circuitous entry paths to faculty positions—no longer almost exclusively directly from graduate school—as well as a more extended "settling-in" period.

Chapter 5 addresses career progression with emphasis on a new mix of career trajectories. This chapter develops, among other ideas, the thesis that deteriorating conditions for the academic profession constrain academic career advancement and, accordingly, most likely will undermine the attractiveness of such careers to those highly talented would-be faculty members, perhaps deflecting prospective faculty to other competing career options (professional and other). It incorporates the authors' analysis of the comparative mobility of faculty associated with various appointment types and career tracks as well as attrition from academic careers. This analysis, as we show, is based largely on the examination of National Science Foundation longitudinal data on natural and social scientists (1993–2013) and a fresh look at data from the 2004 National Study of Postsecondary Faculty. Following these analyses, chapter 6 explores the changing paths leading to exit from academic careers, spanning changes in retirement options in the public and private sectors generally, phased retirement options, and the timing of and preparedness for postretirement plans.

Part 3, consisting of three chapters, explores the world of faculty work. Chapter 7 describes pressing new realities that are reshaping faculty work. These include more attention to the growing impact of technology, especially the outsourcing phenomenon for instructional purposes, as well as the benefits via technology available to individual faculty members and, concomitantly, the purported diminished staffing requirement for traditional full-time faculty. This chapter also explores the changing role of faculty involvement in governance and the most recent trends in collective bargaining among faculty.

Next, chapter 8 examines academic culture and values in transition. More emphasis is placed here than previously on market influences ("academic capitalism") and the apparent sometimes unsettling effects on a range of basic academic issues, for example, the economic viability of traditional yet less popular academic disciplines, the economic challenges attendant to preserving a "core" traditional faculty, and so on (Brint et al. 2012). The chapter includes an examination of the status and prospects for academic freedom and continued professional autonomy, as well as the changing status and outlook for tenure.

Still further, shifting priorities bearing on work-nonwork balance in life issues enter the equation here in a perceptible if measure-resistant fashion. It appears that larger proportions of faculty members and would-be faculty members are striving, often struggling, to achieve more balanced lives characterized by an elusive proportionality in professional and personal priorities. To the extent that non-work-dependent priorities hold sway, it follows that an individual's identity with work and career are thereby leavened (Lancaster and Stillman 2002, 2010; Mason and Ekman 2007).

Chapter 9, "Academic Compensation Trends in a New Era," updates basic compensation data derived mainly from the American Association of University Professors' annual compensation survey. This chapter also provides several additional lenses for assessing pay for part-time and non-tenure-track faculty—US Bureau of Labor Statistics data comparing the compensation of postsecondary faculty to several job categories requiring advanced degrees in a number of disciplines and professional fields outside academe—as well as a more extended analysis of changes in fringe benefits, particularly in the public sector of higher education.

Part 4 of the volume provides a global prism throughout its two chapters. In the past half decade, higher education reform has become a prominent recurring theme in developed and developing countries alike, including the United States, requiring a sharper focus on the global nature of American higher education (Wildavsky 2010; Huang, Finkelstein, and Rostan 2013). That movement toward globalization continues to accelerate. Moreover, countries throughout the world are focusing as never before on their own national systems and what they can learn from the evolving American system to advance their own competitiveness in an increasingly globalized economy (Clotfelter 2010). The central questions in part 4 revolve around just how well the American faculty are poised to enter the swiftly expanding era of globalization and just how high are the stakes.

The first aspect of academic globalization as presented in chapter 10 highlights evidence of trends in importing academic talent to, and exporting from, the US academy. Some emphasis here is placed on science, technology, engineering, and mathematics fields, in particular, and those national interests that are and will be affected. Furthermore, the increasing evidence of cross-national scholarly collaboration and on multinational course and program content are explicated.

Then, in chapter 11, the faculty factor is viewed in comparative perspective alongside the status and prospects of the academic profession in other developed countries. Indicators span the distribution of types of appointments, compensation levels, the presence of female academics, and (to the extent measurable) the relative influence of market forces. These metrics are highlighted to show wherein the American faculty appears to lag but also appears to lead (Cummings and Finkelstein 2011). In addition, we explore briefly comparative data on academic career entry conditions in eight other countries as drawn from a recent international study. Implications for US higher education and for US national interests more generally are discussed.

The concluding two chapters, comprising part 5 ("Prospects for the Academic Profession"), both sum up earlier chapters and peer into the future. Chapter 12 revisits our central themes—the emergence of a new paradigm to describe higher education and the diminution in "clout" of the faculty factor—which are recast and reinforced in these pages. Emphases are on the challenges to traditional academic careers and, accordingly, to the effectiveness of American higher education and the likely consequences for American leadership in the twenty-first century, as well as on the opportunities for regenerating the faculty (Conley 2008). The chapter's organization largely follows the lines of inquiry earlier identified.

Finally, chapter 13 urges strategies for coping with political and economic threats grounded in the recognition that the "old ways" can never be reclaimed, any more so than has been the case in times past. Despite the perils that inhere in a new era fraught with challenges, both known and unknowable, we seek in this culminating chapter to suggest constructive, realistic interventions to help balance long-standing core academic values with the unrelenting economic, political, and sociocultural realities.

There follows a succinct afterword. In this coda the authors reflect on the meaning of our effort to provide a balanced, if sometimes contrarian, commentary about higher learning and its faculty at this pivotal historical juncture.

The Faculty Repurposed: A Concluding Comment

The consequence of the powerful forces that are relentlessly reshaping the faculty's identity and their roles and careers, we contend, add up to nothing less than a reconstituted faculty. Another way to underscore the relevance of recent developments for the future of the academy and its faculty is to recognize that the faculty, in effect, have been *repurposed.* That is, the faculty role has been channeled into a more limited, more narrowly focused scope of responsibilities: their mission—their very purpose—has become more constricted. No longer are "the faculty" a factor in the sense that one could say was more commonly the case two or three decades ago. Deeper into the twenty-first century, the repositioned, more fragmented faculty exert less leverage. In an academy squeezed hard by formidable pressures, the faculty have been relegated—one might even say demoted—to a more junior partnership in the academic enterprise.

That, then, is the central thesis of this volume: the differences have become so great over so short a period, and the implications so far reaching, that a fresh analysis is now necessary. As the sociology and culture of the professoriate continue to morph, the cumulative and still ongoing effects have been emphatic. This is what we have set about to demonstrate.

NOTES

1. Such recent pronouncements include, for example, the American Council on Education's senior vice president Terry Hartle: "The heart of any college or university is its human capital" (as quoted in Tamar Levin, "Gap Widens for Faculty at Colleges, Report Finds," *New York Times*, April 8, 2013, 15).

2. The expression *student-centric* is used in various ways; there is no precise definition. In our use, the term spans both a focus on student learning outcomes and an emphasis on consumerism, particularly amenities (in facilities and activities) intended to attract student enrollment (and thereby enhance revenues) distinct from academic teaching and learning activities.

3. Trow (1974) himself did not claim that the mass-to-universal phase had been achieved, although Kerr (1982), in *The Uses of the University* (154, 163–64), suggests that the stage of "universal access to higher education" has been accomplished.

4. This broad expansion of faculty influence over academic matters did not translate into the acquisition of formal power. The formal authority was still vested in governing boards (although their exercise of control had become "seldom" compared with what it once had been). The faculty role, individually and collectively, though "still . . . largely advisory," had escalated in its de facto influence (Jencks and Riesman 1968, 16). Later Riesman (1980), looking backward, uses the term "faculty dominance" (1, 11).

5. Graham and Diamond (1997) elaborate regarding these "unfaculty": "They include research and visiting faculty, postdoctoral fellows, research associates, administrative staff, technicians, and graduate students" (59).

6. For purposes of these tabulations, graduate student employees have not been included in the total count of instructional staff. Had graduate student employees been included in the denominator, the percentage of full-time tenured plus full-time tenure-track instructional staff would have declined from 35.0% in 1993 to 24.1% in 2011. (American Association of University Professors 2013). See also US Department of Education's National Center for Education Statistics Integrated Postsecondary Education Data Systems (IPEDS), "Human Resources Component," in Snyder and Dillow (2015).

7. These traditional roles are broken out in Finkelstein and Schuster (2011, 3–4).

8. See, generally, the writing of Charles Taylor, particularly *The Ethics of Authenticity* (1991) and Charles Guignon, *On Being Authentic* (2004).

9. "Patch dynamics" is a concept most often used in ecosystem and habitat analysis, underscoring a "mosaic of sub-ecosystems." The term is used here as a metaphor for the numerous dynamic, heterogeneous but interacting subsystems that make up the highly decentralized and complex "nonsystem" that is American higher education.

REFERENCES

Archibald, James. 2010. *Faculty Senate Leader Survey: Preliminary Results of Doctoral Institutions.* Athens: Center for Higher Education, Ohio University.

Archibald, James G., and Valerie M. Conley. 2011. "The Role of Faculty Senate in Budget Planning: Perceptions of Faculty Senate Leaders." *Planning for Higher Education* 39 (July–September): 54–58.

Baldwin, Roger G., and Jay L. Chronister. 2001. *Teaching without Tenure: Policies and Practices for a New Era.* Baltimore, MD: Johns Hopkins University Press.

Bok, Derek C. 2004. *Universities in the Marketplace: The Commercialization of Higher Education.* Princeton, NJ: Princeton University Press.

Bowen, Howard R., and Jack H. Schuster. 1986. *American Professors: A National Resource Imperiled.* New York: Oxford University Press.

Brint, Steven, Kristopher Proctor, Scott P. Murphy, and Robert A Hanneman. 2012. "The Market Model and the Growth and Decline of Academic Fields in US Four-Year Colleges and Universities, 1980–2000." *Sociological Forum* 27 (May): 275–99.

Burgan, Mary. 2009. *Whatever Happened to the Faculty? Drift and Decision in Higher Education.* Baltimore, MD: Johns Hopkins University Press.

Christensen, Clayton M., and Henry J. Eyring. 2011. *The Innovative University: Changing the DNA of Higher Education from Inside Out.* San Francisco, CA: Jossey-Bass.

Clark, Burton R. 1987. *The Academic Life: Small Worlds, Different Worlds.* Princeton, NJ: Carnegie Foundation for the Advancement of Teaching.

Clotfelter, Charles. 2010. *American Universities in a Global Market.* Chicago: University of Chicago Press.

Conley, Valerie Martin. 2008. "Regenerating the Faculty Workforce: A Significant Leadership Challenge and a Public Policy Concern." *TIAA-CREF Institute: Advancing Higher Education*, February, 1–16.

Cross, J. G., and E. N. Goldenberg. 2009. *Off-Track Profs: Non-Tenured Teachers in Higher Education.* Cambridge, MA: MIT Press.

Cummings, William K., and Martin J. Finkelstein. 2011. *Scholars in the Changing American Academy: New Context, New Rules, and New Roles.* Dordrecht, NL: Springer.

Curtis, John W., and Saranna Thornton. 2013. "Here Is the News: The Annual Report on the Economic Status of the Profession, 2012–13." *Academe* 99 (March–April): 7.

Eaton, Judith S. 2012. "The Future of Accreditation." *Planning for Higher Education* 40 (April–June): 8–15.
Eaton, Judith S., and Anne Neal. 2015. "Accreditation's Future." *Change* 47 (January–February): 20–27.
Finkelstein, Martin J., and Jack H. Schuster. 2011. "A New Higher Education: The 'Next Model' Takes Shape." *TIAA-CREF Institute: Advancing Higher Education*, April, 1–9.
Friedman, Thomas. 2005. *The World Is Flat: A Brief History of the Twenty-First Century*. New York: Farrar, Straus and Giroux.
Gaston, Paul L. 2013. *Higher Education Accreditation: How It's Changing, Why It Must*. Sterling, VA: Stylus Publishing.
Gerber, Larry G. 2014. *The Rise and Decline of Faculty Governance: Professionalization and the Modern American University*. Baltimore, MD: Johns Hopkins University Press.
Ginsberg, Benjamin. 2011. *The Fall of the Faculty: The Rise of the All-Administrative University and Why It Matters*. Oxford, UK: Oxford University Press.
Gould, Eric. 2003. *The University in a Corporate Culture*. New Haven, CT: Yale University Press.
Graham, Hugh Davis, and Nancy Diamond. 1997. *The Rise of American Research Universities: Elites and Challengers in the Postwar Era*. Baltimore, MD: Johns Hopkins University Press.
Guignon, Charles. 2004. *On Being Authentic*. New York: Routledge.
Hentschke, Guilbert C., Vincente M. Lechuga, William G. Tierney, and Marc Tucker. 2010. *For-Profit Colleges and Universities: Their Markets, Their Regulation, Performance, and Place in Higher Education*. Sterling, VA: Stylus Publishing.
Huang, Futao, Martin Finkelstein, and Michele Rostand. 2014. *The Internationalization of the Academy: Changes, Realities, and Prospects*. Dordrecht, NL: Springer.
Jencks, Christopher, and David Riesman. 1968. *The Academic Revolution*. Garden City, NY: Doubleday.
Johnstone, Bruce D. 2003. "The International Comparative Study of Higher Education: Lessons from the Contemplation of How Others Might See Us." *Futures Forum 2003: Exploring the Future of Higher Education*, 45–48. Washington, DC: Forum for the Future of Higher Education and the National Association of College and University Business Officers.
Kaplan, Gabriel. 2003. "How Academic Ships Actually Navigate: A Report from the 2001 Survey on Higher Education Governance." In *Governing Academia*, edited by Ronald Ehrenberg, 165–208. Ithaca, NY: Cornell University Press.
Kerr, Clark. 1963. *The Uses of the University*. Berkeley, CA: University of California Press.
———. 1982. *The Uses of the University*. 3rd ed. Cambridge, MA: Harvard University Press.
Kezar, Adrianna, and Cecile Sam. 2010. "Understanding the New Majority of Non-Tenure-Track Faculty in Higher Education: Demographics, Experiences, and Plans of Action." *ASHE Higher Education Report* 36, no. 4 (November): 1–133.
Kirp, David. 2003. *Shakespeare, Einstein, and the Bottom Line: The Marketing of Higher Education*. Cambridge, MA: Harvard University Press.
Lancaster, Lynne C., and David Stillman. 2002. *When Generations Collide: Who They Are, Why They Clash, How to Solve the Generational Puzzle at Work*. New York: Harper Collins.
———. 2010. *The M-Factor: How the Millennial Generation Is Rocking the Workplace*. New York: HarperBusiness.
Mason, Mary Ann, and Eve Mason Ekman. 2007. *Mothers on the Fast Track: How a New Generation Can Balance Family and Careers*. Oxford, UK: Oxford University Press.

Metzger, Walter. 1973. "Academic Tenure in America: A Historical Essay." In *Faculty Tenure: A Report and Recommendations by the Commission on American Tenure in Higher Education*, 93–159. San Francisco, CA: Jossey-Bass.
Musselin, Christine. 2010. *The Market for Academics*. New York: Routledge.
Noam, Eli M. 1995. "Electronics and the Dim Future of the University." *Science* 270 (October): 247–49.
Riesman, David. 1980. *On Higher Education: The Academic Enterprise in an Era of Rising Student Consumerism*. San Francisco, CA: Jossey-Bass.
Rice, Andrew. 2012. "Anatomy of a Campus Coup." *New York Times Magazine*, September 11.
Schrecker, Ellen. 2010. *The Lost Soul of Higher Education: Corporatization, the Assault on Academic Freedom, and the End of the American University*. New York: New Press.
Schuster, Jack H. 2011. "The Professoriate's Perilous Path." Introduction to *The American Academic Profession: Transformation in Contemporary Higher Education*, edited by Joseph Hermanowicz, 1–17. Baltimore, MD: Johns Hopkins University Press.
Schuster, Jack H., and Martin J. Finkelstein. 2006. *The American Faculty: The Restructuring of Academic Work and Careers*. Baltimore, MD: Johns Hopkins University Press.
Schuster, Jack H., Daryl G. Smith, Kathleen Corak, and Myrtle M. Yamada. 1994. *Strategic Governance: How to Make Big Decisions Better*. Phoenix, AZ: American Council on Education and Oryx Press.
Slaughter, Sheila, and Larry L. Leslie. 1997. *Academic Capitalism: Politics, Policies, and the Entrepreneurial University*. Baltimore, MD: Johns Hopkins University Press.
Slaughter, Sheila, and Gary Rhoades. 2004. *Academic Capitalism and the New Economy: Markets, State, and Higher Education*. Baltimore, MD: Johns Hopkins University Press.
Snyder, Thomas D., and Sally A. Dillow. 2015. *Digest of Education Statistics 2013*. NCES 2015-011. National Center for Education Statistics, Institute of Educational Sciences. Washington, DC: US Department of Education.
Taylor, Charles. 1992. *The Ethics of Authenticity*. Cambridge, MA: Harvard University Press.
Tierney, William G., and Guilbert C. Hentschke. 2007. *New Players, Different Game: Understanding the Rise of For-Profit Colleges and Universities*. Baltimore, MD: Johns Hopkins University Press.
Tierney, William G., and James T. Minor. 2003. *Challenges for Governance: A National Report*. Los Angeles: Center for Education Policy Analysis, University of Southern California.
Trow, Martin. 1974. "Problems in the Transition from Elite to Mass Higher Education." In *General Report on the Conference on Future Structures of Postsecondary Education*, 55–101. Paris: OECD. Reprinted in Martin Trow, *Twentieth-Century Higher Education: Elite to Mass to Universal*, edited by Michael Burrage, 88–143. Baltimore: Johns Hopkins University Press.
Wildavsky, Benjamin. 2010. *The Great Brain Race*. Princeton, NJ: Princeton University Press.
Woodhouse, Howard. 2009. *Selling Out: Academic Freedom and the Corporate Market*. Montreal, CAN: McGill-Queens University Press.
Zemsky, Robert. 2011. "The Unwitting Damage Done by the Spellings Commission." *Chronicle of Higher Education*, 58, no. 5 (September 23): A-10.
Zemsky, Robert, Gregory R. Wegner, and William F. Massy. 2005. *Remaking the American University: Market-Smart and Mission-Centered*. New Brunswick, NJ: Rutgers University Press.

2

The American Faculty in Historical Perspective

The Importance of Context

As noted in chapter 1, a confluence of pressures challenge contemporary higher education in the opening years of the twenty-first century.[1] These pressures emanate both from outside academe (the political, economic, and sociocultural environment) and from within (that is, how the higher education system itself, including individual campuses, is responding—or, perhaps more accurately, scrambling to adapt). These adaptations can be seen everywhere: in changes in the composition of the faculty, in the curriculum offered, in the increasingly heterogeneous mix of types of faculty appointments, and in the makeup of, and intensifying competition for, postsecondary education students. Furthermore, and more broadly, the postsecondary enterprise itself is being resculpted by the scarcer resources available to it and, less tangibly (but vitally), by recalibrations in the public's expectations of and support for higher education. These potent forces serve to reconfigure the higher education sector's overall mission and to diminish the prioritization of higher education among the wide array of public services clamoring for the currently reduced amount of government and philanthropic support. Perhaps chief among the change agents should be counted the breathtaking advances in technology that are transforming virtually every dimension of higher education, with momentous consequences for academic work and careers. In all, higher education is indisputably undergoing remarkable, irreversible changes, exciting in potential benefits for the academic enterprise and its effectiveness (perhaps especially for students) but also alarming for these changes' effects, both intended and unintended, on traditional faculty roles.

What might these changes portend specifically for the American faculty? Indeed, what kind of faculty will the nation require to meet these formidable challenges? As we address these overarching questions throughout this volume, it is instructive to begin with the lessons derived from the historical record. That record suggests at least one striking conclusion: when the number and intensity of external social, economic, and political forces impinging on the higher education system reach critical mass, the system is forced to find a new equilibrium to accommodate those pressures, not only responding quantitatively but adapting qualitatively as well. Historically, that has meant that as American higher education itself expanded in response to the nation's transition to a secular, industrial, urban society with an emergent middle class (Veysey 1965), it adopted new purposes, functions, and modes of operation (Trow 1973). And that has invariably meant shifts in faculty roles, work activities, and careers—indeed, a reformulation of the very definition of a college or university faculty member—and, it follows, what the qualifications would be for performing in that role. This chapter provides a concise account of how the faculty of American colleges and universities have evolved over time. It depicts how the faculty slowly, unevenly accrued stature and influence to reach something like a plateau of respected professionalism during the 1960s and 1970s. This upward surge occurred before an assortment of mostly environmental forces (previewed in chapter 1) began to erode the faculty's centrality to the postsecondary enterprise, giving way to a new era of uncertainties for faculty and their institutions. That story begins on these shores soon after Europeans began to colonize the North American continent.[2]

The Beginnings

For nearly four centuries, since the founding of Harvard College in 1636, instructional staff of one sort or another have stood (or sat) in front of a group, large or small, of physically present students. For more than half that period, college teaching changed little and could best be described as an odd job taken on largely by fresh graduates of baccalaureate programs as a way station on the path to some other career, be it the ministry, business, law, medicine, government, or agriculture. Through the first half of the eighteenth century, the predominant model could be described as curriculum centric, by which a changing, unstable corps of tutors delivered the content; their wide-ranging responsibilities spanned mentoring, moral oversight, and figurative hand-holding (as described in more detail below). However, in the mid-nineteenth century an extraordinary change began to set in, leading to a more focused role of academic staffs regarding their responsibilities, backgrounds, and career paths.

This metamorphosis both reflected and made possible the expansion in the United States of, and its uneven transformation to, a mass system of higher education, then progressing toward (albeit not achieving) universal access (Trow 1973).

These historical shifts in the roles and responsibilities of academic staffs have proceeded in two basic phases: professionalization in the nineteenth century and expansion and diversification in the twentieth century (Metzger 1973). Professionalization began in the first quarter of the nineteenth century and gained momentum after the Civil War, roughly paralleling the emergence of the American university (Veysey 1965; Jencks and Riesman 1968; Finkelstein 1983). Expansion and diversification marked the post–World War II period. These trends continue, although the rate of growth, in numbers of institutions, students, and academic staff, has slowed in more recent years (Metzger 1987; Kerr 1991, 2001), as discussed in chapter 3. The past two decades, as we suggest, have witnessed turbulence within higher education and its faculty. This has yielded, for now, an unprecedented set of conditions that, as we assert in chapter 1, constitutes a new model or, in our vernacular, Paradigm Three.

Reviewing such historical transitions provides an important perspective on the historical development of faculty work and careers, allowing us to unfreeze some of our assumptions about the essentialness and invariability of who faculty are and what they do, providing us with the necessary framework within which to contemplate the future. Indeed, it is our belief that this overview of how the academic profession evolved in North America will allow us to interpret more clearly the current condition of academic life—poised, we argue, at the threshold of momentous change—and will enable us as well to discern more reliably the key issues that will reconfigure academic work and careers deeper into the twenty-first century.

The College Teaching Career circa 1800

During the seventeenth and the first half of the eighteenth centuries the teaching staffs of American colleges were composed entirely of tutors, exclusively young men, often no more than twenty years of age, who had just received their own baccalaureate degrees and who were preparing for careers mostly in the ministry (Morison 1936). Their responsibilities were pastoral-custodial, as well as pedagogical, in nature. Ideally, a single tutor was assigned to shepherd a single class through the prescribed four-year curriculum. As Samuel Morison (1936) observed, "Tutors were with their pupils almost every hour of the day [in the classroom recitations, study halls and at meals], and slept in the same chamber with some of them at night. They were responsible not only for the intellectual, but also for the moral and spiritual development of their charges." In reality, however, the tutorship during this era functioned more as a revolving door. At Harvard before 1685, seldom did a tutor see a class through all four years, and only six of the forty-one tutors during this period remained at Harvard for more than three years. Similar dynamics obtained later at Yale, Brown, Dartmouth, and Bowdoin (Finkelstein 1984, 8–9).

During the second half of the eighteenth century, however, these staffs of tutors began to be supplemented by a small cadre of "permanent" faculty; these were the first professors. William Carrell (1968) could identify only 10 professors in all of American higher education as late as 1750. By 1800, the number of colleges had doubled, and professorial ranks had multiplied tenfold to more than 100. All in all, by the onset of the nineteenth century, some 200 or so individuals had served as professors in nineteen American colleges.

The pattern that had developed at Harvard for well over a century and at Yale for more than a half century was adopted almost immediately by those colleges founded during the second half of the eighteenth century. At Brown, for example, within five years of its founding in 1764 a core permanent faculty had already emerged with David Howell's promotion from tutor to professor to join president-cum-professor James Manning. By 1800, Brown's five tutors had been supplemented by three permanent professors (*Historical Catalogue* 1905). At Princeton, by 1767, two decades after the institution's founding, three permanent professors had joined the three tutors (Wertenbaker 1946). At Dartmouth, during the lengthy administration of John Wheelock (1779–1817), several professors were appointed to augment the single professor who, together with two or three tutors, had constituted the entire faculty during the preceding administration of Eleazar Wheelock (Richardson 1932, 820, as cited by Cowley 1980, 80).

While these pioneer professors discharged responsibilities very similar to the tutors in terms of supervising recitations, study halls, chapel, and discipline, they were distinguishable from the tutors in at least three crucial respects. First, these early professors did not take general charge of a whole class of students; rather, they were appointed in a particular *subject* area such as natural philosophy, divinity, or ancient languages, and, for the most part, they provided instruction in that area of specialization. Second, they were generally older than the tutors (by at least five to ten years) and more experienced (the majority had some postbaccalaureate professional preparation in theology, law, or medicine).[3] Third, they stayed on—that is, they were relatively permanent employees.

Carrell's (1968) analysis of 124 biographical sketches of professors during the second half of the eighteenth century illuminates the particular meaning of a "permanent" appointment before 1800. First, a professorship implied a career at a single institution, most frequently one's alma mater. Nearly 40% of Carrell's sample taught at his own alma mater (there were no "hers"), ranging from just over one-third at the College of Philadelphia (later the University of Pennsylvania) to five-sixths at Harvard. Indeed, with few exceptions, almost all—seven-eighths—taught at only one institution during their careers, while a practically invisible one in forty had taught at three or more institutions. Second, a professorial position, although often enduring, was typically a non-exclusive career. In analyzing the lifetime occupational commitment of his sample, Carrell reports that only about 15% identified themselves *exclusively* as professional teachers and roughly 20% described themselves *primarily* as professional teachers but with a secondary occupation in the ministry, medicine, or law, whereas somewhat over half identified themselves primarily as practitioners of one of the traditional professions but only *secondarily* as professional college teachers.

If college teaching typically was not an exclusive career, or even the first choice, of a majority of eighteenth-century professors, it became a long-term commitment for many, once the move had been made. In analyzing indicators of the extent of professors' occupational commitment during their teaching tenure, Carrell finds strikingly varied results: only 45% identified themselves as college teachers exclusively, while another one-quarter identified themselves, as college teachers only primarily or secondarily. In the latter two categories, clergy were heavily represented in the first subset, while physicians and lawyers made up the greater portion of the second subset, suggesting that clergymen were more likely than their counterparts in the other learned professions to develop a primary commitment to the professorial role, once assumed.

An important question remains: to what extent did appointments as tutors lead to professorial appointments, or, alternatively, were these types of appointments typically compartmentalized from each other? In fact, the tutorship remained a separate, *temporary* career track for young people poised to move on to other pursuits. Tutorships rarely led to entrance into the professorial ranks: never at Harvard, only one in five at Brown, and a scant one in ten tutors at Yale progressed to a professorship during this period. The professors were typically drawn from outside the ranks of the tutors, although at a few venues (Yale being one) the majority of the professors at one time or another had served as tutors (Finkelstein 1983).

In sum, by 1800 college teaching was becoming a *bifurcated* occupation. The majority of college teachers were still young, inexperienced tutors, providing general custodial supervision as well as instruction to students for what would be a brief postbaccalaureate engagement before they, the tutors, moved on with their lives and into other careers. An emerging minority were more experienced professionals drawn from other fields (ministry, medicine, law) who transitioned into professorships in a teaching field following a career in their profession, often appointed at their alma mater, and who typically continued in the faculty role as a second or secondary career.

Nineteenth-Century Professionalization

Faculty professionalization during the nineteenth century meant at least four things. First, as already noted, it meant the beginnings of *specialization* in teaching; that is, faculty usually were hired to teach in a particular field rather than to guide a cohort of freshman through the entire prescribed baccalaureate course, as had begun to occur during the second half of the eighteenth century (Carrell 1968). Second, associated with specialization in teaching was the notion that academic staffs should have formal preparation, through graduate education, for the specializations they taught (not merely general preparation in one of the learned professions). And until the last quarter of the nineteenth century, such training was available only in European universities (Veysey 1965; McCaughey 1974; Tobias 1982). Third, the time dedicated to preparation meant that college teaching no longer made sense as a mere transitory position but would ordinarily require and sustain a lifelong career commitment (Carrell 1968; McCaughey 1974). Finally, specialization, coupled with the requisite advanced subject matter preparation, spawned the conception of the academic as expert. This, in turn, provided the basis for subsequently advancing claims to academic freedom and faculty professional autonomy (Scott 1966; Baldridge et al. 1978; Tobias 1982). The professionalization phase proceeded in two relatively distinct stages, two minirevolutions separated by a half century.

Phase One: Professionalization's Beginning

The first quarter of the nineteenth century witnessed the ascent of a core of permanent, specialized professors as the centerpiece of academic staffing, quickly supplanting the tutorship as the modal appointment type at the leading institutions. This new breed of academic staff, as just noted, was older, appointed to teach a particular subject, and quite likely had some "professional training" in theology, law, or medicine. The professors remained still largely independent of the more temporary tutorship, thereby perpetuating a bifurcated staffing system but with this transfiguring feature: the professors replaced the tutors as the primary instructional staff.

How can one account for this first big step in the evolving professionalization of the academic career—the rise of the permanent faculty and the corresponding displacement, in a brief two decades, of the class of temporary, revolving-door tutors as the instructional heart of the academy? Several environmental pressures appear to provide necessary, if not sufficient, conditions for driving the shift. The first is sheer expansion in the opportunity for such careers: growth in size of some of the leading institutions (Yale, for example, doubled its enrollment in twenty years) and growth in the number of institutions as a result of the "college movement," however modest that growth may seem in light of later, more dramatic expansion (Rudolph 1962; Burke 1982).

A second set of factors can be seen in changing church-related careers, the most important occupational sector then competing with colleges for would-be faculty members. Daniel Calhoun (1965), examining the New Hampshire clergy in the late-eighteenth and early-nineteenth centuries, reports a radical shift in clerical career patterns, which he attributes to the increasing secularization and urbanization of the populace. The average terms of service in local parishes, which through the eighteenth century had as often as not been measured in whole adult lifetimes, began to resemble the tenures of modern college and university presidents. This new hazard of job insecurity meant that the challenge of obtaining even so tenuous a position, coupled with the low salaries of clergy hired by rural and small-town congregations, led many ministers to seek to enhance their careers by developing options, such as launching colleges and becoming professors themselves (Tobias 1982). And the correlation of these developments in clerical careers with the ascent of the permanent professorship is lent further credence by the demonstrably greater likelihood that clergymen, as distinguished from their fellow counterparts in law and medicine, would identify themselves primarily as college teachers.

While the "professor movement" had created by 1825 a relatively large cohort of career college faculty, their preparation, the nature of their work, and the characteristics of their careers remained not yet fully professionalized in our contemporary sense. With the exception of Harvard, the postgraduate preparation of faculty in their teaching specialty (as distinguished from the ministry, law, or medicine) remained a rarity. The majority of faculty members continued to be drawn to their initial appointments as professor from nonacademic jobs, primarily in school teaching or the ministry, secondarily in law or medicine. Any semblance of a career grounded in their academic discipline typically ended with their institutional career. That is, the modal pattern at some institutions was for the majority of faculty to move into nonacademic careers following their stints, however lengthy, as college teachers; this transition applied to some 50% of the full professors at Brown and 60% at Bowdoin, although that was not true at Harvard and Yale.[4] And irrespective of their length of institutional service, most faculty members in the first half of the nineteenth century still displayed relatively low engagement with a field of study in terms of their scholarly publication patterns and scholarly associational involvements. Only a single faculty member at Brown, Bowdoin, Harvard, and Yale was involved to any significant extent in the activities of the fledgling learned societies of the day. And, excluding the medical faculty, it was only these same solo faculty members who were engaged in publishing in their areas of academic appointment.[5]

While many professors in the first quarter of the nineteenth century were actively pursuing concurrent "public" careers, virtually none was rooted in their academic specialization. Beyond the budding multifaceted careers of a few men such as Benjamin Silliman at Yale and Parker Cleaveland at Bowdoin, both of whom were visible on the academic public lecture circuit, the vast majority of professors expended their extrainstitutional time in less scholarly pursuits, devoted instead to church-related or civic activities. Fully three-quarters of the professors at Dartmouth, two-thirds of those at Bowdoin, and half of those at Brown were engaged in itinerant preaching and work with missionary societies. Somewhat lower proportions were actively involved in community life, principally by holding political office at the local or even national level, assuming leadership roles in civic associations unrelated to education or intellectual culture (e.g., tree-planting societies), or, in fewer cases, holding membership in state historical societies (Packard 1882; *Historical Catalogue* 1905; Tobias 1982).

Phase Two: Toward Maturation

By the mid-nineteenth century, the confluence of a number of social and intellectual forces gained sufficient momentum to propel (catapult, really) the professionalization process to the next level—a critical step in the shaping of modern academic life. The progressive secularization of American society was penetrating the classical college, subordinating the demands of piety to the secular religion of progress and materialism, reflecting the needs of a growing industrial economy (Hofstadter and Metzger 1955; Brubacher and Rudy 1968). At the same time, the rise of science and the tremendous growth of scientific knowledge were breaking apart the classical curriculum and giving rise to the development of the academic disciplines—distinguishing, thereby, the professional from the amateur—and spawning systematic research and graduate education (Berelson 1960; Veysey 1965; Wolfle 1972; Oleson and Voss 1979). By midcentury, increasingly large numbers of Americans were studying in Germany and were importing their versions of the German university and the German notion of research back into the United States (Hofstadter and Metzger 1955). Once graduate education and disciplinary specialization took hold in earnest in the last quarter of the nineteenth century, it was but a short step to the establishment of the major, now familiar, learned societies and their sponsorship of specialized, disciplinary journals: for example, the American Chemical Society in 1876, the Modern Language Association in 1883, the American Historical Association in 1884, the American Psychological Association in 1892, and on and on (Berelson 1960).

These developments together provided American higher education in the last quarter of the nineteenth century with the capability of producing graduate-trained specialists and created clear career opportunities for these specialists thereby produced. And thus the impetus was provided for furthering—completing in some respects—a second-order restructuring of faculty roles and careers.

This second-order shift saw the emergence of the faculty role as specialist in a discipline. Advanced graduate training in a discipline (in contradistinction to professional training in theology, law, and medicine), together with scholarly publication and participation in the activities of learned societies, was evident at a few institutions, most notably Harvard, well before 1850. By 1845, for example, some 70% of the Bowdoin faculty were publishing in their field of specialization (about half writing primarily textbooks), while nearly one-third of them were active in professional associations (Packard 1882). Also by 1845, about half of Brown's faculty were publishing in their field of specialization, and by the Civil War fully one-half were affiliated with one of the major learned societies of the day. It was not, however, until the second half of the century (the 1860s and 1870s for the most part) that institutions such as Dartmouth and Williams began basing appointments on discipline-related credentials and began hiring individuals directly out of the European and nascent American graduate schools (Finkelstein 1983). It was then, too, that interinstitutional mobility emerged: faculty, trained in a discipline, moving to more attractive positions at other institutions as emergent disciplinary loyalties began to supplant historically local institutional commitments. The center of gravity was shifting.

The professorial role as expert, as it began to take more definitive form in the immediate pre–Civil War period, gave rise to two significant, interrelated developments in the professors' institutional careers during the last quarter of the nineteenth century. First was the emergence of new academic ranks (assistant and associate professor) and the forging of these new roles into a career sequence that at once gave shape to the career course and regulated movement through the more junior ranks to a full professorship. Concomitantly, there was an expansion and professionalization of the junior faculty. Together, these developments served to integrate into a seamless structure the earlier dual-career track system—temporary tutors and a small core of permanent professors—that had characterized the early part of the nineteenth century (McCaughey 1974; Finkelstein 1983).

While the instructorship and assistant professorship made their appearance quite early in the annals of some institutions, such appointments did not become standard practice anywhere until the last quarter of the nineteenth century; nor, initially, did they serve as routes into the senior ranks. These junior faculty roles, however, came to represent not merely changes in nomenclature but the waning of the tutorship, leading at some institutions to the disappearance of the tutorship altogether and at others to its transformation into an instructorship rank. Most critically, these newly created types of appointments came to serve by the 1870s and 1880s at most institutions as feeders to the full professorial ranks. By 1880, the junior faculty grew in number to parity or surpassed in size the senior faculty at many institutions, and such appointees were increasingly entering their academic careers directly from graduate training in their specialties or from junior appointments at other institutions. The essential features of the twentieth-century faculty role by century's end were becoming the norm—a far cry from the composition of faculties in the first quarter of the nineteenth century.

All of these structural changes in the academic career followed from the emergence of the discipline as the central organizing principle of academic life and the university as the dominant organizational form. Beginning in the 1850s, the bare outline of a concurrent public career rooted in a faculty member's disciplinary expertise, as an educator and/or as a proponent of culture (rather than of religion), was becoming discernible at many institutions. At Brown, for example, the immediate pre–Civil War period saw the first instance of a faculty member using his expertise in the service of state government: the appointment of a chemistry professor to head the Rhode Island board of weights and measures. By the end of the Civil War, the proportion of the Brown faculty involved in itinerant preaching and other clerical activities had dropped from over one-third at midcentury to one-eighth. While a large majority (about 75%) of the faculty remained involved in civic and community affairs, a change in the nature of that involvement had taken place: only a single faculty member was directly involved in elective politics, while the majority were engaged in distinctively cultural, academic, or education-related activities such as membership on boards of education, holding office in national honor, art, or historical societies, and service on state and federal government commissions (*Historical Catalogue* 1905). At Bowdoin, by the eve of the Civil War, four of seven faculty members were engaged in extrainstitutional roles as specialists, educators, and public men of letters. Parker Cleaveland was holding public lectures on mineralogy, and Alpheus Packard on education; President James Woods and Professor Packard were engaging in commissioned writing for the Maine Historical Society, and Thomas Upham was producing pamphlets for the American Peace Association (Packard 1882).[6]

The growing centrality of the discipline fortified new professorial claims for a role in college governance that had traditionally been the province of college presidents, especially regarding pivotal academic matters—most notably, faculty appointments and curricular decisions. Such matters had traditionally been driven by religious, as distinguished from scholarly, considerations. These claims were evident during the pre–Civil War period in the struggles, albeit amicable ones, between the old- and new-guard faculty members concerning the relative emphasis on moral development and student discipline versus purely academic concerns (Dwight 1903). The assertions of faculty prerogatives were reflected more dramatically, and less amicably, in the post–Civil War period in the form of veritable faculty revolts at some of the more traditional institutions. At Williams, for example, the faculty, concerned about student performance and academic standards, confronted Mark Hopkins, the prototypical old-time college president, over their determination to enforce regular class attendance via a marking system. Two years earlier the faculty had succeeded in instituting annual written examinations. Then in 1869, at the faculty's insistence, admissions standards were tightened and the practice was initiated of sending lists of class standings (the equivalent of the modern registrar's grade report) to all parents—despite, it should be noted, enrollment shortfalls. By 1872, these conflicts had precipitated Hopkins's resignation and the inauguration of Paul Ansel Chadbourne, who had come to Williams eight years earlier as only the second European-trained specialist on the faculty (Rudolph 1956, 223–24).

At Dartmouth a decade later, fifteen of the twenty-two resident faculty members petitioned the Board of Trustees for the dismissal of President Samuel Colcord Bartlett. At issue was the president's attempt to secure the appointment of a new professor of Greek whose religious qualifications appeared to the faculty to exceed the candidate's scholarly qualifications. While Bartlett survived the challenge and lingered on for another decade, his successor, William Jewett Tucker, recognized in his 1893 inaugural address the emergence of a "New Dartmouth," a new kind of college staffed by a new kind of faculty (Tobias 1982).

The faculty, it could be said, by century's end had scaled one plateau. Consolidation and deeper professionalization lay ahead.

Consolidation and Elaboration in the Early-Twentieth Century

By 1915, one indicator that the new academic profession had turned a collective corner was the founding of the American Association of University Professors (AAUP). The coming together of eighteen academic luminaries from seven of the leading universities to charter the first national organization of professors suggests a newfound sense of collective professorial self-consciousness and a sense of colleagueship or fraternity in the service of scientific progress. As Edwin R. A. Seligman of Columbia, one of the AAUP founders, proclaimed, "Loyalty to our institution is admirable, but if our institution for some unfortunate reason stands athwart the progress of science, or even haltingly follows that path, we must use our best efforts to convince our colleagues and the authorities of the error of their ways. . . . In prosecuting this end, we need both individual and collective efforts. The leisure of the laboratory and of the study accounts for much; but almost equally important is the stimulus derived from contact with our colleagues" (cited in Hofstadter and Metzger 1955, 471). Yet this sense of collective consciousness was, in one important sense, highly restricted in terms of the quite narrow definition of just who was to be included in the collectivity. In the AAUP's initial constitution, membership was limited to "recognized" scholars with at least ten years' experience in the professoriate. Although the base was soon broadened in 1920 to include professors with three or more years of experience, nonetheless the cadre that was conscious of itself collectively still constituted a small, exclusive contingent of professionalized scholars within the expanding professoriate (Hofstadter and Metzger 1955).

Initial membership included 867 research-oriented full professors; seven years later 4,000 faculty members, constituting some 6% of the professoriate, could be counted among the AAUP's members. But among even this select group, strictly professional concerns were secondary to institutional ones. John Dewey sought to direct the energies of the new organization toward developing professional standards for the university-based scholar and away from intervention into faculty-administrative disputes at the institutional level. But the membership clearly saw the association's primary function as that of a grievance committee assisting individual faculty in internal campus disputes, and during the early years, the organization was overwhelmed by the grievances brought to its attention (Hofstadter and Metzger 1955).

The focus on such faculty-administration disputes heralded the persistent, if imperfect, arrival of the modern university scholar. Indeed, the two-decade period between the world wars was largely one of consolidating the gains of the preceding quarter century. Discipline-based graduate study and research grew at an unprecedented rate. The annual production of doctorates ballooned fivefold, from 620 in 1920 to nearly 3,300 in 1940. More discourses and pronouncements on graduate education were published than in any previous or subsequent twenty-year period, excepting the immediate post–World War II era (Berelson 1960). A cycle of intense, second-order specialization was evident in the differentiation of yet more specialized subareas within the disciplines. To illustrate, the social sciences spawned in quick succession the Econometric

Society (1930), the American Association of Physical Anthropologists (1930), the Society for the Psychological Study of Social Issues (1936), the American Society of Criminology (1936), the Rural Sociological Society (1937), the Society for Applied Anthropology (1941), and the Economic History Association (1941), among numerous others. These societies, in turn, sponsored more specialized scholarly journals, for example, the *Journal of Personality* (1932), *Econometrica* (1933), *Sociometry* (1937), and *Public Administration Review* (1940). By the mid-1940s, the dominance of the graduate research model, as we now know it, was clearly established, as was the professoriate's claim to that crucial desideratum of professionalization, specialized expertise (Berelson 1960).

On campus, the recognition of disciplinary expertise as the sine qua non of faculty work translated into gradually relieving the faculty of oversight responsibilities for student discipline; this had been, after all, the major noninstructional function of their faculty counterparts during the eighteenth and nineteenth centuries. While the first deans of students emerged with the advent of the university in the last quarter of the nineteenth century (Brubacher and Rudy 1968, 322), what became known as the student personnel movement began in the 1920s, gaining momentum throughout the 1930s and 1940s. The movement established on campuses across the nation an infrastructure designed to address the nonintellectual, nonacademic needs of college students. This infrastructure, featuring deans of students, counseling, student health services, career development, and so on, was, to be sure, a response to a broad array of convergent forces. These encompassed growth and diversification of student bodies; a reaction against the more narrow German conception of, and influence on, higher education; and expressions of John Dewey's education philosophy. This growth of nonacademic campus specialists nonetheless coincided with a historical responsibility of the faculty that by the interwar period had grown anachronistic and provided the occasion (and organizational means) for the faculty collectively to cast off those nonacademic responsibilities.

The Faculty's Role in Governance and Public Service

The faculty's disciplinary expertise expressed itself on campus not only in the shedding of antiquated responsibilities but also in the addition of new ones. Organizationally, the increasing recognition of the faculty's claim to professional expertise brought an enhanced role in campus decision making. Faculty governance structures had existed statutorily at several leading institutions, including Harvard, Princeton, and Pennsylvania, as early as the mid-eighteenth century, closely paralleling the emergence of the professorship. And by the second half of the nineteenth century, other faculty bodies had developed considerable authority at, for instance, Yale, Cornell, and Wisconsin. However, although precedent may have placed student discipline, admission, and graduation requirements within their purview, faculty prerogatives in key academic areas, such as curriculum, education policy, and, especially, in faculty personnel decisions (appointments and promotions), as well as the selection of academic administrators, were not yet clearly established for the most part at most institutions. Faculty input in these latter areas was often ignored (Cowley 1980).

The 1930s saw the blossoming of faculty committee structures on most leading campuses. By 1939, William Haggerty and George Works (1939) found that two-fifths of faculty members employed by institutions served by the North Central Association of Colleges and Schools were on average sitting on two committees each. While two-thirds of such committees concentrated on administrative functions, a significant minority focused on issues of education policy. These developments culminated in the report of the AAUP's Committee on College and University Government (Committee T) that set forth five overarching principles for faculty participation in institutional governance.[7] Taken together, these principles mandated a role for faculty in the selection of administrators, in the formulation and control of education policy, and in the appointment and promotion processes. While the role promulgated was largely consultative, the AAUP document had as its foundation the premise that "faculty were not hired employees to be manipulated by president and trustees, but were academic professionals whose role involved teaching and contributing to the direction and major decisions of an institution" (Orr 1978, 347–48).

Perhaps even more fundamental, professors' expertise translated on their own campuses into leverage that enabled them to win tenure rights. Throughout the nineteenth century, the professoriate had labored without provisions for job security, as mere employees of their campuses who were subject to the will of presidents and trustees. Many full professors were on indefinite appointments, which simply meant that no length of term had been specified in their contract. Indefinite appointments were never the equivalent of permanent appointments, either in intent or law; and individuals on such appointments could be dismissed at any time (Metzger 1973). Moreover, for junior faculty, neither a recognized set of procedures nor a timetable had yet coalesced for attaining even these indefinite appointments that were the reward of a full professorship. An individual faculty member might serve his institution for fifteen or twenty years and yet be dismissed at any time, without reason and without a hearing. And this possibility was realized time and again, even at those institutions with a tradition of significant faculty influence, such as Yale and Wisconsin (Orr 1978). In its historical 1940 Statement of Principles of Academic Freedom and Tenure, culminating many years of negotiation with the Association of American Colleges, the AAUP articulated the concept of permanent faculty tenure, designed a means for regularizing the flow of decision making leading to tenure (by stipulating a six-year probationary period), and endorsed procedures to ensure due process in instances of nonreappointment (Metzger 1973, 148–55). By that time, the AAUP had sufficient stature to gain widespread institutional acceptance of its pronouncement, and by that time, too, most institutions had already formalized the system of academic ranks to provide the infrastructure for career progression (Orr 1978, v).

Off campus, the growing recognition of the faculty's specialized expertise brought them into public service on a scale theretofore unknown. Although the discipline-based public-service role of the professional scholar had germinated during the Progressive era and World War I, the number of faculty involved had been relatively small and their national exposure highly circumscribed. To illustrate: during the heyday of the Wisconsin Idea (1910–11), some thirty-three University of Wisconsin faculty members held official positions both with the state and with the university, mostly as agricultural experts or with the state railroad or tax commissions; thirteen others were "on call" at the capital as needed, including economists, lawyers, and political scientists.[8] Even so, fewer than 10% of the university faculty participated directly, and this group of participants was drawn from only a handful of disciplines (Veysey 1965).

During World War I, the faculty's public service to the nation was offered primarily through two vehicles: the National Board for Historical Service and the Committee on Public Information. The former, linked to the leadership of the American Historical Association, directed the efforts of several dozen historians to the revision of social studies curricula for secondary schools. Under the Committee on Public Information, some 100 social scientists were commissioned to prepare wartime propaganda pamphlets, while others were employed to monitor foreign-language newspaper editorials to detect disloyalty (Gruber 1976).

The national brain trust assembled by President Franklin Roosevelt to address the social and economic dislocation wrought by the Depression provided on an unprecedented scale a highly visible public showcase for faculty talent.

Between 1930 and 1935, forty-one independent and state-supported universities granted nearly 300 leaves to full-time faculty members for the express purpose of serving the federal government (Orr 1978). A much larger number of faculty served state and local governments "on overload." In the early 1940s, it was to academics that the federal government turned once again in support of the national defense effort associated with World War II. The Manhattan Project, which gave birth to the atomic bomb, is only the most dramatic and famous of innumerable faculty-assisted wartime projects. After the war this newfound visibility contributed to the legitimation of the professional role of the college faculty member. The esteem in which the public held members of the academic profession increased, as did the prestige attached to an academic career.[9]

The growing recognition of faculty as professionals served not only to elevate the profession but also to broaden entry into it. Professionalization permitted (although it by no means assured) the introduction of achievement-related criteria of success and a concomitant reduction in the salience of the ascriptive characteristics of social class and religious preference. Thus by 1940, the presence of Catholics and Jews within the ranks of faculty surged to constitute nearly one-quarter of what had been an exclusively Protestant profession; the sons of farmers and manual laborers were increasingly joining the sons of businessmen and professionals; and daughters were now joining the sons, comprising fully 13% of a sample of faculty affiliated with institutions accredited by the North Central Association (Kunkel 1938; Lipset and Ladd 1979).

By World War II, the various components of the contemporary academic role had at last crystallized into the highly differentiated model of today: teaching, research, and institutional and public service, all rooted in the faculty member's disciplinary expertise. The modern era of faculty roles and academic work had thus begun.

Growth and Diversification, 1940–1969

The thirty-year period between the onset of World War II and the close of the 1960s was characterized by unprecedented growth for American higher education and for faculty members. The rate of expansion, peaking in the late 1960s with the establishment by most states of large and diverse public systems of higher education designed to achieve goals of very broad—even near-universal—access, nearly doubled the ranks of college faculty between 1940 and 1960, from about 120,000 to 236,000 (Harris 1972, 484) and nearly doubled again in a single decade, 1960–70, from 236,00 to 450,000 (US Department of Education 1980).[10] Indeed, the number of new positions created between 1965 and 1970 alone exceeded the total number of positions extant in 1940 (Lipset and Ladd 1979).

This explosive growth was closely associated with diversification. Most critically, faculty members were pursuing careers in institutions with a much wider range of missions. By 1969, seven of ten faculty members were employed in the public (state) sector (home to less than half of them in 1940), and fully one in six faculty were employed at two-year institutions (Harris 1972). While the majority of faculty members were teaching in the liberal arts fields throughout this period, by 1960 the professions were beginning to rival the liberal arts in doctoral degree production (Berelson 1960)—a harbinger of things to come. Demographically, the gradual opening up of faculty ranks to women and to individuals from more diverse religious (non-Protestant) and racial and ethnic (nonwhite, non-European) backgrounds continued to proceed, if, initially, at glacial speed (Steinberg 1974; Oren 1985).

In the midst of such modest, if expanding, diversification of faculty characteristics, we nevertheless find a growing normative homogenization of the profession in at least one crucial aspect: the hold of the academic disciplines on faculty loyalties and commitments. Thus while student enrollments were burgeoning and diversifying, a critical component of what Christopher Jencks and David Riesman (1968) characterize as the "academic revolution," particularly the growing influence of one's field, exercised primarily through the socialization experience of graduate school and later through the disciplinary associations, had been narrowing the definition of the proper scope and standards of academic work. This model of the university scholar and his or her scholarship suffused the early professional socialization experience of that large, dominant cohort of faculty hired to staff the great expansion of higher education during the 1960s; and the broad acceptance of this outlook and orientation had, through the influence of this robust, energetic generation of faculty, largely penetrated the whole American system by the late 1960s.

The Last Quarter of the Twentieth Century and into the Twenty-First

Since the consummation of the academic revolution described by Jencks and Riesman (1968) and the concomitant crystallization of the model of the modern academic, American higher education has been pushed, forcefully, in new directions by the economic and technological changes to which we have alluded. Brief mention must suffice here to describe the expanding role of the federal government in underwriting university-based research activity, predominantly in the natural sciences. This substantial, if uneven, channeling of billions of dollars of funding has had pivotal effects in significantly bolstering and reallocating the research function among faculty at research-intensive institutions of higher education. The effects on faculty work distribution, on the "unbundling" phenomenon (mainly the further separation between research and teaching functions) on faculty status, and indeed on academic careers writ large, have been sweeping (Thelin 2004; Geiger 2004, 2011). Many believe that the face of American higher education has already morphed substantially, perhaps much of it beyond recognition, with much more transformation now under way and in the offing. How are these competing forces of change and stasis being resolved? How are the changes that have already manifested reshaping the nature of faculty work and careers? And how will they do so in the foreseeable future?

We postulated in chapter 1 that the seven decades of immense change in postsecondary education since World War II can be viewed as having progressed through several phases, and, then, in very recent years—indeed, during this past decade—thrust into an unprecedented new era. So great has been the change in environment (social, cultural, political, economic) pressing on postsecondary education, and so dramatic have been the changes in policies and work-a-day practices that reflect institutions' adaptations, that, historically speaking, this unequivocally new era is manifest. We label this unique conjunction of conditions as Paradigm Three. In this chapter we identify the precedents leading to this new model, and in chapter 1 we outline the distinctive characteristics of this newly emergent system.

A decade ago John Thelin (2004) ended his fine history of American higher education with the observation that the challenge confronting higher education, beyond the usual strictures of funding, is "rediscovering essential principles and values" amid a rapidly changing environment. He proposes that "going back to the basics . . . of institutional purpose . . . can once again connect past and present as a prelude to creating an appropriate future" (362). Our undertaking in this volume accepts that challenge by attempting to outline a plausible pathway forward (albeit obstacle strewn). We seek to make a compelling case for preserving traditional strengths (quite apparently too easily underappreciated) while acknowledging the irreversible realities of postsecondary education in an exceedingly fluid, unstable environment. As we have noted, a new era has suffused all dimensions of the postsecondary enterprise. How best can we accommodate these new realities while striving to preserve essential core values? That is our task.

Plentiful evidence, reported in subsequent chapters of this volume and previewed in chapter 1, suggests that the academic revolution of the 1960s, insofar as it crystalized faculty professionalization and expanded faculty influence in matters academic, has been fraying at the edges (Thelin 2004, 332); palpable changes are well under way in the nature of faculty life and work. Faculty careers, for example, appear to be becoming less exclusive, that is, there is increasing traffic between college teaching and other employment, especially between one's campus-based career and one's off-campus professional practice—and also less preemptive, that is, less of a career preoccupation that demands and consumes all available time. For most part-time faculty, this is obviously true, by definition. But increasingly, for regular, full-time faculty, there are competing claims on their time: economic pressures have led some of them to redirect a part of their energies to extramural income-generating pursuits (that is, other concurrent employment); for others, a lack of congruence between individual faculty orientations and changing institutional missions have led to disengagement from institutional life to pursue other life interests. This has led many observers to decry the decline of "academic citizenship" (Cross 1994).

This putative retreat comes anomalously at a time when, first, commitments to enhancing the quality of campus life should be increasing (given the burgeoning contingent of senior faculty, who by virtue of their loyalty and know-how have traditionally been the most valued and valuable academic citizens) and, second, when that interest needs to be intensified (as proportionately fewer full-time faculty positions devolve more institutional responsibility on the now shrinking proportion of regular, full-time faculty). Greater attention has been paid in recent years, an era of increasing student consumerism (Thelin 2004, 330; 2013), to the escalating importance of the faculty's teaching role; and indeed a significant and rapidly growing segment of the faculty—part-time and non-tenure-eligible faculty members—have their on-the-job responsibilities explicitly limited to teaching.

For perspective on the authors' treatment of the American faculty's evolution and current challenges, it will be useful to invoke other scholars' characterizations of the post–World War II era. Perhaps most relevant for present purposes is to consult the work of the prominent education historian Roger L. Geiger (2011, 37–68; 2013). In his much-cited *The Ten Generations of American*

Higher Education, Geiger describes two postwar "generations." His ninth, "The Academic Revolution, 1945–1975," is followed by the tenth such generation, "Regulation, Relevance, and the Steady State, 1975–2010." We find highly instructive his concise concluding comment: "The economic turmoil of 2008–10 almost certainly signaled the passing of generation 10 and the probable inception of new trends as yet too inchoate to identify" (64). And that observation is precisely where our own thesis—of a successive era that we label a third postwar paradigm—embarks. That is to say, Geiger's two postwar eras, the latter characterized as relatively stable, begin to unravel in the tumult occasioned by the recent sharp economic downturn and successive destabilizing waves of technological change. (See also Altbach, Gumport, and Berdahl 2011.)

Issues such as these are relevant not only to the American faculty as an aggregate body but especially to the cohorts of new entrants that colleges and universities have begun hiring in recent years (Finkelstein, Seal, and Schuster 1998) and accelerating markedly during the early years of the twenty-first century. This raises the crucial question: How will these major shifts in the composition of the faculty, especially in the dramatic reallocation of types of appointments (previewed in chapter 1 and explicated in subsequent chapters), play out with respect to this critical group who will, after all, serve as the American faculty of the first decades of the twenty-first century? Will these changes inevitably constitute a further revolution in American academic life? More fundamental, is the very nature of higher education, as some contend, being transformed—its values and priorities, its institutional organization, and, of course, its faculty—into a "system" that will swiftly become barely recognizable from today's vantage point? Or will changes now in motion merely amount to the more transient disjunction that the system fostered after World War II but that can, with effort, be accommodated? And whatever the disruption, will the nation have the faculty—in adequate quantity, requisite expertise, and sufficient commitment—that is required to staff its institutions for years to come? It is to questions such as these that the current volume is addressed, by reassessing the faculty factor and weighing the implications.

NOTES

1. An earlier succinct account of the importance of context is found in Schuster and Finkelstein (2006, chap. 2).

2. The authors acknowledge that standard histories of American higher education, and of its faculty, focus disproportionately on the more established, more prestigious in-

stitutions of higher education; this circumstance reflects in part the quality of accessibility of resource materials, including institutional archives. There are important exceptions, however, that do highlight historical developments in particular subsectors. A few such examples include women's higher education (Solomon, 1986), historically black colleges and universities (Gasman and Tudico 2008), Catholic higher education (Gleason 1995), and two-year institutions (Cohen, Brawer, and Kisker 2014).

3. Seven of the eight professors at Brown during the eighteenth century had such training (*Historical Catalogue* 1905), as did all ten professors at Harvard (Eliot 1848).

4. It should be noted, however, that those full professors who left teaching averaged nearly two decades in their institutional positions (21.2 years at Brown, 18.5 years at Bowdoin), so that college teaching still constituted a significant span in their careers (Finkelstein 1983).

5. The four "active" faculty were Caswell at Brown, Cleaveland at Bowdoin, Peck at Harvard, and, at Yale, Silliman who had in 1824 founded the *American Journal of Science.* While many of their colleagues were publishing *something*, their work consisted chiefly of collections of sermons and addresses made at commencements and other public occasions (Finkelstein 1984, 16).

6. Other institutions lagged a decade or more behind these developments. At Dartmouth, as late as 1851, three-quarters of the faculty continued to participate actively in the community as preachers, licentiates, or ordained ministers and as civic boosters. By the late 1870s, however, the proportion of faculty engaged in clerical activities had plummeted to 15%, while more than half were then significantly engaged in scientific associations in their fields of specialization (Tobias 1982). At Wisconsin, by the early 1870s, professors at the university were called on to head the state geological survey (Curti and Carstensen 1949).

7. That Committee T was the second committee organized by the AAUP (in 1916, one year after the association's founding) indicates the importance the professoriate attached to what came to be called "shared governance." The committee's original name—College and University Government—reflects that the more contemporary "governance" is latter-day terminology; that term was not customarily employed for these purposes until after World War II.

8. The "Wisconsin idea" refers to the use of applied research in the public interest; mutual cooperation of a campus and a state's capital. See Thelin 2004, 137–38.

9. Howard Bowen (1977) has documented the close association of public attitudes toward academe and levels of faculty salaries. He pinpoints World War II as marking a major upturn in both the level and rate of real growth in faculty salaries.

10. The numbers are for faculty at the rank of instructor or above offering resident, degree-credit instruction. This includes both full-time and part-time faculty offering instruction in on-campus degree programs but excludes those offering nondegree instruction or instruction off campus. The figure for 1940 is estimated from the total instructional staff figure (US Department of Education 1980). Further data are provided in chapter 3.

REFERENCES

Altbach, Philip G., Patricia J. Gumport, and Robert O. Berdahl, eds. 2011. *American Higher Education in the Twenty-First Century: Social, Political, and Economic Challenge.* 3rd ed. Baltimore, MD: Johns Hopkins University Press.

Baldridge, J. Victor, David Curtis, George Ecker, and Gary Riley. 1978. *Policy Making and Effective Leadership: A National Study of Academic Management.* San Francisco, CA: Jossey-Bass.

Berelson, Bernard. 1960. *Graduate Education in the United States.* New York: McGraw-Hill.

Bowen, Howard R. 1977. *Investment in Learning: The Individual and Social Value of American Higher Education.* San Francisco, CA: Jossey-Bass.

Brubacher, John, and Willis Rudy. 1968. *Higher Education in Transition.* Rev. ed. New York: Harper and Row.

Burke, Colin. 1982. *American Collegiate Populations.* New York: New York University Press.

Calhoun, Daniel. 1965. *Professional Lives in America.* Cambridge, MA: Harvard University Press.

Carrell, William. 1968. "American College Professors: 1750–1800." *History of Education Quarterly* 8 (Autumn): 289–305.

Cohen, Arthur M., Florence B. Brawer, and Carrie B. Kisker. 2014. *The American Community College.* 6th ed. San Francisco, CA: Jossey-Bass.

Cowley, William H. 1980. *Professors, Presidents, and Trustees.* Edited by Donald Williams. San Francisco, CA: Jossey-Bass.

Cross, K. Patricia. 1994. "Academic Citizenship." *American Association for Higher Education Bulletin 1994–1995* 47 (September): 3–5.

Curti, Merle E., and Vernon Carstensen. 1949. *The University of Wisconsin: A History.* Vol. 2, *1848–1925.* Madison, WI: University of Wisconsin Press.

Dwight, Timothy. 1903. *Memories of Yale Life and Men, 1845–1899.* New York: Dodd, Mead.

Eliot, Samuel. 1848. *A Sketch of the History of Harvard College.* Boston: Little, Brown.

Finkelstein, Martin J. 1983. "From Tutor to Professor: The Development of the Modern Academic Role at Six Institutions during the Nineteenth Century." *History of Higher Education Annual* 3:99–121.

———. 1984. *The American Academic Profession: A Synthesis of Social Scientific Inquiry since World War II.* Columbus, OH: Ohio State University Press.

Finkelstein, Martin J., Robert K. Seal, and Jack H. Schuster. 1998. *The New Academic Generation: A Profession in Transformation.* Baltimore, MD: Johns Hopkins University Press.

Gasman, Marybeth, and Christopher L. Tudico. 2008. *Historically Black Colleges and Universities.* London: Palgrave Macmillan.

Geiger, Roger L. 2004. *Research and Relevant Knowledge: American Research Universities since World War II.* 2nd ed. New Brunswick, NJ: Transaction.

———. 2011. "The Ten Generations of American Higher Education." In *American Higher Education in the Twenty-First Century: Social, Political, and Economic Challenges.* 3rd ed. Edited by Philip G. Altbach, Patricia G. Gumport, and Robert O. Berdahl, 37–68. Baltimore, MD: Johns Hopkins University Press.

———. 2013. "Postmortem for the Current Era: Change in American Higher Education, 1980–2010." *Higher Education Forum* 10 (March): 1–21. Research Institute for Higher Education, Hiroshima University.

Gleason, Philip. 1995. *Contending with Modernity: Catholic Higher Education in the Twentieth Century.* New York: Oxford University.

Grant, Vance W., and Leo J. Elden. 1980. *Digest of Education Statistics 1980.* NCES 80-401. National Center for Education Statistics, Institute of Educational Sciences. Washington, DC: US Department of Education.

Gruber, Marilyn. 1976. *Mars and Minerva.* Baton Rouge, LA: Louisiana State University Press.

Haggerty, William, and George Works. 1939. *Faculties of Colleges and Universities Accredited by the North Central Association of Colleges and Secondary Schools, 1930–1937.* Publication 12. Chicago: Commission on Institutions of Higher Education, North Central Association.

Harris, Seymour E. 1972. *A Statistical Portrait of Higher Education.* New York: McGraw-Hill.

Historical Catalogue of Brown University, 1764–1904. 1905. Providence, RI: Brown University.

Hofstadter, Richard, and Walter Metzger. 1955. *The Development of Academic Freedom in the United States.* New York: Columbia University Press.

Jencks, Christopher, and David Riesman. 1968. *The Academic Revolution.* Garden City, NY: Doubleday.

Kerr, Clark. 1991. *The Great Transformation in Higher Education, 1960–1980.* Albany, NY: State University of New York Press.

———. 2001. *The Uses of the University.* 5th ed. Cambridge, MA: Harvard University Press.

Kunkel, B. W. 1938. "A Survey of College Faculties." *American Association of University Professors Bulletin* 24 (March): 249–62.

Lipset, Seymour, and Everett C. Ladd Jr. 1979. "The Changing Social Origins of American Academics." In *Qualitative and Quantitative Social Research*, edited by Robert Merton, James S. Coleman, and Peter H. Rossi. Glencoe, IL: Free Press.

McCaughey, Robert M. 1974. "The Transformation of American Academic Life: Harvard University, 1821–1892." *Perspectives in American History* 8:239–334.

Metzger, Walter P. 1973. "Academic Tenure in America: A Historical Essay." In *Faculty Tenure: A Report and Recommendations by the Commission on Academic Tenure in Higher Education*, 93–159. San Francisco. CA: Jossey-Bass.

———. 1987. "The Academic Profession in the United States." In *The Academic Profession: National, Disciplinary, and Institutional Settings*, edited by Burton R. Clark, 123–208. Berkeley, CA: University of California Press.

Morison, Samuel E. 1936. *Harvard College in the Seventeenth Century.* Cambridge, MA: Harvard University Press.

Oleson, Alexandra, and John Voss, eds. 1979. *The Organization of Knowledge in Modern America, 1860–1880.* Baltimore, MD: Johns Hopkins University Press.

Oren, Dan A. 1985. *Joining the Club: A History of Jews and Yale.* New Haven, CT: Yale University Press.

Orr, Kenneth B. 1978. "The Impact of the Depression Years, 1929–39, on Faculty in American Colleges and Universities." PhD diss., University of Michigan, Ann Arbor.

Packard, Alpheus, ed. 1882. *History of Bowdoin College.* Boston, MA: James Ripley Osgood and Co.

Richardson, Leon D. 1932. *History of Dartmouth College.* Vol. 2. Hanover, NH: Dartmouth College Publications.

Rudolph, Frederick. 1956. *Mark Hopkins and the Log.* New Haven, CT: Yale University Press.

———. 1962. *The American College and University: A History.* New York: Random House.

Schuster, Jack H., and Martin J. Finkelstein. 2006. *The American Faculty: The Restructuring of Academic Work and Careers.* Baltimore, MD: Johns Hopkins University Press.

Scott, W. Richard. 1966. "Professionals in Bureaucracies: Areas of Conflict." In *Professionalization*, edited by Howard M. Vollmer and D. L. Mills. Englewood Cliffs, NJ: Prentice Hall.

Solomon, Barbara M. 1986. *In the Company of Educated Women: A History of Women in Higher Education in America.* New Haven, CT: Yale University Press.
Steinberg, Stephen. 1974. *The Academic Melting Pot: Catholics and Jews in American Higher Education.* New York: McGraw-Hill.
Thelin, John R. 2004. *A History of American Higher Education.* Baltimore, MD: Johns Hopkins University Press.
———. 2013. *The Rising Costs of Higher Education: A Reference Handbook.* Baltimore, MD: Johns Hopkins University Press.
Tobias, Marilyn. 1982. *Old Dartmouth on Trial.* New York: New York University Press.
Trow, Martin. 1973. "Problems in the Transition from Elite to Mass Higher Education." In *Policies for Higher Education, from the General Report on the Conference on Future Structures of Post-Secondary Education*, 55–101. Paris: Organization for Economic Cooperation and Development.
US Department of Education (USDE). 1980. *Digest of Education Statistics 1980.* Washington, DC: National Center for Education Statistics.
Veysey, Laurence R. 1965. *The Emergence of the American University.* Chicago: University of Chicago Press.
Wertenbaker, Thomas J. 1946. *Princeton, 1746–1896.* Princeton, NJ: Princeton University Press.
Wolfle, Dale. 1972. *The Home of Science.* New York: McGraw-Hill.

3

The Faculty in Profile

We began *The American Faculty* (Schuster and Finkelstein 2006) with the broad characterization of the American professoriate since 1970—much like that of American higher education itself—as massively expanded and diversifying at an accelerating pace. As the number of colleges and university grew between 1979 and 2013 by more than 50%, from about 3,100 to more than 4,700, and enrollments expanded from about 11 million to 20 million students, the instructional staff of colleges and universities more than doubled, from nearly 675,000 to more than 1.5 million. Moreover, unlike previous expansions, which largely saw replication of the status quo ante, this one was distinctive for its associated diversification: most dramatically the restructuring of academic appointments off the historical career ladder, the influx of women, the aging of the faculty, and the shifting center of gravity from the liberal arts to the professions and from the research university sector to the prebaccalaureate sector, including the emergence of for-profit providers.

In what follows, we first extend the portrait of the demographic revolution in the composition of faculty over time by continuing the story beyond the first half decade of the twenty-first century through the advent of the second decade, factoring in any disruptive effects of the Great Recession of 2008, from which the United States was still slowly recovering in 2015. Has expansion and diversification continued at its prerecession pace? Atrophied? Accelerated? Second, we provide a finer and more nuanced examination of how the story has unfolded somewhat idiosyncratically within the distinctive contexts of the increasingly diverse mix of institutional settings defining American higher education. Does the aggregate picture we drew in 2006, overall and across three broad institutional types (two-year, four-year, and university), irrespective of sector, adequately account for system diversification when we now distinguish the private from the public sector and, within the private sector, between the nonprofit and the growing for-profit sector?[1]

In telling this more finely nuanced story, our strategy has been to sharpen and extend the institutional lenses we bring to the analysis while we limit the number of data points we consider within each institutional lens, owing at once to the requirements of manageability as well as some of the limitations of data availability.[2] Before proceeding to our finer-grained analyses of growth and diversification within institutional types and sectors, we begin with a second look at institutional growth in American higher education since 1979—the basic context within which the academic profession has evolved over the past half century.

The Changing Institutional Landscape

Tables 3.1 and 3.2 display the number of institutions and student enrollment from 1979 through 2013, while figure 3.1 displays the total number of full-time and part-time faculty over the same years.[3] The first observation to be made concerns the rate of expansion: while the 1960s and 1970s are usually viewed as a period of unprecedented growth, expansion in faculty numbers continued at only a slightly diminished rate over the next thirty-five years. The number of institutions increased by 50%, from 2,000 to 3,000, during the 1960s and 1970s but by nearly 50% again between 1979 and 2013, from about 3,100 to 4,700. Student enrollments more than tripled during the 1960–80 period, from 3.5 million to 11.5 million, and increased again by more than 50% between 1979 and 2013. The size of instructional staffs increased by nearly 70% between 1960 and 1980 (from 380,000 to 675,000) and more than doubled between 1979 and 2013, from 675,000 to more than 1.5 million (figure 3.1).[4]

A second set of observations relates to diversification. During the 1960s and 1970s, the two-year college sector mushroomed from a barely visible presence to nearly 30% of the institutional sector; during the subsequent thirty-five years (1979–2013), the for-profit providers emerged from relative obscurity to claim their place in the academic sun, representing virtually one-sixth of the institutional sector. The trend in student enrollment has been even more pronounced: while the four-year and university sectors dominated during the 1960s and, to a lesser extent, the 1970s, by 2013 the two-year sector (7.0 million) and the for-profit providers (1.7 million) were claiming more than two-fifths (40%) of all postsecondary student enrollment (table 3.2).

Table 3.1 Number of postsecondary institutions, by type and control of institution, 1979–2013

Institution type	1979	1989	1993	1999	2003	2005	2011	2013	% change, 1979–99	% change, 1999–2013
All	3,134	3,565	3,679	4,048	4,236	4,216	4,599	4,726	29.2	16.7
Public	1,474	1,582	1,647	1,681	1,720	1,700	1,656	1,623	14.0	–3.5
Private	1,564	1,658	1,718	1,695	1,664	1,637	1,630	1,652	8.4	–2.5
For-profit	96	325	314	672	852	879	1,313	1,451	600.0	115.9
Four-year	1,941	2,129	2,237	2,335	2,530	2,533	2,870	3,026	20.3	29.6
Public	550	598	617	612	634	639	678	689	11.3	12.6
Private	1,376	1,478	1,538	1,531	1,546	1,525	1,543	1,555	11.3	1.6
For-profit	15	53	82	192	350	369	649	782	1,180.0	307.3
Two-year	1,193	1,436	1,442	1,713	1,706	1,683	1,729	1,700	43.6	–0.8
Public	924	984	1,030	1,069	1,086	1,061	978	934	15.7	–12.6
Private	188	180	180	164	118	112	87	97	–12.8	–40.9
For-profit	81	272	232	480	502	510	664	669	492.6	39.4

Sources: HEGIS:1966–86; IPEDS-IC:1986–2013. (Refer to appendix A for key.)

Table 3.2 Enrollment in postsecondary education, by type and control of institution, 1979–2013

Institution type	1979	1989	1993	1999	2003	2005	2013	% change, 1979–99	% change, 1999–2013
All combined	11,569,899	13,740,686	14,448,295	14,791,224	16,900,471	17,487,475	20,616,377	27.8	39.4
Public	9,036,822	10,577,963	11,258,203	11,309,399	12,857,059	13,021,834	14,809,682	25.1	31.0
Private	2,533,077	2,960,597	2,982,374	3,051,626	3,340,718	3,454,692	4,108,648	20.5	34.6
For-profit	—	202,126	207,718	430,199	702,694	1,010,949	1,698,047		294.7
Four-year	7,353,233	8,440,212	8,886,646	9,198,525	10,407,553	10,999,420	13,610,136	25.1	48.0
Public	4,980,012	5,694,303	5,908,584	5,969,950	6,649,441	6,837,605	8,174,936	19.9	36.9
Private	2,373,221	2,693,368	2,891,528	2,989,285	3,296,882	3,411,170	4,076,450	26.0	36.4
For-profit	—	52,541	86,534	239,290	461,230	750,645	1,358,750		467.8
Two-year	4,216,666	5,300,474	5,561,649	5,592,699	6,492,918	6,488,055	7,006,241	32.6	25.3
Public	4,056,810	4,883,660	5,349,619	5,339,449	6,207,618	6,184,229	6,634,746	31.6	24.3
Private	159,856	267,229	90,846	62,341	43,836	43,522	32,198	−61.0	−48.4
For-profit	—	149,585	121,184	190,909	241,464	260,304	339,297		77.7

Sources: HEGIS:1979–86; IPEDS-IC:1988–2013. (Refer to appendix A for key.)

Note: For-profit enrollment breakdown not available for 1979 or 1989.

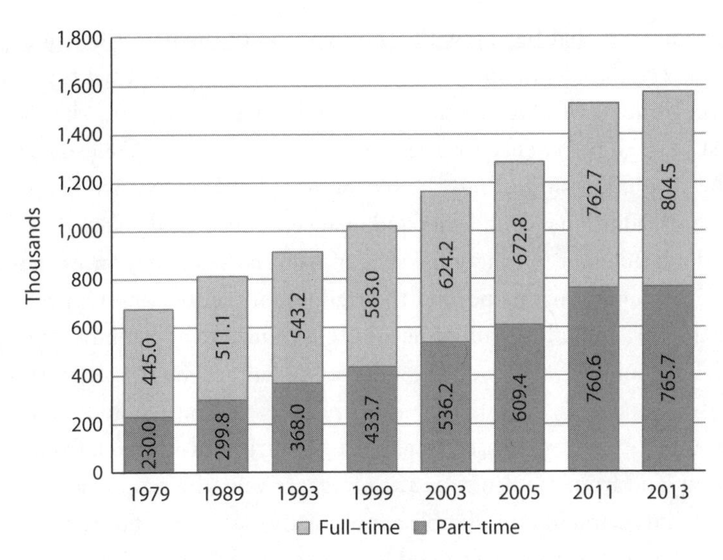

Figure 3.1 Number of faculty (in thousands), by employment status, 1979–2013. *Sources:* HEGIS: 1979–86; IPEDS-IC:1986–2013. (Refer to appendix A for key to data sources.)

The faculty are, however, another story. While for-profits constitute more than one-quarter of all institutions (28.5%), they employ only about 9% of the headcount faculty (3.5% of the full-time faculty). Two-year colleges, on the other hand, which also constitute nearly a quarter of all institutions (23.2%), employ a commensurate proportion of the headcount instructional staff (one-quarter, or 25.0%) but only about one-seventh of the full-time faculty (15.1 %). In stark contrast to both for-profits and the two-year nonprofits, the public and private four-year institutions constitute not quite half of the institutional universe but account for nearly two-thirds (65.9%) of all instructional staff and more than four-fifths (81.5%) of all the full-time faculty. Thus while institutional diversification has continued—even accelerated—over the past thirty years,[5] the plurality of American faculty, especially full-time faculty, remain in the four-year collegiate and university sectors.[6]

The Changing Distribution of Faculty Appointments

Although the past half century is defined by sheer numerical growth in the faculty, there are incipient signs of diversification within that growth in terms of where the faculty work. This aspect of diversification pales, however, in comparison with that fueled by the proliferation of the new kinds of appointments. In *The American Faculty*, we identified such an appointments revolution as transforming the faculty of our colleges and universities during the 1990s and the first years of the twenty-first century.[7] The currently available data suggest that the revolution surges into the second decade of the twenty-first century, adding both additional complexity and nuance. Figure 3.2 displays the percentage of the headcount instructional staff of America's colleges on various kinds of academic appointments beyond the traditional tenured and tenure-earning appointments, including full-time limited-contract (non-tenure-track) and part-time appointments as well as graduate-student teaching assistantships, between 1979 and 2013. While the actual number of tenured and tenure-track faculty appointments increased by about 10% during that period, from 274,890 to 306,737 and from 111,829 to 124,533, respectively, the proportion of all faculty on tenured and tenure-eligible appointments as seen in figure 3.2 declined by nearly half (from 29.0 to 17.2 and from 16.1 to 7.0%, respectively), while the proportion on full-time limited-term (non-tenure-track) appointments increased by half (from 10.3 to 14.9% of the total) and that on part-time appointments increased by 75% from 24.0 to 43.0%.[8] While part-timers had constituted one out of four instructional staff in 1979, by 2013 they accounted for 43% of the corps of 1.5 million instructional staff in the United States. The disjunction between modest growth in numbers and striking proportionate decline of tenured and tenure-eligible appointment reflects, of course, the sheer growth in the total number of faculty appointments over the nearly thirty-five-year period—most of which were of the nontraditional variety.

When we drill down from the aggregate level to examine specifically trends in the new faculty hires (figure 3.3)—those full-time faculty who appear on university payrolls for the first time and who will constitute the core of the faculty in the next generation[9]—we find the trend even more pronounced: non-tenure-track, limited-term appointees continue to constitute a majority of all new full-time hires.[10] This is the case in 2003 and again in 2011, where the trend lines of tenure-track and non-tenure-track new hires begin their most dramatic divergence, defined principally by the accelerated decline in the proportion of new hires on the tenure track. Between 2005 and 2007, that divergence narrowed abruptly, only to reestablish itself in 2009. Similarly, between 2011 and 2013, we see another narrowing of the gap between on- and off-track new hires—and whether the gap is cyclically reestablished or continues to narrow remains to be seen in 2015 and 2017 data to come.

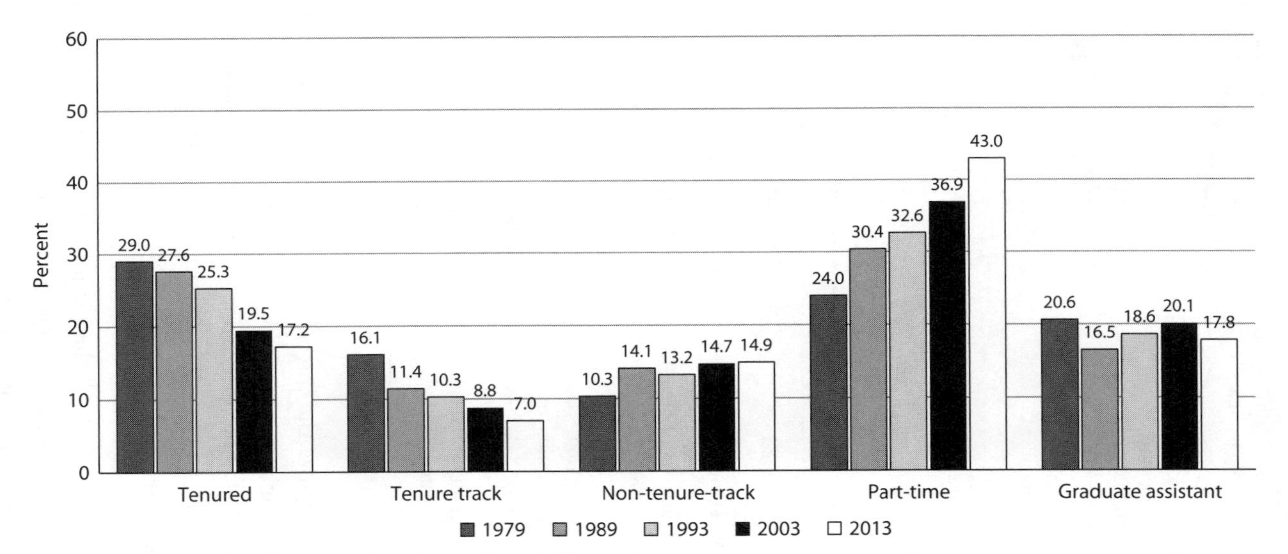

Figure 3.2 Percentage distribution of faculty, by appointment type, 1979–2013. *Source:* Derived from tabulation by AAUP Research Office, based on data from IPEDS. Released April 2013.

Note: Figures are for degree-granting institutions only, but the precise category of the included institutions has changed over time. Graduate assistant includes teaching and research assistants. Graduate assistant totals for 1979 and 1989 are approximate totals.

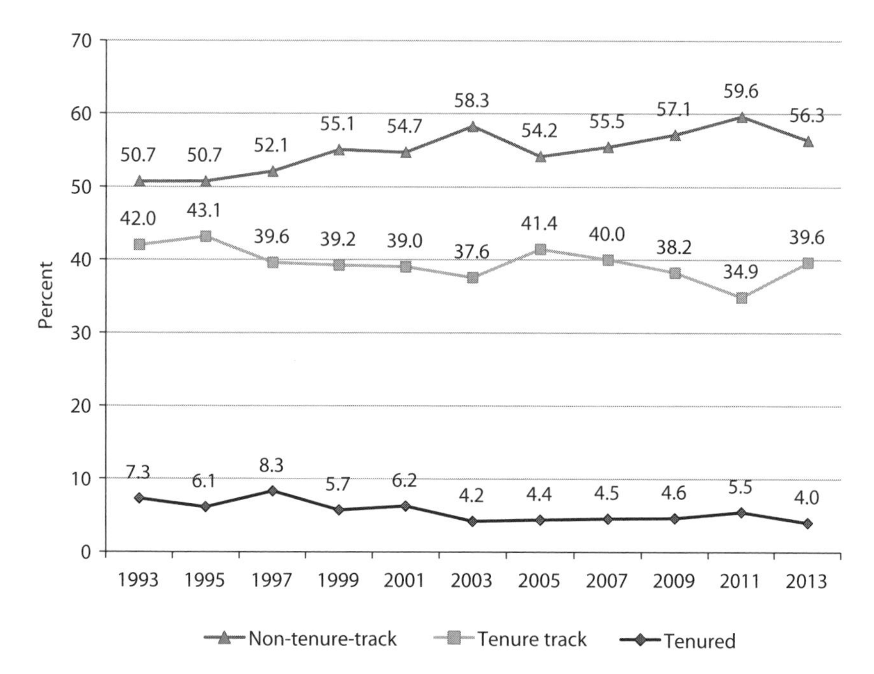

Figure 3.3 Percentage distribution of new full-time faculty hires in Title IV institutions, by appointment type, 1993–2013. *Source:* IPEDS:1993–2013. (Refer to appendix A for key to data sources.)

Note: Title IV (degree-granting) four-year public, four-year private, four-year for-profit, two-year public, two-year private, and two-year for-profit institutions. Title IV institutions have a written agreement with the secretary of education that allows the institution to participate in any of the Title IV federal student financial assistance programs (other than the State Student Incentive Grant [SSIG] and the National Early Intervention Scholarship and Partnership [NEISP] programs).

Figures 3.4 and 3.5 explore the intersection of diversification in appointment types with institutional types by displaying the distribution of appointment categories for each of three institutional types at three points in time: 1993, 2003, and 2013—first in the public (figure 3.4) and then in the private sector (figure 3.5). In 1993, about three-fifths of the faculty in public sector four-year institutions were tenured or on tenure track (ranging from 62.2% at the research universities to 58.9% at the institutions awarding bachelor and master's degrees). By 2003, that majority had shrunk to just over half (53.5%) at the public research universities and dipped to below half (48.7%) at the public bachelor's- and master's-conferring institutions. By 2013, that figure had

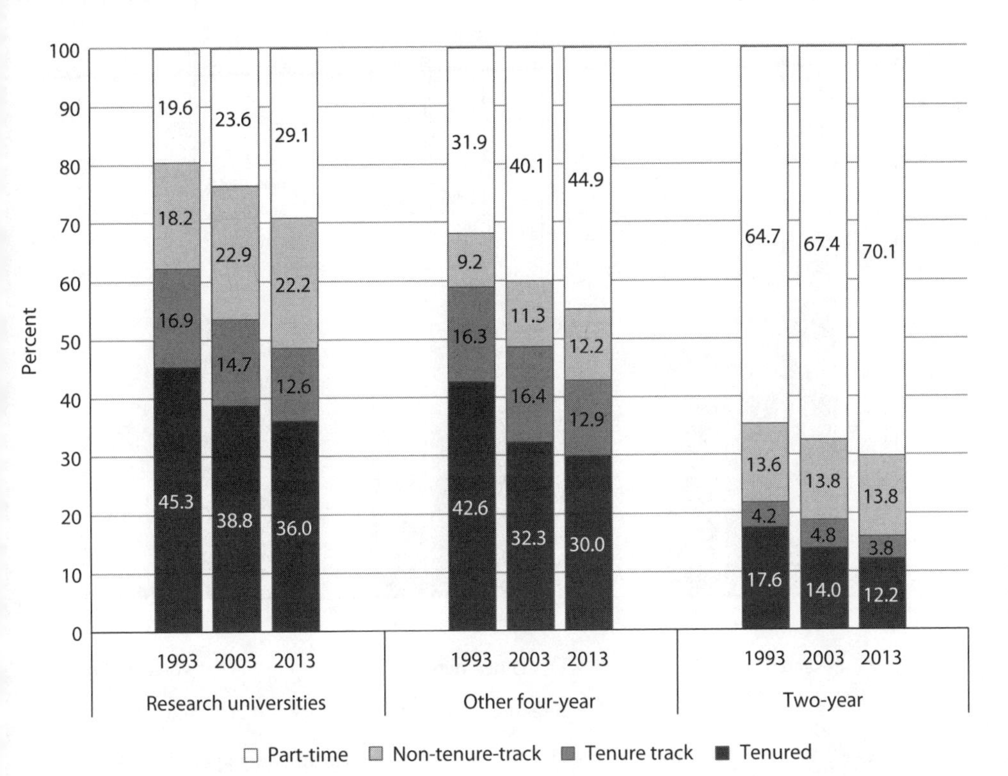

Figure 3.4 Percentage distribution of faculty in public institutions, by appointment type and type of institution, 1993, 2003, and 2013. *Sources:* IPEDS:93; IPEDS:03; IPEDS:13. (Refer to appendix A for key to data sources.)

Note: Includes four-year public and two-year public institutions.

---

shrunk again to just over two-fifths (48.6 and 42.9%, respectively). In the private sector (see figure 3.5), where tenure was already less pervasive, the bare majority of faculty (50.0%) in 1993 were either tenured or on tenure track at the research universities and about 42.1% at the bachelor's- and master's-conferring institutions—lower than where the public sector would "descend" by 2003. By 2003, the proportions of faculty who were tenured or on the tenure-track had dropped precipitously at the private research universities from 50.0 to 38.2% and from 42.1 to 32.0% at the private bachelor's- and master's-conferring institutions, respectively. From 2003 to 2013, the drop was fairly modest, suggesting clearly that in the private, four-year sector, the appointments revolution had largely been consummated by 2003, while, as we have seen, the public

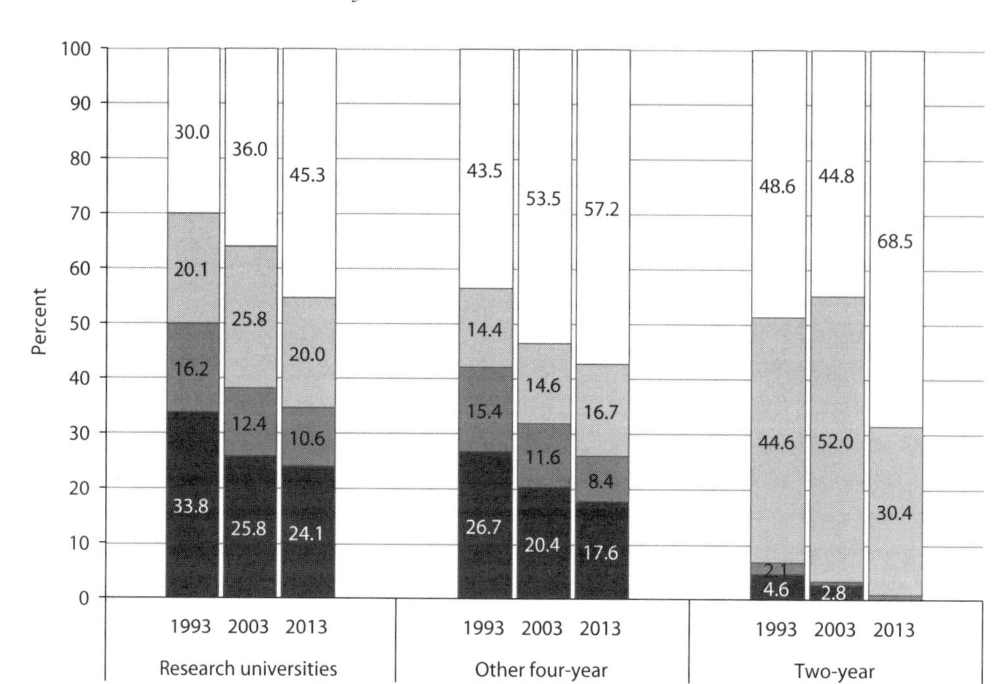

Figure 3.5 Percentage distribution of faculty in private institutions, by appointment type and type of institution, 1993, 2003, and 2013. *Sources:* IPEDS:93; IPEDS:03; IPEDS:13. (Refer to appendix A for key to data sources.)

Note: Includes four-year private nonprofit, four-year for-profit, two-year private nonprofit, and two-year for-profit institutions. Values too small to show on the figure are as follows: two-year tenure-track faculty: 2003, 0.5%, and 2013, 0.1%; two-year tenured faculty 2013, 0.9%.

sector experienced initially less dramatic, but more nearly equal rates of decline in traditional appointments over the two periods.

The two-year institutions in both the public and private sectors tell a somewhat different story. Part-time appointments dominated the two-year public sector in 1993 (nearly two-thirds of all faculty appointments) and very slightly increased that dominance over the ensuing two decades, constituting seven-tenths of faculty appointments by 2013. Concomitantly, the modest proportion of tenured and tenure-track appointments shrunk from about one-fifth (21.8%) to one-sixth (16.0%) of the faculty. In the private, two-year sector, we see a different pattern. While these institutions have always relied on part-time faculty (just under half of the teaching force), between 2003 and 2013 there was a dramatic upswing in part-time appointments (68.5%) and an equally dramatic shrinkage in the small proportion of tenured and tenure-track faculty from about one-twentieth in 1993 (6.7%) to barely 1% by 2013. They continue to rely on a substantial core (nearly one-third of their teaching force) of full-time, fixed-contract faculty.

The appointments revolution has touched on every sector of American higher education without exception, that is, the revolution has spread to the research university as well as the two-year community college sector, although it has swept more quickly and dramatically through the private sector than the public. That was already abundantly clear in 1993; and these developments have only accelerated since. That said, it appears that the type of "new" appointment preferred seems to vary by institutional type if not sector. Among public two-year institutions, part-time appointments have been and remain the dominant form of contingency; that is increasingly true of the private two-year sector, as well. Among research universities in both the public and private sector, one can, however, discern a trend toward stability in the use of full-time non-tenure-track appointments. Indeed, in 1993, the proportion of full-time, non-tenure-track, and part-time appointments was about equal, at about one-fifth of the instructional staff (10% higher in the private sector); by 2013, full-time off-track appointments remained about one-fifth of all appointments at the research universities, while part-time appointments increased their profile by 50% in both the public and private sector, accounting for nearly one-third of appointments in the former and more than two-fifths in the latter. That said, it should be noted that the appointments profile of research universities, both private and public, changes substantially when one factors in the widespread use of graduate teaching assistants who have historically been a backbone of undergraduate instruction, especially in the lower division courses. When factoring graduate teaching assistants as another form of part-time faculty—as in figure 3.6—into the mix, the profile of research universities bears a striking resemblance to that of other four-year institutions and diverges much less dramatically from the profile of the community colleges.

Yet another lens for illuminating the silent revolution before us is to examine ratios among types of faculty appointments. Figure 3.7 specifically displays two ratios—the ratio of full-time to part-time faculty and the ratio of tenured and tenure-track to non-tenure track, fixed-contract faculty—at three points in time for three types of institutions. At the research universities, the ratio of

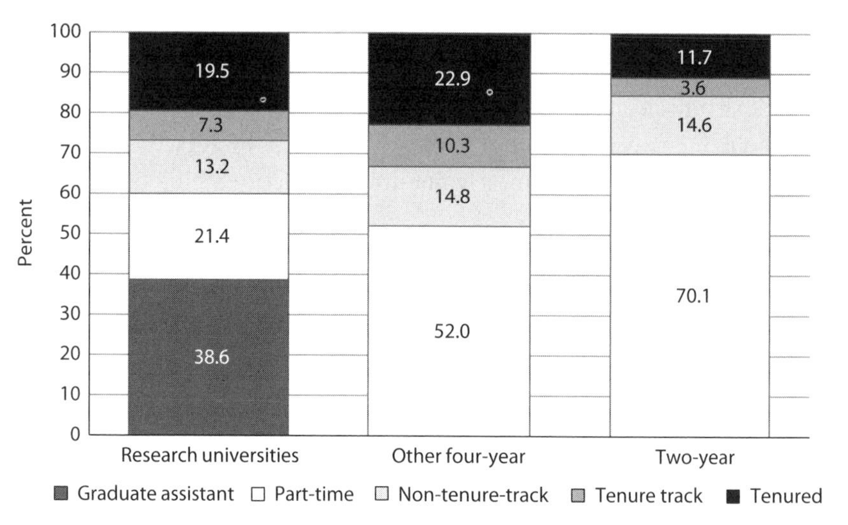

Figure 3.6 Percentage distribution of faculty by appointment type and type of institution, including graduate assistants, 2013. *Sources:* IPEDS:93; IPEDS:03; IPEDS:13. (Refer to appendix A for key to data sources.)

Note: Includes research universities (public); research universities (private); and two-year public, two-year private, and two-year for-profit institutions. Graduate assistants in research universities include both teaching and research assistants.

---

full- to part-time faculty shrunk from 3.4:1 in 1993 to 1.9:1 by 2013, that is, from 3.4 full-time faculty for every part-time faculty member to 1.9 full-time faculty for every part-time faculty member. During that same period, albeit only slightly less dramatically, the ratio of tenured and tenure-track to contract faculty shrank from 3:1 to 2:1—underlining what is the big story at the research universities. At institutions conferring bachelor's and master's degrees, part-time faculty have historically been a more essential part of the instructional staffing picture. In 1993, full-timers outnumbered part-timers by 1.6 to 1; by 2013, part-timers had surpassed the number of full-timers (full-time to part-time ratio under 1.0). At the same time, the dominance of tenured and tenure-track faculty among the full-time staff in 1993 (nearly 4.3:1) had been halved by 2013 (2.2:1). Unlike the research universities, four-year institutions that confer bachelor's and master's degrees have experienced dramatic realignments in both ratios over these two decades. At both levels of the four-year sector, most of the reconfiguration had already occurred by 2003. In the two-year sector, part-timers have maintained their dominance as the majority

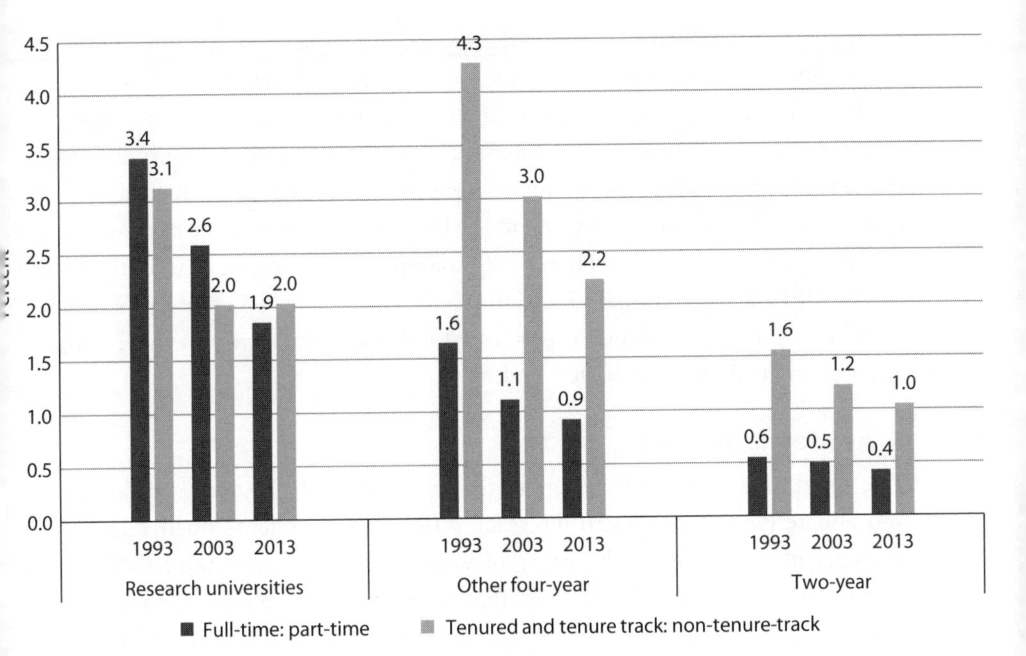

Figure 3.7 Ratios of full-time faculty to part-time faculty and of tenured and tenure-track faculty to non-tenure-track faculty, by type of institution, 1993, 2003 and 2013. *Sources:* IPEDS:93; IPEDS:03; IPEDS:13. (Refer to appendix A for key to data sources.)

Note: Includes four-year public, four-year private, four-year for-profit, two-year public, two-year private, and two-year for-profit institutions.

---

of the instructional staff throughout this period. What has changed—as everywhere else—is the shrinkage among the full-timers of the tenured and tenure-track contingent to virtual parity by 2013 with the full-time contract faculty. In many respects, then, it has been in the nonuniversity four-year sector where we have witnessed the most dramatic impact of the appointments revolution.

We reported in *The American Faculty* that quite beyond institutional type, the new appointments intersected in definable patterns by academic field. The changing center of gravity among the corps of instructional staff away from the traditional arts and science fields (fine arts, humanities, social sciences, physical and biological sciences) and toward the professional fields, including business, the health sciences, and so forth, largely following the pattern of student enrollments, has also paralleled the move toward the new appointments. In general, we reported that the new appointments were most common in these "rising" professional and vocational fields (business, health sciences, other vocations) as well as in selected "service" components of the liberal arts curriculum, including English composition, foreign languages, introductory mathematics, and remedial education and for staffing general education course requirements, more broadly (Schuster and Finkelstein 2006). Conversely, we found that career-ladder appointments were most prevalent in the natural sciences, a trend corroborated by David Leslie (2007) in his analysis of changes in the number of tenured and tenure-eligible appointments based on results of the NSOPF:04 Institutional Questionnaire.[11] While our earlier analyses had been based on fall 1998 data, Leslie's (2007) addition of data five years later (fall 2003) confirmed the same basic trends.

Academic Women

The appointments revolution that we first chronicled in *The American Faculty* and update here continues to intersect with an independent, albeit related, demographic revolution: the entry of women en masse into the academic professions. Earlier, we documented the ascent of women to more than 42.7% of headcount instructional staff and 35.9% of full-time faculty in the aggregate but approaching half among full-time new hires (see Schuster and Finkelstein 2006, chap. 3). At the same time, we found that women tended to be proportionately better represented (relative to men) on the faculties of baccalaureate and two-year institutions and proportionately less well represented than men in the doctoral and research university sector.[12] They tended to be proportionately well represented in the arts and humanities, the less quantitative social sciences (sociology, anthropology, history, American and women's studies, rather than economics and political science) and poorly represented in mathematics and computer science, physical sciences, and engineering (although much better represented in the biomedical and health sciences, including historically gendered fields such as nursing). Even more strikingly, women tended to be underrepresented among full-time career-ladder appointees (either tenured or tenure-eligible) and to be overrepresented among part-time and full-time limited-term appointments. Specifically, we found that 21% of women were on full-time limited-term appointments compared with 10% of the men overall; and among new entrants (defined as those in the first seven years of an academic career), 36% of women compared with 26% of men were on such appointments. Moreover, fully half (52.3%) of academic women were on part-time appointments compared with 43.8% of men (Schuster and Finkelstein 2006).

To what extent have these gender-based demographic trends continued into the second decade of the twenty-first century? Table 3.3 documents the changes in the overall numbers and distribution of male and female faculty in 1993, 2003, and 2013 by appointment type and employment status. While the overall numbers of women more than doubled during this period from 342,000 to 713,000 (compared with a mere 33% increase among males), the data show a still robust, if slightly reduced rate of growth of women faculty between 2003 and 2013 as compared with the decade between 1993 and 2003: 42.4% versus 47.3% in the earlier decade. What they also show is that that the growth has been disproportionately in the full-time, non-tenure-track and in the part-time appointments. Thus while the overall number of women faculty grew by 109% between 1993 and 2013, the growth in full-time faculty was 77.6%, and among full-time faculty, the growth in tenured appointments was 68.3% and the growth in tenure-track appointments half of that, that is, 31.1%. Conversely, the growth in full-time non-tenure-track appointments was 121.8% and in part-time appointments 144.2%. Put another way, the proportion of all women faculty on tenured and tenure-track appointments has shrunk from 64.5% in 1993 to 55.7% by 2013, while, concomitantly, the proportion of all women faculty on full-time non-tenure-track appointments has increased from 35.5 to 44.3%, and that on part-time appointments has increased from 48.2 to 56.1%. In short, while we are witnessing a growing presence of women in the academy, the locus of their increasing presence is shifting away from tenured and tenure track to part-time and off-track appointments.

How does this pattern compare with faculty men during the same period? To what extent does it parallel the male pattern? Or diverge? In terms of basic direction, the data in the bottom half of table 3.3 suggests an overall similarity in the gender patterns: the proportion of both women and men in the tenured and tenure-track ranks has been shrinking; concomitantly, the proportion of both genders in the part-time ranks has been increasing while the proportion of both in the full-time off-track appointments has been relatively stable. That said, as compared with men, women continue to be underrepresented among tenured appointments at the same level as in 2003, 9 % less than men. In 1993, women were about half as likely to be tenured as men and slightly more likely than men to be on the tenure track and on full-time, off-track appointments, while nearly 50%more likely than men to be on part-time appointments (48.2 of women vs. 34.9% of men). By 2003, the gender gap between men and women in tenured appointments had shrunk by half, albeit owing less to gains by

Table 3.3 Percentage distribution of female and male faculty, by appointment type, 1993, 2003, 2013

	Female faculty							
	1993	% of all female faculty	2003	% of all female faculty	2013	% of all female faculty	change N, 1993–2013	% change, 1993–2013
All female faculty	342,059		503,702		717,359		375,300	109.7
Full-time	177,243	51.8	245,914	48.8	314,816	43.9	137,573	77.6
Tenured	68,444	38.6	90,477	36.8	115,182	36.6	46,738	68.3
Tenure track	45,965	25.9	55,969	22.8	60,272	19.1	14,307	31.1
Non-tenure-track	62,834	35.5	99,468	40.4	139,362	44.3	76,528	121.8
Part-time	164,816	48.2	257,788	51.2	402,543	56.1	237,727	144.2
	Male faculty							
	1993	% of all male faculty	2003	% of all male faculty	2013	% of all male faculty	change N, 1993–2013	% change, 1993–2013
All male faculty	543,464		656,602		740,172		196,708	36.2
Full-time	353,295	65.0	378,282	57.6	381,539	51.5	28,244	8.0
Tenured	206,446	58.4	192,345	50.8	191,555	50.2	–14,891	–7.2
Tenure track	65,864	18.6	71,597	18.9	64,261	16.8	–1,603	–2.4
Non-tenure-track	80,985	22.9	114,340	30.2	125,723	33.0	44,738	55.2
Part-time	190,169	35.0	278,320	42.4	358,633	48.5	168,464	88.6

	Percentage difference between male versus female faculty			
	1993	2003	2013	1993–2013
All faculty				
Full-time	13.2	8.8	7.7	–5.5
Tenured	19.8	14.1	13.6	–6.2
Tenure track	–7.3	–3.8	–2.3	5.0
Non-tenure-track	–12.5	–10.2	–11.3	1.2
Part-time	–13.2	–8.8	–7.7	5.5

Sources: IPEDS:93; IPEDS:03; IPEDS:13. (Refer to appendix A for key.)

Notes: Includes four-year public; four-year private nonprofit; four-year for-profit; two-year public; two-year private nonprofit; and two-year for-profit Title IV institutions.

women than losses by men (i.e., retirement as well as an abrupt shrinkage in tenured appointments overall), and the gender gap in part-time appointments had shrunk as well, although less precipitously. Both genders held their own in their proportionate presence among tenure-track and off-track appointments. By 2013, only slight decreases in the proportion of faculty, both men and women, who were tenured and tenure-track are discernable as well as slight increases in the proportion of both men and women in off-track and part-time positions. It appears that most of the appointments reconfiguration had already occurred by 2003 and was merely continuing at a decelerated pace through 2013.

To what extent has this reconfiguration of appointments and associated gender gaps proceeded at an equal or differential pace across the institutional universe, defined by both type and control, especially in light of the punishing decline of funding in the public sector over the past decade? Table 3.4 examines the ratio of male to female faculty by appointment type and type of institution in 1993, 2003, and 2013. Among all institutions, the ratio of men to women in the tenured ranks has been virtually cut in half over twenty years: from three men for every woman in 1993 to 1.7 men for every woman in 2013. Similarly, if less dramatically, the ratio of men to women among tenure-track appointments has shrunk by nearly a third from 1.4 men for every women to near parity: 1.1 men for every women. Moreover, the data suggest that most of the shrinkage in the gender gap in tenured appointments occurred before 2003. That said, the data also demonstrate some striking variation by institutional type. As late as twenty years ago, men outnumbered women in the tenured ranks at research universities by a ratio of 4.4 to 1, that is, 4.4 men for every woman. While that gender gap has shrunk by nearly half over the ensuing twenty years, it nonetheless remains fairly substantial (2.5 men to 1 woman) among tenured appointments at the research universities, especially the private research universities. The gender ratio among tenured appointments has shrunk to 1.5:1 at the bachelor's- and master's-conferring institutions, and women actually outnumber men among the tenured ranks in the two-year sector, especially among the small number of tenured appointments in the for-profit sector.[13] Among tenure-track appointees, the gender gap has been virtually eliminated among all institutional types, except research universities, and there it remains at about 1.3:1. However, that shrinkage comes amid the overall shrinkage in these types of appointments. Among non-tenure-track, full-time appointments, the gender gap, small to begin with, has been eliminated with two

Table 3.4 Ratio of male to female faculty, by type and control of institution and appointment type, 1993, 2003, 2013

	Full-time					
	Tenured			Tenure track		
	1993	2003	2013	1993	2003	2013
N	262,564	269,069	292,064	103,231	117,837	113,896
All institutions	3.0	2.1	1.7	1.4	1.3	1.1
Public	2.9	2.0	1.6	1.4	1.2	1.0
Private	3.3	2.4	1.9	1.5	1.4	1.1
Four-year	3.5	2.5	1.9	1.5	1.4	1.1
Two-year	1.5	1.1	0.9	0.8	0.8	0.7
Research institutions	4.4	3.0	2.3	1.8	1.6	1.3
Public	4.4	3.0	2.2	1.7	1.5	1.2
Private	4.2	3.3	2.5	2.0	1.8	1.4
Master's institutions	2.7	1.8	1.4	1.2	1.1	0.9
Public	2.7	1.9	1.4	1.2	1.1	0.9
Private	2.5	1.8	1.4	1.2	1.1	0.9
Bachelor's institutions	2.8	1.9	1.5	1.3	1.2	1.0
Public	2.4	1.8	1.5	1.5	1.3	1.1
Private	2.9	1.9	1.5	1.3	1.2	1.0
Two-year institutions	1.5	1.1	0.9	0.8	0.8	0.7
Public	1.5	1.1	0.9	0.8	0.8	0.7
Private	0.9	0.9	0.9	0.5	1.4	0.9
For-profit institutions	1.7	1.6	0.6	0.8	0.7	1.8
Two-year, private	3.1	1.6	0.6	0.1	0.7	2.0
Four-year, private	1.4	1.6	0.6	1.1	0.6	1.7

	Non-tenure-track			Part-time		
	1993	2003	2013	1993	2003	2013
N	125,029	195,394	231,530	323,763	514,513	721,647
All institutions	1.3	1.1	0.9	1.1	1.1	0.9
Public	1.2	1.0	0.9	1.1	1.0	0.9
Private	1.4	1.3	1.0	1.3	1.2	1.0
Four-year	1.3	1.2	0.9	1.2	1.1	0.9
Two-year	1.1	0.9	0.8	1.0	1.0	0.8
Research institutions	1.4	1.3	1.0	1.4	1.2	1.0
Public	1.3	1.2	1.0	1.3	1.1	1.0
Private	1.7	1.4	1.0	1.5	1.3	1.1
Master's institutions	1.0	0.9	0.8	1.2	1.0	0.9
Public	1.0	0.8	0.7	1.0	1.0	0.8
Private	1.1	1.0	0.8	1.3	1.1	0.9

(continued)

Table 3.4 (continued)

	Non-tenure-track			Part-time		
	1993	2003	2013	1993	2003	2013
N	125,029	195,394	231,530	323,763	514,513	721,647
Bachelor's	1.3	1.1	1.0	1.1	1.1	0.9
Public	1.4	1.0	1.0	1.2	1.2	0.9
Private	1.3	1.2	1.0	1.1	1.0	0.9
Two-year institutions	1.1	0.9	0.8	1.0	1.0	0.8
Public	1.1	0.9	0.8	1.0	1.0	0.8
Private	1.1	1.0	0.6	1.1	0.7	0.7
For-profit institutions	1.6	1.5	0.8	1.3	1.7	0.7
Two-year, private	1.7	1.3	0.7	0.9	0.9	0.7
Four-year, private	1.5	1.8	0.9	1.4	1.9	0.7

Sources: IPEDS:93; IPEDS:03; IPEDS:13. (Refer to appendix A for key.)

Notes: All institution counts do not include private for-profit institutions. Underrepresented racial minority includes Black, Hispanic, American Indian, and Alaskan Native individuals.

exceptions: the research universities at one extreme (still slight proportionate male dominance) and the private two-year and proprietary sector, at the other, where gender ratios have actually reversed themselves, with women becoming the new majority among fixed-contract, full-time employees. Finally, among part-time appointments, whatever small gender gap existed in 1993 was either eliminated by 2013 or actually reversed—again with the exception of the research universities and the private for-profit institutions.

Taken together, these trends in the distribution of women faculty across institutional and appointment types suggest a pattern of movement, albeit uneven movement, in the direction of broader representation, if not quite increasing equity at the highest levels, largely achieved prior to 2003.[14] The historically large gender gap, especially among tenured appointments, has been reduced substantially, as has the less extreme gender gap also among tenure-track, off-track, and part-time appointments—even as the overall numbers of such appointments (except full-time off track) are declining. While research universities and the private for-profit sector show a shrinking gender gap, it is one that remains stubbornly resistant to elimination.

Racial and Ethnic Diversity

In *The American Faculty*, we documented the gradual growth of a racial and ethnic minority presence in the professoriate from about 5% in 1975 to about

15% by 1998, noting that the proportionate presence among new hires had risen to about 1 in 5 by 2003. While that growth has remained a steady trickle, to what extent have racial and ethnic minorities, like academic women, found themselves disproportionately overrepresented among non-career-ladder or contingent appointments (both full- and part-time)?[15]

In examining race and ethnicity, we followed the lead of Daryl Smith (2012) and sought to identify nonresident aliens (foreign citizens who are in the United States on F-1 or J-1 visas) and distinguish them explicitly from faculty with Asian, Latino, or African-Caribbean backgrounds who were born or educated in the United States and who are either US citizens or permanent residents. The intent is to avoid counting such individuals who have not grown up in the United States as underrepresented racial minorities (URMs, the acronym popularized by the National Science Foundation in its reports)—who, by definition, are US citizens. With that critical distinction between race/ethnicity and nativity in mind—in effect distinguishing between native-born underrepresented minorities and foreign-born and educated faculty—table 3.5 traces the changing distribution of faculty by race/ethnicity and appointment type in 1993, 2003, and 2013. While the number of white headcount faculty increased by 43.3% between 1993 and 2013, the numbers of Asian and URM faculty grew by 170.5 and 142.8%, respectively—three times the rate of growth in white faculty. Moreover, among white faculty, the proportionate presence of women increased from 38.4 to 48.6%, suggesting that women are destined over the next decade, if current trends continue, to become the majority of white faculty. The reversal of fortunes of white versus nonwhite faculty is illustrated most dramatically when we focus on the growth of faculty in tenured and tenure-track appointments. The absolute number of white faculty, men and women combined, on tenured appointments declined from 242,000 to 238,000, while the number on tenure-track appointments declined from 90,000 to 82,000—a negative growth rate. The largest shrinkage in the proportionate representation of whites was among the tenure-track faculty: from four-fifths in 1993 to two-thirds in 2013. During the same period, the number of Asian faculty in tenured and tenure-track appointments more than doubled, from 11,000 to 27,000 and from 6,500 to 14,000, respectively. The number of URM faculty on tenured and tenure-track appointments grew by a much more modest 60 and 30%, respectively, while mushrooming in numbers of non-tenure-track full-time (142.9% growth) and part-time (229.8% growth) appointments. Among URMs, African Americans fared the least well, growing by 40 and 15%

Table 3.5 Number and percentage distribution of female and male faculty by race/ethnicity and appointment type, 1993, 2003, 2013

	1993	% of all faculty	Male *N*	Female *N*	2003
All faculty	885,541		656,751	503,702	1,160,453
White	744,983	84.1	511,226	389,468	900,694
Asian or Pacific Islander	34,469	3.9	37,303	21,550	58,853
Underrepresented racial minority	76,455	8.6	60,626	60,986	121,612
African American	42,911	4.8	30,174	34,114	64,288
Hispanic	30,358	3.4	27,570	24,291	51,861
Native American	3,186	0.4	2,882	2,581	5,463
Two or more	—		—	—	—
Nonresident alien	19,317	2.2	18,720	9,258	27,978
Unknown race	10,317	1.2	28,876	22,440	51,316
All full-time faculty	530,550	59.9	378,324	245,914	624,238
White	450,618	84.9	300,682	194,321	495,003
Asian or Pacific Islander	24,686	4.7	27,395	13,113	40,508
Underrepresented racial minority	43,701	8.2	31,904	29,889	61,793
African American	24,501	4.6	15,938	16,386	32,324
Hispanic	17,373	3.3	14,361	12,188	26,549
Native American	1,827	0.3	1,605	1,315	2,920
Two or more	—		—		—
Nonresident alien	10,677	2.0	14,724	6,157	20,881
Unknown race	868	0.2	3,619	2,434	6,053
Tenured full-time faculty	274,894	51.8	192,354	90,477	282,831
White	242,678	88.3	162,049	74,249	236,298
Asian or Pacific Islander	11,274	4.1	13,094	4,131	17,225
Underrepresented racial minority	19,401	7.1	14,735	11,259	25,994
African American	10,195	3.7	6,994	5,510	12,504
Hispanic	8,478	3.1	7,048	5,305	12,353
Native American	728	0.3	693	444	1,137
Two or more	—		—	—	—
Nonresident alien	1,351	0.5	1,608	435	2,043
Unknown race	190	0.1	868	403	1,271
Tenure-track full-time faculty	111,831	21.1	71,597	55,969	127,566
White	90,286	80.7	51,523	41,847	93,370

% of all faculty	Male N	Female N	2013	% of all faculty	change N, 1999–2013	% change, 1999–2013
	740,333	717,359	1,457,692		572,151	64.6
77.6	548,756	518,912	1,067,668	73.2	322,685	43.3
5.1	51,987	41,235	93,222	6.4	58,753	170.5
10.5	81,790	103,824	185,614	12.7	109,159	142.8
5.5	40,172	60,575	100,747	6.9	57,836	134.8
4.5	38,285	39,575	77,860	5.3	47,502	156.5
0.5	3,333	3,674	7,007	0.5	3,821	119.9
	4,693	5,542	10,235	0.7		
2.4	18,207	12,308	30,515	2.1	11,198	58.0
4.4	34,900	35,538	70,438	4.8	60,121	582.7
53.8	381,586	314,816	696,402	47.8	165,852	31.3
79.3	285,133	233,270	518,403	74.4	67,785	15.0
6.5	36,136	23,564	59,700	8.6	35,014	141.8
9.9	36,958	40,621	77,579	11.1	33,878	77.5
5.2	17,374	21,713	39,087	5.6	14,586	59.5
4.3	18,012	17,309	35,321	5.1	17,948	103.3
0.5	1,572	1,599	3,171	0.5	1,344	73.6
	2,246	2,387	4,633	0.7		
3.3	12,043	7,251	19,294	2.8	8,617	80.7
1.0	9,070	7,723	16,793	2.4	15,925	1834.7
45.3	191,560	115,182	306,742	44.0	31,848	11.6
83.5	149,557	88,971	238,528	77.8	–4,150	–1.7
6.1	18,662	8,318	26,980	8.8	15,706	139.3
9.2	16,952	14,273	31,225	10.2	11,824	60.9
4.4	7,707	6,683	14,390	4.7	4,195	41.1
4.4	8,595	7,034	15,629	5.1	7,151	84.3
0.4	650	556	1,206	0.4	478	65.7
	995	761	1,756	0.6		
0.7	2,307	1,076	3,383	1.1	2,032	150.4
0.4	3,087	1,783	4,870	1.6	4,680	2,463.2
20.4	64,278	60,272	124,550	17.9	12,719	11.4
73.2	41,925	40,471	82,396	66.2	–7,890	–8.7

(continued)

Table 3.5 (continued)

	1993	% of all faculty	Male N	Female N	2003
Asian or Pacific Islander	6,562	5.9	6,628	3,812	10,440
Underrepresented racial minority	11,227	10.0	7,081	7,295	14,376
African American	6,710	6.0	3,613	4,163	7,776
Hispanic	4,079	3.6	3,158	2,829	5,987
Native American	438	0.4	310	303	613
Two or more	—		—	—	—
Nonresident alien	3,396	3.0	5,341	2,246	7,587
Unknown race	360	0.3	1,024	769	1,793
Non-tenure-track full-time faculty	143,825	27.1	114,373	99,468	213,841
White	117,654	81.8	87,110	78,225	165,335
Asian or Pacific Islander	6,850	4.8	7,673	5,170	12,843
Underrepresented racial minority	13,073	9.1	10,088	11,335	21,423
African American	7,596	5.3	5,331	6,713	12,044
Hispanic	4,816	3.3	4,155	4,054	8,209
Native American	661	0.5	602	568	1,170
Two or more	—		—	—	—
Nonresident alien	5,930	4.1	7,775	3,476	11,251
Unknown race	318	0.2	1,727	1,262	2,989
Part-time faculty	354,991	40.1	278,427	257,788	536,215
White	294,365	82.9	210,544	195,147	405,691
Asian or Pacific Islander	9,783	2.8	9,908	8,437	18,345
Underrepresented racial minority	32,754	9.2	28,722	31,097	59,819
African American	18,410	5.2	14,236	17,728	31,964
Hispanic	12,985	3.7	13,209	12,103	25,312
Native American	1,359	0.4	1,277	1,266	2,543
Two or more	—		—	—	—
Nonresident alien	8,640	2.4	3,996	3,101	7,097
Unknown race	9,449	2.7	25,257	20,006	45,263

Sources: IPEDS:93; IPEDS:03; IPEDS:13. (Refer to appendix A for key.)

Notes: Includes four-year public; four-year private; four-year for-profit; two-year public; two-year; private; two-year for-profit. Asian/Pacific (2013) includes Asian and Native Hawaiian or Other Pacific Islander. Two or more races was not indicated on the 1993 and 2003 surveys.

% of all faculty	Male *N*	Female *N*	2013	% of all faculty	change *N*, 1999–2013	% change, 1999–2013
8.2	7,839	6,142	13,981	11.2	7,419	113.1
11.3	6,591	8,013	14,604	11.7	3,377	30.1
6.1	3,180	4,591	7,771	6.2	1,061	15.8
4.7	3,180	3,127	6,307	5.1	2,228	54.6
0.5	231	295	526	0.4	88	20.1
	430	568	998	0.8		
5.9	5,141	3,055	8,196	6.6	4,800	141.3
1.4	2,352	2,023	4,375	3.5	4,015	1115.3
34.3	125,748	139,362	265,110	38.1	121,285	84.3
77.3	93,651	103,828	197,479	74.5	79,825	67.8
6.0	9,635	9,104	18,739	7.1	11,889	173.6
10.0	13,415	18,335	31,750	12.0	18,677	142.9
5.6	6,487	10,439	16,926	6.4	9,330	122.8
3.8	6,237	7,148	13,385	5.0	8,569	177.9
0.5	691	748	1,439	0.5	778	117.7
	821	1,058	1,879	0.7		
5.3	4,595	3,120	7,715	2.9	1,785	30.1
1.4	3,631	3,917	7,548	2.8	7,230	2,273.6
46.2	358,747	402,543	761,290	52.2	406,299	114.5
75.7	263,623	285,642	549,265	72.1	254,900	86.6
3.4	15,851	17,671	33,522	4.4	23,739	242.7
11.2	44,832	63,203	108,035	14.2	75,281	229.8
6.0	22,798	38,862	61,660	8.1	43,250	234.9
4.7	20,273	22,266	42,539	5.6	29,554	227.6
0.5	1,761	2,075	3,836	0.5	2,477	182.3
	2,447	3,155	5,602	0.7		
1.3	6,164	5,057	11,221	1.5	2,581	29.9
8.4	25,830	27,815	53,645	7.0	44,196	467.7

in tenured and tenure-track appointments, respectively, but by 122% and 242%, respectively, in full-time off-track and part-time appointments. Much as we found with academic women, the greatest inroads overall among any racial or ethnic subgroup into tenured and tenure-track appointments was by the foreign-born and foreign-educated nonresident aliens, increasing by nearly 150% in both categories and much less so among non-tenure-track, full-time and part-time appointments (about 30%).

Where are the nonwhite faculty located? The Asian, foreign-born, and foreign-educated nonresident-alien faculty are disproportionately located at research universities: 56.4% of all Asians and Pacific Islanders and 75.9% of all nonresident aliens were so located in 1993, and the corresponding figures for 2009 were 53.5% and 79.1%, respectively (Smith, Tovar, and Garcia, 2012). As for the URM faculty, table 3.6 displays the ratio of white to URM faculty by appointment type across and within institutional types in 1993, 2003 and 2013. Overall, the data show that the 15:1 ratio of whites to URMs among tenured faculty in 1993 had been cut in half to 7.7:1 by 2013. While the ratio had been highest at research universities and at private institutions at all levels in 1993—and this relative position has been maintained—nonetheless the ratio has been halved almost everywhere, with most of that shrinkage occurring by 2003.[16] Among tenure-track appointees, the ratios of white to URM faculty were half as large in 1993—on the order of 8:1—and the shrinkage has been less dramatic (about one-third), especially between 2003 and 2013. Presumably this reflects the decline in the proportion of tenured and tenurable appointments just as URMs are increasingly entering the academic pipeline.

Nonetheless, some progress is clear—although private sector institutions still lag behind public sector institutions. Among full-time contract appointments, the ratio of whites to URMs persists—in initial magnitude and shrinkage—expect for the case of public master's and baccalaureate institutions, where the ratio has actually grown, suggesting that new hires to non-tenure-track appointments have been disproportionately white. Finally, among part-time appointments, white-to-URM ratios began lower and have shrunk proportionately. Again, however, two-year private institutions and the for-profit sector remain outliers—having dramatically shrunk their white-to-URM ratios by one-fifth or more.

In sum, the proportion of whites among full-time faculty has declined by 11% between 1993 and 2013, offset primarily by the growth in Asian American and, to a lesser extent, black and Latino URM faculty. While foreign-born and educated nonresident aliens and Asian American faculty—in addition to

Table 3.6 Ratio of white to underrepresented racial minority faculty by type and control of institution, and appointment type, 1993, 2003, 2013

	Full-time					
	Tenured			Tenure track		
	1993	2003	2013	1993	2003	2013
N	250,365	248,665	256,206	94,199	99,398	88,798
All institutions	15.0	9.2	7.8	8.7	6.6	5.7
Public	13.4	8.3	7.1	7.5	6.2	5.3
Private	20.3	12.7	10.5	11.6	7.7	6.4
Four-year	17.1	10.0	8.5	8.8	6.8	5.9
Two-year	8.9	6.5	5.5	6.9	5.8	4.7
Research institutions	21.1	11.1	9.3	10.6	6.9	6.1
Public	22.8	10.6	8.9	9.6	6.5	5.8
Private	17.3	12.9	10.5	13.9	8.1	6.6
Master's institutions	12.5	9.7	8.0	7.3	7.1	5.9
Public	10.7	8.4	7.0	6.0	6.4	5.2
Private	26.3	14.0	11.1	13.2	8.7	7.5
Bachelor's institutions	16.7	7.0	6.9	7.8	5.9	5.1
Public	8.3	3.2	3.3	5.5	4.9	4.9
Private	21.6	11.3	10.0	8.5	6.3	5.2
Two-year institutions	8.9	6.5	5.5	6.9	5.8	4.7
Public	8.8	6.5	5.5	6.6	5.7	4.7
Private	42.3	13.3	29.0	71.6	—	19.0
For-profit institutions	4.4	1.6	0.2	15.0	3.2	17.0
Two-year, private	3.7	1.5	0.2	11.5	2.8	—
Four-year, private	—	1.7	0.2	—	3.4	14.0
	Non-tenure-track			Part-time		
	1993	2003	2013	1993	2003	2013
N	116,466	160,968	187,569	310,014	400,368	533,434
All institutions	10.2	7.9	6.8	9.9	7.0	5.7
Public	10.3	8.0	7.1	9.0	7.0	5.9
Private	9.7	7.9	6.8	13.1	7.4	6.3
Four-year	9.7	8.1	7.1	10.9	7.8	6.6
Two-year	11.1	7.7	6.7	9.0	6.5	5.4
Research institutions	12.0	9.2	7.8	11.8	9.2	7.3
Public	14.1	10.2	8.3	12.1	9.2	7.9
Private	9.0	7.8	6.9	11.3	9.1	6.6
Master's institutions	6.1	7.4	7.2	9.8	7.4	6.2
Public	4.6	5.6	6.0	7.4	8.2	6.3
Private	12.6	11.2	8.6	15.2	6.8	6.1
Bachelor's institutions	9.4	5.3	5.0	11.6	5.9	5.8
Public	5.8	4.2	5.3	7.4	5.2	5.3
Private	10.4	5.7	4.9	13.1	6.4	6.1

(continued)

Table 3.6 (continued)

	Non-tenure-track			Part-time		
	1993	2003	2013	1993	2003	2013
N	116,466	160,968	187,569	310,014	400,368	533,434
Two-year institutions	11.1	7.7	6.7	9.0	6.5	5.4
Public	11.5	7.6	6.6	8.9	6.4	5.4
Private	7.5	25.1	9.8	14.9	14.9	4.7
For-profit institutions	11.7	5.6	3.1	13.7	4.2	2.2
Two-year, private	12.1	5.1	2.7	10.9	3.7	2.1
Four-year, private	11.1	8.8	5.3	20.7	4.9	2.5

Sources: IPEDS:93; IPEDS:03; IPEDS:13. (Refer to appendix A for key.)

Notes: All institution counts do not include private for-profit institutions. Underrepresented racial minority includes Black, Hispanic, American Indian, and Alaskan Native individuals.

white faculty—are most heavily represented in research universities, the largest absolute number of URM faculty (as distinguished from their proportion) are actually located in research universities and other four-year institutions—given their much larger corps of full-time faculty. The part-time faculty presents a largely similar pattern.

The Intersection of Race and Gender

While the separate stories of women and underrepresented minority faculty in American higher education over the past generation largely parallel each other, a more nuanced story emerges at the intersection of gender and race/ethnicity. Table 3.7 below shows the distribution of female faculty by race/ethnicity and appointment type between 1993 and 2013, again being careful to distinguish between underrepresented minorities and faculty born and educated abroad.[17] Among all headcount faculty, white women have actually benefited the least among all racial subgroups of women—although they remain the dominant majority. Relative to the 109% increase in women between 1993 and 2013, white women increased by 81.5% compared with the 296% increase in Asian women, the 196% in URM women (with Hispanic women outpacing both African American and Native Americans). Indeed, Asian women showed robust growth rates across all appointment types, ranging from 238% (among tenure-track, full-time faculty) to 321% (among tenured faculty and part-time

Table 3.7 Percentage distribution of female faculty by race/ethnicity, and appointment type, 1993, 2003, 2013

	1993	% of all female faculty	2003	% of all female faculty	2013	% of all female faculty	change *N*, 1993–2013	% change, 1993–2013
All female faculty	342,059		503,702		717,359		375,300	109.7
White	285,961	83.6	389,468	77.3	518,912	72.3	232,951	81.5
Asian/Pacific	10,414	3.0	21,550	4.3	41,235	5.7	30,821	296.0
Underrepresented racial minority	35,813	10.5	60,986	12.1	103,824	14.5	68,011	189.9
African American	21,295	6.2	34,114	6.8	60,575	8.4	39,280	184.5
Hispanic	13,122	3.8	24,291	4.8	39,575	5.5	26,453	201.6
Native American	1,396	0.4	2,581	0.5	3,674	0.5	2,278	163.2
Two or more	—		—		5,542	0.8		
Nonresident alien	8,337	2.4	9,258	1.8	12,308	1.7	3,971	47.6
Unknown race	1,534	0.4	22,440	4.5	35,538	5.0	34,004	2216.7
All full-time female faculty	177,243	51.8	245,914	48.8	314,816	43.9	137,573	77.6
White	148,657	83.9	194,321	79.0	233,270	74.1	84,613	56.9
Asian or Pacific Islander	6,220	3.5	13,113	5.3	23,564	7.5	17,344	278.8
Underrepresented racial minority	19,666	11.1	29,889	12.2	40,621	12.9	20,955	106.6
African American	11,662	6.6	16,386	6.7	21,713	6.9	10,051	86.2
Hispanic	7,274	4.1	12,188	5.0	17,309	5.5	10,035	138.0
Native American	730	0.4	1,315	0.5	1,599	0.5	869	119.0
Two or more	—		—		2,387	0.8		
Nonresident alien	2,426	1.4	6,157	2.5	7,251	2.3	4,825	198.9
Unknown race	274	0.2	2,434	1.0	7,723	2.5	7,449	2718.6
Tenured full-time female faculty	68,444	38.6	90,477	36.8	115,182	36.6	46,738	68.3
White	58,404	85.3	74,249	82.1	88,971	77.2	30,567	52.3
Asian or Pacific Islander	1,973	2.9	4,131	4.6	8,318	7.2	6,345	321.6

(continued)

Table 3.7 continued

	1993	% of all female faculty	2003	% of all female faculty	2013	% of all female faculty	change N, 1993–2013	% change, 1993–2013
Underrepresented racial minority	7,855	11.5	11,259	12.4	14,273	12.4	6,418	81.7
African American	4,340	6.3	5,510	6.1	6,683	5.8	2,343	54.0
Hispanic	3,307	4.8	5,305	5.9	7,034	6.1	3,727	112.7
Native American	208	0.3	444	0.5	556	0.5	348	167.3
Two or more	—		—		761	0.7		
Nonresident alien	178	0.3	435	0.5	1,076	0.9	898	504.5
Unknown race	34	0.0	403	0.4	1,783	1.5	1,749	5144.1
Tenure-track full-time female faculty	45,965	25.9	55,969	22.8	60,272	19.1	14,307	31.1
White	38,100	82.9	41,847	74.8	40,471	67.1	2,371	6.2
Asian or Pacific Islander	1,815	3.9	3,812	6.8	6,142	10.2	4,327	238.4
Underrepresented racial minority	5,202	11.3	7,295	13.0	8,013	13.3	2,811	54.0
African American	3,265	7.1	4,163	7.4	4,591	7.6	1,326	40.6
Hispanic	1,716	3.7	2,829	5.1	3,127	5.2	1,411	82.2
Native American	221	0.5	303	0.5	295	0.5	74	33.5
Two or more	—		—		568	0.9		
Nonresident alien	730	1.6	2,246	4.0	3,055	5.1	2,325	318.5
Unknown race	118	0.3	769	1.4	2,023	3.4	1,905	1614.4
Non-tenure-track full-time female faculty	62,834	35.5	99,468	40.4	139,362	44.3	76,528	121.8
White	52,153	83.0	78,225	78.6	103,828	74.5	51,675	99.1
Asian or Pacific Islander	2,432	3.9	5,170	5.2	9,104	6.5	6,672	274.3

Underrepresented racial minority	6,609	10.5	11,335	11.4	18,335	13.2	11,726	177.4
African American	4,057	6.5	6,713	6.7	10,439	7.5	6,382	157.3
Hispanic	2,251	3.6	4,054	4.1	7,148	5.1	4,897	217.5
Native American	301	0.5	568	0.6	748	0.5	447	148.5
Two or more	—		—		1,058	0.8		
Nonresident alien	1,518	2.4	3,476	3.5	3,120	2.2	1,602	105.5
Unknown race	122	0.2	1,262	1.3	3,917	2.8	3,795	3110.7
Part-time female faculty	164,816	48.2	257,788	51.2	402,543	56.1	237,727	144.2
White	137,304	83.3	195,147	75.7	285,642	71.0	148,338	108.0
Asian or Pacific Islander	4,194	2.5	8,437	3.3	17,671	4.4	13,477	321.3
Underrepresented racial minority	16,147	9.8	31,097	12.1	63,203	15.7	47,056	291.4
African American	9,633	5.8	17,728	6.9	38,862	9.7	29,229	303.4
Hispanic	5,848	3.5	12,103	4.7	22,266	5.5	16,418	280.7
Native American	666	0.4	1,266	0.5	2,075	0.5	1,409	211.6
Two or more	—		—		3,155	0.8		
Nonresident alien	5,911	3.6	3,101	1.2	5,057	1.3	–854	–14.4
Unknown race	1,260	0.8	20,006	7.8	27,815	6.9	26,555	2107.5

Sources: IPEDS:93; IPEDS:03; IPEDS:13. (Refer to appendix A for key.)

Notes: Includes four-year public; four-year private; four-year for-profit; two-year public; two-year; private; two-year for-profit. Asian/Pacific (2013) includes Asian and Native Hawaiian or Other Pacific Islander. Tow or more races was indicated in the 1993 and 2003 surveys.

faculty). Similarly, nonresident-alien women increased their presence among tenured faculty appointments fivefold over the twenty-year period and more than threefold among tenure-track appointments. While URM women faculty grew by 196% in total headcount over two decades, their growth in tenured and tenure-track full-time appointments has been much more modest—81.7% among tenured appointments and 51% among tenure-track appointments. Their most robust growth has been among full-time, non-tenure-track appointments (177%) and part-time appointments (238%). Within the URM category, Hispanic women have grown at twice the pace of African American women among tenured (112.7 vs. 54%) and tenure-track appointments (82.2 vs. 40.6%).

While somewhat dizzying, these growth rates must, however, be interpreted in the context of the actual numbers, which remain small, and their proportionate presence among all women faculty, which remains virtually unchanged over the two decade period. It pales, moreover, in comparison to the overall rate of growth in the size of the female professorate as a whole (77.6% growth in full-time women, 109.7% growth in women in all appointment types). Thus African American women have increased their proportionate presence among all women full-time faculty from only 6.6% to 6.9% in two decades; from 7.1 to 7.6% among female tenure-track, full-time faculty during this period, and their proportionate presence among the tenured, full-time female faculty has actually declined, from 6.3 to 5.8%. Latinas have increased their proportionate presence among all women full-time faculty from 4.1 to 5.5% in two decades: from 3.7 to 5.2% among the tenure track, full-time female faculty and from 4.8 to 6.1% of the tenured full-time female faculty. Native American women have increased their proportionate presence among the full-time professoriate from 0.4 to 0.5% over two decades and have remained as 0.5% of the tenure track professoriate and risen from 0.3 to 0.5 of the tenured professoriate. While the proportionate presence of Asian women among all full-time female faculty has nearly doubled from 3.5 to 7.5% (2.9 to 7.2% among tenured, full-time female faculty and 3.9 to 10.2% of all tenure-track, full-time female faculty), the numbers remain relatively small, and the big picture as seen through this prism is relatively static. While the situation of Asian and nonresident-alien women has improved the most, URM women more modestly, and white women the least, the numerical dominance of white women in 1993 continues largely unchanged in 2013. White women remain the vast majority.

Diversification in National Origin

When we now consider faculty teaching in American higher education with international backgrounds, we include not only the category of foreign born and educated nonresident aliens discussed earlier but also permanent residents (noncitizens granted permanent residency status while citizens of another country) and naturalized citizens (who were born abroad but have been granted US citizenship). The key consideration here is aggregating those individuals on academic appointments at US colleges and universities who are foreign born, whether they have been educated in the United States or abroad, and whether they have been granted permanent residence or citizenship. When we do so, the proportion of international scholars on American faculties (by birth) has risen from about one-tenth in 1975 to about one-fifth by 2013, clearly surpassing the presence of underrepresented racial minorities (Kim, Twombley, and Wolf-Wendel 2012). According to the 2008 National Science Foundation's Survey of Doctorate Recipients, nearly two-thirds are actually "naturalized" citizens; about 60% completed their undergraduate education abroad, and about 40% completed their undergraduate education in the United States (Kim, Twombley, and Wolf-Wendel 2012).

In *The American Faculty*, we reported that these international faculty tended to be concentrated in the natural sciences and engineering: 35% of the faculty in engineering and 39% in computer science. In 2009, 33% of doctoral recipients in science and engineering fields overall were foreign-born, but that figure jumped to 57% for engineering, 54% for computer science and 51% for physics (NSF 2012), suggesting that the proportion of foreign-born faculty in the science, technology, engineering, and mathematics fields will continue to grow. Table 3.8 displays the distribution of foreign-born faculty by citizenship status and academic field between 1993 and 2013, ranging from about one-fifth in the life sciences (19.2%), the humanities (20.3%), and the social sciences (22.5%) to 41.3% in engineering. Since 1993, the proportion has grown by fully one-third, from 17.3% overall in 1993 to 25.4% in 2010 as the proportion of native-born citizens has shrunk from 82.7 to 74.6%.

Historically, foreign-born faculty have been concentrated not only in the science, technology, engineering, and mathematics fields but also at research universities. To the extent that they occupy full-time limited-term appointments—and they are less likely to do so that native-born faculty—those tend to be in research (Schuster and Finkelstein 2006). Moreover, foreign-born faculty are

Table 3.8 Number and percentage distribution of foreign-born faculty, by academic field and citizenship status, 1993–2013

	Birth and citizenship										
	Foreign born								Native born		
	Non-US citizens		Naturalized		Foreign born to US citizens		Total foreign born		US citizens		
Academic field/year	*N*	% of total	*N*	% of total	*N*	% of total	*N*	% of total	*N*	% of total	Total
Engineering											
1993	258	20.3	188	14.8	—		446	35.0	828	65.0	1,274
1999	4,169	14.0	5,649	18.9	—		9,818	32.9	20,018	67.1	29,836
2004	4,723	12.6	8,658	23.1	—		13,381	35.7	24,120	64.3	37,501
2006	114	12.0	208	21.9	10	1.1	332	35.0	618	65.1	950
2010	183	19.3	200	21.1	8	1.0	391	41.3	556	58.7	947
2013	137	17.8	192	25.0	9	1.2	338	44.0	431	56.0	769
Computer and math sciences											
1993	202	15.4	168	12.8	—		370	28.2	941	71.8	1,311
1999	5,266	6.5	8,302	10.2	—		13,568	16.7	67,558	83.3	81,126
2004	8,037	9.4	7,026	8.2	—		15,063	17.7	70,156	82.3	85,219
2006	242	16.0	226	15.0	22	1.5	490	32.4	1,022	67.7	1,512
2010	271	18.2	268	18.0	19	3.4	558	37.5	930	62.5	1,488
2013	184	18.9	210	21.6	18	1.9	412	42.4	560	57.6	972
Physical and related sciences											
1993	69	6.1	118	10.5	—		187	16.6	938	83.4	1,125
1999	3,912	10.4	3,862	10.3	—		7,774	20.6	29,922	79.4	37,696
2004	3,907	9.7	5,535	13.7	—		9,442	23.4	30,845	76.6	40,287
2006	134	9.1	141	9.5	18	1.2	293	19.8	1,186	80.2	1,479
2010	212	13.7	180	11.6	26	1.7	418	27.0	1,128	73.0	1,546
2013	162	13.5	140	11.7	19	1.6	321	26.8	878	73.2	1,199

Life-related sciences											
1993	72	3.6	149	7.5	—		221	11.1	1,766	88.9	1,987
1999	7,488	14.5	4,342	8.4	—		11,830	22.8	39,958	77.2	51,788
2004	5,244	10.2	7,080	13.7	—		12,324	23.9	39,348	76.2	51,672
2006	76	5.1	123	8.2	24	1.6	223	14.9	1,274	85.1	1,497
2010	144	8.1	175	9.9	22	1.2	341	19.2	1,432	80.8	1,773
2013	101	6.7	161	10.7	20	1.3	282	18.8	1,216	81.2	1,498
Social and related sciences											
1993	182	7.5	198	8.2	—		380	15.8	2,033	84.3	2,413
1999	4,082	4.0	7,030	6.8	—		11,112	10.8	92,174	89.2	103,286
2004	5,738	5.3	8,577	7.9	—		14,315	13.2	93,973	86.8	108,288
2006	238	8.8	230	8.5	59	2.2	527	19.5	2,170	80.5	2,697
2010	336	11.5	274	9.4	50	1.7	660	22.5	2,271	77.5	2,931
2013	269	11.5	231	9.8	42	1.8	542	23.1	1,807	76.9	2,349
Humanities											
1993	246	5.4	326	7.3	—		572	12.8	3,912	87.2	4,484
1999	7,159	6.3	8,097	7.2	—		15,256	13.5	82,585	73.0	113,097
2004	10,193	6.2	15,456	9.4	—		25,649	15.6	138,778	84.4	164,427
2006	168	5.8	289	9.9	35	1.2	492	17.0	2,399	82.9	2,891
2010	237	7.4	372	11.6	43	1.3	652	20.3	2,556	79.7	3,208
2013	87	12.1	102	14.2	12	1.7	201	28.0	518	72.0	719
All fields											
1993	1,029	8.2	1,147	9.1	—		2,176	17.3	10,418	82.7	12,594
1999	32,076	7.7	37,282	8.9	—		69,358	16.6	332,215	79.7	416,929
2004	37,842	7.8	52,332	10.7	—		90,174	18.5	397,220	81.5	487,394
2006	972	8.8	1,217	11.0	168	1.5	2,357	21.4	8,669	78.6	11,026
2010	1,383	11.6	1,469	12.4	168	1.4	3,020	25.4	8,872	74.6	11,892
2013	940	12.5	1,036	13.8	120	1.6	2,096	27.9	5,410	72.1	7,506

Sources: Selected years from 1993–2013 National Science Foundation "Science & Engineering Indicators—Chapter 5 (Academic Research and Development)."

Notes: Unweighted, public release SDR data. Number of Foreign Born to U.S. Citizens was not indicated in the surveys for 1993, 1999, 2004. Fields follow the groupings derived by NSF-SESTAT. Social/related sciences includes Economics, Political/related sciences, Psychology, Sociology/Anthropology, and other social sciences. The Non-Science & Engineering fields include Art/humanities fields, Education (except science/math), Business: Management/Administration, Sales/Marketing, and Social services/related.

increasingly Asian in origin (from about one-eighth in 1975 to one-third by 2013), most frequently from China, Taiwan, Korea, and India. These numbers reflect a significant shift in the source of foreign-born faculty from Europe in the post–World War II and cold-war periods to Asia (see Finkelstein, Seal, and Schuster 1998).

An Aging Faculty

There remains one additional demographic trend that is reshaping the American professoriate no less than the general population (simultaneously, with some irony, making it less diverse): their rising life expectancy on the job. The faculty aging phenomenon is, of course, in part a simple function (artifact) of the historical pattern of system growth: the great hiring boom in the 1960s and early 1970s that brought an outsize generation of baby boomers into the faculty ranks to meet surging postwar enrollments. More ominously, however, these individuals, like the baby boom generation to which they belong, are no longer subject to mandatory retirement, but—and here's the unique twist—are protected from the vagaries of the market upending other workers by the institution of tenure. More specifically, as a result of the 1994 uncapping of mandatory retirement (i.e., the lapse in 1994 of the initial professorial exception written into federal age-discrimination legislation by Congress in 1986), reinforced, no doubt, by the ripples of the Great Recession, faculty are beginning to retire later, thereby accelerating the clogging of the academic pipeline that began in the 1980s with the shift from a seller's to a buyer's market in academic labor (see chapter 6 for a fuller treatment of the changing exit patterns from academic careers).

Figures 3.8 and 3.9 chart the age distribution of full-time and part-time faculty, respectively, in the four-year college and university sector from 1987 to 2013.[18] In 1987, at the extremes of the age distribution, 4% of full-time faculty were over the age of sixty-five and 10.8% were under the age of thirty-five; by 2013, the over-sixty-five cadre had more than doubled to 9 % of the full-time faculty, and the under-thirty-five group had shrunk to 8.5%. In 1987, full-time faculty between the ages of thirty-five and fifty-four dominated the middle of the distribution (64.7%, or nearly two-thirds), while faculty at the upper range of the middle, that is, fifty-five to sixty-four, constituted only about one-fifth of faculty. By 2013, positions in the middle had been reversed: faculty in the fifty-five to sixty-four band became modal, now constituting nearly one-third of the whole (30.0%), while faculty in the thirty-five to fifty-

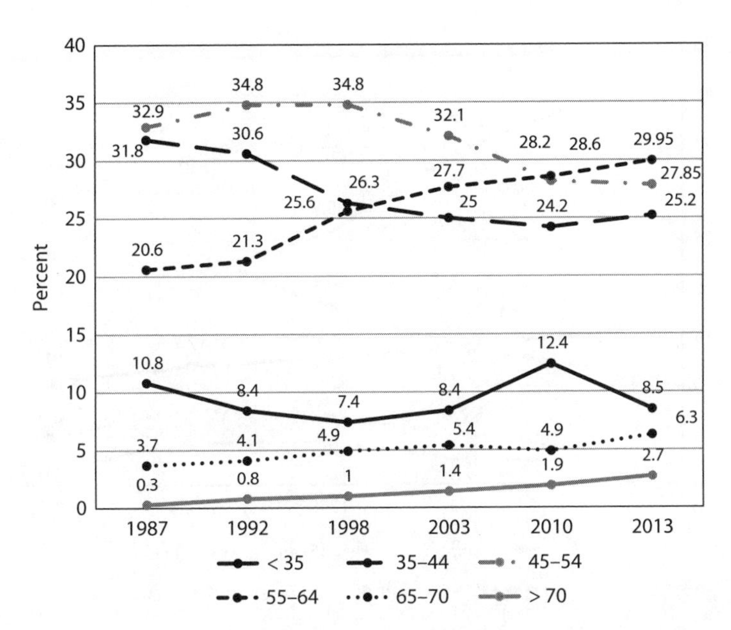

Figure 3.8 Percentage distribution of full-time faculty at four-year institutions, by age, 1987–2013. *Sources:* NSOPF:88; NSOPF:93; NSOPF:99; NSOPF:04; HERI:10; HERI:13. (Refer to appendix A for key to data sources.)

Note: Values for 2013 are estimated from HERI 2013–14 since the age categories are given in years of birth. HERI Faculty Survey changed how age was reported. In 1992–93 and 2004–05, reports used the age categories given above. In 2013–14 age was reported by five-year intervals of birth year starting in 1940.

---

four age band had shrunk from nearly two-thirds to just over half (53.1%). Among part-time faculty (figure 3.9), the pattern is slightly more extreme. While the proportion of faculty in the middle age group (thirty-five to fifty-four) has been shrinking on a par with full-timers, the proportion between fifty-five and sixty-four has increased even more dramatically (threefold), while the proportion under thirty-five has shrunk by half and that over sixty-five has remained the same after a doubling between 1987 and 2003.

The greying of the faculty is visible across all institutional types. While figure 3.10 shows the proportionate growth of faculty between sixty-five and sixty-nine years of age and those older than seventy to be increasing in linear fashion, the increase is greatest at the private universities, where academic work is both more autonomous and more highly compensated. Similarly, while recruitment of scholars under the age of thirty-five has shrunk among all

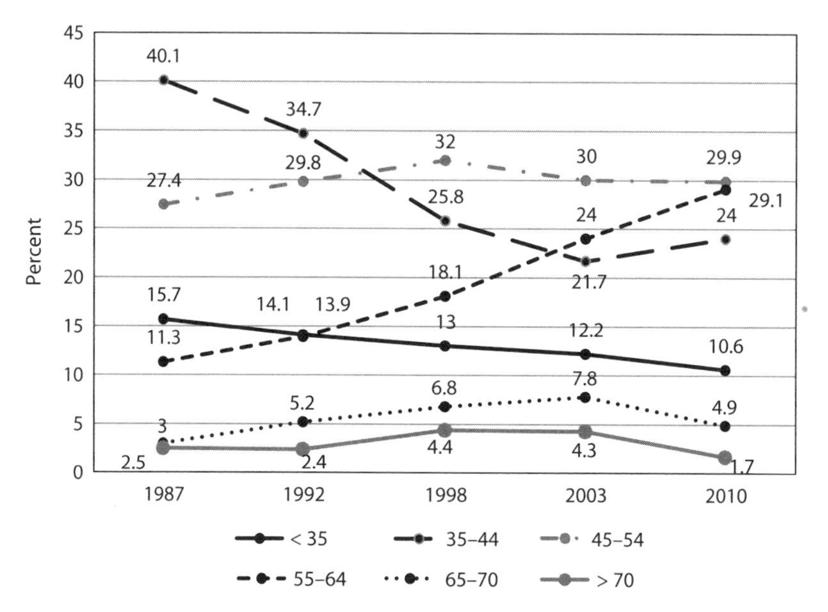

Figure 3.9 Percentage distribution of part-time faculty at four-year institutions, by age, 1987–2010. *Sources:* NSOPF:88; NSOPF:93; NSOPF:99; NSOPF:04; HERI:10. (Refer to appendix A for key to data sources.)

Note: Part-time faculty were not included in the Higher Education Research Institute Faculty Survey Report 2013–14.

institutional types—at least until 2013–14—it may be turning around, with the exception, once again, of the private universities.

Aging differentials are more noticeable, however, when gender and race are taken into account. In 1987 academic women were slightly less likely than academic men to be under the age of thirty-five; by 2013, they were more likely than men to be in this youngest age cohort. Men, moreover, were twice as likely as women to be over fifty-five. Similarly, in 1987 URMs were slightly less likely to be under thirty-five than whites; by 2013, those proportions had reversed themselves, reflecting the differentiated pattern of an aging white, male faculty subgroup contrasted with a younger subgroup that is disproportionately female and more diverse racially or ethnically.

Finally, what can we expect about the relationship between age and appointment type? Are the oldest faculty also those who are most likely to be tenured on traditional appointments? And the youngest faculty disproportionately on limited-term or part-time appointments? While data gaps prevent us from

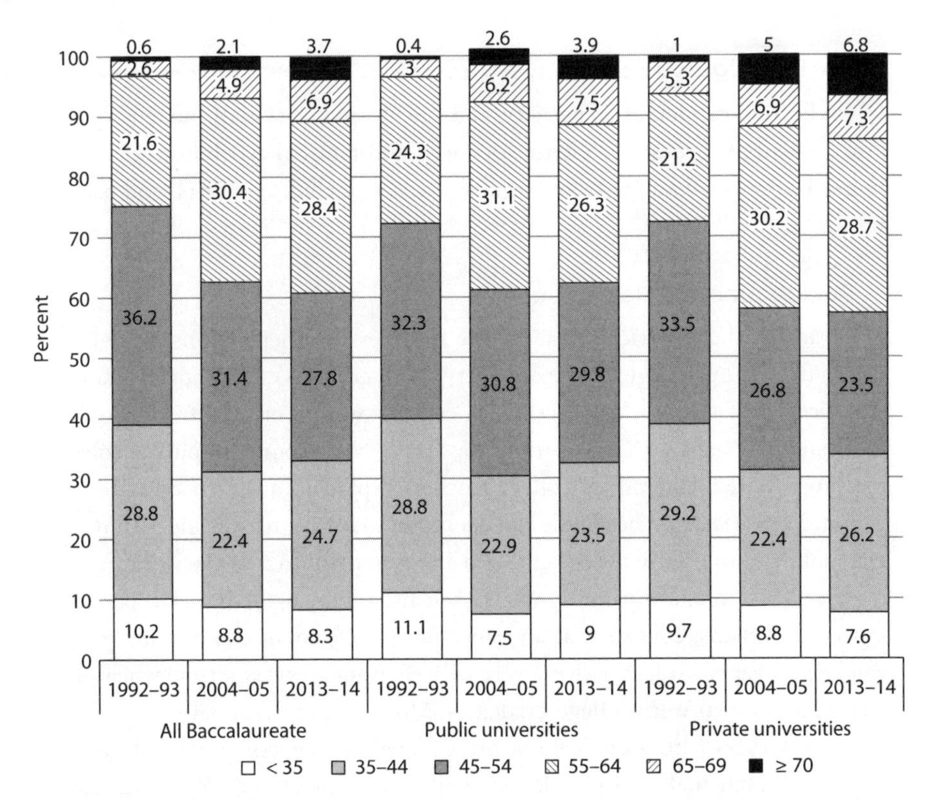

Figure 3.10 Percentage distribution of full-time faculty, by age and type and control of institution: 1992–1993, 2004–2005, 2013–2014. *Sources:* Higher Education Research Institute Faculty Survey, 1992–93, 2004–05, 2013–14.

Note: Values for 2013–14 were estimated from the HERI Faculty Survey 2013–14. HERI Faculty Survey changed how age was reported. In 1992–93 and 2004–05 reports used the age categories given above. In 2013–14 age was reported by five-year intervals of birth year starting in 1940.

---

answering these questions with fully current data, the data yielded by the last National Study of Postsecondary Faculty in 2004 (now a decade old, to be sure) and the Changing Academic Profession Survey of 2007–08 (see chapter 10 and appendix D), together with all the evidence we have about new hires and the new trajectory of academic career entry and early career progression (see chapters 4 and 5), suggest that indeed that newly entering and younger faculty—disproportionately women, URMs, and foreign nationals—are finding themselves increasingly occupying fixed-contract, full-time and part-time appointments.

Social Origins and Family Structure

Quite beyond gender, race, nativity, and age, diversification of the faculty can also be viewed through the lenses of social and familial attributes: socioeconomic background and current family structure, including marital and parental status.

Socioeconomic Background

Historically, the American faculty, like faculties in other nations, have been drawn from the privileged strata of society. As Laurence Veysey(1965) has noted, American professors in the nineteenth century were recruited from those of independent means who could afford, by family background, to pursue college teaching. As the demand for college teachers exploded in the 1960s and compensation rose sharply, academic careers began to offer a reasonable path to social mobility, especially for the children and grandchildren of the working and middle classes, including immigrants (Ladd and Lipset 1979). If we use parents', especially father's, education as an indicator, in 1975 about one in four American faculty reported fathers who were college graduates—at a time when only 12% of adult men were college graduates. More strikingly, about one in seven reported fathers with a graduate or professional degree, compared with about 2% of the adult male US population (Ladd and Lipset 1979). By 2004, those figures had increased substantially, largely, of course, paralleling the increasing educational attainment of the nation. Both then and now, about 25% of the professoriate characterized their socioeconomic background as "working class."

This diversification of socioeconomic background over the past half century, however masks a number of distinctive subgroup patterns. Faculty at universities, especially the elite research universities, have always been drawn from more-privileged social strata than their colleagues in other sectors, and that continues to be the case. Indeed degrees of institutional prestige correlate nearly perfectly with levels of faculty socioeconomic background (Schuster and Finkelstein 2006). Similarly, faculty in the liberal arts fields have been drawn from higher socioeconomic strata than their colleagues in the professions. Among the professions, education and business have tended, and continue, to be among the most proletarian in the social origin of their practitioners (Ladd and Lipset 1979). New hires—both now and then—boasted better-educated parentage than their more senior colleagues, and academic women have consistently been recruited from higher socioeconomic backgrounds than academic men.

Inferences about social origins based on father's education have been basically corroborated by the sparse available data on fathers' occupation. In sum, the current faculty body is being drawn less and less among traditional social-class lines; instead they are increasingly coming from a richer mix of gender, racial and socioeconomic backgrounds than their predecessors.

Current Family Structure

Like the general population, American academics have historically been likely to marry (or form marriage-like relationships): in 1975, about one in seven was single and never married, and that proportion decreased marginally to about one in eight by 2010.[19] What was new by the first decade of the twenty-first century were two developments. First, divorce rates had increased to about one-eighth of the faculty,[20] with women showing slightly higher rates than men. Second, and much more momentous, the rate at which faculty men married declined slightly over the quarter century (1975–2010) from 87 to 80%, while the marriage rate among academic women jumped from 44.7 to 66.7% (and an additional 7.4% living with a partner), yielding a situation of closer gender parity. While the majority of women faculty in the 1960s were single and never married (Dunham et al. 1963) compared with one-eighth of the men, by 2010, 74.1% reported that they were married (or in a marriage-like relationship), while another 10% reported that they were widowed, divorced, or separated; only one of seven reported being single and never married. Together with an increasing marriage rate, academic women in the United States increasingly report that they are members of a dual-career couple, not infrequently a dual-academic couple. Indeed, between one-third and two-fifths of academic women report on recent national surveys that they had an academic spouse (Ward and Wolf-Wendel 2004, 2012).[21]

The increasing convergence of academic men and women in terms of marital status extends to parental status as well. In 1975 about one-third of academic women on full-time appointments reported having one or more children; by 2010 that number had nearly doubled to 63%. In short, the family patterns of male and female faculty have grown more similar, although they may not be experienced in similar ways. Recent studies have reported that in tandem with this change in marital and parental status, academic women are reporting greater conflict between their work and family roles—frequently more severe than among physicians, attorneys, and business executives (Mason and Ekman 2007; Ward and Wolf-Wendel 2004). A recent international survey of the academic profession found that while about one-eighth of full-time faculty overall reported interrupting their career for child or elder care, fully one-quarter of all women reported such interruption compared with only one-twentieth of the men (Cummings and Finkelstein 2011). And women were 10–15% more likely than men to report high levels of stress related to childcare and elder care responsibilities (Hurtado et al. 2012, 5).

Conclusion

This chapter began with a question: Has the expansion and diversification of the instructional staff of America's colleges and universities in the post-2008 period continued on the trajectory that we first identified in great detail in *The American Faculty*? Our updating of the evidence and our application of finer-grained analytical lenses has led us to some rather clear conclusions. First, the first decade of the twenty-first century has seen the consummation of a restructuring of the institutional arena in American higher education: nearly half the enterprise, in terms of institutions and student enrollment, has migrated sequentially to the two-year public sector and the two- and four-year for-profit sector. The faculty, however, has not quite followed: the lion's share of full-timers remain in the four-year sector, especially the university sector; most staffing assignments of the public two-year and for-profit sectors have been part-time. That said, the most striking and consequential development has been the continued—and, in some cases, accelerated—reliance on non-career-ladder faculty, both full- and part-time, to do the instructional "heavy lifting." The divide between the four-year and two-year nonprofit sectors in the preference for full- versus part-time limited-term faculty has remained, with the newly emergent for-profit sector—two-year and four-year—taking the two-year public model one step further in the near complete reliance on part-timers. Similarly, the bifurcation (fragmentation) of the academic landscape in terms of academic field-specific trends in the use of traditional, limited-term, and part-time faculty appears to be continuing.

Second only to the appointments revolution, the continuing demographic diversification of the faculty is the other big story of this chapter. The infusion of women into the faculty ranks continues, as does, to a lesser extent, the infusion of the foreign-born and underrepresented racial minorities. Their integration continues, albeit unevenly, throughout the enterprise, including the research university sector. Indeed, when we focus on pure numbers, more women and URMs are located at research universities than anywhere else, an artifact, of course, of the skewed distribution of full-time faculty over institutional types with high concentrations in the universities, with their large faculties. Women, and URMs as well, however, are distinguishable in terms of their preponderance among the new-hire appointments, especially among the part-time faculty, where they constitute the majority. When we drill down one degree further to the intersection of gender and race, we find a clear pattern: Asian women and URM women have made substantial progress over the past two decades, African American, Latino, and Native American women much less so, while white women have largely maintained their own dominant position. Nonetheless, this internal diversity among academic women suggests that, moving forward, generalizations about gender and academic careers will require disaggregated analyses and a more nuanced approach.

Finally, the aging of the American faculty continues unabated—reinforced at once by the uncapping of mandatory retirement and the lingering effects of the Great Recession of 2008. Tenured academic staff, especially at the research universities, appear to be staying on past the age of seventy in significantly greater numbers, thereby limiting the opportunity of a prospective, new academic generation (see chapter 6).

What do these trends mean for the enterprise, going forward in challenging times? In some sense, of course, the remainder of this volume is focused on addressing this very question. For the moment, by way of preview, we would frame a few broad dilemmas that readers may take with them on their journey. On one hand, there is the continuing diversification in academic appointments: the majority of headcount instructional staff in American higher education are now contingent, and, conversely, the core, career-ladder faculty are an increasingly shrinking portion of the enterprise. In some sense, as we suggest elsewhere (chapters 4 and 5), that represents an expansion of opportunity for access to academic careers, especially for historically underrepresented groups, and brings a much more diverse mix of work and life experience to the academy. That sounds attractive on the face of it. That the shrinking of traditional academic opportunities, however, coincides with the increased entry of women and racial/ethnic minorities into the faculty ranks introduces equity issues into the mix, as historically underrepresented new entrants meet much less promising career prospects and are being offered, in effect, a species of second-class citizenship as a reward for their wait. Beyond the increased opportunity prospect and the equity risk, the appointments revolution results in a fundamental restructuring of the routinized, predictable, and secure academic career as it has evolved over the past half century in the United States—a source we argue later of the US higher education systems' strength over that time (see chapter 11 and also Clotfelter 2010). Chapters 4 and 5 in this volume seek to empirically weight that risk in terms of career mobility and attrition.

The shrinking of the core staff and the heavy reliance on "independent contractors"—amid the concurrent growth in academic administrative ranks—promises to wreak havoc on any semblance of traditional notions of an academic community. This cannot augur well for the shared governance of the enterprise: the fragmentation of the instructional staff and the likely diminution of academic influence on steering the enterprise (a prospect considered in chapter 8). And perhaps no trend is less sanguine than the increased aging of the faculty: the more the faculty age and stay on, the greater the likelihood, absent an infusion of new financial resources, that institutions will be reluctant to hire. And to the extent that they are hesitant, the greater the likelihood that they will hedge their bets by resorting to contingent appointments—a species of closed, self-reinforcing system (see chapter 6).

NOTES

1. Part of the story of the past quarter century in American higher education has been the progressive decline of state support for higher education and the associated decline of faculty compensation and working condition in the public sector (see chapter 7).

2. In terms of limited data availability, we are referring to the demise of the National Study of Postsecondary Faculty (NSOPF) following its last administration in 2004. That, in effect, means that we must draw on either less comprehensive data sources such as The Integrated Postsecondary Data System (IPEDS), the National Science Foundation's Survey of Doctoral Recipients, or the Higher Education Research Institute's Faculty Survey. We have, however, sought to select data points which allow us to isolate insofar as possible developments impacted by the Great Recession of 2008.

3. 2013 is the last year for which reliable national IPEDS data are available before publication.

4. The data on developments in the 1960s and 1970s are presented in detail in Schuster and Finkelstein (2006).

5. These percentages are calculated based on the raw numbers in figure 3.1.

6. More than half of these full-time faculty in the four-year sector are located in the relatively small research university sector of fewer than 400 institutions.

7. See Schuster and Finkelstein (2006), chap. 3.

8. The absolute number of tenure-eligible faculty actually increased during this period. The precipitous proportionate decline reflects the enormous growth in the sheer number of faculty appointments that are increasingly of the nontraditional character.

9. There is no concomitant capacity to track new hires among the part-time faculty.

10. "New Hires" are composed of full-time faculty who are moving from one institution to another as well as those who are entering the academic workforce for the first

time. While we cannot provide precise estimates of the proportion of each subgroup within new hires, the available evidence on limited inter-institutional mobility suggests that the vast majority of these "new hires" are "new" to higher education—and not movers from other colleges and universities.

11. Institutions in the faculty sample for the NSOPF04 survey responded to an Institution Questionnaire that addressed matters of instructional staffing levels and changes therein, faculty recruitment and hiring practices, and retirement policies and rates.

12. Although, given the much larger size of research and doctoral universities and their faculties, the greatest absolute number of women were affiliated with universities.

13. This likely reflects the large number of faculty hired during the great expansion of the community college sector in the 1960s and 1970s, frequently drawing on teachers in the public schools.

14. While the data support a trend of *increasing* equity in the area of faculty appointments, we draw no conclusion that any standard of equity has been achieved in this area, let alone—as we shall see in subsequent chapters, for example, 8 and 9—in other areas such as workload and compensation.

15. In *The American Faculty*, we reported that at least among full-time appointments, minority faculty were actually less likely than white faculty to be on non-career-ladder tracks.

16. The decline has been especially radical in the private two-year, not for profit and the for-profit sector, where URM faculty have become the new majority.

17. We had developed a taxonomy for addressing race/ethnicity in *The American Faculty* (Schuster and Finkelstein 2006) which was described in considerable detail in appendix I in that volume, pp. 441–42. Since that time, the federal government has redefined the categories they use to classify race and ethnicity in federal databases. In light of that change, and following the lead of our colleague, Daryl Smith (Smith, Tovar, and Garcia 2012), we have here reconceived our racial/ethnic taxonomy: a new category of nonresident alien is introduced to include foreign-born faculty who may in the past have been misclassified as URMs (underrepresented racial minorities) owing to their race but ignoring where they were born or educated (i.e., outside the United States, e.g., the case of the African immigrant or the Latin American or Spanish immigrant), native-born Asians and Pacific islanders have been separated out as a category of nonwhites that are nonetheless hardly underrepresented in the academic or scientific workforce, and then African American and non-white Latinos as well as native Americans have been included separately (when possible) but also collectively under the rubric URM, a term employed by the National Science Foundation (1993, 1999, 2004, 2006, 2010, 2013) in their annual *Science and Technology Indicators* publication.

18. The only national data on faculty age after 2003 are available from the UCLA's Higher Education Research Institute Faculty surveys of 2004–05, 2007–08, 2010–11. Since HERI faculty surveys did not fully sample two-year institutions until very recently, data are only displayed for faculty affiliated with four-year colleges and universities.

19. One in seven among academic women.

20. The figure reported in the NSOPF:04 is twelve.

21. Forty-six percent of women respondents to the US component of the Changing Academic Profession survey reported an academic spouse—a rate substantially higher than female colleagues in other nations. The figure was closer to one-third in the 2010–11 HERI Faculty Survey.

REFERENCES

Astin, Alexander W., William S. Korn, and Eric L. Dey. 1990. *The American College Teacher: National Norms for 1989–90 HERI Faculty Survey Report.* Los Angeles: Higher Education Research Institute, UCLA.

Cummings, William K. and Martin J. Finkelstein. 2011. *Scholars in the Changing American Academic: New Roles and New Rules.* Dordrecht, NL: Springer.

Dey, Eric L., Claudia E. Ramirez, William S. Korn, and Alexander W. Astin. 1993. *The American College Teacher: National Norms for 1992–93 HERI Faculty Survey Report.* Los Angeles: Higher Education Research Institute, UCLA.

Finkelstein, Martin J., Robert K. Seal and Jack H. Schuster. 1998. *The New Academic Generation: A Profession in Transformation.* Baltimore, MD: Johns Hopkins University Press.

Hurtado, Sylvia, Kevin Egan, John Pryor, Hannah Whang, and Serge Tran. 2012. *Undergraduate Teaching Faculty: The 2010–11 HERI Faculty Survey.* Los Angeles: Higher Education Research Institute, UCLA.

Kim, Dongbin, Susan Twombley, and Lisa Wolf-Wendel. 2012. "International Faculty in American Universities: Experiences of Academic Life, Productivity, and Career Mobility." *New Directions for Institutional Research* 155 (Fall): 27–46.

Leslie, David. 2007. "The Re-Shaping of America's Academic Workforce." *Research Dialogue.* New York: TIAA-CREF.

Lindholm, Jennifer A., Katalin Szelenyi, Sylvia Hurtado, and William S. Korn. 2005. *The American College Teacher: National Norms for the 2004–2005 HERI Faculty Survey.* Los Angeles: Higher Education Research Institute, UCLA.

National Science Foundation (NSF). 1993. "Academic Research and Development." In *Science and Engineering Indictors.* Washington, DC: National Science Foundation.

———. 1999. "Academic Research and Development." In *Science and Engineering Indicators.* Washington, DC: NSF.

———. 2004. "Academic Research and Development." In *Science and Engineering Indicators.* Washington, DC: NSF.

———. 2006. "Academic Research and Development." In *Science and Engineering Indicators.* Washington, DC: NSF.

———. 2010. "Academic Research and Development." In *Science and Engineering Indicators.* Washington, DC: NSF.

———. 2013. "Academic Research and Development." In *Science and Engineering Indicators.* Washington, DC: NSF.

Sax, L. J., A. W. Astin, W. S. Korn, and S. K. Gilmartin. 1998. *The American College Teacher: National Norms for 1998–99 HERI Faculty Survey Report.* Los Angeles: Higher Education Research Institute, UCLA.

Schuster, Jack, and Martin J. Finkelstein. 2006. *The American Faculty: The Restructuring of Academic Work and Careers.* Baltimore, MD: Johns Hopkins University Press.

Smith, Daryl G., Esau Tovar, and Hugo Garcia. 2012. "Where Are They? A Multilens Examination of the Distribution of Full-Time Faculty by Institutional Type, Race/Ethnicity, Gender, and Citizenship." *New Directions for Institutional Research* 155 (Fall): 5–26.

Veysey, Laurence. 1965. *The Emergence of the American University.* Chicago: University of Chicago Press.

Ward, Kelly, and Lisa Wolf-Wendel. 2004. "Academic Motherhood: Managing Complex Roles in Research Universities." *Review of Higher Education* 27 (Winter): 23–57.

———. 2012. *Academic Motherhood: How Faculty Manage Work and Family.* New Brunswick, NJ: Rutgers University Press.

PART II / The Morphing of Academic Careers

During the second half of the twentieth century, university faculty careers in the United States developed a definition and predictability unprecedented in academic history. Graduate schools produced a ready supply of PhDs in most of the traditional liberal arts fields, who competed in what became, after federal antidiscrimination legislation in the 1960s and 1970s, a relatively open and transparent recruitment process for full-time, probationary entry-level positions.[1] Career progression proceeded along a defined path on a defined schedule: a six- to seven-year probationary period, followed by a high-stakes evaluation that preceded the promotion to an associate professorship and the conferral of "tenure" rights.[2] Incumbents were then eligible for promotion in rank (although not everyone was promoted to full professor, and the schedule and criteria might be ill defined) and might further "branch out" into academic administrative roles, such as department chair or dean, or pursue other academic positions at competing institutions. Very few who entered and were promoted left the fold. Moreover, with great regularity, faculty who reached their institutionally mandated retirement age moved quickly and cleanly into retirement, although a few stayed on informally in some kind of largely honorary "emeritus" role.

Indeed, sociologists of science postulated more than forty years ago what became known as the first law of academic career development: Where you start (in terms of type of institution and type of position) determines where you end up (Cole and Cole 1973; Long 1978; Merton 1968). Those who were fortunate enough to attain the right kind of first position at the right kind of institution progressed successfully career-wise; while those who did not begin at the right place experienced "cumulative" disadvantages (McClelland 1990).

Much of this definition and clarity, and much of the predictability, is now gone for most faculty—except for a rapidly shrinking core (as described in part I, chapter 3)—yielding to a complex and ambiguous ballgame. The majority of new academic appointees take on various contract or part-time assignments, the road to a career-ladder or even stable faculty position is increasingly circuitous and uncertain, careers forged at a single institution are increasingly rare, and career exit more ambiguous and uncertain.

These changes are chronicled in the three chapters that follow. Building on the analytical lens afforded by discussion of the aging of the faculty in chapter 3, we transition in chapters 4 and 5 to a focus on four stages or phases of an academic career: the entry stage (the first one to three years in the first academic job); early career (within the first three to eight year post entry, when incumbents have traditionally pursued tenure); mid-career (the first nine to fifteen years post initial entry, typically after the receipt of tenure); and the late or senior career (at least sixteen years post career entry), stages that are frequently, but not invariably associated with advancing age.[3] Figure 4.1 provides an overview of the relative size of these career-stage groups, based on the 2004 National Survey of Postsecondary Faculty: in 2003, those at the new entrant stage constituted about one-sixth of faculty, those in early career about one-fifth, those in mid-career another one-fifth, and those at the senior stage—the largest of the subgroups—at about two-fifths. Chapter 4 focuses on the first, or entry stage, drawing on two different data sources: the National Study of Postsecondary Faculty 2004 (US Department of Education, 2006) and the Survey of Doctoral Recipients (NSF 2016). It highlights the critical role of education credentials—the research doctoral degree—in shaping patterns of career entry in terms of institutional venues and type of appointments (for those with and without the doctoral degree), and movement among employment statuses and appointment types during the settling-in period. It explicitly considers how career entry varies for those bringing different levels of education credentials with them (PhD or other terminal degree vs. master's and baccalaureate degrees), those in different academic fields with different labor markets, and for distinctive demographic groups such as academic women.

Drawing upon the same two data sources, chapter 5 focuses on the academic career post-entry. It takes as its point of departure the various entry points into academic careers chronicled in chapter 4 and inquires into how careers are navigated going forward, that is, in our terminology, early career, mid-career, and early-advanced or late career. Insofar as most new hires are in nontraditional, non-tenure-track appointments, what do we know about the probabilities and routes to a more stable position? To what extent is there mobility between part-time and full-time positions? Between contract and tenure-track or tenured positions? Once a stable position is achieved (to the extent it is), what do we know about promotion opportunities? What do we know about attrition, that is, individuals prematurely leaving academic careers? Are there identifiable points of "leakage" in the pipeline, for example, pre-tenure? Who is most vulnerable? Finally, how does the navigation of an academic career differ for academic women? For faculty in different academic fields with different nonacademic opportunities? For members of underrepresented racial and ethnic minorities?

Chapter 6 is the realm of the senior faculty, with a particular focus on the process of exiting from academic careers. As a function largely of the uncapping of mandatory retirement, career exit has become an individual rather than a purely institutional decision. And as a function of the trend away from defined-benefit to defined-contribution retirement plans (see chapter 6), prospective retirees are less certain about their level of benefits and more subject to the vagaries of financial markets in making the retirement decision. In light of such greater uncertainties and fears related to health care costs, the chapter examines faculty adaptations to the "new" environment, including extending the transition through alternative employment (often academic) rather than making a clean break from the labor market. To considerations of faculty age and career stage, chapter 6 adds a focus on generations or birth cohort and the complex interaction between age, career stage, and generation or birth cohort in shaping career exit.

Taken together, these three chapters provide a window on what we know about the emerging new contours of academic employment as it metamorphoses before our eyes.

NOTES

1. This is not to suggest that ascriptive characteristics were absent, including prestige of the PhD-granting department and dissertation sponsor, that bifurcated the labor market by prestige of the sending institution (Caplow and McGee 1958). But the search process operated under a series of federal regulations related to availability pools, interview pools, that were enforced—at least ostensibly—by university human resource departments.

2. In defining tenure rights, we follow the lead of Walter Metzger, who clarified that the "right" in question was to a dismissal procedure governed at once by peer review and procedural due process.

3. For faculty holding the doctorate, career stage is calculated in terms of years elapsed since award of the PhD (which historically has been coterminous with entry into an academic position); for faculty who do not hold the doctorate, career stage is calculated in terms of years elapsed since appointment to the first academic position (those

who do not hold the doctorate frequently, as we shall see, typically report work experience following receipt of highest degree before assuming a faculty position).

REFERENCES

Caplow, Theodore and Reece J. McGee. 1958. *The Academic Marketplace.* New York: Basic Books.

Cole, Jonathan R., and Stephen Cole. 1973. *Social Stratification in Science.* Chicago: University of Chicago Press.

Long, John. 1978. "Productivity and Academic Position in the Scientific Career." *American Sociological Review* 43 (December): 899–908.

McClelland, Katherine. 1990. "Cumulative Disadvantage among the Highly Ambitious." *Sociology of Education* 63 (April): 102–21.

Merton, Robert K. 1968. "The Matthew Effect in Science." *Science* 159 (January): 56–63.

National Science Foundation. 2016. *Science and Engineering Indicators.* Washington, DC: NSF.

US Department of Education. 2006. *2004 National Study of Postsecondary Faculty: Methodology Report.* NCES 2006179. Washington, DC: National Center for Education Statistics.

4

Changing Pathways to Career Entry

In chapter 3, we documented the reshaping over the past two to three decades of the opportunity structure for pursuing academic careers (the sustained surge in part-time and non-tenure-track, and the concomitant proportionate decline in tenure-track, appointments) and the changing demographic complexion of the new academic workforce (the rise of a new breed of academic woman, the steady growth in foreign-born and underrepresented racial minorities, and the gradual aging of the academic generation hired to staff the vast expansion of American higher education in the 1960s and 1970s). What have these developments meant for the process of recruitment and entry into academic careers? And what do they mean for the mechanisms of settling into a stable, entry-level job? On the face of it, the increasing diversification of types of appointments seems to be associated with an increasing demographic diversification of the academic workforce—more and different types of opportunities that are suitable for individuals in a richer diversity of life circumstances; and that is, by and large, a good thing. At the same time, diversification has the potential to promote stratification as historically privileged groups continue to move into privileged appointments and less privileged groups are relegated to nontraditional, and less well compensated, roles—what the sociologists refer to as "accumulative disadvantage."[1] What do the data tell us about career entry and how it is changing?

An "Entering Class" of New Faculty

To address that question, we turned first to the most recent National Study of Postsecondary Faculty (NSOPF) and identified a cohort of new entrants to the faculty: respondents who in 2003 reported that they had embarked on their first academic appointment of any sort, full- or part-time and on or off the tenure

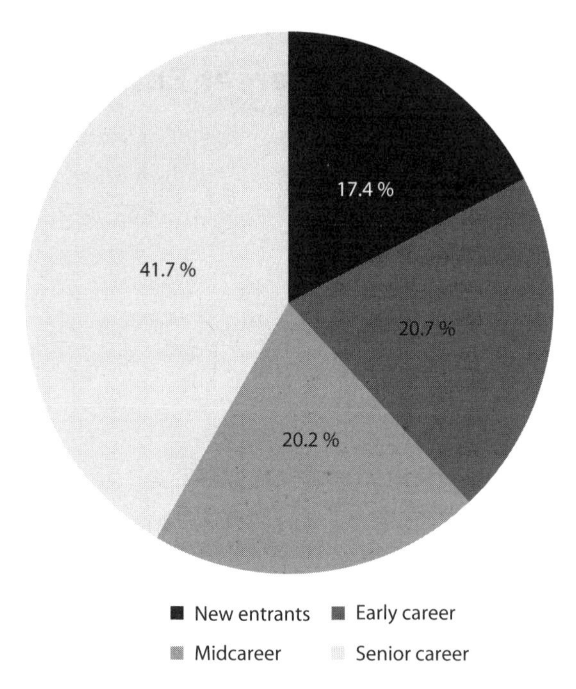

Figure 4.1 Percentage distribution of faculty, by career stage, 2003. *Source:* NSOPF:04. (Refer to appendix A for key to data sources.)

---

track beyond graduate teaching assistant—in the previous three years. This strategy yielded a cohort of some 150,000 individuals (151,409, to be precise) who reported formally entering the academic labor market (workforce) within a three-year window between 2001 and 2003. It promised to provide us with a stable snapshot of the entering class to academic careers at the turn of the twenty-first century, avoiding any aberrations that may have characterized a particularly good or bad recruiting year. Figure 4.1 displays the new-entrant slice of academic appointees—just over one-sixth (17.4%) of the total workforce in that three-year period—who are the focus of this chapter relative to those in the three later career stages (the other 82.6%), who are the focus of chapters 5 and 6.

What did we learn from our entering class? First, over the past quarter century, as the US academic labor market tightened and took on the characteristics of a long-term buyer's market, one substantially restructured and diversified in its mix of career-ladder and temporary opportunities and of institutional and disciplinary venues (higher growth outside the research university sector and the traditional liberal arts and science fields), the PhD has come to no longer constitute the universal entry credential everywhere across the system.[2] Table 4.1 shows the proportion of newly entering faculty in 2003 (the last year for which reliable national data are available), both full- and part-time, who reported holding the PhD degree by employment status, institutional type, academic field, gender, and appointment type. While about one-quarter of the 151,000 newly entering faculty overall hold the PhD (39,000), there are sharp differences in PhD representation between full-time faculty in the four-year and two-year sectors (63.2 to 73.0% in the four-year sector vs. 6.3% in the two-year sector), between full-time faculty in the liberal arts fields (humanities, 70.9%; natural sciences, 86.7%; and social sciences, 82.5%), and faculty in some of the applied professions (health sciences, 21.3%; fine arts, 38.0%; and business, 56.9%), and between full-time faculty in the tenure stream (72.0%) and those off the tenure track (31.0 %). Within the four-year sector, there are vast differences between full-time (67.5%) and part-time faculty (14.9%) in proportion holding the PhD. Finally, there are discernable differences in education credentials by gender: 57.9% of men versus 50.7% of women full-time, new faculty report holding the PhD.

The data further demonstrate how differences in education credentials shape the institutional venue and appointment type through which individuals enter into academic careers. Table 4.2 shows the entry venues of newly entering PhD recipients versus non-doctorate holders embarking on faculty careers in 2003 by institution type and employment status. The basic pattern is one in which PhDs gravitate toward the four-year sector (more than nine-tenths) and toward full-time appointments (about three-quarters), while non-PhDs gravitate toward part-time appointments (about three-quarters), but as much in the four-year as the two- year sector. There remain, however, a substantial minority of PhDs who enter through part-time appointments (about one-quarter) and even through the two-year sector (about one-twelfth). The bottom half of table 4.2 provides an alternative lens on the link at entry between education credentials, on the one hand, and institutional and appointment types, on the other. About one-third of the new faculty recruited by four-year institutions are full-timers with PhDs, another 45% are non-PhD-holding part-timers, and the remaining one-fifth to one-quarter of the entering class in the four-year sector are distributed between full-timers not holding the PhD degree (typically, in the professions) and part-timers with the PhD. More than nine of ten faculty who enter the labor market via the two-year college sector do not hold a PhD, and barely one in twenty is a PhD holder.

Table 4.1 Percentage of newly entering full-time and part-time faculty holding the PhD degree, by type of institution, academic field, gender, and appointment type, Fall 2003

	All new entrants		PhD new entrants		% PhD	
	(*N* = 151,409)		(*N* = 39,273)			
	Full-time	Part-time	Full-time	Part-time	Full-time	Part-time
	(*N* = 54,306)	(*N* = 97,103)	(*N* = 29,660)	(*N* = 9,613)		
Institution type[a]						
Four-year	41,972	45,184	28,332	6,724	67.5	14.9
Research	16,444	8,883	12,007	1,536	73.0	17.3
Doctoral	6,428	6,314	4,168	1,165	64.8	18.5
Comprehensive	13,493	21,534	8,522	3,280	63.2	15.2
Liberal arts	5,607	8,453	3,635	743	64.8	8.8
Two-year	9,938	47,558	626	2,466	6.3	5.2
Academic field (Four-year institutions only)						
Business	2,563	6,822	1,458	449	56.9	6.6
Education	4,676	7,729	3,109	1,230	66.5	15.9
Engineering	3,009	624	2,701	328	89.8	52.6
Fine arts	2,676	4,949	1,018	94	38.0	1.9
Health sciences	4,165	3,767	888	171	21.3	4.5
Humanities	6,804	6,645	4,825	1,598	70.9	24.0
Natural sciences	9,145	5,922	7,930	1,544	86.7	26.1
Social sciences	5,318	5,043	4,390	1,410	82.5	28.0
Other programs	5,108	7,472	2,203	295	43.1	3.9
Gender						
Female	24,866	50,866	12,601	4,391	50.7	8.6
Male	29,441	46,237	17,060	5,222	57.9	11.3
Appointment type						
Tenured or tenure track	31,261	2,740	22,517	118	72.0	4.3
Non-tenure-track or tenure not applicable	23,045	94,362	7,144	9,496	31.0	10.1

Source: NSOPF:04. (Refer to appendix A for key.)

Table 4.2 Employment status of new faculty at career entry, by highest degree and institution sector, Fall 2003

	Non-PhD (N=112,134)		PhD (N=39,274)	
	N	%	N	%
Four-year institutions	57,731	51.0	36,181	92.1
Full-time	15,334	13.6	29,034	73.9
Part-time	42,397	37.5	7,147	18.2
Two-year institutions	54,403	48.1	3,092	7.9
Full-time	9,312	8.2	626	1.6
Part-time	45,091	39.9	2,466	6.3

	Four-year institutions (N=93,912)		Two-year institutions (N=57,496)	
	N	%	N	%
Non-PhD	57,731	61.5	54,404	94.6
Full-time	15,333	16.3	9,312	16.2
Part-time	42,398	45.1	45,092	78.4
PhD	36,181	38.5	3,092	5.4
Full-time	29,034	30.9	626	1.1
Part-time	7,147	7.6	2,466	4.3

Source: NSOPF:04. (Refer to appendix A for key.)
Note: Total of new entrants regardless of highest degree.

For our purposes, this means that there are multiple stories to be told about recruitment and entry into academic careers. The modal story—and certainly the one that dominates the literature on faculty recruitment since at least Alan Cartter's *PhDs and the Academic Marketplace* in 1974—remains that of PhD-trained aspirants filling full-time appointments in the four-year sector in the traditional liberal arts fields. But to that basic leitmotif must be added the more contemporary stories of the entry of fully one-quarter of the newly entering PhDs into nontraditional, part-time appointments; the entry of non-doctorate-holders, typically those with master's and first professional degreess, into the four-year sector, especially in the newer professional fields, such as the health sciences (see table 4.1 row for percentage PhD among full-time health sciences faculty); and, finally, entry of about one-twelfth of PhDs to full-time academic appointments in the two-year, community college sector.

The data infrastructure for telling these stories is, alas, uneven. While the National Science Foundation's Survey of Doctorate Recipients (SDR) provides information over time on the careers of many thousands of PhD recipients through 2013,[3] the data foundation for the study of nondoctored faculty, including part-timers and full-timers, in the "newer" professions is largely limited to the last National Study of Postsecondary Faculty administered by the National Center for Education Statistics in fall 2003. Thus we begin with the richer fabric of our main storyline buttressed by very current National Science Foundation data and draw primarily on what amounts to old data, though we believe the data are largely still valid in their basic essentials. Then we tell the less noticed, albeit no less important story, one heretofore only superficially covered in the literature on academic careers (see Cohen and Brawer 1977; Seidman 1985; Gappa and Leslie 1993; and Lechuga 2005 as rare examples of studies of non-full-time and non-four-year faculty), to illuminate the key minor themes of what amounts to the new majority's career entry.[4]

Market Entry: Historical Context

First, a word by way of historical context. In the halcyon days of the 1960s and 1970s, prospective academics were often plucked out of graduate school by (or before) the age of thirty, while still completing their doctoral dissertations for full-time, tenure-track positions with excellent career prospects. That is no longer the case. Table 4.3 shows the employment sector of new doctoral-degree recipients with definite employment commitments between 1990 and 2013.[5] A glance at the table suggests at least two clear trends. First, in the aggregate, there is remarkable durability in immediate postgraduate employment plans of doctorates over two decades: about half typically enter academe in some capacity, about one-fifth to one-quarter enter business and industry, and less than a tenth enter government or the private, nonprofit sector. Second, there is enormous variation in employment sector by academic field: at one end of the spectrum, more than four-fifths of humanities doctorates enter academe (closely followed by social science doctorates at three-fifths), while at the other end, fewer than one-fifth of engineering doctorates do (closely followed by physical science doctorates at one-third). It is important to note that while half of new PhDs move into academe upon degree receipt, the move is not necessarily into career-ladder faculty positions. In 2013, for example, among 15,000 Science and Engineering doctoral recipients with definite employment commitment, 50.2% were planning to enter academe (the vast majority in postdoctoral study), 19.7% other sectors (elementary and secondary education, government,

Table 4.3 Sector of initial employment of new PhD recipients with definite employment commitments, by gender, 1990–2013

Sector and year of commitment	Total	Life sciences	Physical sciences	Social sciences	Engineering	Education	Humanities
				N			
All U.S. employment commitments							
1990	15,239	1,325	1,780	2,935	1,872	4,020	1,922
1995	15,303	1,456	1,666	2,736	1,890	3,913	2,178
2000	17,246	1,949	2,033	3,116	2,335	3,907	2,575
2005	15,658	1,713	1,785	2,731	2,129	3,550	2,399
2010	14,429	1,763	1,849	2,644	2,025	2,794	1,984
2013	15,008	1,987	2,295	2,590	2,568	2,313	1,897
				%			
Academe							
1990	51.5	48.5	38.7	50.3	26.3	46.4	83.2
1995	52.4	51.4	41.8	53.4	19.1	48.3	82.8
2000	48.6	46.0	33.7	51.6	14.8	47.9	79.3
2005	54.3	53.2	40.6	61.7	18.5	50.2	83.0
2010	52.6	49.0	35.9	59.9	16.9	53.4	81.7
2013	50.2	45.9	30.6	60.3	13.7	58.6	82.8
Government							
1990	8.8	16.3	8.3	12.8	11.9	7.2	2.2
1995	8.1	14.1	8.6	12.5	10.9	6.0	1.8
2000	7.4	13.6	5.8	11.5	9.0	4.6	2.0
2005	6.9	12.7	6.6	10.1	9.3	4.1	2.3
2010	8.9	14.5	9.8	13.9	12.8	3.5	2.3
2013	7.5	12.6	6.1	12.0	9.5	3.2	2.3

(continued)

Table 4.3 (continued)

Sector and year of commitment	Total	Life sciences	Physical sciences	Social sciences	Engineering	Education	Humanities
Business or industry							
1990	21.9	26.4	50.6	18.4	59.1	6.2	4.7
1995	21.7	24.5	45.3	16.4	66.1	6.0	5.1
2000	26.1	28.9	54.7	17.7	72.9	5.7	6.5
2005	22.8	25.3	48.7	14.4	68.7	4.1	4.2
2010	23.2	24.6	48.1	13.7	64.4	4.5	4.9
2013	30.1	29.0	59.4	15.1	73.3	4.5	4.5
Nonprofit organizations							
1990	6.7	7.3	1.6	13.3	2.2	5.7	5.7
1995	6.3	7.3	2.2	11.5	2.2	5.1	5.8
2000	5.9	6.9	2.0	11.5	1.8	4.6	6.0
2005	5.3	7.1	2.5	8.8	2.3	4.3	6.2
2010	5.2	8.4	2.7	7.2	3.2	4.4	4.9
2013	5.6	9.6	2.3	8.8	2.8	5.2	5.2
Other or unknown							
1990	11.1	1.5	0.8	5.2	0.5	34.5	4.1
1995	11.4	2.7	2.1	6.2	1.6	34.6	4.5
2000	12.0	4.6	2.8	7.8	1.5	37.2	6.1
2005	10.7	1.8	1.6	5.0	1.2	37.3	4.3
2010	10.1	3.5	3.5	5.3	2.7	34.1	6.2
2013	6.6	2.9	1.6	3.7	0.7	28.4	5.2

Source: NSF/NIH/USED/USDA/NEH/NASA, 2010 Survey of Earned Doctorates.

Notes: Fields follow the groupings derived by NSF-SESTAT. Social-related sciences includes economics, political-related sciences, psychology, sociology and anthropology, and other social sciences. The non-cience-and-engineering fields include art and humanities fields, education (except science and math), business including management, administration, sales, and marketing, and social services-related fields.

nonprofit), and 30.1% business and industry. Most of the academic-sector employment reported, at least initially, was either in postdoctoral fellowship positions or in other nonregular positions, including part-time and fixed-contract full-time instructional or research positions as well as administrative positions.

Education Credentials and Entry Venues: New PhDs

Table 4.4 presents a descriptive portrait of two subgroups among the entire class of faculty entering academic appointments between 2001 and 2003: PhDs recipients and non-PhD holders.[6] When we compare the doctorate recipient subgroup with non-PhD holders, a few observations are striking. First, doctoral recipients constituted just over one-quarter of all newly entering faculty between 2001 and 2003 (26.4%)—a distinct minority of the entire cohort entering the American professoriate for the first time between 2001 and 2003. Second, the PhDs tend to be disproportionately located at research and doctoral universities (48.1% vs. 17.3% of non-PhDs) and virtually absent from the two-year community colleges (only one-twelfth vs. about half of the non-PhDs). Three out of four are employed in full-time faculty positions compared with 22.4% of the non-PhDs and among the full-timers, predominantly in tenured or tenure-track appointments (57.3% vs. 7.9% of non-PhD new entrants). Two-thirds of the PhD recipients are in the traditional liberal arts fields compared with just over one-third of non-PhD new entrants (35.9%).[7] PhD recipients are more likely than non-PhDs to be under thirty-five years of age (36.8 vs. 29.5% of non-PhDs) and much less likely to be over the age of forty-five (23.4% vs. 39.5% of non-PhDs). Consistent with their relatively greater youth, PhD recipients in the entering class are much less likely to report being six or more years beyond their highest degree (24.6% vs. 56.6% of all new entrants), that is, they report lower levels of post-terminal-degree labor force participation before assuming their current job. Indeed, they are three times as likely as non-PhDs to report having held no previous job (19.6% vs. 5.2%) and half as likely to report having held a job outside of postsecondary education (31.8% vs. 73.0%). Moreover, they are two and a half times as likely as non-PhDs to report no other employment concurrent with their focal position in postsecondary education (80.9 vs. 33.6%). These are the prototypical college and university faculty of the last half of the twentieth century—except, perhaps, that they are more likely than in the past to be female (43.3% of all newly entering PhDs) although less likely to be female than non-PhDs (53.2%).

Table 4.4 Selected characteristics of faculty with and without the PhD, Fall 2003

	All new entrants		PhD		Non-PhD	
	(*N*=151,409)		(*N*= 39,273)		(*N*= 112,135)	
	N	%	*N*	%	*N*	%
Institution type[a]						
Research	25,328	16.7	13,545	34.5	11,637	10.6
Doctoral	12,743	8.4	5,334	13.6	7,352	6.7
Comprehensive	35,027	23.1	11,802	30.1	22,769	20.8
Liberal arts	14,063	9.3	4,379	11.2	9,682	8.8
Two-year	57,497	38.0	3,092	7.9	52,574	48.0
Academic field						
Business	13,064	8.6	1,987	5.1	11,077	10.1
Education	17,660	11.7	4,794	12.2	12,866	11.7
Engineering	5,042	3.3	3,029	7.7	2,013	1.8
Health Sciences	14,671	9.7	1,294	3.3	12,919	11.8
Fine arts	10,922	7.2	1,133	2.9	9,277	8.5
Humanities	22,299	14.7	6,720	17.1	15,579	14.2
Natural sciences	26,420	17.4	10,158	25.9	15,969	14.6
Social sciences	14,518	9.6	6,615	16.8	7,902	7.2
Other rograms	26,817	16.3	3,546	9.0	21,982	20.1
Appointment type						
Part-time	97,103	64.1	9,613	24.5	85,118	77.7
Full-time	54,306	35.9	29,660	75.5	24,466	22.3
Tenured	1,849	1.2	994	2.5	855	0.8
Tenure track	29,412	19.4	21,523	54.8	7,768	7.1
Non-tenure-track	17,969	11.9	6,384	16.3	11,527	10.5
Not tenured or no tenure system	5,077	3.4	760	1.9	4,317	3.9

Years since highest degree						
Post-hire	8,024	5.3	3,441	8.8	4,584	4.1
One year	29,504	19.5	15,734	40.1	13,772	12.3
Two years	19,385	12.8	4,903	12.5	14,482	12.9
Three to five years	30,240	20.0	7,543	19.2	19,549	17.5
Six to ten years	22,900	15.1	3,886	9.9	22,162	19.8
Eleven or more years	38,808	25.6	3,771	9.6	35,038	31.3
Gender						
Female	76,094	50.3	16,991	43.3	58,283	53.2
Male	75,315	49.7	22,282	56.7	51,301	46.8
Age						
<35	47,155	31.1	14,456	36.8	32,276	29.5
>45	53,884	35.6	9,172	23.4	43,328	39.5
Retired from previous position						
Not retired	136,055	89.9	36,793	93.7	96,935	88.5
Retired	15,354	10.1	2,480	6.3	12,649	11.5
Held positions outside postsecondary education	94,049	62.1	12,488	31.8	80,024	73.0
Previous employment, by sector						
No job immediately preceding	13,383	8.8	7,698	19.6	5,685	5.2
Four- or two-year postsecondary institution	25,381	16.8	13,301	33.9	12,048	11.0
Other educational institution	32,849	21.7	6,210	15.8	26,484	24.2
Government or military organization	14,025	9.3	1,926	4.9	11,411	10.4
Foundation or nonprofit organization	12,981	8.6	2,709	6.9	10,272	9.4
For-profit business or industry	42,009	27.7	5,160	13.1	35,656	32.5
Other	10,781	7.1	2,272	5.8	8,028	7.3
Concurrent employment (Fall 2003)						
No	68,956	45.5	31,757	80.9	36,842	33.6
Yes	82,453	52.7	7,234	18.4	70,526	64.3

Source: NSOPF:04. (Refer to appendix A for key.)

[a]Institutions not included are institutions classified as Specialized Institution in NSOPF:04.

Beyond basic confirmation of the traditional pattern of entry of PhDs into academe, table 4.4 suggests that there is a significant minority of newly entering PhDs (24.5%, or just under 10,000) who initially entered academic careers in a part-time role. While precipitously lower than the more than the 77.7% of non-PhDs who enter through the part-time route, this is nonetheless a significant subgroup and raises some pointed questions: What leads some PhDs to pursue part-time entry? Is it simply the lack of availability of full-time positions (lack of market demand)? Or are these individuals consciously and deliberately pursuing different sorts of hybrid careers in their fields? While the 2004 National Study of Postsecondary Faculty (NSOPF:04) does not ask specific questions about the motivation to pursue part-time rather than full-time work, it does ask a number of questions that permit us to make some informed inferences.[8] For example, items include whether respondents view their part-time instructional role as their primary employment, whether they would prefer a full-time position, whether they hold concurrent full-time employment outside of postsecondary education, their previous employment experience, the number of years elapsed since PhD receipt, whether they had retired from another position, and, finally, the number of courses they teach. Table 4.5 provides a portrait of those PhDs who reported entering academic careers in part-time appointments, controlling for broad academic field (a more refined breakdown by academic field is provided in appendix table A-4.1). A glance at the table suggests that three in five (61.7%) do not view their part-time employment as their primary job, and just over half (53.2%) are teaching part-time because they prefer it to full-time. Nearly half (45.1%) report holding a full-time job outside postsecondary education. Fully 55.4% of the part-timers are teaching one course only, and an additional one-third are teaching a second course.[9] Moreover, beyond those one or two courses, nine in ten (89.5) report teaching at no other postsecondary institution. These individuals tend to be older (two-fifths are over the age of forty-five), and one-third have held their PhD degrees longer than five years; nearly three in five (58.4%) have held jobs outside postsecondary education since receiving their PhDs. Presumably, then, this subgroup of PhDs were among those who largely moved rather seamlessly from conferral of their doctorate to nonacademic pursuits and returned to higher education as an "adjunct" to their full-time job—most frequently outside postsecondary education. Indeed, in the case of business, where the majority report that their part-time job is their primary employment, nearly half (47.4%) report that they have retired from another position, and more

Table 4.5 Selected characteristics of PhD recipients whose first academic job is part-time, by academic field, Fall 2003

		Academic field	
	All fields	Professions	Liberal arts
N	9,585	3,615	5,970
Institution type[a]			
Research	16.0	15.6	16.3
Doctoral	11.8	8.0	14.1
Comprehensive	34.2	39.3	31.2
Liberal arts	7.8	4.7	9.6
Two-year	25.7	31.6	22.2
Tenure status			
Tenured	0.0	0.0	0.0
Tenure track	1.2	3.2	0.0
Non-tenure-track	95.2	88.0	99.6
Not tenured or no tenure system	3.5	8.7	0.4
Years since highest degree			
Post-hire	16.1	8.4	20.7
Within one year	17.4	17.1	17.6
Within two years	9.3	11.7	7.8
Within three to five years	23.9	19.1	26.9
Six to ten years	11.8	15.9	6.3
Eleven years or more	21.5	27.8	20.7
Gender			
Female	45.8	50.7	42.9
Male	54.2	49.2	57.1
Age			
< 35	23.3	14.5	28.7
35–44	34.8	31.8	36.6
45–54	24.6	29.0	21.9
55–64	14.3	23.2	8.8
65–70	1.5	1.4	1.6
71 or above	1.4	0.0	2.3
Retirement status			
Not retired	86.7	85.2	87.7
Retired	13.3	14.8	12.3
Previous job outside postsecondary education since highest degree			
No	41.6	36.4	44.7
Yes	58.4	63.5	55.3
Previous employment sector			
No job immediately preceding	9.6	6.0	11.8
Four- or two-year postsecondary institution	20.7	10.4	26.9
Other educational institution	18.9	26.2	14.5

(continued)

Table 4.5 (continued)

		Academic field	
	All fields	Professions	Liberal arts
N	9,585	3,615	5,970
Government or military organization	4.3	8.4	1.9
Foundation or nonprofit organization	11.8	7.6	14.3
For-profit business or industry	22.1	33.3	15.4
Other	12.6	8.2	15.2
Part-time employment is primary employment			
Yes	38.2	30.8	42.8
No	61.7	69.2	57.2
Part-time but full-time preferred			
Yes	46.8	30.3	56.8
No	53.2	69.7	43.2
Number of courses taught			
One	55.4	57.3	54.1
Two	33.4	30.2	35.3
Three or more	11.4	12.8	10.6
Concurrent employment (Fall 2003)			
No	34.3	15.5	45.7
Yes	62.8	81.8	51.3
Other concurrent employment			
Full-time	45.1	56.4	38.4
Part-time	54.8	43.6	61.6
Other concurrent jobs in postsecondary instruction			
Yes	10.5	11.8	9.7
No	89.5	88.1	90.3

Source: NSOPF:04. (Refer to appendix A for key.)
Note: Rounding accounts for percentages not totaling 100.
[a]Institutions classified as Specialized Institution in NSOPF:04 are not included.

than three-quarters (77.1%) report that their part-time status is preferable to full-time.

What is also striking about table 4.5 is the sharp differences between the liberal arts and professional fields. Among all the professional fields, with the notable exception of business,[10] part-time postsecondary appointments are not reported as respondents' primary employment for 69.2% and, with the notable exception of engineering, are perceived as preferable to full-time employment.[11] Among liberal arts fields, with the notable exception of the social sciences, the majority of doctorate holders consider their part-time appointments to be their primary employment (42.8% in the social sciences, 63.7% among humanists and natural scientists alone) and over half (56.8%) would prefer a full-time appointment (including 47.6% of social scientists). Similarly, part-time PhD-holding faculty in the liberal arts are more likely to report that their part-time job is their only job (45.7) than are PhD holders on part-time appointments in the professions (15.5%). While 89.5% of all PhD-holding part-timers hold no other jobs at another college or university, PhD-holding part-timers in the professions are much more likely to hold full-time jobs (56.4 vs. 38.4%) and to hold jobs outside of academe (72.6 vs. 44.7). Finally, part-timers in the professions are likely to be significantly older than their counterparts in the traditional liberal arts: 53.6% of part-timers in the professions were over the age of forty-five versus 34.6% in the liberal arts.

The evidence suggests, then, that the one-quarter of PhDs who enter academic careers in part-time appointments differ in significant ways from their majority counterparts who enter academic careers in full-time appointments. Most striking are the sharp differences among academic fields: among the professions (with the possible exception of business) the majority are pursuing postsecondary teaching as a preferred, supplementary opportunity to their employment outside postsecondary education. However, among the substantially larger numbers of part-timers in the liberal arts fields, especially the humanities, the modal picture is quite different. The majority of these part-timers in the liberal arts fields are not employed full-time elsewhere and express a preference for full-time academic employment.

That said, what about that even smaller minority of PhDs (about 8%) who begin their academic careers in two-year community colleges? Do they resemble their counterparts who enter into part-time roles in terms of their demographic profile and disciplinary and career background? Do PhDs in full-time appointments in the two-year sector resemble more closely their full-time counterparts in the four-year sector? Or their part-time counterparts in the two or four-year sector? Table 4.6 looks at PhDs whose first academic position was in a two-year college setting and compares their characteristics with those teaching in the four-year sector by employment status. The data suggest first

Table 4.6 Selected characteristics of PhD recipients whose first academic job is at a two-year college, Fall 2003 (percentage)

		PhDs in four-year institution		PhDs in two-year institution	
	All PhD recipients	Full-time	Part-time	Full-time	Part-time
N	39,273	29,034	7,150	626	2,466
Academic field					
Business	2.6	5.0	6.3	12.9	0.0
Education	14.7	10.7	17.2	0.0	18.4
Health sciences	7.6	3.1	2.4	8.5	7.4
Fine arts	0.7	3.5	1.3	3.3	0.0
Humanities	9.6	16.6	22.3	19.5	7.1
Natural sciences	22.1	27.3	21.6	30.8	19.9
Social sciences	26.4	15.1	19.7	25.2	26.7
All other programs	16.3	18.7	9.1	0.0	20.5
Gender					
Female	52.4	42.1	43.9	58.9	50.8
Male	47.6	57.9	56.1	41.1	49.2
Age					
Under 35	28.3	41.6	20.8	20.3	30.3
35–44	34.8	41.2	36.6	52.0	30.4
45–54	31.9	12.3	21.5	27.7	33.0
55–64	5.0	4.8	17.0	0.0	6.2
Employment status					
Full-time	20.2	100.0	0.0	100.0	0.0
Part-time	79.8	0.0	100.0	0.0	100.0
Retired from previous position					
Not retired	89.4	96.1	85.7	87.1	89.9
Retired	10.6	3.9	14.3	12.9	10.1
Years since highest degree					
Post-hire	25.5	6.4	11.2	6.7	30.3
Within one year	9.5	47.7	22.3	34.8	3.1
Within two years	12.6	13.3	9.2	24.9	9.5
Within three to five years	18.3	17.7	25.6	15.8	19.0
Six to ten years	12.8	9.2	12.3	12.3	12.9
Eleven years or more	21.3	5.7	19.4	5.4	25.3
Previous job outside postsecondary education since highest degree					
No	37.0	83.4	69.8	49.2	33.9
Yes	63.0	16.6	30.2	50.8	66.1

Table 4.6 (continued)

		PhDs in four-year institution		PhDs in two-year institution	
	All PhD recipients	Full-time	Part-time	Full-time	Part-time
N	39,273	29,034	7,150	626	2,466
Previous employment, by sector					
No job immediately preceding	11.7	23.2	8.5	7.0	12.9
Four- or two-year postsecondary institution	13.9	38.5	23.7	22.7	11.6
Other education institution	8.3	15.0	22.5	8.1	8.3
Government or military organization	6.5	5.0	3.9	10.6	5.5
Foundation or nonprofit organization	12.3	5.3	11.0	5.6	14.0
For-profit business or industry	32.2	9.5	19.7	40.4	30.1
Other	15.2	3.6	10.8	5.6	17.6
Concurrent employment (Fall 2003)					
No	35.6	96.2	38.4	84.0	22.0
Yes	65.4	3.7	61.6	16.0	77.9

Source: NSOPF:04. (Refer to appendix A for key.)

that PhDs entering academic careers through the two-year community college are more than twice as likely to have pursued nonacademic employment immediately following receipt of the PhD (half of those employed full-time and two-thirds of those employed part-time in the two-year sector vs. one-sixth and one-third, respectively, in the four-year sector). Among full-timers, those employed in two-year institutions were four times as likely to report previous work experience in business and industry (two-fifths vs. one-tenth). PhDs in the two-year sector reported later entry to their first academic job after degree receipt and were twice as likely to be over the age of forty-five at entry. They were more likely to report other concurrent employment, including teaching and professional development outside higher education. Finally, they were more likely to be women. Those PhDs entering community college teaching do so later in life as a second career or between first and second careers.

Career Entry of Non-PhDs

Having examined the entry of PhDs into the four-year sector, including mostly full-time appointments, but also part-time appointments, and having briefly described that small subgroup of PhDs who enter into careers in the two-year sector, the "big" question remains of the entry of non-PhDs into the academic workforce. What about these 110,000 new entrants to faculty roles who are not PhD recipients but report the first professional, masters, or baccalaureate as their highest degree? This subgroup constitutes fully two-thirds of the "entering class," an increasingly large—indeed, now the modal—subgroup who have traditionally remained in the shadows of our studies of the pathways to academic careers. Who are these new entrants in terms of demographics and background? What was their route to academic positions? What kinds of appointments do they hold? Do they hold other concurrent employment? And how does their pathway compare with that of doctoral recipients?

Table 4.4 demonstrates that the vast majority of these non-PhDs entered into part-time appointments, albeit primarily in the two-year sector. However, the table also signaled a subgroup of newly entering faculty in four-year institutions—about 50,000—who embarked on their first academic job without the PhD degree. This subgroup is some 25% larger in size than the subgroup of PhD holding new entrants upon which we have been focusing.

Table 4.7 documents the institutional and disciplinary venues, demographics (age and gender), type of appointments, and previous and concurrent employment of those non-PhD faculty entering academic careers in the four-year sector and explicitly compares them to their PhD holding counterparts in the four-years sector and to their non-PhD counterparts in the two-year sector. What do these data show?

First, these non-PhDs in the four-year sector tend to be clustered in a handful of academic fields: one-third are in business and education, another quarter in the humanities and fine arts. They are located predominantly in comprehensive institutions and liberal arts colleges rather than universities. More than two-fifths (42.3%) of these non-PhD new entrants are more than five years beyond receipt of their highest degree, and seven-tenths have held a position outside of postsecondary education during that interim period. More than half (56.3%) are women, and just over a third are over the age of forty-five. In terms of immediately prior employment, one-quarter (26.7%) report K–12 education, another quarter (29.5%) business and industry, and one-sixth

Table 4.7 Selected characteristics of non-PhD faculty whose first job is at a four-year versus two-year institution, Fall 2003

	All new entrants	Non-PhD in four-year institutions	Non-PhD in two-year institutions	PhD in four-year institutions
N	151,409	57,737	54,404	36,181
Academic field				
Business	8.6	13.0	6.6	5.3
Education	11.7	14.0	8.8	12.0
Engineering	3.3	1.0	2.6	8.4
Health sciences	9.7	11.9	12.0	2.9
Fine arts	7.2	11.3	6.0	3.1
Humanities	14.7	12.2	15.7	17.7
Natural sciences	17.4	9.7	19.6	26.2
Social sciences	9.6	7.9	6.1	16.0
Other programs	16.3	19.1	22.5	8.4
Appointment type				
Part-time	64.1	73.4	82.9	19.8
Full-time	35.9	26.6	17.1	80.2
Tenured	1.2	0.7	0.9	2.7
Tenure track	19.4	7.7	6.3	58.3
Non-tenure-track	11.9	16.2	4.1	17.5
Not tenured or no tenure system	3.4	2.0	5.9	1.6
Years since highest degree				
Post-hire	5.3	3.7	4.5	7.3
Within one year	19.5	13.9	10.5	42.7
Within two years	12.8	13.2	12.6	12.5
Within three to five years	17.9	19.5	15.2	19.3
Six to ten years	17.2	18.4	21.2	9.6
Eleven years or more	27.3	30.0	32.6	8.6
Gender				
Female	50.3	52.6	52.8	42.5
Male	49.7	47.4	47.2	57.5
Age				
<35	31.1	29.8	25.5	37.5
>45	35.6	37.6	42.3	22.1
Retired from previous position				
Not retired	89.9	89.6	87.4	94.1
Retired	10.1	10.4	12.6	5.9
Previous job outside postsecondary education since highest degree				
No	37.9	82.5	83.6	70.9
Yes	62.1	17.5	16.4	29.1

(continued)

Table 4.7 (continued)

	All new entrants	Non-PhD in four-year institutions	Non-PhD in two-year institutions	PhD in four-year institutions
N	151,409	57,737	54,404	36,181
Previous employment, by sector				
No job immediately preceding	8.8	6.4	3.7	20.3
Four- or two-year postsecondary institution	16.8	12.9	8.5	35.6
K–12	21.7	22.5	25.1	16.5
Government or military organization	9.3	7.2	14.6	4.8
Foundation or nonprofit organization	8.6	9.8	8.5	6.4
For-profit business or industry	27.7	33.5	32.1	11.5
Other	7.1	7.7	7.5	5.0
Concurrent employment (Fall 2003)				
No	45.5	36.3	29.8	84.8
Yes	54.4	63.7	70.2	15.2

Source: NSOPF:04. (Refer to appendix A for key.)
Notes: Newly entering faculty are defined as those faculty reporting in 2003 that they began their first academic job in 2001 or later. Faculty at for-profit institutions are not included.

(15.4%) report a previous position (but not necessarily academic) in postsecondary education. Nearly three-quarters (73.5%) hold part-time appointments: more than half (55.7%) report other concurrent employment outside postsecondary education, but nearly two-fifths (37.4%) indicate no other concurrent employment. The portrait that emerges is of a subgroup of somewhat specialized faculty in a couple of professional fields and in humanities and the fine arts that have pursued careers in K–12 education, government or the military, or business and industry and are now entering a faculty role for the first time at middle age, most often as a second—and not necessarily exclusive—career. They are very different from the typical PhD new entrant.

Table 4.8 provides a more detailed look at the characteristics of the new-entry non-PhD holders by broad academic field. A glance suggests that a plurality of non-PhD new entrants are clustered in the comprehensive institutions in both full- and part-time appointments, although those in the liberal arts fields, especially the humanities and the natural sciences, are distributed throughout the institutional landscape, with about one-third of the full-time

Table 4.8 Selected characteristics of non-PhD faculty whose first job is at a four-year institution, by academic field and employment status, Fall 2003 (percentage)

	All fields			Academic fields: Professions			Academic fields: Liberal arts		
	Total	Full-time	Part-time	Total	Full-time	Part-time	Total	Full-time	Part-time
N	47,618	12,876	34,742	27,873	7,971	19,902	19,745	4,905	14,840
Institution type[a]									
Research	21.1	29.9	17.7	19.6	27.9	15.4	23.9	33.0	20.8
Doctoral	12.3	13.7	11.8	13.1	12.7	13.2	11.3	15.5	9.9
Comprehensive	39.6	31.5	42.6	38.7	33.8	40.7	40.8	27.9	45.1
Liberal arts	17.5	13.5	19.0	17.2	10.6	20.0	17.9	18.2	17.9
Appointment type									
Tenured	1.1	2.6	0.5	1.1	3.4	0.2	1.1	1.2	1.0
Tenure track	8.6	29.3	0.9	8.0	26.8	0.5	9.5	33.4	1.6
Non-tenure-track	84.1	61.2	92.6	83.5	60.9	92.6	85.0	61.7	92.7
Not tenured or no tenure system	6.2	6.9	5.9	7.4	8.9	6.8	4.5	3.7	4.7
Years since highest degree									
Post-hire	3.3	2.4	3.4	3.6	2.6	4.2	2.5	2.2	2.5
Within one year	14.2	15.2	13.7	11.3	10.2	8.7	18.2	23.5	16.4
Within two years	12.0	9.3	13.0	8.9	9.6	8.9	16.3	8.7	18.8
Within three to five years	20.2	18.2	21.0	20.2	20.2	22.1	20.3	15.0	22.1
Six to ten years	17.8	26.8	14.3	17.9	28.8	14.6	17.3	27.3	14.1
Eleven years or more	31.5	28.0	34.6	38.1	28.6	41.2	25.4	23.3	26.1

(continued)

Table 4.8 (continued)

	All fields			Academic fields					
				Professions			Liberal arts		
	Total	Full-time	Part-time	Total	Full-time	Part-time	Total	Full-time	Part-time
N	47,618	12,876	34,742	27,873	7,971	19,902	19,745	4,905	14,840
Gender									
Female	50.7	49.8	51.0	53.4	53.9	53.2	46.9	43.1	48.2
Male	49.3	50.2	49.0	46.6	46.1	46.8	53.1	56.9	51.8
Age									
<35	32.8	35.8	31.7	26.8	31.0	25.1	41.3	43.6	40.5
35–44	29.0	30.0	28.6	30.8	32.5	30.1	26.5	26.0	26.6
45–54	23.5	21.7	24.1	24.6	22.5	25.4	21.9	20.4	22.4
55–64	12.7	12.2	12.9	15.3	13.6	16.0	9.1	10.0	8.8
65–70	1.4	0.3	1.7	2.2	0.5	2.8	0.2	0.0	0.3
71 or above	0.7	0.0	1.0	0.4	0.0	0.6	1.1	0.0	1.5
Retired from another position									
Not retired	90.4	90.7	90.2	88.7	88.3	88.9	92.7	94.8	91.9
Retired	9.6	9.3	9.8	11.3	11.7	11.1	7.3	5.2	8.1
Previous job outside postsecondary education since degree									
No	26.7	44.7	20.0	21.6	40.1	14.1	33.8	52.2	27.8
Yes	73.3	55.3	80.0	78.4	59.9	85.9	66.2	47.8	72.2

Previous employment, by sector									
No job immediately preceding	75.0	12.2	5.7	4.4	8.0	3.0	11.8	19.1	9.3
Four- or two-year postsecondary institution	8.3	15.4	5.7	5.6	11.1	3.4	12.1	22.4	8.7
Other education institution	22.8	17.1	25.0	23.7	19.7	25.3	21.6	12.7	24.5
Government or military organization	7.3	6.6	7.5	9.5	6.8	10.6	4.1	6.3	3.4
Foundation or nonprofit organization	10.1	8.4	10.7	9.3	9.5	9.3	11.2	6.8	12.6
For-profit business or industry	35.5	30.6	37.4	38.0	34.1	39.5	32.1	24.9	34.5
Other	8.5	9.7	8.1	9.5	10.9	8.9	7.2	7.8	6.9
Concurrent employment									
No	36.5	80.3	20.2	32.0	75.8	14.6	42.7	87.9	27.8
Yes	63.5	19.7	79.8	68.0	24.2	85.4	57.3	12.1	72.2

Source: NSOPF:04. (Refer to appendix A for key.)

Notes: Rounding accounts for percentages not totaling 100.

[a]Institutions classified as Specialized Institution in NSOPF:04 are not included.

non-PhDs at research and doctoral universities. These include both faculty teaching composition and remedial English as well as faculty manning the science laboratories. Non-PhD new entrants in the liberal arts fields tend to be younger (41.3% are under the age of thirty-five) than those in the professions (26.8% under thirty-five), they tend to have earned their highest degree more recently (37% within two years of embarking on their first job vs. 23.8% among the professions), they are less likely to have held jobs outside postsecondary education since receiving that degree (about two-thirds compared with nearly four-fifths in the professions) and are less likely to have retired from another position (7.3 vs. 11.3% in the professions). They are more likely to report no previous employment (one-eighth vs. one-twentieth in the professions) and no concurrent employment (more than two-fifths vs. about one-third). Thus for many non-PhD faculty in the professions, faculty work is clearly a second—if not a late first—career; for those in the liberal arts, it may be a first career but one that is decidedly in positions with less promising career prospects. Indeed, one cannot leave these data without concluding that the pathways to academic work for those not holding the PhD diverge substantially from the paths of PhD holders. Moreover, it seems clear that in no small part, the bifurcation of full-time faculty appointments along tenure-eligible, that is, career-ladder and fixed-term appointments is largely drawn along the lines of entry-level education credentials (PhD or not).

Settling In: Early Shifts in Employment Status and Tenure Status

Whether they enter into full- or part-time faculty appointments, on or off the tenure track, in the four-year or two-year sector, important questions remain about career entry: What is the route new recruits take from their highest degree—whether PhD or not—to their first faculty job? How much time elapses? Are there intermediate steps between receipt of highest degree and first faculty job? To what extent is the move to the higher education sector immediate? Circuitous? And if immediate, are there intermediate steps within higher education before arriving at the first faculty job?

Our earlier analyses based on the NSOPF:04 (see table 4.4) suggested that PhD recipients (as compared with non-PhDs) tend to take a more direct path to their first faculty job: nearly half report having assumed a first faculty job either just before receiving the doctorate (8.8%) or within one year of completing the doctorate (40.1%). Nonetheless, about one-third (31.7%) of the PhDs in newly appointed faculty jobs reported that two to five years had elapsed since PhD receipt and nearly one-fifth (19.5%) more than six years. How do new PhDs who report an extended gap between degree receipt and entry into first faculty job spend that time? Insights into the "transition" period are provided by a national survey of the postdoctorate experience of social science PhDs undertaken by Maresi Nerad in 2003 (earlier in the same year as the NSOPF:04). Nerad (2008) reported that it was only about four years after PhD receipt that three-quarters of social science PhD recipients achieved stable, full-time employment in any sector (academe, industry, government, private nonprofit) and eight years before 90% had done so; less than half had achieved such stable employment in the first two years after receiving the PhD degree.

Nerad's national sample overrepresented aspirants to academic careers (three-quarters aspired to academic careers vs. about half across all fields in the larger population). Moreover, the delayed time to stable, full-time employment was especially acute for those pursuing an academic path. Among the 75% of academic hopefuls, only one-quarter had landed a career-ladder job within six months of degree receipt, and two-fifths within one year. Fully six years out, about three-quarters had secured a tenured or tenure-track faculty position (Nerad 2008). The typical career path began with a temporary position but frequently progressed to a career-ladder position—usually requiring a change of institutional employer and frequently a geographic move. The path to a career-ladder faculty appointment typically went through such part-time or fixed-contracts appointments: the probability of moving from a full-time nonacademic job to a career-ladder position was nearly zero.[12] These results largely match the findings of Ehrenberg et al.'s study of successive cohorts of humanities doctorates during the 1990s for the Andrew Mellon Foundation (Ehrenberg et al. 2010).

In this kind of job market, according to Nerad (2008), about one in five who aspired to an academic job changed their career goals within the first five years post-PhD. Of these post-PhD "goal shifters," 60% had never been in a tenure-track position. To explain their change of heart, goal shifters usually offered "push" factors such as "no positions available in academia" rather than "pull" factors such as attraction to other opportunities. Conversely, people rarely left tenure-track positions. Among those who had ever been on the tenure track, when surveyed, 93% were still in ladder faculty positions. Furthermore, those who began post-PhD careers outside academia entered the academic sector almost exclusively into temporary and part-time positions—the lowest rungs of the ladder.

New Data from the Survey of Doctorate Recipients

Nerad's (2008) and Ehrenberg et al.'s (2010) findings of a circuitous path to a first faculty job for PhDs in the social sciences and humanities, respectively, are largely corroborated by new analyses of three cohorts of new PhD respondents to the National Science Foundation's Survey of Doctorate Recipients in the natural and social sciences and engineering.[13] The survey, repeated every two to three years, provides the broadest swath of data on doctoral recipients in the natural and social science fields at the point of degree receipt and over multiple subsequent administrations (see appendix A).[14] In an effort to document as thoroughly as possible entry and early paths to academic careers, the authors identified three cohorts of new PhD recipients separated by a decade: a cohort of 1993 SDR respondents who had received their PhD between 1990 and 93 and who also responded to the 1996 SDR survey; a second cohort of 2003 SDR respondents who received their PhD between 2000 and 2003 and had responded as well to the 2006 SDR survey; and a third cohort of new PhDs respondents to the 2010 survey (who received their PhD between 2007 and 2010) who also responded to 2013 survey.[15] The new entrant career-stage subgroup across all three SDR cohorts allows us to examine the first reported job post—PhD receipt, its sector, and employment and tenure status as well as changes in these characteristics in the subsequent two- to three-year interval defined by the subsequent SDR survey administration. Moreover, they allow us to track differences by academic field, gender, and race/ethnicity. For purposes of our examination of the new entrants, we examined two data points for each new entrant career-stage subgroup in each survey year cohort: for the 1993 cohort, 1993 and 1997; for the 2003 cohort, 2003 and 2006; for the 2010 cohort, 2010 and 2013.

The data in table 4.9 of actual post-PhD labor market outcomes for new entrants in the 1993, 2003, and 2010 cohorts confirms the historical pattern of stability in the labor market behavior of new PhDs in the social and natural sciences revealed by earlier National Science Foundation surveys. (See table 4.3.) In 1993, 2003, and 2010, about half (plus or minus 5%) of new PhDs initially pursue their postdegree career in academic institutions (although not necessarily in faculty jobs), just about one-third enter business or industry, nearly one-tenth enter government, one-twentieth are unemployed, and a mere 1–2%

Table 4.9 Employment sector at career entry of new PhD recipients, by gender and cohort, 1993, 2003, 2010 (Survey of Doctorate Recipients cohorts)

	All			Male			Female		
	1993	2003	2010	1993	2003	2010	1993	2003	2010
N	29,910	28,411	40,638	20,082	16,449	23,427	9,828	11,962	17,211
Postsecondary education	48.8	54.7	52.9	48.5	51.7	50.9	49.3	58.9	55.7
Four-year	47.0	53.0	50.8	46.3	49.9	49.4	48.5	57.3	52.8
Two-year	1.7	1.7	2.1	2.2	1.8	1.5	0.9	1.5	3.0
Business and industry	37.6	31.7	31.2	39.0	36.3	35.8	34.7	25.4	25.0
Government	8.4	7.1	9.8	8.5	6.7	9.4	8.1	7.7	10.5
K–12	1.1	1.4	1.4	0.4	1.2	0.7	2.4	1.8	2.4
Not working	4.2	5.0	4.5	3.6	4.1	3.2	5.4	6.3	6.4
	White			Asian			URM		
	1993	2003	2010	1993	2003	2010	1993	2003	2010
N	21,698	19,718	23,965	6,480	6,026	11,920	1,731	2,267	3,969
Postsecondary education	48.2	56.5	56.3	48.5	46.2	46.4	56.7	62.7	52.7
Four-year	46.4	54.4	54.1	46.8	46.0	45.0	55.8	60.1	48.4
Two-year	1.8	2.1	2.2	1.7	0.1	1.3	0.9	2.6	4.3
Business and industry	36.5	29.7	27.7	44.4	42.3	39.8	25.2	22.5	26.3
Government	10.2	7.8	10.2	2.3	4.4	7.8	8.8	7.1	12.8
K–12	1.0	1.5	1.7	0.5	0.5	0.6	4.2	1.5	2.7
Not working	4.1	4.5	4.1	4.3	6.6	5.3	5.1	6.2	5.4

Source: SDR:93; SDR:97; SDR:03; SDR:06; SDR:10; SDR:13. (Refer to appendix A for key.)

Note: A "multiple race" race/ethnicity category was available for the 2003 and 2010 SDR cohorts, but these respondents are not included in this analysis.

enter K–12 education. Women are slightly more likely than men to enter academe (about 5%), especially the two-year colleges, and to enter K–12 education, and about 10% less likely than men to enter business and industry; they are nearly twice as likely as men to begin their postdoctoral career unemployed.[16] Among racial and ethnic groups, Asians are less likely to enter academe and more likely to enter business and industry; underrepresented minorities are slightly more likely to enter academe.

Among those PhDs who initially enter the postdoctoral labor market in higher education institutions, the data in table 4.10 show that about half of both the 1993 and 2003 new-entrant group enter in various faculty positions, with the ratio of tenure track to non-tenure-track positions at 1.5 or 2:1; the other half enter into various research or postdoctoral positions. By 2010, the ratio of faculty (on or off track) to postdoc positions had moved from 50:50 to 40:60 (faculty-to-postdoc). Moreover, the proportion of new entrants in tenure-track and non-tenure-track positions, respectively, had declined slightly (from 32.2 and 13.1% to 26.8 and 11.3%, respectively) while the proportion of new entrants in nonfaculty research positions had increased by 7 (compared with 2003) to 10 (compared with 1993)%. Gender differences were barely discernable, except for the 10% lower proportion of women in postdoctoral positions. Racial or ethnic differences were more pronounced: Asians were more likely to begin in nonfaculty-status positions and less likely to begin in tenure-track faculty positions; underrepresented minorities were slightly more likely than white and Asian PhDs to begin in tenure-track faculty positions and less likely than either Asian or white PhDs to begin in nonfaculty-status positions. While these data certainly have their limitations, they suggest that the trend has been toward a slight decline in faculty positions for newly entering PhDs and an increase in various kinds of nonfaculty positions.

If, then, PhDs newly entering higher education institutions begin increasingly in nonfaculty positions, what do we know about the mobility experiences of these new entrants early on in their first jobs? Do those in non-tenure-eligible positions have the opportunity to move onto the career track? Do those in tenure track positions get promoted? Does the situation of the 2010 cohort resemble that of the earlier cohorts? Or are there indicators of deterioration or improvement? Table 4.11 examines the early mobility experiences of the three cohorts of new entrants over a three-year period (1993 cohort: 1993–96; 2003 cohort: 2003–06; 2010 cohort: 2010–13), focusing first on the proportion who remained on and off the tenure track and the proportion who reported different

Table 4.10 Appointment type at career entry of new PhD recipients entering higher education employment by gender and age cohort, 1993, 2003, 2010 (Survey of Doctorate Recipients cohorts)

	All			Male			Female		
	1993	2003	2010	1993	2003	2010	1993	2003	2010
N	14,582	15,545	21,511	9,734	8,504	11,921	4,848	7,041	9,590
Tenured	1.8	1.4	1.2	1.0	1.7	1.4	3.6	1.0	1.0
Tenure track	28.3	32.2	26.8	27.1	31.6	26.6	30.8	32.9	27.0
Non-tenure-track	19.3	13.1	11.3	21.5	12.8	10.2	14.9	13.5	12.8
Non-faculty status	50.5	53.3	60.7	50.5	53.9	61.9	50.7	52.6	59.3
Postdoctural	44.9	38.1	43.2	48.4	42.1	47.1	37.8	33.3	38.3
	White			Asian			Underrepresented minority		
	1993	2003	2010	1993	2003	2010	1993	2003	2010
N	10,461	11,133	13,498	3,140	2,783	5,528	982	1,423	2,089
Tenured	2.2	1.6	1.5	0.7	0.0	0.2	2.1	2.4	1.8
Tenure track	30.3	32.7	27.9	17.1	28.2	20.9	43.0	35.6	34.0
Non-tenure-track	18.9	13.1	13.0	23.0	12.2	8.0	11.7	14.2	10.1
Non-faculty status	48.6	52.6	57.6	59.2	59.6	70.9	43.2	47.9	54.1
Postdoctural	41.6	36.1	39.7	58.6	52.5	56.2	36.3	27.3	31.1

Source: SDR:93; SDR:97; SDR:03; SDR:06; SDR:10; SDR:13. (Refer to appendix A for key.)

Note: A "multiple race" race/ethnicity category was available for the 2003 and 2010 SDR cohorts, but these respondents are not included in this analysis.

Table 4.11 Early mobility across appointment types of new PhD recipients entering higher education employment, by gender and age cohort, 1993, 2003, 2010 (Survey of Doctorate Recipients cohorts)

	All			Male			Female		
	1993	2003	2010	1993	2003	2010	1993	2003	2010
N	14,582	15,545	21,511	9,734	8,504	11,921	4,848	7,041	9,590
Remains the same	35.9	60.8	56.8	33.2	62.1	57.0	41.4	59.3	56.6
Tenured	1.3	1.0	1.0	0.3	1.1	1.0	3.4	0.9	1.0
Tenure track	15.8	27.3	22.7	14.7	26.4	23.1	18.1	28.4	22.1
Not on tenure track	5.9	5.6	4.7	7.0	6.8	5.1	3.5	4.3	4.2
Non-faculty status	12.9	26.8	28.5	11.2	27.7	27.7	16.3	25.7	29.4
Moves	64.1	39.2	43.2	66.8	37.9	43.0	58.7	40.8	43.4
Postdoc to Not on tenure track	7.9	6.3	7.7	9.3	5.1	7.0	5.0	7.8	8.5
Postdoc to tenure track/ tenured	13.0	8.0	7.9	13.8	8.7	9.0	11.4	7.2	6.6
Not on tenure track to tenure-track	4.7	2.3	2.2	4.9	1.7	2.3	4.3	3.1	2.0
Tenure track to tenured	7.1	2.5	1.5	6.6	3.6	1.2	8.0	1.1	1.9
Tenured/Tenure track to not on tenure track	2.2	1.2	1.2	2.1	0.6	1.0	2.2	2.0	1.5
Other	29.2	18.8	22.7	30.0	18.3	22.4	27.7	19.5	22.9
Not on tenure track to out of sector	22.4	14.1	17.8	23.1	13.7	18.5	21.1	14.5	17.1
Other	6.8	0.2	0.2	6.9	4.6	4.0	6.7	5.0	5.9

	White			Asian			URM		
	1993	2003	2010	1993	2003	2010	1993	2003	2010
N	10,461	11,134	13,498	3,141	2,783	5,529	981	1,422	2,089
Remains the same	37.5	61.5	57.6	30.0	60.4	55.6	37.6	56.3	57.8
Tenured	1.6	1.2	1.3	0.0	0.0	0.2	2.1	1.8	1.1
Tenure track	17.4	27.2	24.1	8.3	25.8	17.2	22.9	31.0	27.6
Not on tenure track	5.1	6.4	5.9	9.9	3.3	2.7	1.1	4.6	2.3
Non-faculty status	13.4	26.7	26.3	11.7	31.3	35.5	11.4	19.0	26.8
Moves	62.5	38.5	42.4	70.0	39.6	44.4	62.4	43.7	42.2
Postdoc to Not on tenure track	7.6	6.1	7.1	11.0	7.4	7.8	1.4	6.0	8.8
Postdoc to tenure track/ tenured	11.9	7.5	9.2	13.5	9.0	5.2	22.9	11.2	7.1
Not on tenure track to tenure-track	4.9	2.5	1.7	3.5	1.1	3.0	6.1	2.9	3.4
Tenure track to tenured	7.8	2.8	1.0	4.2	1.1	2.1	8.8	2.7	3.8
Tenured/Tenure track to not on tenure track	1.8	1.4	1.5	3.2	0.3	0.5	3.0	1.8	1.5
Other	28.5	18.2	22.0	34.6	20.6	25.8	20.2	19.0	17.6
Not on tenure track to out of sector	21.6	14.1	16.8	29.4	14.4	22.6	8.9	12.9	11.5
Other	6.9	4.1	5.2	5.1	6.2	3.2	11.3	6.0	6.1

Source: SDR:93; SDR:97; SDR:03; SDR:06; SDR:10; SDR:13. (Refer to appendix A for key.)

Notes: Periods of change are defined as 1993–1997, 2003–2006, 2010–2013. Other moves include Not on tenure track to Non-faculty status; Tenure track to Out of sector; Tenured to Nonfaculty status; and Tenured to tenure-track. Beginning in 2003, the NSF offered a derived "multiple race" race/ethnicity category that is not included in this analysis.

job status moves in their earliest career years. A glance at table 4.11 suggests that among the 1993 cohort, just over one-third (35.9%) reported no change in their job status over their first three years, with women slightly more likely to report nonmobility (stability) than men. Nearly two-thirds (64.1%) reported some kind of mobility: one-fifth (20.9%) moved from some kind of non-faculty status to a faculty position (one-eighth, or 13.0%, to a tenure-track faculty position), one-fourteenth (7.1%) achieved tenure, and more than one-fifth (22.4%) migrated out of academe. Among new entrants in the 2003 cohort, the proportion reporting no early mobility increased sharply from one-third to three-fifths (60.7%); the proportion moving from a non-faculty to a faculty status declined to about one-seventh (from about one-fifth), the miniscule proportion moving from a non-tenure track to a tenure track faculty position declined by half (from 4.7 to 2.3%), the proportion of tenure track faculty achieving tenure declined by 75% (from one-fourteenth to one-fortieth, or from 7.1 to 2.5%), and the proportion migrating out of higher education declined about 25% (from one-fifth to one-seventh). Much the same pattern characterized new entrants in the 2010 cohort when compared with the 1993 cohort. Women were slightly less likely than men to move from nonfaculty statuses (including postdocs) to tenure-track faculty positions, but slightly more likely than men to move from nonfaculty status into non-tenure-track faculty positions. While underrepresented-racial-minority PhDs were more likely than either white or Asian PhDs to move from off to on the tenure track in 1993 (whether from a postdoctorate or other non-tenure-track faculty position), any difference appeared to attenuate by the 2003 cohort amid the general decline in mobility. While is important to stress the limitations of the data and the lack of any statistical significance testing, nonetheless the portrait is one of increasingly limited early mobility within higher education institutions, including movement from nonfaculty to faculty positions, movement from non-tenure-track to tenure track, and movement upward within the tenure track. Both gender and race/ethnicity difference that were discernible in the 1993 cohort were attenuated in the 2003 and 2010 career-entry cohorts, with the notable exception of the continued presence of Asians in nonfaculty-status positions.

Table 4.12 examines the early migration patterns of the three cohorts of newly entering PhDs across job sectors, including out-migration from higher education to business and industry, government, and unemployment as well as in-migration into higher education from these other sectors. We were especially

Table 4.12 Early migration of new PhD recipients into and out of higher education employment, by gender and age cohort, 1993, 2003, 2010 (Survey of Doctorate Recipients cohorts)

	All			Male			Female		
	1993	2003	2010	1993	2003	2010	1993	2003	2010
N	29,910	28,411	40,638	20,082	16,449	23,427	9,828	11,962	17,211
Sector and movement overview									
Remains the same	72.9	80.0	79.8	74.0	81.7	81.4	70.5	77.6	77.5
Moves	27.1	20.0	20.2	26.0	18.3	18.6	29.5	22.4	22.5
Distribution of moves									
From postsecondary education									
to business or industry	9.1	5.5	6.4	9.9	5.6	6.8	7.5	5.4	5.9
to government	2.2	1.4	2.2	2.5	1.2	2.2	1.7	1.7	2.2
to not working	1.3	1.2	1.4	0.8	0.4	1.0	2.3	2.2	1.9
To postsecondary education									
from business or industry	3.8	2.4	2.5	3.0	1.7	2.5	5.4	3.4	2.4
from government	1.1	0.6	1.1	0.7	0.7	1.3	1.7	0.5	0.9
from not working	1.4	1.7	0.9	1.2	1.9	0.6	1.6	1.5	1.3
Within postsecondary education	0.8	0.6	0.6	0.7	0.6	0.3	1.0	0.5	1.1
Within business or government	3.6	2.2	1.6	3.6	2.0	1.7	3.6	2.3	1.4
Other moves									
Into postsecondary education	0.2	0.0	0.3	0.2	0.1	0.0	0.3	0.0	0.6
Out of postsecondary education	0.1	0.3	0.1	0.1	0.5	0.0	0.2	0.1	0.3
Other	3.6	4.0	3.1	3.3	3.5	2.1	4.2	4.8	4.5

(continued)

Table 4.12 (continued)

	White			Asian			Underrepresented minority		
	1993	2003	2010	1993	2003	2010	1993	2003	2010
N	21,699	19,718	23,965	6,481	6,026	11,923	1,728	2,268	3,971
Sector and movement overview									
Remains the same	72.1	79.4	78.9	74.3	82.3	82.1	77.6	80.6	78.2
Moves	27.9	20.6	21.1	25.7	17.7	17.9	22.4	19.4	21.8
Distribution of moves									
From postsecondary education									
to business or industry	8.5	6.1	6.4	12.5	3.9	7.2	4.4	4.3	4.3
to government	2.5	1.6	2.4	1.5	1.3	2.3	1.3	0.5	1.3
to not working	1.2	0.7	1.2	0.9	1.9	1.5	2.7	2.9	1.1
To postsecondary education									
from business or industry	4.6	2.5	2.6	1.5	2.1	1.4	1.4	1.7	4.8
from government	1.2	0.7	1.2	0.1	0.2	0.6	3.2	0.9	2.4
from not working	1.4	2.0	1.0	1.2	1.0	0.5	1.8	1.8	0.8
Within postsecondary education	0.8	0.5	1.0	0.4	0.9	0.0	2.4	0.4	0.8
Within business or government	4.1	2.6	2.0	2.3	0.6	0.9	1.6	1.5	1.2
Other moves									
Into postsecondary education	0.1	0.0	0.2	0.2	0.0	0.1	1.3	0.5	1.0
Out of postsecondary education	0.0	0.4	0.2	0.3	0.0	0.0	1.3	0.4	0.0
Other	3.5	3.5	2.8	4.8	5.8	3.4	1.1	4.5	4.2

Source: SDR:93; SDR:97; SDR:03; SDR:06; SDR:10; SDR:13. (Refer to appendix A for key.)

Notes: Periods of change are defined as 1993–97, 2003–06, and 2010–13. Other moves are defined as Business/Government to K–2; K–12 to Business/Government; Not Working to K–12/Business/Government; an—K–12/Business/Government to Not Working. A "multiple race" race/ethnicity category was available for the 2003 and 2010 SDR cohorts, but these respondents are not included in this analysis.

interested in the extent to which a lack of early career opportunities in higher education might lead new entrants to leave academe. Broadly speaking, the data suggest that new PhDs tend to remain in the sector of their initial employment—whether in or outside higher education: more than seven-tenths of newly entering PhDs in the 1993 cohort, increasing to about eight-tenths in the succeeding 2003 and 2010 cohorts. Among new entrants in the 1993 cohort, about one-eighth (12.6%) migrated out of higher education during their first few career years compared with about one-twelfth (8.1%) in the 2003 cohort and one-tenth in the 2010 cohort, suggesting that out-migration during career entry is actually slowing slightly (that out-migration accelerates in the "early" career phase, following initial entry; see chapter 5). Differences in overall out-migration rates for men and women and for different racial or ethnic groups were negligible, although men were slightly more likely to migrate to business or industry and women to unemployment. Among new entrants in the 1993 cohort, 6.3% reported in-migration to higher education from other sectors, and that declined to less than 5% in the two succeeding cohorts—suggesting a net out-migration in the career entry period (migration out minus migration into higher education) of 3–6% across the three cohorts. There are no marked gender differences in in-migration patterns by gender (indeed, women are as likely as men to in-migrate, albeit less likely to out-migrate to business and industry). Underrepresented minorities, however, appear to show a slightly higher rate of in-migration to higher education, especially from business and industry as well as from government.

In sum, the picture that emerges from the Survey of Doctorate Recipients analyses largely confirms and extends the portrait of PhDs circuitous path to a stable job early in the academic career initially inferred from the experience of PhDs in the social sciences (Nerad 2008) and the humanities (Ehrenberg et al. 2010): while about half of PhD recipients enter higher education employment after receiving their degree (and that has been remarkably stable), the balance has shifted over the past twenty years from a bare majority entering initially into faculty positions to a decisive majority entering initially into nonfaculty positions of one sort or another, including postdocs, primarily in research. Early mobility appears to be declining: among those who enter into tenure-track positions the proportion earning early tenure is shrinking, as is the proportion moving from nonfaculty to faculty status and those moving from off- to on-track faculty positions. These patterns cross gender boundaries, although women are less likely than men to move from nonfaculty positions to tenure-track-faculty positions and more likely to move from nonfaculty positions to non-tenure-track faculty positions. Women are also more likely to begin their career unemployed or move into unemployment early on than men. Among racial groups, Asians are more likely to find their way into nonfaculty status positions and underrepresented minorities slightly more likely to find their way into tenure-track-faculty positions. Migration out of higher education during the career entry years has ranged from about 8–12% of the new entrants, with the data suggesting some modest decline in out-migration, but one that is matched by a decline in in-migration to higher education from other sectors—except perhaps in the case of underrepresented racial minorities. This suggests that while higher education continues to lose more PhDs to other sectors than it gains, the losses—both actual and net—are declining slightly. We are not seeing anything like a mass exodus, at least during career entry; and indeed, out-migration is higher among those who are in nonfaculty and non-career-ladder positions.

Another Lens on Early Mobility: Evidence from the 2004 National Study of Postsecondary Faculty

The 2004 National Study of Postsecondary Faculty (NSOPF:04) offers another lens on mobility during career entry. In one sense, it is a narrower lens, in that it focuses only on those individuals in faculty positions in higher education (a narrower band of university-based knowledge workers). Thus the NSOPF excludes individuals, PhD or non, who are not in faculty positions per se, effectively excluding a variety of new entrants employed in institutions of higher education—many of who are intent on securing faculty positions—but who are, in effect, waiting in the wings. In addition, the NSOPF excludes those individuals who may have migrated out of higher education between entry into a faculty position and the time of the survey. In another sense, the NSOPF offers a much broader lens, that is extending to a much broader swath of those in faculty positions, including those without PhD degrees and those in predominantly part-time faculty roles. Taken together, one would probably expect less mobility in evidence among respondents to NSOPF insofar as they have already achieved a faculty position of one kind or another; and early mobility, whether within higher education and between higher education and other sectors—as we have learned from SDR—tends to be lower among those already in faculty positions. On the other hand, given the larger share of part-timers, one might expect somewhat greater mobility among what are after all "temporary" positions. With a focus on the "entering class" of faculty between 2001 and 2003, the 2004 National Study of Postsecondary Faculty allows us to determine whether new entrants changed jobs, that is, employers, within that brief entry window (as little as one year from entry level for about a third and as much as three years for another third) as well as whether members of the entering class changed their status (from part- to full-time or vice versa) or their appointment type (from off- to on-track and vice versa) with their initial or subsequent employer during the one- to three-year entry period. It provides a second slice of data on PhDs in faculty positions that can be tested against the findings of our analyses of the SDR and adds to that an added light on the early career mobility of the majority of our entering class, the non-PhDs.

What do the data tells us? Table 4.13 provides an overview of early mobility among new entrants, both PhDs and non-PhDs, between 2001 and 2003, including the proportion changing jobs (employers), changing employment status, and changing their appointment type. Overall among the PhDs, one-fifth of the new entrants, women slightly more than men, reported changing jobs or employers during this one- to three-year entry window, meaning their current employer at the time of the fall 2003 NSOPF survey was not their first employer in a faculty job. While half as many (about one-tenth overall) reported changing their employment status during the 2001–03 entry period, women were more likely to do so than men (13.8 vs. 8.5%). Moreover, they were much more likely than men to move from part-time to full-time—not surprising insofar as more women enter into part-time appointments. A slightly lower proportion of PhD new entrants, about one-eighth (8.3%), changed their tenure status, men and women alike, moving almost exclusively in the direction of off to on the tenure track.

Among non-PhD-holding new entrants, rates of job changing were very slightly lower than for PhDs: five-sixths of non-PhD faculty who entered their academic career between 2001 and 2003 were still in their first job, while about one-sixth had changed jobs at least once between 2001 and 2003. While non-PhDs did not differ appreciably in early job or employer changing (17.0% reported changing employers compared with 19.7% of PhDs), non-PhDs were more likely to report changes in their employment status than PhDs, fully 18.1%, nearly identical to the proportion reporting a change in employer. Moreover, the direction of change was opposite that of PhDs: primarily in the direction of full-time to part-time, although most of that pattern is attributable to men—a finding clearly at odds with our conventional expectations

Table 4.13 Early changes in employer, employment, and tenure status of new entrants in both two-year and four-year institutions by highest degree and gender, Fall 2003

	All PhD new entrants		Male		Female	
	(*N*= 39,274)		(*N*= 22,282)		(*N*= 16,992)	
	N	%	*N*	%	*N*	%
Change in job or employer	7,719	19.7	4,002	18.0	3,717	21.9
Change in employment status	4,246	10.8	1,904	8.5	2,342	13.8
Part-time to full-time	3,156	8.0	1,222	5.5	1,934	11.4
Full-time to part-time	1,090	2.8	682	3.1	408	2.4
Change in tenure status	3,252	8.3	1,869	8.4	1,383	8.1
Tenured or tenure track to non-tenure-track	190	0.5	64	0.3	126	0.7
Non-tenure-track to tenured or tenure track	3,062	7.8	1,805	8.1	1,257	7.4
	All non-PhD new entrants		**Male**		**Female**	
	(*N*= 112,135)		(*N*= 53,032)		(*N*= 59,103)	
	N	%	*N*	%	*N*	%
Change in job or employer	19,030	17.0	7,505	14.2	11,525	19.5
Change in employment status	20,329	18.1	10,873	20.5	9,456	16.0
Part-time to full-time	7,082	6.3	3,048	5.7	4,034	6.8
Full-time to part-time	13,247	11.8	7,825	14.8	5,422	9.2
Change in tenure status	2,498	2.2	1,261	2.4	1,237	2.1
Tenured or tenure track to non-tenure-track	1,029	0.9	350	0.7	679	1.1
Non-tenure-track to tenured or tenure track	1,469	1.3	911	1.7	558	0.9

Source: NSOPF:04. (Refer to appendix A for key.)

about career progression. Contrary then to what is considered the ideal or typical pursuit of a better job, it appears that a small but significant contingent of newly entering faculty, primarily those who enter without the PhD, are forsaking fulltime positions for part-time work.[17] Add to that picture one further element: while only a miniscule proportion of non-PhDs reported an early change in tenure status (2.2%)—not surprising insofar as many more than PhDs enter into non-tenure-track positions—the direction of tenure movement differed by gender: while the men are nearly three times as likely to move from off-track to on-track as to move from on-track to off-track (the same pattern as among PhDs), the non-PhD women were slightly more likely to move from on- to off-track as to move from off- to on-track.

Together, these findings suggest that even after landing an initial faculty position—whether full- or part-time—involving as it does a lag between highest degree receipt and academic career entry, some significant proportion of new entrants experience some kind of mobility, changing employer, employment, or tenure status, until they settle in to career entry. The size of this contingent goes well beyond the one-fifth who change employers since many change both employment status or tenure status, or both, without changing employers (see table 4.13). So that estimate is probably more like one-quarter, or even in certain cases, one-third.

How are we to explain this early career mobility? Part of the answer does not appear to lie with any differences by gender observable in table 4.13—at least if we look at women PhDs. A glance back at table 4.13 suggests that while women PhDs were slightly more likely than men to change jobs or employers during their initial career-entry period overall (21.9% of women vs. 18.0% of men), they were one and one-half times as likely as men to change employment status (13.8 vs. 8.5%), and the direction of that change was almost uniformly from part-time to full-time (indeed they were four times as likely to move that way as from full to part-time, while men were only twice as likely to do so). However, newly entering women PhDs were no more or less likely than men to report early changes in their tenure status or in the direction of those changes from off- to on-track. While non-PhD women were slightly less likely to change employment status than non-PhD men, men were much more likely to move from full-time to part-time. While both men and women non-PhDs are equally unlikely to change tenure status (only about 2%), they report moving in opposite directions: the men from off- to on-track and the women from on- to off-track. Thus the puzzling phenomenon of non-PhD men moving disproportionately from full- to part-time roles and non-PhD women moving disproportionately from tenured or tenure-track to non-tenure-track appointments during the entry period.

When we examine patterns by institutional type (table 4.14), we see that PhD faculty beginning their careers at research and doctoral institutions are less likely to report job changes in the entry period: only one in eight new-entrant PhDs at research universities (13.1%) report an entry-period job change compared with about one-quarter of those at comprehensives (23.6%) and two-year community colleges (24.1%) and three-tenths at liberal arts colleges (29.7%). New-entrant PhDs at research universities are less likely to report changes in employment status—one-fourteenth (7.0%) reported a change in employment status compared with one-sixth at two-year community colleges (16.3%)—but no more or less likely than PhD new entrants at other types of institutions to report a change in tenure status. Among institutional types, new PhD hires at the research universities were more likely to be in their first job and were least likely to report any changes in their employment or tenure status between 2001 and 2003. These data suggest that pathways into academic careers at research universities, and, to a lesser extent, at doctoral universities, have remained more stable overall than those at other four-year institutions or the two-year community colleges. Indeed, among non-PhD new entrants as well, those at research universities are less likely to experience a change in employment and tenure status during initial entry. Beyond that exception, table 4.14 suggests no substantial differences across institutional types, except perhaps for the greater elasticity of tenure-status changes at the comprehensive institutions. Much of the tumult associated with settling in that we have been referring to is apparently taking hold outside the research university sector and, in terms of employment status, among non-PhDs—both inside and outside the research university sector.

The differential salience of type of institution in the entry experience of those with and without PhDs is reflected as well in the case of academic field. When we examine variation in entry patterns by academic field for PhDs and non-PhDs (tables 4.15 and 4.16), we find among PhD new entrants greater early stability in selected professions (engineering, business, fine arts) and the natural sciences, where between 85 and 95% report a single early-career job compared with new PhD faculty in the humanities and social sciences, where only about 70% report a single early-career job—thus nearly a third reporting a job change at least once during career entry. Such disciplinary differences are not

Table 4.14 Early changes in employer, employment, and tenure status of new entrants in both two-year and four-year institutions, by highest degree and institution type, Fall 2003

	All PhD new entrants (*N*=39,274)		Institution type: Research (*N*=13,544)		Doctoral (*N*=5,333)		Comprehensive (*N*=11,803)		Liberal arts (*N*=4,378)		Two-year (*N*=4,378)	
	N	%	*N*	%	*N*	%	*N*	%	*N*	%	*N*	%
Change in jobs/employer	7,719	19.7	1,772	13.1	1,041	19.5	2,780	23.6	1,300	29.7	744	24.1
Change in employment status	4,245	10.8	945	7.0	548	10.3	1,419	12.0	592	13.5	504	16.3
Part-time to full-time	3,155	8.0	786	5.8	421	7.9	1,227	10.4	585	13.4	96	3.1
Full-time to part-time	1,090	2.8	159	1.2	127	2.4	192	1.6	7	0.2	408	13.2
Change in tenure status	3,253	8.3	1,090	8.0	353	6.6	1,242	10.5	402	9.2	136	4.4
Tenured or tenure track to non-tenure-track	190	0.5	44	0.3	57	1.1	—		65	1.5	—	
Non-tenure-track to tenured or tenure track	3,063	7.8	1,046	7.7	296	5.6	1,242	10.5	337	7.7	136	4.4

	All non-PhD new entrants (*N*=112,135)		Institution type: Research (*N*=11,784)		Doctoral (*N*=7,409)		Comprehensive (*N*=23,225)		Liberal arts (*N*=9,682)		Two-year (*N*=54,404)	
	N	%	*N*	%	*N*	%	*N*	%	*N*	%	*N*	%
Change in job or employer	19,030	17.0	1,782	15.1	1,549	20.9	4,358	18.8	1,324	13.7	8,917	16.4
Change in employment status	20,329	18.1	1,603	13.6	1,525	20.6	4,183	18.0	1,896	19.6	10,175	18.7
Part-time to full-time	7,082	6.3	768	6.5	698	9.4	1,187	5.1	511	5.3	3,604	6.6
Full-time to part-time	13,247	11.8	835	7.1	827	11.2	2,996	12.9	1,385	14.3	6,571	12.1
Change in tenure status	2,497	2.2	170	1.4	190	2.6	817	3.5	170	1.8	1,011	1.9
Tenured or tenure track to non-tenure-track	1,029	0.9	88	0.7	98	1.3	260	1.1	95	1.0	451	0.8
Non-tenure track-to tenured or tenure track	1,468	1.3	82	0.7	92	1.2	557	2.4	75	0.8	560	1.0

Source: NSOPF:04. (Refer to appendix A for key.)

Table 4.15 Early changes in employer, employment, and tenure status of new entrants in both two-year and four-year institutions by highest degree and academic field, PhD recipients, Fall 2003

	All PhD new entrants (N=39,274)		Academic field: Professions											
			All profession (N=14,650)		Business (N=1,987)		Education (N=4,794)		Engineering (N=3,029)		Health sciences (N=1,294)		All other (N=3,546)	
	N	%	N	%	N	%	N	%	N	%	N	%	N	%
Change in job or employer	7,719	19.7	2,287	15.6	317	16.0	1,032	21.5	233	7.7	378	29.2	327	9.2
Change in employment status	4,245	10.8	1,690	11.5	70	3.5	737	15.4	198	6.5	369	28.5	316	8.9
Part-time to full-time	3,155	8.0	1,221	8.3	70	3.5	599	12.5	198	6.5	215	16.6	139	3.9
Full-time to part-time	1,090	2.8	469	3.2	0	0.0	138	2.9	-	0.0	154	11.9	177	5.0
Change in tenure status	3,253	8.3	2,850	19.5	65	3.3	335	7.0	1,921	63.4	168	13.0	361	10.2
Tenured or tenure track to non-tenure-track	190	0.5	356	2.4	21	1.1	—		—		—		335	9.4
Non-tenure-track to tenured or tenure track	3,063	7.8	2,494	17.0	44	2.2	335	7.0	1,921	63.4	168	13.0	26	0.7

	Academic field: Liberal arts									
	All liberal arts (N=24,624)		Natural sciences (N=10,158)		Fine arts (N=1,132)		Humanities (N=6,719)		Social sciences (N=6,615)	
	N	%	N	%	N	%	N	%	N	%
Change in job or employer	5,432	22.1	1,569	15.4	164	14.5	1,798	26.8	1,901	28.7
Change in employment status	2,559	10.4	562	5.5	153	13.5	901	13.4	943	14.3
Part-time to full-time	1,937	7.9	383	3.8	120	10.6	780	11.6	654	9.9
Full-time to part-time	622	2.5	179	1.8	33	2.9	121	1.8	289	4.4
Change in tenure status	2,181	8.9	1,096	10.8	25	2.2	626	9.3	434	6.6
Tenured or tenure track to non-tenure-track	63	0.3	23	0.2	—		—		40	0.6
Non-tenure-track to tenured or tenure track	2,118	8.6	1,073	10.6	25	2.2	626	9.3	394	6.0

Table 4.10 Early changes in employer, employment, and tenure status of new entrants in both two-year and four-year institutions, by highest degree and academic field, non-PhD recipients, Fall 2003

	All non-PhD new entrants (*N*=112,136)		Academic field: Professions											
			All profession (*N*=62,603)		Business (*N*=11,077)		Education (*N*=12,866)		Engineering (*N*=2,012)		Health sciences (*N*=13,378)		All other (*N*=23,270)	
	N	%	*N*	%	*N*	%	*N*	%	*N*	%	*N*	%	*N*	%
Change in job or employer	19,030	17.0	10,030	16.0	1,884	17.0	2,275	17.7	332	16.5	1,740	13.0	3,799	16.3
Change in employment status	20,329	18.1	11,915	19.0	2,884	26.0	2,006	15.6	362	18.0	2,331	17.4	4,332	18.6
Part-time to full-time	7,082	6.3	3,512	5.6	650	5.9	390	3.0	79	3.9	1,332	10.0	1,061	4.6
Full-time to part-time	13,247	11.8	8,403	13.4	2,234	20.2	1,616	12.6	283	14.1	999	7.5	3,271	14.1
Change in tenure status	2,497	2.2	1,570	2.5	176	1.6	303	2.4	21	1.0	533	4.0	537	2.3
Tenured or tenure track to non-tenure-track	1,029	0.9	602	1.0	0		175	1.4	0		330	2.5	97	0.4
Non-tenure-track to tenured or tenure track	1,468	1.3	968	1.5	176	1.6	128	1.0	21	1.0	203	1.5	440	1.9

	Academic field: Liberal Arts									
	All liberal arts (*N*=49,532)		Natural sciences (*N*=16,262)		Fine arts (*N*=9,789)		Humanities (*N*=15,579)		Social sciences (*N*=7,902)	
	N	%	*N*	%	*N*	%	*N*	%	*N*	%
Change in job or employer	9,001	18.2	2,641	16.2	1,792	18.3	3,210	20.6	1,358	17.2
Change in employment status	8,413	17.0	2,938	18.1	1,394	14.2	2,647	17.0	1,434	18.1
Part-time to full-time	3,570	7.2	1,230	7.6	622	6.4	1,508	9.7	210	2.7
Full-time to part-time	4,843	9.8	1,708	10.5	772	7.9	1,139	7.3	1,224	15.5
Change in tenure status	927	1.9	285	1.8	291	3.0	115	0.7	236	3.0
Tenured or tenure track to non-tenure-track	427	0.9	97	0.6	67	0.7	92	0.6	171	2.2
Non-tenure-track to tenured or tenure track	500	1.0	188	1.2	224	2.3	23	0.1	65	0.8

Source: NSOPF:04. (Refer to appendix A for key.)

clearly discernable among non-PhDs, suggesting that the shaping role of academic field in easing or complicating career entry is a fact of life primarily for those who enter with the PhD in hand. There was fairly wide variation across academic fields in the proportion of new entrants reporting changes in both employment and tenure status during the entry period: more than a quarter of new faculty in the health sciences reported a change in employment status (primarily from full-time to part-time) and one-fifth a change in tenure status (nearly exclusively from on track to off track); at the other extreme, one of twenty new entrants in business and engineering reported a change in either employment or tenure status (primarily in the direction of part-time and non-tenure-track); in the middle, about one-seventh of new entrants in the humanities, social sciences, and education changed their employment or tenure status—again with the dominant direction being toward part-time and off track. What these data suggest is that new entrants into the humanities and social sciences have experienced the rockiest entry into academic careers (the same might be said for those in the health sciences, but the rockiness there is for quiet different reasons); career entry has been most stable in professions such as business and engineering and also in the natural sciences. Most of these disciplinary effects, however, were felt among those entering with the highest educational credentials.

What is the relationship of early patterns of job changing during career entry to early changes in employment and tenure status? That is, to what extent do new entrants change jobs in order to improve—however defined—their employment or appointment status? In *The American Faculty*, based on data furnished from the 1999 National Study of Postsecondary Faculty, we reported that the modal mechanism for improving one's employment or tenure status was clearly and decisively to change jobs or institutions. That was the path to moving from off track to on track and from part-time to full-time; indeed the search to *improve* was the practical equivalent of the search to *move*—with the notable exception of the movement of faculty from part-time to full-time status in the community colleges. Table 4.17 cross-tabulates whether new entrants did or did not change jobs during their entry period and whether they changed employment or tenure status and the direction of those changes by highest degree. A glance at the table suggests the earlier reported equivalence of changing jobs to changing status depends a good bit on educational credentials: among PhDs, those who changed jobs were four times more likely than those who remained in their first job to "upgrade" their employment status from part-time to full-time. One in five PhDs who changed jobs moved to full-time status (21.9%) compared with one-twentieth who did not change jobs (4.6%). Much the same pattern is reflected among PhDs reporting changes in tenure status: four times as many who changed employers moved from off track to on track as compared with those who remained with their original employer (22.9% of movers vs. 4.6% of nonmovers). The association of changing employer with improving employment or tenure status was slightly stronger for men than for women: men who moved were five to six times more likely than men who did not move to upgrade their employment or tenure status, while women who moved were about four times as likely to upgrade both their employment and tenure status. Among non-PhDs, however, the mobility dividend is considerably smaller for upgrading employment status—movers are about twice as likely to upgrade from part-time to full-time as nonmovers—and the mobility dividend is actually greater for women than for men: women non-PhDs are twice as likely to upgrade to full-time by changing employer, while men non-PhD movers are about one and one-half times as likely to upgrade as non-movers. In terms of upgrading tenure status, the data suggest again a very modest mobility dividend for non-PhDs, with the advantage slightly in favor of men.

At the least, these data suggest that the traditional close coupling of inter-institutional mobility and upgrading employment and tenure status is still operative during the entry period overall but is differentiated by education credentials: the mobility dividend is much greater for those new entrants who hold the PhD, and among PhD holders, it favors men. That, of course, may simply reflect the greater freedom that men have to move. There is also some indication of movement in nontraditional directions, especially among non-PhD new entrants, and especially among non-PhD women (see table 4.13). A significant segment of new entrants—disproportionately women, those outside the research university sector, and those in the professions—appear to be experiencing a more complex and uncertain period of career entry.

In sum, what inferences can we draw overall from the evidence provided by the SDR and the National Study of Postsecondary Faculty about pathways to academic careers? First, there is evidence of increasing complexity or circuitousness to the entry path. While the proportion of PhDs entering higher education as first postdegree job remains stable, decreasing proportions are entering initially into faculty positions, let alone career-ladder faculty positions. Those entering into faculty positions are reporting a modest shaking-out period in

Table 4.17 Early employment and tenure status outcomes for new entrants who did and did not change jobs, by highest degree, Fall 2003

		Still in first job					
		Total N=31,554		Male N=18,280		Female N=13,275	
		N	%	*N*	%	*N*	%
PhD (N=39,274)	Change in employment status						
	Part-time to full-time	1,465	4.6	567	3.1	898	6.8
	Full-time to part-time	863	2.7	635	3.5	228	1.7
	Change in tenure status						
	Tenured or tenure track to non-tenure-track	119	0.4	40	0.2	79	0.6
	Non-tenure-track to tenured or tenure track	1,291	4.1	729	4.0	562	4.2
		Changed jobs					
		Total N=7,719		Male N=4,002		Female N=3,717	
		N	%	*N*	%	*N*	%
	Change in employment status						
	Part-time to full-time	1,690	21.9	655	16.4	1,035	27.8
	Full-time to part-time	227	2.9	47	1.2	181	4.9
	Change in tenure status						
	Tenured or tenure track to non-tenure-track	71	0.9	24	0.6	47	1.3
	Non-tenure-track to tenured or tenure track	1,771	22.9	1,075	26.9	695	18.7
		Still in first job					
		Total N=90,802		Male N=45,527		Female N=47,578	
		N	%	*N*	%	*N*	%
Non-PhD (N=109,584)	Change in employment status						
	Part-time to full-time	5,019	5.5	2,456	5.4	2,621	5.5
	Full-time to part-time	11,771	13.0	7,159	15.7	5,077	10.7
	Change in tenure status						
	Tenured or tenure track to non-tenure-track	811	0.9	324	0.7	486	1.0
	Non-tenure-track to tenured or tenure track	886	1.0	527	1.2	408	0.9

Table 4.17 (continued)

	Changed jobs					
	Total $N = 18{,}782$		Male $N = 7{,}505$		Female $N = 11{,}525$	
	N	%	*N*	%	*N*	%
Change in employment status						
Part-time to full-time	2,005	10.7	592	7.9	1,413	12.3
Full-time to part-time	1,011	5.4	666	8.9	345	3.0
Change in tenure status						
Tenured or tenure track to non-tenure-track	218	1.2	25	0.3	193	1.7
Non-tenure-track to tenured or tenure track	533	2.8	383	5.1	150	1.3

Source: NSOPF:04. (Refer to appendix A for key.)

terms of changes in employment and tenure status—and the entry period itself has been lengthening, that is, it simply is taking longer to land and stabilize in an entry-level faculty position. That said, there is evidence that this increasingly unstable entry path is experienced more by women than men, perhaps more by Asians than by either whites or underrepresented racial minorities, more in those institutional sectors outside the research university, and more in the humanities and social sciences than in the natural sciences or the professions. The hegemony of the basic law of early academic careers—to seek at all costs the full-time and preferably the career-ladder position and to use the labor market (job changing) to do so—may remain true, albeit largely for those entering with the PhD credential—who are, after all, the new minority.

Conclusion

Our assemblage and analysis of data from a variety of national data bases paints an updated and much more nuanced picture of entry into academic careers that reflects the broader diversification of the academic workforce we have been documenting and, in particular, the role of education qualifications as a principal axis of differentiation in entry roles, venues, and pathways. Doctorate holders no longer constitute the majority of new entrants to the academic workforce overall and barely retain their majority among the shrinking proportion of full-time appointments (although they do continue to dominate the entry-level tenure-track appointments). While among new PhDs, there remains a prototypical core of traditional new entrants who come to full-time faculty jobs directly from their graduate studies at a young age with no nonacademic work experience, sizable contingents have emerged—perhaps a new majority—who enter higher education in a variety of nonfaculty jobs and spend several years before moving into a first faculty job. There is also a growing contingent of PhDs who embark on careers outside of higher education and engage in academic work on a planned part-time basis and a small contingent who pursue careers in the two-year community college sector. Academic field appears to provide a powerful second axis of differentiation, not infrequently in interaction with education qualifications: new entrants in the professional fields, not infrequently non-PhDs, tend to show a later (delayed) and more circuitous route to a first faculty job—often through previous or concurrent nonacademic employment. However direct or indirect a path to the first faculty job, the available evidence suggests that the entry period (the three-year window as we define it) has come to resemble a multiyear easing or "settling in" more than a single moment in time when an initial career-ladder appointment is offered and accepted as an anchor for the foreseeable future. Depending on academic field, anywhere from 20–25% of new entrants will change jobs during their first two to three postdegree years. The available evidence suggests that while the percentage of new PhDs entering academe is holding remarkably steady, the percentage actually securing faculty positions in higher education is slowly declining, and the prospects for upward mobility—either within the tenure track or between off track and on track—are declining as well.

Among the non-PhDs who increasingly pursue academic careers are individuals not infrequently in the professional fields who pursue academic work in both the four- and two-year sectors in both full-time and part-time roles—typically, after a period of work experience outside the higher education sector and not infrequently in conjunction with other full-time jobs outside higher education. While the numbers of itinerant teachers rushing from campus to campus may reflect the reality of a relatively circumscribed group of PhD or master's holders in the humanities (and their numbers are undeniably large), the new faculty largely reflect a broadening base of professionals who in the past may not have pursued an academic vocation.

So what do these new and increasingly complex patterns of career entry mean? Elsewhere (chapter 11), we argue that the very predictability and routinization of academic careers, achieved by hard-won national organizing, emerged by the mid-twentieth century as one of the major attractions of academic careers in the United States—drawing scholars from around the world who cut a bargain to trade off pecuniary gains for job security and professional autonomy or academic freedom like none other available worldwide. To the extent that the security and predictability of career entry is compromised, clearly a major incentive for recruitment of scientific talent to our universities is threatened—although we have no discernible evidence just yet that American PhDs, at least, are forsaking academic entry-level jobs for other employment sectors. It is not, of course, clear whether that reflects the continued attractiveness of academic work or rather the dimming of employment prospects in the larger economy, especially in those competing sectors, such as law and medicine, that also require advanced degrees. That said, in some sense the multiplication of entry paths and venues may be seen as a welcome democratization in the opportunity structure for joining the academic workforce, opening up heretofore largely unavailable possibilities to those outside the traditional career lockstep of intellectually gifted college graduates proceeding directly into doctoral education and, ultimately, a full-time, tenure-track assistant professorship. New kinds of individuals with nonhomogeneous educational socialization experiences and different kinds of work and life experiences outside academe are now enriching the mix to which we expose the nation's youth. That may be a clear benefit for the nation's youth as well as a benefit for those individuals who would have been effectively excluded from participation by the dominance of a monolithic path to career entry. What is less clear is the extent to which these benefits are offset by the potential of diverse paths becoming, in effect, mere placeholders or, at the extreme, off-ramps to satisfying careers, that is, opportunities that do not lead anywhere. And indeed, it is this very set of issues to which we turn in the next chapter on changing patterns of career progression. While multiple entry points enhance initial opportunity, the larger question is whether these increased opportunities represent dead-ends for the individuals whom they ostensibly enable? Or do they provide a holding pattern, allowing individuals to tread water until the pipeline in their field unclogs? Or do they provide a true diversity of points of entry to a multilaned, promising career highway?

NOTES

1. *Accumulative advantage or disadvantage* is the technical term for "the rich get richer, and the poor get poorer." Coined by Robert Merton (1968) in his early work on the sociology of science, it describes the phenomenon wherein an initial advantaged position in the social system tends to attract more and better opportunities, which in turn lead to the

accumulation of even greater positional advantages. Similarly, an initially disadvantaged position contributes to a dearth of opportunities, leading to progressively greater disadvantage.

2. The NSOPF:04 did not ask whether respondents were currently pursuing a doctoral degree; so non-doctorate holders includes some portion of individuals who, while not holding a doctorate, may be in various stages of pursuing one. The available current evidence from other sources, specifically the HERI Faculty Survey, suggests that in four-year baccalaureate institutions (whose faculty would be less likely than those in research universities to hold the doctorate and therefore more likely to be pursuing a doctoral degree), only about 10% of nondoctored faculty reported that they were actively pursuing a doctoral degree. We would therefore judge that the size of this PhD-in-process group is relatively small.

3. These data can be supplemented with the results of the Mellon Foundation's Graduate Education Surveys of 2003 (Ehrenberg et al. 2010) as well as with the results of Maresi Nerad's 2003 national survey of a cohort of social science doctorates (Nerad 2008).

4. To be clear, the two different sources—the SDR, made up of only PhD recipients, a portion of whom enter academic jobs, and the NSOPF, made up of only individuals holding academic jobs at the time of the survey, a portion of whom hold the doctorate—required establishing a common metric for identifying new entrants. For analyses based on the SDR, *new entrants* were defined based on year of award of the PhD: new entrants were those individuals receiving the PhD within the past three years (2001, 2002, and 2003) who during that same period entered into an initial postdegree teaching or research job in higher education. For analyses based on the NSOPF, which included substantial numbers of individuals who did not hold the doctorate, new faculty were defined based on the year in which they assumed their first academic job beyond teaching assistant, whether full- or part-time: new faculty were those who reported appointment to their first academic job in the three years previous to the time of the survey, fall 2003. Insofar as PhDs entering academe tend to do so either immediately upon or within a year of degree receipt, the two standards yield roughly equivalent results for PhDs.

5. Typically, it should be noted, only about one-third of doctoral recipients annually have "definite employment commitments" on which to report at the time of degree award, so this may not reflect a sample of all PhD recipients.

6. About equal numbers of faculty embarked on their first academic job in 2001 (n=46,896 or 31.0%) and 2002 (n=48,102 or 31.8%), with a somewhat larger number in 2003 (n=56,433 or 37.3%).

7. Traditional liberal arts fields include the humanities and the natural and social sciences, while the professions include agriculture, business, education, engineering, fine arts, health sciences, and other academic programs.

8. Earlier versions of the NSOPF survey posed such a question about the voluntary nature of part-time employment choice.

9. It must be underscored that this limited teaching is only at the focal institution at which they were surveyed. Technically, they could be teaching at other institutions; however, 89.5% were not teaching at another postsecondary institution.

10. In the case of business, an unusually high proportion report having "retired" from a previous position, suggesting that their part-time employment is their primary postretirement employment from an earlier career.

11. Of course, this means that for nearly one-third (30.1%) of PhDs employed part-time, their part-time employment is their "primary" employment.

12. There was, however, some reciprocal flow between the contingent academic labor market and stable, full-time positions in industry, government, and nonprofits as well as to nonfaculty positions in the academic sector. The path to a career-ladder faculty appointment is defined as an appointment on the tenure track with assurance of a tenure review after a fixed term followed by an "up or out" (promotion or termination) decision.

13. The survey excludes PhDs in some of the "softer" social sciences, for example, anthropology and history, as well as all PhDs in the humanities, so the focal sample is not, strictly speaking, comparable to those of Nerad (2008) and Ehrenberg et al. (2010).

14. The SDR began in its current form in 1993 and draws a two-pronged sample in each administration: half are new PhD recipients who received their degree following the last administration of the instrument two to three years earlier; half are PhDs who have responded to previous administrations of the instrument. That allows the possibility of identifying subgroups of PhD recipients who have responded to multiple administrations of the instrument over periods as short as four to six years (two cycles) or twenty years (ten cycles beginning with 1993 and concluding with 2013).

15. At the time of writing, the SDR 2013 data file had just been released. We chose to abbreviate the ten-year period between the 2003 and subsequent cohort—making it 2010 rather than 2013—to permit an examination at two data points of the most recent PhD recipients for whom data was available.

16. These gender differences are less pronounced in the 1993 cohort.

17. While this finding, in and of itself, does not suggest that individual, rather than organizational, choice is operating here, other evidence, including table 4.7, suggests that individual choice may indeed be disproportionately operative.

REFERENCES

Cartter, Allan M. 1976. *PhDs and the Academic Labor Market*. New York: McGraw-Hill.

Cohen, Arthur, and Florence Brawer. 1977. *The Two-Year College Instructor Today*. New York: Praeger.

Ehrenberg, Ronald, Harriet Zuckerman, Jeffrey A. Groen, and Sharon M. Brucker. 2010. *The Education of Scholars*. Princeton, NJ: Princeton University Press.

Gappa, Judith, and David Leslie. 1993. *The Invisible Faculty: Improving the Status of Part-Timers in Higher Education*. San Francisco, CA: Jossey-Bass.

Lechuga, Vicente. 2005. *The Changing Landscape of the Academic Profession: Faculty Culture at For-Profit Colleges and Universities*. New York: Routledge.

Merton, Robert K. 1968. "The Matthew Effect in Science." *Science* 159, no. 3810: 56–63.

Nerad, Maresi. 2008. *Social Science PhDs 5+Years Out: A National Survey of PhDs in Six Fields*. Seattle, WA: Center for Innovation and Research in Graduate Education, University of Washington.

Seidman, Earl. 1985. *In the Words of the Faculty: Perspectives on Improving Teaching and Educational Quality at Community Colleges*. San Francisco, CA: Jossey-Bass.

Twombly, Susan B. 2005. "Values, Policies, and Practices Affecting the Hiring Process for Full-Time Arts and Sciences Faculty in Community Colleges." *Journal of Higher Education* 76 (July–August): 423–47.

5

Career Progression and Mobility

The previous chapter documents the changing pathways leading to an academic career: entrants are arriving at their first jobs slightly older; venues for entry into an increasingly differentiated job market, defined by both institutional type and employment or appointment status, are increasingly tied to education credentials and gender; and entry to a relatively stable faculty job has become much more circuitous. An array of questions follows: Once an initial foothold has been established in higher education, although not necessarily faculty employment, how does one's career unfold? Do multiple starting points lead to different or similar career trajectories and outcomes? Do different entry points have equal holding power, or do they result in differential attrition patterns? That is, to what extent do new entrants persist in academic careers? Which ones? To the extent that they do persist after the initial entry, what are the opportunities for mobility among different entry statuses, between full- and part-time appointments, between contract and tenure-track appointments? Is career trajectory determined by point of entry? For the minority who make it to the tenure track, what are the prospects for tenure and promotion to senior academic rank? How long does that take?

When Jack Schuster and Martin Finkelstein (2006) first documented diversity in appointment status at point of career entry, using 1998 data, they found that initial-entry status largely shaped career trajectory, that is, those who entered into part-time positions tended to lead careers within a part-time track, moving from one part-time appointment to another (with the notable exception of new faculty in the humanities and new faculty in the two-year community college sector, who managed to move into full-time appointments with greater frequency), while those who entered into full-time positions tended to pursue largely separate, full-time career tracks—even suggesting that among full-time appointees, initial tenure eligibility status (tenure eligible vs. non-tenure-track) gave rise to largely separate career subtracks. Since then, our analyses of 2003 data (NSOPF:04; Finkelstein, Schuster, and Iglesias 2013; and chapter 4) and analyses by the Mellon Graduate Education Initiative (Ehrenberg et al. 2010) suggest that greater permeability and flexibility of movement between appointment statuses has become more common. If so, that new reality suggests that after a period of intense disruption of historic, post–World War II career-entry patterns, we may be settling in to a "new normal," with the new appointments taking their place along with traditional appointments in a new and relatively more flexible, albeit still internally stratified, equilibrium.

In what follows, we examine career development through three lens. First, we examine the prospects for career progression for those entering in different statuses, part-time or full-time, on or off track. What are the prospects for, and directional patterns of, mobility between part- and full-time employment? Between off- and on-tenure-track appointments? In short, is the new stratification of appointment types relatively permeable or not? And if so, is movement unidirectional or multidirectional, as it appeared to be for new entrants (see chapter 4)? How does interinstitutional mobility figure into this? Second, for that subgroup of individuals who manage to find their way into full-time traditional appointments, we address a narrower set of questions related to promotion and mobility, including achieving promotion in rank and the awarding of tenure. What proportion of tenure-track faculty achieve promotion to senior ranks (associate and full professor) and the award of tenure? How long does it take? And how has that changed over the past decade or two? Moreover, how does promotion or tenure and its schedule differ by institutional type, academic field, gender, race/ethnicity, and early mobility experience (whether an individual has stayed in his or her first job or moved)? Finally, we examine overall persistence and retention in academic careers. What is the available evidence on patterns of out-migration from academic careers? Who is most likely to leave? What are the most likely points of attrition? Is it primarily early on? And is out-migration stanched once tenured status is achieved, contributing to the immobile, deadwood phenomenon of which we hear so much?

In addressing these three sets of questions on mobility between employment and appointment statuses, on promotion and tenure prospects for those who make their way onto the career ladder, and on the incidence and timing of out-migration, we draw on the 2003 administration of the National Study of

Postsecondary Faculty (NSOPF:04). While we concede that these data are dated, we also argue that they constitute the best broad-based-system status information available. Moreover, to the extent that changes in historic career patterns are already discernible as early as 2003—both before the impact of the Great Recession of 2008 and the full flowering of Paradigm Three (see chapter 1)—there is, we believe, added credibility to the portrait being drawn of change in the second decade of the twenty-first century.

We draw as well, as we do in chapter 4, on successive administrations of the Survey of Doctorate Recipients (SDR) between 1993 and 2013, albeit with a different twist. While in the preceding chapter we were able to narrow our focus to two points in time (over a one- to three- year period after PhD receipt) to gain perspective on the nascent career experiences of those who were newly entering academic employment, we need here to expand our focus to at least three points in time (a ten-year career chunk) as we examine PhD faculty as they move farther along in their academic careers.[1]

Pathways to a Career Ladder: Mobility Patterns among Appointment Types

In chapter 4, we sketched a portrait of contemporary academic career entry as involving an extended settling-in period: that is, a sizable portion of new entrants took an indirect path to a first faculty position (often through an initial nonfaculty position in or outside higher education) and may then have experienced additional jobs changes and employment and tenure statuses changes (with or without job changes) during an initial one- to three-year entry period. Once settled in, we now ask, what pattern (trajectory) do their academic careers take? To what extent do patterns of job changing and movement between different appointment statuses continue well beyond the entry period? What are the prospects for career progression in terms of in-place promotions or movement to better jobs at one's initial or a new institution? Is status at point of entry tantamount to one's destiny? Or is there permeability or mobility across appointment and employment statuses?

As noted earlier, we have two principal sources of evidence on these matters. The 2004 National Study of Postsecondary Faculty provides data on respondents' employment and tenure status in fall 2003 (the time of the survey) as well as their employment and tenure status at their initial appointment (whether that initial appointment was with their current employer or, if they have held more than one job, with another first employer or job). It allows us to document the fact of a job change (or not) between the first and the current (fall 2003) faculty job and whether the current job is the first job. The NSOPF:04 thus allowed respondents to report on changes in their employment and tenure status between their initial hire to a faculty position and their current job; this, in effect, allows the analyst to document movement between first hire and current situation—whether or not there has been a job change—and to construct a profile of those who have changed employment or tenure status and those who have not. The second source is the Survey of Doctorate Recipients, which allows us to identify changes in employment and tenure status for two cohorts (1993 and 2003) of survey respondents over a ten-year period as it varies by career stage and to construct profiles of those who changed status and those who did not.

2004 National Study of Postsecondary Faculty

Table 5.1 below provides an overview of reported changes in job or employer and in employment and tenure status by gender and highest degree. A quick examination shows that the majority of full-time faculty have changed jobs at least once during their career. Interestingly enough, non-PhD holders are decidedly less likely than PhD holders to change jobs (especially women). Much greater stability, however, is evident in both employment and tenure status. Among PhD holders, nearly a quarter reported changes in employment status and tenure status; among non-PhDs, who disproportionately serve on part-time appointments, nearly one-third (30.9%) changed employment status, but only about one of twelve (8.1%) changed their tenure status. Women were more likely than men to change their employment status but not their tenure status.

The 2004 National Study of Postsecondary Faculty (NSOPF:04), in addition to eliciting data about the current employment and tenure status of respondents, also elicits data about the employment and tenure status of the respondents' first job, if the current job is not their first. It thus allows us to examine patterns in first job experience for those in current jobs varying in both employment and tenure status. Of the entire faculty population, about three-fifths reported having had a previous job (67.2 of the PhDs and 57.9% of the non-PhDs, as shown in table 5.1). Figure 5.1 focuses on the nature of the first job of current part-time faculty in 2003. Among the 168,000 part-time faculty who reported having held a previous job, 72.2% reported that their previous job was also part-time, as compared with 27.8% who reported a full-time first job—a nearly 3:1 ratio. That overall 3:1 ratio shrinks, however, to

Table 5.1 Changes in employers, employment, and tenure status of faculty, by highest degree and gender, Fall 2003

	PhD		Non-PhD	
	N	%	*N*	%
Male	247,969		195,574	
Change in jobs or employer	163,536	66.0	113,287	57.9
Change in employment status	52,754	21.3	55,602	28.4
Part-time to full-time	34,615	14.0	33,243	17.0
Full-time to part-time	18,139	7.3	22,359	11.4
Change in tenure status	61,838	24.9	17,026	8.7
Tenured or tenure track to non-tenure-track	13,201	5.3	7,685	3.9
Non-tenure-track to tenured or tenure track	48,637	19.6	9,341	4.8
Female	114,258		160,737	
Change in job or employer	79,959	70.0	93,107	57.9
Change in employment status	32,569	28.5	54,411	33.9
Part-time to full-time	24,055	21.1	37,523	23.3
Full-time to part-time	8,514	7.5	16,888	10.5
Change in tenure status	26,927	23.6	11,887	7.4
Tenured or tenure track to non-tenure-track	6,857	6.0	4,739	2.9
Non-tenure-track to tenured or tenure track	20,070	17.6	7,148	4.4
Male and female combined	362,227		356,311	
Change in job or employer	243,495	67.2	206,394	57.9
Change in employment status	85,323	23.6	110,013	30.9
Part-time to full-time	58,670	16.2	70,766	19.9
Full-time to part-time	26,653	7.4	39,247	11.0
Change in tenure status	88,765	24.5	28,913	8.1
Tenured or tenure track to non-tenure-track	20,058	5.5	12,424	3.5
Non-tenure-track to tenured or tenure track	68,707	19.0	16,489	4.6

Source: NSOPF:04. (Refer to appendix A for key.)

1.2:1 among PhDs, suggesting that among PhD holders, movement from full-time to part-time is relatively common, presumably at later stages of their career.[2] Among the 281,000 full-time faculty in 2003 who reported having had a previous job (figure 5.2), nearly two-thirds (65.7%) characterized that previous job as full-time, while 34.3% reported that previous job as part-time. Thus among current full-timers in 2003, irrespective of education credentials, previous full-time

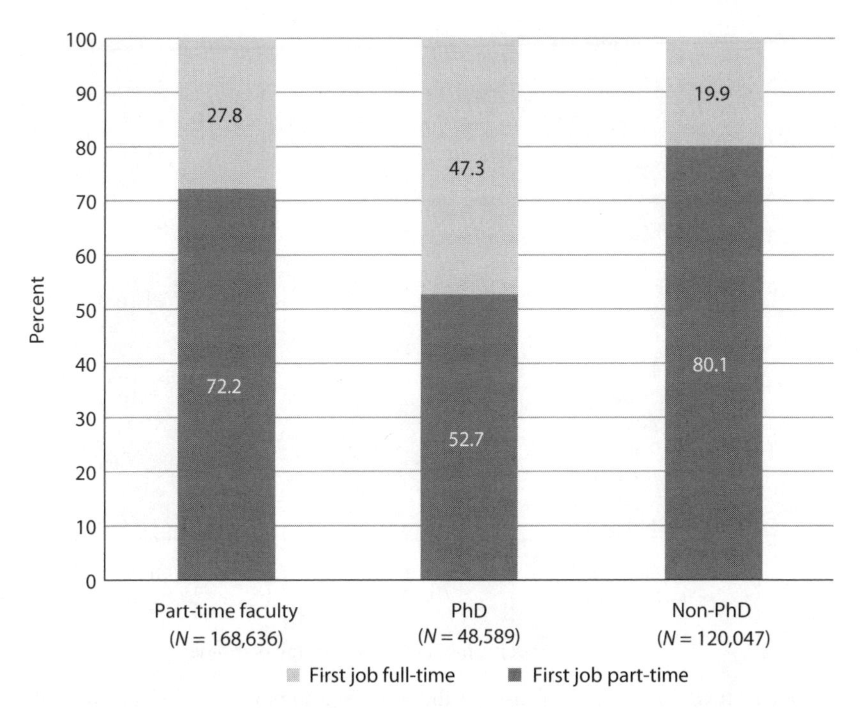

Figure 5.1 Employment status at first academic job for current part-time faculty reporting more than one job, by highest degree, 2003. *Source:* NSOPF:04. (Refer to appendix A for key to data sources.)

Note: Percentage of part-time faculty with at least one previous job.

---

faculty experience prevailed over part-time experience by a 2:1 ratio. Among PhD holders, however, that ratio was 3:1 (74.6% vs. 25.4%), while among non-PhDs, it was closer to 4:5 (45.7% vs. 54.3%), suggesting that for non-PhD holders, part-time appointments are more likely to serve as precursors to full-time appointments—especially at the two-year community colleges. Clearly, education credentials continue to shape mobility from part-time to full-time status.

In an effort to illuminate in greater detail the paths of current full-time faculty from their earlier jobs, figure 5.3 examines concurrently the tenure as well as employment status of their previous work experience. Among the 281,174 full-time faculty in 2003 who reported having had a previous job, nearly two-thirds (64.8%) reported a previous full-time job (5:1 tenure track over non-tenure-track) while just over one-third (34.3%) reported a previous part-time position. Among those tenured or on tenure track in 2003, nearly

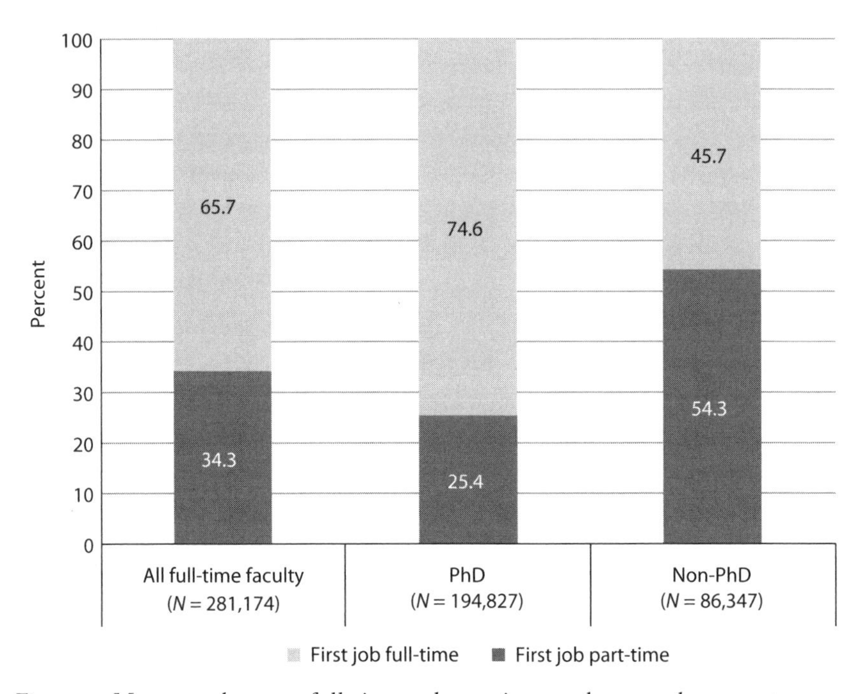

Figure 5.2 Movement between full-time and part-time employment, by current full-time faculty with one or more previous jobs, 2003. *Source:* NSOPF:04. (Refer to appendix A for key to data sources.)

---

three-fifths reported previous tenure-track experience and fewer than one-third (29.8%) part-time experience. That is, tenured or tenure-track faculty were twice as likely to report previous full-time tenure-track experience as to report previous part-time experience and six times more likely to report such tenure-track experience as to report previous non-tenure-track full-time experience. When we control for highest degree, however, we see that the pattern of previous part-time experience is modal primarily for nondoctorate faculty, with just half (51.2%) of current full-time tenured or tenure-track, albeit non-PhD, faculty reporting previous part-time experience compared with about one-quarter (23.2%) of full-time tenure-track faculty holding the doctorate. This at once corroborates, and circumscribes, our earlier findings that the tenure track tended to operate as something of a self-contained and only modestly permeable career path: clearly, it does so for faculty holding the PhD much more so than for those without a doctorate (Schuster and Finkelstein 2006). The relative permeability to previous part-time experience for non-doctorate-holding

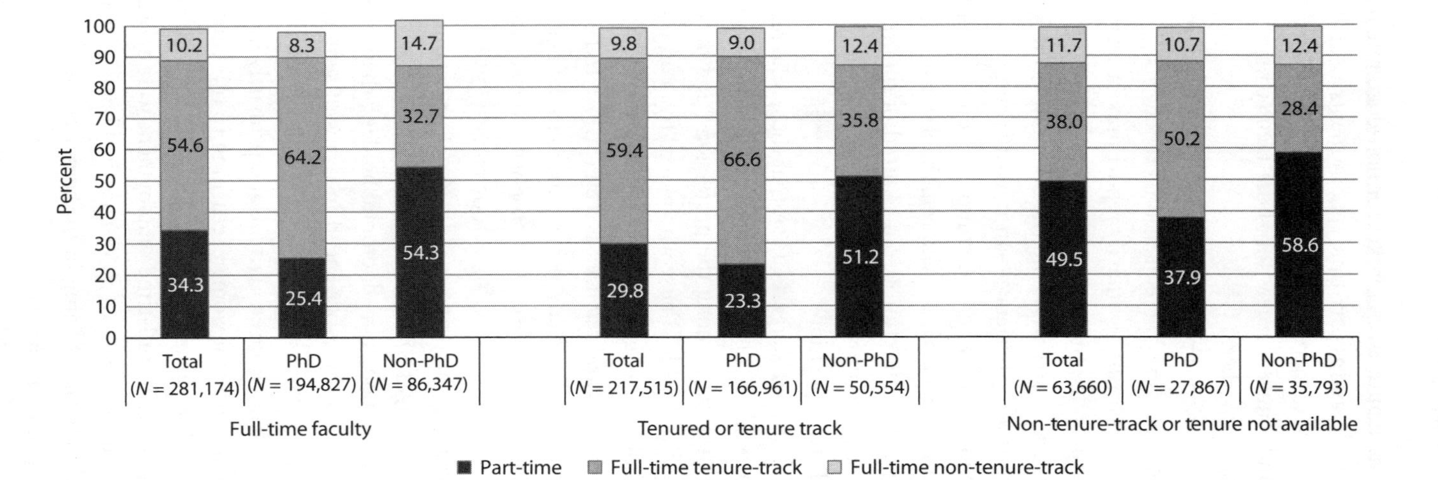

Figure 5.3 Job mobility patterns of current full-time faculty, by appointment type, 2003. *Source:* NSOPF:04. (Refer to appendix A for key to data sources.)

faculty suggests that the tenure-track market for non-doctorate holders may be becoming more permeable, and as part-time appointments assume an ever larger share of the faculty market, there may be increasing flexibility of movement across employment and tenure statuses for those faculty members, especially in the non-doctoral labor market.

The previous job experience patterns of current non-tenure-track faculty similarly differ along the lines of education credentials. Non-doctorate-holding, non-tenure-track faculty primarily report previous part-time experience (presumably disproportionately in the two-year sector), while those current non-tenure-track faculty who hold the doctorate primarily report previous full-time tenure-track experience—an initially counterintuitive finding. These patterns are illuminated when we compare the profile of those faculty who moved from off to on track, those who remained non-tenure-track, those who moved in the opposite direction (from tenured or tenure-track to non-tenure-track), and those who moved from part-time to either tenure track or non-tenure-track, full-time positions.

A careful perusal of table 5.2 suggests, first, that those who remained off the tenure track were more likely to be non-doctorate holders, to be disproportionately in the health sciences among the professions, and in the natural sciences among the liberal arts fields. Those who moved from off track to on track were more likely to hold the doctorate (86%), to be located in the four-year sector (86%), to be in the natural sciences as well (31.2%), to be men (70%), to have published twice as much as any other subgroup defined by movement among tenure and employment statuses. Those who moved from on track to off were more likely to be male (66.7%), senior faculty (77.8%) who held the PhD (63%) and who were age fifty-five or older (63%)—presumably transitioning into retirement. Finally, those who moved from part-time to full-time included two subgroups. Among non-doctorate holders, they were more likely to be women (55.4%), relatively experienced in terms of seniority (46.2% senior career stage), in the two-year sector (55.4%), under age the age of fifty-five (69.2%), with dependent children (43.1%), and primarily in the liberal arts fields (43.1%). This may represent women returning to full-time work following several years devoted to raising families. Among doctorate holders, those who moved from part-time to full-time employment were more likely to be men (58.6%), in the four-year sector (77.6%), in the liberal arts fields (60.3%), relatively experienced in terms of being in the senior career stage (51.7%), but under the age of fifty-five years (62.1%).

Table 5.2 Selected characteristics of full-time faculty who reported various patterns of prior employment and tenure statuses, Fall 2003

	Total	Moved from not tenure-track to tenure or tenure-track		Moved from part-time to full-time: Not-tenure-track		Moved from part-time to full-time: Tenure or tenure-track		Tenure or tenure-track to not tenure-track	
		N	%	*N*	%	*N*	%	*N*	%
Institution type[a]									
Research	74,397	19,986	26.9	5,899	7.9	8,565	11.5	2,945	4.0
Doctoral	34,392	9,202	26.8	3,735	10.9	5,591	16.3	1,107	3.2
Comprehensive	74,590	21,578	28.9	7,125	9.6	18,113	24.3	2,088	2.8
Liberal arts	29,824	7,033	23.6	3,769	12.6	7,557	25.3	1,375	4.6
Two-year	52,403	7,283	13.9	8,081	15.4	21,839	41.7	1,562	3.0
Academic Field									
Professions									
Business	22,730	3,889	17.1	2,848	12.5	4,242	18.7	898	4.0
Education	18,618	3,837	20.6	2,544	13.7	3,824	20.5	495	2.7
Engineering	12,052	3,057	25.4	419	3.5	1,530	12.7	408	3.4
Health sciences	25,081	5,063	20.2	3,669	14.6	4,438	17.7	976	3.9
Liberal arts									
Humanities	49,991	13,421	26.8	6,404	12.8	14,321	28.6	1,432	2.9
Natural sciences	59,346	18,490	31.2	4,759	8.0	10,823	18.2	2,281	3.8
Social sciences	33,332	8,095	24.3	2,822	8.5	8,824	26.5	1,281	3.8
Highest degree									
PhD	194,827	56,024	28.8	10,576	5.4	38,941	20.0	7,267	3.7
First professional degree	9,830	1,924	19.6	1,146	11.7	1,663	16.9	285	2.9

(continued)

Table 5.2 (continued)

	Total	Moved from not tenure-track to tenure or tenure-track		Moved from part-time to full-time				Tenure or tenure-track to not tenure-track	
				Not-tenure-track		Tenure or tenure-track			
		N	%	*N*	%	*N*	%	*N*	%
Master's	70,620	9,354	13.2	18,008	25.5	22,395	31.7	2,246	3.2
Bachelor's or less	5,624	381	6.8	1,692	30.1	1,758	31.3	317	5.6
Career stage									
Early	45,136	10,448	23.1	7,775	17.2	12,056	26.7	1,140	2.5
Mid	63,712	13,866	21.8	9,341	14.7	16,853	26.5	2,360	3.7
Senior	172,326	43,402	25.2	14,419	8.4	35,922	20.8	6,615	3.8
Citizen status									
U.S. citizen	19,826	61,167	308.5	29,931	151.0	61,872	312.1	795	4.0
Not a US citizen	261,348	6,551	2.5	1,604	0.6	2,959	1.1	9,320	3.6
Gender									
Male	177,986	46,446	26.1	15,079	8.5	36,027	20.2	5,875	3.3
Female	103,188	21,270	20.6	16,456	15.9	28,804	27.9	4,240	4.1
Race/ethnicity									
Asian	22,623	5,877	26.0	1,915	8.5	3,582	15.8	974	4.3
URM[b]	30,376	5,663	18.6	3,894	12.8	7,654	25.2	1,504	5.0
White	243,677	59,235	24.3	27,927	11.5	57,784	23.7	8,343	3.4

Marital status and dependent children									
Single without dependent children	46,174	11,643	25.2	6,461	14.0	10,560	22.9	1,478	3.2
Single with dependent children	14,563	3,816	26.2	2,044	14.0	3,144	21.6	648	4.4
Married without dependent children	94,597	20,429	21.6	10,747	11.4	21,753	23.0	3,588	3.8
Married with dependent children	125,841	31,831	25.3	12,283	9.8	19,374	15.4	4,401	3.5
Principal activity									
Teaching	224,859	53,578	23.8	27,156	12.1	58,067	25.8	7,981	3.5
Research	26,727	8,712	32.6	942	3.5	2,131	8.0	818	3.1
Administration	29,588	5,428	18.3	3,438	11.6	4,632	15.7	1,316	4.4
Age									
Under 35	9,376	1,907	20.3	1,946	20.8	2,507	26.7	246	2.6
35–44	59,385	14,954	25.2	7,556	12.7	15,470	26.1	2,035	3.4
45–54	97,022	24,834	25.6	11,755	12.1	23,547	24.3	3,279	3.4
55–64	92,203	21,414	23.2	8,233	8.9	19,565	21.2	3,350	3.6
65 or above	23,187	4,609	19.9	2,045	8.8	3,743	16.1	1,205	5.2
Average number of publications in the last two years	4.6	5.4		2.4		3.7		3.5	

Source: NSOPF:04. (Refer to appendix A for key.)

[a] Institutions classified as Specialized Institution in NSOPF:04 are not included.

[b] Underrepresented racial minority.

Table 5.3 Faculty mobility across employment and tenure statuses, by highest degree, Fall 2003

	Total faculty (*N*=718,538)		PhD (*N*=362,227)		Non-PhD (*N*=356,311)	
	N	%	*N*	%	*N*	%
Moved from part-time to full-time	129,435	18.0	58,669	16.2	70,766	19.9
Moved from full-time to part-time	65,900	9.2	26,653	7.4	39,247	11.0
Moved from on to off tenure	32,482	4.5	20,058	5.5	12,424	3.5
Moved from off to on tenure	85,198	11.9	68,707	19.0	16,488	4.6
Did not move						
Stayed tenured or tenure track	194,202	27.0	155,392	42.9	38,810	10.9
Stayed part-time	194,800	27.1	33,009	9.1	161,791	45.4
Stayed non-tenure-track	82,422	11.5	26,390	7.3	56,033	15.7
No previous job	268,727	37.4	118,811	32.8	149,916	42.1

Source: NSOPF:04. (Refer to appendix A for key.)

Table 5.3 summarizes the movement between part-time and full-time, off track and on-track, and vice versa. Overall, nearly one in five faculty moved from part-time to full-time and about one in ten moved from full-time to part-time, the latter group dominated by men in the late stage of their career. There were relatively small differences in employment status mobility between faculty who held and did not hold the doctoral degree. About one-eighth of faculty moved from off to on the tenure track, and that movement was heavily shaped by education credentials. About one-fifth of doctorate holders made that transition compared with one-twentieth of non-doctorate holders. Similarly, about one of twenty faculty moved from on to off the tenure track. In many respects, what emerges is a portrait of relative stability with mobility in both employment and tenure status not significantly exceeding that experienced by newly entering faculty. As with newly entering faculty, education credentials continue to play a role in shaping career trajectory, particularly movement onto the tenure track.

The Survey of Doctorate Recipients

Table 5.4 documents the employment status and tenure status changes reported by two cohorts (1993, 2003) of PhD recipients responding to the Survey of Doctorate Recipients over a ten-year period by career stage. A glance at the employment status columns suggests that the reported rate of employment

Table 5.4 Percentage of PhD recipients employed in higher education reporting changes in employment or tenure status or both over a ten-year period, by gender and career stage, 1993 and 2003 (Survey of Doctorate Recipients cohorts)

	1993 Cohort						2003 Cohort					
		% changing employment status		% changing tenure status				% changing employment status		% changing tenure status		
	N	Part-time to full-time	Full-time to part-time	Tenure NA to non-tenure-track	Non-tenure-track to tenured or tenure track	Tenured or tenure-track to non-tenure-track	*N*	Part-time to full-time	Full-time to part-time	Tenure NA to non-tenure-track	Non-tenure-track to tenured or tenure track	Tenured or tenure-track to non-tenure-track
Early career	33,642	2.8	4.4	2.1	5.1	1.2	50,577	3.0	4.5	3.2	3.2	1.3
Male	21,873	2.2	2.5	1.0	5.2	0.9	30,424	1.9	2.8	2.4	3.1	1.6
Female	11,769	3.7	7.9	4.1	5.1	1.8	20,153	4.5	7.1	4.4	3.4	1.0
Mid-career	32,941	3.3	4.4	1.7	1.3	1.5	48,406	3.0	3.5	2.9	1.6	1.4
Male	24,077	2.0	3.7	1.3	1.2	1.3	30,178	1.8	2.1	2.2	1.4	1.0
Female	8,864	6.9	6.2	2.6	1.5	2.1	18,228	4.8	5.9	4.0	1.8	2.1
Senior career	65,223	1.5	9.9	1.3	0.3	1.7	102,180	1.3	8.2	1.5	0.4	1.5
Male	56,960	1.3	10.0	1.2	0.4	1.7	80,743	1.0	7.9	1.3	0.3	1.5
Female	8,263	3.1	9.1	2.0	0.0	1.6	21,437	2.1	9.3	2.1	0.7	1.6
All career stages	131,806	2.3	7.1	1.6	1.8	1.5	201,163	2.1	6.2	2.2	1.4	1.4
Male	102,910	1.7	6.9	1.2	1.6	1.4	141,345	1.4	5.6	1.7	1.1	1.4
Female	28,896	4.5	7.7	3.0	2.5	1.8	59,818	3.7	7.5	3.5	2.0	1.5

Sources: SDR:93; SDR:03; SDR:13. (Refer to appendix A for key.)

Notes: Other fields of major include mathematical sciences, computer and information, and health sciences. Tenure NA = Tenure track not applicable. Periods of change are defined as 1993 to 2003 and 2003 to 2013.

status changes is slightly lower than that reported by the broader swath of faculty in the NSOPF:04—under 10%—but, based on what the NSOPF data teaches us, we would expect a group composed solely of PhDs (and PhDs outside the humanities, where part-time employment is more common) to report lower employment status mobility than a larger mixed group with substantial numbers of non-PhD holders (see table 5.1). Consistent with the NSOPF:04 findings, women were at least twice as likely as men to change their employment status, both at the early and mid-career stages; but the direction of change was as likely (or more likely) to be from full- to part-time as from part-time to full-time—the reverse of traditional career-track expectations. Gender differences disappeared at the senior career stage: indeed, employment status change overall was greatest in both the 1993 and 2003 cohorts among the senior faculty, with the direction of that movement predominantly from full-time to part-time. Presumably this represents individuals at the later stages of their careers transitioning into retirement.

As for tenure status, reported changes among early-career faculty were on a par with those of new entrants as reported in the NSOPF (see chapter 4)—about one of twelve early career faculty reported a change in tenure status—and that proportion declined among the mid-career and senior faculty. This suggests clearly that when tenure status changes occur, they tend to occur earlier rather than later in an academic career.[3] Women PhDs reported nearly double the incidence of tenure status changes as men—in both the 1993 and 2003 cohorts—a departure from the NSOPF:04 findings. The direction of that change, however, is as likely to be from positions to which tenure is not applicable (typically postdocs) to non-tenure-track faculty positions as from off- to on-track full-time faculty positions.

When we examine the characteristics of those faculty who changed employment status and those who did not, as in table 5.5, we find that a clear picture emerges among both the 1993 and 2003 SDR respondent cohorts. Faculty at two-year colleges were more than twice as likely as those in the four-year sector to maintain their part-time status (22.2% vs. 7.8% in the 1993 cohort and 49.0% vs. 21.9% in the 2003 cohort); and when movement occurred, those in the two-year sector were more likely to move from part to full-time and those in the four-year sector from full-time to part-time. Women were slightly more likely than men in both cohorts to remain part-time (although only a small minority, one-sixth in the 1993 cohort and one-quarter in the 2003 cohort actually did so); but when they did move, they were more likely than men to

Table 5.5 Selected characteristics of PhD recipients employed in higher education reporting changes in employment status over a ten-year period, by career stage, 1993 and 2003 (Survey of Doctorate Recipients cohorts)

	1993 Cohort (*N*=131,807)				2003 Cohort (*N*=201,163)			
			Moved from				Moved from	
	N	Remain PT	PT to FT	FT to PT	*N*	Remain PT	PT to FT	FT to PT
N		1,195	3,016	9,341		5,352	4,214	12,373
Institution type								
2-year college	999	22.2	28.6	49.1	2,053	49.0	24.9	26.1
4-year college or university	12,553	7.8	21.7	70.5	19,886	21.9	18.6	59.5
Field of degree	13,552	8.8	22.3	68.9	21,938	24.4	19.2	56.4
Computer and math sciences	904	11.5	8.5	80.0	1,607	20.1	22.2	57.7
Life and related sciences	3,954	9.8	22.0	68.2	5,039	24.2	23.5	52.3
Physical and related sciences	2,122	9.0	24.7	66.3	2,877	21.0	12.7	66.3
Social and related sciences	5,364	7.6	25.4	67.0	8,858	29.5	19.5	50.9
Engineering	1,208	8.7	14.9	76.4	1,903	18.5	16.6	64.9
Science and engineering–related fields	—	—	—	—	1,329	14.4	14.7	70.8
Non-science-and-engineering–related fields	—	—	—	—	325	14.5	20.0	65.5
Gender	13,552	8.8	22.3	68.9	21,937	24.4	19.2	56.4
Male	9,392	6.0	18.2	75.8	12,684	22.3	15.6	62.0
Female	4,160	15.2	31.4	53.4	9,253	27.2	24.1	48.7
Age	13,552	8.8	22.3	68.9	21,936	24.4	19.2	56.4
Under 35 years	780	14.1	41.0	44.9	950	18.9	32.4	48.6
35–44 years	3,653	10.6	36.6	52.8	4,063	25.7	42.6	31.7
45–54 years	5,460	8.7	21.0	70.3	6,050	25.7	24.1	50.2
54–64 years	3,659	6.1	5.7	88.2	10,103	23.3	6.6	70.2
65+ years	0	0.0	0.0	0.0	770	29.4	6.9	63.8

(continued)

Table 5.5 (continued)

	1993 Cohort (N=131,807)				2003 Cohort (N=201,163)			
			Moved from				Moved from	
	N	Remain PT	PT to FT	FT to PT	N	Remain PT	PT to FT	FT to PT
N		1,195	3,016	9,341		5,352	4,214	12,373
Career stage	13,552	8.8	22.3	68.9	21,940	24.4	19.2	56.4
Early career	2,778	13.8	33.4	52.8	5,027	24.5	29.7	45.8
Mid-career	2,899	12.5	37.8	49.7	4,181	24.6	34.4	41.0
Senior career	7,875	5.7	12.6	81.7	12,732	24.3	10.1	65.6
Race/ethnicity	13,552	8.8	22.3	68.9	21,935	24.4	19.2	56.4
White	12,022	9.3	21.9	68.7	18,645	24.4	17.5	58.0
Black or African American	244	0.0	39.8	60.2	897	15.1	21.1	63.9
Asian or Pacific Islander	866	3.1	27.5	69.4	1,425	26.7	35.3	38.0
Hispanic	280	16.4	16.1	67.5	698	30.7	32.1	37.2
Native American	140	0.0	0.0	100.0	0	0.0	0.0	0.0
Multiple races	—	—	—	—	270	23.3	9.3	67.4
Marital status	13,552	8.8	22.2	68.9	21,938	24.4	19.2	56.4
Married	10,968	10.2	21.6	68.2	17,097	24.3	19.8	55.9
Marriage-like relationship	0	0.0	0.0	0.0	932	28.1	9.2	62.7
Widowed	82	0.0	0.0	100.0	228	13.2	48.2	38.6
Separated	162	14.8	16.0	69.1	150	43.3	36.0	20.7
Divorced	1,170	2.1	17.9	80.1	1,649	26.6	11.1	62.3
Never married	1,170	2.5	35.1	62.4	1,882	21.4	21.2	57.4
Children in household	13,552	8.8	22.3	68.9	21,937	24.4	19.2	56.4
At least one	6,529	12.5	30.2	57.3	9,928	27.6	25.8	46.5
None	7,023	5.4	14.9	79.8	12,009	21.7	13.7	64.5

Sources: SDR:93; SDR:03; SDR:13. (Refer to appendix A for key.)

Notes: Other fields of major include mathematical sciences, computer and information, and health sciences. PT=part-time, FT=full-time. Periods of change are defined as 1993–2003–2013.

move from part to full-time status, while men were more likely to move from full to part-time status. While not directly displayed in the table, the largest share of men moving from full to part-time status were senior faculty in the fifty-four- to sixty-four-year age group. PhD faculty with children were slightly more likely to stay part-time but, paradoxically, were less likely than those without children to move from full to part-time. These patterns should be interpreted, however, within the context of the relative rarity of employment status change at any career stage for PhD recipients and the irony that such changes are most common in the latter stages of the academic career.

When we consider the profile of those who changed tenure status and those who remained off the tenure track among both cohorts, as shown in table 5.6, we find that faculty in the two-year sector were more likely to remain off the tenure track and less likely to move into the tenure track than faculty at four-year institutions, not surprising given the lower prevalence of tenure systems. Among academic fields, faculty in the social sciences were the least likely in both cohorts to move from off to on track. Younger faculty at the earlier career stages were most likely to change their tenure status, although senior faculty were more likely to make one particular change—that from on to off track. Women were slightly more likely than men to move within non-tenure-track statuses, but no more likely in either cohort to move from off to on track. Underrepresented racial minority faculty were slightly more likely in both cohorts to remain in off-track positions, but in the 2003 cohort they were actually nearly twice as likely as white faculty to move from off to on track (10 vs. more than 20%).

In summary, the portrait that emerges from the SDR is largely congruent with that which emerges from the NSOPF:04 in terms of modest rates of employment and tenure status change across all career stages. Employment status changes occur in both directions (with faculty nearly as likely to move from full-time to part-time as vice versa) and are more common for non-doctorate holders and for women at early and mid-career stages; employment status changes are most common, however, for men at the latter stages of an academic career. Tenure-status changes typically occur during the early and, to a lesser extent, mid-career stages; men are more likely to move from off to on the tenure track than women, and women more likely to move within various non-tenurable appointments. The majority of those who find themselves off the tenure track in the early stages of their career remain off the tenure track, although holding the doctorate facilitates movement between part- and full-time as well as from off to on track. In some respects, the academic career has

Table 5.6 Selected characteristics of PhD recipients employed in higher education reporting changes in tenure status over a ten-year period by career stage, 1993 and 2003 (Survey of Doctorate Recipients cohorts)

	1993 cohort (*N* = 131,807)					2003 cohort (*N* = 201,163)				
				Moved from					Moved from	
	N	Remain NTT/ Ten NA	Ten NA to NTT	NTT to T/ TT	T/TT to NTT	*N*	Remain NTT/ Ten NA	Ten NA to NTT	NTT to T/ TT	T/TT to NTT
N		10,704	2,065	2,375	2,010		20,547	4,524	2,751	2,873
Institution type										
Two-year college	834	77.0	9.7	10.0	3.4	1,779	85.3	9.2	0.0	5.5
Four-year college or university	16,320	61.7	12.2	14.0	12.1	28,916	65.8	15.1	9.5	9.6
Field of degree	17,153	62.4	12.0	13.8	11.7	30,697	66.9	14.7	9.0	9.4
Computer and math sciences	776	41.2	17.0	26.5	15.2	1,455	60.0	8.8	7.1	24.1
Life and related sciences	6,546	62.1	12.5	14.1	11.4	10,843	62.7	16.2	12.4	8.7
Physical and related sciences	4,041	60.3	14.8	14.4	10.5	4,560	72.0	15.7	7.5	4.8
Social and related sciences	4,746	64.9	10.3	10.0	14.7	9,194	70.8	14.4	5.5	9.3
Engineering	1,044	77.0	2.7	18.1	2.2	2,199	68.8	16.8	8.2	6.1
Science and engineering—related fields	—	—	—	—	—	2,101	59.7	10.9	11.9	17.4
Non-science-and-engineering—related fields	—	—	—	—	—	345	91.3	0.0	8.7	0.0
Gender	17,156	62.4	12.0	13.8	11.7	30,695	66.9	14.7	9.0	9.4
Male	11,761	63.4	10.1	14.0	12.6	18,021	66.8	13.6	8.8	10.8
Female	5,395	60.3	16.3	13.6	9.9	12,674	67.1	16.4	9.2	7.3
Age	17,153	62.4	12.0	13.9	11.7	30,693	66.9	14.7	9.0	9.4
Under 35 years	1,974	37.1	16.3	37.5	9.0	2,452	62.4	11.9	19.4	6.2
35–44 years	7,139	64.6	9.6	17.4	8.5	10,907	61.5	16.5	14.1	7.9

45–54 years	6,624	71.1	12.9	6.0	10.1	10,618	75.8	12.1	6.2	5.8
54–64 years	1,416	45.9	14.4	0.0	39.7	6,307	63.3	18.2	1.2	17.3
65+ years	0	0.0	0.0	0.0	0.0	409	63.6	0.0	0.0	36.4
Career stage	17,156	62.4	12.0	13.8	11.7	30,693	66.9	14.7	9.0	9.4
Early career	6,060	53.2	11.6	28.4	6.8	10,731	63.4	15.2	15.2	6.3
Mid-career	5,021	70.5	10.9	8.5	10.1	8,534	66.6	16.6	8.8	8.0
Senior career	6,075	64.9	13.5	3.7	17.9	11,428	70.5	13.0	3.2	13.3
Race/ethnicity	17,154	62.4	12.0	13.8	11.7	30,696	66.9	14.7	9.0	9.4
White	14,900	64.2	11.7	12.6	11.5	25,074	67.8	14.2	8.2	9.8
Black or African American	424	61.8	21.2	5.4	11.6	756	63.9	20.1	10.3	5.7
Asian or Pacific Islander	1,322	48.8	11.0	28.6	11.6	3,611	63.7	16.8	11.7	7.8
Hispanic	441	44.9	20.4	22.7	12.0	893	54.5	17.7	19.0	8.7
Native American	67	43.3	0.0	0.0	56.7	26	100.0	0.0	0.0	0.0
Multiple races	—	—	—	—	—	336	75.9	14.0	8.6	1.5
Marital status	17,156	62.4	12.0	13.8	11.7	30,693	66.9	14.7	9.0	9.4
Married	13,460	61.4	11.9	13.3	13.3	23,077	66.2	14.6	9.3	9.8
Marriage-like Relationship	0	—	—	—	—	1,508	73.0	6.0	10.1	10.9
Widowed	105	75.2	0.0	0.0	24.8	278	77.7	10.8	0.0	11.5
Separated	133	80.5	19.5	0.0	0.0	432	83.8	0.0	7.4	8.8
Divorced	1,056	76.2	10.2	10.8	2.7	1,704	79.9	16.0	3.5	0.6
Never married	2,402	60.0	13.6	19.4	7.0	3,694	60.2	20.4	9.6	9.8
Children in household	17,154	62.4	12.0	13.9	11.7	30,696	66.9	14.7	9.0	9.4
At least one	9,984	65.6	11.1	11.8	11.5	16,377	69.0	14.3	9.4	7.4
None	7,170	58.0	13.3	16.6	12.1	14,319	64.6	15.3	8.5	11.6

Sources: SDR:93; SDR:03; SDR:13. (Refer to appendix A for key.)

Notes: Other fields of major include mathematical sciences, computer and information, and health sciences. Ten NA = Tenure not applicable, NTT = Not tenure track, T/TT = Tenure or tenure track. Periods of change are defined as 1993–2003–2013.

become more elastic, especially in terms of the increased likelihood of moving from part-time to full-time and back, and less predictable.

Moving Up the Career Ladder: Prospects for the Chosen Few

For those who find their way into career-ladder faculty positions—typically, either during the entry period or in the early career stages—the award of tenure has historically constituted the second major career milestone (the first milestone, of course, being the initial appointment to a full-time, tenure-track position).[4] While the overall number of tenured faculty in US higher education has grown by about one-third over the past quarter century as enrollment expanded by one-half (see chapter 3), we have, nonetheless, witnessed a steady decline in the proportion of full-time faculty with tenure, from nearly three-fifths a half century ago to just over two-fifths in 1993 (44.8%) and to about 38.7% in 2013; so the proportion of all faculty appointees with tenure has shrunk dramatically. During this same period, achieving the rank of associate professor has come to coincide at most four-year institutions with the award of tenure.[5] About one-quarter of full-time faculty in US colleges and universities reported holding the rank of associate professor through 1999 (Schuster and Finkelstein 2006), although that figure dropped to about one-fifth by 2013. That the awarding of tenure continues to shrink dramatically as the proportionate representation of associate professors holds steady or declines slowly suggests that there has been some decoupling of tenure from senior rank.[6] Indeed, data from the NSOPF:04 suggests that just over three-quarters (76.3%) of faculty holding associate professor rank reported holding tenure as well, ranging from about seven in ten in the two-year sector and the four-year liberal arts college sector to five-sixths in the doctoral and research university sector.

Figure 5.4 displays the proportion of full-time time faculty who were tenured or held senior ranks of associate or full professor, by gender, in 1993, 2003, and 2013. The data confirm the 32.8% increase in the number of tenured faculty over the twenty-year period, 1993–2013, from 230,000 to 306,000, albeit the concomitant decline in the proportion of full-time faculty who were tenured from 42.3% in 1993 to 38.7% in 2013. While the proportion of men who are tenured has declined, the proportion of women who are tenured has actually increased from just over one-quarter (27.1%) to nearly one-third (32.4%). Similarly, the number of faculty at the associate professor rank increased 37.1% over the twenty year period, from 113,000 to 155,000, while the proportion of all full-time faculty at the associate rank actually shrank from 20.4% to

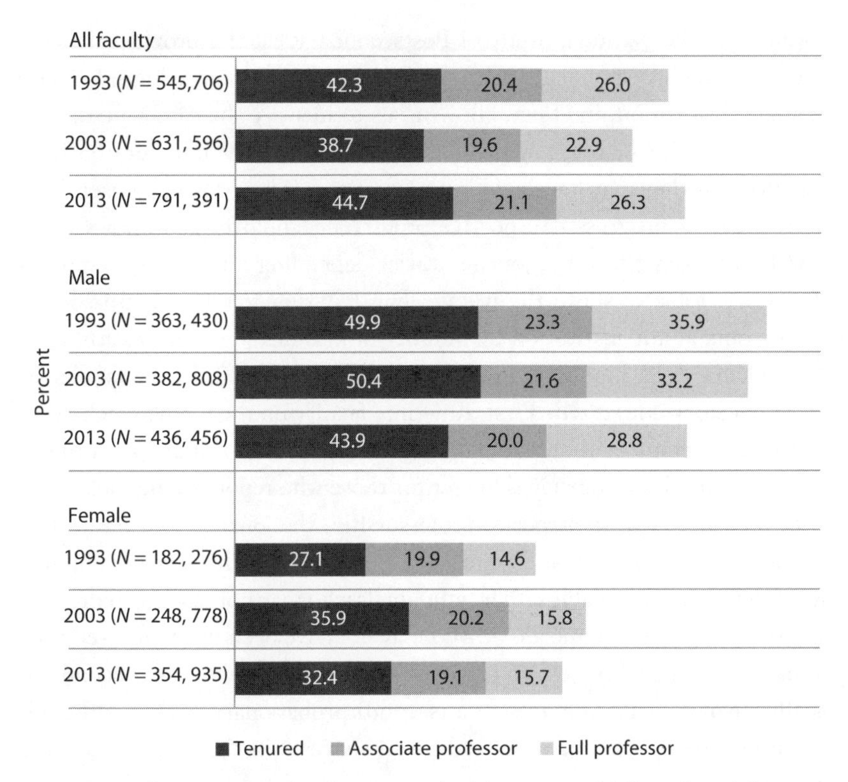

Figure 5.4 Full-time tenured and senior ranks (associate and full professor) for 1993, 2003, and 2011. *Sources:* IPEDS:93; IPEDS:03; IPEDS:13. (Refer to appendix A for key to data sources.)

19.6%. The number of faculty at the full professor rank increased over the twenty-year period from 142,000 to 181,000 or 27.5%, while the proportion holding the highest rank actually shrank from 26.0% to under one-quarter (22.9%). And it here—at the full professor rank—where the situation of women has changed the least: while the numbers have more than doubled from 26,700 to 55,700, the proportion has increased only from 14.6% in 1993 (compared with 35.9% among men) to 15.7% twenty years later (compared with 28.8% for men), although the disparity is clearly shrinking.

Moving Up in Rank and Achieving Tenure

Whatever the outcome of the quest for tenure and senior rank, what can we say about the journey, in particular its length? And what factors seem to affect that journey? The National Study of Postsecondary Faculty provides data on the year in which respondents were first awarded tenure or achieved senior rank at any institution, in effect, allowing us to identify the career marker in the life of the individual faculty member irrespective of the number of different faculty jobs they may have held in their careers. This provides a useful indicator of career progress irrespective of current employer and allows us to look at how the length of the journey varies depending on academic employment history. Table 5.7 shows the average length of time to tenure and associate professor rank at any institution by number of jobs held, gender, institutional type, academic field, highest degree, and career stage for full-time faculty in 2003. What story does it tell? First, full-time faculty on the tenure track overall report an average of about an eight-year journey from initial appointment to tenure.[7] Second, the journey is longer for those who report having held multiple faculty jobs. For an associate professorship, the journey is three to five years longer for those men and women, respectively, who have changed jobs.[8] Most of these are presumably either individuals who may not have been granted tenure in their first academic job or who may not have been in a tenure-eligible appointment in their first job. In either of these cases, moving to a second job typically involves what amounts to a (second) probationary period, although one that may be shorter than the traditional six years in the typical four-year institution.

Moreover, the data further suggest that institutional type, academic field, and career stage all shape the journey to the tenure milestone. In the first place, the road to tenure is shorter by one to two years in the two-year community college sector and the research university sector than in other four-year institutions. Gender disparities of one to two years are evident across institutional types. In the second place, academic field makes a modest difference: overall, time to tenure is shorter in engineering (7.1 years) and the humanities and the natural sciences (7.4 years); it is longer in business (8.2 years) and education (8.5 years). There is an interaction effect of academic field with gender: women report longer journeys than men in engineering and the health sciences among the professions and in the humanities and natural sciences among the liberal arts fields, in contrast to barely discernable differences in business, education, or the social sciences. Finally, there are discernible differences by career stage: among PhDs, time to tenure is longer for the senior career group and shorter for the early and mid-career group. While the comparison is cross-sectional, it does suggest that overall time to tenure has been decreasing for more recent

Table 5.7 Mean years to associate professor rank and to tenure for full-time faculty, by gender, type of institution, academic field, highest degree, and career stage, Fall 2003

	Achieved associate professorship *N*=119,209		Achieved tenure *N*=269,078	
	Male *N*=76,881	Female *N*=42,328	Male *N*=187,846	Female *N*=81,232
All full-time faculty	9.2	10.5	7.9	9.4
Institutional type[a]				
Research	8.1	9.4	7.1	9.1
Doctoral	8.8	10.6	8.1	10.2
Comprehensive	9.9	10.7	8.9	10.2
Liberal arts	10.0	11.4	9.4	10.5
Two-year	11.1	12.0	7.2	8.2
Academic field				
Profession				
Business	9.1	9.6	8.3	8.1
Education	8.9	9.8	8.2	8.7
Engineering	8.1	9.8	7.1	10.6
Health sciences	9.1	11.5	7.8	10.4
Liberal arts				
Humanities	10.3	10.7	7.4	9.7
Natural sciences	8.7	10.1	7.4	9.0
Social sciences	9.5	8.7	8.0	8.9
Achieved* at first job	7.1	7.0	5.7	6.2
Achieved at subsequent job	10.7	12.5	9.5	11.6
Highest degree				
PhD	8.7	10.0	8.0	9.6
First professional degree	8.4	9.9	7.0	9.2
Master's	11.8	12.5	7.9	9.4
Bachelor's or less	12.2	5.5	6.3	5.6
Career stage				
Early	4.4	4.2	4.6	4.5
Mid-career	7.2	7.5	6.5	7.0
Senior	12.0	14.2	8.5	11.0
Race/ethnicity[b]				
White	9.3	10.3	7.9	9.4
Asian or Pacific Islander	7.8	10.6	7.3	9.9
URM	10.2	11.5	8.6	9.6

Source: NSOPF:04. (Refer to appendix A for key.)

[a]Institutions classified as Specialized Institution in NSOPF:04 are not included.

[b]NSOPF:04 Race/ethnicity allowed for multiple responses. The categories used for this table utilized a recoded variable X03Q74. Underrepresented minority (URM) includes Black/African American, Hispanic (Black and White), and American Indian/Alaska Native.

entrants to academic careers—a somewhat surprising finding, although gender disparities may be attenuating.

A second lens through which to view progress to tenure, albeit only for those faculty holding doctoral degrees in the natural and social sciences, is provided by the SDR. The SDR allows us to identify not the precise year but the precise triennium—the period between triennial administrations of the surveys—at which tenure was achieved. Thus for the 1993 cohort we can identify those respondents at each career stage—early, middle, and senior—who reported having achieved tenure at the baseline survey year of 1993 and who reported achieving tenure during each of the next two subsequent trienniums. We can do precisely the same for the 2003 cohort. Table 5.8 reports the proportion of PhD faculty who had already achieved tenure in the baseline year and who subsequently achieved tenure during each half of the ensuing decade. The table shows that among faculty at the early career stage, about one-eighth—13.5% in the 1993 cohort and 12.0% in the 2003 cohort—had achieved tenure at the baseline administration of the SDR (during the first three to eight years following PhD receipt) and an additional two-fifths (44.9% of the 1993 cohort and 39.2% of the 2003 cohort) achieved it during the next decade. Overall, more than half of each early-career cohort (58.4% for 1993 and 51.2% for 2003) had achieved tenure ten years after they first responded to the SDR, although the rate was perceptibly lower (7.2%) among the 2003 cohort. Indeed, those in the 1993 cohort were not only more likely to earn tenure, but on average, they appeared to earn tenure more quickly. Among the 1993 cohort, the modal point of tenure award was in the first third of the decade after baseline, while for the 2003 cohort, it was in the second two-thirds of the decade after baseline.[9] Early-career males in the 1993 cohort were slightly more likely to have been awarded tenure early—that is, at baseline and in the first (rather than the second) half of the decade—than women, but those differences decreased in the 2003 cohort. Among those at the mid-career stage (nine to fifteen years after PhD award), about half reported receiving tenure at baseline, with an additional one-sixth (about 16–17%) achieving tenure during the decade following baseline for a total tenure rate of about two-thirds. Once again, men earned tenure earlier than women: men were 11.2% (2003 cohort) to 16.7% (1993 cohort) more likely than women to report tenure at baseline; however, they earned tenure in the subsequent decade post baseline at the same pace as woman. Among senior faculty, 70% reported the award of tenure at baseline, with only an additional 5% reporting the award of tenure in the decade post

Table 5.8 Percentage of PhD recipients employed in higher education achieving tenure at three points in time over a decade, by career stage and gender, 1993 and 2003 (Survey of Doctorate Recipients cohorts)

	1993 cohort					2003 cohort				
			Percentage achieved tenure					Percentage achieved tenure		
	N	Tenured in 1993	1993–97	97–2003	1993–2003	*N*	Tenured in 2003	2003–06	2006–13	2003–13
Early career	33,644	13.5	27.5	17.4	44.8	50,575	12.0	13.8	25.4	39.2
Gender										
Male	21,874	15.0	29.8	17.4	47.3	30,423	13.5	13.7	27.6	41.3
Female	11,770	10.8	23.0	17.3	40.3	20,152	9.8	13.8	22.1	35.9
Race/ethnicity										
White	26,954	13.9	26.8	17.6	44.4	37,776	12.9	14.0	25.3	39.4
Asian or Pacific Islander	4,273	12.2	30.3	13.2	43.5	7,937	6.9	10.5	25.4	35.8
URM	2,416	11.5	30.2	22.3	52.4	4,355	13.5	17.4	25.8	43.2
Mid-career	32,941	52.2	11.6	5.0	16.6	48,404	49.4	7.5	9.9	17.4
Gender										
Male	24,078	56.7	10.8	4.4	15.2	30,177	53.6	8.4	10.0	18.4
Female	8,863	40.0	13.7	6.5	20.3	18,227	42.4	5.9	9.9	15.8
Race/ethnicity										
White	28,956	52.6	11.7	4.7	16.4	37,571	50.1	7.0	9.5	16.5
Asian or Pacific Islander	2,453	47.6	9.5	4.6	14.2	6,499	48.5	8.0	10.2	18.2
URM	1,530	52.9	12.8	9.8	22.6	3,601	45.5	10.3	13.8	24.0
Senior career	65,222	72.1	2.7	2.0	4.7	102,182	67.9	1.7	1.9	3.6
Gender										
Male	56,960	74.0	2.4	2.0	4.4	80,745	70.1	1.7	1.7	3.3
Female	8,262	59.2	4.3	2.1	6.4	21,437	59.8	2.0	2.7	4.7

(continued)

Table 5.8 (continued)

	1993 cohort					2003 cohort				
			Percentage achieved tenure					Percentage achieved tenure		
	N	Tenured in 1993	1993–97	97–2003	1993–2003	*N*	Tenured in 2003	2003–06	2006–13	2003–13
Race/ethnicity										
White	58,694	71.8	2.7	1.4	4.1	90,587	67.7	1.6	2.0	3.6
Asian or Pacific Islander	3,865	75.7	0.9	0.4	1.3	6,456	72.3	1.9	0.5	2.4
URM	2,664	73.4	3.7	0.8	4.4	4,193	67.2	4.1	2.6	6.7
All career stages	131,807	52.2	11.2	6.7	17.9	201,161	49.4	6.1	9.7	15.9
Gender										
Male	102,912	57.4	10.2	5.8	16.0	141,345	54.4	5.7	9.0	14.7
Female	28,895	33.6	14.8	9.6	24.5	59,816	37.6	7.2	11.4	18.6
Race/ethnicity										
White	114,603	50.5	5.5	1.9	7.4	165,933	48.6	3.0	4.5	7.4
Asian or Pacific Islander	10,593	41.2	9.4	3.2	12.7	20,893	40.2	6.7	8.7	15.4
URM	6,612	41.8	4.4	1.5	5.9	12,149	37.3	5.1	6.2	11.3

Sources: SDR:93; SDR:97; SDR:03; SDR:06; SDR:13. (Refer to appendix A for key.)

Note: For 1993, underrepresented racial minority (URM) includes Hispanic, Black, and Native American. For 2003, URM includes Native American/American Indian, Black, and Hispanic. Beginning in 2003, NSF offered a derived "multiple race" race/ethnicity category that is not included in this analysis.

baseline. The tenure gap between men and women faculty remains and is only slightly larger than among mid-career faculty.

In sum, considering the evidence from multiple sources, we can say that while the road to tenure continues to be tread by a larger number of individuals, it has become a proportionately narrower road open to a smaller proportion of overall academic labor market traffic. Moreover, it is a longer road for non-doctorate holders, for those who change jobs, for women (although the gender gap is narrowing), for those in nonresearch four-year institutions, and for those in certain academic fields. It is a road that senior faculty negotiated more slowly than their current junior and early-career colleagues. While the road to tenure remains paved and continues to support traffic, increasingly large portions of the staffing action are elsewhere.

Promotion to Full Professor

While full professor is the modal academic rank, that is, proportionately more full-time faculty hold it than any other rank (22.9% of full-time faculty in 2013), ladder or nonladder, it constitutes at the same time the ultimate career milestone that many entering academic careers aspire to but never quite achieve.[10] Indeed, in terms of status as reflected in compensation, the move from associate to full professor represents a quantum leap vis-à-vis the move from assistant to associate or from instructor to assistant (see chapter 9). That said, what do we know about the journey to full professor?

The National Study of Postsecondary Faculty asked respondents in 2003 to report the year in which they first attained the rank of full professor (if they had done so) at any institution—in effect allowing us to identify the career marker in the life of individual faculty members irrespective of the number of different faculty jobs they may have held in their careers. This provides a useful indicator of the "ultimate" career progress irrespective of current employer as well as allowing us to look at how the length of the journey varies depending on academic employment history. Table 5.9 shows the average length of time to full professor rank by number of jobs, gender, institutional type, academic field, highest degree and career stage for full-time faculty in 2003. A glance at the table shows that male faculty report on average a 12.7-year journey to full professor, while women report on average a 15.0-year journey. For those in their second or subsequent job, the journey is three (men) or four (women) years longer. The picture that emerges, then, of career progression for those entering on the career ladder is one of a two-stage journey at roughly equal

Table 5.9 Mean years to full professor rank for full-time faculty, by gender, type of institution, academic field, highest degree, and career stage, Fall 2003

	Achieved full professor N= 157,228	
	Male N= 120,276	Female N= 36,965
All full-time faculty	12.7	15.0
Institutional type[a]		
Research	11.7	14.4
Doctoral	13.2	16.5
Comprehensive	13.8	15.9
Liberal arts	15.1	16.9
Two-year	11.8	13.6
Academic field		
Profession		
Business	12.7	14.4
Education	12.3	14.3
Engineering	11.3	12.6
Health sciences	12.1	15.7
Liberal arts		
Humanities	14.4	16.7
Natural sciences	11.9	14.0
Social sciences	13.3	14.7
Achieved at first job	10.9	12.3
Achieved at subsequent job	13.9	16.4
Highest degree		
PhD	12.9	15.1
First professional degree	10.2	12.1
Master's	12.9	15.5
Bachelor's or less	12.0	6.8
Career stage		
Early	3.2	3.3
Mid-career	8.4	8.7
Senior	13.5	16.4
Race/ethnicity[b]		
White	12.9	15.0
Asian or Pacific Islander	11.1	14.7
URM	12.6	15.1

Source: NSOPF:04. (Refer to appendix A for key.)

[a]Institutions classified as Specialized Institution in NSOPF:04 are not included.

[b]NSOPF:04 Race/ethnicity allowed for multiple responses. The categories used for this table utilized a recoded variable X03Q74. Underrepresented racial minority (URM) includes Black/African American, Hispanic (Black and White), and American Indian/Alaska Native.

intervals: after securing an initial faculty appointment, a seven- to nine-year sprint for tenure (and, concomitantly, most often, associate professor, see table 5.7) followed by a five- to six-year sprint (depending on gender) for those who have stayed in their initial position but eight to ten years (depending on gender) for those who have moved to one or more subsequent positions.

The second stage of that journey, much as the first stage, may be further shaped by institutional type, academic field type, and career stage, as these may interact with gender and education credentials. The data in table 5.9 show that time to full professor does vary substantially across institutional types—shorter for those in the two-year sector and in the research universities (as it was for tenure) and longer for those in the freestanding four-year liberal arts sector. It is a longer road for women and for those who have changed jobs. In terms of academic field, the road is longer for faculty in the humanities and shorter for those in the natural sciences and the professions. In terms of career stage, senior faculty report the longest journeys to full professor; the small contingent of early-career full professors, the shortest; and gender disparities are greatest for the senior faculty.

If we turn to the evidence furnished by the Survey of Doctorate Recipients, as shown in table 5.10, we see that the senior—and to a lesser extent, the mid-career—stage are the arena for attaining the full professorship. Nearly three-fifths of the PhD senior faculty were full professors at baseline, and only about 10% more achieved that rank in the ensuing decade, for a total of 70% during the first twenty-five years of their academic career. Approximately one-seventh of the mid-career-stage faculty held the rank of full professor at baseline with 35% (2003 cohort) to 40% (1993 cohort) more earning it during the postbaseline decade. That translates into just about half of the mid-career-stage PhD faculty (nine to fifteen years following PhD receipt) achieving full professor rank by their eighteenth to twenty-fourth after PhD receipt. Once again, gender disparities are substantial—on the order of 16–22% fewer PhD women attaining that rank during that period.

Attrition in Academic Careers

While students of academic careers have provided some largely "qualitative" evidence of attrition early on in the pursuit of academic careers (Gappa, Austin, and Trice 2007; Nerad 2008; Trower 2012; Ward and Wolf-Wendel 2012)—especially among women and underrepresented minorities—there has been little by way of actual documentation of attrition rates among new entrants to

Table 5.10 Percent of PhD recipients employed in higher education achieving full professor rank at three points in time over a decade, by career stage and gender, 1993 and 2003 (Survey of Doctorate Recipients cohorts)

	1993 Cohort					2003 Cohort				
			Percent Achieved Full Professor Rank					Percent Achieved Full Professor Rank		
	N	Full Professor in 1993	1993–97	97–2003	93–03	*N*	Full Professor in 2003	2003–06	2006–13	03–13
Early Career	33,644	1.5	5.2	26.9	32.0	50,575	1.8	2.0	20.5	22.5
Gender										
Male	21,874	1.4	6.4	30.6	37.0	30,423	1.6	2.4	22.1	24.4
Female	11,770	1.6	2.9	20.0	22.8	20,152	2.1	1.4	18.2	19.6
Race/Ethnicity										
White	26,954	1.5	5.3	25.8	31.1	37,776	1.8	2.1	20.5	22.7
Asian/Pacific Islander	4,273	1.3	2.9	30.9	33.8	7,937	1.2	1.1	21.2	22.4
URM	2,416	1.8	7.7	31.6	39.2	4,355	3.0	1.7	19.1	20.8
Mid-Career	32,941	16.2	19.8	19.6	39.4	48,404	15.0	10.7	25.2	35.9
Gender										
Male	24,078	18.8	21.0	19.2	40.2	30,177	16.7	11.8	28.2	40.1
Female	8,863	8.8	16.7	20.6	37.3	18,227	12.2	8.8	20.2	29.0
Race/Ethnicity										
White	28,956	16.2	19.5	19.7	39.2	37,571	15.0	10.7	25.1	35.7
Asian/Pacific Islander	2,453	13.9	26.0	17.5	43.5	6,499	15.8	10.8	27.7	38.4
URM	1,530	18.6	16.7	20.6	37.3	3,601	12.2	11.3	24.6	35.9

Senior Career	65,222	60.1	5.5	5.3	10.9	102,182	57.8	3.9	5.7	9.6
Gender										
Male	56,960	62.5	5.1	4.9	10.1	80,745	60.7	3.6	5.1	8.7
Female	8,262	43.1	8.3	3.1	11.4	21,437	47.1	4.9	8.1	13.0
Race/Ethnicity										
White	58,694	59.9	5.3	3.4	8.7	90,587	57.9	3.8	5.4	9.2
Asian/Pacific Islander	3,865	64.4	6.6	2.3	8.9	6,456	60.4	4.2	9.4	13.6
URM	2,664	57.5	8.6	5.7	14.3	4,193	52.6	5.7	7.3	13.0
All Combined	131,807	34.1	9.0	9.4	18.4	201,161	33.4	5.0	14.1	19.2
Gender										
Male	102,912	39.3	9.1	10.0	19.1	141,345	38.6	5.1	13.7	18.8
Female	28,895	15.7	8.7	8.1	16.8	59,816	21.3	4.9	15.2	20.1
Race/Ethnicity										
White	114,603	35.1	8.9	9.5	18.4	165,933	35.4	5.0	13.3	18.3
Asian/Pacific Islander	10,593	27.2	9.6	9.1	18.7	20,893	24.1	5.1	19.6	24.7
URM	6,612	28.1	10.1	10.8	21.0	12,149	22.8	5.9	16.7	22.6

Sources: SDR:93; SDR:97; SDR:03; SDR:06; SDR:13. (Refer to Appendix A for key.)

Notes: For 1993, URM includes Hispanic, Black, and Native American. For 2003, URM includes Native American/American Indian, Black, and Hispanic. Beginning in 2003, NSF offered a derived "multiple race" race/ethnicity category that is not included in this analysis.

academic careers. Moreover, there has been little by way of documentation of the trajectory of attrition over the course of an academic career. The prevailing assumption has been that what attrition may occur, occurs early on; once a tenure-track appointment—or, especially, tenure itself—has been achieved, there is little movement out of academic life (Nerad 2008). That conventional wisdom largely evolved before the ascent of non-traditional appointments and the shift of the center of gravity from the liberal arts fields to the professions. The declining prevalence and hence "pull" of tenured appointments and the flexibility of the professions where movement between employment sectors (in and out of academe) is more common suggest that whatever the historic merits of the conventional view, patterns of out-migration from academic careers may well be in flux.

Indeed, chapter 4 began that examination of attrition and out-migration for newly entering PhDs, those in the first three years after PhD receipt. We reported that about one-tenth left higher education employment in the first three years after receiving the PhD, with women showing a very slightly lower attrition rate and those off the tenure track showing a much higher attrition rate (closer to one in five). What happens to out-migration rates over a decade when we examine the career experience of two cohorts of PhD respondents to the Survey of Doctorate Recipients (1993 and 2003) at three later career stages: in early career (within the first three to eight career years post PhD); in mid-career (within the first nine to fifteen years post PhD); and in the late-career or senior stage (at least sixteen years post PhD)? Does attrition abruptly halt? To what extent is this initial "leakage" in the pipeline a near-term adjustment to a perceived mismatch that becomes apparent early on and is quickly and permanently sealed off? Or to what extent is out-migration from higher education employment a persistent pattern, albeit with different motives and opportunities, at multiple career stages? Do gender differences persist? Do differences by appointment type persist? The Survey of Doctoral Recipients offers an unparalleled opportunity to examine out-migration from higher education employment for PhD recipients in the natural and social sciences over an extended period.

Table 5.11 displays the attrition rates from the higher education sector (and concomitant movement to either the business or industry, government, the private nonprofit sector, K–12, or unemployment) for the 1993 and 2003 cohorts of SDR respondents over a ten-year period by gender and career stage. The focal ten-year period is divided into two segments: three to four years from the baseline year defining the cohort (1993 or 2003) and six to seven years after that. Thus for the original 1993 cohort of respondents (*N*=131,807 across three career stages), there is a snapshot of the proportion who had left academe by 1997 and by 2003; and for the original 2003 cohort of SDR respondents (*N*=201,161 across the three career stages), there is a snapshot of the proportion who had left academe by 2006 and by 2013—in both cases broken out by gender and career stage. Thus, for example, among the early-career-stage subgroup of the 1993 cohort (*N*=33,644), 15.1% had left the academic sector by 1997 and an additional 12.3% of the 33,644 early-career subgroup in that 1993 cohort had left by 2003—yielding a total attrition over a ten-year period of 27.5% of the original early-career group.

What, then, do the data in table 5.11 tell us? First, the data suggest that attrition continued at about 25%, although declining ever so slightly, for both the 1993 and 2003 cohorts during the early-career period: about one-quarter (27.5% in 1993; 26.0% in 2003) of early career stage PhD recipients (three to eight years post PhD) employed initially in higher education leave academe within the first decade; with women at early career—in contrast to women at career entry (see chapter 4)—slightly (4–7%) more likely to depart in both cohorts. Attrition declines to about 16–18% in the mid-career stage for both cohorts (18.1% for the 1993 cohort, 16.5% for the 2003 cohort), although women continue to out-migrate at a higher rate than men and their attrition tends to be later in the mid-career period than that of men, that is, in the second segment of the focal ten-year period. Among the senior cohort, attrition rises dramatically to about 35%, largely accounted for by retirement, with gender differences attenuating, if not disappearing (see chapter 6 for a full treatment of retirement or career exit). What emerges is a picture of significant and steady attrition during the first career decade, followed by a dip (but not a block) in mid-career and then by a surge in late career largely representing, we suspect, retirement; and during most of that trajectory (after the initial entry period), women leave at a higher rate (as much as 25% higher) than men. Across both early- and mid-career stages, attrition was slightly lower among the 2003 compared with the 1993 cohort—likely reflecting in no small measure the chilling effect of the Great Recession of 2008 in the larger economy.

When we factor in appointment or tenure status (table 5.12), we see a testament to the "retentive" impact of tenure. At all career stages, PhD recipients in non-tenure-track positions, or positions without faculty status (tenure not applicable, in NSF jargon), report attrition rates of 1.5 to 4.0 times that of PhD

Table 5.11 Percentage of PhD recipients migrating from higher education to other nonacademic employment over a decade, by career stage and gender, 1993 and 2003 (Survey of Doctorate Recipients cohorts)

	1993 cohort				2003 cohort			
	1993 N	1993–97 %	1997–2003 %	1993–03 %	2003 N	2003–06 %	2006–13 %	2003–13 %
Early career	33,644	15.1	12.3	27.5	50,575	11.8	14.2	26.0
Gender								
Male	21,874	14.7	11.3	26.0	30,423	10.2	12.9	23.1
Female	11,770	16.0	14.2	30.2	20,152	14.2	16.3	30.5
Race/ethnicity								
White	26,953	14.7	11.8	26.5	37,775	11.0	14.2	25.2
Asian or Pacific Islander	4,274	20.8	18.7	39.6	7,937	17.7	16.7	34.5
URM	2,417	10.2	7.4	17.6	4,356	7.8	11.0	18.8
Mid-career	32,941	8.9	9.1	18.1	48,404	6.9	9.6	16.5
Gender								
Male	24,078	8.5	7.1	15.6	30,177	5.9	7.8	13.7
Female	8,863	10.1	14.9	25.0	18,227	8.4	12.7	21.1
Race/ethnicity								
White	28,957	8.6	9.3	18.0	37,571	6.9	10.4	17.3
Asian or Pacific Islander	2,453	10.8	8.2	19.0	6,499	7.3	5.1	12.5
URM	1,530	9.7	9.0	18.7	3,601	6.3	10.3	16.6

Senior career	65,222	10.9	25.0	35.8	102,182	11.0	24.7	35.7
Gender								
Male	56,960	10.8	25.7	36.5	80,745	11.2	24.8	36.0
Female	8,262	11.4	19.9	31.4	21,437	10.6	24.2	34.8
Race/ethnicity								
White	58,693	10.9	25.8	36.7	90,587	11.1	25.4	36.5
Asian or Pacific Islander	3,865	13.2	20.1	33.3	6,456	8.7	20.0	28.7
URM	2,665	7.6	13.4	21.0	4,193	11.3	17.2	28.5
All career stages	131,807	11.5	17.8	29.3	201,161	10.2	18.3	28.6
Gender								
Male	102,912	11.1	18.3	29.4	141,345	9.8	18.5	28.3
Female	28,895	12.9	16.1	29.0	59,816	11.1	18.0	29.2
Race/ethnicity								
White	114,603	11.2	18.4	29.6	165,933	10.1	19.3	29.5
Asian or Pacific Islander	10,592	15.7	16.7	32.4	20,892	11.7	14.0	25.7
URM	6,612	9.0	10.2	19.3	12,150	8.6	12.9	21.4

Sources: SDR:93; SDR:97; SDR:03; SDR:06; SDR:13. (Refer to appendix A for key.)

For 1993, underrepresented racial minority (URM) includes Hispanic, Black, and Native American. For 2003, URM includes Native American/American Indian, Black, and Hispanic. Beginning in 2003, NSF offered a derived "multiple race" race/ethnicity category that is not included in this analysis.

Table 5.12 Percentage of PhD recipients migrating from higher education to other nonacademic employment, by career stage and appointment type, 1993 and 2003 (Survey of Doctorate Recipients cohorts)

	1993 cohort				2003 cohort			
	1993 N	1993–97 %	1997–2003 %	1993–2003 %	2003 N	2003–06 %	2006–13 %	2003–13 %
Early career	33,645	15.2	12.3	27.5	50,575	11.8	23.0	34.8
Tenured or tenure track	20,379	6.4	8.7	15.1	27,094	3.1	7.9	11.0
Gender								
Male	13,896	6.2	7.6	13.8	17,354	2.9	6.4	9.3
Female	6,483	6.8	10.9	17.7	9,740	3.5	10.6	14.1
Race/ethnicity								
White	16,407	5.9	8.7	14.6	20,602	3.1	8.4	11.5
Asian or Pacific Islander	2,296	9.2	10.8	20.0	3,703	4.0	4.6	8.6
URM	1,675	7.3	5.2	12.4	2,508	2.0	8.4	10.4
Non-tenure-track or tenure n.a.	13,266	28.6	19.7	48.3	23,481	21.7	39.9	61.7
Gender								
Male	7,979	29.4	20.0	49.4	13,070	19.8	38.6	58.4
Female	5,287	27.4	19.2	46.6	10,411	24.1	41.7	65.8
Race/ethnicity								
White	10,546	28.3	18.2	46.6	17,173	20.6	22.6	43.2
Asian or Pacific Islander	1,978	34.4	31.4	65.7	4,234	29.7	31.3	61.0
URM	741	16.7	13.0	29.7	1,847	15.6	15.1	30.8
Mid-career	32,941	8.9	9.1	18.1	48,406	6.9	9.6	16.5
Tenured or tenure track	24,203	4.0	6.1	10.0	33,501	2.4	5.6	8.0
Gender								
Male	18,310	3.6	5.0	8.6	22,084	1.7	3.7	5.4
Female	5,893	5.2	9.5	14.7	11,417	3.9	9.2	13.2
Race/ethnicity								
White	21,435	4.1	6.1	10.2	26,020	2.4	5.9	8.2

Asian or Pacific Islander	1,637	3.0	5.2	8.2	4,503	4.2	2.3	6.6
URM	1,131	3.3	6.6	9.9	2,467	0.5	8.0	8.5
Non-tenure-track or tenure n.a.	8,738	22.6	19.8	42.4	14,905	16.8	20.4	37.2
Gender								
Male	5,768	24.1	15.5	39.6	8,095	17.5	21.3	38.8
Female	2,970	19.9	27.5	47.4	6,810	16.0	19.3	35.3
Race/ethnicity								
White	7,522	22.0	20.2	42.1	11,551	17.1	22.3	39.4
Asian or Pacific Islander	816	26.3	16.3	42.7	1,996	14.4	12.1	26.5
URM	399	27.8	18.4	46.2	1,133	19.0	16.4	35.4
Senior career	65,222	10.9	25.0	35.8	102,181	11.0	24.7	35.7
Tenured or tenure track	54,991	7.8	24.6	32.5	78,818	6.0	23.2	29.2
Gender								
Male	48,909	7.9	25.4	33.4	63,906	6.2	23.4	29.6
Female	6,082	7.1	18.3	25.4	14,912	5.1	22.5	27.6
Race/ethnicity								
White	49,574	8.1	25.7	33.8	69,723	6.2	24.2	30.4
Asian or Pacific Islander	3,201	6.2	18.0	24.2	5,152	2.9	17.5	20.4
URM	2,217	4.3	11.0	15.3	3,269	3.8	14.2	18.0
Non-tenure-track or tenure n.a.	10,231	27.2	27.2	54.4	23,363	28.1	31.0	59.1
Gender								
Male	8,051	28.2	27.7	55.9	16,838	30.1	31.9	61.9
Female	2,180	23.6	25.3	48.9	6,525	23.2	28.9	52.1
Race/ethnicity								
White	9,120	26.0	26.6	52.5	20,863	27.2	30.6	57.9
Asian or Pacific Islander	664	47.0	38.1	85.1	1,304	31.5	34.4	65.9
URM	448	24.1	27.9	52.0	924	37.6	33.6	71.2

(continued)

Table 5.12 (continued)

	1993 cohort				2003 cohort			
	1993 N	1993–97 %	1997–2003 %	1993–2003 %	2003 N	2003–06 %	2006–13 %	2003–13 %
All career stages	131,808	11.5	17.8	29.3	201,162	10.2	20.6	30.8
Tenured or tenure track	99,573	6.6	16.7	23.3	139,413	4.6	15.9	20.4
Gender								
Male	81,115	6.7	17.6	24.3	103,344	4.7	16.2	20.8
Female	18,458	6.4	12.9	19.3	36,069	4.3	15.1	19.4
Race/ethnicity								
White	87,416	6.7	17.6	24.3	116,345	4.8	17.1	21.9
Asian or Pacific Islander	7,134	6.4	12.7	19.1	13,358	3.7	8.9	12.5
URM	5,023	5.1	8.1	13.2	8,244	2.3	10.6	12.8
Non-tenure-track or tenure n.a.	32,235	26.6	22.0	48.6	61,749	23.0	32.5	55.4
Gender								
Male	21,798	27.6	21.6	49.1	38,003	23.9	32.4	56.2
Female	10,437	24.5	23.0	47.5	23,746	21.5	32.6	54.2
Race/ethnicity								
White	27,188	25.8	21.6	47.4	49,587	22.6	25.7	48.3
Asian or Pacific Islander	3,458	34.9	28.4	63.3	7,534	25.9	25.9	51.8
URM	1,588	21.6	18.3	39.9	3,904	21.8	19.0	40.8

Sources: SDR:93; SDR:97; SDR:03; SDR:06; SDR:13. (Refer to appendix A for key.)

Notes: For 1993, underrepresented racial minority (URM) includes Hispanic, Black, and Native American. For 2003, URM includes Native American/American Indian, Black, and Hispanic. Beginning in 2003, NSF offered a derived "multiple race" race/ethnicity category that is not included in this analysis.

recipients in tenured or tenure-track positions—with the sole exception of senior faculty at the later stages of their career. Among early career faculty, for example, the differences are stark: in the 1993 cohort, about 13.8% of the tenure-track or tenured male faculty and 17.7% of the female tenure-track or tenured faculty left higher education over the first post-PhD decade compared with nearly *half* (49.4% male, 46.6% female) of the non-tenure-track faculty; in the 2003 cohort, the corresponding differential was 9.4% of the male tenured or tenure track (14.9% of the female) versus 41.1% of the male (46.6% of the female) non-tenure-track. Moreover, in controlling for gender, it becomes apparent that appointment type trumps gender as a driver of out-migration: gender differences in attrition are fairly small among non-tenure-track faculty, with the possible exception of the mid-career stage subgroup in the 1993 cohort. It appears, then, that the new appointments may be providing a second order "selection process" for career progression within a more elastic and accessible career space.

Where do those faculty who leave higher education go? Table 5.13 shows the destination of those leaving academic employment by gender and career stage for the 1993 and 2003 cohorts of SDR respondents. Far and away the largest proportion of leavers among the early- and mid-career-stage groups depart academe for business and industry, with much lower proportions going into the government, the nonprofit sector, and K–12 education. Among the senior faculty, retirement accounts for the largest share (about one-quarter), although the outflow to business and government persists as a steady trickle of about one-sixth of seniors in the 1993 cohort and nearly a quarter (23.8%) in the 2003 cohort compared with two-thirds of the early-career-stage and half of the mid-career-stage out-migrants.[11] Across all career stages, women are less likely to out-migrate to the business and industry sector and more likely to exit employment altogether—presumably to assume a greater share of family and childcare responsibilities. It is notable that while early- and mid-career women PhDs were three times more likely to move to unemployment in the 1993 cohort of SDR respondents, the size of that gender differential shrinks substantially among the 2003 cohort. While the interpretation of this shrinkage is not unambiguous, it would appear likely that academic women are becoming less likely to forsake academic employment for a period of full-time family responsibilities. Unemployment, however, remains a destination for fewer than one in twenty faculty. Among the senior-career-stage subgroup, "not working" predominantly reflects retirement; and when it comes to moving into retirement, men are better represented than women (see chapter 6).

Table 5.13 Destination of PhD recipients out-migrating from higher education, by career stage and gender, 1993 and 2003 (Survey of Doctorate Recipients cohorts)

	1993 cohort						2003 cohort					
	N	Business or industry	Government	K–12	Not working	Retired	*N*	Business or industry	Government	K–12	Not working	Retired
Early career	7,671	61.7	19.2	5.1	9.8	4.2	10,912	66.4	13.1	2.9	8.7	8.9
Gender												
Male	4,826	69.6	19.5	3.7	5.7	1.4	5,742	73.6	12.1	2.1	7.9	4.3
Female	2,845	48.3	18.6	7.4	16.6	9.1	5,170	58.5	14.2	3.7	9.5	14.1
Children <18	5,501	66.1	16.4	6.1	8.3	3.1	7,466	70.0	13.6	3.8	9.5	3.1
Children <12	4,815	67.1	16.7	6.0	8.6	1.6	6,723	70.8	14.6	3.1	10.6	0.9
Race/ethnicity												
White	5,968	61.1	19.7	5.5	9.4	4.3	8,086	66.9	12.8	3.3	6.6	10.5
Asian or Pacific Islander	1,398	69.7	15.0	0.0	11.2	4.1	2,066	67.0	15.1	0.0	15.1	2.8
URM	304	38.5	28.6	20.1	9.5	3.3	688	62.5	10.3	6.8	10.3	10.0
Mid-career	4,987	50.2	19.8	1.1	9.7	19.2	6,964	51.6	15.0	4.2	12.5	16.7
Gender												
Male	3,081	57.7	25.3	1.6	4.4	11.1	3,568	62.2	17.5	2.8	11.1	6.4
Female	1,906	38.1	10.9	0.3	18.4	32.3	3,396	40.5	12.4	5.7	13.9	27.6
Children <18	3,222	60.1	21.4	1.7	8.3	8.5	4,343	63.1	17.6	4.9	9.4	5.1
Children <12	2,790	64.2	20.4	1.1	8.5	5.8	3,162	64.4	16.8	5.7	11.1	2.0
Race/ethnicity												
White	4,390	51.2	19.2	1.1	10.1	18.4	5,652	49.8	16.2	5.2	11.8	17.0
Asian or Pacific Islander	340	57.1	24.1	1.8	9.1	7.9	657	59.7	13.5	0.0	20.7	6.1
URM	257	24.5	24.1	0.0	4.3	47.1	565	60.0	1.9	0.0	9.2	28.8

Senior career	20,686	17.0	5.8	0.5	2.3	74.5	32,326	23.8	4.0	0.2	1.2	70.9
Gender												
Male	18,388	16.2	5.9	0.4	2.0	75.5	25,857	23.6	3.8	0.0	1.1	71.4
Female	2,298	23.1	4.6	1.0	4.6	66.6	6,469	24.3	4.9	0.7	1.6	68.6
Children <18	8,576	21.3	9.2	0.6	3.0	66.0	10,039	33.8	7.8	0.1	2.8	55.5
Children <12	1,569	33.3	15.2	3.2	5.1	43.2	2,109	53.6	18.9	0.0	4.6	22.9
Race/ethnicity												
White	19,129	16.7	5.7	0.5	1.9	75.1	29,216	23.1	4.0	0.1	0.7	72.1
Asian or Pacific Islander	1,036	16.9	5.7	0.0	8.3	69.1	1,732	36.8	0.6	0.0	6.6	56.0
URM	520	26.0	9.6	0.0	2.3	62.1	998	25.1	5.1	2.6	4.4	62.8
All career stages	33,344	32.2	10.9	1.6	5.1	50.1	50,202	36.9	7.5	1.3	4.4	49.9
Gender												
Male	26,295	30.9	10.7	1.2	2.9	54.3	35,167	35.7	6.6	0.7	3.2	53.9
Female	7,049	37.4	11.9	3.4	13.2	34.1	15,035	39.7	9.8	2.9	7.1	40.6
Children <18	17,299	42.7	13.7	2.6	5.7	35.3	21,848	52.0	11.7	2.3	6.4	27.5
Children <12	9,174	60.5	17.5	4.0	7.9	10.0	11,994	66.1	15.9	3.2	9.6	5.1
Race/ethnicity												
White	29,487	30.8	10.5	1.6	4.7	52.4	42,954	34.8	7.3	1.4	3.2	53.3
Asian or Pacific Islander	2,774	48.4	12.7	0.2	9.8	28.9	4,455	54.2	9.2	0.0	12.6	24.0
URM	1,081	29.1	18.4	5.6	4.8	42.0	2,251	45.3	5.9	3.2	7.4	38.2

Sources: SDR:93; SDR:03; SDR:13. (Refer to appendix A for key.)

Note: Children in the household during 93–97–03 and 03–06–13; not the number of children. For 1993, underrepresented racial minority (URM) includes Hispanic, Black, and Native American. For 2003, URM includes Native American/American Indian, Black, and Hispanic. Beginning in 2003, NSF offered a derived "multiple race" race/ethnicity category that is not included in this analysis.

It should be noted that the pattern of fluctuating, albeit persistent, attrition we have sketched ranging from 20–25% early on to 16–18% at mid-career and ballooning to 35% in the later phases of the senior career stage is one based only on PhD recipients. As noted in chapter 4, non-PhD-holding faculty were more likely to embark on their first academic job with work experience outside postsecondary education and were more likely to be employed part-time and to hold concurrent employment outside postsecondary education. That greater permeability of sector boundaries for non-PhDs might suggest on the face of it that out-migration may be even higher among this subgroup of non-PhD faculty. That said, we recognize that a substantial portion of these non-doctored faculty have entered higher education employment not directly from their graduate education but rather after a period of extended employment outside academe. Indeed, a substantial subgroup may have retired from, or otherwise permanently left, an earlier career trajectory, in effect embarking in higher education as their second career. Out-migration, then, may be considerably lower in this second career—except for retirement.

Conclusion

In chapter 4, we sketched a portrait of entry into academic careers that represents a significant departure from earlier post–World War II prototypes. In the first place, entry patterns differed sharply by education credentials: doctorate holders were more likely to gravitate to full-time appointments, to the four-year sector, and to the tenure track; non-doctorate holders were more likely to gravitate to part-time or non-tenure-eligible, full-time appointments and to the two-year sector. Indeed, education credentials drove the nontraditional appointments. While among doctorate holders, there was no discernible retreat from pursuing immediate postdegree employment in the higher education sector, the road to a full-time, tenure-eligible faculty position proved circuitous: modal first jobs immediately postdegree were not to tenure-track appointments or even appointments with faculty status. There was considerable mobility (one-fifth) among jobs, employment, and tenure status during the entry period of up to three years. The emerging portrait was one of a newfound unpredictability but at the same time, one of diversification of opportunities and democratization of access to individuals with diverse education credentials and work and life experience.

What did we learn in chapter 5 about how an academic career path plays out in the post-entry period? Do all points of entry lead to opportunities that, however different in specific conditions, allow for career progression, growth, and satisfaction? In the first place, we learned that, at least for doctorate holders, initial appointment type matters. Those in off-track appointments were four to six times as likely to leave higher education during the first career decade as those on the tenure track; yet even among those on the tenure track, about one-fourth left higher education during the first post-PhD decade—about twice the rate of those doctorate holders in-migrating to higher education from business or industry, government, and the nonprofit sector. Women left higher education at a higher rate than men, irrespective of tenure status, but tenure status clearly trumped gender as a "push" factor. While out-migration slowed at mid-career, it by no means disappeared. Indeed, we see a steady, albeit diminished, stream of out-migration to business and industry throughout mid-career, culminating in the final episode of out-migration—retirement—among senior faculty (the subject of the next chapter). We know much less about the staying power of non-doctorate holders. What we do know is that they are much more likely than their doctorate-holding counterparts to move into academic careers directly from stints in business and industry and to arrive in academe as second careers (indeed a sizable contingent, as many as one-seventh, arrive following retirement from a previous job: see chapter 4); so they are more likely to be in-migrants than doctorate holders. Women and practitioners of the professions (business, education, and health) are overrepresented among such non-doctorate holders.

What these patterns of out-migration mean for the health of the enterprise is unclear. Some substantial degree of early out-migration seems, on the face of it, a healthy sign: individuals who find that they are less suited to academic work than they had expected probably should be leaving, rather than persisting in a career that is discovered early on to be unsuitable. That some modicum of attrition continues through mid-career also suggests a degree of healthy turnover and contradicts those who insist that tenured faculty are like barnacles on the bough of the academic ship of state. This assumes, of course, that it is those who are disaffected or ill-suited to academic life who are amply represented among those who leave midcourse (rather than those academic stars who are being raided by business, industry, or government). It is obviously a less sanguine development if those overrepresent the best and the brightest; but we have no way of assessing that from the available data. What may be more troubling is the early flight of those who do not land a tenure-eligible position early on. One can argue, of course, that this represents the academic version of social Darwinism: those least adapted for the rigors fall by the wayside. The problem with this interpretation is that those who fall by the wayside are disproportionately women and to a lesser extent racial and ethnic minorities. Moreover, insofar as non-tenure-track appointments are clustered mostly in certain fields, it is prospective faculty in those fields who are being sacrificed—not necessarily as a result of their competence or fit but simply the happenstance of the socioeconomic value of their field of interest (i.e., the prevailing marketplace at a particular moment in history).

Second, we learned that mobility among employment and tenure statuses remains modest: no more than one-seventh move from part-time to full-time or vice versa; less than one in ten changes tenure status. Thus to a considerable extent, status at the point of career entry—in terms of employment and tenure status—remains destiny: that is, where you begin largely shapes where you wind up. The majority of then-current part-time faculty in 2003 began their careers in part-time appointments. Similarly, the majority of then-current full-time, off-track faculty began in full-time off-track roles; and the majority of full-time tenure-track or tenured faculty who reported a job change came from previous full-time, tenure-track jobs. The 2003 NSOPF data suggest, however, that we may be seeing more permeability among employment and tenure statuses; in particular, a much larger proportion of then-current full-time, tenured or tenure-track faculty in 2003 reported moving from part-time positions than had been the case in 1998 (Finkelstein, Schuster, and Iglesias 2013). Moreover, other sources, including the Mellon Graduate Education Initiative (Ehrenberg et al. 2010), suggest that the movement from part-time to full-time tenure track may be especially common in the humanities fields—and, not incidentally, among the products of the elite graduate schools. While changes in employment status occur across all career stages (indeed, they are most common among early-career and senior faculty, albeit in different directions and for different reasons), changes in tenure status tend to occur early on and are relatively rare afterward. Women are more likely than men to report changes in employment status, and men are more likely to report changes in tenure status. Changes in employment status are most common in the two-year sector, and changes in tenure status in the four-year sector.

For those who gain access to the tenure track—and this is a proportionately smaller core than ever before—career progression remains fairly regularized: a six- to seven-year journey to associate professor with tenure (once on the tenure track) and a second-stage journey of about equal duration to full professor. It appears, based on cross-sectional data, to be sure, that the journey may actually be shorter for newer entrants as compared with their senior colleagues. The first leg of the journey is shaped, to some extent, by institutional type, gender, education credentials, and job history: those in the four-year sector, those without doctoral degrees, women, and those who change jobs at least once take a bit longer. The second leg is shaped even more so by these contextual factors: the journey is much longer for those who change jobs, especially in the case of women; and it is much longer for non-PhDs. In some cases, albeit not reflected in the data we have marshaled here, branching out into administration after having received tenure may further complicate and prolong the process. And, of course, some percentage of tenured associate professors never receive the promotion to full professor. The available evidence suggests that while tenure certainly acts as a "pull" factor in keeping faculty in the higher education sector, there is a steady stream of out-migration (much more significant than the stream of in-migration) at least among PhD holders in the natural and social sciences.

All in all, there has indeed been a sea change in the differentiation of the academic job market along the lines of appointment type. And, as we have demonstrated, the road to career-ladder appointments is open to proportionately fewer, who navigate increasingly circuitous and unpredictable routes. But and here is the main point: the structure of the traditional career ladder, if and when reached, seems largely unaltered. If one can make it there—and depending on one's academic field and the ranking of one's graduate school, that is most likely no better than a fifty-fifty proposition—the road ahead holds promise. Promise, yes, but of a different kind. As the next chapter shows, that road, too, is no longer entirely linear, moving inexorably toward a clear and decisive end game, retirement. Indeed, the later stages of an academic career are coming to increasingly resemble an individualized, improvised, and largely unpredictable—journey, thereby further complicating the faculty factor.

NOTES

1. In expanding our analysis to three points in time, we have reconstructed our three SDR cohorts of new entrants (1993, 2003, 2010) presented in chapter 4 into two cohorts of SDR respondents (1993 and 2003) divided along the lines of more-advanced career-stage subgroups (early career, mid-career, and senior, in contrast to new entrants), with each cohort including data at three points in time spanning a ten-year period. For the 1993 cohort of respondents, that includes baseline data at 1993, followed by data in 1997

and 2003; for the 2003 cohort of SDR respondents, that includes baseline data at 2003, followed by data in 2006 and 2013. At each data point, respondents are categorized by career stage defined by year of PhD receipt. For the 1993 cohort, early career respondents are defined as those who received their PhD between 1985 and 1990; mid-career those who received their PhD between 1978 and 1984; and senior those who received their PhD in 1977 or earlier. For the 2003 cohort, early career respondents are those who received their PhD between 1995 and 2000; mid-career, those who received their PhD between 1988 and 1994; and senior those who received their PhD in 1987 or before. The same respondents may appear at one career stage in the 1993 cohort and in a later stage in the 2003 cohort.

2. Nearly one-quarter (23.8%) of part-time faculty reported that they had retired from other, first careers, although in certain fields, such as business, that proportion is much higher. Nearly half of the part-time faculty among new entrants in business had retired from another position (see appendix table A-4.1).

3. We recognize, of course, the likely effect of attrition here, as those off the tenure track tend to depart earlier and at a much higher rate that their on-track colleagues (see table 5.12).

4. Our earlier analysis especially in chapter 4 suggests that the homogeneity of this cultural expectation is indeed in flux.

5. Together with the nearly one-fifth of the full-time faculty at the full professor rank, these faculty at the associate and full professor rank constitute nearly the entire complement of "tenured" full-time faculty. As we learned from NSOPF:04, about one tenth of part-time faculty report that they have granted tenure in their part-time positions, which tend to "fractional" (of full-time) rather than course-based positions.

6. That de-coupling is largely the result of hiring at the senior ranks initially without tenure in a species of "advanced" probationary period.

7. On average, the journey is about one year longer to associate professor.

8. Among PhD holders, three years for men, five for women; among those holding master's degrees or less, five years on average, irrespective of gender.

9. While the second half of the postbaseline decade for the 2003 cohort was one year longer than for the 1993 cohort—seven versus six years—that seems unlikely to account for the stark difference in the two patterns.

10. Historically, about 65–70% of senior faculty holding the PhD have ultimately achieved the full professor rank. (See table 5.11.)

11. It should be noted that while the proportion of seniors out-migrating to business declines markedly from earlier career stages, the actual number of out-migrants among the senior-career-stage group is higher than the number of out-migrants to business among the early- and mid-career-stage faculty combined—a function of the sheer greater size of the senior group.

REFERENCES

Dooris, Michael, and Louis Sandmeyer. 2006. "Planning for Improvement in the Academic Department." *Effective Practices for Academic Leaders* 1 (October): 1–16.

Ehrenberg, Ronald, Harriet Zuckerman, Jeffrey A. Groen, and Sharon M. Brucker. 2010. *The Education of Scholars*. Princeton, NJ: Princeton University Press.

Finkelstein, Martin J., and Jack H. Schuster. 2011. "A New Higher Education: The 'Next Model' Takes Shape." *TIAA-CREF Institute: Advancing Higher Education*, April, 1–9.

Finkelstein, Martin J., Jack H. Schuster, and Kevin Iglesias. 2013. "Faculty Careers in Rapid Transition: The Salience of the Redistribution of Faculty Appointments." *TIAA-CREF Research Dialogues* 108 (June): 1–21.

Gappa, Judith, Ann Austin, and Andrea Trice. 2007. *Rethinking Faculty Work: Higher Education's Strategic Imperative*. San Francisco, CA: Jossey-Bass.

National Science Foundation (NSF). 1993. *Survey of Earned Doctorates*. Washington, DC: National Science Foundation.

———. 1993. *Survey of Earned Doctorates*. Washington, DC: NSF.

———. 1997. *Survey of Earned Doctorates*. Washington, DC: NSF.

———. 2003. *Survey of Earned Doctorates*. Washington, DC: NSF.

———. 2006. *Survey of Earned Doctorates*. Washington, DC: NSF.

———. 2013. *Survey of Earned Doctorates*. Washington, DC: NSF.

Nerad, Maresi. 2008. *Social Science PhDs 5+ Years Out: A National Survey of PhDs in Six Fields*. Seattle, WA: Center for Innovation and Research in Graduate Education, University of Washington.

Schuster, Jack H., and Martin J. Finkelstein. 2006. *The American Faculty*. Baltimore, MD: Johns Hopkins University Press.

Trower, Cathy A. 2012. *Success on the Tenure Track: Five Keys to Faculty Job Satisfaction*. Baltimore, MD: Johns Hopkins University Press.

US Department of Education. 2008. *The National Study of Postsecondary Faculty 2004*. Washington, DC: National Center for Education Statistics.

Ward, Kelly, and Lisa Wolf-Wendell. 2012. *Academic Motherhood: How Faculty Manage Work and Family*. New Brunswick, NJ: Rutgers University Press.

6

Academic Career Exit

Faculty Retirement Viewed Anew

We have premised this volume on the proposition that the faculty has been restructured and repurposed in recent years, exacerbated by the economic downturn in 2008–09. We have provided evidence in the preceding chapters about ways in which the academic profession has been transforming, and continues to do so. In the preceding chapter, chapter 5, we provided data on outmigration from academic careers by career stage. Not surprisingly, a significant portion of senior faculty leaving academic careers did so through retirement. This chapter focuses specifically on this less often studied aspect of the academic career—career exit—and the ways in which retirement, in particular, is contributing to the transformation of the faculty factor. [1]

The retirement landscape for faculty has changed significantly in the past two decades, in part because of the aging of the population (demographics) but also because of the shifting political and economic environment. A key political driver is the Age Discrimination in Employment Act of 1967 (ADEA) and its subsequent amendments. In the first part of the chapter, we provide a brief account of the events leading up to the decision to eliminate mandatory retirement for tenured faculty. Next, detailed data on the age of faculty by gender and selected other characteristics (including tenure status) provide a backdrop for understanding the emerging distribution of faculty by appointment type and the emerging complexity of retirement decision making across the generations in this new environment. We examine the changing pathways to retirement after the ADEA legislation took effect and uncapping[2] occurred. We provide descriptions of what we know about the timing of retirement decisions among senior faculty; the prevalence of postponed, early, and phased retirement; retirement incentives; and the nature of postretirement employment.

Additionally the chapter examines complexity of retirement plan design, and the shift from defined benefit to defined contribution plans in the public sector. These financial factors impact confidence and financial readiness for retirement in the new, third paradigm, era. Finally, a comment on retirement patterns and prospects for faculty on different appointment types is provided.

A Strikingly New Environment

The stage was set for faculty retirement to change fundamentally when the federal Age Discrimination in Employment Act was passed in 1967. The legislation prohibits arbitrary age discrimination in employment. The original legislation allowed a few exceptions, including "tenured teaching personnel" (faculty). Three major amendments followed in 1978, 1986, and 1990. Initially, the legislation established sixty-five as the mandatory retirement age. The age was increased to seventy in 1978, the year of the first major amendment. Mandatory retirement was eliminated altogether in 1986, the year of the second major amendment, with an exemption provided for tenured teaching personnel until January 1, 1994.

Before passage of the ADEA, retiring from an academic career was a fairly straightforward process. Most institutions had mandatory retirement ages (Rees and Smith 1991). This meant that there was a high degree of certainty for both individuals and institutions regarding the timing of retirement, and staffing plans were relatively simple to manage. Of course there were always exceptions to the rule, but for the most part retirement was an institutional decision and was considered an event that could be acknowledged and celebrated to culminate an academic career.

Today, retiring from an academic career is a complicated process, a web of individual, institutional, and government decisions. The process involves a labyrinth of regulations (state and federal) and institutional policies that many retirees and potential retirees are left to navigate on their own.[3]

The ADEA exemption for tenured teaching personnel was enacted, in part, because the higher education community was divided on the question of whether or not eliminating mandatory retirement for tenured faculty would make any difference. Several research studies were published around the time policy makers were debating the issue (e.g., Gray 1989; Lozier and Dooris 1989; Rees and Smith 1991; Epstein and MacLane 1991). A seminal study conducted by Albert Rees and Sharon Smith (1991) looked at disciplines within arts and sciences in thirty-three colleges and universities. They found little evidence to continue the exemption. Others argued for keeping mandatory retirement because they believed that there was too much uncertainty about the potential outcomes and not enough definitive evidence to support eliminating it. For example, Richard Epstein and Saunders MacLane (1991, 95) asserted "if Congress adheres to its present course, it will commit us to a statutory regime that not only favors the past over the future, and the old over the young, but also reduces the effectiveness and vitality of universities."

The American Association of University Professors (AAUP) supported the elimination of mandatory retirement, citing research suggesting that while there were small differences, most faculty members would choose to retire at about the same time anyway, regardless of the elimination of mandatory retirement.

Representatives from higher education organizations, selective private institutions, and prestigious research institutions expressed opposition to eliminating mandatory retirement ages, or "uncapping," citing research suggesting that in the absence of mandatory retirement ages many faculty members (particularly those with light teaching loads or those who exercised the right to teach specialized courses because of seniority in the department) would postpone retirement indefinitely, leading to constraints on the institutions' ability to hire new talented tenure-track faculty members, especially women and faculty of color (Hammond and Morgan 1991). For example, Rees and Smith (1991, 21–22) found that "the mean age at retirement was 1.45 years higher for research university faculty than for the faculty at other universities and liberal arts colleges." They also pointed out that the more meaningful projection was not average retirement age but rather the percentage of tenured faculty members who would postpone retirement in the absence of a mandatory retirement age.

Second, many argued that an aging professoriate would grow increasingly ineffective but irremovable because of tenure. Some projections indicated that there would be an oversupply of tenured older professors because of the number of faculty members hired during the expansion of higher education in the 1950s and the 1960s. Others argued that if mandatory retirement was abolished or the upper age limit was raised, tenure would be threatened. "Some faculty and administrators expressed concern that colleges and universities would abolish the tenure system rather than allow it to shelter poorly performing faculty working past age 70" (Hammond and Morgan 1991, p. xiii–xiv).

To inform its decision about whether or not to continue the exemption, Congress directed the Equal Opportunity Commission to request that the

National Academy of Sciences undertake a study aimed at understanding "the potential consequences of the elimination of mandatory retirement in institutions of higher education" (ADEA, 1986, sec. 12[c]). A committee comprising thirteen members and staff, supported by consultants, guided this comprehensive study, including the editors—Brett Hammond and Harriet Morgan (1991)—of the committee's final report, *Ending Mandatory Retirement for Tenured Faculty*, published in 1991. The study's two key conclusions have been widely cited.

> —*At most colleges and universities, few tenured faculty would continue working past the age of seventy if mandatory retirement were eliminated.* Most faculty retire before the age of seventy. The few uncapped colleges and universities with data report that the proportion of faculty over age seventy is no more than 1.6%.
>
> —*At some research universities, a high proportion of faculty would choose to work past the age of seventy if mandatory retirement were eliminated.* At a small number of research universities, more than 40% of the faculty who retire each year have done so at the current mandatory retirement age of seventy. Evidence suggests that faculty who are research oriented, enjoy inspiring students, have light teaching loads, and are covered by pension plans that reward later retirement would be more likely to work past age seventy (2).

So what has happened since? Twenty years after the exemption expired, the resounding answer to the question of whether eliminating mandatory retirement for tenured faculty would make any difference is yes, it most certainly has made a difference, although perhaps not precisely as predicted. More choice has been one outcome of eliminating mandatory retirement. There are now many more options available to individuals, including phased retirement and opportunities for postretirement employment, either at the same institution or at a different one. On the other hand, some higher education leaders lament not being able to control the timing of the retirement decision. An *Inside Higher Ed* article published after the Great Recession reports that "ever since higher education lost its exemption from laws against mandatory retirement ages, and especially since the economic downturn, college leaders have worried that not enough faculty members are retiring" (Basu 2012). One of the most frequent questions is, how has ending mandatory retirement affected the timing of the retirement decision for tenured faculty members in particular? In this chapter, we review available evidence related to age and retirement to provide a context for understanding the timing of retirement decision making in the current environment and to provide support for our assertion that the elimination of mandatory retirement for tenured faculty members has contributed to the transformation of the faculty factor.

An Aging Tenured Professoriate

As noted earlier in this volume, the "graying" of the professoriate has been visible across all institutional types and academic disciplines since the late 1980s. The percentage of full-time faculty in four-year institutions who were over age seventy has increased steadily since fall 1987, from a negligible 0.3% to 2.7% in 2013, and the percentage of full-time faculty between sixty-five and seventy teaching in four-year institutions increased from 3.7% in 1987 to 6.3% in 2013 (see figure 3.8). In addition, we suggested that faculty members are working longer, which is contributing to a clogging of the academic pipeline, at least in part, as a result of the elimination of mandatory retirement. We also suggested that there are important nuanced differences in the age distribution of faculty when gender and race/ethnicity are taken into account and that various staffing models are being employed at different types of institutions, resulting in a proliferation of faculty on non-tenure-track appointments.

Chapters 3 to 5 provide detailed evidence that representation of women and members of underrepresented racial/ethnic groups is higher among younger faculty than older faculty. However, many of these individuals hold contingent appointments rather than tenure-track appointments.

In this chapter we extend this narrative as we seek to provide a description of the characteristics of older faculty and their retirement patterns using a generational lens. Not only do different generations approach retirement differently, but different generations were affected by the economic downturn differently also. A report published from the Economic Mobility Project sponsored by Pew Charitable Trusts described how the economic downturn affected baby boomers in the general population relative to younger and older cohorts of Americans, by comparing wealth at similar ages for the different cohorts and by tracking the wealth of each cohort over time (Pew 2013).[4] The findings showed Americans in the younger cohorts were impacted the most by the economic downturn and that the older generations of Americans may be the last to have more accumulated wealth than the preceding generation (Pew 2013). These data have implications for how Americans approach retirement and their receptivity to retirement.

What about faculty? Although we do not have comparable data on wealth for faculty members, in chapter 9 we show that faculty salaries are not keep-

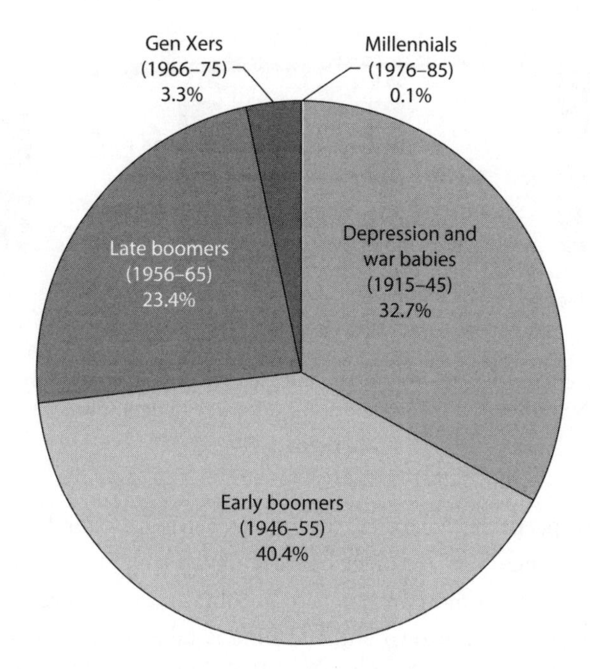

Figure 6.1 Percentage distribution of tenured faculty, by birth cohort, Fall 2003.
Source: NSOPF:04.

ing pace with inflation or with other professions. Taken together, the elimination of mandatory retirement, an aging tenured professoriate, and an uncertain economic environment have created a strikingly new environment for academic career exit.

Figure 6.1 shows the distribution of tenured faculty by birth cohort. In fall 2003, the overwhelming majority of tenured faculty members were at least approaching forty years of age, the threshold for protection under the ADEA. Fewer than 5% were born after 1965.

In fall 2003, about one-third (32.7%) of all faculty members in the oldest generational cohort (Depression and war babies), ranging in age from approximately fifty-eight to eighty-eight years old, were tenured men. An additional 40% were early boomers, born between 1946 and 1955 and ranging in age from about forty-eight to fifty-seven years old; and almost one-quarter (23.4%) were late boomers, born between 1956 and 1965 and ranging from thirty-eight to forty-seven years old.

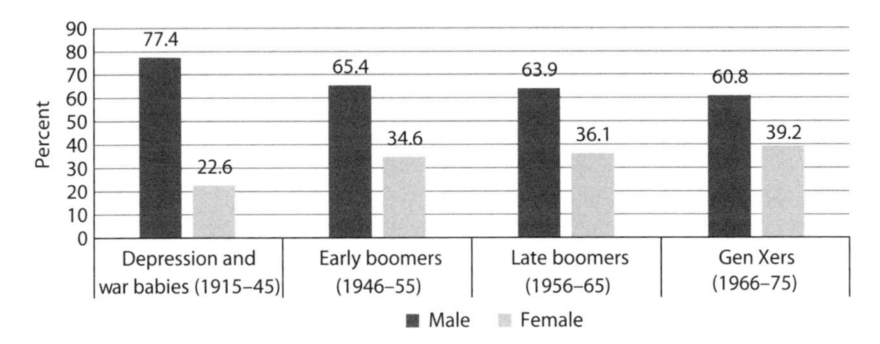

Figure 6.2 Percentage distribution of tenured faculty, by gender and birth cohort, Fall 2003. *Source:* NSOPF:04. (Refer to appendix A for key to data sources.)

In some respects these patterns are not surprising. It stands to reason that tenured faculty members are older because of the time it takes to complete a doctoral degree (a common prerequisite for obtaining a tenure-track position in most four-year institutions) and the time it takes to complete the tenure process. If in the absence of mandatory retirement these older tenured faculty members choose to postpone retirement—even for a short time—the impact on higher education's goals to diversify the faculty could be substantial.

Figure 6.2 provides a visual representation of the percentage of tenured faculty by gender and birth cohort. Although the percentage of women among tenured faculty has increased for each successive birth cohort, the majority of tenured faculty members, still, are men, by a substantial margin.

The differences by type of institution are even more striking. Table 6.1 shows the tenure status and gender of faculty by birth cohort and type of institution in fall 2003. One half of the Depression and war babies in doctoral institutions were tenured men. About one-third (35%) of tenured early boomers and approaching one-quarter (22.7%) of late boomers were tenured men. The comparable percentages for tenured women draw a sharp contrast. Only about 10% of the Depression and war babies (9.4%), early boomers (12.5%), and late boomers (22.7%) in doctoral institutions were tenured women. With the exception of Depression and war babies, the percentages are much closer for those not on the tenure track. About one-quarter of early boomers not on tenure track were men (24.1%) and another quarter women (22.3%), and the pattern was essentially the same for late boomers (see table 6.1). Put another way, three-quarters of tenured faculty born between 1915 and 1945 were men.

Table 6.1 Percentage distribution of tenure status and gender, by type of institution and birth cohort, Fall 2003

	Tenured		Tenure track		Non-tenure-track	
	Male	Female	Male	Female	Male	Female
All institutions	19.3	8.7	7.1	5.2	31.1	28.7
Birth cohorts						
Depression and war babies (1915–45)	32.6	9.5	2.0	1.4	33.0	21.6
Early boomers (1946–55)	22.8	12.1	3.7	3.7	29.2	28.5
Late boomers (1956–65)	15.6	8.8	10.4	6.6	29.2	29.5
Gen Xers (1966–75)	3.4	2.2	15.5	10.8	33.5	34.6
Millennials (1976–85)	1.3[a]	0.01[a]	3.2[b]	2.8	45.1	47.6
Doctoral	28.6	8.5	9.5	5.2	26.1	22.1
Birth cohorts						
Depression and war babies (1915–45)	50.0	9.4	1.3	0.7	26.4	12.2
Early boomers (1946–55)	35.0	12.5	3.3	2.7	24.1	22.3
Late boomers (1956–65)	22.7	8.4	13.9	6.9	25.0	23.1
Gen Xers (1966–75)	4.2	1.4	23.5	12.6	29.1	29.3
Millennials (1976–85)	0.7[a]	0	2.5[a]	2.2[b]	46.7	47.9
Four-year	18.1	9.3	8.2	6.8	29.9	27.6
Birth cohorts						
Depression and war babies (1915–45)	30.8	10.5	3.0	2.3	32.1	21.3
Early boomers (1946–55)	21.8	12.4	5.4	5.3	28.2	26.8
Late boomers (1956–65)	13.2	9.7	11.7	8.6	27.8	29.0
Gen Xers (1966–75)	2.5	1.7	16.5	13.4	31.8	34.0
Millennials (1976–85)	0	0	2.6[b]	4.2[b]	46.7	46.5
Two-year	9.8	8.4	3.1	3.3	38.0	37.4
Birth cohorts						
Depression and war babies (1915–45)	13.9	8.4	1.6	1.0[b]	42.0	33.0
Early boomers (1946–55)	11.3	11.3	2.3	3.2	35.3	36.6
Late boomers (1956–65)	9.1	8.3	4.6	3.8	36.0	38.1
Gen Xers (1966–75)	3.4	3.7	4.0	5.7	41.1	42.1
Millennials (1976–85)	3.0[a]	0.01[a]	4.2[b]	2.1[b]	42.6	48.2

Source: NSOPF:04. (Refer to appendix A for key.)

[a]Interpret data with caution. Estimate is unstable because the standard error represents more than 50 percent of the estimate.

[b]Interpret data with caution. Estimate is unstable because the standard error represents more than 30 percent of the estimate.

Among early boomers the percentage of tenured faculty who were women was higher than in the cohort of Depression and war babies (35% compared with 23%, respectively). The percentage did not change significantly for late boomers or Gen Xers, however, suggesting that the increase in appointments off the tenure track is slowing the progress for women in reducing the tenure gap.

Next we look at the distribution for all faculty members, not just those who are tenured. Figure 6.3 shows the distribution of all faculty members by tenure status, gender, and birth cohort. Faculty members born between 1915 and 1945 were predominately male (67.6%), and about one-third (32.6%) were male and tenured. While the stark contrast between the percentage of tenured men and women is evident in each of the three birth cohorts, the gap narrows in each successive generation. Tenured female faculty members increased their share of the faculty ranks from 10% (9.5%) among the Depression and war babies to 12% in the early boomers cohort. However, the percentage of tenured female faculty declined to 9% of the late boomer cohort.

As earlier chapters have demonstrated, the story line is complicated. Figure 6.3 shows also the relative increase in the share of female faculty not on tenure track, from 22% (21.6%) of Depression and war babies to 30% (29.5%) of the late-boomer cohort.

Tenured male faculty decreased their share within the faculty ranks from 33% (32.6%) of Depression and war babies to 23% (22.8%) of the early-boomer cohort and to 16% (15.6%) of the late-boomer cohort. The share of male faculty not on tenure track did not increase commensurately, though. The percentage of male faculty not on tenure track declined from 33% of the Depression and war babies to 29% of the late boomers. And the percentage of male faculty on tenure track in the late-boomer cohort (10.4%) was higher than the percentage of female faculty on tenure track (6.6%), leaving little hope for women in the youngest of the older cohorts to increase their share of the tenured faculty ranks among senior faculty.

The pattern for underrepresented minority faculty by tenure status, gender, and birth cohort (figure 6.4) is similar to the distribution for all faculty members in fall 2003. Female underrepresented minority faculty members hold a smaller share of tenured positions than male underrepresented minority faculty members in each of the three birth cohorts.

Table 6.2 displays the distribution of tenure status and gender by teaching or research field and birth cohort in fall 2003. A higher proportion of faculty members born between 1915 and 1945 were tenured men in natural sciences

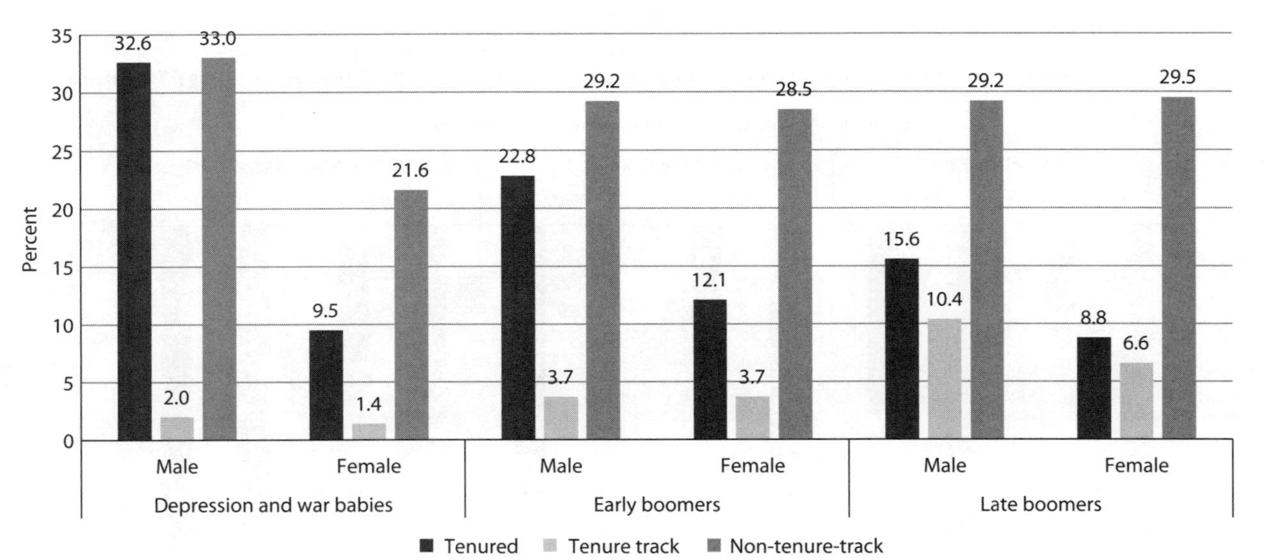

Figure 6.3 Tenure status and gender, by birth cohort, Fall 2003. *Source:* NSOPF:04. (Refer to appendix A for key to data sources.)

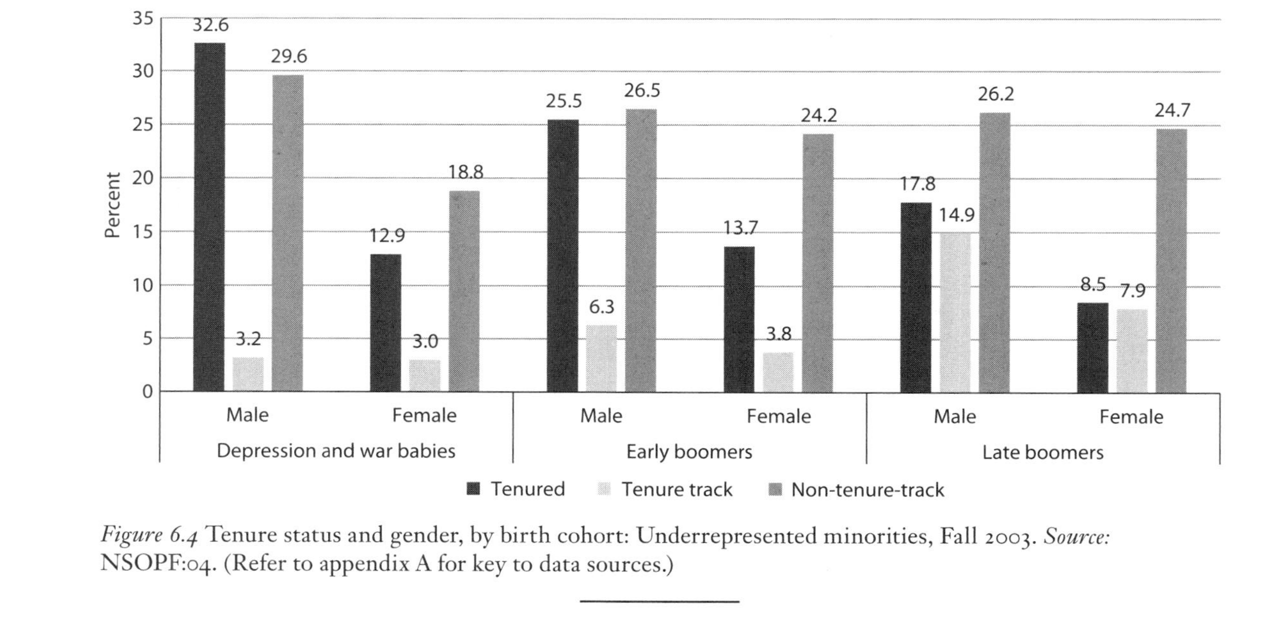

Figure 6.4 Tenure status and gender, by birth cohort: Underrepresented minorities, Fall 2003. *Source:* NSOPF:04. (Refer to appendix A for key to data sources.)

Table 6.2 Percentage distribution of tenure status and gender, by academic field and birth cohort, Fall 2003

	Tenured		Tenure track		Non-tenure-track	
	Male	Female	Male	Female	Male	Female
All program areas	19.3	8.7	7.1	5.2	31.1	28.7
Birth cohorts						
Depression and war babies (1915–45)	32.6	9.5	2.0	1.4	33.0	21.6
Early boomers (1946–55)	22.8	12.1	3.7	3.7	29.2	28.5
Late boomers (1956–65)	15.6	8.8	10.4	6.6	29.2	29.5
Gen Xers (1966–75)	3.4	2.2	15.5	10.8	33.5	34.6
Millennials (1976–85)	1.4[a]	0.01[a]	3.2[b]	2.8	45.1	47.6
Business, law, and communications	18.6	7.6	6.6	4.4	39.8	22.9
Birth cohorts						
Depression and war babies (1915–45)	29.3	5.1	2.3	1.2[b]	48.0	14.1
Early boomers (1946–55)	22.4	10.0	3.5	2.2	40.5	21.3
Late boomers (1956–65)	14.3	10.5	9.1	5.9	33.4	26.8
Gen Xers (1966–75)	3.1	1.4[b]	16.8	11.8	37.1	29.8
Millennials (1976–85)	1.4[a]	0	0	5.9[a]	44.7	48.0
Health sciences	10.9	9.7	5.9	7.0	25.3	41.2
Birth cohorts						
Depression and war babies (1915–45)	24.4	15.8	2.8	1.5[b]	25.3	30.3
Early boomers (1946–55)	14.4	15.2	3.5	7.4	21.1	38.4
Late boomers (1956–65)	6.4	5.9	8.0	8.0	26.1	45.6
Gen Xers (1966–75)	0.8[a]	1.2[b]	10.5	9.7	31.7	46.0
Millennials (1976–85)	0	0	0	1.2[a]	30.9[b]	68.0
Humanities	18.7	11.0	5.9	5.6	24.5	34.3
Birth cohorts						
Depression and war babies (1915–45)	33.7	13.2	1.2[b]	0.5[b]	22.9	28.4
Early boomers (1946–55)	20.3	14.2	2.5	3.4	22.2	37.4
Late boomers (1956–65)	15.1	11.6	9.5	8.2	24.5	31.0
Gen Xers (1966–75)	2.8	3.2	13.4	12.9	28.0	39.6
Millennials (1976–85)	0	0	1.3[a]	1.9[a]	42.8	54.0
Natural sciences and engineering	29.4	6.9	9.5	3.1	33.8	17.2
Birth cohorts						
Depression and war babies (1915–45)	44.0	5.9	1.8	0.5[b]	37.5	10.3
Early boomers (1946–55)	34.8	10.0	4.2	0.9	32.4	17.7
Late boomers (1956–65)	26.9	8.0	13.9	4.0	30.1	17.1

(continued)

Table 6.2 (continued)

	Tenured		Tenure track		Non-tenure-track	
	Male	Female	Male	Female	Male	Female
Gen Xers (1966–75)	6.2	2.2	23.3	9.6	35.2	23.5
Millennials (1976–85)	3.4[a]	0.02[a]	4.0[a]	2.0[b]	51.3	39.3
Social sciences and education	17.0	9.9	5.9	7.4	24.4	35.5
Birth cohorts						
Depression and war babies (1915–45)	27.1	9.7	2.1	2.4	29.0	29.7
Early boomers (1946–55)	19.3	13.5	3.4	5.8	22.6	35.3
Late boomers (1956–65)	13.5	11.2	8.0	9.4	21.0	36.9
Gen Xers (1966–75)	3.6	2.6[b]	13.4	15.4	25.1	39.9
Millennials (1976–85)	0	0	5.7[a]	2.7[a]	29.4[b]	62.2
Occupationally specific, other, and none specified	15.5	8.1	7.1	4.4	37.4	27.5
Birth cohorts						
Depression and war babies (1915–45)	27.1	11.4	2.2[b]	2.3	34.7	22.3
Early boomers (1946–55)	21.0	10.8	4.3	3.5	34.6	25.8
Late boomers (1956–65)	10.7	7.2	10.9	5.7	37.3	28.2
Gen Xers (1966–75)	2.1	2.1[b]	12.2	6.3	43.7	33.7
Millennials (1976–85)	1.5[b]	0	4.4[b]	3.3[b]	54.5	36.3

Source: NSOPF:04. (Refer to appendix A for key.)

[a]Interpret data with caution. Estimate is unstable because the standard error represents more than 50 percent of the estimate.

[b]Interpret data with caution. Estimate is unstable because the standard error represents more than 30 percent of the estimate.

and engineering (44%) than in the humanities (34%) or in the social sciences and education (27%).

The percentage of tenured women born between 1915 and 1945 was higher in health sciences (16%), humanities (13%), and social sciences and education (10%) than business, law, and communications (5%) and natural sciences and engineering (6%). The patterns were similar for men and women born between 1946 and 1955 and between 1956 and 1965, respectively. In spite of efforts to diversify the faculty, disciplinary patterns remain largely unchanged for each successive generation.

Table 6.3 provides breakouts by academic rank. One half of the Depression and war babies in doctoral institutions were tenured male full professors.

Table 6.3 Percentage distribution of gender and rank, by academic field and birth cohort, Fall 2003

	Full professor		Associate professor		Assistant professor		Instructor/ lecturer		Other title		No rank	
	Male	Female	Male	Female	Male	Female	Male	Female	Male	Female	Male	Female
All program areas	13.6	4.4	8.6	4.9	8.1	6.6	13.4	14.1	12.5	11.2	1.3	1.3
Birth cohorts												
Depression and war babies (1915–45)	28.5	6.9	7.9	3.4	2.9	2.6	12.5	10.5	14.5	7.9	1.3	1.2
Early boomers (1946–55)	16.0	6.2	10.1	6.5	4.1	5.1	12.4	13.8	11.7	11.4	1.4	1.3
Late boomers (1956–65)	7.0	2.8	11.4	6.6	11.5	8.5	13.2	15.2	10.7	10.7	1.4	1.1
Gen Xers (1966–75)	1.5	0.6	3.3	1.8	17.5	12.5	15.9	16.9	13.2	14.3	1.0	1.4
Millennials (1976–85)	1.1[a]	0.3[a]	0.6[a]	1.0[b]	2.0[b]	2.0[b]	20.8	19.4	22.9	25.3	2.3[b]	2.3
Business, law, and communication	14.2	3.8	8.2	3.8	6.9	4.2	15.5	11.6	18.6	10.3	1.6	1.2
Birth cohorts												
Depression and war babies (1915–45)	28.4	3.3	9.9	1.6[b]	3.2	1.6[b]	17.8	6.6	18.2	6.4	2.0[b]	1.0[a]
Early boomers (1946–55)	15.6	5.5	9.1	4.4	4.2	2.6	15.3	10.4	20.0	9.6	2.2	1.1[b]
Late boomers (1956–65)	7.5	4.1	8.0	6.3	9.5	4.9	13.7	14.7	17.0	11.9	1.2[b]	1.4[b]
Gen Xers (1966–75)	3.2[b]	0.8[a]	4.6	1.7[b]	14.5	10.4	15.7	15.9	18.5	13.2	0.5[a]	1.0[a]
Millennials (1976–85)	3.4[a]	0	0	0	0.0	5.9[a]	18.8[b]	15.2[b]	23.9[b]	28.5	0.0	4.2[a]
Health Sciences	10.0	4.4	8.9	7.7	11.0	14.7	7.0	19.3	4.5	10.7	0.7	1.1
Birth cohorts												
Depression and war babies (1915–45)	26.7	9.8	9.1	8.5	6.7	8.0	4.0[b]	13.3	6.0	6.9	0.02[a]	1.0[b]
Early boomers (1946–55)	13.5	7.2	10.7	11.3	5.9	13.3	5.0	18.3	3.2	9.8	0.7[b]	1.1[b]
Late boomers (1956–65)	3.8	1.2[b]	11.4	7.2	14.2	18.0	6.0	21.0	3.9	11.3	1.2[b]	0.9[b]

(continued)

Table 6.3 (continued)

	Full professor		Associate professor		Assistant professor		Instructor/ lecturer		Other title		No rank	
	Male	Female	Male	Female	Male	Female	Male	Female	Male	Female	Male	Female
Gen Xers (1966–75)	0.5[a]	0.2[a]	0.9[b]	1.1[b]	20.3	18.4	14.3	22.8	7.0	12.6	0.1[a]	1.9[b]
Millennials (1976–85)	0	0	4.5[a]	0.2[a]	0.0	4.8[b]	22.7[b]	27.7[b]	3.7[a]	36.4	0.0	0.0
Humanities	12.2	5.1	6.7	5.5	6.7	6.3	12.2	21.2	10.2	11.5	1.1	1.4
Birth cohorts												
Depression and war babies (1915–45)	26.8	8.7	6.1	3.8	2.0[b]	1.1[b]	12.2	17.7	9.9	9.0	0.9[b]	1.9[b]
Early boomers (1946–55)	13.3	7.1	7.8	6.6	2.6	3.9	10.0	21.5	9.7	14.6	1.5[b]	1.4[b]
Late boomers (1956–65)	5.0	2.6	9.8	8.8	10.3	9.3	12.7	20.6	10.0	9.0	1.4[a]	0.5[a]
Gen Xers (1966–75)	1.5[b]	0.6[a]	2.2	2.4	15.3	13.5	13.8	25.3	10.9	12.4	0.5[b]	1.7[b]
Millennials (1976–85)	0	1.8[a]	1.0[a]	0	1.0[a]	0.9[a]	24.2	31.4	17.2[b]	18.2	0.6[a]	3.7[a]
Natural sciences and engineering	19.9	3.4	12.6	3.5	10.1	4.2	13.5	8.4	14.9	6.7	1.8	1.1
Birth cohorts												
Depression and war babies (1915–45)	37.5	4.3	9.8	1.2	2.1	1.1	13.6	5.9	19.1	3.4	1.3[b]	0.7[b]
Early boomers (1946–55)	24.5	5.4	13.9	4.7	5.0	2.2	12.7	8.1	13.6	6.8	1.8	1.3
Late boomers (1956–65)	12.6	2.6	18.7	5.2	14.1	5.4	12.0	8.7	11.6	6.3	2.0	0.8
Gen Xers (1966–75)	1.5[b]	0.4[b]	5.8	2.0	24.7	10.6	16.9	10.5	13.8	10.3	2.1[b]	1.3
Millennials (1976–85)	2.2[a]	0.0	0.2[a]	0.3[a]	1.3[a]	0.8[a]	17.0	16.9	37.0	19.9	0.9[a]	3.5[a]

Social sciences and education	12.2	5.7	6.5	5.3	6.6	7.8	9.7	15.9	11.1	16.6	1.1	1.4
Birth cohorts												
Depression and war babies (1915–45)	23.6	8.5	6.9	3.3	2.5	3.2	9.2	12.3	14.3	13.7	1.6	0.8[b]
Early boomers (1946–55)	14.1	7.4	7.0	7.1	3.5	6.3	9.0	15.5	10.7	16.3	1.0[b]	2.2
Late boomers (1956–65)	5.8	4.3	8.7	7.9	8.5	10.3	10.1	19.3	8.4	14.9	1.0[b]	0.8
Gen Xers (1966–75)	1.2[b]	0.7[b]	3.0	1.9	16.1	15.0	10.4	17.5	10.7	21.2	0.7[a]	1.5[b]
Millennials (1976–85)	0.0	0.5[a]	0.0	1.7[a]	5.9[a]	1.7[a]	18.3[b]	19.0	9.7[b]	42.0	1.3[a]	0.0
Occupationally specific, other, and non-specified	10.0	4.0	7.1	4.8	6.8	5.0	20.6	12.5	14.1	12.3	1.3	1.4
Birth cohorts												
Depression and war babies (1915–45)	23.4	8.1	5.7	5.2	3.7	3.1	16.3	9.6	13.5	8.0	1.5[b]	2.1
Early boomers (1946–55)	12.7	5.1	10.5	6.0	3.4	3.8	19.6	12.6	12.6	11.9	1.0[b]	0.8
Late boomers (1956–65)	4.2	2.2	7.3	5.3	10.8	5.7	22.6	12.9	12.9	12.9	1.2[b]	2.0[b]
Gen Xers (1966–75)	1.7[b]	0.9[a]	2.2	1.3	11.5	8.9	23.2	14.2	18.2	15.6	1.2[b]	1.2[b]
Millennials (1976–85)	0.9[a]	0.0	0.0	2.3[a]	2.2[b]	1.5[a]	24.2	14.2	26.4	19.8	6.7[a]	1.9[a]

Source: NSOPF:04. (Refer to appendix A for key.)

[a]Interpret data with caution. Estimate is unstable because the standard error represents more than 50 percent of the estimate.

[b]Interpret data with caution. Estimate is unstable because the standard error represents more than 30 percent of the estimate.

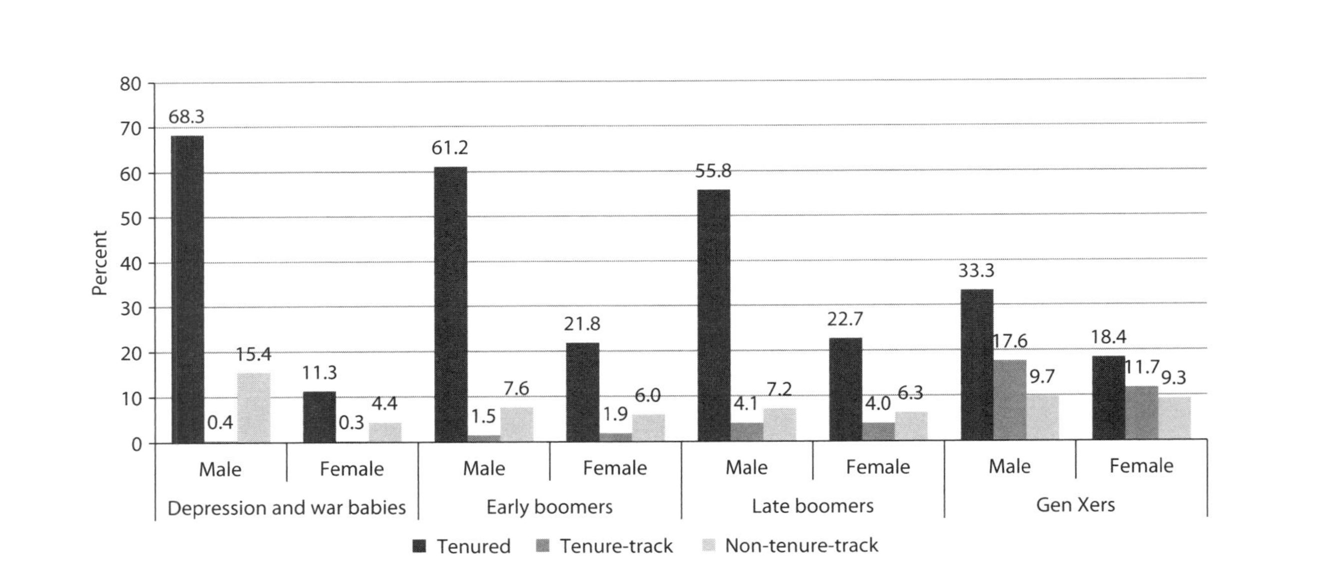

Figure 6.5 Tenure status and gender, by birth cohort, science and engineering, 2013. *Source:* SDR:13. (Refer to appendix A for key to data sources.)

About one-third (35%) of early boomers and approaching one-quarter (22.7%) of late boomers were tenured male professors. The comparable percentages for female full professors draw a sharp contrast. About 10% (9.4%) of the Depression and war babies in doctoral institutions were tenured female full professors. About one-quarter of faculty members in natural sciences and engineering were full professors. Twenty percent of these full professors were men, and 3% were women. More than one-third (37.5%) of faculty born between 1915 and 1945 were full professors in natural sciences and engineering in fall 2003. Four percent were women.

A little more than one-third (35.5%) of female full professors were Depression and war babies. Almost one-half (48.5%) were early boomers, and 15.1% were late boomers (see table 6.1). The pattern is similar across different types of institutions.

A decade later, the pattern is essentially the same. The Survey of Doctorate Recipients is a source of information for faculty in science and engineering fields. Figure 6.5 shows the distribution of tenure status and gender by birth cohort for 2013. More than two-thirds (68.3%) of faculty members born between 1915 and 1945 were tenured men compared to 11.3% who were tenured women. While the tenure gap has been reduced in each successive birth cohort, among early boomers (39.4%); late boomers (33.1%); and Gen Xers (14.8%), the decline in the proportion of tenure-track positions available has impacted progress toward diversification of the faculty.

Taken together, these data suggest some support for the assertion of the researchers who projected that there would be an oversupply of older tenured (male) professors and the lobbyists who argued that if mandatory retirement were abolished or the upper age limit were was raised, tenure would be threatened. Less than 10% of full-time faculty left their institution between fall 2002 and fall 2003, and only about one-third of those who left retired (see table 6.4).

Timing and the Retirement Decision

As a result of the ADEA, timing of the decision about when to retire shifted from institutions to individuals. This means that institutional staffing plans went from having a high degree of certainty to almost no degree of certainty virtually overnight. Timing of the now individual retirement decision became an important variable to consider. In light of Rees and Smith's (1991) findings, one of the more salient questions on many higher education leaders' minds today is, how many tenured faculty members are postponing retirement in the

Table 6.4 Percentage of full-time faculty who left institutions and percent distribution, by reason for leaving, by type of institution, Fall 2002 to Fall 2003

Institution type	Full-time faculty who left	Of those who left, reason for leaving	
		Retired	Other reason
All institutions[a]	6.9	35.6	64.4
Public doctoral[b]	8.0	29.9	70.1
Private not-for-profit doctoral[c]	7.5	24.0	76.0
Public master's	8.0	43.2	56.8
Private not-for-profit master's	6.0	31.0	69.0
Private not-for-profit baccalaureate	7.8	16.8	83.3
Public associate's	6.4	46.1	53.9
Other[3]	6.8	36.9	63.1

Source: NSOPF:04. (Refer to appendix A for key.)

Note: Faculty includes all faculty and instructional staff.

[a]All public and private not-for-profit Title IV degree-granting institutions in the 50 states and the District of Columbia.

[b]Doctoral includes research/doctoral institutions and specialized medical schools and medical centers as classified by the 2000 Carnegie Classification.

[c]Includes public baccalaureate, private not-for-profit associate's, and other specialized institutions except medical schools and medical centers.

absence of a mandatory retirement age? Data to answer this question are hard to find. Most studies focus on a single institution. For example, Sharon Weinberg and Marc Scott (2013) studied a single institution and found that before the elimination of mandatory retirement only 11% of faculty remained after age seventy, but after the law changed 60% of faculty expect to remain employed after age seventy, and 15% will not retire until age eighty or older. A study of three institutions in North Carolina found retirement rates were low for faculty members aged sixty-two and that the retirement rates declined for faculty aged sixty-nine and seventy after mandatory retirement ended.[5] As noted in previous chapters, more current data representative of the faculty population as a whole are not available. Two sources in addition to the National Study of Postsecondary Faculty (NSOPF:04) are informative however: the Higher Education Research Institute's Biennial Faculty Survey and the National Science Foundation's Survey of Doctorate Recipients (SDR). All three of these sources (NSOPF, HERI, and SDR) have information regarding plans for retirement. In addition, the SDR has information about the actual year individual faculty members retired and their postretirement employment.

Table 6.5 displays information regarding planned retirement age for tenured faculty by birth cohort, based on data from the NSOPF:04. While the median retirement age for each birth cohort except for the oldest, Depression and war babies, born between 1915 and 1945, was sixty-five years old, there is more to the story. One-third of the faculty members born between 1915 and 1945 reported a planned retirement age greater than seventy years old. These most senior of the tenured faculty also reported planning to work six more years on average before they would retire. Three-quarters of early boomers reported planning to work more than five more years before retiring, and almost one-half (47%) reported planning to work more than ten years before retiring. These numbers suggest there may be little turnover from retirement in the tenured academic workforce.

Figure 6.6 shows the percentage of full-time faculty with retirement plans by type of institution, based on another source on retirement plans, the 2013 HERI Faculty Survey. Between 10 and 13% of faculty at all baccalaureate institutions and public universities reported having plans to retire in the next three years. Consistent with other findings, the percentage was lower at private universities (9%) than at four-year public colleges (12.9%).

Figure 6.6 also shows the percentage of full-time faculty who reported that they had considered early retirement in the past two years.[6] The percentage ranged from 16% at four-year Catholic colleges to 23% (22.9%) at public four-year colleges. Overall, 21% (20.6%) of full-time faculty reported considering early retirement in the past two years.

Postretirement Employment

The Survey of Doctorate Recipients has the most detailed information available regarding actual retirement decisions and postretirement employment. Figure 6.7 shows the percentage of faculty members who were retired but still working in 2013. Understandably, the percentage of Gen Xers and millennials who were retired is negligible. A small percentage (2.7%) of late boomers had retired but were still working in higher education. Among Depression and war babies and early boomers, substantial percentages had retired but were continuing to work in higher education as of 2013. More than one-third (37.5%) of the oldest birth cohort (those born between 1915 and 1945) and 12% (12.5%) of the next oldest birth cohort (early boomers) were working, retired from another position (see figure 6.7).

Table 6.5 Tenured faculty retirement plans, by birth cohort and retirement status, Fall 2003

	Average planned retirement age	Planned retirement age (% > 70)	Average years until retirement (avg. > 0)	Years until retirement (% > 1)	Years until retirement (% > 3)	Years until retirement (% > 5)	Years until retirement (% > 10)
All tenured faculty	66.4	13.2	18.1	91.8	86.9	80.9	66.1
Birth cohorts							
Depression and war babies (1915–45)	69.0	23.9	6.4	68.4	51.0	34.3	10.7
Early boomers (1946–55)	66.0	10.5	12.9	96.7	93.5	86.6	60.1
Late boomers (1956–65)	65.6	9.9	21.9	99.4	99.2	98.8	94.8
Gen Xers (1966–75)	65.1	9.7	30.9	99.6	99.5	99.5	99.3
Millennials (1976–85)	64.7	13.7	38.5	99.8	99.2	99.2	99.2
Retired from another position = Not retired	66.1	11.6	19.0	94.2	90.2	85.2	71.2
Birth cohorts							
Depression and war babies (1915–45)	68.4	19.2	6.6	72.3	54.6	37.6	11.7
Early boomers (1946–55)	66.0	10.4	13.0	96.8	93.8	87.4	61.5
Late boomers (1956–65)	65.6	9.9	21.9	99.5	99.2	98.9	95.0
Gen Xers (1966–75)	65.1	9.5	30.9	99.6	99.5	99.5	99.3
Millennials (1976–85)	64.7	13.7	38.5	99.8	99.2	99.2	99.2
Retired from another position = Retired	68.5	25.5	10.2	73.6	61.6	48.3	27.4
Birth cohorts							
Depression and war babies (1915–45)	70.0	33.0	6.0	60.8	43.9	28.0	8.9
Early boomers (1946–55)	65.9	12.0	11.5	95.6	90.6	78.4	46.6
Late boomers (1956–65)	64.9	10.7	21.1	97.6	97.5	96.4	89.6
Gen Xers (1966–75)	67.6	21.8[b]	33.3	100.0	100.0	100.0	100.0
Millennials (1976–85)[c]	—	—	—	—	—	—	—

Source: NSOPF:04. (Refer to appendix A for key.)

[a]Interpret data with caution. Estimate is unstable because the standard error represents more than 50 percent of the estimate.

[b]Interpret data with caution. Estimate is unstable because the standard error represents more than 30 percent of the estimate.

[c]Reporting standards not met.

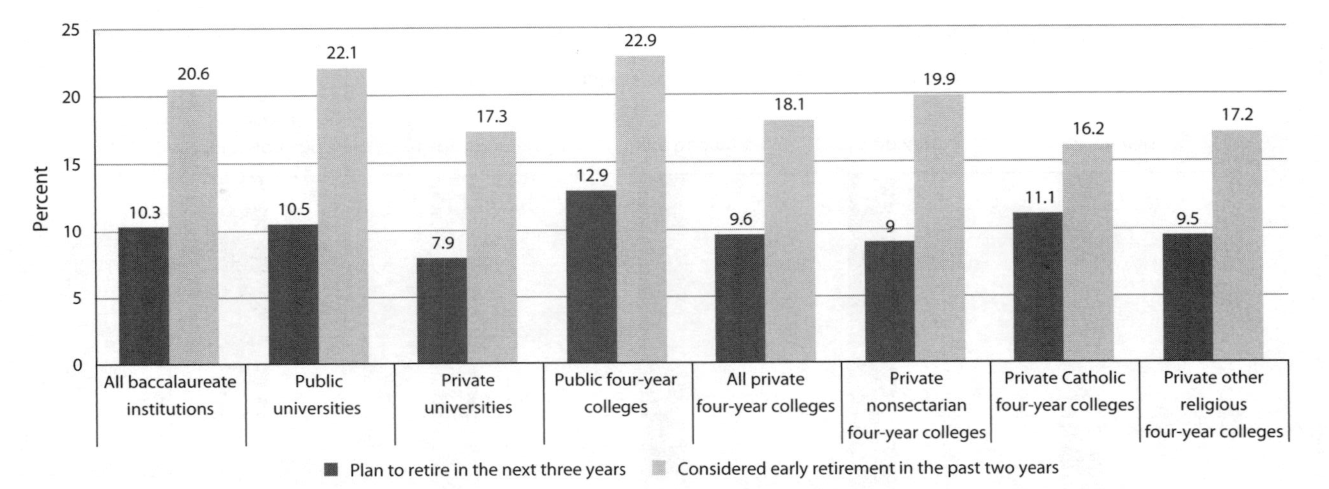

Figure 6.6 Percentage of full-time faculty with retirement plans, by type of institution, 2010. *Source:* HERI:11. (Refer to appendix A for key to data sources.)

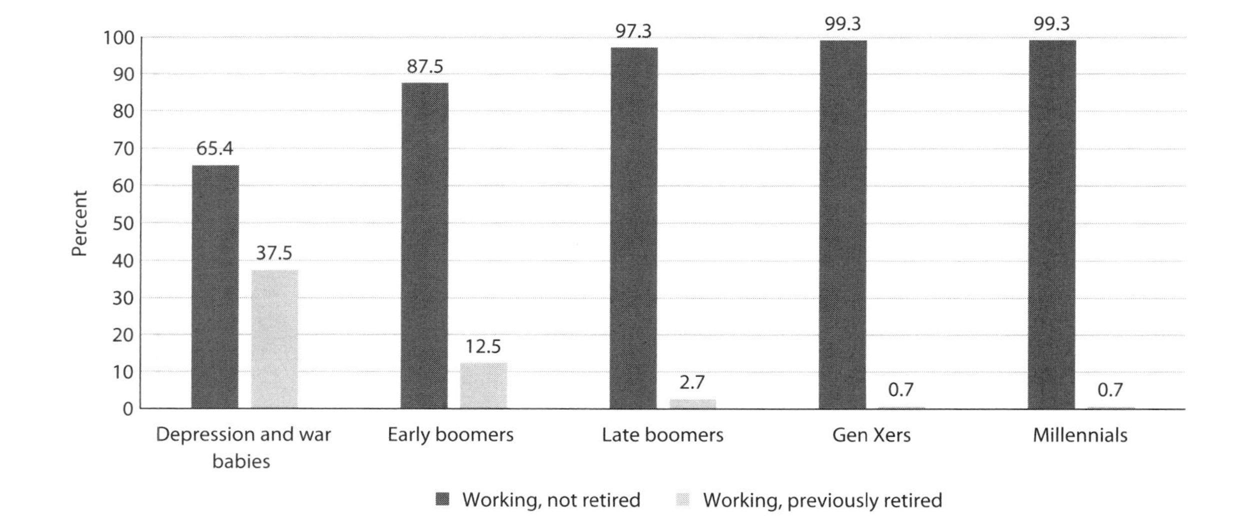

Figure 6.7 Percentage faculty, by retirement status, science and engineering, 2013. *Source:* SDR:13. (Refer to appendix A for key to data sources.)

Receptivity and Readiness

The economic downturn—the Great Recession–has focused more attention on faculty retirement issues in higher education. Individuals are concerned that they may not have enough money to provide for a financially secure retirement. Many states have legislated substantial pension reform, and the definition of retirement is becoming more and more ambiguous. To pinpoint exactly when someone is "retired" is not an easy proposition. Individuals sometimes retire from one position only to accept another full- or part-time position at a different institution. Some retire from an institution and are rehired by the same institution, referred to in some states (such as Florida) as "double dipping." Many faculty members continue working well past the traditional retirement age of sixty-five or seventy, while others choose to phase into retirement by reducing their work commitments gradually over time. Figure 6.8 provides a visual depiction of the complexity of the question about the prospective timing of retirement. While the largest percentage expected to retire on time (defined as between the ages of sixty-five and sixty-seven), about one-quarter of faculty members reported expecting to retire early (fifty-five to sixty-four) and nearly one-third reported expecting to retire either late (sixty-eight to seventy-four) or very late (after seventy-four).

Given the current economic environment, one reason more people may postpone retirement is declining confidence that they will be able to afford a comfortable retirement. Given the aging of full- and part-time faculty, attempts to identify innovative strategies to entice senior faculty members to retire may be all the timelier given the current economic climate. Work being undertaken by the American Council on Education is focusing on policies and practices at institutions specifically designed to support an aging academic workforce.

Stagnant salaries exacerbate the issue (see chapter 9). At the same time that responsibility for funding retirement is shifting away from governments and employers to employees, salaries have not kept pace—leaving individuals without the resources to save, even if they had the wherewithal to do so. The problem is even more pronounced when we consider different appointment types. While part-time faculty members are eligible to participate in retirement plans in many institutions, there is little evidence to indicate the extent to which they do so. Relatively low salaries most certainly impact the ability to contribute to retirement savings.

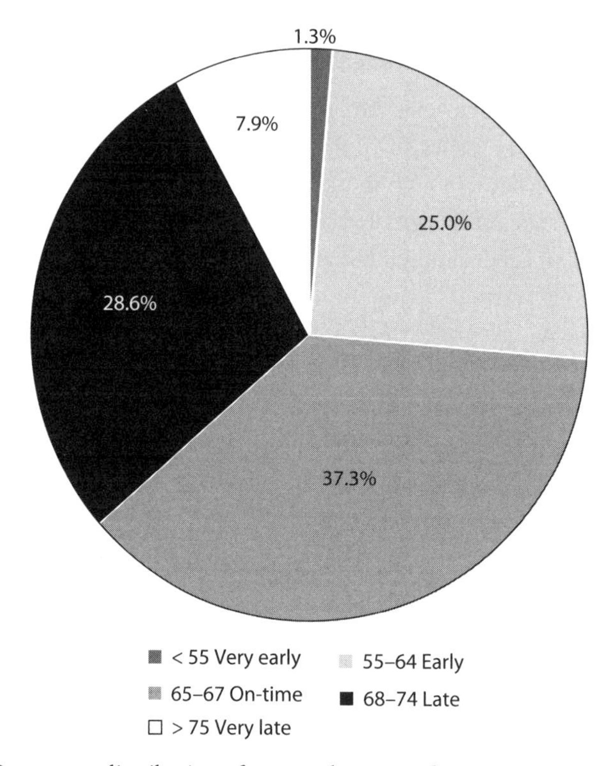

Figure 6.8 Percentage distribution of expected timing of retirement of full-time instructional faculty, by type and control of institution, Fall 2003. *Source:* NSOPF:04. (Refer to appendix A for key to data sources.)

Taken together these issues are converging to create a crisis for higher education. One indicator is the growing number of faculty members who are postponing retirement. The TIAA-CREF Institute refers to these individuals as either "reluctantly reluctant" to retire or "reluctant by choice" (Yakoboski 2011). Early retirement incentives, so-called buyouts, can only go so far to entice older faculty members to retire, especially those who are reluctant by choice. Sixty-one percent of institutions reported that they had offered an early-retirement buyout to full-time tenured faculty since 2007 (Yakoboski and Conley 2013). Alternative strategies such as life planning are needed to complement early-retirement incentive packages and phased retirement (Yakoboski 2011). Another emerging complexity is postretirement employment.

The data in table 6.6 show movement out of higher education, including retirement for senior career-stage faculty, by birth cohort, for 1993, 2003, and 2010

Table 6.6 Distribution of out-migration venues of senior career stage faculty from higher education, including retirement, 1993, 2003, 2010 (Survey of Doctorate Recipients cohorts)

	All combined			Male			Female		
	1993	2003	2010	1993	2003	2010	1993	2003	2010
N	65,222	102,183	135,277	56,961	80,746	99,364	8,263	21,437	35,913
Movement overview									
Remained in higher education	66.9	67.0	90.0	66.3	66.8	89.6	70.9	67.8	91.0
Move	33.1	33.0	10.0	33.7	33.2	10.4	29.1	32.2	9.0
Retired[a]	5.5	22.4	6.0	5.5	22.9	6.4	5.0	20.7	5.1
Other	27.6	10.6	4.0	28.2	10.3	4.0	24.1	11.5	3.9
Average age at retirement (yrs)	63.2	64.2	65.7	63.3	64.4	65.8	62.1	63.6	65.2
Birth cohorts									
Depression and war babies (1915–45)	98.6	70.0	57.1	99.3	71.9	60.5	91.7	62.4	45.5
Early boomers (1946–55)	1.4	29.5	41.8	0.7	27.9	38.3	8.3	36.2	53.9
Late boomers (1956–65)	—	0.5	1.0	—	—	1.2	—	1.4	—
Gen Xers (1966–75)	—	—	—	—	—	—	—	—	—
Millennials (1976–85)	—	—	—	—	—	—	—	—	—
Rank at retirement[b]									
Full professor	55.1	53.0	65.3	57.2	54.3	67.9	36.4	47.7	56.1
Associate professor	11.8	10.4	13.2	11.3	9.5	12.8	17.2	14.2	14.6
Other	33.1	36.6	21.5	31.5	36.2	19.3	46.4	38.1	29.3

Sources: SDR:93; SDR:97: SDR:03; SDR:06; SDR:10; SDR:13. (Refer to appendix A for key.)

Note: Periods of change are defined as 1993–97-03, 2003–06-10, and 2010–13.

[a]Retired indicates the faculty that are not working and retired.

[b]Rank attained before retirement was indicated during the times that change was measured.

cohorts of SDR respondents. The average age at retirement has been edging upward for each successive cohort. For senior career-stage faculty in the 1993 cohort, the average age at retirement was 63.2. The average at retirement for the 2003 cohort was 64.2, and for the 2010 cohort it was 65.7. The upward trend toward an older average retirement age held for both men and women. Women, however, tend to retire at a slightly younger age on average than men. The average age at retirement for women in the 2010 cohort was 65 and the average for men was 66 years old.

Retirement Incentives

It is evident, then, why institutions feel compelled to develop strategies to entice senior faculty to pinpoint the timing of the retirement decision—and to retire. Over time, more certainty has begun to reemerge. But this certainty has come with a price tag for institutions in the form of retirement incentives, or buyouts. The aging of the population has prompted many institutions to consider offering these retirement incentives. Sixty-one percent of institutions reported offering an early retirement buy-out to full-time tenured faculty since the beginning of 2007 (Yakoboski and Conley 2013). The success of these programs varies, particularly with respect to the extent to which the individuals that institutional leaders would like to see opt for a buyout do so. Many institutions have established regular or ad-hoc phased retirement options as well. Research indicates broad receptivity to opportunities for phased retirement (Conley 2006). Patterns in the shifts in appointment types away from tenure-eligible positions to part-time and full-time off-track appointments may have been another strategy that institutions employed to gain more flexibility and control over staffing. As noted elsewhere in this volume, we believe the rate of change has accelerated after the economic downturn of 2008–09. Data from a survey about retirement plans offered at colleges and universities across the United States highlight the fact that phased retirement programs have emerged as a strategy to support senior faculty members' transition to retirement, particularly in private institutions, where phased retirement programs have been more prevalent than in public institutions (Yakoboski and Conley 2013).

Figures 6.9, 6.10, and 6.11 provide the distribution of timing of the retirement decision for those respondents who were retired, by birth cohort. Less than 5% of Depression and war babies who had retired had already done so before the exemption for uncapping occurred (2.2%), and less than 10% retired in the years immediately following the elimination of mandatory retirement

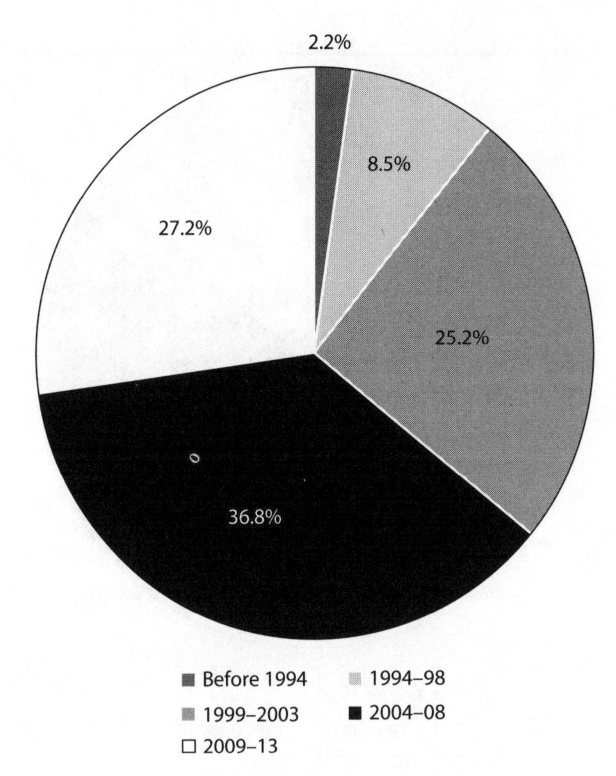

Figure 6.9 Timing of retirement decision by birth cohort: Depression and war babies (1915–1945), science and engineering, 2013. *Source:* SDR:13. (Refer to appendix A for key to data sources.)

(8.5 percent). One-quarter reported retiring between 1999 and 2003 (25.2%), and more than one-third (36.8%) retired between 2004 and 2008. About one-quarter of the faculty who had retired reported doing so after the economic downturn (between 2009 and 2013).

More than one-half of working early boomers who had retired did so after the economic downturn (57.3%). Similar to the Depression and war babies, only a small percentage of working retired early boomers did so before the exemption for uncapping occurred (1.6%) or immediately following uncapping (3.1%). Less than 10% retired (8.6%) between 1999 and 2003. Similarly, about one-half of working late boomers who had already retired did so after the economic downturn (50.8%). One-quarter reported retiring between 2004 and 2008 (24.7%).

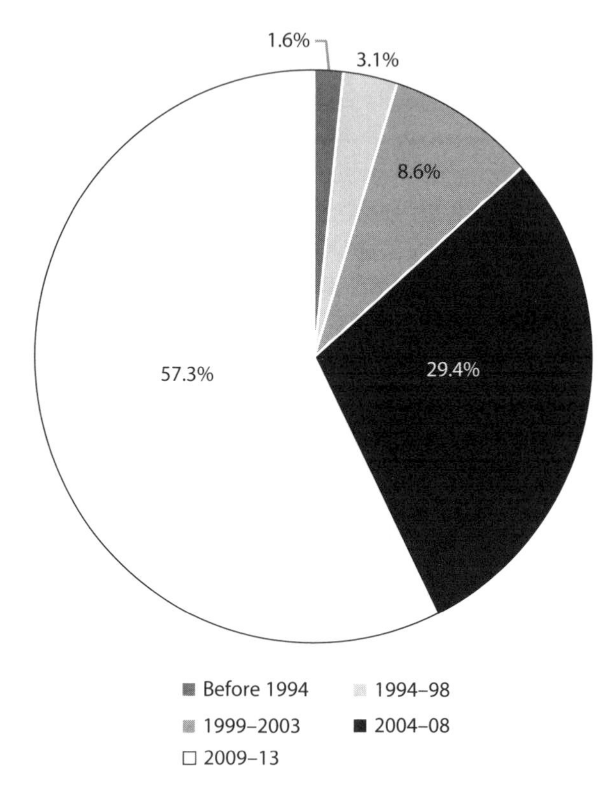

Figure 6.10 Timing of retirement decision, by birth cohort: Early boomers (1946–1955), science and engineering, 2013. *Source:* SDR:13. (Refer to appendix A for key to data sources.)

Age is the single most important predictor of retirement, followed by health and wealth. There is a positive correlation between education and health. Although specific data on faculty health are not available, individuals with higher levels of education tend to have better health, and individuals in good health tend to work longer.

Retirement Plan Design and Pension Reform

Responsibility for funding retirement has been shifting away from governments and employers to individuals or employees (that is, faculty members themselves). This shift is most pronounced in the public sector and is most often discussed within the context of the shift to defined-contribution retirement plans away from defined-benefit or pension plans. The primary differ-

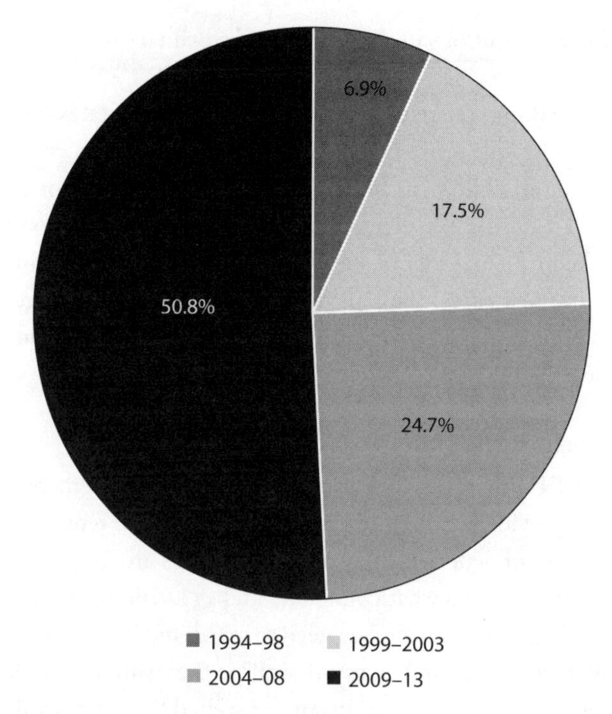

Figure 6.11 Timing of retirement decision, by birth cohort: Late boomers (1956–1965), science and engineering, 2013. *Source:* SDR:13. (Refer to appendix A for key to data sources.)

---

ence between defined-contribution and defined-benefit plans is in how the value of the accumulated wealth of the plan due to be paid out to the employee is determined. In defined-contribution plans, the value of the plan is determined by the contributions made into it, either by the individual or by the institution or, as in most cases, both the employee and the institution. In defined-benefit plans, the value of the benefit is based on a formula that typically takes into consideration the number of years of service of the faculty member and final salary. The latter is commonly referred to as a pension and has historically been the norm in public institutions, while private not-for-profit institutions have relied on defined contribution plans as the vehicle to support faculty members during retirement. Data collected in 2011 and 2012 from a sample of institutions nationwide reveal that only 22% of public institutions relied exclusively on a primary defined-benefit plan and that the majority (67%) had both primary defined-benefit and primary defined-contribution plans. Almost all of the private institutions in the sample had a primary defined-contribution plan (95%).

Generally speaking, retirement policy in the United States has been moving toward an older full retirement age, also referred to as normal retirement age.[7] Changes in eligibility for full Social Security benefits, for example, are one indicator. Following the economic downturn, public pension reform has been undertaken by a majority of states. Although the reforms will not impact near retirees in most cases, the long-term effects of these changes will most certainly have consequences for retirement security for individuals in the years to come.

Retirement Confidence

The TIAA-CREF Institute's 2014 Faculty Career and Retirement Survey provides compelling evidence that the vast majority (83%) of tenured and tenure-track faculty felt confident that their retirement plans are sufficient. About half (52%) said they were "somewhat confident" and 31% said they were "very confident" they will have the money they need to retire and live comfortably. About half (48%) say that "saving and investing well" is the main reason for their confidence. Age and confidence are positively correlated. In other words, older faculty are more confident they will have enough money to retire and live comfortably in retirement than younger faculty. Fifty-nine percent of faculty members age seventy or older were "very confident" they would have enough money to live comfortably throughout retirement compared with only 20% of those less than fifty years old. Furthermore, faculty members are generally more confident than American workers overall in their prospects for a financially secure retirement (Yakoboski 2015).

Retirement from the "Other" Academy

The huge expansion of different appointment types has created a bifurcated academic labor market. We refer to the "other academy" as shorthand to draw distinction between the circumstances those with tenure-line positions hold compared with those employed in different types of positions. Eligibility for benefits may depend on the nature of the employment relationship with the institution. Retirement plan designs have grown increasingly varied, with different employees being eligible for different benefits depending on when they were hired, even if they are in the same employee group. The variation in plan design stems, at least in part, from the shift from defined-benefit to defined-contribution plans (particularly among public institutions). At first, public institutions offered defined-contribution plans as an option to encourage supplemental savings, as an alternative to the defined-benefit plan, or both. Among the relatively few private institutions with multiple vendors, the norm is two vendors. By contrast, 40% of public institutions with multiple vendors report using three, and 45% report more than three. Over time, state governments began to look at defined-benefit plans as a place to cut costs and help to balance state budgets, especially when compared with the higher cost of defined-contribution plans.

Conclusion

Exiting from an academic career is a complex process. There is no doubt that ending mandatory retirement has contributed to this complexity. Tenured faculty members are now free to say when they will leave (retire), but there are myriad factors that go into making that decision. Have the concerns expressed during the deliberations of ending mandatory retirement been realized? Evidence suggests we do have an older tenured faculty workforce. While tenure is still alive and well and the overall number of tenured faculty has continued to grow, hiring for positions other than tenure-track has outpaced hiring of tenure-track positions. We are not suggesting cause and effect, rather a multitude of consequences, intended and unintended, that has contributed to the strikingly new environment for retirement for tenured faculty that mirrors almost no other profession.

There is also compelling evidence to suggest that ending mandatory retirement has stalled progress for women and members of underrepresented groups. While there has been progress, some may even say remarkable progress, in the number of women in particular, who have secured academic appointments in higher education over the past twenty to thirty years, the proportion of tenured and tenure-track appointments remains relatively low. What are the implications?

On one hand, having more options for exiting an academic career is positive. As our society ages and recognizes the vitality of older workers, higher education leaders have an opportunity to harness the benefit of age and experience of older faculty (Bland and Bergquist 1997). On the other hand, concerns about the productivity of senior faculty persist. “Changing student characteristics require that higher education not only *replace* current faculty as they retire, but also *regenerate* the faculty workforce for the twenty-first century" (Conley 2008, 1). Assuring, insofar as possible, a new faculty cohort better attuned to rapidly emerging technological opportunities, cross-disciplinary collaboration, and a more global orientation, is necessary to transforming academic programs and institutions to serve the changing workforce requirements of a knowledge economy and for regenerating the faculty.

At the extreme, it is possible that uncapping, particularly when coupled with an aging tenured faculty population and the Great Recession, has pushed institutions into the marketplace in unprecedented ways. This environment has created significant tension on many campuses across the United States, particularly for resource-challenged institutions and community colleges.

NOTES

1. People voluntarily leave, or exit, academic careers for a variety of reasons. Generally, these voluntary reasons can be grouped into two categories: resignation and retirement. Resignation typically involves changing jobs, whether to accept a different job within the same academic institution (as in the case of moving from an academic to an administrative position) or to move to accept an appointment in a different location. Career exit may also result from involuntary separation. Examples of involuntary separation include dismissal for cause or death, both relatively rare. This chapter focuses only on voluntary separation and retirement. For purposes of our volume, movement between jobs is considered mobility and is treated in chapter 5.

2. *Uncapping* is a term used to refer to the elimination of a mandatory retirement age.

3. The extent to which institutions provide guidance varies considerably, although there have been some recent initiatives to help individuals and institutions. For example, the American Council on Education, with support from the Sloan Foundation, has been gathering information and convening institutional leaders interested in identifying best practices on faculty retirement transitions (Van Ummersen, McLaughlin, and Duranleau 2014).

4. Faculty born between 1915 and 1945 are referred to here as Depression and war babies. Baby boomers are separated into two categories: early boomers, born between 1946 and 1955, and late boomers, born between 1956 and 1965. Faculty born between 1966 and 1975 are called Gen Xers, and the youngest group of faculty, born after 1976, is referred to as millennials. Wealth was measured three ways: net worth, financial net worth, and home equity. Net worth included all assets less debt. Financial net worth is a subset of net worth made up only of financial assets (savings accounts, 401[k]'s, pensions, and individual retirement accounts) (Pew 2013).

5. The three institutions were Duke University, University of North Carolina, and North Carolina State University.

6. The item was not included in the 2013 HERI Report, so data are included for 2010.

7. Social Security Administration, "Retirement Planner: Benefits by Year of Birth" (https://www.ssa.gov/planners/retire/agereduction.html).

REFERENCES

Age Discrimination in Employment Act. 1967 Amendments (Pub. L. 90-202).

Basu, Kaustuv. 2012. "Easing the Path to Retirement: Colleges Honored for Creative Approaches to Encouraging Professors to Consider Going Emeritus." *Inside Higher Ed*, June 19. https://www.insidehighered.com/news/2012/06/19/faculty-retirement-and-innovative-practices.

Bland, C. J., and W. H. Bergquist. 1997. *The Vitality of Senior Faculty Members: Snow on the Roof, Fire in the Furnace.* ASHE-ERIC Higher Education Report 25, no. 7. Washington, DC: George Washington University, Graduate School of Education and Human Development.

Conley, Valerie M. 2006. "Demographics and Motives Affecting Faculty Retirement." In *New Ways to Phase into Retirement: Options for Faculty and Institutions; New Directions for Higher Education*, edited by David W. Leslie and Valerie M. Conley. San Francisco, CA: Jossey-Bass.

Epstein, Richard A., and Saunders MacLane. 1991. "Keep Mandatory Retirement for Tenured Faculty." *Regulation* 85 (Spring): 85–96.

Finkin, Matthew W., M. C. Bernstein, M. Eymonerie, W. Hammerle, W. L. Hansen, T. P. Schultz and P. O. Steiner. 1978. "The Impact of Federal Retirement-Age Legislation on Higher Education: A Report of the Special Committee on Age Discrimination and Retirement American Association of University Professors." *AAUP Bulletin* 64 (September): 181–92.

Gray, Kevin. 1989. *Retirement Plans and Expectations of TIAA-CREF Policyholders.* New York: Teachers Insurance and Annuity Association College Retirement Equities Fund.

Hammond, P. Brett, and Harriet P. Morgan, eds. 1991. *Ending Mandatory Retirement in Higher Education.* Committee on Mandatory Retirement in Higher Education, Commission on Behavioral and Social Sciences and Education, National Research Council. Washington, DC: National Academy Press.

Lozier, G. G., and M. J. Dooris, eds. 1989. "Managing Faculty Resources." *New Directions for Institutional Research* 63 (Fall): 1–102. San Francisco, CA: Jossey-Bass.

———. 1991. "Projecting Faculty Retirement: Factors Influencing Individual Decisions." *AEA Papers and Proceedings* 81, no. 2: 101–05.

Rees, Albert, and Sharon P. Smith. 1991. *Faculty Retirement in the Arts and Sciences.* Princeton, NJ: Princeton University Press.

Social Security Administration. "Retirement Planner: Benefits by Year of Birth." https://www.ssa.gov/planners/retire/agereduction.html.

The Pew Charitable Trusts. 2013. "Retirement Security Across Generations: Are Americans Prepared for Their Golden Years?" *Economic Mobility Project*: 1–32. http://www.pewtrusts.org/~/media/legacy/uploadedfiles/pcs_assets/2013/empretirementv4051013finalforwebpdf.pdf

Van Ummersen, Claire, Jeanne M. McLaughlin, and Lauren Duranleau. 2014. *Faculty Retirement: Best Practices for Navigating the Transition*. Sterling, VA: Stylus.

Weinberg, Sharon L. and Marc A. Scott. 2013. "The Impact of Uncapping of Mandatory Retirement on Postsecondary Institutions." *Educational Researcher* 42, no. 6: 338–48.

Yakoboski, Paul J. 2015. "Retirement Planning and Confidence among Tenured and Tenure-Track Faculty: 2014 Faculty Career and Retirement Survey." Data summary. September.

Yakoboski, Paul J., and Valerie M. Conley. 2013. "Retirement Plans, Policies, and Practices in Higher Education." TIAA-CREF Institute, *Trends and Issues*, March, 1–13.

PART III / The Changing Complexion of Faculty Work and Professional Identity

The three chapters in part 3 focus on faculty work, academic climate and culture, and compensation. Taken together they provide a snapshot of the work environment for faculty. Why does this matter? It is increasingly important to understand the work environment for faculty because higher education in the United States has grown increasingly important to the nation's continued security, growth, and prosperity. So much so that the competitiveness and success of the US economy and society is now inextricably linked to the education attainment levels and success of students in postsecondary education. At the same time, higher education has grown increasingly complex and diverse. It stands to reason that student learning outcomes and environments across institutional settings have garnered so much attention in recent years. What is less understandable is why there has been almost no attention paid to those individuals who directly impact the learning environment for students—the faculty—or any real discussion about the working environment of the individuals who educate and support the students—faculty and staff. Chapter 7, "Faculty Work under Pressure," provides basic data on what faculty do, including the distribution of effort across the three traditional areas of faculty work: teaching, research, and service. Yet we know that these data are insufficient. Even those within higher education struggle to understand faculty work and to develop policies that can be used to equitably distribute workload across individuals and departments. Part of the reason may be that faculty work is highly individualized and the measures that we use to describe it are crude at best. Put simply: Academic work in higher education is complex.

Chapter 8, "Academic Culture and Values in Transition," looks at three traditional core values central to faculty professional identity: academic freedom, autonomy, and shared governance. Higher education is being called upon to embrace the complexity of academic work in this new era by providing flexible options for students to succeed. This creates tension within the academy. For example, students' desire to take courses online, in the evenings, and on weekends puts pressure on faculty to offer courses at times other than during the regular workday. This schedule potentially conflicts with research and service commitments requiring them to be present on-campus during the regular workday. In the absence of clear guidelines and policies designed to ensure equitable workloads among faculty, tensions may emerge. One way to look at this tension may be to identify the push and pull factors that contribute to solidarity (collegiality) versus stratification (dissension) among faculty and the extent to which the relationship between faculty and administration, broadly defined, is cooperative versus adversarial. A highly visible example of the tension is the resignation and reinstatement of the president of the University of Virginia, Theresa Sullivan, in June 2012. This case demonstrates both threats to shared governance and how shared governance can prevail. The chapter concludes with a discussion of the important role of tenure in protecting academic core values, especially academic freedom, and the tensions stoked by the new realities of higher education, which create what we refer to as "the tenure dilemma."

An economic lens provides a window into the status of the profession. The American Association of University Professors (AAUP) publishes "The Annual Report of the Economic Status of the Profession" in the March–April issue of *Academe*. Chapter 9, "Academic Compensation Trends in a New Era," draws on these data to provide an overview of recent salary trends and the changing determinants of faculty salaries, including the widening gap between institutional types and fields and the persistent unexplained wage gap between men and women. Stratification within the academic workforce is clearly identified, particularly between full-time and part-time faculty. Generally speaking, high wages and good working conditions result in a positive work environment. The role of benefits and unions is also considered, historically providing a buffer for those fields with a less strong non-academic labor market. Finally, an effort is made to contextualize faculty salary more broadly in terms of trends in median family income and comparison with compensation for the other learned professions. To be sure, it is difficult to make salary comparisons when there is not consensus around the tasks associated with the job. The greater the complexity or lack of consistency in the position, the more difficult it is to do comparisons. Wages, working conditions, and quality of life for workers in higher education and the professions are susceptible to the quest for greater efficiency and control, in metro areas in particular, as the knowledge economy becomes central to the future of the nation.

7

Faculty Work under Pressure

The nature of academic work has changed (beginning before the Great Recession of 2007–08 and gaining momentum afterward) so significantly and so rapidly that we believe the new conditions constitute a new paradigm. In this chapter we provide evidence of the confluence of pressures being put on faculty work and argue that higher education must not only embrace the complexity of academic work in this new era but also provide flexible options for faculty for them to succeed. Called into question in ways never before imagined—at least not since the time after World War II that Jencks and Riesman (1968) branded *The Academic Revolution*—is the very essence of what it means to be faculty. The core functions remain: teaching, research, and service. However, each of these functions has become more complex, more diffused, and more specialized. For example, instructional delivery now routinely extends beyond the classroom. Tools to enhance instructional design require specialized expertise. Assessment of learning outcomes has become more sophisticated and is required at more detailed levels of analysis by state agencies and disciplinary and regional accrediting bodies. Entrepreneurial faculty members succeed in institutions that embrace Slaughter and Leslie's (1999) theory of academic capitalism. Institutions are setting aside pots of money to incentivize this behavior. The University of Colorado Boulder, for example, offers CU–Boulder Campus Entrepreneurship Seed Awards. The proposal guidelines invite proposals for projects involving "entrepreneurship or a problem-solving mindset" (University of Colorado Boulder "2016–2016 CU–Boulder Campus Entrepreneurship Initiative Seed Awards Proposal Guidelines"). The stated purpose of the awards is "to inspire faculty and staff to take risks, develop new projects and to encourage entrepreneurial initiative.[1]

Additionally, the vast array of appointment types now available for pursuing an academic career exert pressure on individuals to make informed choices about the repercussions of accepting different appointment types on long-term career potential (see chapter 5 for a discussion of career progression). The pressures extend to the institution level also. "Mission creep" and "upward striving" for institutional prestige have blurred the lines between types of institutions. Calls for increased accountability to government and consumers touch all providers of postsecondary education. For-profit institutions have received intense scrutiny because of high student-loan default rates and failure to meet gainful employment standards, but not-for-profit higher education institutions are not immune from scrutiny, most especially Title IV participating institutions.[2] It takes resources to respond to requests for information and to remain in compliance with state and federal regulations, and there is growing evidence to suggest that faculty members are viewed as the primary lever for realizing "efficiencies" in a resource-strapped environment.

For example, in some cases, public and private, four-year and two-year not-for-profit institutions are augmenting revenue and offsetting budget cuts by adopting "for-profit-like" revenue-generating models of instructional delivery. "Extended university" is a common label used to describe these endeavors. In some cases these units were established to further the access mission of the institution. For example, the University of New Mexico's Extended University coordinates the institution's distance education offerings. The stated mission of UNM's Extended University is to create "statewide access to the highest quality education, made convenient and affordable through innovative pedagogies and technologies" (Dominguez 2012, 1). As the demographics of the population continue to change and demand for postsecondary education increases among nontraditional students, units established to enhance the access mission of colleges and universities may find themselves at the core of the enterprise, and budget models that incorporate this complexity are needed to ensure adequate resources are distributed throughout the university.

The recent proliferation of private for-profit institutions adds even more complexity. As previously noted (see chapter 3), the number of for-profit institutions in 1993–94 was 320. By 2011–12 the number had more than quadrupled to 1,404. These institutions operate using alternative rather than traditional staffing models and contribute to an increasingly competitive environment. The combined effect of these complexities on the core functions of colleges and universities in the United States impacts faculty work in important ways and contributes to an environment that we call faculty work under pressure.

This characterization provides a stark contrast to the one described by Susan Adams (2013) in *Forbes Magazine*. Adams, a staff writer reporting on the results of an annual ranking of best and worst jobs compiled by CareerCast, received a barrage of comments when she reported "university professor" as being high on the list of least stressful jobs. An addendum was quickly issued. Perhaps it is not so surprising, though. It is striking how little the general public understands about faculty work. Even those within higher education struggle to understand faculty work and to develop policies that can be used to equitably distribute workload across individuals and departments. Part of the reason may be that faculty work is highly individualized, and the measures that we use to describe it are crude at best. Put simply, academic work in higher education is complex. Chad Wellmon put it succinctly in an interview with *Inside Higher Ed*: "Knowledge is not just an inert object to be efficiently distributed. It is rather an activity that one engages in—and into which one is cultivated" (Jaschik 2015).

To understand faculty work today, it is necessary to assemble a patchwork narrative that draws on a variety of sources. Schuster and Finkelstein (2006) draw on available data to provide compelling evidence that academic work and careers were being restructured. To construct trend lines they combined data from multiple sources. At the time the book went to press, the US Department of Education had not yet released the 2004 National Study of Postsecondary Faculty. So we begin this chapter with an update of key trends related to faculty work, including the 2004 National Study of Postsecondary Faculty (NSOPF:04). Following this description, we turn to a review of trends available from the University of California Los Angeles (UCLA) Higher Education Research Institute (HERI) triennial Faculty Survey and a discussion of the specific context within which faculty members are experiencing pressure on their work in the contemporary academic work environment. Because of the explosion in the use and impact of technology, especially the outsourcing phenomenon and massive open online courses (MOOCs), we devote special attention to this topic as it relates to faculty work. Next, we endeavor to describe the current work environment from the perspective of faculty members themselves, using attitudinal and perception data from the Collaborative on Academic Careers in Higher Education (COACHE) Tenure-Track Faculty Job Satisfaction Survey and the COACHE Faculty Job Satisfaction Survey. Finally, we conclude the chapter with an interpretive comment on pressures on faculty work, including a discussion of three career stress points that roughly coincide with career stages described in chapters 4–6.

Schuster and Finkelstein (2006, 75) posed a question: "Has faculty work—what faculty members actually do on the job—changed substantially, or perhaps just at the edges, during the past three decades?" Their answer, presented over the ensuing pages, was that faculty work effort (measured in average hours worked per week reported by individual faculty members) increased about 20% over the period studied (approximately late sixties through the late nineties) and that there were modest shifts in preference for research over teaching. "The largest aggregate proportionate shifts in preference from teaching to research" were found among underrepresented groups in the academy, namely women and African American faculty members (Schuster and Finkelstein 2006, 89). In actual allocation of effort, too, there was a decline in the percentage of time spent on teaching between 1984 and 1997, but then the percentage "rose again in the mid-1990s to approach former levels" (89). The increase in faculty work effort devoted to research was not directly attributable to a decrease in time spent on teaching. Furthermore, women reported spending more time on teaching than men, regardless of type of institution. This is especially interesting given the increase in preference for research among women. Indeed, the ratio of teaching to research effort for full-time female faculty in the fall of 1998 looked very similar to that of males (91). If the increased research effort did not come at the expense of teaching, then from where had it come? "To the extent that both teaching and research pressures have increased, the resolution of those forces has apparently been achieved via a combination of decreased time allocated to administration and a greater aggregated volume of work effort" (97).

In terms of publication productivity, patterns clearly showed an increase in publication activity for new faculty (from first through sixth years). The proportion of those not publishing decreased from about one-half to one-third of the faculty. The authors concluded, "Not only are more faculty publishing, but more faculty are publishing *more*" (103). Finally, they draw attention to "two key external developments that promised to reshape the faculty role to an extent not seen since the emergence of graduate education in the nineteenth century or the birth of Big Science during and after World War II:

—Ubiquitous computing capability (24/7 availability via PC or laptop) for communication and access to information, and

—the Internet as a source of global content accessible to anyone.

These developments together change the relationship between faculty and learners and promise to recast the role of college faculty as experts and gatekeepers—the great addition to academic work in the twentieth century (107).

Yet in spite of the positive change made possible by these IT developments, the authors foresaw that the breakthroughs in technology would lead to more delineation of roles and specialization. For example, we have seen the emergence of new kinds of professionals (e.g., instructional designers and facilitators, or "coaches" for online courses).

We turn now to the question, what has happened since?

Key Trends

Table 7.1 shows that the trend of increasing faculty work effort (measured in average hours worked per week within the faculty member's home institution) has continued, although the rate of change has slowed. Faculty members reported working, on average, forty-nine hours per week in the fall of 2003. Faculty in research universities reported working the most (fifty-one hours per week).

Evidence suggests the additional hours spent working per week is a result of effort spent on research activities, except in two-year colleges. Table 7.2 shows the ratio of high to low teaching loads among full-time faculty from 1988 to 2004. High teaching loads are defined as greater than or equal to nine hours per week. Low teaching loads are defined as six hours or less per week. While the ratio did increase in other four-year institutions over the period, this ratio has not changed in universities in more than thirty years (Schuster and Finkelstein 2006). There has been a great deal of change in two-year colleges,

Table 7.1 Weekly hours full-time faculty worked inside home institution by institution type, 1988–2004

	1988	1993	1999	2004
Mean total hours worked in institution (all faculty)	46.4	47.1	48.6	49.2
Institutional type				
Universities	50.2	50.6	50.6	51.1
Other four-year institutions	45.6	46.8	48.3	48.8
Two-year colleges	40.0	41.8	45.1	46.5

Sources: NSOPF:88, NSOPF:93, NSOPF:99, NSoPF:04. (Refer to appendix A for key.)

Table 7.2 Ratio of high to low teaching loads among full-time faculty, by gender and institution type, 1988–2004

	1988	1993	1999	2004	Difference 1988–2004
All faculty	1.7	1.8	2.0	1.8	0.1
Gender					
Female	2.2	2.2	2.5	2.2	0.0
Male	1.5	1.6	1.8	1.6	0.1
Institutional type					
Universities	0.6	0.5	0.7	0.6	0.0
Other four-year institutions	3.6	3.6	3.9	3.7	0.1
Two-year colleges	8.1	7.6	11.9	11.3	3.2
Institution type					
Universities	0.6	0.5	0.7	0.6	0.0
Female	0.9	0.7	0.8	0.8	−0.1
Male	0.5	0.4	0.6	0.6	0.1
Other four-year institutions	3.6	3.6	3.9	3.7	0.1
Female	3.1	3.1	3.8	3.4	0.3
Male	3.7	3.9	4.0	3.9	0.2
Two-year colleges	8.1	7.6	11.9	11.3	3.2
Female	6.0	5.8	7.8	8.3	2.3
Male	0.1	9.7	21.7	15.8	15.7

Sources: NSOPF:88, NSOPF:93, NSOPF:99, NSOPF:04. (Refer to appendix A for key.)

Note: High teaching load or more credit hours a week; low teaching load 6 or fewer credit hours a week.

however. The ratio of high to low teaching loads in two-year colleges increased from 8.1 to 11.3 between 1988 and 2004. Most of the change was attributable to the teaching load of men. In 2004 the ratio in two-year colleges was 15.8 for men and 8.3 for women. Faculty members often receive additional compensation for teaching courses above the number considered to be the regular teaching load. These data raise questions about equitable access to additional teaching opportunities for men and women.

Table 7.3 displays research and publication activity of full-time faculty. The downward trend in the percentage of faculty with no publications also continued. In the fall of 2003, 32% of full-time faculty reported having no publications. This is a marked decrease from the fall of 1987, when more than one-half of full-time faculty (54.7%) reported having no publications in the previous two years, and a slight decrease from the fall of 1998, when one-third (33%) reported having no publications.

Table 7.3 Percentage distribution of full-time faculty research and publication activity by institution type, 1988–2004

	1988	1993	1999	2004
All faculty				
No publications in past two years	54.7	40.4	33.4	32.0
Five or more publications in past two years	14.2	12.7	22.5	21.6
Engaged in funded research in past two years	21.9	27.4	33.9	31.8
No publications in past two years				
Universities	29.1	21.0	14.0	14.8
Other four-year institutions	64.4	40.1	35.1	33.3
Two-year colleges	91.8	73.4	69.1	66.6
Five or more publications in past two years				
Universities	28.6	26.4	40.9	33.8
Other four-year institutions	4.5	5.5	3.5	16.1
Two-year colleges	0.9	1.2	3.3	5.0
Engaged in funded research in past two years				
Universities	37.9	49.3	52.4	47.2
Other four-year institutions	12.4	18.2	26.3	26.0
Two-year colleges	6.1	5.7	13.6	8.8

Sources: NSOPF:88, NSOPF:93, NSOPF:99, NSOPF:04. (Refer to appendix A for key.)

Also noteworthy is the decline in the percentage of full-time faculty engaged in funded research in the previous two years in universities, where the expectation for engaging in funded research is great. In the fall of 2003, 47% of full-time faculty in universities reported having engaged in funded research in the previous two years. In the fall of 1998, that portion was 52%. In contrast, the percentage of faculty members engaged in funded research in other types of institutions increased during that five-year span: for other four-year institutions from 23% to 26%, and in two-year colleges from 5% to 9%. The marked decline in the availability of research funding and the increased competition for scarce dollars to support it are certainly contributing to the environment we refer to as faculty work under pressure.

Faculty Work Post–Great Recession

Since the NSOPF has not been conducted since fall 2003, we endeavor to describe what has been happening with regard to faculty work since the Great Recession, using other sources. The Higher Education Research Institute conducts a triennial faculty survey, which differs from the NSOPF in a number of ways. The HERI Faculty Survey is designed to provide institutions with information, including an institutional profile report and benchmark data (comparisons with other similar institutions), rather than to provide general access to information for research purposes. The HERI Faculty Survey is not based on a systematically drawn sample; rather, institutions elect to participate in the survey and pay a fee for participation. Nonetheless, a large number of institutions (about 1,100) have participated in the survey since its inception in 1989, and the descriptive data compiled from these surveys provide valuable information about key aspects of the faculty experience. While not directly comparable to data collected through NSOPF, staff members at the Higher Education Research Institute have taken steps to ensure that estimates approximate the faculty population.[3]

Figures 7.1 to 7.12 and appendix E tables A-7.1 through A-7.6 show summary data on selected work activity items derived from the publicly available HERI Faculty Survey reports for full-time undergraduate faculty at American colleges and universities (Eagan et al. 2014). The HERI reports focus on teaching, research activities, and professional development as well as issues related to job satisfaction and stress.

Figure 7.1 shows hours per week that faculty in baccalaureate institutions spent on scheduled teaching. In 2013–14, 55% of faculty in baccalaureate institutions reported spending less than nine hours per week on scheduled teaching, 30% reported spending nine to twelve hours per week, and 15% reported spending more than twelve hours per week. There has been a marked increase in the percentage of faculty in baccalaureate institutions reporting spending less than nine hours per week on scheduled teaching since 1989–90 (from 41% to 55 %).

In all types of institutions except private four-year colleges, a higher percentage of women than men reported more than twelve hours of scheduled teaching per week (see appendix E, table A-7.1). Furthermore, this pattern has been consistent throughout the life of the survey. Figure 7.2 shows that the pattern for men and women faculty in all baccalaureate institutions is similar, although a higher percentage of male faculty than female faculty reported spending less than nine hours on scheduled teaching per week; and a correspondingly higher percentage of female faculty than male faculty reported spending more than twelve hours on scheduled teaching per week.

As might be expected, the percentage of men and women who reported more than twelve hours of scheduled teaching per week was lower in the universities—public and private—than in all baccalaureate institutions. Looked at another

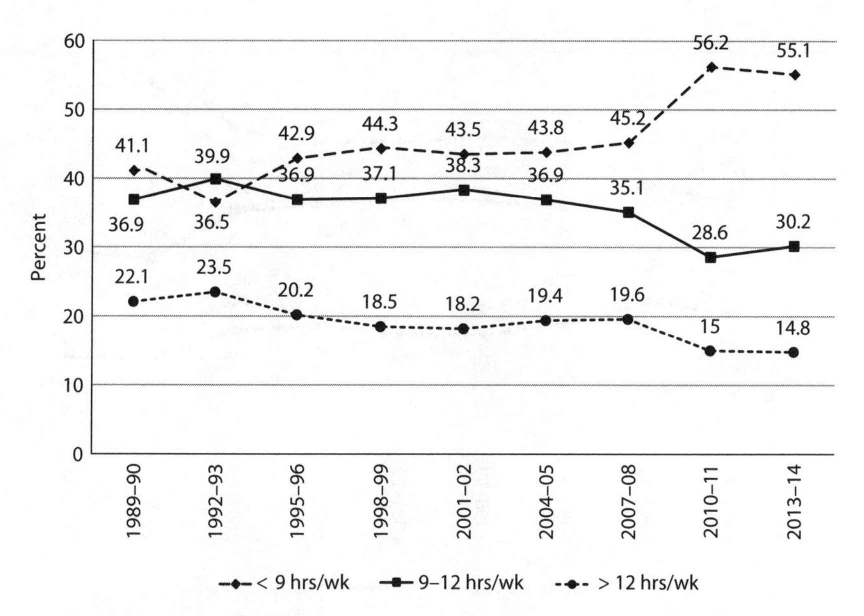

Figure 7.1 Hours per week spent on scheduled teaching in baccalaureate institutions, 1989–2014. *Sources:* HERI:89; HERI:92; HERI:95; HERI:98; HERI:01; HERI:04; HERI:07; HERI:10; HERI:13. (Refer to appendix A for key to data sources.)

---

way, male faculty were more likely than female faculty to report less than nine hours of scheduled teaching per week across the board in all baccalaureate institutions, public universities, and private universities participating in the HERI Faculty Survey between 1989–90 and 2013–14 (see appendix E, table A-7.1).

However, patterns are more difficult to discern in participating public and private four-year colleges. Generally speaking, the pattern holds for men and women spending more than twelve hours of scheduled teaching per week in public four-year colleges, though notably in 2013–14 there was no discernable difference between men and women faculty reporting this level of scheduled teaching activity (23.0% and 22.2%, respectively). There also was no discernable difference in the percentage of male and female faculty reporting less than nine hours of scheduled teaching per week in public four-year colleges in 2013–14. The lack of difference may be a result of many public institutions establishing workload policies that govern instructional load. Overall, the general trend in private four-year colleges has been toward lighter teaching

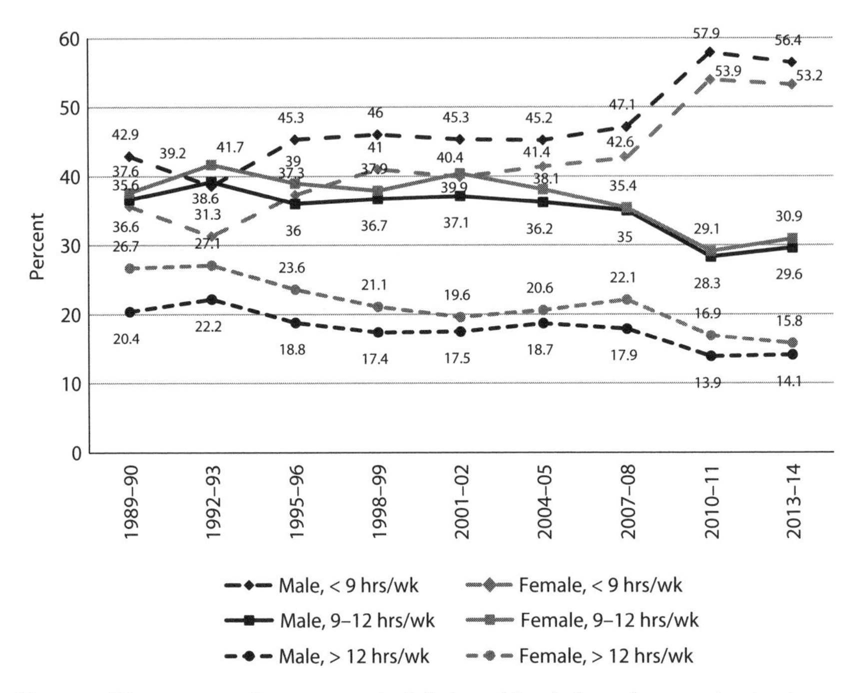

Figure 7.2 Hours per week spent on scheduled teaching in baccalaureate institutions, by gender, 1989–2014. *Sources:* HERI:89; HERI:92; HERI:95; HERI:98; HERI:01; HERI:04; HERI:07; HERI:10; HERI:13. (Refer to appendix A for key to data sources.)

---

loads for all faculty members. This has not been the case in other types of institutions (see appendix E, table A-7.1).

Anyone who has taught a higher education course knows that hours spent on scheduled teaching, or in the classroom, tells only part of the story. Figure 7.3 shows the hours per week spent by faculty in baccalaureate institutions on preparing for teaching. Findings are consistent with patterns for time spent on scheduled teaching. Overall, faculty members reported spending less time preparing for teaching in 2013–14 than they had in 1989–90.

Figure 7.4 shows that the percentage of men and women faculty in all baccalaureate institutions who reported spending more than twelve hours per week preparing for teaching has declined from 41.7% for men and 48.3% for women in 1989–90 to 30.8% for men and 39.2% for women in 2013–14. This is an area where efficiencies gained from technology may have been realized, but in the absence of additional data there is no way to know for sure.

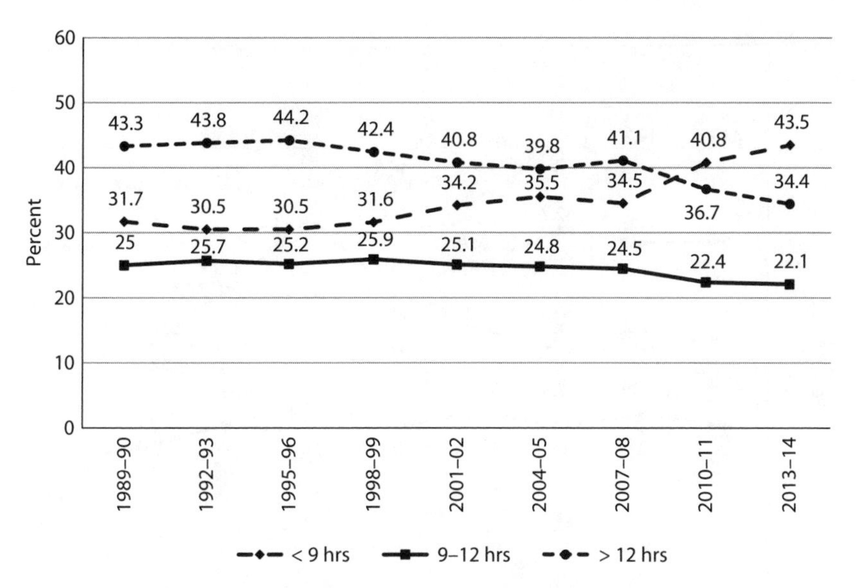

Figure 7.3 Hours per week spent on preparing for teaching in baccalaureate institutions, 1989–2014. *Sources:* HERI:89; HERI:92; HERI:95; HERI:98; HERI:01; HERI:04; HERI:07; HERI:10; HERI:13. (Refer to appendix A for key to data sources.)

In public and private universities, the change has been even more dramatic. The percentage of men and women faculty in public universities who reported spending more than twelve hours per week preparing for teaching in 1989–90 declined from 35.6% for men and 42.9% for women to 22.9% for men and 29.6% for women in 2013–14 (see appendix E, table A-7.2). In private universities the percentage of men and women who reported spending more than twelve hours per week preparing for teaching declined from 32.5% for men and 50.2% for women in 1989–90 to 27.7% for men and 31.5% for women in 2013–14 (see appendix E, table A-7.2). Still, the gap between men and women has persisted over time. Only in private universities has the gap narrowed substantially; and in public and private four-year colleges the gap has actually increased. The percentage of men and women faculty in public four-year colleges who reported spending more than twelve hours per week preparing for teaching declined for men between 1989–90 and 2013–14 from 44.5% to 39.7%, while it increased for women (from 47.5% to 48.4%, respectively). The gap between men and women increased from three to nine percentage points. The percentage of men and women faculty in private four-year colleges who reported spending more than

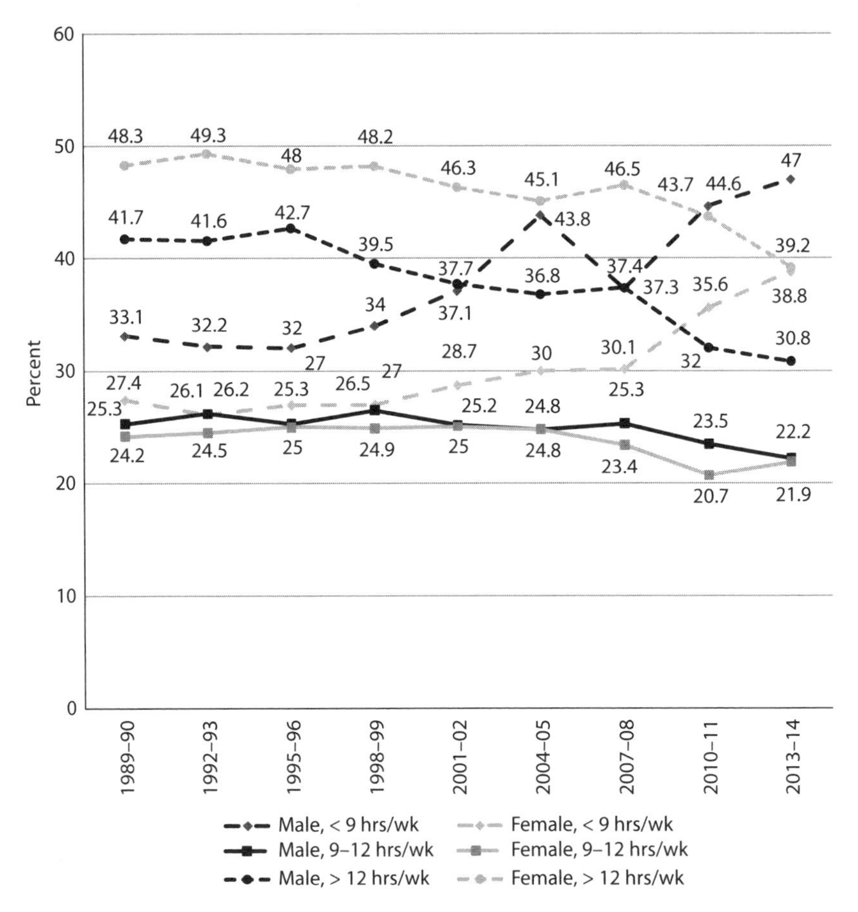

Figure 7.4 Hours per week spent on preparing for teaching in baccalaureate institutions, by gender, 1989–2014. *Sources:* HERI:89; HERI:92; HERI:95; HERI:98; HERI:01; HERI:04; HERI:07; HERI:10; HERI:13. (Refer to appendix A for key to data sources.)

---

twelve hours per week preparing for teaching declined from 52.7% for men and 54.3% for women in 1989–90 to 41.4% for men and 50.7% for women in 2013–14. The gap between men and women increased over the period from two to nine percentage points (see appendix E, table A-7.2).

Another measure of teaching—time spent outside of the classroom advising or counseling students—provides additional information about how faculty members spend their time. Figure 7.5 shows the hours faculty in baccalaureate institutions spent per week advising or counseling students. The patterns have

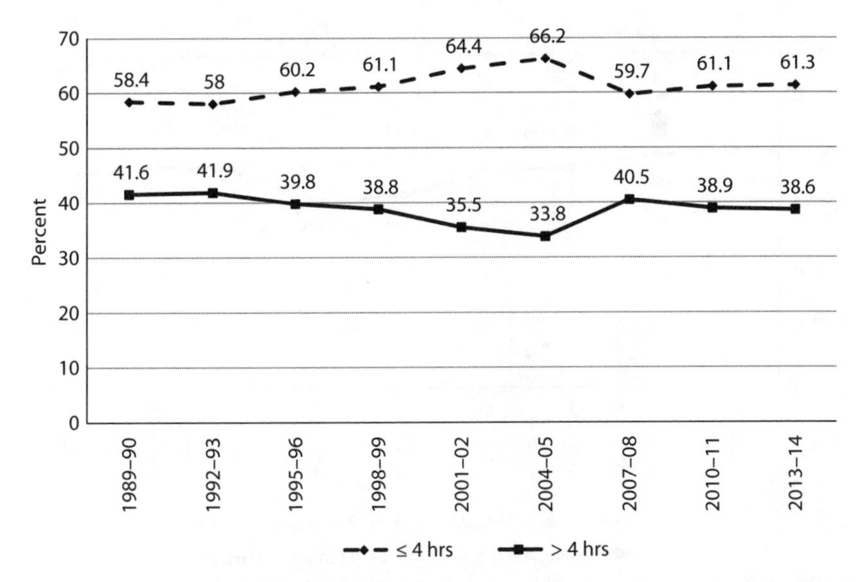

Figure 7.5 Hours per week spent on advising and counseling students in baccalaureate institutions, 1989–2014. *Sources:* HERI:89; HERI:92; HERI:95; HERI:98; HERI:01; HERI:04; HERI:07; HERI:10; HERI:13. (Refer to appendix A for key to data sources.)

---

been remarkably consistent over time. Approximately 60% of faculty members in baccalaureate institutions report spending four hours or less advising or counseling students, while about 40% report spending more than four hours on this activity.

Figure 7.6 displays data derived from the HERI reports on hours per week spent on advising or counseling students by gender. Higher percentages of men than women reported spending four hours or less per week advising or counseling students, and higher percentages of women than men reported spending more than four hours per week on this activity.

Taken together, figures 7.1 to 7.6 show that women faculty members still spend more time teaching and on teaching-related activities than male faculty members do, in terms of scheduled time, preparation, and advising or counseling students, and that they do so in all types of institutions with the possible exception of private four-year colleges.

Figure 7.7 displays hours per week spent on research and scholarly writing. There has been an increase in the percentage of faculty in baccalaureate

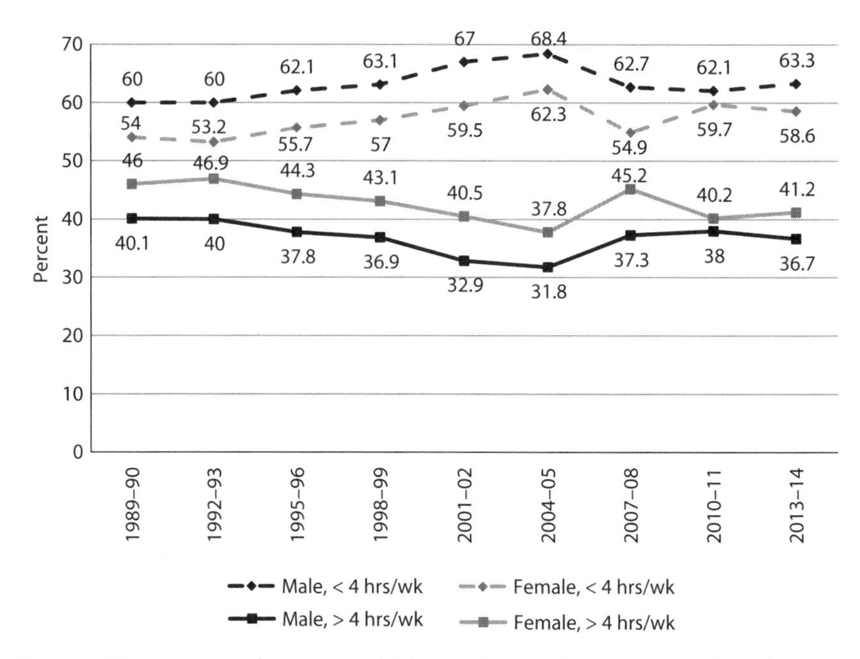

Figure 7.6 Hours per week spent on advising and counseling students in baccalaureate institutions, by gender, 1989–2014. *Sources:* HERI:89; HERI:92; HERI:95; HERI:98; HERI:01; HERI:04; HERI:07; HERI:10; HERI:13. (Refer to appendix A for key to data sources.)

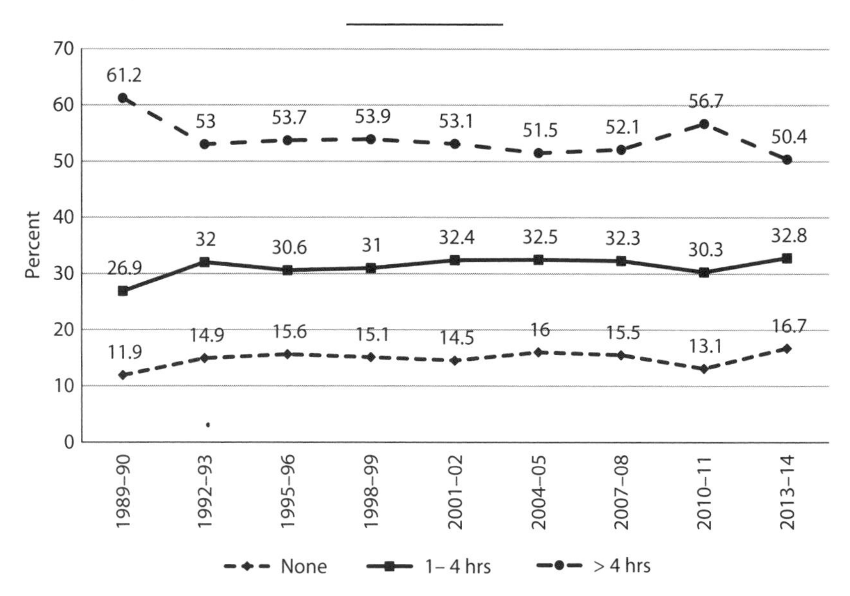

Figure 7.7 Hours per week spent on research and scholarly writing in baccalaureate institutions, 1989–2014. *Sources:* HERI:89; HERI:92; HERI:95; HERI:98; HERI:01; HERI:04; HERI:07; HERI:10; HERI:13. (Refer to appendix A for key to data sources.)

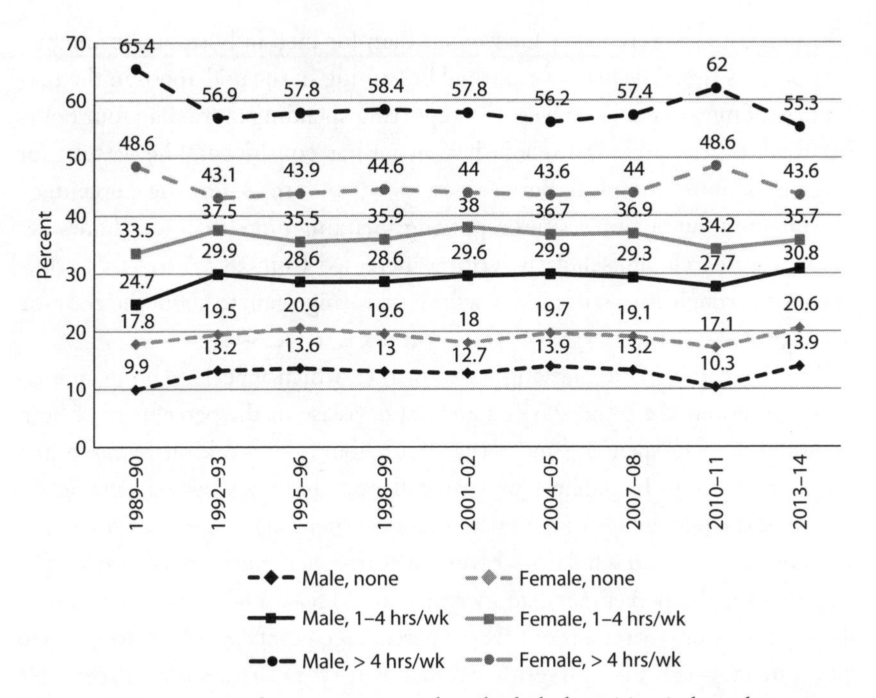

Figure 7.8 Hours per week spent on research and scholarly writing in baccalaureate institutions, by gender, 1989–2014. *Sources:* HERI:89; HERI:92; HERI:95; HERI:98; HERI:01; HERI:04; HERI:07; HERI:10; HERI:13. (Refer to appendix A for key to data sources.)

---

institutions reporting spending no time on research and scholarly writing (11.9% in 1989–90 to 16.7% in 2013–14); and a decline in the percentage of faculty in these institutions reporting spending more than four hours on this activity per week (61.2% in 1989–90 to 50.4% in 2013–14).

In 2013–14, about one-third of men (30.8%) and women (35.7%) reported spending one to four hours per week on research and scholarly writing (see figure 7.8). More than half of men (55.3%) reported spending more than four hours per week on research and scholarly writing, while 43.6% of women reported doing so (see figure 7.8).

In public and private universities, where research is an important part of the mission of the institution, high percentages of men (66.4% in public universities and 69.5% in private universities) and women (56.8% in public universities and 57.7% in private universities) reported spending more than four hours per week on research and scholarly writing (see appendix E, table A-7.4).

The percentages were lower for women than for men in both public and private universities. The downward trend beginning in the mid-1990s in the percentage of men in public universities reporting spending more than four hours per week on research and scholarly writing has continued. The pattern for women is more complex. Between 1992–93 and 1998–99, the percentage of women in public universities reporting spending more than four hours per week on research and scholarly writing increased from 58.5% to 63.2%, then declined through 2010–11 (54.6%) before increasing again to about the 2001–02 level (58.4%) in 2013–14 (56.8%) (see appendix E, table A-7.4).

In private universities, leaving aside 2010–11, which appears to be an anomalous data point, the trend shows a general decrease in the percentage of both men and women spending more than four hours per week on research and scholarly writing. In public four-year colleges, there has been a notable increase in the percentage of men who reported spending one to four hours per week on research and scholarly writing. In 2007–08, the percentage was 34.5%. By 2013–14, the percentage had increased to 44.4%. The change for women during the same period was only three percentage points (41.7% in 2007–08 to 45.3% in 2013–14). The end result was that in 2013–14 there was no discernable difference in the percentage of men and women in public four-year colleges who spent one to four hours per week on research and scholarly writing. On the other hand, in private four-year colleges, the gap between men and women spending more than four hours per week on research and scholarly writing in 2013–14 was eight percentage points. The trend line for change over time in the percentage reporting that they spent one to four hours per week on research and scholarly writing followed approximately the same pattern for men and women, and the gap between men and women remained steady at about three percentage points. Taken together, these data suggest faculty members are engaging in scholarship more frequently in all types of four-year institutions and that patterns of difference are changing in some contexts but not in others (see appendix E, table A-7.4).

In sum, faculty work effort (measured in average hours worked per week reported by individual faculty members) has not changed much since the late 1990s, and for the most part the gaps between men and women in time spent on various activities have not diminished. The available data are insufficient to discern contextual differences in faculty work and shed little if any light on the new realities of faculty work. What is discernable is that there has been a blurring of lines between institutional types. Higher percentages of faculty members in institutions other than universities are spending more hours per week on activities related to research, while faculty in universities are spending more time on activities related to teaching, especially in public universities. Women continued to report spending more time on teaching than men. Increased effort on both teaching and research has continued. The trend toward decreased time allocated to administration also continued. In addition, faculty reported spending fewer hours per week preparing for classes and counseling and advising students. This latter trend could suggest greater efficiencies realized through technological advances and more specialization. The fastest-growing occupational category in higher education has been "other professionals," including, among others, student affairs professionals, many of whom provide student advising. On the other hand, caution should be taken to ensure that quality is not being sacrificed as faculty members spread their time ever more thinly.

Service

Up to this point in the chapter we have focused on two of the primary functional responsibilities of the faculty: teaching and research. In the next section, we turn to a specific functional responsibility that is fundamental to faculty identity: service. Service is a complex construct to disentangle because it encompasses many facets of a faculty member's role and the specific activities that are counted as service vary in different contexts. At one end of the continuum is service to the community, or public service. Also included is service to the profession, which can include anything from serving as a reviewer for a refereed journal to providing pro bono tax-accounting support to low-income members of the community. At the other end of the spectrum is service to the institution, which includes the day-to-day operations necessary to administer the curriculum as well as engaging in decision making processes, adhering to the culture of the institution with respect to shared governance. A more extensive treatment of the latter construct—the faculty role in shared governance—is provided in chapter 8. For now, we turn to a review of available evidence about faculty members' work related to service.

Figure 7.9 shows that there has been an increase in the time faculty in baccalaureate institutions report spending on committee work and meetings between 1989–90 and 2013–14. More than one-third (37.1%) of faculty in baccalaureate institutions reported spending more than four hours per week on this activity in 2013–14, an increase from 28.8% in 1989–90. The percentage

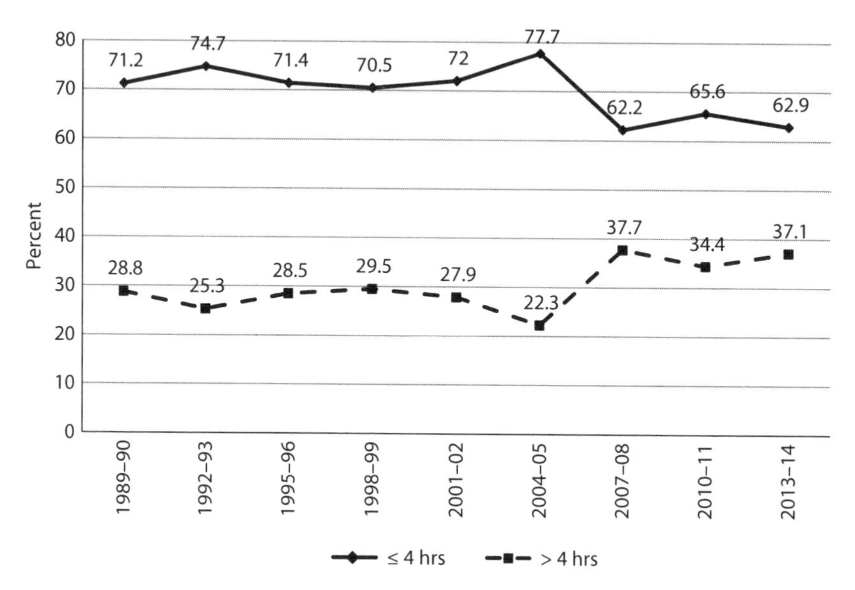

Figure 7.9 Hours per week spent on committee work and meetings in baccalaureate institutions, 1989–2014. *Sources:* HERI:89; HERI:92; HERI:95; HERI:98; HERI:01; HERI:04; HERI:07; HERI:10; HERI:13. (Refer to appendix A for key to data sources.)

---

of faculty reporting spending four hours or less on committee work and meetings declined from 71.2% in 1989–90 to 62.9% in 2013–14.

Forty percent of women in all baccalaureate institutions participating in the survey in 2013–14 reported spending more than four hours per week on committee work and meeting. This was a higher percentage than for men (34.8%) (figure 7.10).

This general pattern held across institutional types; however, the magnitude of the difference between men and women reporting this level of effort varied from two percentage points in public universities to ten percentage points in public four-year colleges, a striking difference (see appendix E, table A-7.5).

Figure 7.11 displays trends in responses about time spent on community and public service from 1992–93 to 2013–14 for all faculty members in baccalaureate institutions.[4] Overall, the trend has been to spend less time on community and public service. In 2013–14, about 40% (42.8%) reported spending no time on this activity compared with about 30% (32.2%) in 1992–93.

Figure 7.12 shows that in general, the trend to spend less time on community and public service held for both men and women. In 2013–14, less than

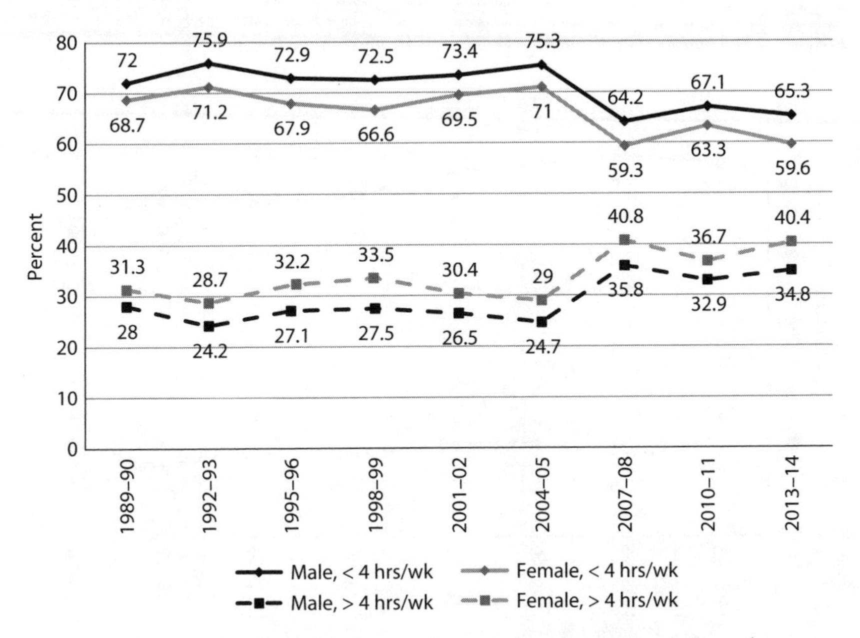

Figure 7.10 Hours per week spent on committee work and meetings in baccalaureate institutions, by gender, 1989–2014. *Sources:* HERI:89; HERI:92; HERI:95; HERI:98; HERI:01; HERI:04; HERI:07; HERI:10; HERI:13. (Refer to appendix A for key to data sources.)

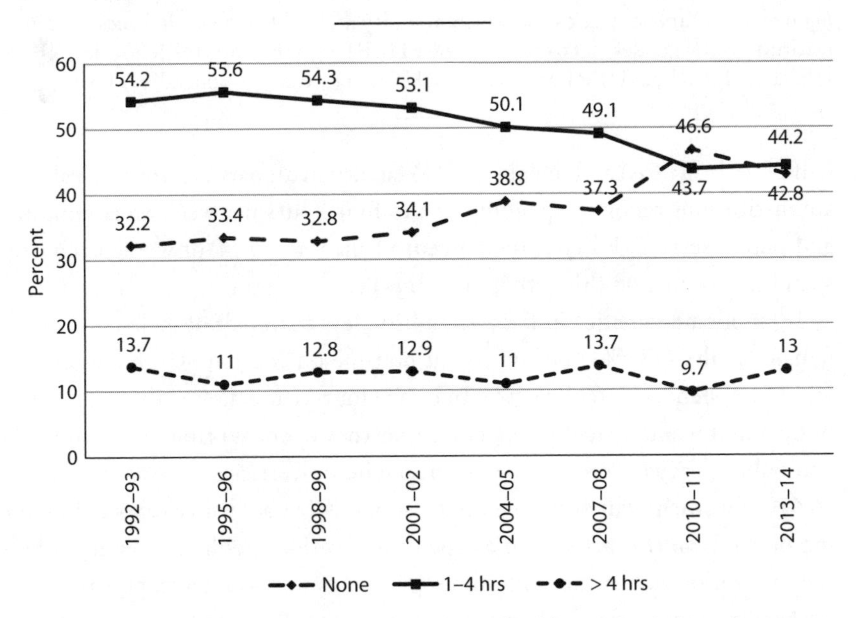

Figure 7.11 Hours per week spent on community and public service in baccalaureate institutions, 1989–2014. *Sources:* HERI:89; HERI:92; HERI:95; HERI:98; HERI:01; HERI:04; HERI:07; HERI:10; HERI:13. (Refer to appendix A for key to data sources.)

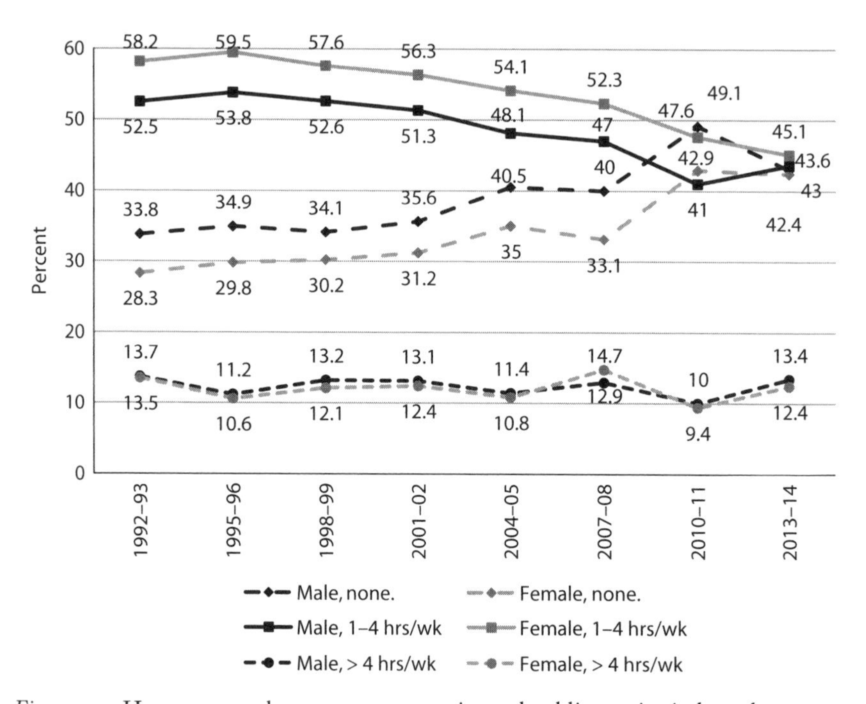

Figure 7.12 Hours per week spent on community and public service in baccalaureate institutions, by gender, 1989–2014. *Sources:* HERI:89; HERI:92; HERI:95; HERI:98; HERI:01; HERI:04; HERI:07; HERI:10; HERI:13. (Refer to appendix A for key.)

---

half of male (43.6%) and female (45.1%) faculty in all participating baccalaureate institutions reported spending one to four hours per week on community and public service. Forty-three percent of men and 42% of women reported spending no time on this activity in 2013–14.

In public universities in 2013–14, a little less than half of male (47.8%) and female faculty (48.0%) said they spent no time on community and public service (see appendix E, table A-7.6). In public four-year colleges, the percentages of men and women faculty reporting that they spent no time on community and public service were lower than in public universities (34.6% of men and 36.6% of women), but even so more than one-third of faculty reported spending no time on this activity in a type of institution (public university) where the mission of the institution would suggest this was an important expectation for faculty work. In fact, the percentage of male (47.8%) and female (48.0%) faculty who reported spending no time on community and public service in public universities in 2013–14 was higher than in private universities (43.4% for men and 46.3% for women, respectively). The gap between men and women faculty reporting spending no time on community and public service was the greatest in private four-year colleges—four percentage points (see appendix E, table A-7.6).

In all, trends in the amount of time faculty spend on the three traditional areas of faculty work—teaching, research, and service—provide one lens through which to view the current environment for faculty work. There is little doubt that technology has had an impact on faculty work. In the next section we devote special attention to the role advances in technology has played in faculty work, particularly since Schuster and Finkelstein's 2006 assertions. To what extent do these assertions ring true today?

Distance Education

The desire to "take education to the people" and the recognition that many potential students could not, or would not, leave home to study in residence at a college or university led early pioneers in distance education to develop correspondence courses. Chautauqua College of Liberal Arts in western New York was the first institution to confer academic degrees to students who completed their coursework entirely through correspondence courses. The year was 1883 (Schlosser and Simonson 2006). Although considered a legitimate form of instructional delivery, little innovation occurred in delivery modes of distance education until the 1980s, when instructional television (ITV) made its debut. Instructional television has many similarities to modern twenty-first-century massive open online courses (MOOCs)—prominently, there is a visual component. "With ITV, professors could broadcast their lectures to their students via cable channels, public broadcasting or satellite links. In addition to viewing the broadcast, some instructors would allow their students to call them during a live broadcast to ask questions" (Reisslein, Seeling, and Reisslein 2005, 26).

Fast forward to today. In spite of all of the technological advances, in fall 2003 less than 10% of all faculty and instructional staff reported teaching any distance education courses (data not shown in tables). Table 7.4 provides basic information for faculty with at least some instructional duties related to credit courses or activities, by the number of distance education courses taught. The vast majority (93%) of faculty with at least some instructional duties related to credit courses or activities reported teaching no distance education courses. Of those who did report teaching distance education courses, the most common number of courses taught was one.

Table 7.4 Percentage distribution of distance education classes taught by full-time and part-time faculty, by gender, race/ethnicity, and academic field, Fall 2003

	All faculty			Full-time faculty			Part-time faculty		
Number of distance education classes taught	No classes	One class	More than one class	No classes	One class	More than one class	No classes	One class	More than one class
Total	92.8	4.4	2.8	91.7	5.2	3.1	94.1	3.4	2.4
Gender									
Male	93.3	4.2	2.5	92.6	4.7	2.7	94.3	3.4	2.3
Female	92.1	4.7	3.2	90.4	5.8	3.7	93.9	3.5	2.6
Race/ethnicity recoded									
American Indian or Alaska Native	89.4	4.7	5.9	87.3	5.2[a]	7.5	91.5	4.2[a]	4.3[b]
Asian or Pacific Islander	94.5	3.6	1.9	94.4	3.6	2.0	94.5	3.6[a]	1.9[a]
Black or African American non-Hispanic	93.5	4.0	2.4	92.8	4.8	2.4	94.5	3.0	2.5[a]
Hispanic White or Hispanic Black	92.2	4.6	3.2	90.4	6.2	3.4	94.7	2.4	2.9[b]
White non-Hispanic	92.7	4.5	2.8	91.5	5.3	3.2	94.1	3.5	2.4
Age									
Under 35	93.9	3.5	2.6	93.9	3.4	2.6	94.0	3.5	2.5
35–44	93.2	3.9	3.0	92.7	4.4	2.9	93.8	3.1	3.1

45–54	92.5	4.8	2.7	91.2	5.6	3.2	94.3	3.6	2.1
55–64	92.2	4.9	2.9	90.4	6.1	3.5	95.0	3.0	2.0
65–70	94.5	3.7	1.8	94.3	3.4	2.2[a]	94.6	3.9[a]	1.4[a]
71 or above	90.2	5.5	4.2[a]	93.4	5.1[a]	1.4[b]	88.9	5.7	5.4[a]
Principal field of teaching, vocational included									
No principal teaching field[c]	—	—	—	—	—	—	—	—	—
Business, law, and communications	90.8	5.4	3.8	88.5	7.0	4.6	93.1	3.9	3.1
Health sciences	91.2	5.7	3.1	90.8	6.1	3.2	91.8	5.2	3.0
Humanities	93.7	4.2	2.2	92.8	4.5	2.7	94.7	3.8	1.5
Natural sciences and engineering	93.8	3.9	2.3	92.8	4.5	2.7	95.6	2.9	1.5
Social sciences and education	91.5	5.0	3.6	90.4	6.0	3.6	92.8	3.7	3.5
Occupationally specific programs	93.7	4.0	2.4	91.8	5.6	2.6	95.2	2.6	2.2[a]
All other programs	94.8	2.9	2.3	93.9	3.6	2.4	95.7	2.1	2.1

Source: NSOPF:04. (Refer to appendix A for key.)

[a]Interpret data with caution. Estimate is unstable because the standard error represents more than 30 percent of the estimate.

[b]Interpret data with caution. Estimate is unstable because the standard error represents more than 50 percent of the estimate.

[c]Reporting standards not met.

Men and women were just as likely to teach distance education courses. A higher percentage of American Indian/Alaska Native faculty reported teaching at least one class at a distance than faculty from other racial ethnic groups (Black/African American, non-Hispanic, and White). The data do not support assertions that older faculty members are less receptive to teaching distance education courses. Six percent of the oldest faculty (aged seventy-one or above) reported teaching at least one distance education course. There also were differences across academic fields. Faculty members in business, law, and communications and in health sciences were more engaged in distance education than faculty in the humanities or in the natural sciences and engineering.

Massive Open Online Courses

Much has changed in the world of technology since the fall of 1993, however. As has been pointed out repeatedly in this volume, the lack of national data on faculty to inform our understanding of the postsecondary teaching and learning environment makes it difficult to determine the impact of innovations made possible because of technological advances. In an attempt to fill this void, we focus on MOOCs as one example of the wider impact of distance education and technology on faculty work. An interesting point to begin: as MOOCs were initially conceptualized by faculty, the goal was to expand access by providing free versions of courses via the Internet. They debuted in 2008 but began to gain popularity in 2012. The term was born out of a brainstorming online Skype chat conversation between Dave Cormier and George Siemens, the co-instructors for Connectivism and Connective Knowledge (also known as CCK08), attributed as the first MOOC. Now, several years later, both the higher education and more generalized media are still replete with accolades about the bright future promised by these kinds of technological breakthroughs, as well as lamentations citing the supposed undermining and depreciation of face-to-face traditional education. What have we learned over these past several years? What are the implications for higher education and for faculty? The answer to such questions at this juncture is inescapably fluid, preliminary, and premature, for the MOOC phenomenon is still in its infancy. The range of possible scenarios pertaining to the role of MOOCs (or related interventions) in the short term, not to mention in the longer run, is essentially limitless. Given that threshold precaution, we nonetheless venture a few interim propositions.

First, MOOCs are, of course, one expression of technology's effect on the teaching-learning experience. MOOC-abetted pedagogy is a form of, and a natural outgrowth or extension of, processes long in play. In a more generic pedagogical sense, MOOCs and related pedagogies are but a newish expression of long-established trends in distance learning.

Second, the MOOC phenomenon has shown, from its onset, that despite its rich ancestry, it nevertheless has revolutionary potential. It is the distinctiveness of MOOCs, among the profusion of technological innovations, that has commanded such disproportionate attention. The "revolution" inheres in the prospect that low- to minimal-cost higher education content can be distributed on a scale unprecedented (leaving aside, for the moment, the earlier revolutionary properties of content being delivered by radio and, of course, subsequently by television and, more recently, via the computer and the Internet). Despite such obvious precedents, the potential for disrupting business-as-usual education is manifest.

Third is the embryonic nature of the MOOC phenomenon—and this aspect is crucial. The experience to date clearly is in its earliest, highly experimental stage: basic, crude, dynamic, and unformed. As the experiment unfolds, as more is learned about what works well and what works less well, the efficacy of the teaching-learning process will inevitably improve. Given the onrush of unending technological waves, who can say how primitive the current state of the art will be judged, a mere five years hence, much less a decade or two from now? Meanwhile, explorations to assess differences in actual student outcomes linked to such pedagogies are beginning to emerge as study designs that take into account control and intervention groups are examined.

A fourth aspect is inextricably linked to the third, namely, the movement toward a workable business model or, more likely, models. In this early-on highly experimental stage, with just the beginnings of research under way to gauge effects, institutions of higher education and MOOC organizers and providers (such as Coursera, edX, and Udacity, to name three prominent players) alike are working out, and learning from, the malleable financial arrangements. And for the colleges and universities that are already collaborating with the platform providers, the effects of such campus involvement on various aspects of the campus itself, from decisions about what courses to offer via MOOCs to sorting out the consequent recalibrated status of participating faculty and the comparable role of regular faculty are just beginning to be evaluated. There are economic consequences for both involved and uninvolved campus faculty and important considerations for the institution's assessment of how its brand may be affected by, for example, becoming more or less universally accessible to all comers, the rigor and quality of its course and program offerings, and so on. Numerous variables will be shaping an institution's decisions about its priorities and the inevitable trade-offs.

Fifth, and relatedly, as many institutions grapple with the unavoidable tasks of how best to balance more traditional teaching and learning with rich, new technological pedagogies, there will inevitably be on-campus clashes of cultures. For example, an early indicator of faculty guardedness at elite institutions is seen in calls by some faculty for closer oversight of MOOCs (Kolowich 2013).

A sixth dimension, explored in other chapters, is the extent to which the essentially democratic and egalitarian values of access and affordability that inhere in the basic MOOC conception will serve, however unintentionally, to reinforce—some would say exacerbate—the polarization between more elite haves and less affluent have-nots in the astonishing variety of postsecondary institutions and their student learners. Here is not the best place to examine the prospective effects of a MOOC-laden future on inequities evident in the prevailing higher education diverse intensive system. But macro effects there surely will be; the presumed trade-offs between high-tech face-to-face teaching and learning and varying degrees of remoteness in the pedagogical process will and must be weighed. So, despite the presumed egalitarian appeal of MOOC-accessible courses, viewed through a wider lens the potential for further distinguishing the elite institutions (with their capacities to augment high-touch pedagogy with MOOC or other remote-delivered courses) from more ordinary postsecondary institutions is evident.

Thus the emergence is apparent at some resource-affluent campuses of what are sometimes referred to as flipped or inverted classrooms that would appear to bring significant advantages to the education process: namely, the potential of augmenting remotely accessibly high-quality lectures (with the inherent flexibility of fitting such lectures and graphics to the learner's timetable, along with the capacity for revisiting the lecture multiple times). Another fundamental feature of such a pedagogy flows from the advantage of freeing up traditional classroom lecture time to use instead for deeper, follow-on probing and clarification via access to faculty (or aides and teaching assistants, as the case may be).

What do the dramatically new working conditions, economic stringencies, and increased political and governmental involvement mean for the faculty factor? The MOOC (and related phenomena) are bursting with consequences that are further reshaping the academic profession. Yes, technological-grounded pedagogy is nothing new. But this new MOOC phenomenon has far broader, deeper implications. As a recent Association of Governing Boards of Universities and Colleges report puts the reality bluntly: "**This revaluation is not about IT** [information technology]. **It is about teaching and learning**" (Voss 2013, 1). Beyond teaching, these advances have the potential to reshape collaborative research. We would go a step further: this revolution is remaking the faculty in the process—who they are, what they do, and how they do it.

These are some of the conundrums that demand exploration and which promise to affect widely and deeply how higher education will be practiced in a future featuring successively more sophisticated versions of today's MOOC start-ups. More to the point, the MOOC phenomenon will without doubt influence—and potentially even reconfigure—the faculty factor in numerous ways, both directly and indirectly. Kenneth C. Green's (2014) Campus Computing "suggests that 'MOOC Madness' is beginning to decline."

The splintering of the faculty by appointment type may be only an early suggestion of changes in the faculty factor as greater and greater specialization begins to take hold, driven, at least in part, by technology. The 2014 Campus Computing Project also found "a small but significant (and slowly growing) number of campuses are contracting with third party providers for various services (recruitment, curricular development, student services) to help develop or expand their online programs" (Green 2014). We endorse the earlier bold assertions, evident in *The American Faculty* (Schuster and Finkelstein 2006) and elsewhere, that the breakthroughs in technology would lead to more stratification. The confluence of pressures on higher education and, in particular, on faculty work is leading to the emergence of "multiple academies" and many ways to pursue an academic career. This is most readily visible in the world of distance education but, we contend, not exclusively so. Our language to describe *The Faculty Factor* in these multiple academies is woefully inadequate. Indeed, a thorough read of *The American Faculty* finds little reference to the characteristics, work, and careers of faculty off the tenure track, with the exception of references to the growth in their numbers. Today, a volume dedicated to faculty work and careers would be incomplete without it. In the next section we turn our attention to describing what we know about the work of individuals who are off the tenure track.

Faculty Work in the "Other" Academy

In previous chapters we documented the increase in different appointment types and the preponderance of part-time and full-time non-tenure-track faculty as

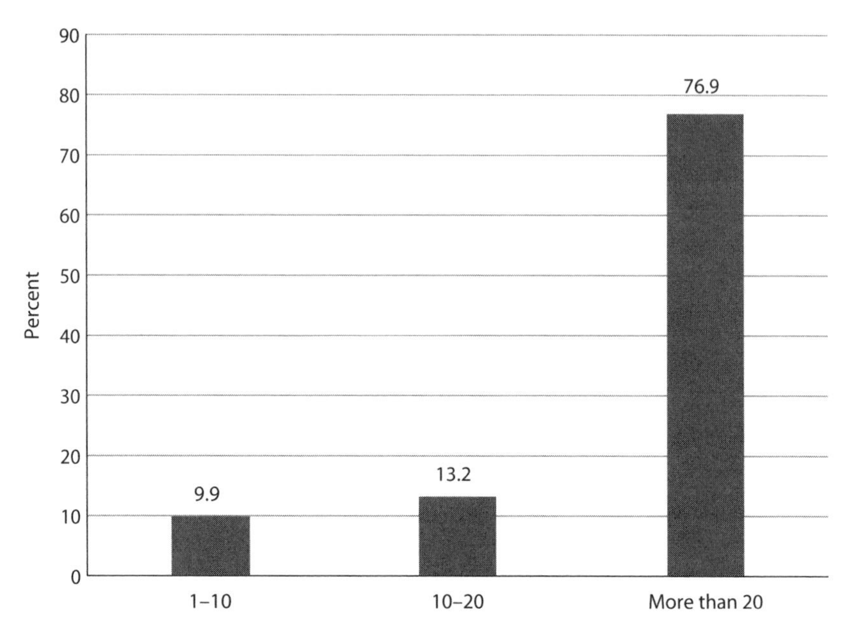

Figure 7.13 Percentage distribution of part-time faculty who taught classes for credit, by average number of hours worked, Fall 2003. *Source:* NSOPF:04. (Refer to appendix A for key to data sources.)

---

a proportion of all faculty members. What do we know about the work of faculty, who now make up the majority of all faculty and instructional staff nationwide? Figure 7.13 shows the percentage distribution of part-time faculty who taught classes for credit by the average number of hours worked in fall 2003. Three-quarters of part-time faculty (77%) reported working more than twenty hours per week. If a typical course is three credit hours and one hour is spent preparing for each credit hour taught, then these numbers contradict conventional wisdom that a substantial portion of part-time faculty is teaching only one course at a time. A meager 10% of part-time faculty reported working from one to ten hours per week, and 13% reported working between ten and twenty hours per week.

The data are inconclusive and somewhat contradictory however. Table 7.5 shows the percentage distribution of part-time faculty by total hours per week teaching for-credit classes. About one-third of part-time faculty reported teaching credit classes one to three hours per week (32%), four to seven hours per week (33%), and more than seven hours per week (35%).

Table 7.5 Percentage distribution of hours per week part-time faculty worked by gender, race/ethnicity, and academic field, Fall 2003

Total hours per week teaching credit classes	One to three hours	Four to seven hours	More than seven hours
Total	32.1	32.9	35.0
Gender			
Male	32.0	32.9	35.1
Female	32.2	33.0	34.8
Race/ethnicity recoded			
American Indian or Alaska Native	22.6[a]	39.1	38.3
Asian or Pacific Islander	31.3	32.6	36.1
Black or African American non-Hispanic	30.3	33.6	36.1
Hispanic White or Hispanic Black	28.7	36.3	35.0
White non-Hispanic	32.6	32.7	34.8
Age			
Under 35	31.4	33.9	34.7
35–44	34.8	29.7	35.5
45–54	34.2	32.8	33.0
55–64	30.1	34.8	35.1
65–70	26.7	35.5	37.8
71 or above	25.5	32.7	41.8
Principal field of teaching, vocational included			
No principal teaching field[b]	—	—	—
Business, law, and communications	39.8	29.2	31.1
Health sciences	29.5	26.8	43.6
Humanities	28.0	37.5	34.5
Natural sciences and engineering	23.9	38.6	37.5
Social sciences and education	39.1	32.1	28.8
Occupationally specific programs	30.4	28.5	41.2
All other programs	33.2	30.9	35.9

Source: NSOPF:04. (Refer to appendix A for key.)

[a]Interpret data with caution. Estimate is unstable because the standard error represents more than 30 percent of the estimate.

[b]Reporting standards not met.

These data suggest that part-time faculty members are doing more than just teaching for-credit classes. Table 7.6 displays the percentage distribution of part-time faculty members by their reported hours e-mailing students in the fall of 2003. Two-thirds of part-time faculty members (69%) reported that

Table 7.6 Percentage distribution of time spent by part-time faculty e-mailing students, by gender, race/ethnicity, and academic field, Fall 2003

Hours per week, e-mailing students	One hour or less	Two to three hours	More than three hours
Total	69.5	20.1	10.4
Gender			
Male	71.8	19.3	8.9
Female	66.8	21.0	12.2
Race/ethnicity recoded			
American Indian or Alaska Native	70.1	14.9[a]	15.0
Asian or Pacific Islander	63.0	25.0	12.1
Black or African American non-Hispanic	63.0	23.9	13.0
Hispanic White or Hispanic Black	69.1	18.9	12.0
White non-Hispanic	70.3	19.7	10.0
Age			
Under 35	65.1	24.1	10.7
35–44	71.9	18.0	10.2
45–54	67.3	21.9	10.8
55–64	72.0	18.0	10.0
65–70	70.7	19.6	9.8
71 or above	69.9	19.0	11.1
Principal field of teaching, vocational included			
No principal teaching field[b]	—	—	—
Business, law, and communications	67.4	22.4	10.2
Health sciences	74.4	16.8	8.8
Humanities	64.4	22.6	13.0
Natural sciences and engineering	73.1	18.7	8.2
Social sciences and education	64.2	22.5	13.4
Occupationally specific programs	84.8	8.7	6.4
All other programs	69.1	21.2	9.7

Source: NSOPF:04. (Refer to appendix A for key.)

[a]Interpret data with caution. Estimate is unstable because the standard error represents more than 30 percent of the estimate.

[b]Reporting standards not met.

they spent one hour or less per week on e-mail communication with students. About one-fifth spent two to three hours, and 10% spent more than three hours per week e-mailing students. A lot has changed since the fall of 2003, and while it is purely speculative, the likelihood is high that the time spent on this activity for all types of faculty members has increased.

Figure 7.14 shows the distribution by gender. On average, women spent more time than men e-mailing students.

Table 7.7 displays the distribution of full-time non-tenure-track faculty by total hours per week teaching credit classes. Fifty-four percent of full-time non-tenure-track faculty members reported teaching credit classes more than seven hours per week (53.6%).

Figure 7.15 shows the distribution by academic field. Two-thirds of full-time non-tenure-track faculty members in humanities reported teaching credit classes more than seven hours per week.

One-quarter of full-time non-tenure-track faculty members (27%) reported that they spent more than three hours per week on e-mail communication with students (table 7.8). Table 7.9 displays the percentage distribution of full-time non-tenure-track faculty by the number of distance education courses taught.

The distribution of full-time non-tenure-track faculty with at least some instructional duties related to credit courses or activities by the number of distance education taught was similar to the distribution for all full-time faculty (see table 7.4). Taken together these data reveal that, for the most part,

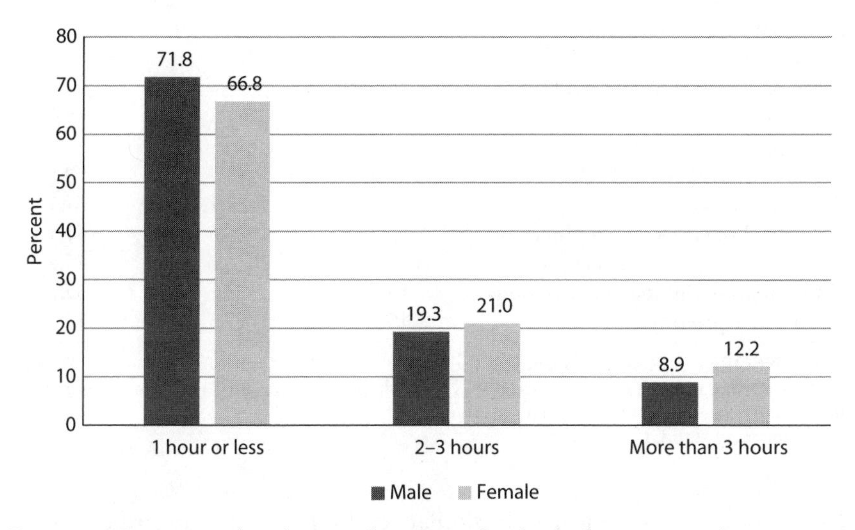

Figure 7.14 Percentage distribution of part-time faculty, by hours per week spent e-mailing students, Fall 2003. *Source:* NSOPF:04. (Refer to appendix A for key to data sources.)

Table 7.7 Percentage distribution of full-time non-tenure-track faculty total hours teaching per week, by gender, race/ethnicity, and academic field, Fall 2003

Total hours per week teaching credit classes	One to three hours	Four to seven hours	More than seven hours
Total	21.6	24.8	53.6
Gender			
Male	23.2	23.7	53.0
Female	20.0	25.8	54.1
Race/ethnicity recoded			
American Indian or Alaska Native	11.2[a]	20.8[a]	68.1
Asian or Pacific Islander	27.3	23.7	49.0
Black or African American non-Hispanic	24.5	22.9	52.6
Hispanic White or Hispanic Black	21.7	23.2	55.0
White non-Hispanic	21.0	25.2	53.8
Age			
Under 35	23.7	27.4	48.9
35–44	22.2	26.5	51.3
45–54	22.0	23.6	54.4
55–64	20.0	23.6	56.4
65–70	17.9	15.5	66.6
71 or above[b]	—	—	—
Principal field of teaching, vocational included			
No principal teaching field[b]	—	—	—
Business, law, and communications	23.0	21.5	55.5
Health sciences	25.5	24.4	50.1
Humanities	10.5	22.1	67.5
Natural sciences and engineering	22.0	26.5	51.5
Social sciences and education	28.6	26.0	45.5
Occupationally specific programs	18.6	23.8	57.7
All other programs	19.1	27.5	53.3

Source: NSOPF:04. (Refer to appendix A for key.)

[a]Interpret data with caution. Estimate is unstable because the standard error represents more than 30 percent of the estimate.

[b]Reporting standards not met.

faculty members are engaged in similar teaching activities regardless of appointment type. The story is an incomplete one, however. There are many aspects of faculty work that these basic data fail to illuminate. In an effort to fill this void, the Coalition on the Academic Workforce undertook an ambitious

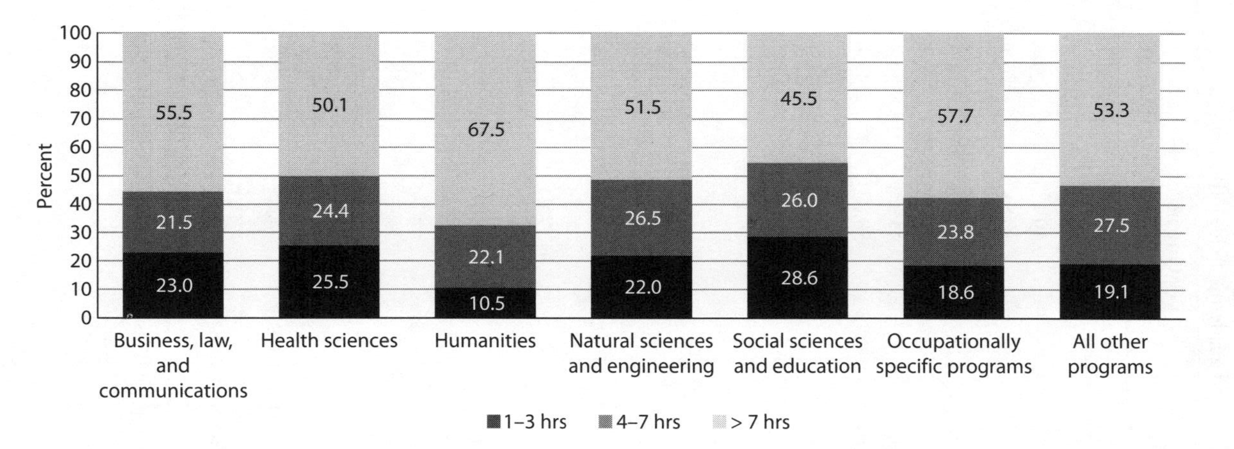

Figure 7.15 Percentage distribution of full-time non-tenure-track faculty, by total hours per week teaching credit classes and academic field, Fall 2003. *Source:* NSOPF:04. (Refer to appendix A for key to data sources.)

Table 7.8 Percentage distribution of full-time non-tenure-track faculty hours per week spent e-mailing students, by gender, race/ethnicity, and academic field, Fall 2003

Hours per week,	One hour or less	Two to three hours	More than three hours
Total	45.1	28.1	26.7
Gender			
Male	49.3	29.6	21.1
Female	40.9	26.7	32.5
Race/ethnicity recoded			
American Indian or Alaska Native	40.5	28.7	30.8
Asian or Pacific Islander	52.4	20.5	27.1
Black or African American non-Hispanic	50.8	19.1	30.1
Hispanic White or Hispanic Black	42.9	32.7	24.3
White non-Hispanic	44.1	29.4	26.5
Age, matches NSOPF:93 distribution			
Under 35	41.4	34.1	24.5
35–44	48.6	25.4	26.0
45–54	45.0	27.3	27.7
55–64	43.2	29.7	27.1
65–70	47.4	21.5	31.1
71 or above[a]	—	—	—
Principal field of teaching, vocational included			
No principal teaching field[a]	—	—	—
Business, law, and communications	33.4	28.3	38.4
Health sciences	61.8	20.0	18.2
Humanities	30.0	39.6	30.3
Natural sciences and engineering	43.7	29.9	26.4
Social sciences and education	37.2	27.9	34.9
Occupationally specific programs	60.2	21.1	18.7
All other programs	53.9	27.4	18.6

Source: NSOPF:04. (Refer to appendix A for key.)

[a]Reporting standards not met.

Table 7.9 Percentage distribution of full-time non-tenure-track faculty teaching distance education classes, by gender, race/ethnicity, and academic field, Fall 2003

Number of classes	No classes	One class	More than one class
Total	93.2	4.4	2.4
Gender			
Male	93.9	4.0	2.0
Female	92.5	4.7	2.8
Race/ethnicity recoded			
American Indian or Alaska Native	86.5	4.2[a]	9.3[a]
Asian or Pacific Islander	97.2	0.5[a]	2.3[b]
Black or African American non-Hispanic	96.2	2.7[b]	1.1[a]
Hispanic White or Hispanic Black	89.8	7.7[b]	2.5[b]
White non-Hispanic	92.8	4.7	2.4
Age, matches NSOPF:93 distribution			
Under 35	95.3	3.5	1.3[b]
35–44	92.8	4.3	2.9
45–54	93.1	4.9	2.0
55–64	91.9	4.7	3.4
65–70	96.6	1.4[a]	2.0[a]
71 or above[c]	—	—	—
Principal field of teaching, vocational included			
No principal teaching field[c]	—	—	—
Business, law, and communications	94.4	2.8[b]	2.9[b]
Health sciences	91.1	6.2	2.6
Humanities	94.1	3.7	2.2[b]
Natural sciences and engineering	95.1	3.8[b]	1.0[b]
Social sciences and education	90.0	5.3	4.7
Occupationally specific programs	93.3	4.5[b]	2.3[a]
All other programs	95.4	3.3[b]	1.3[b]

Source: NSOPF:04. (Refer to appendix A for key.)

[a]Interpret data with caution. Estimate is unstable because the standard error represents more than 50 percent of the estimate.

[b]Interpret data with caution. Estimate is unstable because the standard error represents more than 30 percent of the estimate.

[c]Reporting standards not met.

project to document the working conditions of part-time and full-time non-tenure-track faculty. The next section provides a summary of the findings.

Coalition on the Academic Workforce

Another source of information on part-time and full-time non-tenure-track faculty is the Coalition on the Academic Workforce (CAW). Though CAW was established in 1997, before the suspension of the NSOPF, because of its commitment "to addressing issues associated with deteriorating faculty working conditions and their effect on college and university students in the United States" it has emerged as a go-to source for information on contingent faculty especially since NSOPF was discontinued.

In 1999 CAW organized a survey of staffing practices of humanities and social science disciplines and found "compelling new evidence about the use and treatment of part-time and adjunct faculty, highlighting the dwindling proportion of full-time tenure-track faculty members teaching in undergraduate classrooms, and providing solid evidence of the second-class status of part-time and adjunct employees in the academy" (Coalition on the Academic Workforce 1999, par. 1). Among the key findings from the 1999 CAW Survey, "Notably, full-time tenure-track faculty members taught less than half of the introductory undergraduate courses in all but two of the disciplines. Art history departments reported the largest proportion of introductory classes taught by full-time tenure-track faculty, with 52.3%. Freestanding composition programs reported the smallest proportion, with less than 7% of the introductory courses being taught by full-time tenure-track faculty" (Coalition on the Academic Workforce 1999, par. 8).

Another notable finding is the large proportion of classes taught by graduate students. Graduate students taught between 7% and 34% of the undergraduate courses taught. Graduate students were predominantly teaching introductory classes, where they accounted for from 12% (in art history) to 42.5% (in freestanding composition programs) of the classes taught. Graduate students taught a smaller, but still significant, portion of classes above the introductory or first-year level. Graduate students taught more than 5% of the other undergraduate courses in all of the disciplines (Coalition on the Academic Workforce 1999, par. 9).

The data confirmed some long-held beliefs. The proportions of instructional staff in the classroom varied significantly depending on the type of program and discipline. PhD-granting programs relied heavily on graduate students, and liberal arts and community colleges relied more heavily on part-time and adjunct faculty. "Graduate students taught anywhere from 25 to 60% of the undergraduate classes at PhD programs in all of the reporting disciplines, while part-time faculty taught from 32 to 57% of the undergraduate classes at programs conferring associates degrees" (Coalition on the Academic Workforce 1999, par. 10).

In 2010 CAW took a less systematic approach to data collection: "The survey was open to any faculty member or instructor who wished to complete a questionnaire; respondents therefore do not constitute a strictly representative sample of faculty members working in contingent positions. Nevertheless, the response provides the basis for a more detailed portrait of the work patterns, remuneration, and employment conditions for what has long been the fastest-growing and is now the largest part of the academic workforce. The coalition was seeking information about "the courses part-time faculty members were teaching that term, where they were teaching them, and for what pay and benefits. The survey received close to 30,000 responses, with just over 20,000 coming from individuals who identified themselves as working in a contingent position at an institution or institutions of higher education in fall 2010" (Coalition on the Academic Workforce 2012, 1).

What did they find? One of the key findings was that "part-time teaching is not necessarily temporary employment, and those teaching part-time do not necessarily prefer a part-time to a full-time position. Over 80% of respondents reported teaching part-time for more than three years, and over half for more than six years. Furthermore, over three-quarters of respondents said they have sought, are now seeking, or will be seeking a full-time tenure-track position, and nearly three-quarters said they would definitely or probably accept a full-time tenure-track position at the institution at which they were currently teaching if such a position were offered (Coalition on the Academic Workforce 2012, 2). Moreover, "course loads varied significantly among respondents. Slightly more than half taught one course or two courses during the fall 2010 term, while slightly fewer than half taught three or more courses" (2). Responses by institutions in some states—for example, Ohio and Pennsylvania—to limit the number of courses part-time faculty members teach to avoid offering benefits in compliance with the Affordable Care Act added fuel to the fire.

Concern about working conditions for these individuals is leading to a resurgence in collective bargaining catapulted by an unconventional method, at least for higher education. The Service Employees International Union Adjunct Action campaigns in Boston, Connecticut, Los Angeles, Maryland, Minneapolis–St. Paul, New York, the San Francisco Bay Area, St. Louis, Vermont, Washington DC, and Washington State is using a "metro strategy" to organize adjuncts. The union's Local 500 sees a "metro union" or regional union as a market strategy to respond to a market problem—too many adjuncts for too few jobs (Flaherty 2012): "Key aspects of the union's plan include a citywide contract for adjuncts offered through a central employer with a central hiring database; a push for compensation and working conditions that are equivalent to those of full-time faculty; job security; portability of benefits between institutions; and an academic worker's center where adjuncts can meet with students and prepare for classes (par. 5).

These data speak to the complexity of faculty work in the academy today and provide evidence supporting our contention that a third paradigm has emerged consisting of multiple "academies" characterized not only by institutional type and discipline but also by appointment type. Faculty work varies in each of these academies, and faculty work is subject to different pressures, depending on where within the infrastructure of the multiple academies faculty members are carrying out their work.

Job Satisfaction

Attitudinal and perception data provide a glimpse into the current work environment from the perspective of faculty members themselves. The Collaborative on Academic Careers in Higher Education (COACHE) is a research-based membership organization. More than 200 colleges and universities nationwide have participated in COACHE since its launch in 2002. For the first ten years, COACHE fielded its Tenure-Track Faculty Job Satisfaction Survey. Data from this survey have been used at four-year institutions nationwide to inform decision making regarding changes in the work environment for tenure-seeking faculty. The COACHE Highlights Report 2008 covers three years of data collection: 2005–06, 2006–07, and 2007–08. It provides breakouts by gender, race/ethnicity, and university control for participating four-year colleges and universities. Survey items are clustered around five themes: tenure; nature of the work; policies and practices; climate, culture, and collegiality; and global satisfaction.

Findings reveal that tenure-track faculty members expressed higher levels of satisfaction overall with some aspects of the nature of the work than with others. For example, the average derived teaching composite score was higher (4.00) than the derived research composite score (3.42). The composite scores represent the mean satisfaction levels on the various scales.[5] There were differences by gender and by race/ethnicity as well. Figure 7.16 displays the mean ratings of satisfaction with the nature-of-the-work teaching composite score overall, by dimension, and by gender. Tenure-track men were more satisfied than tenure-track women with the number of courses they taught, the degree of influence they had over the courses they taught, and the number of students they taught. Women on the tenure track were more satisfied than men on the tenure track with the quality of the undergraduate and graduate students they taught.

Figure 7.17 displays the mean ratings of satisfaction with the nature-of-the-work research composite score overall, by dimension, and by gender. Tenure-track men expressed higher levels of satisfaction than tenure-track women on all of the measured dimensions related to research: amount of time allowed to conduct research and produce creative work, the amount of external funding they were expected to find, and their influence over the focus of their research and creative work.

Tables 7.10 and 7.11 display the mean ratings of satisfaction with nature-of-work composites for teaching and research overall, by dimension, and by race/ethnicity. Asian faculty on the tenure track reported significantly less satisfaction than did white faculty with all of the items in the teaching composite except one: the number of students they taught. Asian faculty, on the other hand, reported significantly more satisfaction than did white faculty with the amount of time they had to conduct research. African American faculty on the tenure track reported significantly more satisfaction than did white faculty with the number of courses they taught and the number of students they taught. African American faculty and Hispanic faculty on the tenure track reported significantly less satisfaction than white faculty on the COACHE research composite.

University faculty reported significantly less satisfaction than did college faculty with the COACHE teaching composite, in particular, with the quality of undergraduate students. Figure 7.18 displays the mean ratings of satisfaction with nature-of-the-work teaching composite score overall, by dimension, institutional type, and gender. Similar to the results overall, tenure-track men were more satisfied than tenure-track women with the number of courses they taught, the degree of influence they had over the courses they taught, and the number of students they taught. Women on the tenure track in four-year colleges reported higher levels of satisfaction than men with the quality of undergraduate students.

Men on the tenure track in universities and in four-year colleges reported higher levels of satisfaction than women on the overall composite measure for nature of the-work related to research and for each of the dimensions. Men were more satisfied than women with the amount of time they had to conduct research or produce creative work, the amount of external funding they were

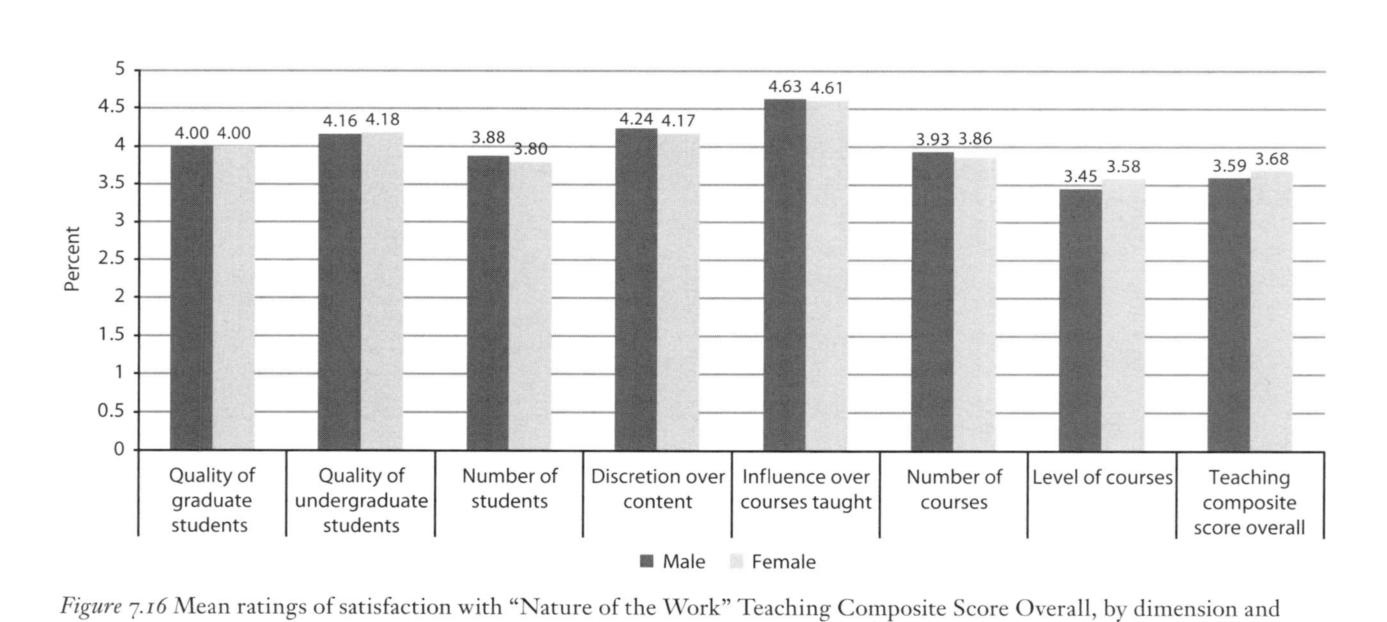

Figure 7.16 Mean ratings of satisfaction with "Nature of the Work" Teaching Composite Score Overall, by dimension and gender, 2005–2007. *Sources:* COACHE:05; COACHE:06; COACHE:07. (Refer to appendix A for key to data sources.)

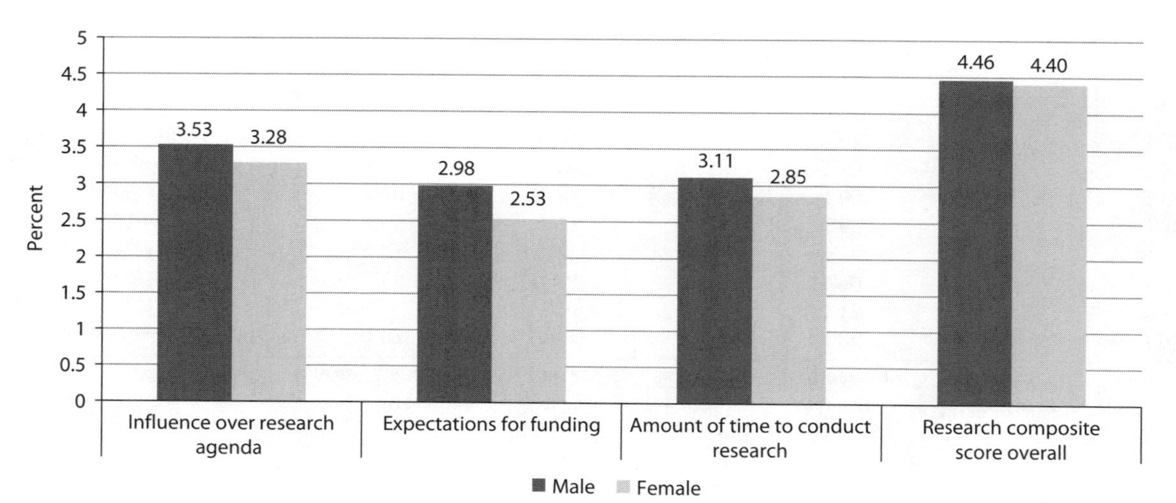

Figure 7.17 Mean ratings of satisfaction with "Nature of the Work" Research Composite Score Overall, by dimension and gender, 2005–2007. *Sources:* COACHE:05; COACHE:06; COACHE:07. (Refer to appendix A for key to data sources.)

Table 7.10 Mean ratings of satisfaction with "Nature of the Work" Teaching Composite Score Overall, by dimension, and by race/ethnicity, 2005–2006, 2006–2007, 2007–2008

	White, non-Hispanic	American Indian or Native Alaskan	Asian or Pacific Islander	Black or African American	Hispanic or Latino	Other or multiracial
Teaching Composite Score Overall	4.02	3.94	3.87	4.06	4.01	3.97
Level of courses	4.19	4.00	4.02	4.17	4.07	4.12
Number of courses	3.86	3.88	3.73	3.99	3.79	3.85
Influence over courses taught	4.23	3.93	4.08	4.20	4.21	4.33
Discretion over content	4.65	4.49	4.41	4.67	4.64	4.58
Number of students	3.90	3.93	3.85	4.02	3.91	4.06
Quality of undergraduates	3.53	3.49	3.35	3.50	3.54	3.32
Quality of graduate students	3.65	3.79	3.51	3.66	3.67	3.27

Sources: COACHE:06; COACHE:07; COACHE:08. (Refer to appendix A for key.)

Table 7.11 Mean ratings of satisfaction with "Nature of the Work" Research Composite Score Overall, by dimension, and by race/ethnicity, 2005–2006, 2006–2007, 2007–2008

	White, non-Hispanic	American Indian or Native Alaskan	Asian or Pacific Islander	Black or African American	Hispanic or Latino	Other or multiracial
Research Composite Score Overall	3.43	3.21	3.46	3.31	3.34	3.28
Amount of time to conduct research	2.73	2.48	3.14	2.72	2.72	2.61
Expectations for funding	3.01	2.78	3.05	2.79	2.86	2.67
Influence over research agenda	4.49	4.33	4.14	4.33	4.42	4.43

Sources: COACHE:06; COACHE:07; COACHE:08. (Refer to appendix A for key.)

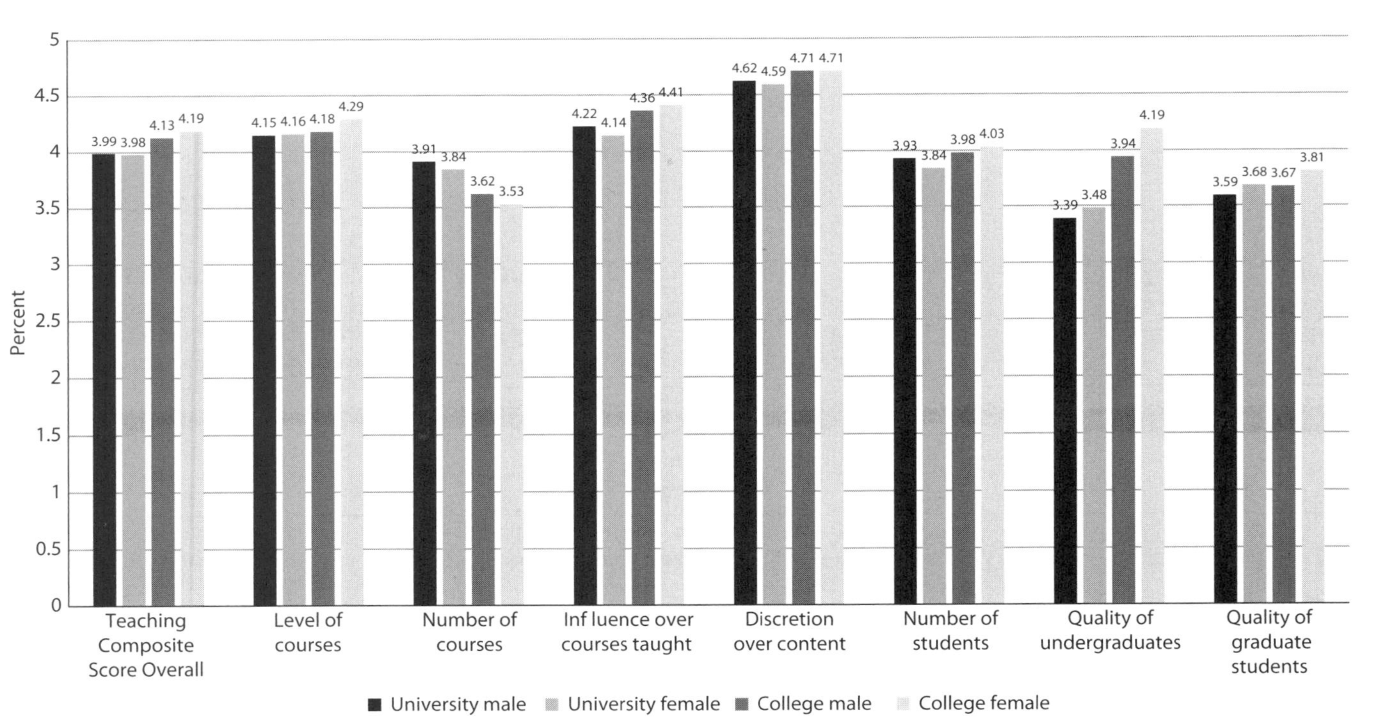

Figure 7.18 Mean ratings of satisfaction with "Nature of the Work" Teaching Composite Score Overall, by dimension, institutional type, and gender, 2005–2007. *Sources:* COACHE:05; COACHE:06; COACHE:07. (Refer to appendix A for key to data sources.)

expected to find, and the influence they had over the focus of their research or creative work (see figure 7.19).

Given these data, perhaps it is not surprising that women on the tenure track reported lower levels of satisfaction than men with both their institutions and departments as places to work.

In 2011, nearly a decade after COACHE launched its Tenure-Track Faculty Job Satisfaction Survey, COACHE distributed a comprehensive survey focused on understanding the experience of tenured and tenure-track faculty—the Faculty Job Satisfaction Survey. Among the most important factors affecting satisfaction among tenured faculty members were colleagues and collaboration, engagement in departmental activities, having good mentors, departmental climate, equitable distribution of work (e.g., teaching load, committee assignments), attractiveness of the work expected, and an appropriate (and, ideally, rewarded) mix of research, teaching, and service. Senior faculty, in particular, felt pressure to be "all things to all people" and with increasingly less institutional support to do so (Trower 2011).

An Interpretive Comment: Faculty Work under Pressure

Regardless of institutional type, the basic mantra that defines faculty work today is, Do more with less. The mantra is manifest in several ways: state mandates to increase teaching loads, increasing expectations for tenure and promotion, institutional administrators' expectations for faculty to bring in outside money from grants and contracts, and engaging in revenue-generating programs through distance learning across institutional type.

In the years since the Great Recession there is more and more of an expectation that faculty will align with the mission and core values of the institution and a greater emphasis on productivity. Interest in faculty productivity is not new, however. The National Study of Instructional Cost and Productivity (known as the Delaware Study) was launched in 1992 to give academic administrators comparative information from similar institutions about who was teaching what to whom, at what cost. Since 1996, nearly 600 institutions nationwide have used the data collected to compare teaching workloads, instructional costs, and productivity by academic discipline.

As part of its response to a requirement in the 1998 reauthorization of the Higher Education Act that the National Center for Education Statistics conduct a study of higher education costs, the agency asked the founding director of the Delaware Study, Michael Middaugh, along with coauthors Rosalinda

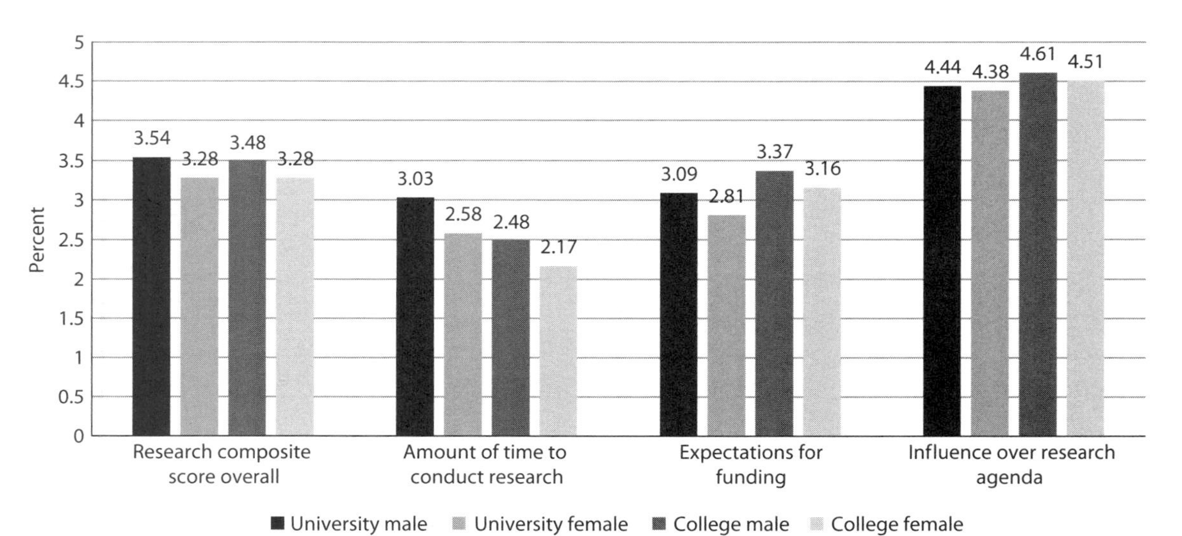

Figure 7.19 Mean ratings of satisfaction with "Nature of the Work" Research Composite Score Overall, by dimension, institutional type, and gender, 2005–2007. *Sources:* COACHE:05; COACHE:06; COACHE:07. (Refer to appendix A for key to data sources.)

Graham and Abdus Shahid (Middaugh, Graham, and Shahid 2003) to conduct an analysis of the aggregate data collected from all participating institutions. Two key findings emerged from their analysis of 1998, 2000, and 2001 data. First, disciplinary mix accounted for most of the variance in instructional expenditures across institutions. Second, there is variation in instructional expenditures within disciplines across institutional types and across disciplines within an institution. What this means is that the mission of the institution drives instructional expenditures and, by extension, faculty work.[6]

Another way to look at faculty work under pressure is through the lens of career stage. The next section describes faculty work during key stress points of a traditional faculty career.

Career Stress Points

The confluence of pressures related to faculty work is perhaps most prominently exhibited during career stress points. For tenure-track faculty, career stress points coincide roughly with career stages discussed in more detail in part 2 of this volume, in chapters 4–6. For example, four obvious career stress points during an academic career are entry, the tenure decision (where applicable), promotion to a higher rank (associate professor or professor), and retirement. Each of these stress points offers unique challenges and opportunities for faculty members pursuing an academic research and teaching career.

Career Entry

Stratification within higher education has been linked to entry into (access to) an academic career and to factors influencing career productivity (Breneman and Youn 1988). Robert. McGinnis and J. Scott Long (1988, 30) acknowledge that "the specific process of determining the prestige of the first position and the effects on the later career is complex." Nonetheless, the evidence presented by these researchers is compelling. Their results suggest that gaining admission to the top graduate schools, at least in science, is an important first step to pursuing an academic research career.[7] Detailed evidence is provided in chapter 4 suggesting that different types of faculty appointments at different types of institutions adhere to different career-entry opportunity structures. The well-documented growth in part-time and non-tenure-track positions begs for an updated understanding of the pressures associated with finding and negotiating the first academic job. While there is more job mobility today than twenty-five years ago, and there are many more pathways of opportunity to pursue a faculty career, conventional wisdom still holds. There is a premium on the doctoral student who graduates from a prestigious graduate program and has held a postdoctoral fellowship. This puts a tremendous amount of pressure on individuals to know that decisions they make about where to attend graduate school may have lasting impact on their entire career.

Faculty members on the tenure track consistently report their desire for clear and reasonable expectations for success through COACHE. Trower (2012) identifies five keys to tenure-track faculty job satisfaction: tenure clarity; work-life integration; support for teaching and research; culture, climate, and collegiality; and engaging leaders across the campus.

The Tenure Process

Once having landed a coveted tenure-track position, faculty members set about developing a tenure portfolio (also referred to as a dossier) that will demonstrate their competence across the three areas of teaching, research, and service. There is no denying that going up for tenure is one of the most stressful times in a faculty member's career. Stress associated with the tenure decision comes from a variety of sources, but at its crux the stress derives from the uncertainty of knowing whether or not the decision will be positive or negative. What goes into a positive or negative decision? It depends. The tenure process varies from institution to institution and often from department to department within an institution. The tenure process has been described as a rite of passage and a socialization process during which new faculty members learn about their roles within their department, institution, and their broader academic community (Tierney and Rhoades 1994). Ambiguity around the tenure process is one of the key sources of stress, anxiety, and dissatisfaction among tenure-track faculty members (Trower 2012). Relationships (culture, climate, and collegiality) are instrumental in reducing career stress and enhancing job satisfaction (Trower 2012). Luis Ponjuan, Valerie Martin Conley, and Cathy Trower (2011) found differences in the levels of tenure-track faculty members' satisfaction with their relationships with peers and with senior colleagues. They offer recommendations for strategies to help tenure-track faculty members develop positive relationships with senior and peer colleagues, thereby mitigating some of the stress associated with career entry and the tenure process.

Promotion to Professor

A third career stress point occurs in mid-career as faculty members contemplate promotion to professor. Roger Baldwin is one of only a handful of higher education researchers who has focused attention on faculty members at mid-career. In an effort to increase representation and advancement of women in academic careers in science and engineering, institution-specific studies have been funded by the National Science Foundation through ADVANCE grants. Understanding what contributes to women's success in attaining the rank of professor is an important piece of the ADVANCE work, and it is an area where lessons learned have contributed to broader impacts for women in the academy and for the academic enterprise as a whole. Still the majority of the research conducted has been focused on recruitment and retention of early-career faculty. Less attention has been given to women at mid-career stage.

Career Exit: Retirement

The fourth career stress point is retirement. Compared with faculty members at other stages of the academic career, senior faculty members experience similar and different pressures on their work than their junior colleagues do. Salary compression issues aside, senior faculty members earn higher average salaries than associate and assistant professors. Senior faculty members are looked to for leadership, mentorship, and, increasingly, enhanced productivity. Expectations for performance should be clearly stated for all faculty ranks. A shift in expectations without time to adjust creates a stressful environment for senior faculty members. Stock market investments performance, especially for the growing number of faculty members in defined-contribution plans (see chapter 6) impacts decision making about when to retire.

Given the complexity of academic careers, it is also important to consider career stress points that faculty members face in the context of different institutional settings, including the for-profit sector of postsecondary education, and in different employment situations. Although a thorough examination is outside of the scope of this volume, in the next section we offer an abbreviated discussion and analysis of these stress points for faculty pursuing an academic research and teaching career.

What do career stress points look like for the "other academy"? For part-time faculty members, career stress points are literally term to term. Results from the CAW Survey highlight the concerns of part-time faculty with no job security, low wages, and few if any benefits. This employment relationship creates constant uncertainty for part-time faculty. Full-time, non-tenure-track faculty members also have career stress points coinciding with contract renewal. These career stress points may be exacerbated as these individuals progress through careers without the benefit of job security afforded their colleagues who are tenured or on the tenure track.

Conclusion

In the preceding pages we have provided evidence from a variety of sources. We reported descriptive data on the core functions of faculty work—teaching, research, and service—and we sought to elucidate the confluence of pressures being put on faculty work. We began the chapter with an assertion that the nature of academic work has changed (beginning before the Great Recession of 2007–08 and gaining momentum afterward) so significantly—and so rapidly—that we believe the new conditions constitute a new paradigm.

Several trends support our assertion. The trend of increasing faculty work effort (measured in average hours worked per week within the faculty member's home institution) has continued, although at a slower pace than in previous years. In the aggregate, faculty work effort has not changed much since the late 1990s, and for the most part the gaps between men and women in time spent on various activities have not diminished. Faculty work is more varied and more complex across all types of institutions. There has been a blurring of lines between institutional types. Higher percentages of faculty members in institutions other than research universities are spending more hours per week on activities related to research, while faculty in research universities are spending more time on activities related to teaching, especially in public universities. Women continued to report spending more time on teaching than men.

Increased effort on both teaching and research has continued. The trend toward decreased time allocated to administration also continued. In addition, faculty reported spending fewer hours per week preparing for classes and counseling or advising students. This latter trend could suggest greater efficiencies realized through technological advances and more specialization. The fastest-growing occupational category in higher education has been other professionals, encompassing among others, student affairs professionals, many of whom provide student advising. On the other hand, caution should be taken to ensure that quality is not being sacrificed as faculty members spread their time ever more thinly.

The extent to which workload policies attend to variation and complexity is not uniform across institutions. Faculty members often receive additional compensation for teaching courses above the number considered to be the regular teaching load. These data raise questions about equitable access to additional teaching opportunities.

There is an almost universal expectation to publish across all types of institutions. Even in public two-year institutions where the mission does not include research, many faculty members are engaged in some kind of scholarly activity, which sometimes leads to publication. The extent to which this is a result of professional socialization, internal motivation, and derived intrinsic value is unknown. In many four-year institutions, there is an expectation to publish. This expectation is tied to a push to increase external funding as a means to enhance revenue. There may be negative consequences associated with this push, especially if the level of anxiety produced by pressure to publish and bring in grant money when availability of funding is limited is high. Is the data indicating less time spent on preparing for teaching evidence of greater efficiencies, for example, those gained from technology, or has the pressure to do more with less permeated academic work to the point that faculty are choosing between multiple priorities?

Higher education should focus more attention on the Faculty Factor and look for ways to relieve some of the pressures being put on faculty work. We argue that there has been a confluence of pressures from both within and outside of the academy that have exerted immense pressure on higher education to change the nature of faculty work, often intensifying expectations for increased productivity. These forces have gained momentum since the Great Recession and, we maintain, constitute an important dimension of the new paradigm for higher education. Embracing the complexity of academic work and identifying ways to increase flexibility are two critical strategies for navigating these choppy waters but call into question the nature of culture and values. In the next chapter we take a closer look at academic culture and values in transition.

NOTES

1. University of Colorado Boulder, "2015–2016 CU–Boulder Campus Entrepreneurship Initiative Seed Awards Proposal Guidelines"; University of Colorado Boulder, "Calling All Faculty and Staff to Think Entrepreneurially."

2. Higher education officials typically view legislative requirements for reporting and disclosure, primarily through the Higher Education Act of 1965 and its amendments, as

"too burdensome" (Nelson 2011). With more than $136 billion in federal student aid in fiscal year 2013 alone, it is fairly safe to say that there is little chance of a reduction in oversight of institutions and accrediting bodies any time soon (US Government Accountability Office 2014).

3. HERI Faculty Survey data have been weighted to provide a normative picture of the American college full-time undergraduate faculty. For more information see *Research Methodology* in *Undergraduate Teaching Faculty: The 2013–2014 HERI Faculty Survey* (http://www.heri.ucla.edu/monographs/HERI-FAC2014-monograph.pdf).

4. The item asking about hours per week spent on community and public service was added to the survey instrument in 1992–93.

5. Clarity scale: 5=Very clear, 4=Fairly clear, 3=Neither clear nor unclear, 2=Fairly unclear, 1=Very unclear; *Agreement scale*: 5=Strongly agree, 4=Somewhat agree, 3=Neither agree nor disagree, 2=Somewhat disagree, 1=Strongly disagree; *Reasonableness scale*: 5=Very reasonable, 4=Fairly reasonable, 3=Neither reasonable nor unreasonable, 2=Fairly unreasonable, 1=Very unreasonable; *Satisfaction scale*: 5=Very satisfied, 4=Satisfied, 3=Neither satisfied nor dissatisfied, 2=Dissatisfied, 1=Very dissatisfied.

6. Similarly, the Kansas Study of Community College Instructional Cost and Productivity (known as the Kansas Study) was designed to elicit information about community colleges, again to give academic administrators in the community college sector comparative (benchmark) data to inform decision making at the participating institutions. Aggregate data sketch a portrait of faculty work in approximately 450 community colleges nationwide. The increasing complexities of faculty work and emerging multiple academies in which faculty perform their work beg for more in-depth analysis.

7. McGinnis and Long's (1988) analyses were delimited to male biochemists who received PhDs in the United States in 1957, 1958, 1962, and 1963 and were employed in a faculty position at the time of the study.

REFERENCES

Adams, Susan. 2013. "The Least Stressful Jobs of 2013." *Forbes*, January 3. http://www.forbes.com/sites/susanadams/2013/01/03/the-least-stressful-jobs-of-2013/.

Astin, Alexander W., William S. Korn, and Eric L. Dey. 1990. *The American College Teacher: National Norms for 1989–90 HERI Faculty Survey Report*. Los Angeles: Higher Education Research Institute, UCLA.

Breneman, David W., and Ted I. K. Youn. 1988. *Academic Labor Markets and Careers*. New York: Falmer Press.

Carey, Kevin. 2013. "MOOCs, Robots, and the Secret of Life." NewAmerica EdCentral Foundation. June 5. http://www.edcentral.org/moocs-robots-secret-life.

Coalition on the Academic Workfoce. 1999. *Who Is Teaching in US College Classrooms? A Coalition on the Academic Workforce Study of Undergraduate Faculty (1999)*. https://www.historians.org/about-aha-and-membership/aha-history-and-archives/archives/who-is-teaching-in-us-college-classrooms.

———. 2012. *A Portrait of Part-Time Faculty Members: A Summary of the Findings on Part-Time Faculty Respondents to the Coalition on the Academic Workforce Survey of Contingent Faculty Members and Instructors*. Coalition on the Academic Workforce. June. http://www.academicworkforce.org/CAW_portrait_2012.pdf.

Dey, Eric L., Claudia E. Ramirez, William S. Korn, and Alexander W. Astin. 1993. *The American College Teacher: National Norms for 1992–93 HERI Faculty Survey Report*. Los Angeles: Higher Education Research Institute, UCLA.

Dominguez, Jeronimo. 2012. *UNM Extended University: Annual Report, 2011–2012.* Albuquerque: University of New Mexico. http://statewide.unm.edu/common/pdf/viceprovost/distance-education-annual-report.pdf.

Eagan, Kevin, Ellen B. Stolzenberg, Jennifer B. Lozano, Melissa C. Aragon, Maria R. Suchard, and Sylvia Hurtado. 2014. "Undergraduate Teaching Faculty: The 2013–2014 HERI Faculty Survey." Los Angeles: Higher Education Research Institute, UCLA.

Flaherty, Colleen. 2012. "A Market Strategy." *Inside Higher Ed.* https://www.insidehighered.com/news/2012/12/03/adjuncts-across-washington-region-plan-unionize-fight-market-problem.

Green, Kenneth C. 2014. "The Campus Computing Project." Encino, CA: Campus Computing. http://www.campuscomputing.net/item/campus-computing-2014, paras. 8–9.

HERI *Research Methodology.* In *Undergraduate Teaching Faculty: The 2013–2014 HERI Faculty Survey.* http://www.heri.ucla.edu/monographs/HERI-FAC2014-monograph.pdf.

Hurtado, Sylvia, Kevin Egan, John Pryor, Hannah Whang, and Serge Tran. 2012. *Undergraduate Teaching Faculty: The 2010–11 HERI Faculty Survey.* Los Angeles: Higher Education Research Institute, UCLA.

Jaschik, Scott. 2015. "Organizing Enlightenment." *Inside Higher Ed.* https://www.insidehighered.com/news/2015/05/08/scholar-discusses-his-book-creation-research-university-and-disciplines.

Jencks, Christopher, and David Riesman. 1968. *The Academic Revolution.* Garden City, NY: Doubleday.

Kolowich, Steve. 2013. "Harvard Professors Call for Greater Oversight of MOOCs." *Chronicle of Higher Education*, May 24. http://chronicle.com/blogs/wiredcampus/harvard-professors-call-for-greater-oversight-of-moocs/43953.

Lindholm, Jennifer A., Katalin Szelenyi, Sylvia Hurtado, and William S. Korn. 2005. *The American College Teacher: National Norms for the 2004–2005 HERI Faculty Survey.* Los Angeles: Higher Education Research Institute, UCLA.

McGinnis, Robert., and J. Scott. Long, eds. 1988. "Entry into Academia: Effects of Stratification, Geography, and Ecology." In *Academic Labor Markets and Academic Careers in American Higher Education*, edited by D. W. Breneman and T. I. K. Youn, 28–51. New York: Farmers Press.

Middaugh, Michael F., Rosalinda Graham, and Abdus Shahid. 2003. *A Study of Higher Education Instructional Expenditures: The Delaware Study of Instructional Costs and Productivity.* NCES 2003-161. National Center for Education Statistics, Institute of Educational Sciences. Washington, DC: US Department of Education.

National Center for Education Statistics (NCES). 2004. *National Study of Postsecondary Faculty.* Washington, DC: National Center for Education Statistics.

Nelson, Libby A. 2011. "Too Many Rules." *Inside Higher Ed.* https://www.insidehighered.com/news/2011/09/29/report_examines_regulatory_burden_on_colleges_for_financial_aid.

Ponjuan, Luis, Valerie M. Conley, and Cathy Trower. 2011. "Career Stage Differences in Pre-Tenure Track Faculty Perceptions of Professional and Personal Relationships with Colleagues." *Journal of Higher Education* 82 (May–June): 319–46.

Reisslein, Jana, Patrick Seeling, and Martin Reisslein. 2005. "Video in Distance Education: ITFS vs. Web-Streaming: Evaluation of Student Attitudes." *The Internet and Higher Education* 8, quarter 1: 25–44.

Sax, L. J., A. W. Astin, W. S. Korn, and S. K. Gilmartin. 1998. *The American College Teacher: National Norms for 1998–99 HERI Faculty Survey Report.* Los Angeles: Higher Education Research Institute, UCLA.

Schlosser, Lee Ayers and Michael Simonson. 2006. *Distance Education: Definitions and Glossary of Terms.* 2nd Edition. Greenwich, CT: Information Age Publishing, Inc.
Schuster, Jack H., and Martin J. Finkelstein. 2006. *The American Faculty: The Restructuring of Academic Work and Careers.* Baltimore, MD: Johns Hopkins University Press.
Slaughter, S. and Larry L. Leslie. 1997. *Academic Capitalism: Politics, Policies, and the Entrepreneurial University.* Baltimore, MD: Johns Hopkins University Press.
Tierney, W. G., and Gary Rhoades. 1994. *Faculty Socialization as Cultural Process: A Mirror of Institutional Commitment.* Washington, DC: George Washington University.
Trower, Cathy A. 2011. "Senior Faculty Vitality." In TIAA-CREF Institute, *Advancing Higher Education,* June, 1–13.
———. 2012. *Success on the Tenure Track: Five Keys to Faculty Job Satisfaction.* Baltimore, MD: Johns Hopkins University Press.
University of Colorado, Boulder. "2015–2016 CU–Boulder Campus Entrepreneurship Initiative Seed Awards Proposal Guidelines." http://www.colorado.edu/law/sites/default/files/Entrepreneurship%20%20Initiative%20Seed%20Award%20RFP.pdf.
———. "Calling All Faculty and Staff to Think Entrepreneurially." University of Colorado News Center. http://www.colorado.edu/news/features/calling-all-faculty-and-staff-think-entrepreneurially.
US Government Accountability Office. 2014. *Education Should Strengthen Oversight of Schools and Accreditors.* GAO-15-59. Washington, DC: US Government Printing Office.
Voss, Brian D. 2013. "Massive Open Online Courses: A Primer for University and College Board Members." *AGB White Paper,* March. Washington, DC: Association of Governing Boards of Universities and Colleges.

8

Academic Culture and Values in Transition

In chapter 7, we described the changing complexion of academic work as college and university faculty respond to external and internal pressures, especially since 2008. We explored how increased demands for efficiency and effectiveness are exerting unprecedented pressures on faculty to adapt. We also provided data on key trends related to the core areas of faculty work: teaching, research, and service. A passing glance at these trends might prompt one to conclude that the more things change, the more they stay the same. Yet we assert that the new sets of working conditions discernable in the emerging "multiple academies," characterized not only by type and control of institution and discipline but also by appointment type, are recasting what it means to be "faculty" and are creating tensions reflective of academic culture and values in transition.

This chapter extends our examination of the status of the academic profession by focusing on three traditional core values central to faculty professional identity: academic freedom, autonomy, and shared governance. We examine the role of faculty in governance and the most recent trends in collective bargaining among faculty. We present basic data on faculty members' perceptions of climate, culture, and collegiality. Selected differences by gender, race/ethnicity, and institutional type are noted. Finally, because of the unique context it creates in the academy, the chapter includes a discussion of tenure and describes the vexing tenure dilemma—issues surrounding policies and practices of tenure.

To begin, we examine fundamental faculty core values through a review of the literature and by displaying measures of satisfaction with key aspects of academic culture. We acknowledge the limitations associated with the crude metrics of satisfaction available, but we also assert that the perceptions of individual faculty members provide an important lens for understanding what is important to them and as such are appropriate indicators to gauge transitions in academic culture and values.

We describe the contemporary environment related to shared governance and collective bargaining in higher education as a barometer for change, paying particular attention to the uptick in bargaining by different groups including part-time faculty, full-time non-tenure-track faculty, and graduate assistants.

Finally, we examine tenure. A key aspect of academic culture is marked by the tenure system. The decline in the proportion of all faculty holding tenured or tenure-track appointments was documented in chapter 3. In this chapter we focus attention on tenure as a reflection of academic culture and core values. Perhaps more than any other single aspect of academic culture, tenure encapsulates the core values of the Faculty Factor in US higher education. We seek to shed light on the impact of trends related to tenure described in chapter 3 and offer an examination of the tenure dilemma along with a recommendation (see chapter 13).

Academic Core Values

Gappa, Austin, and Trice (2007, 140–41) identified five core values that define academic work and careers: the need for academic freedom and professional autonomy to pursue truth with independence and integrity; the value of collegiality and consensus as the basis for shared governance of an academic community; the value of merit as the basis for career advancement, albeit with a concern for equitable treatment of all social groups; continued opportunities to broaden knowledge and skills through professional growth that lead to deeper satisfaction; and flexibility in constructing work arrangements to maximize contributions to the institution and result in meaningfulness in their work and personal lives.

These core values are echoed among the most important factors affecting satisfaction among tenured faculty members. These factors include colleagues and collaboration; engagement in departmental activities; having and being good mentors; departmental climate; equitable distribution of work (e.g., teaching load, committee assignments); attractiveness of the work expected; and an appropriate (and, ideally, rewarded) mix of research, teaching, and service. The extent to which the contemporary higher education work environment provides opportunities for faculty members to pursue careers adhering to these core values varies and contributes to faculty members' feeling torn between serving students, their institutions, their discipline, and the profession. Senior faculty, in particular, feel pressure to be "all things to all people" and with decreasing institutional support to do so (Trower 2011).

To what extent and in what ways has the complexity of academic work and careers affected professional norms? We endeavor to explore this question by describing evidence of the changing normative structure of academic life (see chapters 3–7), complemented by examining, in this chapter, faculty perceptions of the higher education enterprise and the role of the professoriate, using surveys from two primary sources: the University of California Los Angeles (UCLA) Higher Education Research Institute (HERI) and the Collaborative on Academic Careers in Higher Education (COACHE). These two sources provide the best available data on faculty perceptions. Specifically, we use published data from HERI's triennial Faculty Survey and COACHE's Tenure-Track Faculty Job Satisfaction Survey and Faculty Job Satisfaction Survey. We describe trends related to academic culture and values available from HERI followed by a discussion of culture, climate, and collegiality, using attitudinal and perception data from COACHE. These sources are derived from surveys of individuals representing predominately tenured and tenure-eligible faculty at a subset of institutions and may reflect a relatively homogenous portion of the overall faculty population. We acknowledge that these views may not necessarily represent the views of a substantial portion of the faculty, indeed a majority of all faculty members by headcount.

Academic Freedom

Academic freedom is the right of individual faculty members to express their ideas related to their expertise—verbally and in writing—in the classroom and in publication, regardless of whether the ideas are unpopular or go against the political agenda of interested parties (Metzger 1973). Academic freedom is fundamental to the mission of higher education, and thus is arguably the most indispensable academic core value. Academic freedom is operationalized most visibly in faculty control over the curriculum. Although there are exceptions, for the most part decisions about course content are left up to individual faculty members, and faculty express high levels of satisfaction with this discretion. Figure 8.1 shows faculty satisfaction with the level of discretion they have over course content.

Indeed, the vast majority of responding faculty members reported being "satisfied" or "very satisfied" with the freedom they have to determine course

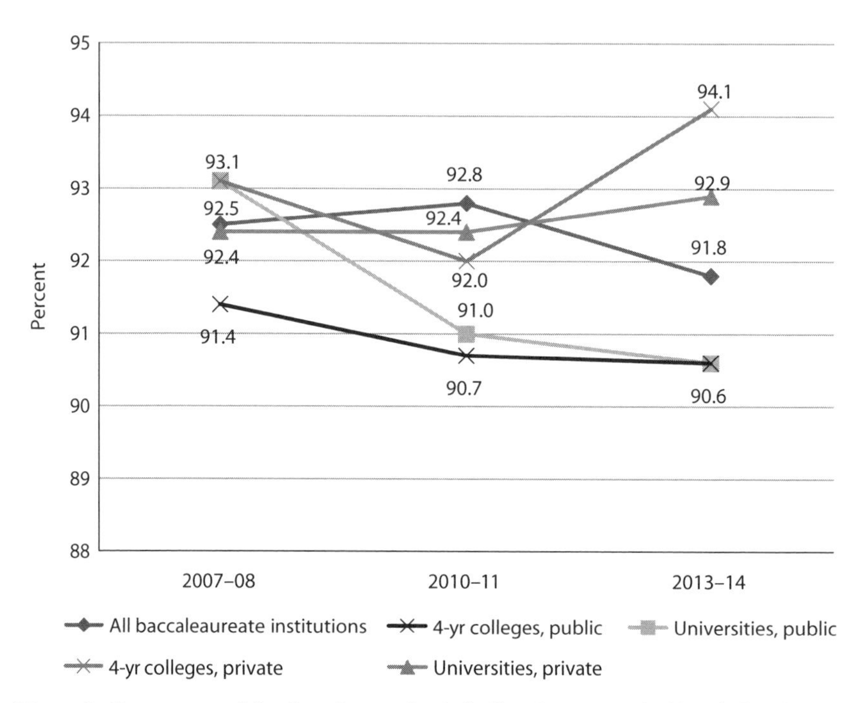

Figure 8.1 Percentage of faculty who are "satisfied" or "very satisfied" with freedom to determine course content, by type of institution, 2007–2014, selected years. *Sources:* HERI:07; HERI:10; HERI:13. (Refer to appendix A for key to data sources.)

---

content. In 2007–08, the first year the item was collected by HERI, 93% of faculty reported being "satisfied" or "very satisfied" with the freedom they had to determine course content. In 2013–14, the percentage fell slightly, to 92%. Thus the overwhelming majority of faculty members participating in these surveys over time have expressed satisfaction with their discretion to determine course content. These data suggest acceptance of faculty authority within the context of the classroom. However, the data also suggest the trend among public institutions may be declining slightly, while in private institutions the reverse may be true.

There are slight differences in perception by men and women, however. Figure 8.2 displays the percentage of men and women by academic rank who reported being "satisfied" or "very satisfied" with the freedom they had to determine course content. Gender differences were more discernable at lower academic ranks and in non-tenure-eligible positions.

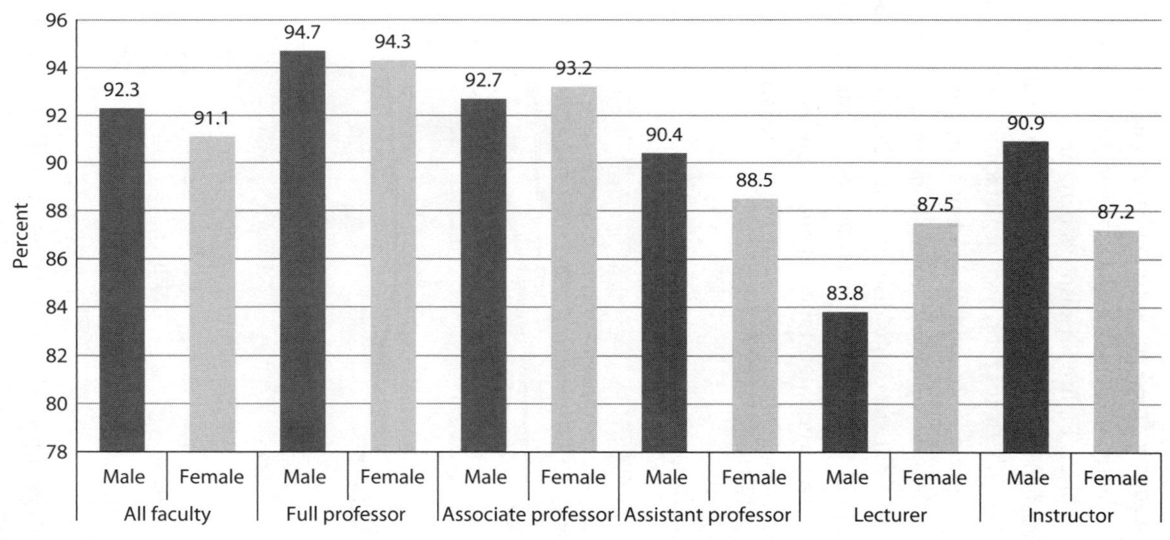

Figure 8.2 Percentage of faculty who are "satisfied" or "very satisfied" with freedom to determine course content, by gender and rank, 2013. *Source:* HERI:13. (Refer to appendix A for key to data sources.)

Autonomy

Another core value of the academic profession is autonomy. Autonomy is closely related to academic freedom. Autonomy refers to the faculty member's right to act independently, without close supervision, by virtue of their unique expertise in their subject. Figure 8.3 displays percentages of faculty who said that they were "satisfied" or "very satisfied" with their level of autonomy and independence in their job. In 2013–14, 85% of all faculty, and 86% of faculty in public universities, reported autonomy and independence as a satisfying aspect of their job. While these percentages are very high, the percentage of faculty members expressing dissatisfaction is disconcerting. Pressures associated with the changing nature of academic work and declining resources may be contributing factors. Given the importance of autonomy as a core value of the academic profession, more information about why some faculty express dissatisfaction is needed.

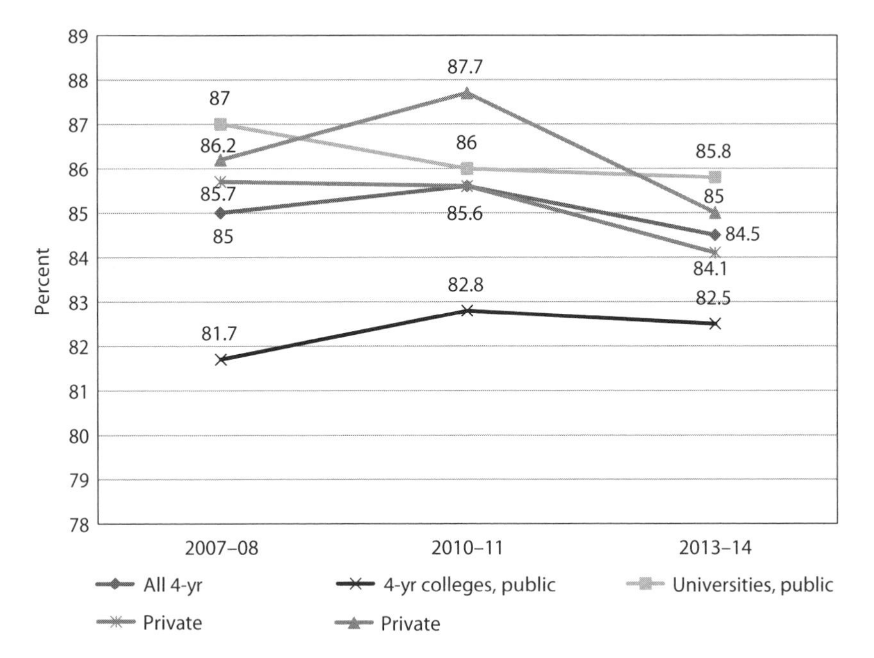

Figure 8.3 Aspects of job with which respondent is "satisfied" or "very satisfied": Autonomy and independence, 2007–2014, selected years. *Sources:* HERI:07; HERI:10; HERI:13. (Refer to appendix A for key to data sources.)

Note: This question was asked for the first time in the 2007–08 Faculty Survey.

Shared Governance

At its heart, shared governance is about including faculty members in decision-making processes of the institution. According to the American Association of University Professors (AAUP), "An institution's system of governance is the structure according to which authority and responsibilities are allocated to the various offices and divisions within the institution" (AAUP, "On the Relationship of Faculty Governance to Academic Freedom," par. 4). The AAUP's first statement on shared governance, published in 1920, argued for faculty involvement in specific areas: personnel decisions, selection of administrators, preparation of the budget, and determination of educational policies (AAUP, "Shared Governance"). The 1966 Statement on Government of Colleges and Universities jointly issued by AAUP, the American Council on Education and the Association of Governing Boards of Universities and Colleges calls for "shared responsibility" and "cooperative action" among the major stakeholders of institutional government, including governing boards, administrations, and faculty. The statement, still considered the gold standard by many higher education leaders and stakeholders, identifies three spheres of decision making. "The faculty has primary responsibility for subject matter, curriculum, methods of instruction, research, faculty status and aspects of student life clearly related to the education process" (Dill 2014, 171). "The governing board and administration have primary responsibility for finances, including maintaining the endowment and obtaining needed capital and operating funds" (Dill 2014, 171). Strategic issues, such as drafting long-range plans, determining priorities, budgeting, and the selection of a president, fall within the scope of shared responsibility. In spite of the clearly articulated standard, there exists considerable "hierarchical differentiation of 'shared governance' in the American system of higher education: 'that is, the distribution of authority among the board of trustees, administration, as well as members of the faculty varies by type of college and university'" (Dill 2014, 172), and this has been the case for decades.

Burton Clark (1987) documented this variation using responses to Carnegie Foundation surveys and interviews with faculty. He described "authority environments" using characteristics of individual versus collegial control and decentralized (department based, bottom-up) versus centralized (bureaucratic) decision-making processes. Figure 8-4 illustrates this matrix by type of institution.

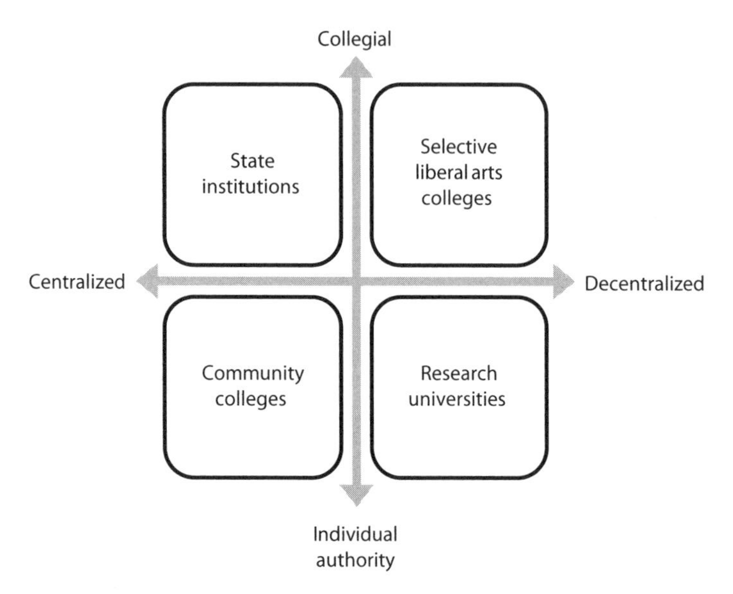

Figure 8.4 Matrix depicting authority environments' hierarchy, by type of institution. Derived from Clark (1987).

What do recent data tell us about faculty members' participation in and perceptions of their role in shared governance? Based on results from a 2001 survey on higher education governance, Kaplan (2004) found increases in faculty control in traditional areas of authority: content of curriculum; degree offerings and requirements; appointment, promotion, and tenure; and selection of department chairs. Indeed, Kaplan's findings refuted the oft-touted notion of the demise of shared governance. The 2007–08 international Changing Academic Profession (CAP) Survey included a sample of US faculty and a number of questions on academic governance. Based on the responses, Finkelstein, Ming, and Cummings (2010) concluded that faculty members have maintained a significant role in the selection of new faculty and in promotion and tenure decisions, but not in the areas of administrator selection, budget, and new academic programs.

Figure 8.5 displays the percentage of faculty who "somewhat agree" or "agree strongly" that faculty are sufficiently involved in campus decision making. Only about one-half of faculty members responding to the HERI triennial Faculty Survey agreed that faculty are sufficiently involved in campus decision making, and the trend appears to be going down slightly over time.

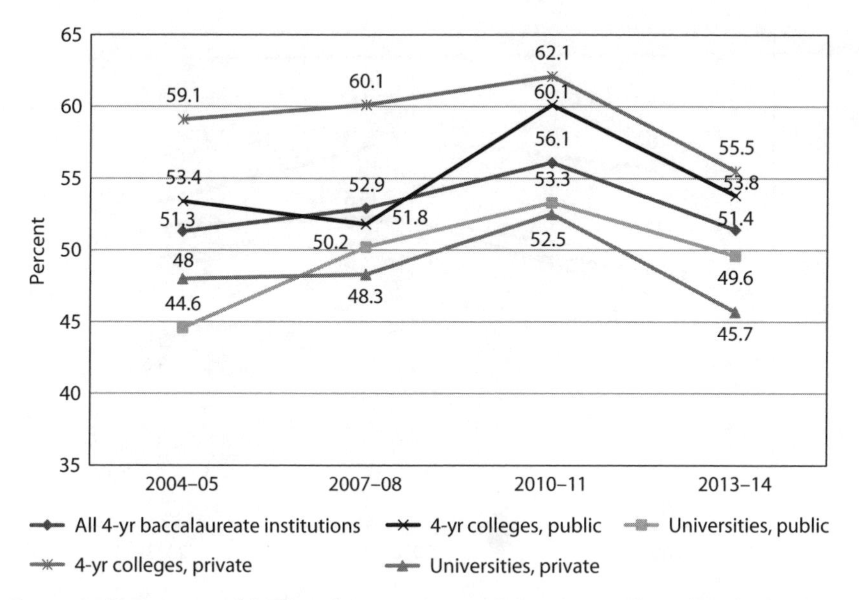

Figure 8.5 Percentage of faculty who agree "strongly" or "somewhat" that the faculty are involved in campus decision making, 2007–2014, selected years. *Sources:* HERI:04; HERI:07; HERI:10; HERI:13. (Refer to appendix A for key to data sources.)

Note: This question was added to the HERI survey in 2004–05.

Figure 8.6 shows the percentage of faculty who agree strongly or somewhat that administrators consider faculty concerns when making policy. There is much lower agreement among faculty across types of institutions, and again, the trend appears to be going down slightly over time.

Generally, the less prestigious the institution the less authority in institutional decision making afforded to the faculty. The complexity of large research institutions makes collective collegial decision making more difficult to achieve. In these institutions, faculty members may be more content to focus on their research and leave administration to administrators. A quote from interviews conducted by sociologist Burton R. Clark (1987) perhaps best expresses an attitude on the skeptical end of the continuum:

> A natural scientist at the same college joined the refrain of mixed feelings with the often-heard view that faculty members "who would like to spend all of their time running the college" do not have anything better to do. They can be seen as campus politicians, even as "street people" who spend their time gossiping in the hallways: What I do know is that the faculty who are most engaged by college

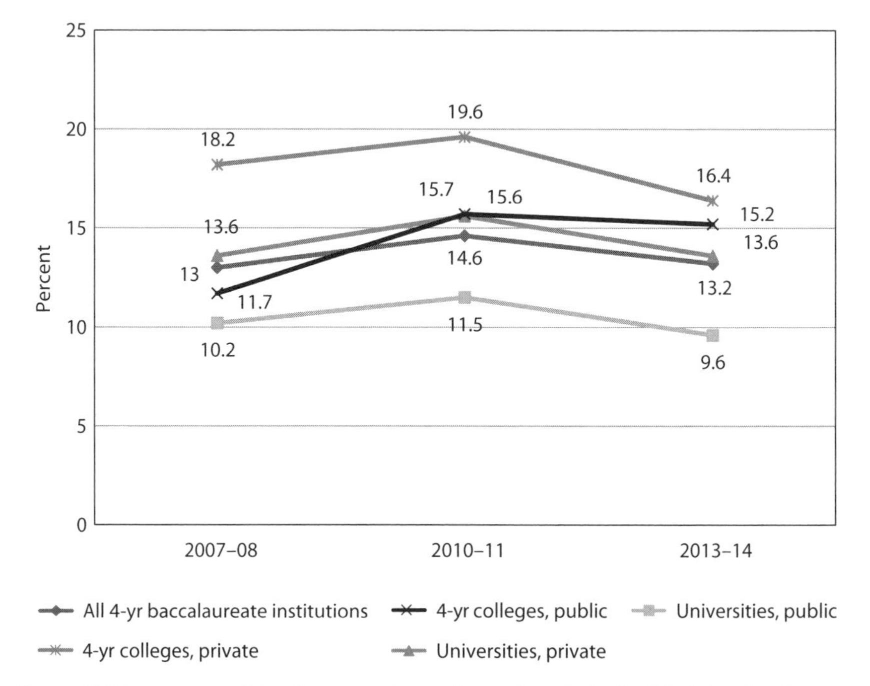

Figure 8.6 Percentage of faculty reporting as "very descriptive" of their institution that "administrators consider faculty concerns when making policy," 2007–2014, selected years. *Sources:* HERI:07; HERI:10; HERI:13. (Refer to appendix A for key to data sources.)

---

governance are the people whose intelligence and opinions I respect the least. They are people with time on their hands very often because they are not doing anything else, so I don't know, I have mixed feelings. I think we have a reasonably competent administration and for the most part I am happy to let them go ahead and do it, with occasionally keeping an eye on them or harassing them when necessary. I guess I think the faculty is certainly as involved as it needs to be. (163)

There is an inherent catch-22 here. Institutional prestige is correlated with academic reputation. Competition for the best faculty creates an incentive to provide more independence and autonomy to faculty, which in turn decreases involvement in collective collegial decision making.

Critics of shared governance say that it hinders an institution's ability to be responsive to the needs of students and the economic interests of the nation.

Administrators and governing boards lament the amount of time it takes to invoke shared governance processes and the snail's pace of committees. Adrianna Kezar and Peter Eckel (2004) argue that it is during periods of transition and rapid change that we need more focused research on what improves institutional decision making and response time. They synthesize governance literature and identify gaps. They document the appeal of increasingly bureaucratic systems and the disadvantages of these systems. They cite Sporn (1999), for example, who found "lowered morale, interpersonal and organizational conflict, and loss of institutional values and integrity" in "corporate-like" environments (Kezar and Eckel 2004, 372). Additionally, they assert that there is growing evidence of tension among higher education stakeholders regarding what constitutes "public interest."

One highly visible example of the tension is the resignation and reinstatement of the President of the University of Virginia, Teresa Sullivan, in June 2012. A *University of Virginia Magazine* (2012) special report documents the events.

> The resignation and reinstatement of President Teresa Sullivan during a tumultuous June were part of a series of events unprecedented at the University of Virginia, and for that matter, in all of higher education. The drama that unfolded on Grounds attracted the national media spotlight, not only for the controversy surrounding the conflict between the president and the Board of Visitors, but also for the passionate support for U.Va. that the University community and alumni displayed. The University was called "Ground Zero for Change," where many of the issues that threaten public colleges across the country took center stage. Debate centered on governance issues involving the Board of Visitors, online learning, pace of change, health care, budget and funding challenges, and faculty recruitment and retention. Other principles near and dear to U.Va., including honor and Jeffersonian ideals, were reaffirmed in the crucible of the leadership crisis. (11)[1]

The report includes a time line of events, which reads like the script for a network drama on par with ABC's hit television series *Scandal.* Beginning June 10, 2012, when Helen Dragas, rector of the University of Virginia Board of Visitors, slid down a slippery slope: "Helen Dragas announces Teresa Sullivan's resignation to U.Va. vice presidents and deans. Helen Dragas gathers U.Va. deans and vice presidents together to announce that Teresa Sullivan has agreed to resign, effective Aug. 15" (*University of Virginia Magazine* 2012, 12). The report quotes Dragas as saying "The Board feels the need for a bold leader who can help develop, articulate and implement a concrete and achievable strategic plan to re-elevate the University to its highest potential. We need a leader with a great willingness to adapt the way we deliver our teaching, research and patient care to the realities of the external environment" (*University of Virginia Magazine* 2012, 12).

On June 15 the Alumni Association invited comments to pass along to the Board of Visitors. The volume is so heavy it crashed the association's servers, and more than 5,500 comments were forwarded in a matter of days (*University of Virginia Magazine* 2012, 12). On June 17 the faculty senate held an emergency meeting: "The Faculty Senate meets at the Darden School to ratify its Executive Committee's earlier resolution declaring no confidence in the Board. Eight hundred people attend the meeting, and John Simon [then executive vice president and provost, now president of Lehigh University] speaks out against the Board's actions" (*University of Virginia Magazine* 2012, 12). The next day, June 18, the Board of Visitors met: "The Board holds a special meeting in the Rotunda to determine an interim president. Meanwhile, more than 2,000 people gather on the Lawn for the 'Rally for Transparency' in support of President Sullivan" (*University of Virginia Magazine* 2012, 12).

On June 21, the deans request that President Sullivan be reinstated: "The University's deans sign a letter to the Board asking for Sullivan's reinstatement" (*University of Virginia Magazine* 2012, 12). The letter says: "It is clear after nearly two weeks of outrage, indignation, upset, threats of withdrawal of support and loyalty, that the people of the University of Virginia, and their ideas, which together comprise the University much more than buildings or landscapes, regard the decision as a mistake made in the absence of open discourse and courtesy" (*University of Virginia Magazine* 2012, 12).

On June 26 the saga comes to a close. The Board of Visitors unanimously votes to reinstate Teresa Sullivan. The Board also votes to affirm a motion supporting Helen Dragas. "After Sullivan's reinstatement, Heywood Fralin [University of Virginia board member and former rector] makes a motion in support of Helen Dragas. 'There has never been any question regarding her integrity,' he says. The Board votes unanimously in support of the motion. Dragas says she is humbled by their support. Sullivan speaks to the Board, thanking them for renewing their confidence in her. 'All of us seek only one thing: what is best for our University,' she says" (*University of Virginia Magazine* 2012, 12).

There are multiple takeaway messages from the UVA case. Faculty members, at least at research universities, have the power to make their voices heard, es-

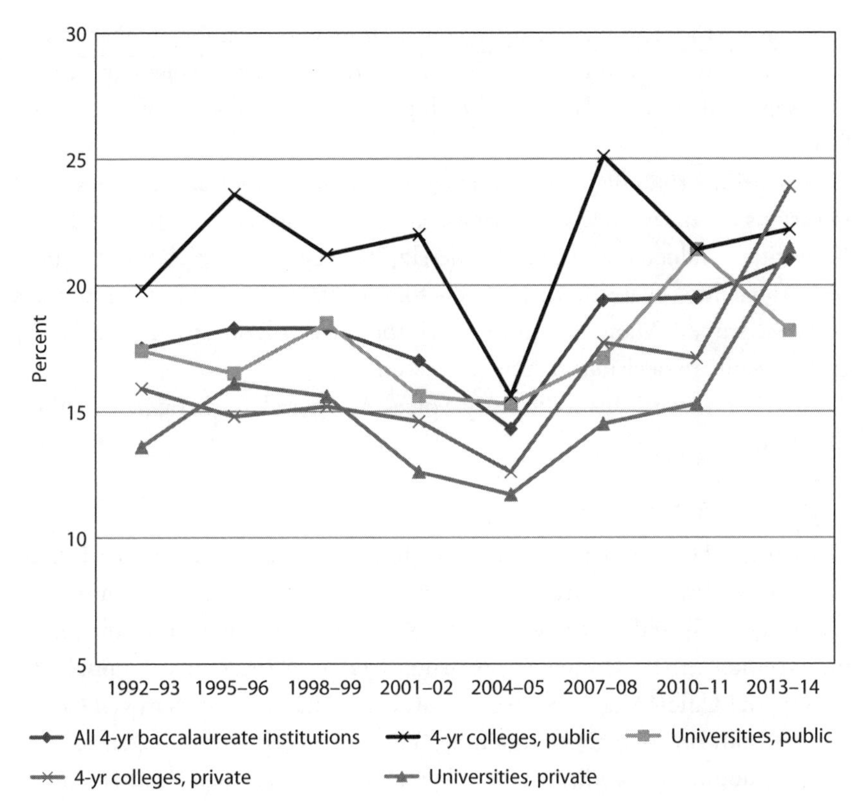

Figure 8.7 Percentage of faculty reporting as "very descriptive" of their institution that "faculty are typically at odds with campus administration," 1992–2014, selected years. *Sources:* HERI:92; HERI:95; HERI:98; HERI:01; HERI:04; HERI:07; HERI:10; HERI:13. (Refer to appendix A for key to data sources.)

pecially when those voices form a chorus including alumni and students. There are serious consequences when shared governance processes are sidestepped. There are distinct differences in point of view regarding what constitutes "public interest" and is illustrative of tensions playing out at institutions all over the country, some with not so happily-ever-after endings.

Figure 8.7 displays percentages of faculty who agree strongly or somewhat strongly that faculty members are typically at odds with campus administration. A quick glance at the figure shows differences by type of institution and an upward trend, providing further evidence of tension.

What are the factors that may be contributing tension among higher education stakeholders? And how do we best ensure that faculty voices are heard? One way is to cultivate faculty leadership and leadership development among faculty.

In an effort to understand the extent to which faculty leaders are included in various institutional level decisions, the Ohio University Center for Higher Education conducted a Faculty Leadership Survey. The survey was administered to faculty senate chairs of all doctoral institutions. Among the findings from the survey: Many institutions lack the infrastructure to engage faculty meaningfully in decision-making processes.

Another way to ensure faculty voices are heard is through collective bargaining.

Collective Bargaining

The National Center for the Study of Collective Bargaining in Higher Education and the Professions tracks information about the prevalence of unions in the academy. Sproul, Bucklew, and Houghton (2014) compiled information on unionization in the United States using data from the Current Population Survey, the Union Membership and Coverage Database, and National Center for the Study of Collective Bargaining. They found "education in general, and higher education specifically, has slowly, methodically, and rather quietly become one of the most heavily unionized segments, with much greater representation than traditional labor segments such as steel and mining" (Sproul, Bucklew, and Houghton 2014, 1). Taken as a whole, the education services industry, including elementary and middle school teachers, secondary school teachers, librarians, and counselors, is "very large" and "very heavily unionized" (4). They go so far as to refer to higher education as a "sleeping giant" (2) and document the size of the proportion of all US faculty members (including graduate students) represented by collective bargaining agreements at more than one-quarter (27%) (1). There is variation by type of institution and sector. The 2012 *Directory of US Faculty Contracts and Bargaining Agents in Institutions of Higher Education* (Berry and Savarese 2012) documents these differences. For example, 42% of faculty members in public two-year institutions are unionized. One-quarter of faculty members in four-year institutions are unionized, while 7% of faculty members in private four-year institutions are unionized. Twenty percent of graduate students are unionized, and two-thirds of this group has become unionized since 1995. States with larger proportions of unionized faculty include California, New York, New Jersey, Illinois, Michigan, Massachusetts, Florida, Pennsylvania, and Washington. The most prevalent national unions representing faculty are the American Association of University Professors, the American Federation of Teachers, and the National Education Association. The United Automobile Workers Union and the American Federation of Teachers represent the majority of the unionized graduate students. There have been 120 new bargaining units in higher education established since 2000 (Berry and Savarese 2012). In sum, academic collective bargaining "is expanding at a faster rate than overall union growth" and "the expansion of graduate student employee unionization is an area of special activity" (Sproul, Bucklew, and Houghton 2014, 9).

Some states have sought to limit the role of collective bargaining, however. The"Wisconsin uprising" and Ohio's Senate Bill 5 stand out as high-profile examples with different outcomes. In Wisconsin, Act 10, which holds wage negotiations to the rate of inflation, ends automatic union dues deductions and requires annual union recertification votes, was upheld by the state Supreme Court. In Ohio, Senate Bill 5 would have prevented unions from charging fair-share dues to employees who opt out, would have restricted the ability to strike, and would have limited public employees ability to collectively bargain for wages, preventing them from collectively bargaining for health insurance and pensions. Voters, through a veto referendum, repealed SB5. Teachers, firefighters, and police officers led the campaign. To what extent has this climate of tension impacted faculty job satisfaction? The next section provides a snapshot of data related to faculty perceptions of climate, culture, and collegiality.

Climate, Culture, and Collegiality

One of the five themes addressed in the COACHE Tenure-Track Faculty Job Satisfaction Survey is climate, culture, and collegiality. Survey items include tenure-track faculty members' perception of the fairness with which their immediate supervisors evaluate their work; the interest tenured faculty members take in tenure-track faculty members' professional development; and the opportunities available to tenure-track faculty to collaborate with tenured faculty. Questions also elicit responses regarding perceptions of the amount of personal and professional interactions tenure-track faculty members have with pretenure and tenured colleagues; their level of satisfaction with how well they fit (e.g., their sense of belonging, their comfort level) in their departments; and the intellectual vitality of tenured colleagues in their departments. The survey section ends by asking faculty to rate their agreement with the statement, "On the whole, my department treats pre-tenure faculty fairly compared to one another." Overall findings from the *COACHE Highlights Report* (2008) reveal that "faculty reported the greatest satisfaction with the fairness with which their immediate supervisors evaluate their work and the amount of personal interaction with pre-tenure colleagues, and the least satisfaction with the intellectual vitality of tenured faculty in their departments" (6).

Figure 8.8 displays the mean ratings of satisfaction with ten dimensions of culture, climate, and collegiality by gender. Tenure-track men were more satisfied than tenure-track women on almost every dimension.

Men on the tenure track expressed higher levels of satisfaction with the fairness with which their supervisor evaluates their work, the interest tenured faculty members take in their professional development, opportunities to collaborate with tenured faculty, professional interaction with tenured colleagues, and sense of belonging in the department. Men on the tenure track also expressed higher mean ratings of satisfaction than female faculty on the tenure track with the extent to which pretenured faculty were treated fairly compared with one another. Both men and women expressed overall lowest satisfaction in three areas: opportunities to interact and collaborate with tenured colleagues and intellectual vitality of tenured colleagues.

Women on the tenure track were significantly more satisfied than men on the tenure track with only one dimension: personal interaction with pretenured colleagues.

Table 8.1 displays the mean ratings of satisfaction with ten dimensions of culture, climate, and collegiality and by race/ethnicity. White non-Hispanic faculty on the tenure track reported significantly more satisfaction than members of other racial/ethnic groups.

Yet when faculty members are asked whether or not they would choose an academic career if they had it to go over again, or whether they still wanted to be a college professor, they respond positively and have consistently done so over time. Figure 8.9 shows the percentages of faculty responding "definitely yes" or "probably yes" to the question, Do you still want to be a college professor? An overwhelming majority of faculty in all four-year institutions (85.4%) said yes. Faculty members in universities, both public and private, are slightly less certain after the economic downturn.

What does this mean for the future of the academic profession? Taken together, the decline in the proportion of faculty holding tenured or tenure-

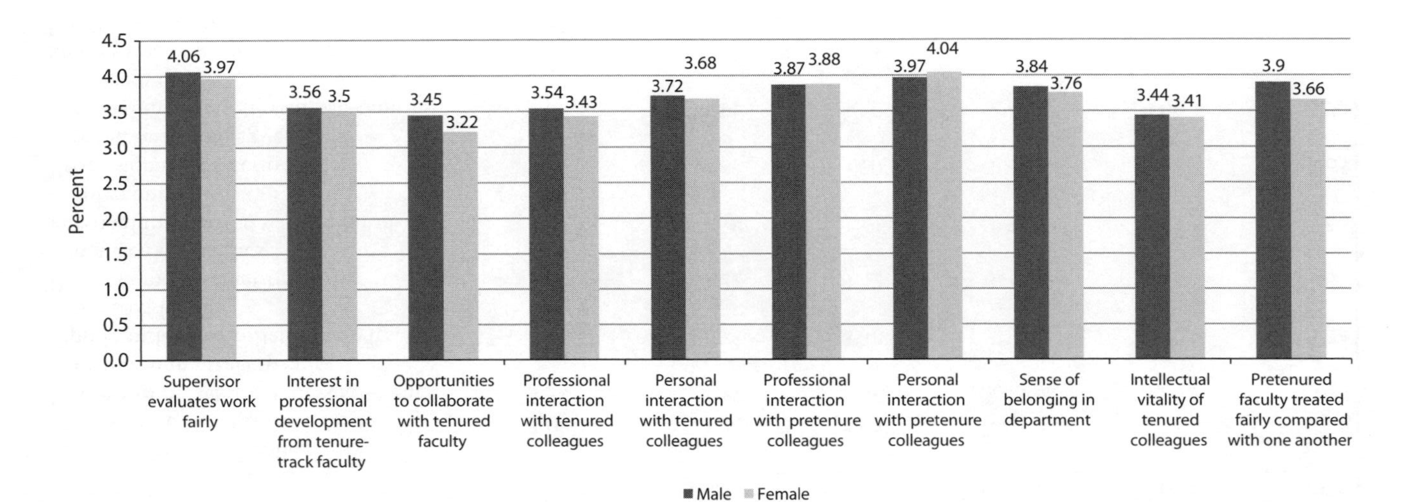

Figure 8.8 Mean ratings of satisfaction with "Culture, Climate, and Collegiality," by dimension and gender, 2005–2006, 2006–2007, 2007–2008. *Sources:* COACHE:05; COACHE:06; COACHE:07. (Refer to appendix A for key to data sources.)

Table 8.1 Mean ratings of satisfaction with "Culture, Climate, and Collegiality," by dimension and race/ethnicity, 2005–2006, 2006–2007, 2007–2008

	White, non-Hispanic	American Indian or Native Alaskan	Asian or Pacific Islander	Black or African American	Hispanic or Latino	Other or multiracial
Culture, climate, and collegiality						
Supervisor evaluates work fairly	4.04	3.94	3.92	3.96	4.05	4.08
Interest in professional development from tenure-track faculty	3.54	3.14	3.56	3.45	3.49	3.33
Opportunities to collaborate with tenured faculty	3.36	2.85	3.38	3.17	3.30	3.14
Professional interaction with tenured colleagues	3.51	3.22	3.42	3.42	3.55	3.33
Personal interaction with tenured colleagues	3.74	3.38	3.61	3.58	3.65	3.56
Professional interaction with pre-tenure colleagues	3.90	3.87	3.70	3.83	3.88	3.65
Personal interaction with pre-tenure colleagues	4.04	4.11	3.82	3.92	4.00	3.70
Sense of belonging in department	3.84	3.47	3.73	3.55	3.83	3.72
Intellectual vitality of tenured colleagues	3.45	3.07	3.39	3.49	3.34	3.07

Sources: COACHE:06; COACHE:07; COACHE:08. (Refer to appendix A for key.)

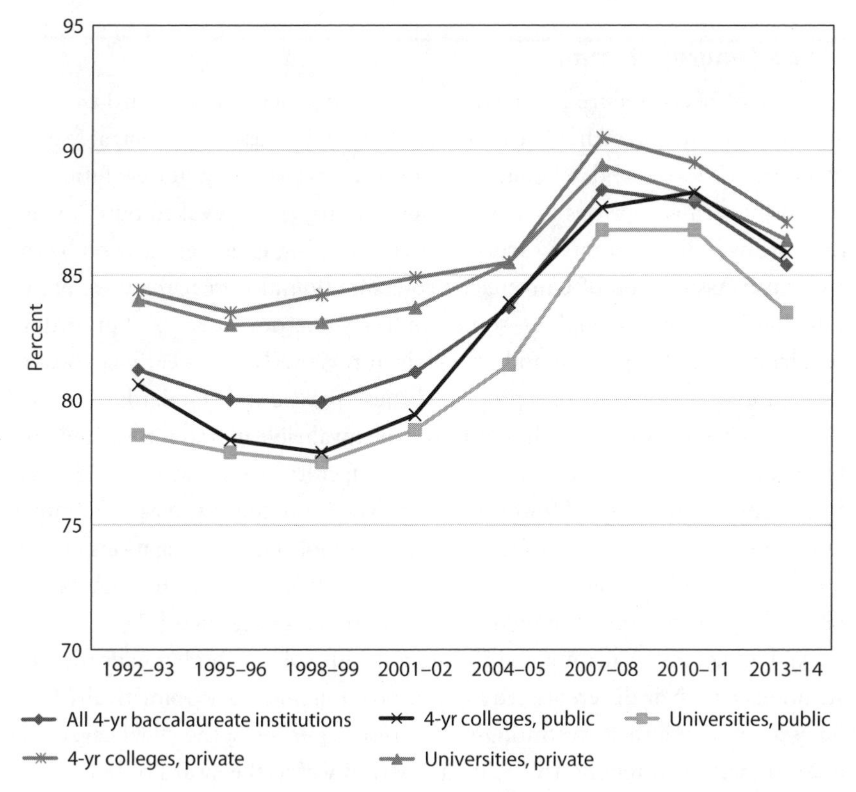

Figure 8.9 Percentage of faculty responding "definitely yes" or "probably yes" to "still want to be a college professor," 1992–2014, selected years. *Sources:* HERI:92; HERI:95; HERI:98; HERI:01; HERI:04; HERI:07; HERI:10; HERI:13. (Refer to appendix A for key to data sources.)

track appointments (documented in chapter 3) and tensions surrounding fundamental core values of what it means to "be faculty" (described in this chapter) converge to create challenges and opportunities for higher education.

To say that in contemporary higher education tenure is contentious is an understatement. Some observers foresee the death of tenure, proclaiming that elements of a terminal illness are palpable (Wilson 2010). Some speak to tenure's vulnerability, its weakening as a norm (Trower 2008), a ripe target of a siege mentality. Still others are resigned to its inevitable decline (Zemsky 2008). Is tenure still necessary? We believe the answer is yes. What, then, is the tenure dilemma?

The Tenure Dilemma

In many respects, tenure is the structural arrangement to safeguard the core values faculty members hold dear. Tenure for faculty has been a central feature of much of postsecondary education for nearly a century. Its evolution, as traced by such authorities as Walter Metzger (1973), has evoked outpourings of praise as well as torrents of scorn. Tenure's origins, endorsed early on by the American Association of University Professors (founded in 1915), were predicated on requiring a complex—some would say onerous—dismissal procedure requiring both due process and peer-driven review. Tenure's early advocates, to ensure academic freedom, promoted these procedural standards. That rationale for tenure, over time, has proved to be invaluable in promoting academic freedom without which untold numbers of faculty could have (would have) faced censure and worse. However, tenure was never conceived as a guarantee of lifelong job security or the freehold right to a job against allegations of serious misconduct (of whatever kind) (Metzger 1973). To reiterate: Tenure was never intended to protect individuals who were not doing their jobs.

And, of course, as maintained throughout this volume, higher education institutions and their differentiated institutional missions vary dramatically from one setting to another. Accordingly, for present purposes, the usual caveat applies to matters of tenure: the contexts (within which the award of tenure and the associated characteristics of implementation) are far from homogenous.

We start as our point of departure with a renewed (if qualified) commitment to the preservation of tenure described in the classic AAUP Statement on Academic Freedom and Tenure as refined and re-promulgated in 1940. But the new realities of higher education, economic and otherwise, and the complexity of academic careers militate strongly in favor of a reconsideration of the trade-offs prompted by institutional policies and practices in the award of and implementation of tenure. These several factors compel a reexamination of assumptions embraced by tenure's advocates.

The Clogged Academic Pipeline Factor

The changing retirement landscape, and the pressures faculty members feel to delay retirement decisions in the face of economic uncertainties, has led to the increasing average age of faculty retirement (see chapter 6). Correspondingly, this development directly and significantly constrains the number of available points of entry at the metaphorical pipeline's entry end—that is, the quantity of prospective new appointments available to those aspirants seeking to embark on academic careers.

As one consequence of the end of mandatory retirement (uncapping), reinforced by subsequent anxieties about the economy, fewer openings, as noted, exist for new appointments, and this development comes at a time when the academic labor market in most academic fields (but clearly not all) is heavily skewed on the side of employers (general low demand for academic appointments) rather than job seekers (ample supply of available position seekers). The net effect is that more full-time academic employees stay put longer, occupying precious academic lines that contribute to the congestion in the pipeline, with highly consequential (admittedly unmeasurable but real) deleterious consequences. These effects are described below.

Academic Quality

Recognizing that lifespans have increased significantly during past decades, a consequence is that larger proportions of the workforce-at-large are capable, physically and mentally, of performing well on the job at a later age than their predecessors (Sheehy 1995). That is a given. Indeed there are countless examples of colleagues of advanced age who continue to excel in their work and who bring historical perspective and wisdom to the workplace that would otherwise be scarcer. Concomitantly, there are many instances (the proportions are indeterminable) in which older faculty may bring less energy and cutting-edge discipline awareness to their classrooms, research, and mentoring roles. These instances of marginality, characterized by slipping currency or productivity, often, it appears, are buffered by the protection of tenure—in the absence of clear malfeasance or conspicuously limited performance.

Grappling with issues of quality and corresponding reasonable expectations of productivity in its various forms surely constitute the most controversial aspect of the tenure issue. After all, just how is adequate performance to be determined? There are no easy answers, but systematic reviews of individual faculty members' performance, as noted subsequently, are crucial.

While critics of tenure abound, there have been few head-on attacks on tenure itself, either by governing boards of institutions or higher education systems, by the respected Association of Governing Boards of Universities and Colleges, or by campus-based senior administrators. But as political criticisms of higher education intensify (challenging, e.g., sharp increases in costs to students; consequent large, debilitating student indebtedness; insufficient attention to academic programs sufficiently well linked to job market needs, and so on), tenure appears to be more vulnerable than usual to criticisms by political foes as an anachronism. Even so, the curious fact remains that, despite widespread economic stringencies and concurrent management and administrative pleas for increased staffing flexibility, there have been few visible or audible frontal assaults on tenure. Perhaps more such clashes lie ahead.

And just maybe there is an unspoken contributing factor in the form of recognizing, by friends of tenure and foes alike, that in some respects tenure as a presence on campuses is being diminished by the explosive redistribution of types of academic appointments. That is to say, as shown elsewhere in these pages, full-time off-track appointments and part-time, adjunct appointments are displacing regular tenure-track appointments, and this unmistakable trend may be gaining momentum as a greying professoriate phases into retirement. Thus tenure is to some degree simply evaporating. Accordingly, some critics of tenure might argue that the political costs of attacking tenure head-on militate in favor of a (seemingly) nonconfrontational stance insofar as the "problem" of a heavily tenured-in faculty is currently dissipating and being succeeded by a much more nimble and irresistibly less expensive deployment of relatively risk-free contingent faculty appointments. Thus some critics of tenure might conclude that the problem is solved—or, at least, is about to be solved; patience, not combat, is the preferred path.

Faculty Evaluation and Accountability

It is important to delineate those matters that are tenure and promotion issues from those that are human resources management concerns. Tenure and promotion committees have the responsibility for judging the merits of candidates' dossiers regarding teaching, research, and service. They do not have supervisory responsibility over employees of the institution.

Some would argue that faculty members are not supervised in the same sense that regular employees are supervised. It is true that faculty members hold special status within the organizational structure of colleges and universities. A question often asked is, Does the individual hold faculty status? The response provides some context for understanding the individual's role in the institution. Similar to partners in a law firm, tenured faculty members hold a vested interest in the mission of the institution and the overall success of the organization. This special status affords faculty members certain privileges.

For example, faculty members enjoy a great deal of autonomy in pursuing their work. Professional ethics dictate that faculty members not abuse the privilege. So what happens if someone does abuse the privilege? This is a serious concern. From a management perspective, granting tenure is a multimillion dollar investment and requires that meticulous care be taken in the decision. From a faculty perspective, granting tenure is an affirmation that the individual is someone who is seen as a colleague and who will contribute to the life of the academic program and department over the course of a career.

The processes governing tenure and promotion decisions are meant to safeguard abuse from happening and to ensure that good decisions are made. The tenure and promotion process is designed to provide individuals with the opportunity to demonstrate competence in accordance with the mission of the institution across the three primary areas of faculty work: teaching, research, and service. Demonstrating competence across the three areas takes time. Time also provides an opportunity for administrators and other faculty members to get a sense of the commitment of the individual to the institution and to the ethics of the profession.

In most institutions, individuals who are on the tenure track have multiyear contracts culminating in a penultimate year after they have submitted their dossier for tenure and promotion. If the vote of the committee is affirmative, then the odds are that the individual will be granted tenure at the institution.

In the prototypical model, if the vote is not in favor of granting tenure, barring an intervention where evidence is presented that there has been a violation of due process, inadequate consideration, or discrimination, the individual has a year to find a new position. The length of time it takes to go through the tenure process varies by individual and by institution (sometimes referred to as the tenure clock), but according to AAUP guidelines it should not exceed six years, with the seventh year as a definitive final year. In extreme cases, if someone is not performing their assigned duties, then the institution can initiate early termination of the contract while the individual is still on the tenure track. Most institutions have policies governing the timing for notification that a contract will not be renewed.

Many institutions have a midpoint tenure review, which is meant to alert the individual to any concerns that the tenure and promotion committee may have regarding their candidacy for tenure or promotion—again, in the specific areas of teaching, research, and service. Although evidence is sparse, there is at least anecdotal information to suggest that tenure and promotion committees have become the vehicle for communicating dissatisfaction with the overall performance of the candidate during the midpoint review. After receiving this information, the individual may choose to redouble efforts to address the areas of concern or may begin to seek another position at a different higher education institution or outside of academe.

Department chairs typically are required to perform annual evaluations of employees and to provide feedback on individuals' progress toward tenure or promotion. In many institutions the department chair receives input from the tenure and promotion committee or from a separate salary committee, regarding evaluations. Performance evaluation is a human resources management function and an important academic administrative responsibility for which many department chairs have not received training.[2] As such, it is separate from the tenure and promotion process. Or is it? Literature is plentiful suggesting that more training is needed for department chairs to equip them to perform tasks such as annual evaluations. More research is needed to understand the roles and responsibilities of the tenure and promotion committee and the department chair and the relationship between the committee and the chair and to develop processes to govern interactions. This is complicated by the fact that the role of the chair is not consistent across institutions. In some institutions, the chair is elected. In others, the chair is appointed. In some institutions, the chair has a vote in tenure and promotion decisions. In others, the chair does not have a vote but is expected to provide an independent judgment that is forwarded to the dean of the college or school. These variations impact the ability of chairs to perform management functions, particularly related to supervision.

We have made the point that change in higher education has accelerated, particularly since the economic downturn. We need a way to reconcile the need to give candidates and committees time to recommend good decisions regarding tenure and promotion with the need to accelerate the pace of change.

Evaluation is just one example. Federal and state employment and labor laws such as the Family Medical Leave Act and regulations addressing equal employment opportunity, sexual harassment, and hostile work environment apply to all employees, including faculty, and need to be considered separate of tenure and promotion. Dysfunctional tenure and promotion committees and department chairs that practice conflict avoidance are extreme examples of what is wrong with the system. Tenure and promotion has become muddled with issues that would be more appropriately handled through human resources management procedures. On many college campuses, however, human resources management professionals steer clear of academic units and seldom interact with department chairs. Has the tenure system become the scapegoat for poor decision making and benign neglect of supervision of faculty employees? Perhaps. Again: Tenure was never intended to protect individuals who were not doing the job.

A number of factors, including the affordability of a college degree, job security in the public sector, and a marked decrease in state and federal appropriations for public higher education, have begun to have an increasingly significant impact on higher education. There is also the growing perception that tenured faculty in American colleges and universities enjoy a privileged lifestyle—sinecure—no matter how well or poorly they perform. As a result of this perception, tenure has come under fierce attack by a number of constituencies inside, as well as outside of academia. Moreover, mandatory retirement of tenured faculty, which at one point occurred when an individual reached the age of seventy, can no longer be invoked according to federal anti–age discrimination statutes; therefore, faculty members currently have tenure until they choose to retire, absent cause for dismissal or financial exigency (see chapter 6 for a fuller treatment of events leading up to the elimination of mandatory retirement).

This is nothing new, however. Throughout the 1990s, the concept of tenure for faculty members at universities and colleges came under fire from state legislators, boards of trustees, and the public at large. Legislatures and taxpayers were particularly concerned that tenure had become a lifetime guarantee of employment at a time when jobs in the corporate, government, and nonprofit sectors were no longer secure. It was also difficult for the academy to communicate the rigor of the tenure process and the constant, ongoing review that takes place in academe through grants, refereed articles, invited and competitive presentations, national awards, sabbatical leaves, and the achievement of full-rank status.

Many public representatives took tenure as a cause of the seemingly low productivity of higher education. Experts on the issue say that many parents are dissatisfied with what their children are or are not getting out of college coursework. Employers have weighed in as well, sometimes complaining about the quality of recent graduates.

Post-Tenure Review

Post-tenure review emerged as one answer to the public's demand for standards and accountability in faculty work. The National Commission on

Higher Education recommended in its summary report *To Strengthen Higher Education*, published in 1982, the adoption of a post-tenure review process and suggested that post-tenure review was one of the most urgent issues facing the academic community (Goodman 1990).[3] Post-tenure review was heralded as a safeguard for tenure and as a mechanism to ensure continued competence, individual renewal, and institutional quality (Goodman 1990).

These ideas were carefully considered at a 1983 meeting of national leaders (the Wingspread Group on Higher Education) cosponsored by the American Council on Education and the American Association of University Professors, resulting in a statement issued by the AAUP, which reaffirmed traditional methods of tenured faculty review. Licata and Morreale (1997) defined post-tenure review as a systematic, comprehensive process, separate from the annual review, aimed specifically at assessing performance and nurturing faculty growth and development. In 1999, and in response to growing pressure for post tenure review, the AAUP advanced minimum standards for good practice in establishing a formal system of post-tenure review (AAUP 1999).

Even though the AAUP supported this recommendation in the 1990s, most state-mandated post-tenure review policies were adopted in American graduate institutions only after mandatory retirement was uncapped. Debates about what post-tenure review means and even whether it should exist have cooled somewhat since the heated battles of the late 1990s, when the adoption of post-tenure review policies at several major public university systems forced administrators and professors at institutions of all types to consider how the trend might affect them. Since then, colleges have adopted a range of policies. Some institutions focus on giving faculty members the resources to meet individual goals; others include mechanisms to judge whether professors have met certain goals, which can lead to dismissal if they have not.

Post-tenure review has two fundamental purposes, one summative and the other formative. The summative purpose seeks to provide assurances of accountability to the institution and to the external public, serving as a developmental tool by triggering rehabilitation efforts on the part of the institution and the faculty member. It can also help to weed out deadwood and to shame a few others into voluntarily taking early retirement. The formative purpose aims to promote continuing growth and development in faculty members' professional skills and to encourage faculty to explore new ways to promote academic excellence.

Post-tenure review policies can be separated into two basic categories: comprehensive periodic review of all tenured faculty, usually at five- to seven-year intervals, and selective review of some faculty, triggered by extant review processes (usually the annual review), which can show ongoing substandard performance in one or more areas. Several state systems have comprehensive post-tenure review processes, including California, Colorado, Florida, Georgia, Hawaii, Maryland, North Carolina, and Wisconsin. The 1994 national survey on the reexamination of faculty roles and rewards by the Carnegie Foundation for the Advancement of Teaching found that 46% of all institutions had regular post-tenure review of faculty and another 28% indicated it was currently under consideration. In 1996 a study showed that 61% of the 680 participating public and private institutions had post-tenure review policies in place, and another 9% were in the midst of policy development (Licata and Morreale 1997).

The divergence of misinformed views has contributed to the formation of two opposing blocs: post-tenure review antagonists and post-tenure review proponents. Advocates think post-tenure review is valuable for addressing accountability issues, improving faculty development and morale, linking mission and individual performance, and identifying unproductive tenured faculty members. Proponents believe that, when approached developmentally, post tenure review can sustain career energy and assist in career enhancement (Association of American Universities 2001). Furthermore, it can enhance faculty performance by guaranteeing systematic, continuous, and comprehensive feedback and opportunities for professional growth (Lees, Hook, and Powers 1999; Licata and Morreale 1997; Plater 2001). O'Meara (2004) asserts that post-tenure review offers the opportunity for faculty to reflect on future career directions, get up to speed on current issues in their disciplines, and interact with and reinvest in their department. It can also hold faculty accountable for future plans and can positively influence the productivity of faculty who have slowed down. Supporters like it, they say, because the faculty, rather than being imposed from above, crafted the system, and because it gives professors the tools—such as personal attention and travel to conferences—to meet professional goals. It is also voluntary, and completion of the three-year process, whose terms are tailored to each faculty member's aspirations, nets participants a raise in base pay.

Post-tenure review advocates contend that once a faculty member receives tenure, he or she too often slides into semiretirement. This belief is supported by several studies that have indicated a decline in faculty research productivity after receiving tenure, which is not accompanied by a commensurate increase in teaching proficiency. Other researchers found that faculty productivity was "saddle shaped"—that is to say, productivity declines immediately after receiving tenure but increases again before attaining the rank of full professor and levels off at the latter stages of career (Bayer and Dutton 1977).

Critics, on the other hand, think post-tenure review will not change faculty performance because faculty members are intrinsically motivated. Many of post-tenure review's antagonists claim that post-tenure review is little more than a veiled attempt to overemphasize faculty duties and eliminate academic freedom by eroding the protection afforded faculty through tenure. The process has the potential to undermine or even destroy hard-won faculty rights of tenure and academic freedom, is excessively costly in time and money needed for other important endeavors, and may erode tenure, academic freedom, and faculty collegiality (Association of American Universities 2001). Some think that the reviews are unwarranted, punitive in nature, and a veiled threat to undermine tenure by narrowing the threshold for what constitutes incompetence—shifting the burden of proof from administration to faculty. Many of the institutions that have adopted post-tenure review are now struggling with the intricacies of implementing a review system that is fair, not overly burdensome, and balances the rights of the faculty member—particularly for due process and academic freedom—against the legitimate need for the institution to certify to its constituents that all faculty are meeting at least a minimal standard.

Little is known about the actual impact of post-tenure review within large state systems. Only recently have scholars been able to demonstrate empirically the longer-term outcomes of post-tenure review (Wood and Des Jarlais 2006). Goodman (1994) studied the outcomes of post-tenure review at the University of Hawaii, Manoa, and found that the program tended to enhance faculty morale and sense of purpose and engagement in their disciplines. Other research suggests that faculty think post-tenure review is unnecessary, yield little to no benefit, and often experience it as a threat (Licata 1986; Wesson and Johnson 1989; Harris 1996).

Conclusion

Academic careers are increasingly complex. Concomitantly, there is no longer a homogeneous academic culture—if there ever truly was one. Unpacking elements of academic culture in these emerging "multiple academies" is critical to understanding the extent to which the new reality inherent in this environment has altered the professional norms and guiding principles that have maintained the foundation of academic life and work in the United States for almost 100 years and that have historically guided individual faculty members in their institutional and professional lives since the days of the medieval university in Europe. We desperately need a framework to help us understand tensions within the academy stemming from different appointment types and evidence that informs our understanding of the confluence of pressures being put on faculty and faculty work resulting from new realities. Higher education must embrace the complexity of academic work in this new environment by providing flexible options for faculty and students in order to succeed. This creates tension within the academy. One way to look at this tension may be to identify the push and pull factors that contribute to cohesion (collegiality) versus stratification (dissension) among faculty. From a structural perspective, what are the policies and procedures in place at our institutions that promote or detract from solidarity or stratification?

A range of vexing issues remain. For example, there has been some momentum for institutions to recognize the contributions of off-track faculty by providing possibility for promotion. To what extent has this created more cohesion among the faculty and to what extent has it contributed to, or furthered, a caste system among faculty members?

Another structural conundrum: Who votes in elections? A faculty handbook typically specifies who is eligible to vote. What is the tipping point in an academic department when it becomes noticeable that a group of individuals are excluded from shared governance processes? How might climate studies be constructed to elicit information about the lived experiences of faculty on different appointment types? What policies and procedures are in place in institutions that either promote or detract from cohesion (a positive culture and climate) among faculty members with different employment appointment types?

Beyond eligibility for voting, what constitutes a majority vote for a policy to pass, and a majority of whom? If it is a policy that focuses on promotion for full-time non-tenure-track faculty, for example, is it necessary to have a majority of tenured and tenure-track faculty support it? To date, our climate surveys have inadequately assessed the culture and climate for employees of different appointment types. The evidence suggesting we are beginning to see declines in autonomy and in participation in governance is important to consider. Furthermore, it is vitally important to the mission of higher education to understand the extent to which external and internal pressures are affecting the most basic values that faculty bring to their daily responsibilities. Confronting the tenure dilemma by engaging in needed tenure reform, while drawing attention to its positive attributes, its role in contributing to the socialization process of new faculty members, and its importance in the development of professional identity is a necessary step in ensuring the future of the faculty factor for generations to come.

NOTES

1. The Board of Visitors is the governing board for the University of Virginia.
2. Human resources management functions are distinct from human resources personnel.
3. The National Commission on Higher Education (1982) released a summary report entitled "To Strengthen Quality in Higher Education," including recommendations for improving educational quality and strengthening public confidence in American higher education.

REFERENCES

American Association of University Professors. 1999. "Post-Tenure Review: An AAUP Response." http://www.aaup.org/report/post-tenure-review-aaup-response.

———. "Shared Governance." http://www.aaup.org/our-programs/shared-governance.

———. "On the Relationship of Faculty Governance to Academic Freedom." http://www.aaup.org/report/relationship-faculty-governance-academic-freedom.

Association of American Universities. 2001. "AAU: Post-Tenure Review." https://www.aau.edu/WorkArea/DownloadAsset.aspx?id=470

Bayer, Alan E., and Jeffrey E. Dutton. 1977. "Career Age and Research-Professional Activities of Academic Scientists: Tests of Alternative Nonlinear Models and Some Implications for Higher Education Faculty Policies." *Journal of Higher Education* 48 (May–June): 259–82.

Berry, Joe, and Michelle Savarese. 2012. *Directory of U.S. Faculty Contracts and Bargaining Agents in Institutions of Higher Education.* Edited by Richard Boris. New York: National Center for the Study of Collective Bargaining in Higher Education and the Professions.

Clark, Burton R. 1987. *The Academic Life. Small Worlds, Different Worlds.* Princeton, NJ: Carnegie Foundation for the Advancement of Teaching.

Collaborative on Academic Careers in Higher Education (COACHE). 2008. *COACHE Highlights Report 2008.* Cambridge, MA: COACHE.

Dill, David D. 2014. "Academic Governance in the US Implications of a 'Commons' Perspective." In *International Trends in University Governance: Autonomy, Self-Government and the Distribution of Authority*, edited by Michael Shattock. New York: Routledge.

Finkelstein, Martin J., Ju Ming, and William K. Cummings. 2010. "The United States of America: Perspectives on Faculty Governance, 1992–2007." In *Changing Governance and Management in Higher Education*, edited by W. Locke, William Cummings, and Donald Fisher. Dordrecht, NL: Springer.

Gappa, Judith M., Ann E. Austin, and Andrea G. Trice. 2007. *Rethinking Faculty Work: Higher Education's Strategic Imperative.* San Francisco, CA: Jossey-Bass.

Goodman, Madeleine J. 1990. "The Review of Tenured Faculty: A Collegial Model." *Journal of Higher Education* 61, no. 4: 408–24.

———. 1994. "The Review of Tenured Faculty at a Research University: Outcomes and Appraisals." *Review of Higher Education* 18, no. 1: 83–94.

Harris, B. J. 1996. "The Relationship between and among Policy Variables, Type of Institution, and Perceptions of Academic Administrators with Regard to Post-Tenure Review." PhD diss., West Virginia University.

Kaplan, Gabriel E. 2004. "Do Governance Structures Matter?" *New Directions for Higher Education* 127 (Autumn–Fall): 23–34.

Kezar, Adrianna J., and Peter D. Eckel. 2004. "Meeting Today's Governance Challenges: A Synthesis of the Literature and Examination of a Future Agenda for Scholarship." *Journal of Higher Education* 75 (July–August): 371–99.

Lees, Douglas N., Sara A. Hook, and Gerald Powers. 1999. "Post-Tenure Review: Changes for Faculty and Challenges for Department Chairs." *Department Chair* 10, no. 4: 7–8.

Licata, Christine M. 1986. *Post-Tenure Faculty Evaluation: Threat or Opportunity?* ASHE Higher Education Report 1. Washington, DC: Association for the Study of Higher Education.

Licata, Christine M., and Joseph C. Morreale. 1997. *Post-Tenure Review: Policies, Practices, Precautions.* Forum on Faculty Roles and Rewards, New Pathways Project. Working Paper Series, no. 12. Washington, DC: American Association for Higher Education.

Metzger, Walter. 1973. "Academic Tenure in America: A Historical Essay." In *Faculty Tenure: A Report and Recommendations by the Commission on Academic Tenure in Higher Education*, edited by William R. Keast and John W. Macy, Jr., 93–159. San Francisco, CA: Jossey-Bass.

National Commission on Higher Education. 1982. "To Strengthen Quality in Higher Education." Washington, DC: American Council on Education.

O'Meara, Kerry Ann. 2004. "Beliefs about Post-Tenure Review: The Influence of Autonomy, Collegiality, Career Stage, and Institutional Context." *Journal of Higher Education* 75 (March–April): 178–202.

Plater, William M. 2001. "A Profession at Risk: Using Post-Tenure Review to Save Tenure and Create an Intentional Future for Academic Community." *Change: The Magazine of Higher Learning* 33, no. 4: 52–57.

Sheehy, Gail. 1995. *New Passages: Mapping Your Life across Time.* New York: Random House.

Sporn, B. 1999. *Responsive University Structures: An Analysis of Adaptation to Socioeconomic Environments of US and European Universities.* London: Jessica Kingsley.

Sproul, Curtis R., Neal Bucklew, and Jeffrey D. Houghton. 2014. "Academic Collective Bargaining: Patterns and Trends." *Journal of Collective Bargaining in the Academy*, vol. 6, art. 5.

Trower, Cathy A. 2008. "Amending Higher Education's Constitution." *Academe* 95 (September–October): 16–18.

———. 2011. "Senior Faculty Vitality." In TIAA-CREF Institute *Advancing Higher Education*, June, 1–13.

University of Virginia Magazine. 2012. "A University of Virginia Magazine Special Report. University Digest: From Resignation to Reinstatement; A Timeline of the Events of June 2012." *University of Virginia Magazine* (Fall): 11–13.

Wesson, Marianne, and Sandra Johnson. 1989. *A Study of Post-Tenure Peer Review at the University of Colorado.* Richmond, VA: Association for the Study of Higher Education.
Wilson, Robin. 2010. "Tenure, RIP: What the Vanishing Status Means for the Future of Education." *Chronicle of Higher Education*, July 4. http://chronicle.com/article/Tenure-RIP/66114/
Wood, Melinda, and Christine Des Jarlais. 2006. "When Post-Tenure Review Policy and Practice Diverge: Make the Case for Congruence." *Journal of Higher Education* 77 (July–August): 561–88.
Zemsky, Robert. 2008. "Tenure Wild Cards." *Academe* 94 (September–October): 19–21.

9

Academic Compensation Trends in a New Era

"They're not in it for the money!" That capsule characterization has been employed to explain the puzzling pecuniary behavior of college and university faculty in America almost uninterruptedly for more than three and a half centuries. Indeed, in his groundbreaking study, *The Emergence of the American University*, Veysey (1965) observed that tutors and professors throughout the eighteenth and nineteenth centuries were typically men of "independent means" who could afford to subsist on their meager academic salaries.[1] And in *American Professors*, Bowen and Schuster (1986) observed that it was only after World War II that academic compensation rose sufficiently quickly and robustly to afford a middle- or even upper-middle-class life style to its incumbents. That rise, of course, fell victim to the stagflation of the 1970s, and it was only in the 1990s that "real" faculty salaries recovered their pre-1970 gloss—only to be savaged a decade later as a result of the Great Recession of 2008. It is with that defining event in mind that this chapter seeks to provide a fresh examination of the status of academic compensation in the post-recession period. Beyond simply updating the basic national data supplied annually by the American Association of University Professors, we seek to determine whether the "marketization" of faculty salaries—by discipline, institutional type and sector (public versus private), and collective bargaining status—has persisted. Attenuated? Accelerated?

More important, we seek to report the results of new analyses in a number of areas of compensation that were not touched on in our earlier work but which have assumed much greater importance in light of recent trends. These include compensation of part-time and full-time, non-tenure-track (fixed-term contract) faculty based on recent research by labor and professional organizations, including the Coalition on the Academic Workforce, the results of recent salary equity studies seeking to assess the magnitude and persistence of gender-based disparities in academic compensation, and the results of new analyses of comparative compensation, that is, how academic compensation compares with compensation in other sectors of the economy (government and industry, public and private) when we compare advanced degree holders across sectors but within common subfields and job categories, drawing on recent data from the US Bureau of Labor Statistics. Finally, we examine new analyses of the changing status of academic fringe benefits as a key but frequently overlooked component of total compensation and the rewards of an academic career.

We begin by reminding the reader that for the vast majority of American academics—unlike, for instance, their Latin American colleagues—salary from their primary institutional employer typically constitutes the major component of their income. That includes, of course, not only their base institutional salary (typically for a nine- or ten-month contract) but also base salary supplements from their institution for overload and summer teaching as well as other special tasks. More than one-third of faculty members receive supplemental salary or stipends. Beyond remuneration from their primary employing institution, as many as one in five US faculty receive income from consulting fees or paid work at other colleges and universities, about one in seven from royalties and speaking fee honoraria, and about one in four from employment outside the academic sector altogether (Schuster and Finkelstein 2006). Getting reliable information on these external sources is difficult; so, in this chapter we limit our focus to income received from the primary employing institution, usually base salary, but, when available, supplementary institutional income typically in the form of overloads or special stipends as well as fringe benefits.

An Overview of Recent Salary Trends

In higher education, where education credentials have historically tended to be relatively uniform at least in the four-year sector, salary levels tend to be based heavily, as in most other industries or sectors, on some mix of seniority and performance: not merely years on the job, but more especially on the academic rank ultimately achieved and perhaps years in that rank.[2] As in any industry, then, in examining salaries, one needs to encompass both ends of the spectrum: entry level and middle or later career.[3] Figure 9.1 displays average salaries of full-time instructional faculty between 1970 and 2014 in current and constant 1970 dollars.[4] A glance at the figure suggests that the steady linear increase in current-dollars salaries over the past four decades conceals a decline in inflation-adjusted"

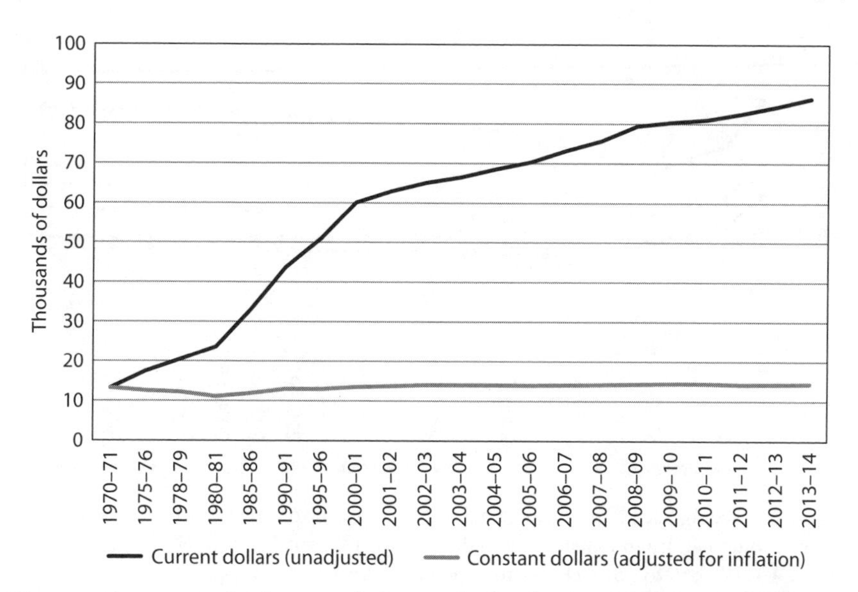

Figure 9.1 Average academic-year salaries standardized to nine months of all full-time instructional faculty in current and constant 1970 dollars, 1970–2014. *Source:* Selected years, AAUP:1970 to 2014. (Refer to appendix A for key to data sources.)

Note: Adjusted for inflation using 1970 average Consumer Price Index for All Urban Consumers.

---

dollars throughout the 1970s and a slow and steady uptick beginning in the 1980s, with recovery to pre-1970 levels in real dollars not achieved until 1995–96. Since then, growth in real terms has been miniscule through 2009–10, when it was halted in the aftermath of the Great Recession. In all, the hard reality is that faculty salaries have remained virtually stagnant for a four-decade period.

Decline and subsequent recovery have not, however, proceeded evenly across the academic ranks. As shown in figure 9.2, the initial decline in real compensation was steepest for full professors, although they recovered more quickly. Moreover, the gap between the real salaries of full professors, on one hand, and those of associate and assistant professors, on the other, has grown steadily since the mid-1990s recovery and shows no signs of abating. At the same time, the relatively small gap between associate and assistant professors, on one hand, and between the latter and instructors or lecturers, on the other, has remain unchanged, suggesting a clear and increasing stratification of compensation between the most senior faculty (full professors) and everyone else.[5]

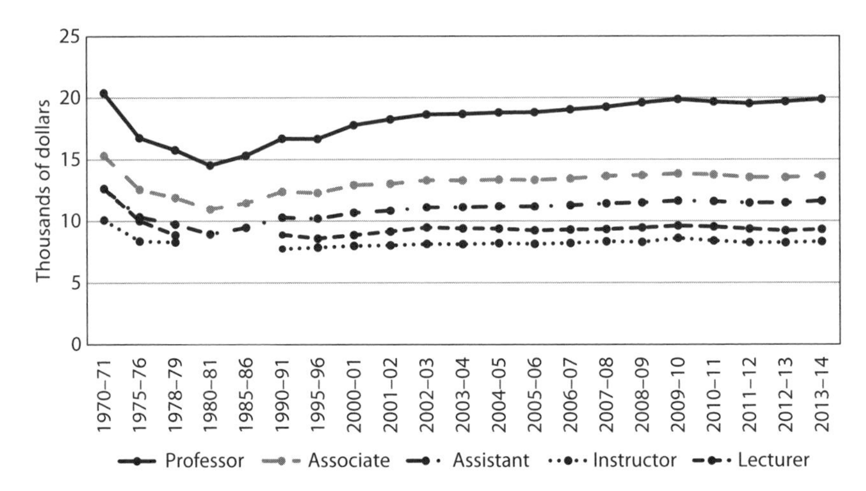

Figure 9.2 Average academic-year salaries standardized to nine months of full-time instructional faculty in constant 1970 dollars by rank, 1970–2014. *Source:* Selected years, AAUP:1970 to 2013. (Refer to appendix A for key to data sources.)

Note: Adjusted for inflation using 1970 average Consumer Price Index for All Urban Consumers. Information for instructor and lecturer categories was not available for 1980–81 and 1985–86. While we report lecturer and instructor ranks, it should be noted that the *N*s are small, and these ranks are not used consistently across institutions.

In an effort to pinpoint the impact of the 2008 recession on salaries, table 9.1 displays the percent change in inflation-adjusted salary for full-time faculty annually from 2007 to 2013. A glance at the table shows a relatively robust inflation-adjusted increase of 3.3% between 2007–08 and 2008–09, followed by a sharp drop in annual increments in succeeding years. Indeed, it was only in the 2013–14 academic year that real salary increases exceeded the rise in the Consumer Price Index, but even then, not for associate professors, who lagged behind their prerecession levels. This remains in stark contrast to the situation of college presidents and other senior administrators. Table 9.2 compares the inflation-adjusted salary increments for college presidents and senior executives with those for faculty by institutional category. Presidents and senior executives weathered the recession remaining securely on the positive side of the Consumer Price Index, while most faculty across institutional types lost ground. This reflects the general trend in higher education and the economy as a whole of increasing distance between senior executives and production workers (Erwin and Wood 2014).

Table 9.1 Percentage change from prior year in current and constant (inflation-adjusted) salary for all full-time faculty, 2007–2008 to 2014–2015

Year	Current salary					Constant salary					Change in CPI-U[a]
	Professor	Associate professor	Assistant professor	Instructor	All ranks	Professor	Associate professor	Assistant professor	Instructor	All ranks	
2007–08 to 2008–09	3.8	3.6	3.6	3.3	3.4	3.7	3.5	3.5	3.2	3.3	0.1
2008–09 to 2009–10	1.0	0.8	1.1	1.4	1.2	–1.7	–1.9	–1.6	–1.3	–1.5	2.7
2009–10 to 2010–11	1.4	1.2	1.5	0.9	1.4	–0.1	–0.3	0.0	–0.6	–0.1	1.5
2010–11 to 2011–12	2.2	1.6	2.1	1.7	1.8	–0.8	–1.4	–0.9	–1.3	–1.2	3.0
2011–12 to 2012–13	2.1	1.7	2.1	2.0	1.7	0.4	0.0	0.4	0.3	0.0	1.7
2012–13 to 2013–14	2.4	2.1	2.3	2.0	2.2	0.9	0.6	0.8	0.5	0.7	1.5
2013–14 to 2014–15	2.6	2.4	2.6	2.4	2.2	1.8	1.6	1.8	1.6	1.4	0.8

Source: Derived from AAUP, *The Annual Report on the Economic Status of the Profession, 2014–15*, table A, 6.

[a]CPI-U is the Consumer Price Index for all Urban Consumers (from the US Bureau of Labor Statistics). Change is calculated from December to December. While we report lecturer and instructor ranks, it should be noted that the *N*s are small, and these ranks are not used consistently across institutions.

Table 9.2 Change in average salary for senior administrators and full-time faculty, by institution type, 2007–2008 to 2013–2014

	Public				Private		
	Doctoral	Master's	Baccalaureate	Associate's	Doctoral	Master's	Baccalaureate
President	11.3	8.6	9.9	6.8	17.3	21.5	13.5
Chief academic officer	12.6	9.2	1.9	2.7	23.1	13.5	8.1
Chief financial officer	15.0	6.2	4.2	3.8	15.2	11.6	7.6
Professor	2.2	–1.6	–0.2	–0.8	7.2	–0.1	–0.8
Associate professor	0.5	–1.7	–1.5	–1.0	3.2	0.0	–0.6
Assistant professor	2.6	0.7	0.7	–1.6	4.6	1.7	0.3
Number of institutions	80	123	44	54	15	88	167

Source: Reproduced with permission from the March–April issue of *Academe*, the magazine of the American Association of University Professors. Copyright © 2014 AAUP.

Note: Percentage change controlled for inflation. Institutions submitting data for at least one administrative position and one faculty rank in both years. Private includes both independent and religiously affiliated institutions. Private Associate's institutions are not included.

Changing Determinants of Faculty Salaries

In earlier analyses, Bowen and Schuster (1986) and Schuster and Finkelstein (2006) reported on how academic salaries were shaped by institutional and disciplinary markets: salaries are generally higher at research universities than at other four-year institutions or two-year colleges; they are higher in the private than in the public sector, and they are higher in those academic fields with robust nonacademic employment prospects in which colleges must compete with industry and government for talent. Moreover, Schuster and Finkelstein (2006) reported that within institutions and academic fields, appointment type—even within ranks—was a further differentiator of salary: salaries were higher for tenured or tenure-track faculty than for other full-time faculty off the tenure track, and full-time salaries were enormously higher than for those teaching part-time on a per-course basis. Beyond these structural factors, they further reported that institutional governance characteristics (primarily reflected in whether or not an institution's faculty were part of a collective bargaining unit) as well as individual demographic characteristics, for example, gender, shaped salary level.[6]

The salary premium for union membership appeared to be small overall and varied considerably by field: from substantial differences on the order of 10–20% in the humanities and health sciences outside nursing to no difference in some fields with robust nonacademic labor markets. In terms of gender, women with similar credentials frequently earned less at similar experience levels than men. To what extent have these trends persisted, abated, or intensified?

Institutional Type and Control

Figure 9.3 and 9.4 display the average salaries of faculty by rank, from 1979 to 2013, for doctoral institutions and for all other (nondoctoral) institutions in both the public and private sector.[7] A glance at the figures shows that faculty at doctoral universities across all ranks earn a premium of anywhere from 1 to 92% over faculty teaching at master's- or baccalaureate-granting institutions or two-year community colleges. While the premium averaged 16% in 1979, by 2013–14 it had increased to 29%. When we examine the institutional type premium by rank, we see that that it tends to be lowest at the entry point for assistant professors and to increase appreciably with seniority, with the largest disparities between full professors at the four-year institutions and those at the doctoral universities. The premium for full professors is slightly higher in the private sector: about 60% versus about 50% in the public sector.

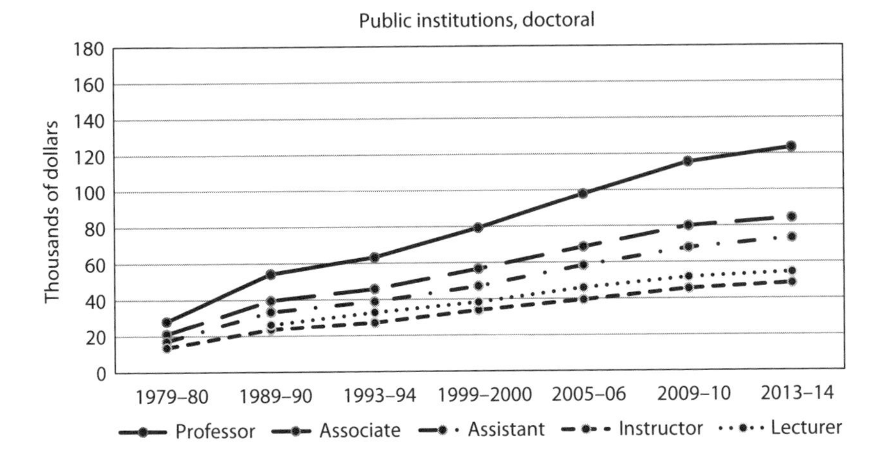

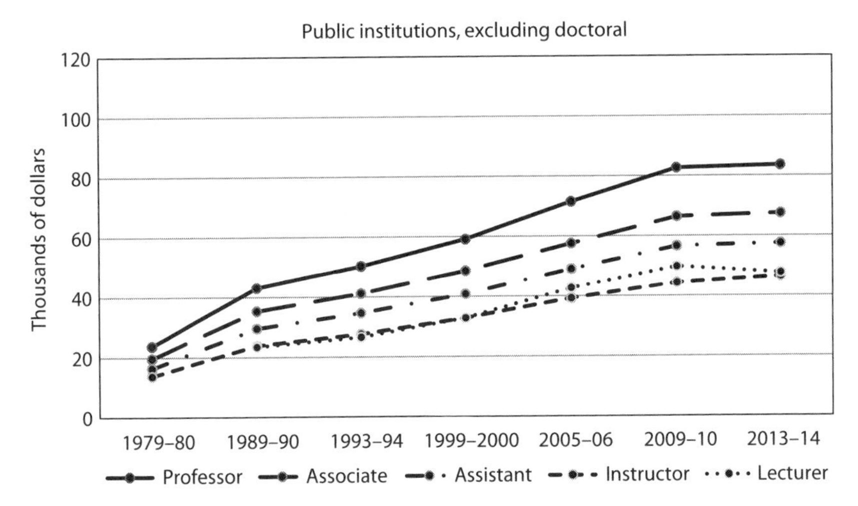

Figure 9.3 Average faculty salaries (unadjusted) for faculty in public doctoral and all other public institutions, by rank, 1979–1980 to 2013–2014, selected years. *Source:* Selected years AAUP:1970 to 2013. (Refer to appendix A for key to data sources.)

Note: While we report lecturer and instructor ranks as per AAUP, it should be noted that the *N*s are small, and these ranks are not used consistently across institutions.

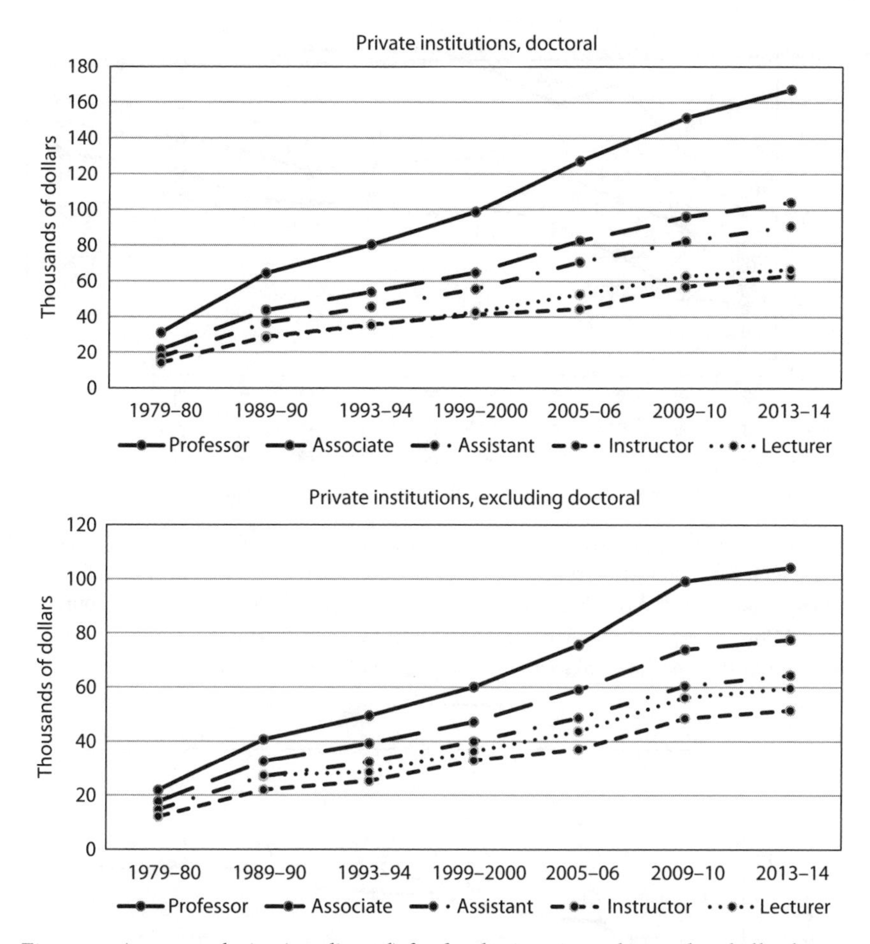

Figure 9.4 Average salaries (unadjusted) for faculty in private doctoral and all other public institutions, by rank, 1979–1980 to 2013–2014, selected years. *Source:* Selected years AAUP:1970 to 2013. (Refer to appendix A for key to data sources.)

Note: While we report lecturer and instructor ranks as per AAUP, it should be noted that the *N*s are small, and these ranks are not used consistently across institutions.

The Widening Gap between the Public and Private Sectors

Beyond the sharp differences between doctoral institutions and the rest, figures 9.3 and 9.4 show sharp differences in salary levels between the public and private sectors, in particular, at the doctoral level.[8] Note especially that these differences have steadily increased over time. In 1979, differences were barely discernable between the public and private sector, either overall or at

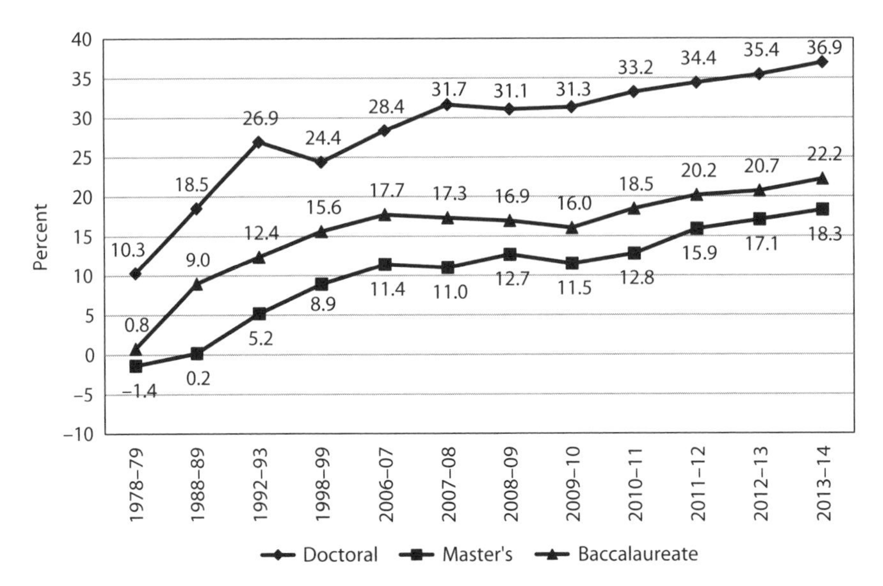

Figure 9.5 Average salary disadvantage (unadjusted) for full professors in public versus private sector, by institution type (degree level), 1978–1979 to 2013–2014, selected years. *Source:* Selected years AAUP:1970 to 2014. (Refer to appendix A for key to data sources.)

Note: While we report lecturer and instructor ranks as per AAUP, it should be noted that the *N*s are small, and these ranks are not used consistently across institutions.

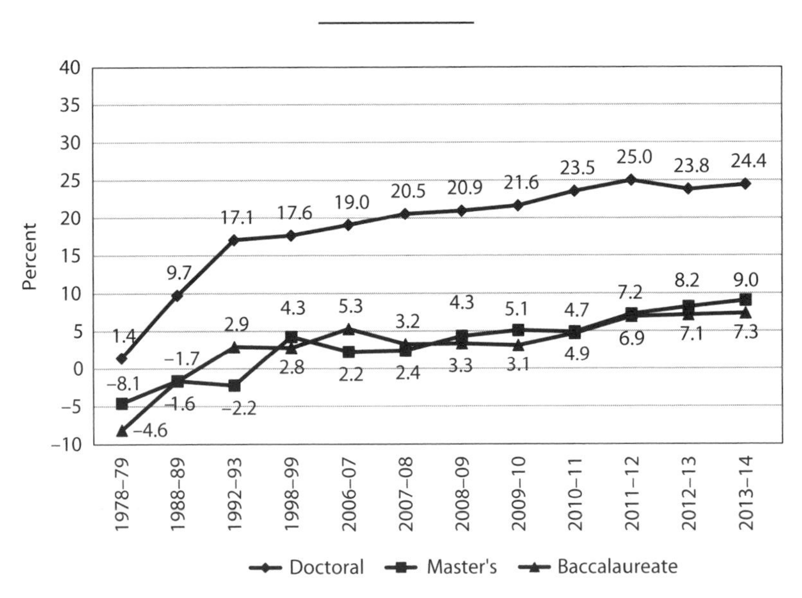

Figure 9.6 Average salary disadvantage (unadjusted) for assistant professors in public versus private sector, by institution type (degree level), 1978–1979 to 2013–2014, selected years. *Source:* Selected years AAUP:1970 to 2014. (Refer to appendix A for key to data sources.)

the doctoral level. By 2013–14, salaries had quadrupled in the public sector but quintupled in the private sector overall (and by a ratio of 5.5:1 in private doctoral institutions). The magnitude of those differences is clearly underscored in figures 9.5 and 9.6, which display the average salary disadvantage of full and assistant professors, respectively, at public and private institutions since 1978–79. The data suggest, first, that while salaries in the public sector closely paralleled those in the private sector—at least in the doctoral universities—just before 1980, over the past thirty-five years we have seen first a steady and then an accelerating public sector disadvantage by 2013–14. The gap—always largest at the doctoral universities—has been relatively smaller at the entry level. Among full professors, the gap more than doubled to an emphatic 37% disadvantage by 2013–14, exacerbating the challenge for public doctoral universities to retain their best professors, let alone to recruit senior faculty from other institutions.

Continued Growth in Disciplinary Disparities

The American Association of University Professors (AAUP), long the gold standard for reporting on academic compensation, does not collect data by academic field. The primary sources of such discipline-based salary data are either proprietary (College and University Personnel Association), with restricted data access, or are limited in scope (the Oklahoma State University Office of Institutional Research Salary Survey). The latter collects discipline-specific salary data but primarily for land-grant universities that are members of the National Association of State Universities and Land-Grant Colleges, now known as the Association of Public and Land-Grant Universities. Earlier data sources including the 2003–04 academic year, that is, the National Center for Education Statistics' National Study of Postsecondary Faculty, are now defunct. Thus it has been difficult to document recent disciplinary trends with confidence and without a variety of caveats.

Until the mid-1970s, disparities in the salaries of faculty in different academic fields were small, and those that existed had remained quite stable over time (Bowen and Schuster 1986). Beginning in the mid-1970s, however, a sharp differentiation in salaries surfaced: faculty in certain fields that were in high demand in the general economy (e.g., engineering, computer science, accounting) began to be recruited at "market" salaries that diverged increasingly from that of their colleagues in fields less prized in the larger economy (e.g., English literature, the performing arts, music, sociology, philosophy, library science).

Table 9.3 Average salaries of full and assistant professors in thirteen disciplines as a percentage of average salaries of professors of English, 1980–1981 to 2013–2014

	Full professors salaries as percentage of English language and literature							
Discipline[a]	1980–81	1985–86	1991–92	1996–97	2001–02	2005–06	2009–10	2013–14
English language and literature	100.0	100.0	100.0	100.0	100.0	100.0	100.0	100.0
Business administration and management	111.4	115.2	133.8	138.7	140.8	146.5	150.9	162.8
Communications	96.7	93.3	102.6	101.9	97.1	96.7	96.8	88.3
Computer and information sciences	113.4	117.6	132.2	128.1	128.7	127.5	128.4	127.2
Economics	113.9	111.3	128.4	125.7	126.4	132.4	141.2	144.4
Education	96.0	92.0	98.8	99.2	97.5	96.2	95.7	104.2
Engineering	108.1	114.3	129.0	127.8	124.0	124.3	125.2	133.4
Fine arts: visual and performing	91.2	90.4	92.1	90.3	88.9	87.8	87.6	83.1
Foreign language and literature	100.9	98.2	98.5	100.5	96.1	95.5	95.9	96.5
Health professions and related sciences	120.3	119.8	134.3	136.4	131.3	118.1	118.9	117.2
Law and legal studies	133.2	141.0	154.2	158.4	153.5	154.0	159.5	157.3
Library science	98.5	99.4	109.9	106.6	103.5	97.9	103.6	95.7
Mathematics	107.6	104.4	111.0	111.5	106.8	106.8	107.2	105.7
Philosophy	102.3	95.2	102.0	101.1	97.1	100.0	102.1	99.9
Physical sciences	107.7	108.0	114.9	114.5	112.8	112.1	112.9	132.9
Psychology	105.0	101.6	109.5	109.7	108.3	109.0	108.9	113.2
Social sciences	104.8	103.2	109.0	108.7	109.2	114.1	116.8	140.9
All discipline average	106.5	106.2	115.3	115.3	113.0	112.9	114.8	117.8

Discipline	Assistant professor salary as percentage of English language and literature							
	1980–81	1985–86	1991–92	1996–97	2001–02	2005–06	2009–10	2013–14
English language and literature	100.0	100.0	100.0	100.0	100.0	100.0	100.0	100.0
Business administration and management	131.8	148.5	169.4	166.4	189.8	201.9	214.6	218.9
Communications	107.9	109.0	109.0	104.6	105.5	104.8	106.0	108.8
Computer and information sciences	126.9	149.8	148.2	143.8	161.6	159.5	153.2	149.3
Economics	116.1	124.8	132.8	131.0	140.8	151.4	159.7	167.6
Education	109.4	105.5	105.4	102.6	104.9	104.3	104.3	110.1
Engineering	125.3	144.0	144.9	136.5	142.6	144.2	142.3	144.8
Fine arts: visual and performing	99.5	98.9	97.0	93.7	95.4	96.4	95.1	95.6
Foreign language and literature	102.7	101.3	101.0	97.4	98.3	98.5	100.1	96.8
Health professions and related sciences	126.5	133.5	146.2	148.8	154.9	139.4	139.0	138.2
Law and legal studies	156.7	164.6	179.2	173.9	165.5	165.9	171.6	156.7
Library science	102.9	108.9	112.1	105.5	113.0	109.1	114.1	112.1
Mathematics	106.6	113.0	116.1	112.3	114.7	116.2	118.8	115.4
Philosophy	101.5	98.7	99.7	95.8	95.3	97.7	99.8	99.5
Physical sciences	111.8	116.6	117.2	113.8	117.5	118.4	120.3	142.4
Psychology	104.1	103.5	109.1	107.3	109.7	110.0	112.4	115.1
Social sciences	106.7	108.2	109.5	107.0	110.2	118.0	120.7	150.2
All discipline average	113.9	119.3	123.4	120.0	124.7	125.6	127.8	130.7

Source: OSU:1980–81 to 2013–14

Note: 2013–14 included 114 institutions including many belonging to the Association of Public and Land-Grant Universities.

[a]Disciplines CIP codes may be combined at different levels if there are fewer than three institutions in the disciplinary code.

The available evidence suggests that the trend has only accelerated in recent years. Table 9.3 reports the average salaries of faculty in sixteen fields (including business, law, economics, foreign language, philosophy, fine arts, and education) as a percentage of the salary of an English faculty member, controlling for academic rank (full professor and assistant professor) at about 100 public, primarily land-grant, universities.[9] The data show substantial disparities among fields at the full professor level as early as 1980, which have only accelerated in recent years. In 1980, the lowest-paid field for full professors (fine arts) differed by 8.8% from English, and only four fields differed by as much as 25% (law, business, engineering, and health sciences). By 2014, the largest spread had mushroomed to 62.8% (business) with law close behind (57.3%), and seven fields surpassed English by more than 20%. Moreover, salaries in the fine arts (83.1%), music in particular, and communications (88.3%) had fallen behind perceptibly, as did those in foreign languages (96.5%) and library science (95.7%). At the assistant professor level, the typical point of recruitment where market sensitivity is likely to be highest, the disciplinary disparities grew even more dramatically: entry-level business faculty were by 2014 being recruited into faculty positions at more than twice the salary of entry-level English professors (and sometimes higher than full professors of English). Assistant professors of economics (167.6%) and law (156.7%) were decisively behind business faculty, and just ahead of new recruits in computer science (149.3%), engineering (144.8%), and the health sciences (138.2%). There is a notably sharp uptick in the social sciences: 150.2% up from 118.5% a decade earlier.

When we examine interdisciplinary differences for a much broader array of institutions for 2012–13 (table 9.4), we find much the same overall pattern. While the magnitude of the differentials are in most cases slightly lower, they tend to be greater at research universities, which are more similar than the general institutional population to the land-grant universities surveyed by Oklahoma State University.

Impact of Appointment Type

Several new sources on the salaries of full-time, non-tenure-track, and part-time faculty have become available since 2006. In 2007 the Modern Language Association (2007) undertook a survey of salaries for part-time instructors in humanities fields, and the following year JBL Associates (2008) published the result of a study of part-time and full-time, off-track salaries commissioned by the American Federation of Teachers, albeit based on the 2004 National Study

Table 9.4 Average salaries of tenured and tenure-track full and assistant professors in thirty academic fields as a percentage of average salaries for full and assistant professors of English, all institutions and research universities, 2012–2013

	All Institutions				Research Institutions			
Academic field	Professor ($)	As % of English	Assistant professor ($)	As % of English	Professor ($)	As % of English	Assistant professor ($)	As % of English
English language and literature and letters	82,840		54,084		97,253		58,403	
Agriculture, agriculture operations, and related sciences	94,432	114.0	64,868	119.9	102,626	105.5	69,567	119.1
Architecture and related services	102,902	124.2	64,903	120.0	105,603	108.6	65,262	111.7
Area, ethnic, cultural, gender and group studies	96,312	116.3	60,356	111.6	105,669	108.7	61,512	105.3
Biological and biomedical sciences	96,241	116.2	61,861	114.4	118,048	121.4	72,488	124.1
Business, management, marketing, and related support services	118,344	142.9	95,268	176.1	153,267	157.6	122,314	209.4
Communication, journalism, and related programs	87,353	105.4	55,995	103.5	105,011	108.0	59,802	102.4
Communications technologies and technicians and support services	85,051	102.7	57,819	106.9	n.a.	n.a.	n.a.	n.a.

(continued)

Table 9.4 (continued)

Academic field	All Institutions				Research Institutions			
	Professor ($)	As % of English	Assistant professor ($)	As % of English	Professor ($)	As % of English	Assistant professor ($)	As % of English
Computer and information sciences and support services	106,568	128.6	75,294	139.2	131,036	134.7	89,890	153.9
Education	86,630	104.6	57,617	106.5	101,744	104.6	61,404	105.1
Engineering	119,951	144.8	80,078	148.1	130,844	134.5	83,667	143.3
Engineering technologies and engineering related fields	94,164	113.7	67,053	124.0	121,999	125.4	73,526	125.9
Family and consumer sciences and human sciences	92,783	112.0	59,849	110.7	104,817	107.8	64,495	110.4
Foreign languages, literatures, and linguistics	87,952	106.2	56,486	104.4	98,159	100.9	59,314	101.6
Health professions and related programs	100,901	121.8	67,160	124.2	118,693	122.0	74,238	127.1
History general	84,805	102.4	55,270	102.2	99,817	102.6	59,373	101.7
Homeland security, law enforcement, firefighting, and related protective services	88,577	106.9	57,299	105.9	111,652	114.8	63,433	108.6

Legal professions and studies	142,033	171.5	91,783	169.7	159,879	164.4	104,924	179.7
Liberal arts and sciences, general studies, and humanities	85,162	102.8	57,811	106.9	95,859	98.6	60,672	103.9
Library science	87,861	106.1	57,956	107.2	98,553	101.3	63,148	108.1
Mathematics and statistics	88,057	106.3	58,917	108.9	106,095	109.1	69,874	119.6
Multidisciplinary and interdisciplinary studies	97,464	117.7	61,646	114.0	120,029	123.4	65,840	112.7
Natural resources and conservation	93,540	112.9	61,790	114.2	101,804	104.7	65,725	112.5
Parks, recreation, leisure, and fitness studies	82,996	100.2	56,543	104.5	103,378	106.3	64,474	110.4
Philosophy and religious studies	88,711	107.1	55,844	103.3	102,280	105.2	59,359	101.6
Physical sciences	92,452	111.6	60,404	111.7	113,188	116.4	70,466	120.7
Psychology	87,500	105.6	57,695	106.7	109,012	112.1	65,900	112.8
Public administration and social service professions	93,098	112.4	59,650	110.3	111,405	114.6	66,385	113.7
Social sciences	92,864	112.1	61,155	113.1	110,032	113.1	67,731	116.0
Theology and religious vocations	73,942	89.3	53,802	99.5	107,141	110.2	65,276	111.8
Visual and performing arts	82,601	99.7	54,138	100.1	91,433	94.0	56,471	96.7

Source: Derived from Faculty in Higher Education Salary Survey 2012–13 Executive Summary, College and University Professional Association for Human Resources, 26–28.

Note: All dollar and percentages are rounded. Total of 794 participating institutions.

of Postsecondary Faculty (JBL Associates 2008). More recently, the Coalition on the Academic Workforce, a loose federation of faculty, and higher education associations located in Washington, DC, including the American Association of University Professors, the American Federation of Teachers, the National Education Association, and the Association of American Colleges and Universities, invited "contingent faculty" across the nation to respond to a jointly developed survey that yielded a very large number of responses (*N*=28,974) from a "convenience" sample. Those data, bolstered by more systematic studies of the College and University Personnel Association that now break down full-time faculty salaries by appointment type, allow us to draw some reasonably conclusive inferences about this elusive category.

Table 9.5 displays the average academic year salary as of fall 2003 for full-time faculty in the public sector only, by appointment and type of institution. The data show substantial differences on the order of 20–40%, with the differences clearly greater at the research universities. Moreover, the appointment type differential increases when we examine "supplemental" institutional income, that is, salary over and above the base awarded for overload, summer teaching, and so on, suggesting that non-tenure-track, full-time faculty are further disadvantaged when it comes to access to opportunities for salary supplements from institutional sources.[10]

The College and University Personnel Association provides comparative and more recent data on the two types of full-time appointments, controlling for rank or seniority and academic field in 2012–13. In addition, they control for whether a non-tenure-track appointment focuses on teaching or research.[11] Data in tables 9.6 and 9.7 show a somewhat more complex pattern. First, as shown in table 9.6, it appears that the magnitude of the differential varies by rank or seniority: it is generally higher at the senior ranks and lower at the junior ranks. Second, the magnitude of differentials between appointment types varies by academic field (table 9.6): it is higher in foreign languages (non-tenure-track as 72.8% of tenure track) and mathematics (non-tenure-track as 81.6% of tenure-track) and lower in education (non-tenure-track as 89.2% of tenure track)—all at the full professor rank.

If the pattern of differences among full-timers holding different kinds of academic appointments are complex and allow for some ambiguity in interpretation, the data in table 9.8 showing the median pay per course for part-time faculty members are quite conclusive. These data suggest that most institutions paid less than $3,000 for teaching a three-credit course (and some even less

Table 9.5 Average salaries of full-time faculty, by appointment and institutional type, Fall 2003

	Basic annual salary			Other salary from institution[a]		
	Tenured or tenure track	Non-tenure-track	Non-tenure-track as % of tenured or tenure-track	Tenured or tenure track	Non-tenure-track	Non-tenure-track as % of tenured or tenure track
Public two-year	58,645	40,117	68.4	5,814	2,625	45.2
Public four-year comprehensive	64,435	41,033	63.7	4,585	3,010	65.6
Public research university	78,409	46,975	59.9	6,765	3,475	51.4

Source: NSOPF:04. (Refer to appendix A for key.)

Note: All dollar and percentages are rounded.

[a] May include summer session, overload courses, administration, research, coaching sports, etc.

Table 9.6 Average salaries of tenured and tenure-track faculty versus non-tenure-track faculty and percent differential by rank and academic field, full-time faculty whose principal activity is instruction, 2012–2013

Academic field	Professor			Associate professor			Assistant professor		
	Tenured or tenure track	Non-tenure-track	Non-tenure-track as % of tenured or tenure track	Tenured or tenure track	Non-tenure-track	Non-tenure-track as % of tenured or tenure track	Tenured or tenure track	Non-tenure-track	Non-tenure-track as % of tenured or tenure track
Education	86,630	77,310	89.2	67,831	65,477	96.5	57,617	55,669	96.6
Engineering	119,951	99,781	83.2	91,707	80,988	88.3	80,078	67,824	84.7
Foreign languages, linguistics	87,952	63,993	72.8	67,745	56,956	84.1	56,486	50,206	88.9
English language, literature, and studies	82,840	70,405	85.0	64,009	58,477	91.4	54,084	49,939	92.3
Mathematics and statistics	88,057	71,824	81.6	68,510	62,501	91.2	58,917	53,045	90.0

Source: Derived from Faculty in Higher Education Salary Survey 2012–13 Executive Summary, College and University Professional Association for Human Resources, 26–29.

Note: Percentages have been rounded.

Table 9.7 Average salaries of tenured and tenure-track faculty versus non-tenure-track faculty and percent differential by rank and academic field, full-time research faculty in all institutions and research institutions, 2012–2013

	Professor			Associate professor			Assistant professor		
	Tenure track	Non-tenure-track	Non-tenure-track as % of tenured or tenure track	Tenure track	Non-tenure-track	Non-tenure-track as % of tenured or tenure track	Tenure track	Non-tenure-track	Non-tenure-track as % of tenured or tenure track
Biological and biomedical sciences	96,241	101,776	105.8	72,104	74,860	103.8	61,861	55,403	89.6
Physical sciences	92,452	91,746	99.2	70,255	71,062	101.1	60,404	55,167	91.3
Social sciences	92,864	80,365	86.5	71,723	67,846	94.6	61,155	62,099	101.5
Medicine, medical clinical sciences, graduate medical studies[a]	100,901	116,555	115.5	78,739	72,346	91.9	67,160	57,774	86.0

Source: Derived from Faculty in Higher Education Salary Survey 2012–13 Executive Summary, College and University Professional Association for Human Resources, 26–29.

[a]Non-tenure-track research faculty were not reported for only research institutions; therefore, percent difference is comparing non-tenure-track research faculty in all institutions to tenure-track faculty at research institutions.

Table 9.8 Average and median salary per course for part-time and adjunct faculty, by institution type, 2003 and 2010

Institution type	2003 average	2010 median
Public associate's	2,486	2,250
Private associate's	—	2,238
Public four-year master's	2,645	3,000
Private four-year master's	—	2,904
Public doctoral and research	4,245	3,200
Private doctoral and research	—	3,800

Source: Data for 2003 derived from JBL Associates Report, table 4, p. 9; data for 2010 derived from Coalition of Academic Workforce, A Portrait of Part-time Faculty Members, 2012, table 22, p. 33.

Note: All dollar are rounded. 2003 data was not presented for private institutions. For 2010 Private institutions exclude for-profit institutions.

than $2,000), and only research universities paid as high as $4,000 and more. While these data are dated or draw on a convenience sample, they nonetheless are consistent across different data sources as well as convergent with experience. What that means is that those individuals who try to make a living by cobbling together five or more courses across multiple institutional employers—variously estimated at 25–30% of the part-time workforce (HERI 2014)—quite likely do not earn a sufficient total teaching income to surpass the federal poverty level of $15,700 for a family of two ($23,850 for a family of four) (Department of Health and Human Services 2014). Indeed, based on the median pay per course for contingent faculty in New England, the Service Employees International Union estimated that:

- an adjunct professor must teach between 17 and 24 classes a year to afford a home and utilities in Boston, and
- an adjunct professor would need to teach up to four classes per year just to cover the cost of groceries for a family of four (Kingkade 2013).

In short, an adjunct faculty member in today's economic environment cannot count on earning an income solely from their teaching, sufficient to escape the poverty line.

The Continuing Impact of Unionization

In earlier analyses based on 1998 data (NSOPF:99), Schuster and Finkelstein (2006) found the impact of unionization on salaries to be modest and mixed, varying substantially by academic field. Faculty in those fields with less robust

Table 9.9 Average salaries for full-time faculty, by unionization status, institution type, and rank, 2010–2011

	Public			Private		
	Not unionized Average salary	Unionized Average salary	Unionized as % of not unionized	Not unionized Average salary	Unionized Average salary	Unionized as % of not unionized
Doctoral						
Professor	118,628	116,376	98	152,710	137,173	90
Associate	80,784	82,896	103	95,958	99,027	103
Assistant	70,093	68,943	98	83,332	77,245	93
Other ranks	49,707	53,665	108	65,123	77,292	119
All	87,256	85,003	97	110,325	104,153	94
Master's						
Professor	83,181	94,714	114	96,420	106,755	111
Associate	67,147	75,609	113	73,268	86,414	118
Assistant	57,735	63,962	111	61,374	70,822	115
Other ranks	44,394	51,832	117	53,706	58,008	108
All	63,791	75,539	118	73,751	85,332	116
Baccalaureate						
Professor	82,471	89,309	108	88,147	99,103	112
Associate	67,104	73,849	110	67,342	77,871	116
Assistant	55,729	62,144	112	55,726	63,196	113
Other ranks	47,514	52,624	111	49,966	53,955	108
All	62,863	70,875	113	68,501	78,725	115
Associates with Ranks						
Professor	68,696	81,062	118	—	—	—
Associate	57,907	67,454	116	—	—	—
Assistant	51,189	58,994	115	—	—	—
Other ranks	44,592	52,961	119	—	—	—
All	56,377	66,710	118	—	—	—
Associates without ranks	54,617	60,393	10	—	—	—

Source: Derived from AAUP Annual Report of the Economic Status of the Profession 2011–12, table C, p. 12.

Note: All dollar and percentages are rounded. No data was reported for Associates private institutions.

nonacademic labor markets (e.g., the humanities) seemed to benefit more from membership in a collective bargaining unit, while those in fields with robust nonacademic markets were apparently bolstered by the market itself.[12] Table 9.9 displays the mean salaries for full-time faculty by unionization status and institutional type in 2010–11. The most striking observation is the apparent power of institutional type: the union premium to faculty salaries is greatest at the two-year institutions (a solid 15%), slightly lower in baccalaureate and master's institutions (about 10–15%), and much weaker in the doctoral institutions. Indeed, at the doctoral institutions, irrespective of sector (public or private), unionization effects are actually negative at the full and assistant professor level and only marginally positive at the associate professor level.[13] The greatest union effect is at the "other ranks"—presumably non-tenure-eligible ranks, where faculty members might be expected to experience greater vulnerability and less negotiating power, and where they earn the least. What we can say in summary is that historically unionization has bolstered salaries in those fields without their own strong, nonacademic labor market, in those types of institutions where faculty can lay fewer claims to expert power and in those types of appointments that are most organizationally vulnerable (not included in the traditional career ladder). That said, to what extent the unionization effect is continuing to shape salaries in its historical pattern remains an open question.

Evidence on Salary Equity

It is a well-known fact that, on average, working women earn less than men. The reasons why these disparities persist in spite of efforts to attenuate the problem are more elusive. Researchers interested in understanding the disparities between the conditions of men and women working in academe have sought to identify the unexplained salary gap—that is, the portion of the salary gap that cannot be explained by differences in worker characteristics that should affect salary, for example, seniority, productivity, education credentials, and rank. Barbezat (2002) traces the history of salary equity studies in higher education beginning with legislative actions including the Equal Pay Act, and she reviews early pay-equity studies. Her synthesis of the findings showed that individual institutional case studies yielded mixed results and raised many methodological questions. She notes, "By the end of the 1970s, a consensus had developed regarding the use of multiple regression analysis as the preferred method of estimating pay equity" (16). The availability of national survey data allowed researchers to generate more representative results and to discern pat-

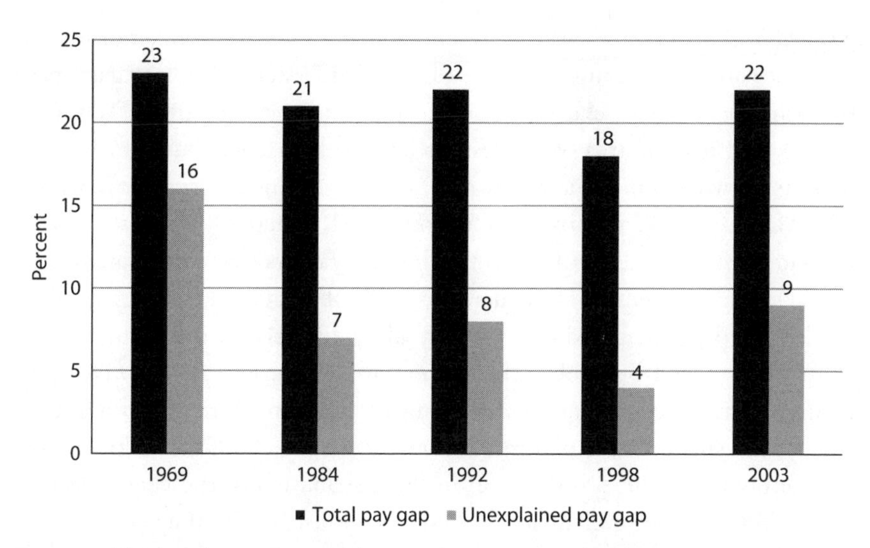

Figure 9.7 Total and unexplained salary gap between men and women in academe, 1969–2003, selected years. *Sources:* CFAT:69; CFAT:84; NSOPF:93; NSOPF:99; NSOPF:04. (Refer to appendix A for key to data sources.)

Note: The total wage gap represents the percentage difference in average salaries for male and female faculty based on the national faculty surveys, respectively. The unexplained wage gap is based on the model specified by Barbezat (2002).

terns by key contextual variables important for understanding academic labor markets such as institutional type and academic field. The National Study of Postsecondary Faculty became a credible source for analyzing faculty salary data. Toutkoushian and Conley (2005) used data from the NSOPF:99 to measure the unexplained salary gap between men and women faculty and compared their results to earlier published studies drawing on national surveys. They found that over time the gap had lessened overall but persisted in some segments of the academy. We updated the Toutkoushian and Conley models using data from NSOPF:04. Figure 9.7 shows that the observed gains in closing the total salary gap and in reducing the magnitude of the *unexplained* salary gap between men and women in the late 1990s were lost by 2003.

In the absence of NSOPF data, institutions committed to identifying and remediating salary equity problems must rely on institutional case studies without the benefit of national benchmarks to gauge their progress. One federal government program that has contributed resources to these efforts is the National Science Foundation's ADVANCE program. The purpose of

ADVANCE is to increase the representation and the advancement of women in science and engineering academic careers. Understanding salary gaps, particularly unexplained salary gaps, is an important piece of the ADVANCE agenda, and it is an area where lessons learned have contributed to broader impacts for women in the academy and for the academic enterprise as a whole. The ADVANCE portal hosted by Virginia Tech includes links to studies related to faculty salaries. Still, disentangling the factors that contribute to academic salary differentials is challenging, and robust national survey data are needed to fully understand the trends in salary differentials over time.

As can be seen from tables 9.10 and 9.11, women's salaries as of 2013–14 remained on average at about 80–82% of men's, following a trend that has stubbornly persisted over the past forty years. These overall numbers do not take into account, of course, differences in the distribution of the genders across institutional types as well as across academic ranks. Nor do they take into account differences in the distribution of the genders across academic fields with their starkly diverging labor markets. Figure 9.8 seeks to account for effects of institutional type by charting women's salaries as a percentage of men's controlling for both institutional type and control. A glance at the figure suggests two clear patterns: first, the gender differential is largest by far at the doctoral institutions, where women earn less than 80% of men's salaries, shrinks significantly at the master's and baccalaureate level institutions to nearly 90%,

Table 9.10 Average salaries of female versus male faculty and percentage gender differential, selected years, 1972–1973 to 2011–2012

	Male	Female	Difference	Female salaries as % of Male salaries
1972–73	14,422	11,925	–2,497	82.7
1980–91	24,499	19,996	–4,503	81.6
1990–91	45,065	35,881	–9,184	79.6
1999–2000	60,084	48,997	–11,087	81.5
2003–04	67,485	55,378	–12,107	82.1
2004–05	69,337	56,926	–12,411	82.1
2005–06	71,569	58,665	–12,904	82.0
2008–09	79,706	65,638	–14,068	82.4
2009–10	80,885	66,653	–14,232	82.4
2010–11	81,868	67,461	–14,407	82.4
2011–12	83,154	68,470	–14,684	82.3

Sources: Selected years IPEDS:1972–2012.

Note: Figures indicate all faculty for all institutions (two- and four-year institutions).

Table 9.11 Average salaries of female versus male faculty and percentage gender differential, selected years, 1999 to 2014

	Male	Female	Difference	Female salaries as % of Male salaries
1999–2000	62,727	50,000	−12,727	79.7
2004–05	74,004	59,508	−14,496	80.4
2009–10	87,206	70,600	−16,606	81.0
2011–12	89,916	72,480	−17,436	80.6
2012–13	91,994	73,932	−18,062	80.4
2013–14	93,692	75,554	−18,138	80.6

Sources: AAUP:99; AAUP:04; AAUP:09; AAUP:11; AAUP:12; AAUP:13. (Refer to appendix A for key.)

Note: Figures indicate all faculty for all institutions (two- and four-year institutions).

and virtually disappears at the associate degree institutions; second, the differential is slightly lower in the public sector across all institutional types. When we focus on gender differentials across academic ranks (figure 9.9), we find that the differentials are indeed greater at full professor and have remained so over the past twenty years. Moreover, we see as well that what progress had been made at the assistant and associate ranks in shrinking the differential (i.e., increasing the percentage of men's salaries received by women) has basically been attenuated, with an abrupt climb in 2009–10 as a temporary blip in a progressive flattening. While differentials are largely imperceptible at the instructor and lecturer ranks, suggesting greater equity here, it should be remembered that salaries are lowest at these ranks, and women tend to be disproportionately overrepresented at these ranks. Finally, when we examine differentials by rank, controlling for institutional control (figure 9.10), we further corroborate the highest differentials among full professors. Indeed, the public sector has become increasingly similar to the private sector over time in that respect. While the public-private divide virtually disappears as well at the associate professor level, it remains persistent at the assistant professor rank with women in the private sector at just over 90% of men compared with about 93% of men in the public sector.

Unfortunately, the data on gender differentials controlling for academic field are impossible to obtain at the national level.

While the differentials we have documented have focused on full-time faculty in the aggregate, when we factor in appointment type and disaggregate

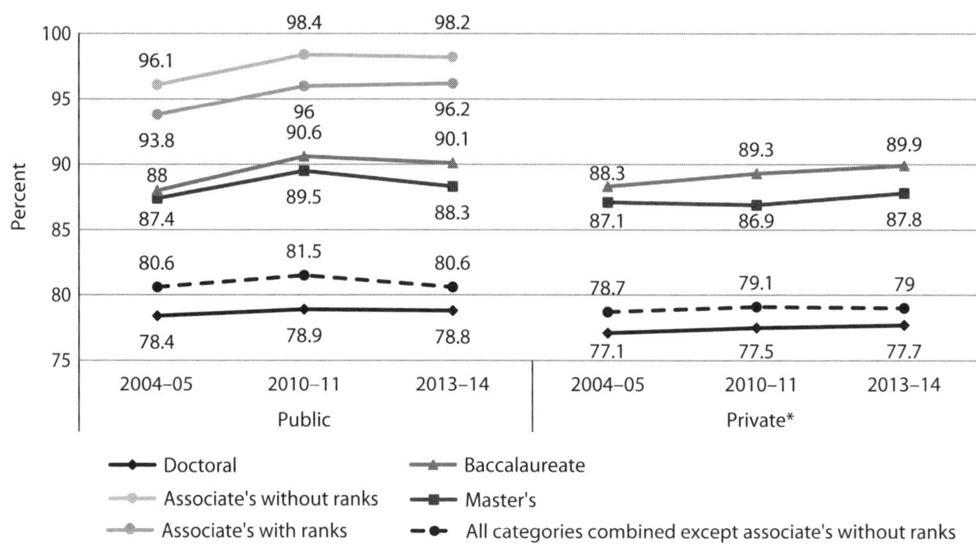

Figure 9.8 Women's average salary as percentage of men's average salary, by institution type, selected years, 2004–2005 to 2013–2014. *Sources:* AAUP:04; AAUP:10; AAUP:13. (Refer to appendix A for key to data sources.)

*Data were not reported by AAUP for Associate's with and without ranks in the private sector for 2010–11 and 2013–14; thus no trend lines are displayed here. The percentages reported for 2004-05 were 96.0 and 96.4 %, respectively.

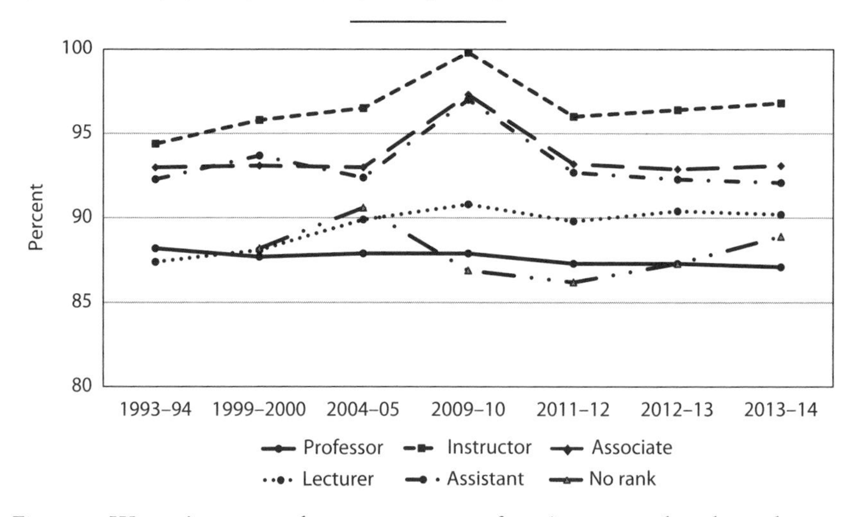

Figure 9.9 Women's average salary as percentage of men's average salary, by rank, 1993–1994 to 2013–2014, selected years. *Sources:* Selected years AAUP:1993 to 2014. (Refer to appendix A for key to data sources.)

Note: While we report lecturer and instructor ranks, it should be noted that the *N*s are small, and these ranks are not used consistently across institutions.

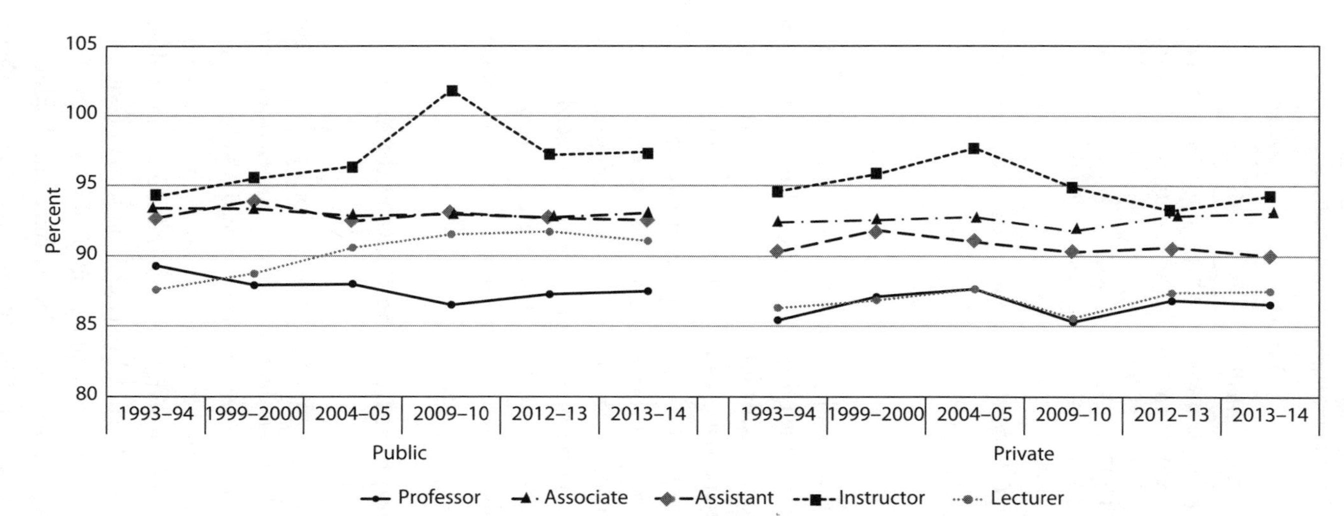

Figure 9.10 Salaries of female faculty as percentage of male faculty, by rank and control of institution, 1993–1994 to 2013–2014, selected years. *Sources:* Selected years AAUP:1993 to 2014. (Refer to appendix A for key to data sources.)

Note: While we report lecturer and instructor ranks, it should be noted that the *N*s are small, and these ranks are not used consistently across institutions.

Table 9.12 Differentials in median salary for full-time non-tenure-track faculty, by gender and institution type, 2010 (dollars)

Institution	All		Female		Male		% difference female of male
	Median	*N*	Median	*N*	Median	*N*	
All institutions	46,588	6,331	46,350	3,771	49,000	2,214	–5.4
Associates	47,000	550	46,000	307	50,000	191	–8.0
Baccalaureate	48,633	549	50,000	324	49,400	193	1.2
Master's	44,333	1,407	44,000	842	45,000	495	–2.2
Doctoral or research	48,833	3,410	47,500	2,058	50,000	1,204	–5.0

Source: Derived from AAUP Annual Report of the Economic Status of the Profession 2012–13, table E, p. 12.

Note: All dollar and percentages are rounded.

non-tenure-track full-time faculty from their tenured and tenure-track colleagues—as in table 9.12, which displays salaries of non-tenure-track faculty by gender, based on the 2010 Coalition on the Academic Workforce survey—we find that gender differentials shrink to about 5%, among non-tenure-track, full-time faculty—a small, but still perceptible, difference. Ironically, the gender differential is largest at associate degree institutions (where differences among academic field and ranks tend typically to be minimized), closely followed by research and doctoral universities. While these results need to be interpreted cautiously given the relatively small *N*s, they are consistent with the broader finding that differentials are lowest at the lowest ranks where women tend to be overrepresented.

Comparative Compensation: The Costs and Benefits of Being a Professor

To understand the power of compensation to lure prospective recruits into an academic career (or at least not deter them), or compensation's power to encourage persistence in that career once commenced, requires that we contextualize academic compensation in at least two respects. First is the matter of the broader socioeconomic context, that is, to what extent do academic salaries allow one to afford a middle-class lifestyle? The second considers academic employment as one alternative to employment in other sectors of the economy in one's field of interest or preparation. That is, once a field of interest has been selected, what are the costs and benefits of pursuing a career in that field in the academic compared with other sectors of the economy (industry, government, nonprofit, etc.) where career opportunities may be available?

Academic Salaries in the Larger Economy: Prospects for a Middle-Class Lifestyle

Figure 9.11 displays the ratio of the average salary of assistant professors to the median family income—a marker, in some respects, of access to the middle class (Schuster and Finkelstein 2006). An examination of the data shows that assistant professors in the first years of the 1970s "beat" the median family income by nearly 15% but lost ground by the early 1980s, to less than 90% of the median family income. While they returned to parity by the early 1990s, they gradually lost ground in the later years of the 1990s through 2007, recovering parity with the median family income only in 2008 and actually achieving a modest 5% advantage by 2010. The pattern is a volatile one—declines alternate with brief rises; and while parity with the median family income has returned, it is not clear to what extent such "recovery" is attributable as much to the flattening of median family income during the Great Recession and slow recovery as to increases in the "real" entry-level academic compensation.

Another lens—and an *intra*-education one—on assessing access to the middle-class is provided by figure 9.12, which traces the ratio of the salaries of

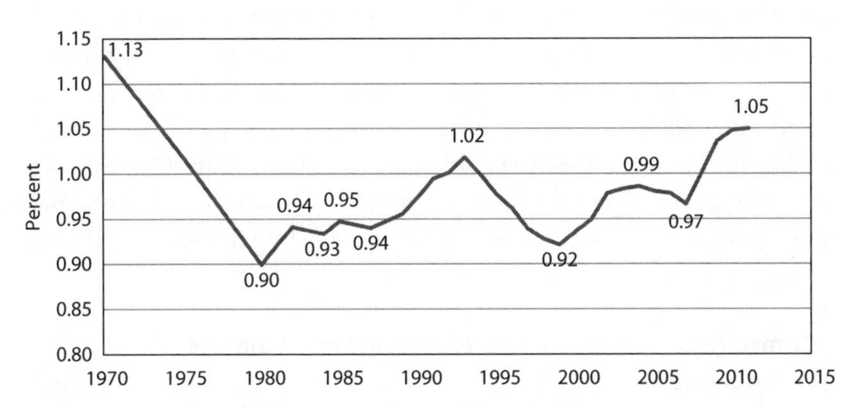

Figure 9.11 Ratio of the average salary of assistant professors to median family income, 1970–2010. *Source:* Derived from *The American Faculty* (Shuster and Finkelstein 2006), figure 8.4, 246; 2010 AAUP and data on median family income from U.S. Census, 2012, table F-8 (http://www.census.gov/hhes/www/income/data/historical/families/2012/F08AR_2012.xls).

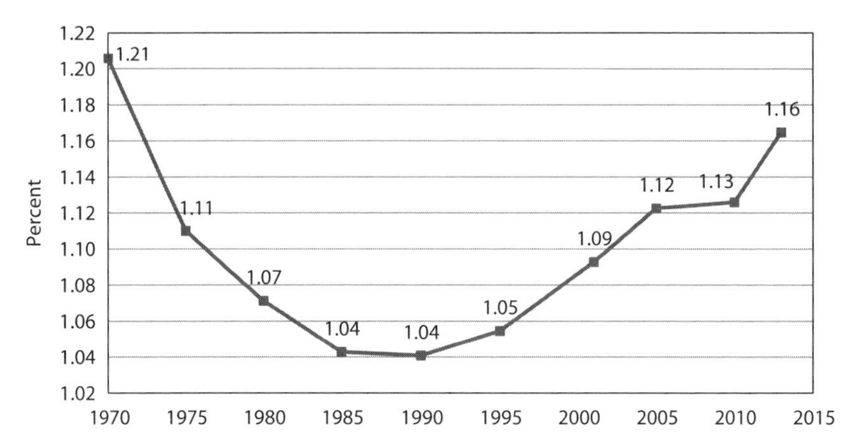

Figure 9.12 Ratio of average salaries of assistant professors in postsecondary institutions to elementary and secondary school teachers in public schools, 1970–2013. *Sources:* Derived from *The American Faculty* (Shuster and Finkelstein 2006), fig. 8.5, 247 and teachers data from NCES, *Digest of Education Statistics*, table 83, estimated average annual salary of teachers in public elementary and secondary schools: Selected years, 1959–60 through 2013–14, table 83 (https://nces.ed.gov/programs/digest/d14/tables/dt14_211.50.asp)

---

assistant professors to those of elementary and secondary school teachers, from 1970 to 2010. The data show that assistant professors outearned public school teachers by more than 20% in 1970 but slid precipitously to virtual parity with school teachers by the late 1980s, recovering only half of their 1970 advantage during the first decade of the twenty-first century. Again, the recovery must be contextualized in terms of the declining fortunes of K–12 teachers over the past decade. Taken together, the most accurate description may be that entry-level faculty as a group have managed, if barely, to hold their own in economic terms—not a disaster, but certainly not an encouraging harbinger of the relative attractiveness of academic rewards.

Comparing Academic and Nonacademic Salaries in the Same Field

Table 9.13 shows the median basic annual salary for new doctoral recipients in 2013 by field of study and employment sector, probably the best single indicator of relative "attractiveness" in pecuniary terms of academic careers relative to careers in industry, government, and the nonprofit sector at the moment of career entry.

Table 9.13 Median basic annual salary for doctorate recipients with definite postgraduation plans for employment in the United States, by field of study and employment sector, 2013 (dollars)

Field of study	Academe	Business and industry[a]	Government	Not for profit organization	Other or unknown[b]
All fields	60,000	97,700	82,000	72,500	70,000
Science and engineering	60,000	98,000	82,000	78,000	62,050
Life sciences	61,000	80,000	78,800	75,000	52,000
Agricultural sciences	56,000	80,000	70,000	67,000	D
Biological, biomedical sciences	50,200	80,000	65,000	60,000	42,000
Health sciences	70,000	90,000	94,000	98,000	81,500
Physical sciences	56,000	101,000	82,000	96,000	57,500
Chemistry	48,000	85,000	70,000	65,000	55,000
Geosciences	59,000	110,000	75,000	D	D
Mathematics and computer and information sciences	60,000	115,000	95,300	100,000	52,000
Physics and astronomy	55,000	95,500	85,000	90,000	D
Social sciences and psychology	60,000	83,000	77,500	65,000	67,000
Economics	82,000	115,000	112,500	100,000	100,155
Psychology	55,000	71,000	65,000	60,000	61,000
Social sciences[c]	57,000	81,000	78,000	70,000	73,000
Engineering	79,000	98,000	96,500	98,000	62,500
Nonscience and engineering	57,000	82,500	81,500	67,000	70,529
Education	60,000	80,000	78,000	75,500	74,000
Humanities	50,000	50,000	77,250	50,000	53,500
Business management and administration	110,001	135,000	96,590	105,000	D
Other nonscience and engineering fields[d]	57,000	78,000	85,000	70,500	62,000

Source: NSF, NIH, USED, USDA, NEH, NASA, Survey of Earned Doctorates, 2013.

D = suppressed to avoid disclosure of confidential information.

[a] Includes doctorate recipients who indicated self-employment.

[b] "Other" is mainly composed of elementary and secondary schools.

[c] Excludes economics.

[d] Excludes business management and administration.

When we examine the salaries paid to new doctorates (table 9.13) across sectors (from academe to industry to government and the nonprofit sector), we see a clear pattern of overall academic disadvantage. At the most extreme, new doctorates entering directly into the business and industry sector report a whopping 63.8% salary premium over those entering academe; while at the lower end, new doctorates entering the private, nonprofit sector nonetheless report a considerable 34.5% premium over those entering academe.[14]

When we examine individual fields, we find much wider gaps in some fields than others. In the physical sciences, the salary premium accruing to new doctorates who choose industry over the academy for their first job is 81.8% (up to 104.7% in the geosciences), while in the social sciences, the premium accruing to new doctorates choosing a first job in industry rather than academe is a more modest (but still substantial) 50.8% and in the humanities, a mere 14.3%. These data suggest that, across different academic fields, the US academy occupies a range of positions vis-à-vis recruiting the next generation of PhDs. The competitive compensation challenges remain greatest in the physical and life sciences and engineering and least formidable in the humanities, education, and the social sciences.

When we move to consider the competitiveness of salary levels at the point of entry to the first career-ladder position—the assistant professorship, which typically occurs three to six years after receipt of the PhD (Nerad 2008; Ehrenberg et al. 2010)—the most reliable and widely available source of data is the American Association of University Professors' Annual Survey of the Economic Status of the Profession. In 2013–14, according to the survey, the average salary of assistant professors across all four-year institutions was in the range of $64,129 to $71,536, although there remained considerable variation by type of institution, with perhaps a 15–20% premium for those employed in the research university sector, especially in the private sector. Impressionistically speaking, that compares with what a newly minted baccalaureate-level nurse or mechanical engineer would be offered in their entry level job or what a newly minted attorney (with at JD degree) would be offered in the public sector (US Department of Labor 2014). Moreover, as we reported earlier, recent studies suggest that these entry-level salaries (for those who secure career-ladder positions) are considerably higher than those received by either full-time, fixed-contract faculty or part-time faculty. This means that the comparisons we are drawing here are to the best-paid and most-advantaged new academic appointees, rather than to the average ones.

Data comparing academic salaries with nonacademic salaries within fields are hard to come by. For instance, national higher education organizations such as the American Association of University Professors, the Modern Language Association, or the American Federation of Teachers studies do not provide a detailed breakdown by academic field nor is it possible to compare such salaries to those of comparably educated professionals outside academe.[15] Therefore, we have employed data from the US Bureau of Labor Statistics to compare individuals serving as postsecondary teachers (in four-year colleges and universities, excluding two-year community colleges and proprietary institutions) to counterparts working in positions in the same field that are outside academe but that typically require the terminal degree (most often the PhD).[16] To focus on individuals at the early stages (but not the very beginning) of their careers—roughly equivalent to the assistant professor stage—we have examined comparative salaries at the 25th percentile rather than the simple median, with the understanding that any differences at that relatively early stage may be either accentuated or attenuated at later career stages. Accordingly, table 9.14 presents the salaries of early-stage postsecondary teachers (with 25th percentile as our proxy) to equivalent positions in government, industry, and the private sector in three occupational fields: chemistry, psychology, and law.[17]

Beginning with chemistry, in the public sector, postsecondary teachers at the 25th percentile earn 8.3% more than bench chemists; in the private sector, the figure is 5.9% more. In psychology, in the public sector, postsecondary teachers at the 25th percentile earn 21.5% less than the average for all other psychology job categories, 8.7% less than organizational and industrial psychologists, but 3.7% more than clinical, counseling, or school psychologists; in the private sector, they earn 26.2% less than industrial and organizational psychologists and 7.5% less than psychologists in the all other category, but 11.5% more than clinical, counseling, and school psychologists. In law, in the public sector, postsecondary teachers at the 25th percentile earn 5.7% more than early-career attorneys and 24.3% more than judges and magistrates; in the private sector, they earn 21.8% less than early-career attorneys. What these initial comparisons suggest is that there are large differences among fields and between the public and private sector. In chemistry, young postsecondary teachers do quite well compared with entry-level bench chemists in contrast to entry-level postsecondary teachers in psychology, who do markedly less well. The situation in law is mixed and inconclusive, varying markedly between the public and private sectors. When considered in the context of the relatively greater security of academic

Table 9.14 Salaries of Postsecondary teachers (mean and 25th percentile) and nonacademic professionals in three fields, and percentage academic differential, 2013

Occupation	Private		Academic as % of nonacademic salary		Public		Academic as % of nonacademic salary	
	Mean salary	25th percentile	Mean salary	25th percentile	Mean salary	25th percentile	Mean salary	25th percentile
Chemistry occupations								
Chemists	77,380	52,850	113.8	105.9	79,650	50,620	108.5	109.0
Chemistry teachers, postsecondary	88,080	55,980			86,400	55,200		
Psychology occupations								
Clinical, counseling, and school psychologist	72,770	45,000	106.1	113.0	72,660	53,050	110.0	103.9
Industrial or organizational psychologist	92,610	64,200	83.4	79.2	76,160	59,880	105.0	92.0
Psychologists, all other	92,360	54,660	83.6	93.0	86,730	66,960	92.2	82.3
Psychology teachers, postsecondary	77,220	50,860			79,960	55,110		
Legal occupations								
Lawyers	140,170	77,440	88.7	82.1	102,110	70,600	124.6	106.0
Judges, magistrate judges, and magistrates	—	—			105,380	56,680	120.7	132.1
Law teachers, postsecondary	124,380	63,580			127,220	74,850		

Source: US Bureau of Labor Statistics, May 2013.

Note: Judges, magistrate judges, and magistrates are not in the private sector.

employment (despite "up or out" tenure decisions where they exist), what differences exist seem rather small and would not seem, at least in the early years, to be a substantial deterrent to pursuit of an academic career. That may change considerably, however, in the later career years to be sure; but there is little evidence currently or historically that academic career choice has been based primarily on a cold-blooded calculus of economic returns. Moreover, in addition to salary, most universities offer attractive and competitive fringe-benefit packages. In the public sector, those benefits parallel those of public employees and include generous pension programs, health insurance, and so on, not infrequently achieved by collective bargaining. In the private sector, benefits may also include tuition benefits for spouses and children as well as subsidized day care. There is some emerging evidence, however, that benefits packages are shrinking (Conley 2014).

Shrinking Fringe Benefits

Benefits, including those related to retirement (see chapter 6), are a sizable portion of higher education employees' total compensation. Figure 9.13 shows the slow, steadily growing size of fringe benefits relative to salary as a proportion of total faculty compensation—rising over the past decade from about 28% to about 32% of wages and salaries. Medical and dental plans and Social Security taxes were the highest reported expenditure categories and, together with retirement plans (see chapter 6), were the largest individual components of such fringe benefit packages and largely drove their recent growth (Schuster and Finkelstein 2006).

A longer term perspective is provided by figure 9.14, which displays the thirty-five-year trend in expenditures for faculty benefits, both overall and by benefit category. Those data demonstrate the sevenfold increase in fringe benefits in current dollars, which translates into a doubling of expenditures for fringe benefits in constant 2011–12 dollars, since 1977. The major components of the actual dollar increase include retirement plans, health insurance, tuition and housing benefits, and Social Security taxes. When focusing on "real" growth, that is, increases in constant dollars, however, it is the areas of health insurance and housing benefits that have seen the largest increase.

Table 9.15 displays recent trends in the proportion of faculty receiving various benefits based on data both from the 2004 National Study of Postsecondary Faculty's Institution Questionnaire as well the Integrated Postsecondary Information System. Included are the typical components of a faculty fringe-benefit package and the number and proportion of full-time faculty receiving

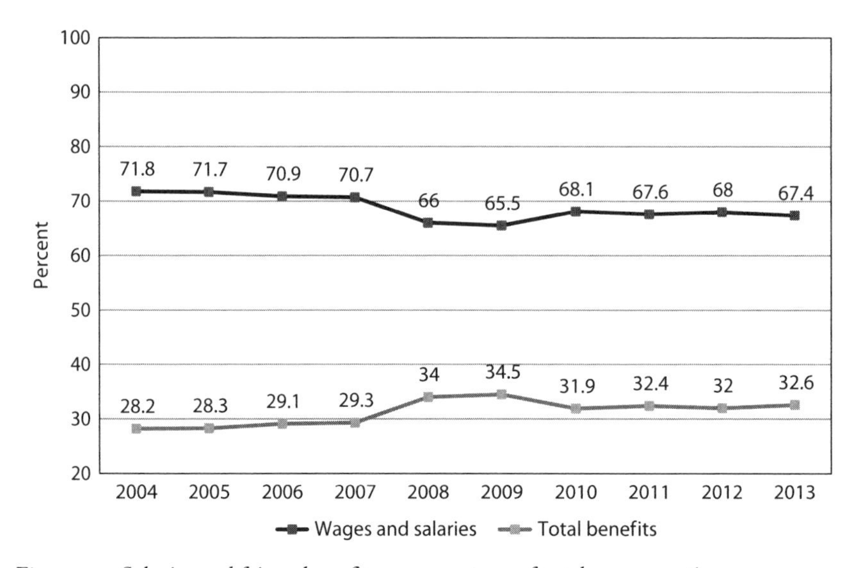

Figure 9.13 Salaries and fringe benefits as percentage of total compensation, 2004–2013. *Source:* Derived from ftp://ftp.bls.gov/pub/special.requests/ocwc/ect/ececqrtn.pdf, table 8.

Note: Excludes federal employees. National Compensation Survey (Bureau of Labor Statistics, U.S. Department of Labor).

---

such a benefit.[18] A glance at the table suggests first that beyond government-mandated benefits (Social Security taxes, unemployment compensation), most full-time faculty receive retirement and health benefits as well as a variety of insurance benefits; proportionately few faculty receive tuition and housing benefits. Second, and directly related to this, most of these benefits and their increased costs, which boost overall compensation levels, do not contribute directly to visible improvement in a faculty's members economic status; higher retirement contributions, contributions to Social Security and health insurance increase institutional costs, but the individual benefits are largely invisible (Conley 2014).

As states battle budget shortfall after budget shortfall and economic struggles continue to plague higher education institutions, reducing such benefits, including retirement benefits in particular, has emerged as a preferred strategy. After all, national and state policy has been moving in the direction of shifting responsibility for retirement from government, taxpayers, and employers to individuals for more than a decade. What kinds of benefit reductions are occur-

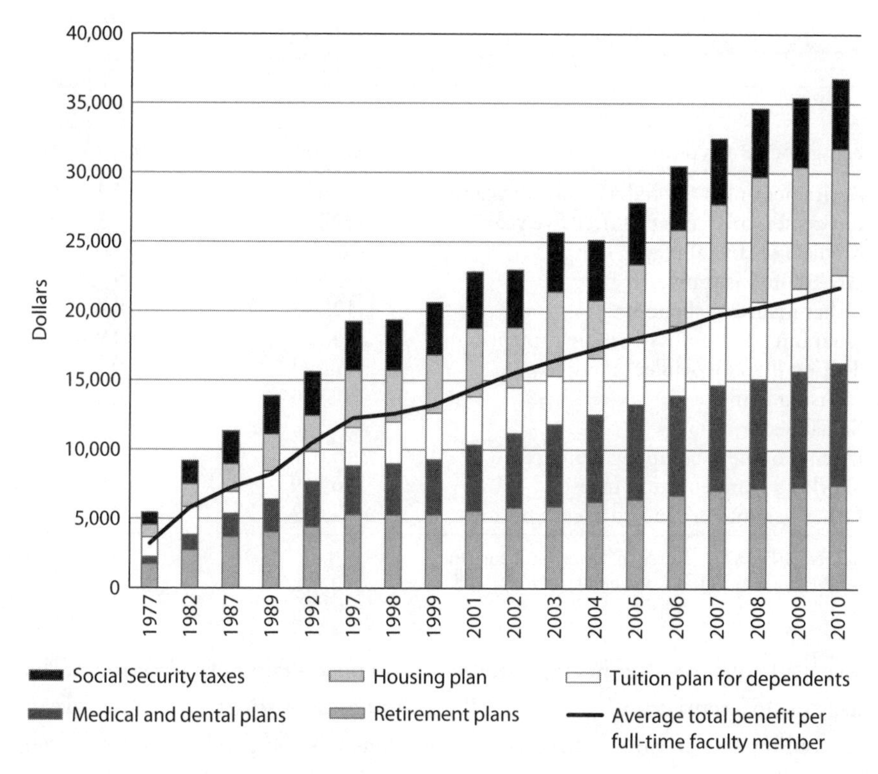

Figure 9.14 Trends in expenditure in real 2011 dollars for various fringe benefits, 1977–2011. *Source: Digest of Education Statistics 2012*, Table 304.

---

ring? The available evidence suggests a variety of developments, including increasing across-the-board faculty-member monthly contributions for health and other insurance (as well as retirement), transitioning to "cafeteria-style" benefits, where institutions agree to cap their level of contribution to individual fringe benefit packages and allow individual faculty to select among the benefits with assigned costs that remain under the cap, offering scaled-down versions of fringe benefits to new employees and even "voluntary" benefits, where the employee covers 100% of the cost (Conley 2014).

Conclusion

The foregoing analysis of faculty compensation suggests a complex picture demanding that inferences be drawn with considerable nuance. While faculty salaries, in general, have sagged over the past five years in response to the Great

Table 9.15 Availability of fringe benefits for full-time faculty on nine- or ten-month contracts, 2010

	Full-time faculty	
Fringe benefit type	Number	% (all institutions)
Retirement plan (vested within five years)	326,494	67.4
Retirement plan (vested after five years)	132,124	27.3
Medical or dental plans	447,555	92.4
Group life insurance	382,841	79
Other insurance benefits	40,693	8.4
Guaranteed disability income protection	294,828	60.9
Tuition plan (dependents only)	47,004	9.7
Housing plan	1,880	0.4
Social Security taxes		92.2
Unemployment compensation taxes	346,077	71.4
Worker's compensation taxes	396,769	81.9
Other benefits in kind with cash options	42,542	8.8

Source: IPEDS:10. (Refer to appendix A for key.)
Note: Total Full-Time Faculty *N*=484,488

Recession of 2008 after having gathered steam once again in the late 1990s, the axes of differentiation have, generally speaking, intensified: the gap between the public and private sectors has increased, as has the gap between research universities, on one hand, and associate- and baccalaureate-level institutions, on the other; the gap among academic fields has widened over the past generation, especially at the entry level, to the point where new recruits in selected professional fields earn more than twice that of their similarly situated colleagues in liberal arts fields; the gap between full-time (or at least certain categories of full-time) and part-time faculty has also widened, with per-course levels of compensation for the latter having changed little in decades and all too often bordering on poverty-level wages. Moreover, the available evidence suggests that salary disparities by gender stubbornly persist. While varying, to be sure, across types of institutions, the gap nonetheless remains essentially unchanged over the past two decades.

When, however, we cast a broader view of academic compensation in the context of overall income trends in the general economy and control for academic field, a dazzlingly complex tableau emerges. First, we must conclude that entry-level compensation overall for new academics has declined as a proportion of the median family income in the United States, suggesting that the economic situation for academics is not as good as it was thirty or forty years go. Much the same, of course, might be said about auto workers, physicians, or attorneys. However, when we drill down to academic field, and compare entry-level options for new recruits with similar education credentials, we see a mixed pattern: in certain fields, new academics actually outearn their colleagues in the public sector (and, in a few cases, the private sector), while in others the opposite holds; and those comparisons may even reverse themselves with increasing seniority (although that is quite rare). Overall, faculty—at least full-time academics on the career ladder—do not do badly in terms of salary compared with their counterparts in nonacademic sectors, especially when one considers the offsetting benefits of a high degree of professional autonomy and, for those diminishing few, the security of tenure.

Quite beyond salary, while expenditures for faculty fringe benefits have been increasing overall, the faculty's share of those expenditures has increased (proportionately and in absolute terms) with little visible improvement in economic status (purchasing power). Moreover, the largest proportion of the profession—the part-timers—has been largely excluded from any fringe benefits at all. Both pension reform initiatives in the states and the implementation of the Affordable Care Act will add confusion and uncertainty to the mix for the foreseeable future.

In all, historically, compensation has never been academe's strong suit in attracting and retaining highly competent and suitably dedicated faculty. Indeed, the evidence is clearly that other aspects of academic life have supplied the magnetic draw. In the decade since compensation was examined in *The American Faculty*, not much has changed—with one notable exception: the increasing marketization of the salaries of full-time faculty, both along the lines of the market value of individual academic fields and the relative vulnerability among different types of academic appointments. Differentiation as shaped by market forces has only increased; and there is no sign that the trend is abating. For full-time faculty and with even greater vengeance for part-time faculty, the market rules. And as we see in chapter 11, that is a unique situation viewed globally, one that leaves the American faculty running the risks of fragmentation and internal stratification in ways not seen elsewhere. The implications for the future of those less "valued" fields, for example, the humanities, remains unclear, but it is hardly sanguine.

NOTES

1. Men, indeed—as we learned in chapter 3.

2. While, strictly speaking, seniority and performance are independent factors, the awarding of higher academic rank typically reflects some kind of assessment of performance, while seniority assumes greater importance in terms of salary increases within ranks. Pure performance approaches to determining faculty salary increases, typically referred to as "merit pay," are a decidedly minor factor in faculty compensation on the whole, in terms both of pervasiveness and of magnitude.

3. This probably excludes the financial sector (Wall Street) as well as the technology sector and other entrepreneurial areas of the economy.

4. This includes not only nine-month contracts but ten- and twelve-month contracts adjusted to a nine-month academic year.

5. The *N*s for the instructor and lecturer ranks are small, and the ranks are not used consistently across institutions. Thus inferences about the gap with assistant professors need to be interpreted with caution.

6. Several researchers have suggested that membership in an underrepresented racial or ethnic minority group may also be associated with salary differentials. Generally speaking, owing to inconsistencies in classification of minority status as well as low sample sizes, the evidence remains inconclusive.

7. *N*s for each of the nondoctoral institutional categories were solicited from the American Association of University Professors and uses to calculate a weighted nondoctoral institution average.

8. While there is some recent evidence that salary increases have been larger in the public than the private sector, the magnitude of the gap largely remains intact, especially at the higher ranks (Clery 2015).

9. The listed fields vary in their inclusivity, ranging from individual academic disciplines to clusters of related disciplines aggregated for purposes of analysis. Operationally, this reflects differences in the use of four- versus 6-digit Classification of Instructional Programs codes. Thus in several cases, data are not, from a technical perspective, purely comparable.

10. It should be noted that since many two-year community colleges have not established tenure systems, it is not clear how to interpret these findings in the case of the two-year colleges.

11. In the natural sciences, non-tenure-track appointments are more likely than in the humanities and social sciences to focus on the research function.

12. Most collective bargaining contracts as reported recognize that institutions take into account external labor market conditions in differentiating especially entry-level salaries for faculty in different fields.

13. That may reflect the fact that unionized doctoral institutions are likely to be public institutions and we have already documented the depressing effect of public control on salaries.

14. It should be noted that new PhDs who enter academic positions typically do so at the entry level while those PhDs entering positions outside the academic sector, i.e. in government or industry, may enter into mid-level (or, at least, non-entry-level) positions. Thus, for example, PhDs enter employment in the federal government as GS-15s. Thus, part of the salary premium of the nonacademic sector may be attributable to level of entry differences across sectors rather than pure sector differences.

15. The College and University Personnel Association does collect salary data by academic field, but its data is proprietary.

16. Insofar as compensation tends to be based on education credentials and years of experience, we have sought to control for both in our comparisons. We have sought to optimize the comparability of education credentials across sectors by targeting job classifications in the focal fields outside the higher education sector that are most likely to require advanced degrees, although not necessarily research doctorates (PhDs). Thus, for example, in psychology, we included only the clinical, counseling, and school psychologist job classifications. Individuals in this category are usually licensed (requiring some kind of advanced graduate degree) and sometimes hold the PhD (indeed, in some states, clinical psychologists are required to hold the doctoral degree to be a candidate for licensure). In chemistry, we included only those individuals categorized as chemists rather than chemical technicians or "other" categories that are likely to require only a baccalaureate degree. We recognize that only some proportion of the clinical, counseling, and school psychologists and only some proportion of the chemists will hold doctoral degrees, and, in the case of the psychologists, at least, even those who hold the doctorate may hold a professional or clinical doctorate (EdD, PsyD, etc.) rather than a research doctorate or PhD. In the case of lawyers, of course, the JD represents a professional rather than a research doctorate, and many law school faculty hold no degrees beyond the JD. That said, we would hasten to point out that, as illustrated in chapter 4, while a majority of full-time, four-year faculty hold the research doctorate, a substantial minority, at least one-third, do not. Nonetheless, the case for the "strict" equivalence of education credentials is certainly debatable. We have endeavored to take that fact into account in our interpretations of any salary differentials between postsecondary teachers and other professionals in the various fields by assuming that education credentials on average most likely favor the postsecondary teachers, who should on that account be earning more than their nonacademic counterparts.

We have employed the mean rather than the median salary to take account more effectively of outliers in the distribution in each job classification—encompassing the full range of salaries. We selected the 25th percentile (bottom quarter) of the distribution as a rough indicator of entry level, although we recognize that the bottom quarter may, to some extent, represent simply the lowest-paid and lowest-skilled individuals within the job classification. This, nonetheless, seemed preferable to employing the median as such an indicator.

17. These fields were chosen because they fulfill two conditions: each offers plentiful nonacademic career opportunities for PhDs; and nonacademic opportunities typically require a PhD or other terminal degree (JD), allowing comparisons to equate for education credentials—a principal determinant of salary.

18. Retirement benefits are not discussed here as they are treated comprehensively in chapter 6.

REFERENCES

American Association of University Professors [AAUP]. 2010. "It's Not Over Yet: The Annual Report on the Economic Status of the Profession: 2010–11." *Academe* 97 (March-April): 4–36.

Barbezat, Debra A. 2002. "History of Pay Equity Studies." *New Directions for Institutional Research* 2002 (Fall): 9–39.

Bowen, Howard, and Jack Schuster. 1986. *American Professors: A National Resource Imperiled?* New York: Oxford University Press.

Clery, Suzanne B. 2014. "Tuition and Expenditures Up, Faculty Salaries Lag." *NEA Almanac of Higher Education.* Washington, DC: National Education Association.

Coalition on the Academic Workforce [CAW]. 2012. *A Portrait of Part-Time Faculty Members: A Summary of the Findings on Part-Time Faculty Respondents to the Coalition on the Academic Workforce Survey of Contingent Faculty Members and Instructors.* Coalition on the Academic Workforce (June).

College and University Professional Association for Human Resources [CUPA]. 2013. *Faculty in Higher Education Salary Survey for the 2012–13 Academic Year.* Knoxville, TN: CUPA.

Conley, Valerie M. 2012. "Eroding Retirement and Benefits: The Wrong Response to Fiscal Crises." *The NEA 2012 Almanac of Higher Education.* Washington, DC: National Education Association, 97-111.

———. 2014. "Retirement and Benefits: The Long Road to Recovery." In *The NEA 2014 Almanac of Higher Education*, 65–81. Washington, DC: National Education Association.

Curtis, John and Saranna Thornton. 2013. "Here's the News: The Annual Report on the Economic Status of the Profession: 2012–13." *Academe* 99 (March-April): 4–19.

Department of Health and Human Services. 2014. "Annual Update of the HHS Poverty Guidelines." *Federal Register* 79, no. 14 (January 22): 3593. http://www.gpo.gov/fdsys/pkg/FR-2014-01-22/html/2014-01303.htm.

Ehrenberg, Ronald, Harriet Zuckerman, Jeffrey A. Groen, and Sharon M. Brucker. 2010. *Educating Scholars: Doctoral Education in the Humanities.* Princeton, NJ: Princeton University Press.

Erwin, Andrew, and Marjorie Wood. 2014. *The One Percent at State U: How University Presidents Profit from Rising Student Debt and Low-Wage Faculty Labor.* Washington, DC: Institute for Policy Studies.

Higher Education Research Institute. 2014. *Undergraduate Teaching Faculty: The 2013–2014 HERI Faculty Survey.* http://www.heri.ucla.edu/monographs/HERI-FAC2014-monograph.pdf.

JBL Associates. 2008. *Reversing Course: The Troubled State of Academic Staffing and a Path Forward.* Washington, DC: American Federation of Teachers.

Kingkade, Tyler. 2013. "Nine Reasons Why Being an Adjunct Faculty Member Is Terrible." *Huffington Post.* http://www.huffingtonpost.com/2013/11/11/adjunct-faculty_n_4255139.html.

Modern Language Association (MLA). 2008. *Education in the Balance: A Report on the Academic Workforce in English.* New York: MLA.

Nerad, Maresi. 2008. *Social Science PhDs 5+ Years Out: A National Survey of PhDs in Six Fields.* Seattle, WA: Center for Innovation and Research in Graduate Education, University of Washington.

Oklahoma State University. 2014. *Faculty Salary Survey by Discipline.* Stillwater, OK: Office of Institutional Research and Information Management.

Schuster, Jack, and Martin Finkelstein. 2006. *The American Faculty: The Restructuring of Academic Work and Careers.* Baltimore, MD: Johns Hopkins University Press.

Thornton, Saranna, and John Curtis. 2012. "A Very Slow Recovery: The Annual Report on the Economic Status of the Profession, 2011–12." *Academe* 99 (March-April): 4–15.

Toutkoushian, Robert, and Valerie M. Conley. 2005. "Progress for Women in Academe, yet Inequities Persist: Evidence from NSOPF:99." *Research in Higher Education* 46 (February): 1–28.

US Department of Labor, Bureau of Labor Statistics. 2014. *Labor Force Characteristics, 2013.* Report 1050, Washington, DC.

Veysey, Laurence. 1965. *The Emergence of the American University.* Chicago: University of Chicago Press.

PART IV / American Academics in Global Perspective

Today, the American academy is recognized as the benchmark that sets the global "gold standard" for cutting-edge research, innovation, and graduate education. With the exception of a few subspecialty areas (e.g., ceramic engineering; arctic oceanography), American scholars and researchers have led the world in refereed journal publications, citations, patents, Nobel Prizes, and so on, and, as a result, many look to American higher education as something of a model for the identification, incubation, and support of academic talent (Goodwin and Nacht 1991). Indeed, for scholars across the globe, American universities still serve as a magnet in the increasingly global academic marketplace.

It is useful to remember that it has not always been so. Indeed, the United States only rose to a dominant global position in higher education (graduate education and research) after World War II. It is thus a relatively recent development. In accounting for this rise of the United States to academic preeminence over the past half century, several explanations are typically offered, most frequently focusing on the high degree of decentralization of the US system and the resulting autonomy from government control (Clotfelter 2010). In effect, the argument here is that academic distinction follows institutional independence. American universities, both public and private, are autonomous corporations chartered by state government to pursue their educational missions and governed by a board of lay trustees. While they may be subject to general government regulations, they are nonetheless independent actors that are free to pursue their ambitions and act to enhance their competitive position in the market for the best faculty and the best students. Among other advantages, this allows considerable institutional flexibility in competing with business, industry, and the professions in recruiting the best talent. The very strength of the private sector in the United States—more independent and insulated from government than the public sector—argues in favor of this hypothesis.

The second most frequent explanation for American prominence focuses on the pattern of sustained and large-scale government support. American research universities began their global ascent largely as a result of the infusion of research support from the federal government's war-related defense efforts in the mid-twentieth century. Until quite recently, that support has been sustained and even grown, fueled by the establishment of the National Institute of Health in 1887 and the National Science Foundation in 1958. Research support was supplemented, beginning in the 1960s, by state governments that invested heavily in the establishment of public university systems, building upon one or two major universities and extending the system by converting former teacher's colleges and normal schools.

A third explanation focuses on the "magnetlike" capacity of the US system to develop and draw in academic talent from across the globe. Historically, this capacity is illustrated by successive waves of emigrating scholars from Nazi Germany, the former Soviet Union, and developing economies such as China and India, seeking opportunities for academic careers in a context supporting academic and individual freedom. The key concept here is *opportunity*; indeed, it is the opportunity structure that developed in the post–World War II period, offering at once a highly structured and predictable career track defined by the American Association of University Professors' 1940 Statement on Academic Freedom and Tenure and a robust job market offering increasingly "competitive" salaries, that would allow academics to join the growing American middle class (Bowen and Schuster 1986). That magnetism, while surely a function of general political and academic freedom (absent McCarthyism in the 1950s) was then, we would argue, also a function of a robust academic marketplace with the flexibility to "recognize" the market value of faculty in certain fields and with certain accomplishments and an established career track that promised a safe and secure road to sustained, if not spectacularly well paid, employment—irrespective of the results of the next national election or political coup.

In the past few years, however, alarms have begun to sound in the United States about gathering threats to American academic hegemony—parallel to the alarms about gathering threats to America's global economic and political hegemony with the rise of the BRICS (Zakaria 2009). Indicators of emergent trouble abound: a documented decline in the proportionate number of referred scientific articles produced by American scholars; a proportionate decline in American representation in global scientific citations indexes; and a decline in the US federal government's expenditures for basic scientific research as a percentage of GDP—all amid a sharp proportionate increase elsewhere in R&D

expenditures and scientific publications, especially in East Asia and Western Europe (Cummings 2008; Clotfelter 2010). More ominously, these indicators of incipiently declining productivity seem rooted in declines in those very conditions that produced American preeminence. And while sociological theories of "accumulative advantage" suggest that privileged groups, by virtue of their initial privilege, enjoy a substantial advantage in maintaining their position even as the playing field changes, nonetheless the prospects for continued supremacy of the American academic professions, especially in the longer term, are anything but certain (Clotfelter 2010).

In the next two chapters, we explicitly explore American academics' place in the changing global order. In doing so, we draw primarily on the 2007–08 Changing Academic Profession Survey, designed as a fifteen-year follow-up to the 1992 International Survey of the Academic Profession, which was directed by Philip Altbach and Ernest Boyer of the Carnegie Foundation for the Advancement of Teaching. When possible, we draw comparisons with the 1992 results. The 2007–08 survey was a collaborative effort of research teams from twenty countries, half of which had been included in the 1992 Carnegie survey. It yielded some 25,000 responses from mostly full-time academics in the twenty countries, who were selected by a stratified random sampling procedure and shared a common instrument.[1]

Chapter 10 focuses explicitly on American academics' engagement in teaching and research and publication on the global stage and their integration of global perspectives into their teaching and research at home. Specifically, we examine the available evidence on the level and scope of US faculty's international activities, in comparison historically with the level and scope of their international activity reported in 1992 and concurrently with the level and scope of such activity among their counterparts in other English-speaking countries, continental Europe, and East Asia. Beyond reporting on such basic comparisons, we also seek to explain the extent and nature of international activity as a function of the US context but also faculty professional characteristics.

In chapter 11, drawing on the 2007–08 Changing Academic Profession Survey more fully, we seek to provide a broad perspective on the distinctive features of the American academic profession, their demographics, their work, their careers and compensation in comparison to counterparts in other mature economies, both Western and Eastern. To what extent are the trends in academic work and careers in the United States distinctive? Or reflective more broadly of global developments? How significant a role do US academics play in the operation of their institutions and broader national policy on higher education? To what extent, and in what ways, is it true that US academics are among the most secure, best compensated, and most powerful in the world? While our answers may surprise you, they will certainly provide a unique perspective on the condition of the American faculty.

NOTES

1. Methodological details on the survey, including sampling, instrument construction, data file construction, and vetting and analysis, are included in appendix A. A fuller description is available in Cummings and Finkelstein (2011).

REFERENCES

Bowen, Howard R., and Jack H. Schuster. 1986. *American Professors: A National Resource Imperiled*. New York: Oxford University Press.

Clotfelter, Charles T., ed. 2010. *American Universities in a Global Market*. Chicago: University of Chicago Press.

Cummings, William K. 2008. "Globalization, Social Capital, and Values: The Case of the Pacific Basin." *Education and Society* 26, no. 2: 23–44.

Cummings, William K., and Martin J. Finkelstein. 2011. *Scholars in the Changing American Academy: New Roles and New Rules*. Dordrecht, NL: Springer.

Goodwin, Craufurd D., and Michael Nacht. 1991. *Missing the Boat: The Failure to Internationalize American Higher Education*. Cambridge, UK: Cambridge University Press.

Zakaria, Fareed. 2009. *The Post-American World—And the Rise of the Rest*. W.W. Norton and Company.

10

The American Faculty in a Newly Globalized Higher Education Environment

This volume began with the proposition that that we have entered a new era, one distinguished by the rapidity of technological and economic change.[1] An essential driver of that accelerated rate of change is globalization, the increasing interconnectedness between economies and industries across the globe. An event in a single locality in a single country is now knowable, and part of the context for action almost instantaneously everywhere else on the globe, with a high-speed Internet connection (Friedman 2005). Nowhere is globalization or interconnectedness more evident than in the knowledge industry, whose center is the university. This has led us to the concept of the delocalized or global university: the notion that institutional markets have expanded beyond the traditional student catchment area, indeed beyond national borders. Thus former New York University president John Sexton has argued that in this globalized environment, a major research university such as NYU is as much obliged to offer its brand of undergraduate education in Shanghai or Abu Dhabi as in New York as well as to bring students in these cities to New York (Wildavsky 2010). The global university self-consciously seeks to join a fraternity of "world-class" universities competing for an ever growing corps of students worldwide who are actively seeking out the best education money will buy wherever it may be (Altbach and Salmi, 2011). On the for-profit side, it has led to the rapid growth of global education and training corporations such as the Apollo Group and the Corinthian Group, whose certificate and degree programs are increasingly dominating tertiary enrollments in Latin America, South Asia, and China (Wildavsky 2010). In Europe, the so-called Bologna Process has removed barriers to student and faculty mobility and is beginning to open up a new brand of European or continent-wide higher education.[2]

At the same time, the world of research and scholarship is expanding beyond the historically limited "core" countries (dominated by the United States and, to a lesser extent, the United Kingdom and Germany) to a mushrooming secondary core in East Asia and the "new" Europe. The dominant position of the United States in global research production is weakening as scholars in East Asia and Europe increase their proportionate presence in academic journals and science citation indexes (Cummings 2008; Adams 2010). Most major academic journals in Europe and Asia now publish in English, and scholars at aspiring world-class universities across the globe are increasingly expected to publish in English. American professors' historic (and those in the United Kingdom and Australia) dominance of the language and organs of scholarly production and communication is waning (Borghans and Corvers 2010). In major regions of the world, national and regional government entities are promoting mobility among scholars through programs such as the Erasmus Project in Europe and the M-I-T Student Mobility Program in Southeast Asia (Yavaprabhas 2011; Huang, Finkelstein, and Rostan 2013).[3]

A fundamental piece of the story of the transformation of the higher education enterprise generally, and its faculty, in particular, is wrapped up in the process of globalization of the "industry." What role is the American faculty—the key players, after all, in internationalizing teaching and research on the ground—playing in the globalization of the higher education enterprise at home? Historically, of course, the American faculty have been a strategic and resourceful importer of academic talent from across the globe. The American university served as a haven for refugees, first from the Nazis during World War II and thereafter from the Soviets during the cold war. Since then, the American academic profession has liberally stocked itself (as shown in chapter 3) with aspiring scholars (graduate students) and actively practicing scholars, especially from China and India and especially in the science, technology, engineering, and mathematics (STEM) fields (Clotfelter 2010). While the latest solid empirical evidence suggests that the influx of foreign scholars is continuing, especially at the graduate level, and "stay rates" in the United States, at least five years following receipt of the PhD, remain overwhelmingly and persistently high (Finn 2010, 2012), there are incipient indicators that a momentum shift may be on its way.[4] Certainly, graduate education in East Asia is booming: China now rivals the United States in PhD production and its expansion in student enrollment, graduate as well as undergraduate (indeed, China now surpasses the United States as the top global provider of postsecondary education, with 22.5 million students overall), and its quest to develop world-class universities promises in the next ten years to provide a reasonably solid infrastructure for the preparation and pursuit of indigenous academic careers (Wang, Li and Liu 2015). Indeed, according to Chinese government sources, the ratio of students leaving China for graduate education in the United States to those returning to work postdegree in China has shrunk precipitously from about 2.4:1 to 1.4:1 over the past decade alone.[5] Moreover, a program begun in 2008 called the Recruitment Program of Global Experts or more generically the One Thousand Talents Plan (Wang, 2013a, 2013b) is luring back prominent Chinese-born academics tenured in Western universities in their prime years of productivity—with President Xi Jinping promising full support and "guaranteeing them the freedom to come and go as they wish."[6]

Similarly, other BRICS countries (Brazil, Russia, India, China, and South Africa) are focusing on the development of their academic infrastructures, as are the major economies of Europe, including, increasingly, the offering of graduate programs in English (Borghans and Corvers 2010), just as the academic infrastructure in the United States, subjected to relentless fiscal duress, is increasingly threatened and fraying at the seams (see chapter 4). Indeed, recent comparative studies of both academic compensation (Altbach et al. 2012)—one indicator of the attractiveness of academic careers—and the opportunity structure into which new faculty enter (Yudkevich and Altbach, 2015) suggest that the relative attractiveness of academic careers is actually on the upswing in several countries (albeit starting perhaps at a lower point of departure) while it is on the downswing in the United States. So, while the preeminence of US graduate education and research products remains high, they are now subject, for the first time in a half century, to serious competition; and our dominant position as the importer of choice is no longer assured by any means in the medium to long term.

While the United States has functioned unambiguously to date as an importer of global academic talent (a veritable magnet), its historic role as an exporter of American academic talent is less clear. In their pioneering 1991 study, Goodwin and Nacht (1991) found that American professors were reluctant to work and study overseas in the preglobalized world for a variety of reasons, including fear, logistical challenges (moving and family matters), career challenges (the ambiguous recognition and rewards for overseas involvement, especially in the pretenure years), and not infrequently as a function of hubris (or, scientific reality, as some would put it). Americans were likely to see the United States as the global center of scholarship in their field and saw no powerful professional need to travel to the "periphery." The major exceptions were scholars in a few fields where the substance of the field required international study and travel (archeology, art history, oceanography, arctic studies) or where the centers of scholarship by virtue of special equipment were generally acknowledged to reside outside the United States (ceramic engineering, high-energy physics). Other exceptions included scholars in agriculture and economic development who contributed through agencies such as the US Information Agency and other federal programs to projects supporting economic development in emerging economies—characterized by some observers as the faculty "altruists" (Goodwin and Nacht 1991).

In the past, such border crossing has been traditionally supported by US government–sponsored programs, including most prominently the Fulbright Scholar Program through which annually nearly a thousand U.S. faculty travel for up to one year to teach and conduct research in forty-five countries worldwide and through which another thousand foreign scholars come to the United States (O'Hara 2009). Other more specialized government programs of technical assistance, such as agricultural assistance coordinated by federal agencies, for example, USAID and institutionally based study-abroad programs abound (Goodwin and Nacht 1991). Since at least the 1990s, internationalization initiatives in American higher education have broadened and localized to include not only physical mobility but also what is referred to in the literature as "internationalization at home" activities. These include the integration of international perspectives into the traditional content of college curricula (Crowther et al. 2000; Joris et al. 2003; Wächter 2003), the revitalization of foreign language and area studies, and international knowledge transfer, that is, international research collaborations and copublication activity with foreign colleagues (Knight 2004; Huang 2007a, 2007b; Huang, Finkelstein, and Rostan 2013). These kinds of activities, rather than physical border crossing, now constitute the latest and in many respects the most cost-effective and scalable strategies for US faculty to respond to the challenges of globalization.

One major previous snapshot of the nature and extent of internationalization of the American faculty, a kind of preglobalization baseline, is the 1992 Carnegie Foundation for the Advancement of Teaching's International Academic Profession survey. Based on those survey data, Altbach and Lewis (1996) reported that about one-third of American faculty had taken at least one trip abroad for study or research, securing for the United States a position in "last place" among the fourteen countries studied, just behind Russia and Brazil. Moreover, the United States also came in dead last in the proportion of faculty reporting that "connections with scholars in other countries are very important to my professional work" (about half compared with more than four-fifths in all other countries except the United Kingdom).

Over two decades have passed since the original 1992 Carnegie International survey and the Goodwin and Nacht (1991) study cited earlier. O'Hara's (2009) review of the field discovered only a single broad-based investigation that addressed the international activities of American faculty (Finkelstein, Walker, and Chen 2009, 2013). That exploratory study, built upon a new international survey, the Changing Academic Profession, undertaken in 2007–08, sought to estimate the extent of faculty international academic activity as well as identify potential predictors of international activity.

Building on the above described work, the current chapter seeks to address three clusters of questions designed to help us estimate the role of the American faculty in the increasingly global higher education marketplace:

1. What is the current scope and nature of US faculty engagement in international teaching and research activities? What are the trends in the physical mobility (border crossing) of US faculty for teaching and research? Are more faculty pursuing teaching and research (study) trips abroad than in the preglobalization era? To what extent do these trends vary by academic field, institutional type, career stage, and gender? Quite beyond physical border crossing, to what extent are US faculty internationalizing "at home," that is, integrating international perspectives and content into their teaching? Teaching more international students? Or engaging in international research collaboration and international dissemination?
2. How can we explain the extent and pattern of faculty engagement in international teaching and research—border crossing as well as "internationalization at home"? What drives it or deters it? and
3. What are the consequences of faculty engagement in international teaching and research activities for the broader arena of overall faculty work performance—and, ultimately, for American higher education's place in the global enterprise? Is engagement in international teaching

and research a diversion or a distraction from productivity in traditional areas of responsibility at home?

US Faculty Engagement in International Teaching and Research

We have already established that historically, American faculty as a whole have not been prone, relatively speaking, to establish linkages with scholars abroad and travel abroad for teaching and study. The 2007–08 Changing Academic Profession Survey allows us to take a more current snapshot of such activity, including

1. physical mobility reflected in time spent abroad following receipt of the BA degree and time spent teaching abroad as a practicing academic;
2. physical or virtual mobility reflected in research collaboration and copublication with colleagues abroad or publication in a foreign language or a foreign country; and
3. internationalization at home, including integrating international content or perspectives into one's teaching and research agenda and teaching increasing numbers of foreign students.

Physical Mobility

Table 10.1 provides data on the proportion of US professors who report teaching abroad compared with faculty in other English-speaking countries, continental Europe, and East Asia.[7] The data suggest that in 2007–08 about one-tenth of US faculty were teaching abroad during the previous three years—falling midway between the one-sixth of European academics (at the high end) and the one-twelfth of Asian academics (at the low end). Moreover, that one-tenth tends to disproportionately represent senior as opposed to junior faculty and men as opposed to women. Natural scientists are among the least likely to teach abroad.[8]

Table 10.2 reports the percentage of American faculty that have spent one year or more abroad for study following receipt of their baccalaureate degree. Most generally, the data suggest that about one-third of US faculty report extended stays abroad sometime after receiving their baccalaureate degree compared with about two-fifths in Asia and other English-speaking countries (but on a par with European colleagues). The table suggests that such "export" of American academic talent varies by institution type, gender, and career stage

Table 10.1 Percentage of full-time faculty in the United States and elsewhere who have taught abroad, by institution type, academic field, rank, and gender, 2007–2008

	United States		Other English-speaking countries		Continental Europe[a]		East Asia	
	N	%	*N*	%	*N*	%	*N*	%
Institution type								
University	89	10.5	364	14.5	804	14.9	138	11.1
Other four-year	32	10.7	68	18.5	164	14.1	91	5.0
All	1,146	10.6	2,877	15.1	6,571	14.7	3,065	7.5
Academic field								
Education and humanities	46	11.6	92	13.4	187	17.9	59	8.0
Social sciences, business, and law	38	13.7	125	17.1	231	16.7	44	7.6
Physical and life sciences	11	6.1	49	10.0	167	11.1	29	7.0
Engineering, manufacturing, construction, and architecture	10	10.1	32	12.6	122	10.4	25	4.0
Health sciences	12	8.2	72	15.1	139	17.2	36	8.3
All	1,137	10.3	2,717	13.6	6,133	13.8	2,969	6.5
Academic rank								
Senior	90	12.4	276	17.8	648	21.4	173	8.0
Junior	31	7.4	157	11.3	310	8.9	54	6.0
All	1,146	10.6	2,941	14.7	6,517	14.7	3,046	7.5
Gender								
Male	76	11.5	252	17.0	649	16.4	190	7.6
Female	44	9.3	161	12.5	301	12.6	37	6.9
All	1,135	10.6	2,778	14.9	6,355	14.9	3,036	7.5

Source: CAP:07. (Refer to appendix A for key.)

[a]Excludes the United Kingdom, which is included under "Other English-speaking countries."

Table 10.2 Percentage of full-time faculty in the United States and elsewhere who have studied abroad for one or more years after receipt of baccalaureate degree, by type of institution, academic field, rank, and gender, 2007–2008

	United States		Other English-speaking countries		Continental Europe[a]		East Asia	
	N	%	*N*	%	*N*	%	*N*	%
Institution type								
University	306	36.6	1,124	42.2	2,034	38.2	644	52.8
Other four-year	81	27.5	122	32.0	179	18.9	582	34.8
All	1,132	34.2	3,043	40.9	6,274	35.3	2,891	42.4
Academic field								
Education and humanities	144	36.9	276	39.0	334	34.8	256	37.3
Social sciences, business, and law	90	32.7	306	39.8	428	34.1	235	42.8
Physical and life sciences	69	38.8	280	52.7	644	42.0	184	46.3
Engineering, manufacturing, construction, and architecture	38	39.6	106	37.7	326	29.5	241	41.4
Health sciences	32	21.9	174	34.7	292	37.1	190	45.1
All	1,123	33.2	2,861	39.9	5,881	34.4	2,799	39.5
Academic rank								
Senior	268	37.2	732	47.3	1,254	45.0	887	44.4
Junior	119	29.0	542	35.1	947	27.5	330	37.7
All	1,132	34.2	3,089	41.2	6,228	35.3	2,872	42.4
Gender								
Male	259	39.4	775	44.8	1,491	38.0	1,012	42.8
Female	128	26.9	533	35.1	728	31.2	210	40.6
All	1,132	34.2	3,249	40.3	6,254	35.5	2,882	42.4

Source: CAP:07. (Refer to appendix A for key.)
[a]Excludes the United Kingdom.

and, to a lesser extent, by academic field. Faculty at universities and at senior ranks as well as male faculty are at least 10% more likely to report such experience than their nonuniversity, junior, and female colleagues. Natural scientists and engineers are slightly more likely than nonscientists to report such travel abroad for study.

Tables 10.3 to 10.6 examine the extent to which faculty have collaborated on research with international colleagues (table 10.3), copublished with them (table 10.4), or published in a foreign country (table 10.5) or foreign language (table 10.6) over the past three years. Together, these data suggest that about one-third of US faculty were collaborating with international colleagues in 2007–08—a figure similar to that fifteen years earlier in 1992—while about one-fifth were copublishing with international colleagues, about one-quarter publishing in a foreign country, and only one-twelfth publishing in a foreign language. Overall, American faculty show the lowest rates of international collaboration, copublication, and foreign publication among world regions. There is considerable variation, however, among subgroups of faculty. Most prominently, scientists and engineers, who were much less likely to teach abroad, were nonetheless twice as likely to collaborate on research and copublish and more likely to publish in a foreign country. As might be expected, research and doctoral university faculty were much more likely than nonuniversity faculty to collaborate and copublish with international scholars; similarly, senior faculty were much more likely that junior faculty and men more likely than women.

Internationalization at Home

Tables 10.7 to 10.9 show the percentage of American faculty in 2007–08 who reported integrating international content into their courses, international perspectives into their research, and teaching increased numbers of international students. Overall, about half of US faculty reported that they integrated international content into their courses (table 10.7)—about 10–15% less than anywhere else in the world. Natural scientists and engineers were 20% less likely than their nonscience colleagues to do so, while academic women were 10% more likely to do so than academic men. There were no differences among faculty by institution type and by academic rank. About 45% of US faculty reported an increase in the presence of international students on their campuses (table 10.8)—less than the three-fifths in Europe and other English-speaking countries but more than in Asia. This disproportionately

Table 10.3 Percentage of full-time faculty in the United States and elsewhere who have collaborated on research with international colleagues, by type of institution, academic field, rank, and gender, 2007–2008

	United States		Other English-speaking countries		Continental Europe		East Asia	
	N	%	*N*	%	*N*	%	*N*	%
Institution type								
University	268	38.5	1,587	63.1	3,560	63.2	607	52.6
Other four-year	38	17.0	180	50.1	289	39.4	389	22.0
All	919	33.3	2,931	60.3	6,329	60.8	2,906	34.3
Academic field								
Education and humanities	71	22.5	354	53.7	528	54.7	168	24.6
Social sciences, business, and law	66	28.1	428	59.0	686	52.9	203	37.5
Physical and life sciences	76	52.8	354	71.7	1,118	70.6	177	43.7
Engineering, manufacturing, construction, and architecture	47	55.3	179	70.5	653	59.3	194	31.2
Health sciences	38	35.5	276	58.5	484	60.2	158	37.9
All	919	32.4	2,931	54.3	6,329	54.8	2,906	31.0
Academic rank								
Senior	237	39.0	1,040	69.6	1,923	65.8	719	34.2
Junior	69	22.2	763	53.1	1,902	55.8	270	33.6
All	919	33.3	2,931	61.5	6,329	60.4	2,906	34.0
Gender								
Male	201	36.7	1,009	67.5	2,463	63.7	808	33.6
Female	102	27.9	710	54.5	1,321	57.3	181	36.6
All	919	33.0	2,931	58.6	6,329	59.8	2,906	34.0

Source: CAP:07. (Refer to appendix A for key.)

[a] Excludes the United Kingdom.

Table 10.4 Percentage of full-time faculty in the United States and elsewhere who have cowritten publications with international colleagues, by type of institution, academic field, rank, and gender, 2007–2008

	United States		Other English-speaking countries		Continental Europe[a]		East Asia	
	N	%	*N*	%	*N*	%	*N*	%
Institution type								
University	184	25.4	1,024	43.3	2,513	47.7	502	46.0
Other four-year	20	9.0	104	31.8	159	28.8	370	23.3
All	947	21.5	2,694	41.9	5,821	45.9	2,680	32.5
Academic field								
Education and humanities	44	13.7	169	28.0	206	23.8	106	17.3
Social sciences, business, and law	33	14.4	266	39.3	387	33.7	162	32.7
Physical and life sciences	58	40.0	283	59.2	968	64.3	184	47.8
Engineering, manufacturing, construction, and architecture	32	34.8	127	52.3	471	46.2	188	32.9
Health sciences	33	26.6	188	42.6	403	53.1	140	35.4
All	947	21.1	2,694	38.3	5,821	41.8	2,680	29.1
Academic rank								
Senior	163	26.0	686	48.1	1,372	49.9	624	32.6
Junior	41	12.8	470	35.6	1,279	42.1	241	32.1
All	947	21.5	2,694	42.9	5,821	45.5	2,680	32.3
Gender								
Male	142	25.2	700	49.3	1,804	49.3	737	33.2
Female	61	16.3	405	33.7	840	39.7	130	4.9
All	947	21.4	2,694	41.0	5,821	45.4	2,680	32.4

Source: CAP:07. (Refer to appendix A for key.)

[a]Excludes the United Kingdom.

Table 10.5 Percentage of full-time faculty in the United States and elsewhere who have published in a foreign country, by type of institution, academic field, rank, and gender, 2007–2008

	United States		Other English-speaking countries		Continental Europe[a]		East Asia	
	N	%	*N*	%	*N*	%	*N*	%
Institution type								
University	221	30.5	1,395	58.9	3,499	72.5	820	75.1
Other four-year	35	15.8	163	49.8	237	53.3	601	37.8
All	947	27.0	2,694	57.8	5,269	70.9	2,680	53.0
Academic field								
Education and humanities	90	28.0	355	58.8	446	58.8	256	41.9
Social sciences, business, and law	56	24.5	369	54.5	584	60.0	246	49.6
Physical and life sciences	44	30.3	317	66.3	1,134	82.9	272	70.6
Engineering, manufacturing, construction, and architecture	29	31.5	145	59.7	707	74.3	290	50.7
Health sciences	29	23.4	228	51.7	520	73.4	238	60.3
All	938	26.4	2,510	56.3	4,954	68.4	2,605	50.0
Academic rank								
Senior	190	30.3	880	61.8	1,812	73.3	966	50.4
Junior	66	20.6	707	53.6	1,901	68.8	446	59.4
All	947	27.0	2,744	57.8	5,236	70.9	2,666	53.0
Gender								
Male	168	29.8	901	63.5	2,479	74.7	1,156	52.1
Female	84	22.5	617	51.3	1,256	64.6	257	58.1
All	938	26.9	2,622	57.9	5,262	71.0	2,662	53.1

Source: CAP:07. (Refer to appendix A for key.)
[a]Excludes the United Kingdom.

Table 10.6 Percentage of full-time faculty in the United States and elsewhere who have published in a foreign language, by type of institution, academic field, rank, and gender, 2007–2008

	United States		Other English-speaking countries		Continental Europe[a]		East Asia	
	N	%	*N*	%	*N*	%	*N*	%
Institution type								
University	75	10.3	462	19.5	4,354	82.6	539	49.4
Other four-year	9	4.1	19	5.8	342	61.8	964	60.7
All	947	8.9	2,694	17.9	5,821	80.7	2,680	56.1
Academic field								
Education and humanities	38	11.8	132	21.9	576	66.5	250	40.9
Social sciences, business, and law	19	8.3	134	19.8	825	71.7	191	38.5
Physical and life sciences	5	3.4	71	14.9	1,356	90.1	274	71.2
Engineering, manufacturing, construction, and architecture	9	9.8	44	18.1	870	85.3	393	68.7
Health sciences	10	8.1	48	10.9	667	87.9	267	67.6
All	938	8.6	2,510	17.1	5,500	78.1	2,605	52.8
Academic rank								
Senior	62	9.9	346	24.3	2,275	82.7	1,128	58.9
Junior	22	6.9	141	10.7	2,391	78.7	372	49.5
All	947	8.9	2,744	17.7	5,788	80.6	2,666	56.3
Gender								
Male	52	9.2	276	19.5	3,028	82.8	1,294	58.3
Female	30	8.0	192	16.0	1,625	76.8	202	45.7
All	938	8.7	2,622	17.8	5,773	80.6	2,662	56.2

Source: CAP:07. (Refer to appendix A for key.)
[a]Excludes the United Kingdom.

Table 10.7 Percentage of full-time faculty in the United States and elsewhere emphasizing an international perspective in their courses, by type of institution, academic field, rank, and gender, 2007–2008

	United States		Other English-speaking countries		Continental Europe[a]		East Asia	
	N	%	*N*	%	*N*	%	*N*	%
Institution type								
University	443	52.4	1,570	64.6	3,235	63.1	844	68.7
Other four-year	161	54.0	244	68.0	619	55.2	1,070	59.3
All	1,144	52.8	2,790	65.0	6,252	61.6	3,031	63.1
Academic field								
Education and humanities	252	63.3	469	70.0	698	69.1	518	70.6
Social sciences, business, and law	160	57.8	517	72.4	881	66.8	416	72.9
Physical and life sciences	57	32.0	256	54.6	792	57.2	223	54.4
Engineering, manufacturing, construction, and architecture	31	31.6	119	48.6	533	47.7	248	39.7
Health sciences	66	45.2	255	55.0	443	56.8	242	57.1
All	1,135	49.9	2,635	61.3	5,827	57.4	2,936	56.1
Academic rank								
Senior	387	53.3	990	65.8	1,922	66.4	1,331	62.5
Junior	217	51.9	870	64.4	1,900	57.5	569	64.5
All	1,144	52.8	2,856	65.2	6,199	61.7	3,013	63.1
Gender								
Male	322	48.9	953	65.4	2,352	61.8	1,532	61.9
Female	274	57.7	826	65.5	1,434	62.3	373	70.1
All	1,133	52.6	2,719	65.4	6,110	62.0	3,008	63.3

Source: CAP:07. (Refer to appendix A for key.)
[a]Excludes the United Kingdom.

Table 10.8 Percentage of full-time faculty in the United States and elsewhere who characterize their research as "international in scope," by type of institution, academic field, rank, and gender, 2007–2008

	United States		Other English-speaking countries		Continental Europe[a]		East Asia	
	N	%	*N*	%	*N*	%	*N*	%
Institution type								
University	298	42.4	1,516	63.9	3,401	67.5	635	57.8
Other four-year	78	35.1	198	58.9	286	44.3	671	40.1
All	925	40.6	2,708	63.3	5,685	64.9	2,771	47.1
Academic field								
Education and humanities	152	47.1	400	65.7	535	63.5	308	46.7
Social sciences, business, and law	88	37.3	444	64.2	771	66.6	290	57.2
Physical and life sciences	57	40.1	317	67.3	1,012	70.6	156	41.1
Engineering, manufacturing, construction, and architecture	36	42.9	147	59.8	615	61.3	252	42.4
Health sciences	28	26.2	246	55.5	449	64.1	183	46.4
All	919	39.3	2,531	61.4	5,345	63.3	2,692	44.2
Academic rank								
Senior	275	45.3	931	66.6	1,828	71.8	967	48.6
Junior	101	31.8	824	60.4	1,831	59.1	331	43.2
All	925	40.6	2,763	63.5	5,644	64.8	2,756	47.1
Gender								
Male	247	44.8	971	68.0	2,356	66.6	1,076	46.8
Female	126	34.3	708	58.7	1,267	61.5	223	49.4
All	918	40.6	2,635	63.7	5,600	64.7	2,749	47.3

Source: CAP:07. (Refer to appendix A for key.)

[a]Excludes the United Kingdom.

low perception no doubt reflects enrollment declines in foreign students in the United States after September 11, 2001. Scientists were more likely to report such increases, those in the humanities and education least likely; senior faculty were more likely to report them than junior faculty, and women slightly more likely than men.

In terms of research, two-fifths of US faculty reported that international perspectives had penetrated their research and scholarship (table 10.9)—slightly less than the half who reported such integration in their teaching and more than the one-third who reported collaborating or copublishing with colleagues abroad. This compared with substantially more faculty in European and other English-speaking nations (about two-thirds) and, to a lesser extent, faculty in Asian countries (about half). Such adoption of international perspectives in research was more common among university faculty, senior faculty, and male faculty; it was most common in education and the humanities as contrasted to the social and health sciences.

In sum, the involvement of American professors in international teaching and research does not appear by 2007–08 to have increased significantly during the decade and a half since the 1992 Carnegie survey, despite the personal computing and Internet revolutions of the past generation. This is a startling example of apparent inertia in the midst of economic turbulence, despite evidence of a growing presence of foreign-born scholars in our graduate programs and among our faculty. Nevertheless, the good news is that about half of the US faculty reports bringing international perspectives into their courses and teaching and interacting with more international students. On the other hand, the bad news is that only about two-fifths report bringing international perspectives into their research, a third report international collaborations, and about one-fifth international publications—at a time when the US share of both journal publications and citations is declining.

Explaining US Faculty Engagement in International Teaching and Research

How can we account for the persistent relatively low level (by international standards) of internationalization of the American faculty as well as the considerable variation among them? Employing data from the 2007–08 Changing Academic Profession Survey, Finkelstein, Walker, and Chen (2013) sought to explain the extent of US faculty collaboration with international colleagues and their relatively limited infusion of international perspectives in their research

Table 10.9 Percentage of full-time faculty in the United States and elsewhere reporting more international students in their courses, by type of institution, academic field, rank, and gender, 2007–2008

	United States		Other English-speaking countries		Continental Europe[a]		East Asia	
	N	%	*N*	%	*N*	%	*N*	%
Institution type								
University	387	45.7	1,481	61.4	2,826	55.6	495	41.0
Other four-year	126	42.3	203	57.2	591	54.1	276	15.5
All	1,144	44.8	2,768	60.8	6,177	55.4	2,986	25.8
Academic field								
Education and humanities	153	38.4	359	54.1	549	55.3	214	29.8
Social sciences, business, and law	129	46.6	467	66.0	784	60.7	232	41.5
Physical and life sciences	83	46.4	289	61.5	705	50.6	87	21.5
Engineering, manufacturing, construction, and architecture	35	35.7	130	53.5	528	47.6	80	13.0
Health sciences	79	54.5	279	60.7	399	52.2	61	14.4
All	1,135	42.2	2,616	58.3	5,766	51.4	2,891	23.3
Academic rank								
Senior	363	49.9	984	65.4	1,686	58.2	527	25.0
Junior	150	36.0	748	56.2	1,697	52.6	235	27.3
All	1,144	44.8	2,836	61.1	6,122	55.2	2,969	25.7
Gender								
Male	306	46.4	895	61.4	2,159	56.9	580	23.7
Female	202	42.6	756	60.9	1,179	52.5	184	35.2
All	1,133	44.8	2,700	61.1	6,039	55.3	2,965	25.8

Source: CAP:07. (Refer to appendix A for key.)
[a]Excludes the United Kingdom.

by testing a model of faculty behavior derived from Blackburn and Lawrence (1995). Drawing broadly on motivation theory, these authors posit that faculty behavior is shaped by two broad sets of factors: individual factors, including sociodemographic characteristics, career characteristics, a set of professional predispositions and values that they label self-knowledge, and a set of factors they label as social knowledge, which translate roughly into faculty perceptions of institutional values and expectations for what constitutes acceptable performance.

More specifically, the model assumes that sociodemographic characteristics (such as gender), career characteristics (such as type of institution, choice of discipline), faculty social knowledge (i.e., their perceptions of institutional priorities, pressures, and rewards), and faculty self-knowledge (teaching vs. research orientation, allocation of work effort, research involvement) shape faculty behavior. Faculty behaviors, in turn, yield tangible outcomes, including publication, grants, and awards (Finkelstein, Walker, and Chen 2013).

Based on the above, their study conceptualized faculty internationalization in the focus and content of their research and in their collaboration and networking patterns as a function of sociodemographic and career characteristics and as a function of their self-knowledge (personal value orientation) and their social knowledge (perception of institutional expectations). The outcome variables included two dimensions of faculty research collaboration, including whether faculty reported collaborating with foreign colleagues on research in the past three years and the extent to which faculty characterized their research as "international in scope." These were conceived to reflect the social networks and content of faculty research.

What did they find? Table A-10.1 (see appendix E) summarizes the results of a logistic regression analysis for the outcome variable collaboration in research with international colleagues.[9] The results confirm the relatively fewer significant effects of sociodemographic factors in contrast to the importance of aspects of both social knowledge and personal knowledge in shaping cross-border collaboration patterns. As between the effects of social (institutional expectations) and personal knowledge (orientation to teaching vs. research), the latter appear more pervasive. The only sociodemographic predictor found to be significant is the years since the first faculty appointment: the longer the time serving as a faculty member, the more likely is collaboration with international colleagues in research.[10]

A large and persistent effect of career characteristics, such as number of years spent abroad postbaccalaureate, discipline, and tenure status, is evident in predicting research collaboration. For example, the odds of international collaboration in research for those US faculty who reported spending between one and two years abroad following receipt of their undergraduate degree were almost three times that of faculty who had not spent any postbaccalaureate time abroad for study or research (odds ratio = 2.817, $p < 0.001$). For those faculty spending three or more years abroad, the odds of international collaboration were somewhat less than 2.5 times that of nonborder crossers, suggesting that beyond a certain threshold, incremental border crossing experience brought diminishing returns (odds ratio = 2.364, $p < 0.005$). There is also a disciplinary effect on the odds of international collaboration in research. Those who work in investigative fields (e.g., physical and life sciences) tended to be more likely to collaborate with international scholars than those working in social fields (e.g., social sciences) (odds ratio = 2.405, $p < 0.005$). However, institution type did not emerge as a statistically significant predictor, suggesting that affiliation with a research university, somewhat unexpectedly, did not contribute independently to the odds of cross-border research collaborations.

One dimension of social knowledge is found to significantly predict collaboration with international colleagues: the perception that faculty themselves (rather than administrators) drove campus internationalization initiatives. The odds ratio for this predictor is 1.97, indicating that for faculty affiliated with institutions in which the faculty are perceived as driving internationalization initiatives, the odds of collaborating with international colleagues on research are nearly two times that of faculty working in institutions where internalization initiatives are perceived as administratively driven. The emergence of this "faculty leadership" predictor is a key distinguishing feature. In terms of personal knowledge, the odds for research collaboration across borders for those whose self-reported orientation is primarily to teaching was less than half of those faculty who are primarily oriented to research. Moreover, one finds that the odds for collaborating across borders for those participants whose research is more oriented to commercial applications and technology transfer and those whose research is more basic were twice that of their counterparts not engaged in basic research or research focused on commercial applications. Finally, the odds of international collaboration in research for those US faculty who are highly involved in research were nearly three times that of faculty who are not so intensively involved (odds ratio=2.871, $p < 0.001$), a not entirely surprising finding!

The results of the logistic regression model for the outcome variable, "The emphasis of your primary research this year is international in scope" are presented in table A-10.2 (see appendix E). Unlike research collaboration with international colleagues, this outcome explicitly focuses on the substantive content rather than the social network development and maintenance aspects of US faculty internationalization. As such, it may provide a window on understanding the similarities and differences in factors shaping the content of faculty work as distinguished from the social networks in which faculty work is embedded.

A review of table A-10.2 reveals both common and distinctive elements. In terms of commonality, the analysis demonstrates that sociodemographic characteristics are only to a limited extent significantly related to the international content of research. Those who had longer careers since their first faculty appointment tended to be more likely to characterize their research as international in scope. The results also demonstrate the powerful shaping influence of faculty's years abroad and faculty self-knowledge (teaching vs. research orientation, intensity of research involvement, type of research undertaken) on international activity. Those whose primary orientation is not in teaching, who are highly active in research, and whose primary research is multidisciplinary—whether it can be described as basic, socially oriented, or commercially oriented—are more likely than their peers to bring an international focus to the content of their research. This synergy seems entirely sensible in light of the increasing globalization of the knowledge industry: more research than ever is driven by economic concerns and passed seamlessly across national and disciplinary borders; more basic research is undertaken by international teams. What is distinctive about faculty infusion of international content and perspectives into their research in contradistinction to their scholarly networks is twofold. First is the virtual disappearance of major career characteristics, including disciplinary differences. Second, a different dimension of social knowledge emerged as a significant predictor of internationalization of research content: whether institutions consider research quality in making personnel decisions. At first glance, it may appear surprising that those who reported their institutions to consider research quality in personnel decision making tended to have lower probabilities of characterizing their research as international in focus or scope (odds ratio=0.483, $p < 0.05$). This may, however, reflect the tendency for American scholars to prefer English-language and American-based research journals as the desideratum of quality and a concern about the prestige or ranking of dissemination venues.

As predicted by the Blackburn and Lawrence (1995) framework, sociodemographic factors, including gender and nativity, were largely insignificant when controlling for faculty career characteristics, personal or self knowledge, and social knowledge, suggesting that the internationalization of academic work does not automatically proceed from the increasing internationalization of the birth origin of US faculty. This finding becomes particularly significant as we witness the increasing presence of women in newly entering academic career cohorts across most fields and as, too, those women, are more likely than ever to be married and have primary responsibility for child (and later elder) care. It is not clear how American higher education's drive to internationalize, especially insofar as that may require increased border crossing and extended stays abroad, will take into account (accommodate) the realities of the growing corps of married academic women. To date, however, all things being equal, gender has not served as a primary obstacle.

If demographics are not destiny, neither are career characteristics. While research on American academics since at least Burton Clark's oft-quoted "small worlds, little worlds" (Clark 1987) has been founded on the premise that institutional and disciplinary affiliation are the major arbiters of academic work and careers, the Blackburn and Lawrence (1995) framework is singular in arguing that both impact faculty behavior indirectly through their mediating effects on self-knowledge and social knowledge. Affiliation with a research or PhD-granting university was only modestly predictive of faculty internationalization. To some extent, the relatively minor discernable impact of institutional type per se may be understood in the context of the powerful role of institutional expectations as perceived by faculty, and reflected in Blackburn and Lawrence's terms, in their social knowledge. Among institutional expectations, one surprisingly strong predictor was the extent to which faculty, rather than administrators, drive campus internationalization. It appears that research intensive universities—quite beyond their place in any Carnegie taxonomy—differ in that regard.

Much like institutional type, the impact of academic field on the internationalization of faculty work was largely limited to research collaboration. In that regard, faculty associated with more investigative fields, that is, those fields emphasizing empirical observation, quantitative analysis, and precision, were more likely to collaborate internationally than those in other fields. It should be noted, however, that the minimal significance of discipline may be attributable as much to the fairly gross taxonomy employed in the study. Earlier research (e.g., Goodwin and Nacht 1991) has shown that disciplinary effects on international activities of American faculty are extremely localized and nuanced with substantial variation in the intrinsic motivation for international activity even among subfields of a single discipline. This suggests that a finer categorization of academic fields and subfields might have uncovered effects that were, in effect, camouflaged by gross taxonomic categories. The generally muted impact of career characteristics boasts two exceptions. First is the matter of career age. "Years of professional service" was modestly, if significantly, associated with a broadening in the scope of faculty research contentwise and in terms of collegial networks. Senior faculty were more likely to lend an international focus to their research, while newer entrants were less likely to do so. It is not clear to what extent this finding represents a developmental maturation process: as they age and mature as scholars, faculty turn their sights outward and broaden their perspectives, a trend noted in the literature (Finkelstein 1988; Baldwin and Blackburn 1981; Hermanowicz 2009) or rather the operation of the ever more narrow academic reward system that is in effect deterring junior faculty from engaging in international activities and cultivating international relationships insofar as that may require extended stays abroad—something that may be incompatible with pretenure pressures as well as family obligations (Fairweather 1996).

More than institutional type and expectations (social knowledge) and discipline, however, it was faculty self-knowledge—the professional values, orientations, and self-concept developed over a career within particular institutional contexts—that emerged as the most powerful and pervasive predictor of the two dimensions of faculty internationalization. High faculty research involvement and involvement in a synergistic intersection of basic, multidisciplinary, and commercially oriented research (the driver of the global knowledge-based economy) significantly predicted not only the participation of faculty in international research networks (the social aspect of internationalization) but also the focus on international elements in the substantive content of faculty research. This reinforces that basic truism of a half century of research on the modern American faculty: that academic behavior is disproportionately shaped by deeply ingrained individual values and predilections and amenable only at the margins to the shaping influence of institutions (Finkelstein 1988) and academic fields.[11]

It may be that time spent abroad following receipt of the baccalaureate degree (i.e., as an adult), while strictly speaking a career characteristic in the Blackburn and Lawrence (1995) framework, constitutes one such deep desideratum of ingrained values and predilections. It was somewhat surprising that adult years spent abroad trumped all but high research involvement as perhaps the most pervasive and powerful predictor of US faculty internationalization in research content and networks. While we were unable to specify either the nature or timing of such border crossing, what is clear is that such sustained border-crossing experience as an adult is key and that such experience requires some substantial duration to have an impact (at least one year). Such a finding provides some solid quantitative empirical support to the value of national initiatives such as the Fulbright Scholars Program. It provides as well a solid justification for institutional and extrainstitutional initiatives to provide graduate students and faculty with extended border-crossing experiences. The Internet may not be an adequate generic substitute for such a place-bound experience.[12]

New Evidence on the Drivers of Faculty Internationalists

More recently, Finkelstein and Sethi (2013) sought to examine faculty engagement in international activity more broadly, including teaching as well as research and publication and physical border crossing both before and after receipt of highest degree, and extending their sample to include faculty from eighteen countries as well as the United States that allowed them to speak at the more macro level about the impact of national context (country characteristics) as well as institutional and faculty career and demographic characteristics on international engagement writ large. The size and diversity of their sample of nearly 25,000 faculty worldwide allowed them to undertake a factor analysis to identify the underlying structure of faculty international activities (nineteen specific activity items ranging across teaching, research, publication, and physical and educational mobility). They identified seven factors or dimensions that accounted for nearly two-thirds of the variance in faculty international activity worldwide. They used scores on the seven factors to construct a seven-dimension profile of individual faculty international activity and subjected those profiles to a cluster analysis, seeking to maximize the "distance" between mutually exclusive subgroups of faculty respondents. That cluster analysis yielded two groups of faculty across all nineteen nations, roughly equal in size, who showed relatively high and relatively low engagement in international activity. Those 6,666 academic staff in the first cluster or subgroup were characterized by relatively high index scores on international collaboration, co-publication and foreign publication and were more likely to have taught abroad and experienced a more international student presence at home. They were more likely to consider international job moves, and were less likely to have been educated in the country of their current employment. The 6,465 academic staff in the second cluster were characterized by lower means scores on international collaboration, copublication and foreign publication, teaching abroad, and perceiving an increased presence of foreign students at home. Faculty who placed in the second cluster were more likely than those in the first to report being educated in the country of their current employment. In sum, the first cluster represented a relatively internationalized faculty, the second cluster a relatively insular one.

The two clusters served as a dichotomous outcome variable in a logistic regression analysis, drawing heavily on the earlier work of Finkelstein, Walker, and Chen (2009, 2013) cited above now with five sets of predictors: *country characteristics*, including size, economic development, language tradition (English vs. non-English), and cultural tradition (Asian vs. Western); *institutional characteristics* (a.k.a. *social knowledge)*, including institutional type (research university vs. other), role of faculty in institutional internationalization initiatives, and undergraduate (vs. graduate) programs focus; *individual career characteristics*, including academic field, academic rank, years since first appointment; *faculty self-knowledge*, including orientation to teaching or research, nature of primary research (e.g. applied/practical, multidisciplinary, articles published in an academic book or journal, research reports/monographs written for a funded project, and papers presented at a scholarly conferences); and *demographic characteristics*, including age, gender, nativity (country of birth same as current country of employment), place of training (country earned degree same as current country of employment) and years of research and study abroad post first degree.

The results of the logistic regression are displayed in table A-10.3 (see appendix E). They suggest that both country characteristics and institutional characteristics exerted powerful independent effects on faculty international activity. Among the former, country size and cultural tradition (Asian or not) as well as language (English or not) were significant, while level of economic development was not. Faculty in large countries and those in English-speaking countries (e.g., the United States), were significantly less likely to be involved internationally. Among organizational characteristics, both institutional type and faculty-centric shaping of campus international initiatives significantly predicted international activity. Academic staff affiliated with universities were 1.5 times as likely to fall in the "high" internationalist group as were those affiliated with nonuniversity postsecondary institutions and faculty at institutions where the faculty drove internationalization initiatives were also 1.5 times as likely to be in the high internationalization cluster as those in which administrators drove internationalization initiatives.

Among the professional and personal characteristics, thirteen out of sixteen proved significant predictors, although only two yielded substantial odds ratios. Academic staff in the "hard" disciplines (life sciences, physical sciences including mathematics and computer science, engineering, architecture, agriculture, medical, and health sciences) were 2.3 times as likely as those outside these fields to be members of the high internationalization cluster. Faculty who were primarily oriented to teaching were half as likely to belong to the high-internationalization group as those primarily oriented to research. Beyond these key professional variables, faculty who were more involved in research and publication showed a slightly (but statistically significant) higher involvement in international activity. Among demographic characteristics both study time spent abroad and gender proved significant predictors. Male faculty and those who spent time abroad were 1.2 times as likely to be highly involved international activity as their opposites. Thus mobility for study emerged as a significant predictor of membership in the high-internationalization cluster.

Perhaps the most telling finding from that analysis is the power of institutional type and academic field, on one hand, to shape the internationalization of academic work and careers (a confirmation yet again of the basic principle that Burton Clark (1987) identified thirty years ago as the structural arbiters of academic life) and the near equal power of national context, on the other, to shape faculty internationalization activity. Disciplinary membership shapes the orientation of faculty to international activity: faculty in the natural sciences and in certain fields where the substantive content of the field requires the crossing of borders (whether physically or mentally). At the same time, nationality factors—whether a faculty member works in a large or small country, whether one in which English dominates or not, and whether in a Western or Asian culture—all to a considerable degree contribute to the motivation and opportunity to engage in international activity. Indeed, it is within these national and disciplinary parameters that institutional type (in terms primarily of research-oriented mission) further channels faculty toward or away from international activity. Beyond these factors, personal characteristics, including gender, time spent abroad for study, academic rank, and an individual faculty member's focus between research and teaching, have less pronounced, although statistically significant, effects.

These analyses suggest that the relatively limited involvement of American faculty in international teaching and research is, in some sense, quite predictable based on the national context in which they work: a large, English-speaking country that offers many opportunities for intranational collaboration and publication in English, the lingua franca of global scholarship. Insofar as they have abundant opportunities, and some of the highest-quality resources at home, there seems little payoff to looking abroad, especially when career risk and convenience are factored in. Nonetheless, it is clear that different institutional and disciplinary contexts shape the predisposition for US faculty to look outward as does their interest in and performance in research and their actual extended experience abroad.

The Consequences of Faculty Engagement in International Research and Teaching

Why worry about the international engagement of American faculty? The source of concern is simply that international engagement has consequences—for individual faculty members, their students and institutions, and the competitiveness of the American economy and, ultimately, the higher education enterprise itself. In their recent volume focusing on higher education internationalization worldwide, Huang, Finkelstein, and Rostan (2013) sought to sum up what we have learned about the substantive consequences of faculty mobility across borders and engagement in international teaching and research. They concluded first that faculty international engagement does make a difference because it is associated with one crucial aspect of the academic profession, that is, academic productivity. Their findings suggest a clear correlation between the individual engagement in international activities at large and the number of articles published in academic books or journals, research reports written for funded project, and papers presented at scholarly conferences (Huang, Finkelstein, and Rostan 2013). More specifically, when the relationship between international research collaboration and research performance in the form of scholarly articles and conference papers is examined, the results show that, across all fields, academics collaborating with international colleagues had published or presented almost twice as many articles or papers as their colleagues in the same field who did not collaborate internationally.[13] While the direction of the relationship between international engagement and scholarly productivity may not be entirely unidirectional,[14] nonetheless it is clear that extending scholarly networks beyond national borders increases opportunities for collaboration, and those are certainly associated with increased productivity. As research and graduate education continue to develop outside the United States and the "core" Western countries, and as the center of gravity of global knowledge production begins to move eastward toward Europe and Asia, such international connections will quite likely become increasingly crucial to the career prospects of American academics in an expanding array of academic fields.

Finally, there is the matter of American students. As national boundaries become more porous through immigration, technology, and business and cultural exchanges, more and more American college graduates will find themselves needing new knowledge and skills to succeed in a global environment, which will place a premium on cultural knowledge and sensitivity. While the new global economy requires that individuals be multicultural in understanding and better informed about international issues, youth in the United States have frequently been characterized as "multi-culturally uninformed" (Bell-Rose and Desai 2005). Indeed, when students enter American colleges and universities in the second decade of the twenty-first century, they find a curricular landscape—at least in terms of global exposure—that has not fundamentally changed over the past generation. While there is much recent discourse on internationalization of the academy promoting both its desirability and inevitability (Altbach 2004; Knight 2004; Welch 2005; Green 2008; American Council on Education 2012), concrete action belies the rhetoric. A recent study of the internationalization of US universities and colleges conducted by the American Council on Education (2012) concludes that the improvements in internationalization efforts as surveyed in 2011 as compared with 2006 and even 2001 are rather modest. The most remarkable area of improvement over the decade is a big jump in the share of the surveyed institutions that offered study-abroad programs (91% vs. 65%), while there were only slight increases in the proportion of campuses who have developed a plan for internationalization (just over a third) and who have established campus infrastructures (offices and officers) to coordinate international activity (about four in ten by 2011). While the proportion of institutions requiring a general education course that features global trends has increased marginally from 24% to 28% over the past decade (albeit still a clear minority), the percentage of institutions requiring undergraduates to take courses that focus primarily on issues or perspectives from countries or regions outside the United States has declined from 37% to 29%. Moreover, the share of institutions that have undergraduate foreign language requirements continued to declined steadily over the past decade (37% in 2011 compared with 53% in 2001). While data show that increasing numbers of institutions are considering international experience in the faculty hiring process, fewer than one in ten institutions build in guidelines specifically considering international work in the promotion and tenure process—representing no change over the past decade (American Council on Education 2012)—even though international faculty collaborations and the incorporation of global perspectives in courses are believed to enhance the quality of teaching and research (see, e.g., Ray and Solem 2009). Support for faculty engagement in international activity, ranging from conference attendance to overseas study and teaching, has largely remained steady. Given the heightened importance of internationalization promoted by prominent US national groups such as the American Council on Education and the Association of International Educators (NAFSA), support of the study-abroad opportunities for undergraduate students through the recently introduced Simon Study Abroad Act and the national security initiatives that promote critical languages learning, the performance of the US universities and colleges on various aspects of internationalization, according to the American Council on Education (2012) survey, is less then lustrous.

Another set of studies by the International Association of Universities (IAU) surveys the importance, rationales, risks, and benefits of internationalization among higher education institutions across the world. According to the surveys conducted in 2003 and 2005, about three-quarters (73%) of the surveyed institutions considered internationalization a high priority for their own institution and fewer than half (46%) considered it as governmental policy priority (Knight 2003, 2006). At the same time 52% viewed faculty as the primary catalysts for internationalization versus 24% for administrators and 20%

for students (Knight 2003). According to the 2009 IAU survey (IAU 2010), there were some shifts in rankings of the perceived top benefits of internationalization as compared with the 2005 IAU survey: while international awareness of the internationalization of students and staff remained the top benefit, strengthened research and knowledge production as the benefit of internationalization moved to the second position in 2009, and more symbolic benefits of internationalization such as cooperation and solidarity as well as enhanced institutional prestige moved up in the ranking of internationalization benefits (Knight 2006; Egron-Polak and Hudson 2010). While the American Council on Education and IAU studies suggest recent shifts in the rationale for internationalization, they do not provide strong evidence for changes in actual practice in the United States, or elsewhere for that matter, short of more focused initiatives at regional cooperation reflected in the European Commission and the Association of Southeast Asian Nations.

Conclusion

Where then does the American faculty stand in the face of the transformative sweep of globalization? The analyses reviewed here suggest first that American academics have historically been, and continue to be, quite inward looking and insular in their orientation. They are US-centric in a way that reflects the realities of the world in the second half of the twentieth century. We have suggested that changing circumstances—the emergence of the knowledge economy and globalization of the knowledge industry—render what had historically been a functional stance increasingly less functional, both for institutions of higher education in the United States and for American college graduates. As knowledge and knowledge-building capacity worldwide disperses, universities and the academic workforce in the United States will need to recalibrate their geographic horizons. A robust minority of the American academic workforce, variously estimated at 30–40%, are doing so. The available evidence suggests that they disproportionately reflect some of our most research-oriented and productive faculty, those in the more investigative academic fields (the natural sciences and engineering) or those in fields that require geographic mobility and those that have had the benefit of previous study abroad experience. To date, the American academic enterprise has been sluggish in its internationalization initiatives; and this is one key area in which the faculty factor will be critical for promoting change.

NOTES

1. An earlier version of parts of this chapter first appeared in Huang, Finkelstein, and Rostan (2013).

2. The Bologna Process represents an initiative of ministers of education in European Union countries to align degree levels and programs across national boundaries, allowing free movement of students within the European area. See, for example, Keeling (2006).

3. The Erasmus Program was initiated by the European Union in 1987. The Association of Southeast Asian Nations (ASEAN) Education Ministers Organization launched the student mobility program in 2010, initially including twenty-three universities from Malaysia, Indonesia, and Thailand (Yavaprabhas 2011).

4. It should be noted that "stay rates" have been generally calculated five years out, that is, five years beyond PhD receipt, and only exceptionally ten years out. It is likely that fifteen- or twenty-year stay rates, if available, would be much lower or reflect back and forth mobility.

5. Yang and Welch (2010) reported that about 25% of the more than 1 million Chinese students departing for US universities between 1976 and 2006 actually returned, representing ratio of 2.4 departing for every one returning to China. The Chinese Ministry of Education reported 800,000 students returning across the five years from 2008 through 2013 (scaling up to 292,700 in 2012 alone), closing the ratio of sent to returning to 1.37 from 2.42 a decade earlier (Wang Hongyi 2013a). These data were reported by Richard Harrington, doctoral student in higher education at Claremont Graduate University (hereafter Harrington n.d.).

6. While it seems nearly impossible to get accurate numbers of Americans holding positions in the Chinese professoriate, according to the Chinese press the number of annual "foreign expert certificates" issued to all countries had reached 540,000 annually by 2013 (Harrington, n.d.), which compares with the cumulative grand total of 740,000 by 2002 reported by the State Administration of Foreign Expert Affairs (2002). According to data gathered for a recent doctoral dissertation, in the twenty years leading up to the new recruitment initiatives of 2008, Chinese tertiary institutions (universities and colleges) had employed 40,000 foreign experts, presumably in a variety of lines but with a preponderance in language instruction. By 2007, the central government was distributing 63 million US dollars annually in support of 799 programs that employ foreign experts. Numbers of foreign experts in universities grew from 1,350 in 1978 to 70,000 in 1998. By 2008 the number had grown to 34,000 new experts annually (Harrington n.d.).

7. The other English-speaking counties include Australia, Canada, and the United Kingdom. Continental Europe includes Finland, Germany, Italy, the Netherlands, Norway, and Portugal. Asia includes Hong Kong (a Special Administrative Region of China), Japan, and South Korea.

8. Although, as we shall see, natural scientists are among the most likely to collaborate on research with colleagues abroad.

9. Logistic regression is a multivariate technique (form of multiple regression analysis) applied to dichotomous outcome variables that computes odds ratios for the various independent or predictor variables, that is, the extent to which an independent variable increases or decreases the odds of the outcome variable having a certain value. The subsequent text discussion are this organized around the "odds ratios" yielded by the various predictors as reported in the appendix tables.

10. It should be noted, however, that the negative squared term of this variable indicates that the appointment year effect decreases as the duration of faculty service increases, that is, the relationship is curvilinear.

11. Although to be sure there is an element of self-selection of faculty into relatively "compatible" academic fields and institutional settings.

12. Just how research and study abroad affect faculty values and worldviews, what durations seem necessary, and the relative substitutability of simulated digital experiences constitute an important arena for future research.

13. While questions may be raised about differential acceptance rates for US-sponsored and foreign-sponsored journals—suggesting that increased productivity of those who publish internationally may be an artifact of this less competitive context—the available evidence does not support that explanation (Borghans and Corvers 2010).

14. That is, academics who are highly productive and visible in their field are likely to have expansive collegial networks that promote such collaboration.

REFERENCES

Adams, James D. 2010. "Is the United States Losing Its Preeminence in Higher Education?" In *American Universities in a Global Market*, edited by Charles T. Clotfelter, 33–68. Chicago: University of Chicago Press.

Altbach, Philip G. 2004. "Globalization and the University: Myths and Realities in an Unequal World." *Tertiary Education and Management* 10 (March): 3–25.

Altbach, Philip G., and Lionel S. Lewis. 1996. "The Academic Profession in International Perspective." In *The International Academic Profession: Portraits of Fourteen Countries*, edited by Philip G Altbach, 3–50. Princeton, NJ: Carnegie Foundation for the Advancement of Teaching.

Altbach, Philip G., Liz Reisberg, Maria Yudkevich, Gregory Androushchak, and Ivan F. Pacheco. 2012. *Paying the Professoriate: A Global Comparison of Academic Compensation and Contracts*. New York: Routledge.

Altbach, Philip G., and Jamil Salmi. 2011. *The Road to Academic Excellence: The Making of World-Class Research Universities*. Washington, DC: World Bank.

American Council on Education. 2012. *Mapping Internationalization on U.S. Campuses: 2012 Edition*. Washington, DC: Center for Internationalization and Global Engagement, American Council on Education.

Baldwin, Roger, and Robert T. Blackburn. 1981. "The Academic Career as a Developmental Process: Implications for Higher Education." *Journal of Higher Education* 52 (November–December): 598–614.

Bell-Rose, Stephanie, and Vishakha Desai. 2005. *Educating Leaders for a Global Society*. New York: Goldman Sachs Foundation and Asia Society.

Blackburn, Robert T., and Janet Lawrence. 1995. *Faculty at Work*. Baltimore, MD: Johns Hopkins University Press.

Borghans, Lex, and Frank Corvers. 2010. "The Americanization of European Higher Education and Research." In *American Universities in a Global Market*, edited by Charles T. Clotfelter, 231–67. Chicago: University of Chicago Press.

Clark, Burton R. 1987. *Academic Life: Small Worlds, Different Worlds*. Princeton, NJ: Carnegie Foundation for the Advancement of Teaching.

Clotfelter, Charles T. 2010. Introduction to *American Universities in a Global Market*, edited by Charles T. Clotfelter, 1–29. Chicago: University of Chicago Press.

Crowther, Paul, Michael Joris, Matthias Otten, Bengt Nilsson, Hanneke Teekens, and Bernard Wächter. 2000. *Internationalisation at Home: A Position Paper.* Amsterdam, NL: European Association for International Education, with the Academic Cooperation Association, IAK, IÉSEG, Nuffic, Katholieke Hogeschool Limburg, and Malmö University.

Cummings, William K. 2008. "The Context for the Changing Academic Profession: A Survey of International Indicators." In *The Changing Academic Profession in International Comparative and Quantitative Perspectives,* RIHE International Seminar Report 12, 35–55. Hiroshima, JP: RIHE Hiroshima University.

Egron-Polak, Eva, and Ross Hudson. 2010. *Internationalization of Higher Education: Global Trends, Regional Perspectives.* IAU 3rd Global Survey Report. Paris: IAU.

Fairweather, James S. 1996. *Faculty Work and Public Trust: Restoring the Value of Teaching and Public Service in American Life.* Needham Heights, MA: Simon and Schuster.

Finkelstein, Martin J. 1988. *The American Academic Profession: A Synthesis of Social Science Research since World War II.* Columbus, OH: Ohio State University Press.

Finkelstein, Martin J., and Wendiann Sethi. 2013. "Predictors of the Internationalization of Academic Work." In *The Internationalization of the Academy: Changes, Realities, and Prospects,* edited by Futao Huang, Martin Finkelstein, and Michele Rostan, 237–58. Dordrecht, NL: Springer.

Finkelstein, Martin J., Elaine Walker, and Rong Chen. 2009. "The Internationalization of the American Faculty: Where Are We, What Drives or Deters Us?" In *The Changing Academic Profession over 1992–2007: International Comparative and Quantitative Perspectives.* RIHE International Seminar Report 13, 113–44. Hiroshima, JP: RIHE Hiroshima University.

———. 2013. "The American Faculty in an Age of Globalization: Predictors of Internationalization of Research Content and Networks." *Higher Education* 66, no. 3: 325–40.

Finn, Michael G. 2010. *Stay Rates of Foreign Doctorate Recipients from US Universities, 2007.* Oak Ridge, TN: Oak Ridge Institute of Science and Education.

———. 2012. *Stay Rates of Foreign Doctorate Recipients from US Universities, 2009.* Oak Ridge, TN: Oak Ridge Institute of Science and Education.

Friedman, Thomas. 2005. *The World Is Flat: A Brief History of the Twenty-First Century.* New York: Farrar, Straus and Giroux.

Goodwin, Craufurd D., and Michael Nacht. 1991. *Missing the Boat: The Failure to Internationalize American Higher Education.* Cambridge, UK: Cambridge University Press.

Greene, Madelyn F. 2008. *Mapping Internationalization on US Campuses: 2008 Edition.* Washington, DC: American Council on Education.

Hermanowicz, Joseph C. 2009. *Lives in Science: How Institutions Affect Academic Careers.* Chicago: University of Chicago Press.

Huang, Fuato. 2007a. "Internationalization of Higher Education in the Developing and Emerging Countries: A Focus on Transnational Higher Education in Asia." *Journal of Studies in International Education* 11 (Fall–Winter): 421–32.

———. 2007b. "Internationalization of Higher Education in the Era of Globalization: What Have Been Its Implications in China and Japan?" *Higher Education Management and Policy* 19 (May): 47–61.

Huang, Fuato, Martin J. Finkelstein, and Michele Rostan. 2013. *The Internationalization of the Academy: Changes, Realities, and Prospects.* Dordrecht, NL: Springer.

International Association of Universities (IAU). 2010. *Internationalization of Higher Education: Global Trends Regional Perspectives.* IAU 3rd Global Survey Report. Paris: IAU.

Joris, M., Christiaan van den Berg, and Stefaan van Ryssen. 2003. "Home, but Not Alone: Information and Communication Technology and Internationalisation at Home." *Journal of Studies in International Education* 71 (March): 94–107.

Keeling, R. 2006. "The Bologna Process and the Lisbon Research Agenda: The European Commission's Expanding Role in Educational Discourse." *European Journal of Education* 41, no. 2 (2006): 203–22.

Knight, Jane. 2003. *Internationalization of Higher Education Practices and Priorities.* 2003 IAU Global Survey Report. Paris: IAU.

———. 2004. "Internationalization Remodeled: Definition, Approaches, and Rationales." *Journal of Studies in International Education* 8 (March): 5–31.

———. 2006. *IAU 2005 Internationalization Survey: Preliminary Findings Report.* Paris: IAU.

O'Hara, Sabine. 2009. "Internationalizing the Academy: The Impact of Scholar Mobility." In *Higher Education on the Move: New Developments in Global Mobility,* edited by Rajika Bhandari, 29–47. New York: Institute for International Education.

Ray, W. and M. Solem (2009). "Gauging Disciplinary Engagement with Internationalization: A Survey of Geographers in the United States. *Journal of Geography in Higher Education* 33, no. 1: 103–21.

Wächter, Bernd. 2003. "An Introduction: Internationalisation at Home in Context." *Journal of Studies in International Education* 7, no. 1 (March): 5–11.

Wang Hongyi. 2013a. *Annual Report of Development of Chinese Returnees.* Report 2. Beijing, CN: Social Sciences Academic Press.

———. 2013b. "More Chinese Students Return to Find Work after Studying Abroad." *China Daily (English Web).* October 17. http://en.people.cn/90882/8427452.html.

Wang, Qi, Yi Li, and Nian Cai Liu. 2015. "Entering Academia: Conditions and Opportunities for New Faculty in Higher Education in Mainland China." In *Young Faculty in the Twenty-First Century: International Perspectives,* edited by Maria Yudkevich, Philip G. Altbach, and Laura E. Rumbley, 53–81. Albany: State University of New York Press.

Welch, Anthony. 2005. "From Peregrinatio Academica to Global Academic: The Internationalization of the Profession." *Professoriate: Portrait of a Profession,* edited by Anthony Welch, 71–96. Dordrecht, NL: Springer.

Wildavsky, Benjamin. 2010. *The Great Brain Race: How Global Universities Are Reshaping the World.* Princeton, NJ: Princeton University Press.

Yang, Rui, and Anthony R. Welch. 2010. "Globalisation, Transnational Academic Mobility, and the Chinese Knowledge Diaspora: An Australian Case Study." *Discourse: Studies in the Cultural Politics of Education* 31, no. 5 (December): 593–607.

Yavaprabhas, Supachai. 2011. "Connect ASEAN: Pushing Forward Harmonization of Higher Education in Southeast Asia Region." In *The Changing Academic Profession in Asia: Contexts, Realities, and Trends,* RIHE International Seminar Report 17. Hiroshima, JP: RIHE Hiroshima University.

Yudkevich, Maria and Philip G. Altbach (eds). 2015. *Young Faculty in the Twenty-First Century: International Perspectives.* Albany, NY: State University of New York Press.

11

American Faculty in an International Perspective

One of the challenges we face as we seek to take the measure of the American faculty—and, in particular, to assess the changing place of the faculty factor in American higher education—is to provide the context within which to interpret the changes we are documenting.[1] Typically, American academic history has served as our context. In a period of such disruptive change as this, however, a traditional historical framework—even relatively recent history, much less hearkening back to the golden age of the 1960s and 1970s—will prove to be inadequate; a more global framework is necessary to comprehend the status and outlook for the American faculty. Comparing the faculty factor in 2013 with that even as recently as twenty years ago, in 1993 (before personal computers, the Internet revolution, and certainly the emergence of MOOCs) may be fundamentally misleading, at best, and irrelevant, at worst. Thus we are seeking in this chapter to juxtapose the American faculty today to academic professionals in other mature economies in 2013 by asking the questions: How does the faculty factor in the United States compare with that in other English-speaking countries, continental Europe, and the mature economies of East Asia? What can we learn about the meaning of current developments in the United States by viewing them in the context of similar developments and economic forces at play elsewhere in the developed world?

To that end, we have been able to draw on a number of recent studies of academics globally. The largest source of data is provided by the Changing Academic Profession (CAP) survey of 2007–08 spanning nineteen countries on five continents (see appendix D for an overview of survey sample and methods). Those data are supplemented by the findings of the Higher School of Economics—Boston College 2010 survey of academic compensation in twenty-eight countries and their subsequent 2012 study of the prospects of new recruits to the academy in ten countries (Altbach et al. 2012; Yudkevich and Altbach 2015).[2] These data are further supplemented by the European Commission's 2012 Mobility of Academic Researchers in Europe survey, known as MORE II (European Commission 2013), when available.[3]

The data that are available from these sources include basic faculty demographics, workload, working conditions, faculty evaluation, career mobility, the faculty role in university governance, compensation, and faculty job and career satisfaction. Before examining the data, a few words are necessary by way of establishing the context, that is, identifying some basic parameters within which the US system differs from other national systems, that must inform any interpretation of such comparative data.

The Distinctiveness of American Higher Education

In some sense, the most obvious distinguishing characteristic of the US system is its size—in terms of numbers of institutions, faculty, and students. Only China is larger, and only Russia is even close; Germany's is half the size—at least in terms of full-time faculty—the United Kingdom one-third, and Japan one-fourth (Altbach et al. 2012). Beyond the sheer scale of higher education in the United States, the single most significant difference with other countries is its basic organization. In the United States, colleges and universities are independent, self-governing corporate entities.[4] Within the context of their charters, they function relatively autonomously from government authority (Ben-David 1977; Cowley 1980; Clark 1983; Duryea 1973). Universities in nearly every other country of the world are branches of national government and are administered by national ministries of education.[5] Historically, they have been funded nearly exclusively by national (or regional, or both) governments, while institutions in the United States, especially those in our large private (not-for-profit) sector, have historically maintained diverse revenue streams, including student tuition, other private sources (especially gifts), grants and contracts, and auxiliary enterprises.

Many of the defining features of academic work and careers in the United States flow directly from these central organizational facts. Accordingly, although ultimate authority for each campus is vested in a governing board, that board typically delegates to a chief executive officer (a president or chancellor) operational, day-to-day responsibility. In turn, the CEO has over the past century, in varying degrees, delegated authority to the institution's faculty in the areas of curriculum and academic appointments. By contrast, in the continental universities of Europe and in East Asia, the senior administrator typically is (or was) faculty elected and served as a relatively weak "pass through" between the individual faculties and the ministry of education.[6] Most immediately, faculty in the United States are employees of corporate entities, rather than civil servants of the national government; and that distinction contributes to a certain inherent vulnerability of American faculty to corporate action, despite the protections of a tenure system. On the other hand, the corporate character of academic employment in the United States has provided considerable insulation from direct government control: unlike their colleagues in nationally centralized systems, faculty in the United States are free to define academic basics, for example, the content covered in their courses, their reading lists, and degree requirements for a major or concentration in their field.[7]

Another characterization flowing from this organizational fact is the historic prominence of market forces in the American system. As independent entities, colleges and universities are free to compete for students and faculty (and have done so for the past three hundred years). This culture of interinstitutional competition (or "responsiveness," as Bruce Johnstone [2003] calls it) and the capacity of institutions to freely establish their niche in the marketplace has contributed to at least two distinctive characteristics of the US academic career: the development of a competitive marketplace for faculty talent and the autonomy to use faculty compensation as an instrument in that competition.[8] Thus we see in the United States the balkanization of faculty compensation by academic discipline (see chapter 9), whereby colleges and universities compete with business and industry (the "private" sector) and government to attract faculty in those fields with significant nonacademic employment prospects.

Related to this market orientation is the extraordinary institutional differentiation in the United States vis-à-vis other national systems. Well ahead of the onset of massification in the 1950s and 1960s, the American system had already given birth to an array of distinctive institutional types. In Europe (as in East Asia) traditionally, one university has looked very much like another. It is only in the past twenty years that other nations have begun to accelerate institutional-type diversification in their national systems, primarily with technical or vocational institutions as a single alternative model to the university (or in the recent spawning of a private sector in otherwise entirely public systems).[9] This means that academic work in the United States has proceeded in very different institutional settings driven by very different missions, expectations, and resources. Thus in the United States, academic work has traditionally been more diversified—in terms of the balance between research and teaching (indeed, whether any research is expected at all), the academic credentials, the backgrounds of faculty, and so on—requiring a great deal more nuance in its description and analysis. That is, in the United States all professors are far from alike in their backgrounds, the work they do as faculty members, and their career trajectories.[10]

A final distinctive characteristic of the US system for our purposes is related to the academic career structure. While it has been true that most national systems offer a modicum of long-term stability to academic staff in employment arrangements (in many countries academics in the public sector, as noted, are members of the civil service), in the United States, thanks in large part to the system's corporate character as well as the American Association of University Professors's 1940 Statement of Academic Freedom and Tenure, the trajectory of academic careers is quite structured in terms of timing and sequence: a fixed, prespecified probationary period, followed by a high-stakes evaluation that often leads to relatively secure indefinite appointment as well as a sequence of ranks through which faculty incumbents move in a regularized flow. It is also, and this is a distinctive feature, institutionally anchored. Historically, in the continental systems of Europe, for example, Germany and France, vacancies have been listed by academic field at the national level where competitions for these positions are conducted by national disciplinary committees. The most highly rated candidates in particular fields are "offered" vacancies—even if they do not precisely meet the needs of the academic unit in which the position exists. Most practically, that has meant that a faculty member must apply for a higher-level position (promotion) at the national level, making it usually necessary to change institutions to advance academically (Musselin 2010). There is less an institutional (and more a disciplinary) anchoring of the career or a defined, sequential system of ranks through which an individual can proceed on a more-or-less accepted schedule.[11] Such institutional anchorage is, however, not associated with inbreeding. Quite the opposite. While inbreeding is typical of many academic systems in East Asia and parts of Eastern Europe and Russia, where promising students are tapped for doctoral study and subsequently for postdoctoral employment by their mentors at their alma mater, most doctoral universities in the United States proscribe hiring their own graduates and insist, by contrast, that graduates "cut the cord" and find another institution within which to pursue their careers, thereby reinforcing academic mobility (Caplow and McGee 1958).

In sum, academic careers in the United States tend to be highly predictable and regularized, institutionally based, subject to market forces, and supportive of interinstitutional mobility; that is to say, US academicians and their career pathways display almost infinite variety. Within the context of that distinctive organizational matrix, we now ask, How do American faculty compare with their global counterparts—in their demographic profile, their institutional and disciplinary venues, their working conditions and workload, their relationship with their employing institution, and their job and career satisfaction? In making such comparisons, we draw primarily on the Changing Academic Profession Survey of 2007–08, which, as noted above, was conducted in nineteen countries on five continents. In contextualizing the situation and views of American faculty, we seek to relate them to three general comparison groups or clusters of faculty members: faculty in other English-speaking systems, including Australia, the United Kingdom, and Canada;[12] faculty in continental Europe, including both the northern countries of Germany, the Netherlands, Norway, and Finland and the southern countries, including Italy and Portugal; and faculty in the advanced economies of East Asia, that is, Japan, South Korea, and Hong Kong.

Comparative Demographics

Table 11.1 provides a basic comparative demographic overview of the American faculty. The data suggest, first, as we averred earlier, that American professors are less likely to be situated in research-intensive universities than their counterparts almost anywhere else. Insofar as institutional mission and type shape academic work and careers (Clark 1987; Schuster and Finkelstein 2006), that means that American professors on average show much greater variation in the kind of work they do and the careers they pursue than do their global counterparts. And this diversity is captured by the relatively lower research orientation of American professors in the aggregate vis-à-vis their global counterparts. Further reflecting the multidimensional system in which they work, they are much more likely to be focused on teaching and their instructional duties. American faculty are more diverse as well in their range of disciplinary backgrounds; they are more likely to be found in the liberal arts fields (the humanities and social sciences) than are their global counterparts. However, that gap may be closing insofar as American universities over the past several decades have been growing primarily in the professions and ap-

Table 11.1 Percentage distribution of selected demographic and career characteristics of full-time faculty, by country/region, 2007–2008

		Other English-speaking countries				Continental Europe[a]		East Asia	
	United States	Australia	Canada	United Kingdom	All other English-speaking countries	Germany	All continental Europe	Japan	All East Asia
University	76	71	100	96	88	89	73	21	38
Heavily oriented toward research	43	70	69	68	69	65	64	71	68
Disciplines									
Professions[b]	37	55	47	33	46	56	52	64	58
Humanities and arts	19	15	17	17	16	12	11	15	18
Female	38	57	34	46	46	33	38	17	21
With academic spouse (all)	43	22	39	31	31	30	35	6	16
Males with academic spouse	41	23	37	28	30	23	33	3	13
Females with academic spouse	46	21	44	34	33	44	39	30	36
40 years and under	18	31	33	40	34	47	43	15	21
40–55 years	42	47	47	43	46	36	38	49	57
Over 55 years	40	22	22	17	21	16	19	35	22
Senior rank	51	22	64	32	38	21	36	79	65
With two or more jobs since highest degree									
In higher education	63	55	53	55	54	36	38	54	55
Outside higher education	18	12	9	22	14	8	11	3	4
Doctorate	83	67	91	58	71	77	57	77	84

Source: CAP:07. (Refer to appendix A for key.)

[a]Excludes the United Kingdom.

[b]Professions includes the following disciplines: medicine, engineering, law, business administration, economics, and agriculture.

Table 11.2 Percentage of full-time faculty reporting various contractual conditions, by country/region, 2007–2008

	United States (*N*= 1,146)		Other English-speaking countries: Australia (*N*= 1,227)		Canada (*N*= 1,148)		United Kingdom (*N*= 1,226)	
	N	%	*N*	%	*N*	%	*N*	%
Permanently employed (tenured)	659	57.5	609	49.6	812	70.7	1,024	83.5
Continuously employed (no preset term but no guarantee of permanence)	133	11.6	147	12.0	25	2.2	95	7.7
Fixed-term employment with permanent or continuous employment prospects (tenure track)	242	21.1	134	10.9	272	23.7	86	7.0
Fixed-term employment without permanent or continuous employment prospects	92	8.0	330	26.9	33	2.9	21	1.7
Other	20	1.7	7	0.6	6	0.5	0	0

Source: CAP:07. (Refer to appendix A for key.)
[a]Excludes the United Kingdom.

plied fields (indeed, the majority of new hires are now in those more pragmatic areas rather than in the traditional arts and sciences, see chapter 3).

Beyond its relatively distinctive institutional and disciplinary venues, the American professoriate shares one basic demographic with most of its global counterparts: the rapidly increasing presence of women in the profession. Indeed, the data show that the United States actually trails many of the European countries in the proportion of women faculty. What may be distinctive, however, about the American case is the high proportion of such women who are married to other academics. The phenomenon of dual-career academic couples is a particularly American phenomenon.

In terms of age and rank distribution, the American faculty is generally older and more senior—and, moreover, is among the very few national professoriates (besides Canada and now the United Kingdom) without a system of

All other English-speaking countries (*N*=3,601)		Continental Europe[a]				East Asia			
		Germany (*N*=1,252)		All continental Europe (*N*=6,017)		Japan (*N*=1,401)		All East Asia (*N*=3,090)	
N	%	*N*	%	*N*	%	*N*	%	*N*	%
2,445	67.9	531	42.4	3,133	52.1	1,050	74.9	1,370	44.3
267	7.4	194	15.5	414	6.9	216	15.4	741	24.0
492	13.7	56	4.5	586	9.7	89	6.4	642	20.8
384	10.7	454	36.3	1,561	25.9	37	2.6	308	10.0
13	0.4	17	1.4	323	5.4	9	0.6	29	0.9

mandatory retirement. While it is relatively top-heavy in terms of age and rank among thirteen developed nations, it is much less so than Japan, or even Canada. Nonetheless, as a system, there is considerable cause for concern in the United States, as underscored in chapters 4, 6, and 13, about the limited availability of opportunities for those seeking entry-level positions owing to congestion in the academic pipeline at the exit level.

Comparing Career Entry and Prospects

Like the United States, most national systems of higher education across the globe have responded to the acute fiscal pressures associated with massification by accelerating the number of fixed contract, non-career-ladder appointments, both full-time and part-time, for faculty. Table 11.2 shows that the United States is about in the middle of the distribution in terms of the proportion of full-time faculty who are on permanent or tenured appointments: about 57% compared with more than 70% in Japan, the United Kingdom, and Canada but slipping to about 40% in Germany and Asia.

The United States is also in about the middle of the distribution in the proportion of faculty on fixed-term, non-career-ladder appointments—one-fifth of the full-time faculty overall as compared with one-half in Germany and two-fifths in Australia and less than 10% in Canada and the United Kingdom.[13] The US position, however, represents a persistent trend of steady decline over the past thirty years in permanent appointments (and a concomitant steady increase in non-career-ladder appointments), while the trend in Germany is in the opposite direction. Indeed, Germany has recently established the new professorial rank of Junior Professor to provide some modicum of a career ladder.[14] Both Canada and the United Kingdom have remained relatively stable, despite the abolition of tenure during the Thatcher years.

Comparing Workload and Support for Academic Work

Workload

Table 11.3 shows the mean hours devoted weekly by faculty to teaching, research, service, and administration.[15] American faculty report the highest mean hours spent on teaching (21.2) compared with faculty in Continental Europe (17.4) at the other extreme, a differential of nearly 20%, with faculty in other English-speaking countries and East Asia between the two. Conversely, Amer-

Table 11.3 Mean weekly hours full-time faculty spend on various work activities, by country/region, 2007–2008

Number of hours in a typical week, when classes are in session, that you spend on . . .	United States (*N*= 1,112)		Other English-speaking countries (*N*= 2,862)		Continental Europe[a] (*N*= 7,017)		East Asia (*N*= 2,960)	
	Mean	SD	Mean	SD	Mean	SD	Mean	SD
Teaching	21.2	11.5	18.7	11.3	17.4	11.8	20.4	11.5
Research	12.4	10.3	14.0	11.5	14.7	12.3	16.7	12.1
Service	4.6	5.5	2.8	5.4	2.7	6.8	4.1	6.6
Administration	7.7	7.8	8.9	8.2	4.6	6.0	7.0	7.1
Other	2.8	4.0	3.0	4.1	2.5	4.4	3.1	4.0

Source: CAP:07. (Refer to appendix A for key.)
[a]Excludes the United Kingdom.

Table 11.4 Ratio of weekly hours full-time faculty spend on teaching versus on research, by country/region, 2007–2008

	United States	Other English-speaking countries	Continental Europe[a]	East Asia
Teaching:research	1.7:1	1.3:1	1.2:1	1.2:1

Source: CAP:07. (Refer to appendix A for key.)
[a]Excludes the United Kingdom.

ican faculty report the lowest mean number of hours spent on research: 12.4 compared with 16.7 in East Asia, at the other extreme, a nearly one-third differential, with Europe and other English-speaking countries in between (14.7 and 14.0, respectively).

Another lens on the contrasting balance between teaching and research in faculty work is provided by table 11.4, which reports the ratio of the median hours spent in teaching to those spent in research for faculty in the United States versus their counterparts elsewhere. The data show that the ratio of median teaching to research effort among American faculty is about 1.7—that is, 1.7 times the effort is spent in teaching as in research—compared with roughly 1.2 in continental Europe, and East Asia and 1.3 in other English-speaking countries. In sum, American professors in the aggregate spend more time on teaching and less on research than their global counterparts, although, of course, the distribution of time among American faculty varies strikingly according to the type of institution where they work.

In terms of service and administration, table 11.3 shows that American faculty spend more time on local community and disciplinary service than their European (almost twice as much) or other English-speaking country counterparts, although still a relatively modest amount. Differences in time devoted to administration (including governance) show American faculty somewhere in the middle: 7.7 hours on average compared with European faculty's 4.6 hours, at the other extreme, with faculty in other English-speaking countries even higher (8.9 hours) and those in Asia slightly lower (7.0 hours).

While American faculty may teach relatively more than their global counterparts, their teaching is distributed in a somewhat distinctive pattern, as illustrated in table 11.5. Like their colleagues in other English-speaking countries, about 60% of their teaching is undergraduate and the remainder graduate. At the other extreme, their Asian counterparts devote more of their

Table 11.5 Mean allocation of full-time faculty teaching effort at various degree levels, by country/region, 2007–2008

	United States (*N*=1,112)		Other English-speaking countries (*N*=2,826)		Continental Europe (*N*=5,537)[a]		East Asia (*N*=2,967)	
Percentage teaching at level	Mean	SD	Mean	SD	Mean	SD	Mean	SD
Undergraduate	61.6	37.5	61.4	34.3	50.4	35.4	76.5	27.6
Master's	20.8	29.1	21.9	27.0	36.8	32.3	13.6	20.1
Doctoral	13.2	24.8	11.7	20.1	7.6	15.9	4.8	12.3

Source: CAP:07. (Refer to appendix A for key.)
[a]Excludes the United Kingdom and Norway.

effort (fully three-quarters) to undergraduate education and a much smaller proportion to graduate education. Their European counterparts not only teach less (table 11.3), but they devote less effort to teaching undergraduates (about half) while more to teaching graduate students. Most of their graduate education effort, however, is devoted to master's-level education in contrast to US faculty, whose effort in graduate education is targeted mostly on doctoral education (more than other English-speaking faculty, twice as much as European faculty, and three times as much as Asian faculty).

Moreover, as table 11.6 shows, American professors are much more likely than their global counterparts to engage in a number of nontraditional pedagogical practices, including, for example, distance education, e-mail communication with students, and group-based projects. More generally, a much larger proportion of American faculty are engaged in curriculum development and outside-of-class interaction with students. These data suggest not only that American faculty in the aggregate teach more, but also that they engage in teaching in a different way that appears to focus more on individual interaction with their students.

In terms of their professional and research activities, the data in table 11.7 suggest that American faculty are more likely to work "individually" on research projects and that their collaborative efforts are less likely to cross national borders (this point has been elaborated on at length in chapter 10). While a majority of US faculty have engaged in writing academic papers and writing proposals for research grants, a majority have not engaged in several activities associated with funded research, including managing a research team, research contracts, and purchasing equipment (all activities in which a majority of their global colleagues report being engaged). Thus American faculty are less likely to be engaged in research and in those activities associated with funded research. Moreover, the data on faculty publications presented in table 11.8 suggest that in every publication category, American academics are less prolific than their counterparts in other developed countries.[16]

In terms of broader professional activities (table 11.9), American faculty are distinguishable from their global colleagues in their participation in political and community life. Nearly half (48.6%) were involved in a community organization or project compared with less than one-fourth of faculty in Asia and a mere 14.7% in Europe. Similarly, 20.5% of American faculty worked with local, national, or international social service agencies compared with 10.4% of faculty in Europe and only 12.9% of faculty in Asia. Still further, one in seven American

Table 11.6 Percentage of full-time faculty engaged in various teaching activities, by country/region, 2007–2008

Have you been involved in any of the following teaching activities:[a]	United States		Other English-speaking countries		Continental Europe[b]		East Asia	
	N	%	*N*	%	*N*	%	*N*	%
Classroom instruction	1,098	96.0	2,866	95.9	6,264	94.6	2,995	98.2
Individualized instruction	911	79.6	1,487	49.8	4,433	66.9	2,221	72.8
Learning in project groups	605	52.9	931	31.2	2,865	43.2	1,230	40.3
Practice instruction or laboratory work	428	37.4	754	25.2	3,389	51.2	1,599	52.4
ICT-based learning[c]	272	23.8	808	27.0	1,570	23.7	765	25.1
Distance education	279	24.4	392	13.1	856	12.9	240	7.9
Development of course materials	973	85.1	1,631	54.6	4,587	69.2	1,566	51.3
Curriculum or program development	845	73.9	1,263	42.3	3,566	53.8	1,315	43.1
Face-to-face interaction with students outside of class	1,028	89.9	1,622	54.3	4,733	71.4	2,390	78.4
Electronic communications (e-mail) with students	1,046	91.4	1,760	58.9	5,216	78.7	2,060	67.5

Source: CAP:07. (Refer to appendix A for key.)

[a]Indicates an affirmative response.

[b]Excludes the United Kingdom.

[c]Information and communication technologies.

Table 11.7 Percentage of full-time faculty participating in various research activities, by country/region, 2007–2008

	United States		Other English-speaking countries		Continental Europe[b]		East Asia	
Research activities[a]	*N*	%	*N*	%	*N*	%	*N*	%
Working individually	678	73.8	2,046	68.1	2,760	42.5	1,360	46.5
Having collaborators	717	78.0	2,557	85.1	5,104	78.5	2,072	70.9
Collaborating with persons in the United States	556	60.5	2,045	68.1	4,451	68.5	1,647	56.3
Collaborating with international colleagues	306	33.3	1,848	61.5	3,910	60.2	996	34.1
Preparing and conducting experiments	476	44.9	1,729	56.4	3,989	60.9	1,741	58.7
Supervising a research team	475	44.8	1,695	55.3	3,321	50.7	1,557	52.5
Writing academic papers	772	72.8	2,699	88.0	5,337	81.5	2,563	86.4
Technology transfer	151	14.2	571	18.6	1,219	18.6	390	13.2
Writing proposals or research grants	569	53.7	2,119	69.1	4,069	62.1	2,293	77.3
Managing research contracts and budgets	348	32.8	1,604	52.3	2,539	38.8	1,647	55.5
Purchasing or selecting equipment and supplies	371	35.0	1,381	45.0	2,968	45.3	1,708	57.6

Source: CAP:07. (Refer to appendix A for key.)

[a]Indicates an affirmative response.

[b]Excludes the United Kingdom.

Table 11.8 Mean number of publications of full-time faculty, by country/region, 2007–2008

How many of the following have you written, cowritten, edited, or presented in the past three years:	United States (N= 1,043)		Other English-speaking countries (N= 2,946)		Continental Europe[a] (N=6,246)		East Asia (N= 2,902)	
	Mean	SD	Mean	SD	Mean	SD	Mean	SD
Scholarly book you wrote or cowrote	0.2	0.6	0.3	0.7	0.6	1.5	1.2	2.4
Scholarly book you edited or coedited	0.2	0.9	0.3	0.7	0.4	1.4	0.5	1.6
Article or chapter	4.3	7.4	6.5	9.5	7.0	9.1	9.7	12.9
Research report or monographs	1.2	3.7	1.4	3.8	1.5	3.2	1.7	4.0
Paper presented at a scholarly conference	5.7	11.2	6.6	8.8	6.2	8.5	6.6	11.8

Source: CAP:07. (Refer to appendix A for key.)
[a]Excludes the United Kingdom.

Table 11.9 Percentage of full-time faculty participating in various professional activities, by country/region, 2007–2008

Professional activities[a]	United States		Other English-speaking countries		Continental Europe[b]		East Asia	
	N	%	*N*	%	*N*	%	*N*	%
Member of committee, board, or body	333	29.4	1,257	34.8	2,623	34.1	1,662	53.4
Peer reviewer	748	66.0	2,712	75.1	3,478	45.2	2,128	68.4
Editor of journal or book series	222	19.6	838	23.2	1,180	15.3	1,140	36.7
Elected officer or leader in association	322	28.4	919	25.4	1,472	19.1	1,637	52.6
Elected officer or leader in union	26	2.3	176	4.9	519	6.7	126	4.1
Participated in local, national, or international politics	155	13.7	169	4.7	305	4.0	83	2.7
Member of a community organization or project	551	48.6	1,816	50.3	1,134	14.7	767	24.7
Worked with local, national, or international social service agency	232	20.5	480	13.3	804	10.4	400	12.9

Source: CAP:07. (Refer to appendix A for key.)
[a]Indicates an affirmative response.
[b]Excludes the United Kingdom.

faculty participated in political activity at some level, in contrast to less than 5% (one in twenty) elsewhere across the globe. US faculty were about in the middle of the distribution in terms of the proportion participating as officers in professional associations, editors, and peer reviewers. In all, American faculty tend to be more heavily engaged in community- and political-oriented activities, beyond their more narrow professionally defined responsibilities, than are their counterparts elsewhere.

Working Conditions

The 2007–08 CAP survey asked academics how they felt about different facets of their working conditions. Concerning most items the respondents were about equally divided between those who felt the conditions were excellent or good and those who felt they were in need of improvement. Interestingly, telecommunications, classrooms, and the technology for teaching tended to get

Table 11.10 Percentage of full-time faculty rating facilities as "excellent" or "very good" by selected countries, 1992, 2007

Percent age saying the following are excellent or very good at their institution	United States			Australia			United Kingdom		
	1992	2007	Change 1992–2007	1992	2007	Change 1992–2007	1992	2007	Change 1992–2007
Classrooms	55	53	–2	31	47	16	31	32	1
Technology for teaching	49	60	11	35	52	17	32	39	7
Laboratories	54	25	–29	33	41	8	32	39	7
Research equipment and instruments	53	27	–26	28	42	14	22	34	12
Computer facilities	68	61	–7	53	62	9	43	43	0
Library facilities and services	62	57	–5	40	75	35	39	55	16
Your office space	45	57	12	40	62	22	34	42	8
Secretarial support	44	41	–3	36	27	–9	33	28	–5
Telecommunications		72	72		67	67		42	42
Teaching support staff		28	28		28	28		35	35
Research support staff		17	17		26	26		34	34
Research funding		16	16		23	23		17	17
All (mean)	54	48	–6	37	51	14	33	39	6

Source: CAP:07 (Refer to appendix A for key.)

the highest ratings, whereas research equipment and support for research and teaching tended to get lower ratings. In the 1992 International Survey of the Academic Profession administered by the Carnegie Foundation for the Advancement of Teaching, a similar question was asked. Comparing the recent findings with those for 1992, the academics in those countries with more-advanced economies, such as the United States, the United Kingdom, and Japan, reported little improvement, whereas academics in several of the emerging societies reported significant improvement (table 11.10). Overall, academics in Hong Kong gave the highest rating to their facilities, resources, and personnel.

The Evaluation of Faculty Work

An essential component of the work life of academic staff is the role peers play in the evaluation or assessment of the basic work of teaching, research, and service. In the United States, the American Association of University Professors

Germany			Japan			South Korea			Hong Kong		
1992	2007	Change 1992–2007	1992	2007	Change 1992–2007	1992	2007	Change 1992–2007	1992	2007	Change 1992–2007
43	51	8	15	33	18	19	48	29	51	68	17
42	56	14	14	53	39	9	44	35	60	82	22
48	64	16	12	9	–3	9	2	–7	42	50	8
46	62	16	14	9	–5	7	24	17	38	52	14
60	72	12	25	37	12	13	40	27	69	76	7
53	56	3	31	39	8	7	43	36	49	82	33
37	68	31	17	35	18	21	48	27	50	59	9
44	50	6	12	16	4	6	19	13	40	47	7
	84	84		53	53		73	73		80	80
	26	26		9	9		14	14		36	36
	38	38		9	9		11	11		29	29
	34	34		18	18		14	14		30	30
47	60	13	18	29	11	11	33	22	50	64	14

and the various disciplinary and professional associations have established the parameters and infrastructure for ensuring peer review of faculty work as the ultimate desideratum of professionalism. To what extent do peers actually dominate the evaluation of faculty work in the United States ? And how does the role of peers in the US context compare with that in other nations? Tables 11.11 to 11.13 report on faculty perceptions of the locus of faculty evaluation in their teaching (table 11.11), research (table 11.12), and service activities (table 11.13).

With respect to teaching (table 11.11), three findings seem particularly striking, if not entirely surprising. First is the pervasive, albeit not necessarily decisive, participation (role) of students, both in the United States, where 90% of faculty indicate that students have at least some role in evaluating teaching, and nearly everywhere else—with the notable exception of Japan.[17] Second is the relatively pervasive role of individual faculty and faculty bodies (peers) in evaluating teaching in the United States. Half of US faculty (50.7%) identify the involvement of other faculty or faculty bodies in evaluating teaching, second only to the United Kingdom's 63%, and significantly higher than levels in the other English-speaking countries (Australia and Canada), and higher than East Asia, and all of continental Europe. Third is the distinctively pervasive role of deans and chairs: more than four-fifths (81.2%) of US faculty attest to the pervasive involvement of deans and chairs, significantly higher than even Canada and Australia and higher than all the continental European and East Asian countries. The pervasive role of academic "middle management" in the United States is buttressed by the relatively greater role of central administration (chief academic officers and provosts) in the United States: 33.4% of faculty report central administrative involvement in teaching evaluation roughly on a par with Canada and the East Asian countries but significantly greater than continental Europe. This may be interpreted to reflect a broader pattern of increasingly decentralized managerialism in the governance of US higher education as described elsewhere (Finkelstein, Ju, and Cummings 2010).

In the case of research, we find a similarly pervasive role of deans and chairs (academic middle management) in evaluation of faculty work in the US.: nearly two-thirds (64.6%) report decanal or chair involvement in the evaluation of faculty research. This pattern is replicated in the other English-speaking countries (Canada, Australia, United Kingdom) but not in continental Europe and East Asia.

Faculty committees and individual faculty peers are second mostly likely to be involved in the evaluation of faculty research in the United States, a pat-

Table 11.11 Percentage of full-time faculty reporting that various stakeholders are involved in evaluating their teaching by country/region, 2007–2008

		Other English-speaking countries				Continental Europe[a]		Asia	
	United States (*N*=1,107)	Australia (*N*=840)	Canada (*N*=984)	United Kingdom (*N*=732)	All other English-speaking countries (*N*=2,556)	Germany (*N*=992)	All continental Europe (*N*=6,213)	Japan (*N*=1,057)	All East Asia (*N*=2,501)
Government/external stakeholders	7.9	5.9	7.9	31.5	14.0	4.3	15.3	9.0	10.80
Central admin	33.4	17.0	28.7	9.0	19.2	11.1	12.9	32.1	31.34
Deans/dept. chairs	81.2	67.2	69.8	50.5	63.4	16.9	37.5	30.0	36.72
Faculty committees/unions	50.7	32.9	34.6	63.8	42.4	21.1	30.2	20.2	24.68
Individual faculty	41.1	52.5	38.7	56.6	48.4	46.3	40.4	20.7	31.13
Students	90.7	85.6	91.5	92.1	89.7	76.5	81.0	49.6	69.97

Source: CAP:07. (Refer to appendix A for key.)
[a]Excludes the United Kingdom.

Table 11.12 Percentage of full-time faculty reporting that various stakeholders are involved in evaluating their research, by country/region, 2007–2008

		Other English-speaking countries				Continental Europe[a]		East Asia	
	United States (*N* = 1,085)	Australia (*N* = 956)	Canada (*N* = 978)	United Kingdom (*N* = 737)	All other English-speaking countries (*N* = 2,671)	Germany (*N* = 985)	All continental Europe (*N* = 5,980)	Japan (*N* = 1,040)	All East Asia (*N* = 2,417)
Government/external stakeholders	38.5	55.1	59.8	62.3	58.8	37.1	40.9	14.6	30.9
Central admin	30.8	21.8	31.1	21.2	25.0	18.6	11.3	38.0	39.5
Deans/dept. chairs	64.6	70.3	60.9	63.5	65.0	17.1	34.5	31.1	36.7
Faculty committees/unions	40.8	34.9	41.3	46.5	40.5	46.6	41.3	17.3	25.5
Individual faculty	37.2	43.4	35.6	50.7	42.6	48.0	40.5	28.6	33.8
Students	2.7	4.0	2.7	5.4	3.9	3.0	10.5	2.2	2.6

Source: CAP:07. (Refer to appendix A for key.)

[a]Excludes the United Kingdom.

Table 11.13 Percentage of full-time faculty reporting that various stakeholders are involved in evaluating their institutional and public service, by country/region, 2007–2008

		Other English-speaking countries				Continental Europe[a]		East Asia	
	United States (*N*=1,099)	Australia (*N*=842)	Canada (*N*=930)	United Kingdom (*N*=620)	All other English-speaking countries (*N*=2,392)	Germany (*N*=806)	All Europe (*N*=4,723)	Japan (*N*=1,045)	All Asia (*N*=2,297)
Government/external stakeholders	6.5	6.6	7.7	12.1	8.5	5.6	8.4	10.2	10.7
Central admin	36.9	23.2	30.8	24.4	26.4	16.3	16.1	34.2	37.4
Deans/dept. chairs	72.8	75.8	70.1	67.6	71.5	13.3	26.4	25.5	33.3
Faculty committees/unions	45.3	26.8	42.5	34.2	34.8	31.8	26.5	11.0	15.8
Individual faculty	30.6	38.3	31.2	47.6	38.0	40.5	34.3	18.9	25.5
Students	4.7	10.7	3.8	21.0	10.7	10.4	13.2	0.7	1.6

Source: CAP:07. (Refer to appendix A for key.)
[a]Excludes the United Kingdom.

tern fairly typical of most of the nineteen CAP countries, with the exception of the East Asian countries (especially Japan). While governmental and other external stakeholders are reported by US faculty to be nearly as pervasively involved in evaluating research as faculty peers (nearly four in ten report such involvement), this is actually considerably less than for all CAP countries except for Japan.[18] Central administration, however, is more likely to participate in the evaluation of faculty research in the United States (nearly one-third—30.8%—report such involvement) than almost anywhere else outside Asia and Canada. Finally, students are notably absent from evaluation, as they are everywhere else. The pattern of participation in the evaluation of faculty service activities almost precisely replicated the pattern for research: dominated by academic middle management (deans and chairs), followed by faculty peers and central administrators. Government and other external stakeholders as well as students are relatively absent from the equation.

In sum, then, while faculty peers in the United States are relatively strongly involved in the evaluation of faculty work across the board, their involvement tends to be second to that of academic middle management, including deans and department chairs. Central administration has a relatively larger role in faculty evaluation in the United States compared with other non-Asian nations; however, the role of both government and external stakeholders in evaluating faculty work tends to be less pervasive in the highly decentralized US academic system than almost anywhere else.

The Changing Status of American Faculty in Their Institutions

As we have already suggested, anchoring the academic career in an institutional setting—albeit without resorting to inbreeding—is a distinctive, almost defining, characteristic of the American professor and the academic career. How faculty perceive their organizational life is perhaps more critical, then, to the career prospects and satisfaction of academics in the United States than anywhere else in the world. Specifically, we examine here the following aspects of institutional life:

1. The faculty role in institutional governance, including

- perceptions of influence at the institutional, school or college, and departmental levels as well as across various decision areas
- perceptions of administrative leadership and communication as well as support for academic freedom

2. The self-reported locus of faculty loyalties as between their discipline, their department, and their institution, especially in cross-sectional comparison to identically constructed self-reports in 1992.

Comparing Faculty Roles in Governance

In an effort to further contextualize the US CAP data regarding the faculty's self-reported role in governance, we used the international dataset prepared by colleagues at Kassel University in Germany to compare our findings for the United States with the findings for faculty in five other developed countries—Canada, Australia, the United Kingdom, Germany, and Japan, each with historically strong academic systems. Table 11.14 compares faculty perceptions of the primary decision maker in five traditional governance areas: administrator selection, faculty appointment, faculty promotion, establishing budget priorities, and launching new academic programs across the six countries. The data suggest that the decisive role of US faculty in academic appointments and promotion is somewhat distinctive, equaled or surpassed only in Japan and possibly Canada. To the contrary, however, the US faculty's role in the selection of administrators, in establishing budget priorities, and in approving new academic programs tends to be less influential than that of faculty in other developed countries.

Another perspective emerges when we compare the percentage of faculty in each nation who report that faculty have the primary influence in each decision area (see table 11.15). In the area of their greatest perceived influence—faculty appointments and promotion—the US faculty fall about in the middle of the international distribution: while more influential than faculty in Germany and, to a lesser extent, Australia (about two-fifths report that faculty are the prime "deciders"), they are about on par with faculty in the United Kingdom but not nearly as influential as faculty in Canada and Japan (where 66–75% report primary faculty influence). In the area of lowest perceived faculty influence—selecting administrators and determining budgetary priorities—US faculty are at or near the bottom of the international distribution. They are slightly below faculty in Canada and Germany but well below those in Australia, the United Kingdom, and Japan. Finally, in the area of new academic programs, US faculty rate themselves at the lower end of the international distribution. Just over a third (35.6%) of US faculty report a primary decision role here as compared with about two-fifths of faculty in Canada (40.3%) and Australia (46.0 %), ranging upward to about three-fifths in the United Kingdom and Japan. German faculty report less influence in this area than the faculty in United States.

Table 11.14 Percentage of full-time faculty rating various constituencies as "influential" or "very influential" on five selected governance areas, by country/region, 2007–2008

		Other English-speaking countries				Continental Europe[a]		East Asia	
	United States	Australia	Canada	United Kingdom	All other English-speaking countries	Germany	All continental Europe	Japan	All East Asia
Selecting key administrators									
Faculty bodies	8.4	18.5	34.7	29.0	27.3	25.3	17.3	43.8	27.3
Central Administration/ external stakeholders	70.9	65.1	46.7	55.2	55.8	49.8	61.8	38.6	53.8
Deans/chairs	14.7	14.3	13.7	13.7	13.9	15.7	14.4	16.3	13.3
Total *N*	1,020	939	909	961	2,809	977	5,745	1,305	2,898
Choosing new faculty									
Faculty bodies	61.4	42.9	85.3	54.0	60.3	46.7	56.1	83.1	59.8
Central Administration/ external stakeholders	5.5	7.9	3.3	15.9	9.2	26.1	13.7	8.8	15.2
Deans/chairs	33.1	30.8	11.2	29.1	24.0	23.0	28.2	7.8	24.0
Total *N*	1,137	970	922	996	2,888	1,005	5,995	1,347	2,986

Making faculty promotion and tenure decisions									
Faculty bodies	51.1	50.8	65.8	52.4	56.2	38.4	46.0	75.6	54.4
Central Administration/ external stakeholders	18.4	33.2	12.1	30.2	25.4	23.6	21.0	16.4	27.0
Deans/chairs	30.5	15.9	21.6	16.8	18.0	35.7	30.8	8.0	18.1
Total *N*	1,137	968	932	982	2,882	1,000	5,890	1,319	2,958
Determining budget priorities									
Faculty bodies	2.3	22.2	6.9	29.5	19.7	13.0	21.0	35.5	23.3
Central Administration/ external stakeholders	53.1	55.4	57.9	52.0	55.1	62.8	48.4	45.9	52.6
Deans/chairs	42.4	20.5	31.9	14.9	22.3	18.9	26.8	18.4	22.4
Total *N*	1,098	955	926	966	2,847	986	5,863	1,330	2,922
Approving new academic programs									
Faculty bodies	35.6	46.0	40.3	60.8	49.1	28.2	—	64.8	52.8
Central Administration/ external stakeholders	31.9	39.5	36.2	41.1	39.0	44.7	23.4	17.3	25.5
Deans/chairs	15.9	12.9	16.5	16.6	15.3	18.5	18.0	16.8	19.5
Total *N*	1,096	957	913	950	2,820	964	5,887	1,301	2,896

Source: CAP:07. (Refer to appendix A for key.)
[a]Excludes the United Kingdom.

Table 11.15 Percentage full-time faculty reporting that faculty have "primary" influence on selected governance areas, by country/region, 2007–2008

		Other English-speaking countries				Continental Europe[a]		East Asia	
	United States	Australia	Canada	United Kingdom	All other English-speaking countries	Germany	All continental Europe	Japan	All East Asia
Selecting key administrators	8.4	18.5	34.7	29.0	27.5	25.3	17.3	43.8	27.4
Choosing new faculty	61.4	42.9	85.3	54.0	61.0	46.7	56.1	83.1	60.2
Making faculty promotion and tenure decisions	51.1	50.8	65.8	52.4	56.4	38.4	46.0	75.6	54.8
Determining budget priorities	2.3	22.2	6.9	29.5	19.5	13.0	21.0	35.5	23.3
Determining the overall teaching load of faculty	11.0	37.5	21.0	39.4	32.6	0.0	38.1	68.0	44.7
Setting admission standards for undergraduates	21.6	32.1	38.5	50.4	40.4	32.1	46.5	66.9	48.8
Approving new academic programs	35.6	46.0	40.3	60.8	49.6	28.2	42.8	64.8	52.7
Evaluating teaching	27.3	33.1	23.2	50.7	35.6	29.1	38.8	39.6	26.0
Setting internal research priorities	43.1	44.6	51.9	53.3	50.0	63.9	59.3	42.3	39.9
Evaluating research	53.1	39.7	56.9	41.7	46.2	40.7	45.7	41.4	46.1
Establishing international linkages	41.4	51.4	51.3	56.2	52.9	62.2	63.4	36.4	31.0

Source: CAP:07. (Refer to appendix A for key.)
[a]Excludes the United Kingdom.

When we examine weekly hours spent in governance or administration alongside the faculty's perceptions of their personal influence at the departmental, school or college, and institutional levels, we see that US faculty are at about the middle of the distribution in weekly time spent on governance matters (table 11.16). They report spending about 3.0 hours weekly as compared with about 4.5 hours in the United Kingdom and Australia, at one extreme, and 1.4 to 2.0 hours weekly in Germany and Japan, at the other. In terms of perceived influence, however, American academics see themselves as more influential at most organizational levels than do academics in any other nation. Only Germany and Canada are on par at the departmental level, with about two-thirds reporting that they are influential or very influential.[19]

In no nation do a majority of faculty see themselves as being influential beyond their own departments; indeed barely one in three or four report considerable influence at the school or faculty level, while barely one in ten do so at the institutional level.[20] However, it is worth noting that the US faculty score themselves higher than do the faculty from any other nation in wielding influence at both the faculty or school and institutional levels.

When, as in table 11.17, we compare US faculty perceptions of administrative competence and faculty institutional engagement with those of colleagues in Australia, Canada, Germany, Japan, and the United Kingdom, American faculty and their UK counterparts are among the least likely to describe administrative leadership as competent (just over one-third) as compared with more than two-fifths of their counterparts in Australia (40.8%), Canada (44.8%), and Japan (45.4%) and nearly three-fifths in Germany (57.3%). At the same time, US faculty are in the "middle of the pack" in terms of being kept informed about developments at their home institution (46.2% compared with over half in the United Kingdom and Canada but well ahead of German and Japanese faculty, at about one-third) and also in terms of reporting a lack of faculty involvement as a real problem. Thirty-eight percent report that a lack of faculty involvement is "a real problem here" (compared with two-fifths elsewhere), one of only two nations with less than 40% agreement.[21] The United States also finds itself in the middle position on perceived administrative support of academic freedom: just over 40% (41.1%) of US faculty agree that the "administration supports academic freedom," roughly on a par with the totals for the United Kingdom (39.2%) and Japan (37.7%), significantly higher than the 23.9% in Australia, but significantly lower than the two-thirds in Canada and about 55% in Germany—a relatively creditable, but absolutely disturbing picture.

Table 11.16 Mean weekly hours full-time faculty spend in governance and perceived level of personal influence at various organizational levels, by country/region, 2007–2008

		Other English-speaking countries				Continental Europe[a]		East Asia	
	United States (*N*= 1,106)	Canada (*N*=984)	Australia (*N*= 1,021)	United Kingdom (*N*=839)	All other English-speaking countries (*N*=2844)	Germany (*N*= 1,073)	All continental Europe (*N*=6,641)	Japan (*N*= 1,088)	All East Asia (*N*=2,553)
Involvement (mean hours weekly)	3.0	3.4	4.4	4.5	4.1	1.4	2.0	2.0	2.6
Perceived personal influence									
at the department level									
Very influential	33.5	20.3	13.4	12.6	15.6	21.3	14.1	7.4	11.8
Influential	33.1	41.8	32.1	28.7	34.5	40.5	36.7	42.2	39.8
at the faculty and school level									
Very influential	10.3	6.3	3.5	5.0	4.9	5.8	3.9	4.2	3.7
Influential	32.5	22.2	15.5	15.9	18.0	20.0	19.4	25.1	23.8
at the institutional level									
Very nfluential	3.3	2.6	0.9	1.0	1.5	2.1	2.0	2.6	3.3
Influential	15.8	9.9	6.7	8.0	8.2	9.3	8.7	11.4	12.4

Source: CAP:07. (Refer to appendix A for key.)
[a]Excludes the United Kingdom.

Table 11.17 Percentage of full-time faculty agreeing that administrators are "competent" and "support academic freedom" and that faculty are institutionally "informed" and "engaged," by country/region, 2007–2008

		Other English-speaking countries				Continental Europe[a]		East Asia	
	United States (*N*=1,104)	Canada (*N*=978)	Australia (*N*=1,005)	United Kingdom (*N*=825)	All other English-speaking countries (*N*=2,808)	Germany (*N*=1,056)	All continental Europe (*N*=6,643)	Japan (*N*=1,092)	All East Asia (*N*=2,564)
Top level administrators are providing competent leadership									
Strongly agree	3.9	7.0	6.5	5.1	6.2	15.0	8.3	12.3	8.4
Agree	31.5	37.8	34.3	30.2	34.3	42.3	33.6	33.1	31.9
I am kept informed about what is going on at this institution									
Strongly agree	7.4	9.0	7.5	10.6	8.9	3.9	6.8	8.7	6.6
Agree	38.8	42.8	40.6	40.9	41.4	27.9	36.8	26.6	34.0
Lack of faculty involvement is really a problem here									
Strongly agree	15.9	14.5	10.7	15.1	13.3	13.4	11.8	23.5	17.5
Agree	22.1	27.4	26.0	34.1	28.9	31.1	29.8	32.7	29.2
The administration supports academic freedom									
Strongly agree	7.0	19.3	3.1	6.1	9.6	15.3	11.3	7.7	9.3
Agree	34.1	48.3	20.8	33.1	34.0	42.8	37.5	30.0	37.0

Source: CAP:07. (Refer to appendix A for key.)

[a]Excludes the United Kingdom.

Table 11.18 Percentage of full-time faculty rating their commitment to their department, institution, and discipline as "strong," selected countries, 1992, 2007

	United States			Australia			United Kingdom		
	1992	2007	Change 1992–2007	1992	2007	Change 1992–2007	1992	2007	Change 1992–2007
Discipline	96	92	−4	94	89	−5	93	81	−12
Department	89	78	−11	74	67	−7	66	56	−10
Institution	90	61	−29	87	51	−36	84	38	−46

Source: CAP:07. (Refer to appendix A for key.)

Trends in the Locus of Faculty Loyalties

While most of the published research has focused on differences in faculty commitment and loyalty *within* nations, there may also be interesting differences *among* nations. In national settings where there is a strong research tradition and professors are very influential in steering their institutions, it might be presumed that academics lean towards the cosmopolitan pole.[22] In contrast, in a society like Japan where workplace identity is highly valued, it might be presumed that academics lean to the local pole (Cummings and Amano 1977).

Table 11.18 compares the percentage of academics who express a strong sense of commitment respectively to their disciplines, their academic departments, and their institutions in both 1992 and 2007–08. In both years, over nine of every ten US academics indicated a strong or moderate sense of commitment to their discipline, as do academics in the other countries studied with the exception of the United Kingdom. Similarly in 1992, nearly nine in ten American academics indicated a strong or moderate sense of loyalty to their academic department, the institutional home of their academic discipline, and, more broadly, to their employing institution. However, by 2007, only eight out of ten US academics indicated a strong or moderate sense of department loyalty, while only six out of ten expressed strong or moderate institutional loyalty—a drop of nearly 30%. The 2007 proportions in the United States, the United Kingdom, and Australia are among the lowest for the nineteen countries in the 2007–08 CAP study, and the decreases relative to 1992 are among the steepest. While disciplinary loyalties persist among faculty in the United States and abroad, the faculty–institution compact that has cemented academic life, especially in the United States, as well as the United Kingdom and Australia, is clearly in transition.

Germany			Japan			South Korea			Hong Kong		
1992	2007	Change 1992–2007	1992	2007	Change 1992–2007	1992	2007	Change 1992–2007	1992	2007	Change 1992–2007
91	90	−1	96	93	−3	99	89	−10	93	90	−3
52	51	−1	85	69	−16	88	89	1	87	72	−15
34	51	17	80	63	−17	97	74	−23	78	60	−18

How US Salaries Compare

Across the globe, academic salaries are a "complex construction of basic salary and supplements, bonuses, allowances and subsidies" (Altbach et al. 2012, 8), making it extremely difficult to compare internationally. In some countries, such as the United States, the base institutional salary remains the primary component by far of total professional compensation for most faculty in most fields. Elsewhere, institutional base salary is a pittance and is supplemented, as in Mexico, by full-time professional employment or stipends from the National Researcher System or, as in China, by a variety of subsidies for housing, health care, dependent's education, performance bonuses, and so on. There are thus formidable limitations built into any comparison of base institutional salaries. Moreover, beyond the differing composition of overall academic compensation, nations differ enormously in the "purchasing power" of that compensation in local currency. Altbach et al. (2012) sought to employ the purchasing parity index (PPI) to adjust the purchasing power of local currencies to that of the United States as a reference country—thus allowing a uniform tool for comparison.

Figure 11.1, drawn directly from Altbach et al. (2012), shows the entry-level, senior-level, and overall average monthly salaries for faculty in the public sector in twenty-eight countries using the purchasing power parity index in 2009 US dollars. A glance at the figure suggests, first, that US salaries in the public sector are at the upper end of the monthly salary continuum, albeit by no means the highest. The figure shows, furthermore, that it is at the entry level, where salary levels in the US public sector stand out, second only to Canada. Indeed, at the senior level, US public sector salaries appear much more modest. As figure 11.2 shows, in the United States the ratio of senior- to entry-level

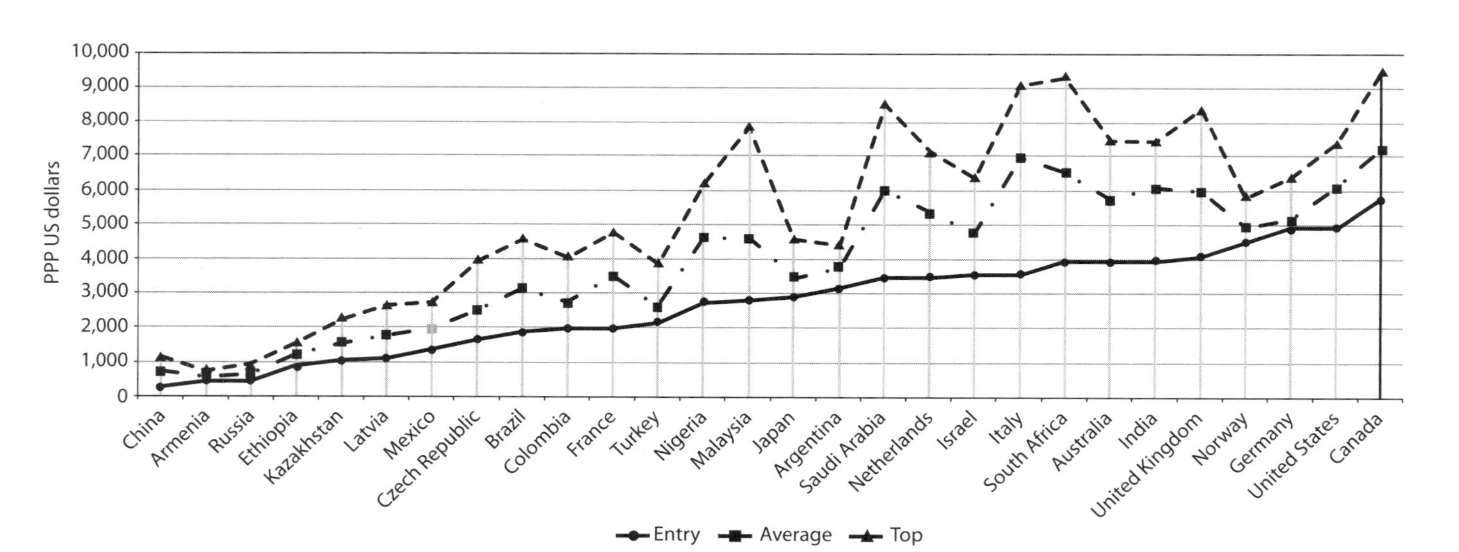

Figure 11.1 Entry-level, mid-level, and senior-level rank salary ranges for full-time faculty, by country, 2010. *Source:* Philip Altbach, Liz Reisberg, and Ivan Pachceco, "Academic Remuneration and Contracts." In *Paying the Professoriate: A Global Comparison of Compensation and Contracts*, ed. Philip Altbach et al., p.10. New York: Routledge, 2012. Copyright © 2012 by Taylor and Francis. Used with permission.

Note: PPP=purchasing power parity.

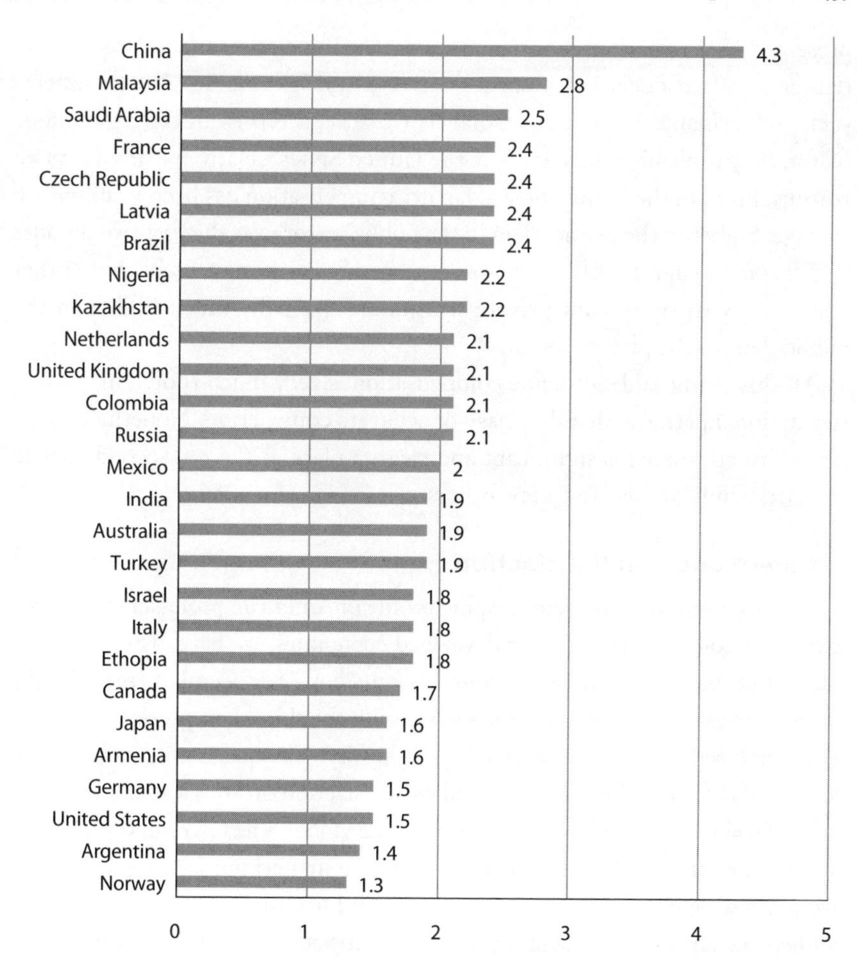

Figure 11.2 Ratio of senior-level to entry-level salaries of full-time faculty, by country, 2010. *Source:* Gregory Androushchak and Maria Yudkevich, "Quantitative Analysis." In *Paying the Professoriate: A Global Comparison of Compensation and Contracts*, ed. Philip Altbach et al., p. 29. New York: Routledge, 2012. Copyright © 2012 by Taylor and Francis. Used with permission.

---

salaries is 1.5:1 compared with 4.3:1 in China, 2.8:1 in Malaysia, and 2.1:1 in the United Kingdom. One interpretation of these variations in entry-level to top-level ratios is that American academics are, relatively speaking, well compensated throughout the traditional faculty ranks and levels of seniority.[23]

In interpreting these differences, it is important to note first that given the extraordinary institutional differentiation in the United States, the averages presented here, whether at entry or senior level, include a much larger range (larger standard deviation) than less diverse and less market driven systems such as Germany. Moreover, insofar as these data represent only the public sector, they probably underestimate the United States' relative position for two reasons. First, in the United States, faculty compensation has been trending, on average, higher in the private than in the public sector over the past two decades (see chapter 9 supra). At the same time, academic compensation in those other countries with significant private sectors are typically much higher in the public than in the private sector.

All this being said, academic compensation is very much rooted in distinctive national patterns that defy easy or accurate comparison. Nonetheless, the American advantage is significant and clear: a place at the top second only to Canada, Saudi Arabia, and a few others.

Career and Job Satisfaction

As we have examined the demographic profile of American professors compared with their counterparts in other developed economies, we have also considered their place in their own institutions—the anchor of academic careers in the United States—including their roles in steering the ship, their perceptions of institutional leadership, and their feelings of loyalty. The question remains: What does all of this mean for the career and job satisfaction of American academics in comparison with their counterparts around the globe? The CAP survey included two items related to these summative issues: the first asking for agreement on a five-point scale in response to the statement, "If I had to do it over again, I would not become an academic" (a proxy for career satisfaction); and the second asking for a rating of the degree of satisfaction with their current job at their home institution. The results, displayed in table 11.19, are instructive.

It is remarkable that majorities of faculty in all surveyed countries indicated that they would choose an academic career again: more than 60% in nine of the thirteen countries. The US faculty (at 75.1%) was one of four nations (including Canada) where at least three-quarters of academics disagreed or strongly disagreed with the first statement. These responses suggest in comparative terms a very high level of career satisfaction among American faculty.

The consistently high levels of career satisfaction indicated by these faculty responses to the first question are, on the whole, reinforced by responses to the second item, asking about overall job satisfaction, albeit, generally, at somewhat lower rates (table 11.20). Among American faculty, the 75.1% who would opt again

Table 11.19 Percentage of full-time faculty reporting that they would not become an academic again, by country/region, 2007–2008

		Other English-speaking countries				Continental Europe[a]		East Asia	
Would not become an academic again	United States (*N*= 1,109)	Canada (*N*= 1,082)	Australia (*N*= 1,109)	United Kingdom (*N*= 935)	All other English-speaking countries (*N*= 3,126)	Germany (*N*= 1,136)	All continental Europe (*N*= 7,250)	Japan (*N*= 1,098)	All East Asia (*N*= 2,580)
Strongly agree/ agree	10.4	11.2	21.4	25.3	19.1	17.9	16.0	12.4	11.4
Strongly isagree/ disagree	75.1	75.9	58.2	54.6	63.3	67.6	67.2	54.7	65.6

Source: CAP:07. (Refer to appendix A for key.)
[a]Excludes the United Kingdom.

Table 11.20 Percentage of full-time faculty reporting that they are "satisfied" or "very satisfied" and "unsatisfied" or "very unsatisfied" with their current job, by country/region, 2007–2008

		Other English-speaking countries				Continental Europe[a]		East Asia	
Overall satisfaction with your current job	United States (*N*=1,109)	Canada (*N*=1,082)	Australia (*N*=1,109)	United Kingdom (*N*=935)	All other English-speaking countries (*N*=3,126)	Germany (*N*=1,136)	All continental Europe (*N*=7,250)	Japan (*N*=1,098)	All East Asia (*N*=2,580)
Very satisfied/ satisfied	64.2	74.8	54.8	45.7	59.0	56.3	62.7	68.3	69.7
Very unsatisfied/ unsatisfied	10.3	8.7	19.9	17.9	15.4	15.7	12.0	13.3	9.5

Source: CAP:07. (Refer to appendix A for key.)
[a]Excludes the United Kingdom.

for an academic career drops to 64.2% who report being satisfied or very satisfied with their current jobs. This pattern of a modest decline in satisfaction is apparent in most of the countries when the focus narrows to the current job. The unavoidable conclusion is clear: most faculty (that is, full-time faculty) in all thirteen countries with developed economies report strong to very strong levels of satisfaction with their careers and, to a slightly lower extent, with their current jobs.[24]

Conclusion

It may well be that these dualities reflect directly the distinctive organizational situation of the American faculty: as employees of relatively autonomous corporate entities, both public and private, they are subject to corporate authority, especially in matters of financial resources and subordination to senior executives; at the same time, they exercise considerable influence in the very limited domains of their expertise, namely, academic affairs.[25] The peculiar significance of their institution as an anchor to their careers may lead them, alternatively, to overestimate their general influence or induce frustration at the limitations to their actual influence. At all events, what influence American faculty exercise tends to be largely concentrated in their individual academic departments and, to a lesser extent, limited to the larger discipline-related academic units with which they are affiliated.

Beyond the ambiguity in the American faculty role, what these data clearly establish is the pervasive role of middle managers, that is, department chairs and deans, even in matters of academic personnel. The significance of middle management is reflected in the decanal or chair role in setting budgets, new program development, and administrator selection. Moreover, the decisive and rather distinctive role of middle management in the American academy extends to the critical area of the evaluation of faculty work. While peer review continues to function in some form in teaching, research, and service, especially in personnel processes, the role of middle management—and even central institutional administration—seems to be relatively more pervasive in the United States than in other national systems.

This somewhat ambiguous, highly circumscribed and slightly fragile institutional role of American faculty appears to be reflected in faculty loyalties and in their career and job satisfaction. Compared with the faculties of other developed nations, American faculty demonstrate a declining loyalty to their employing institutions over the past fifteen years (1992–2007)—an issue that is particularly problematic for those whose career infrastructure is so distinctively and closely tied to their employing institutions. While they maintain their very high career satisfaction vis-à-vis their global counterparts—largely, we would argue, as a function of the historically high degree of predictability of academic careers in the United States—faculty satisfaction with their current job varies and places them in about the middle of the global distribution.

In sum, while Americans have always assumed that the academics staffing our higher education system are the most productive, best compensated, and most powerful in the world, the CAP data strongly suggest otherwise, at least in the matter of organizational power and influence. Japanese, German, and Canadian faculty appear to play a more prominent role in steering their institutions than American faculty do; and academic managerialism may be more decentralized, but no less prominent and decisive, here in the United States. While American academics seem to appreciate the relatively well developed infrastructure for academic careers in the United States, they are no more likely than professors elsewhere to be content with their jobs and their place in their universities.

NOTES

1. Earlier versions of this chapter appeared in *The NEA 2012 Almanac of Higher Education* (Finkelstein 2012) and *Change: The Magazine of Higher Learning* (Finkelstein and Cummings 2012).

2. The Higher School of Economics is Russia's newest research university focusing on the social sciences. It has been collaborating on several studies with Boston College's Center for International Higher Education.

3. The MORE II survey was sponsored by the European Commission and sought to gather data on scientific careers in and outside the academy in the countries of the European Union as well as some of its competitors, including the United States, Canada, and China. It represented a five-year follow-up to the original Mobility of Researchers in Europe study of 2008.

4. This is true even for public institutions in the United States, which are chartered as public corporations with their own boards of governors. The independence and self-governing aspects of public institutions of higher education must be understood within the political dynamics of each state's government—or, in the instance of many two-year community colleges, within the relevant political subdivision.

5. While there is a discernable trend in Europe and Asia toward increasing institutional autonomy, that trend is associated with declines in public financing and increasing diversification of funding sources.

6. *Faculty* is used here in the European sense of an academic unit within the university analogous to "school" or "college" within the American university context.

7. Subject usually, of course, to the prescriptions laid down by their peers in disciplinary or professional associations.

8. Thus faculty mobility is fairly common in the US system, especially in the research university sector—in stark contrast to traditions of inbreeding and stability in most national systems across the globe (Altbach et al. 2012).

9. In contrast to the United States, the private sector functions in most national systems to "absorb excess demand" that cannot be accommodated in the public sector. As such, it is typically for-profit rather than the US typically not-for-profit, although the rise of a for-profit sector in the United States in recent decades is notable (Hentschke et al. 2010).

10. Most recently, however, large systems such as China and Brazil are beginning to match the diversification in the US system, as institutional diversification and stratification becomes a basic concomitant of massification.

11. In several Asian nations, most notably Japan but also China, academic staff may have become tethered to their institutions as graduate students and remained as faculty members. Such inbreeding certainly links faculty to their institutions but in a more personal way rather than in an organizational, career-structural, fashion.

12. Canada is, of course, a primarily English system, outside Quebec province.

13. Strictly speaking, of course, the United Kingdom abolished tenure, or a system of permanent appointment, in the late 1980s.

14. Although preliminary data suggests that implementation has been less robust than expected (Kehm 2014).

15. The CAP survey distinguished between administration, explicitly referring to the campus committee work involved in department and institutional governance as well as academic program administration, and service, in terms of off-campus professional and community activities.

16. This, of course, leaves aside the quality or caliber of journals in which American faculty publish.

17. While the pervasiveness of participation is clear, the actual weight of the student voice is not and no doubt varies substantially across national settings.

18. These "external" stakeholders in the United States are not explicitly identified. It would appear that these would include not-for-profit philanthropic foundations, government agencies, and others that may indeed employ peer review as part of the evaluation process.

19. Although American academics are equally likely to rate themselves as "very influential" (33.5%) and as "influential" (33.1%), German and Canadian faculty are much less likely to rate themselves as "very" influential (about 20%).

20. We use the term *faculty* here to designate an intermediate organizational level between the academic department or program, at the local level, and the central administrative level—roughly equivalent to school or college.

21. Australia is the other.

22. This cosmopolitan-local distinction draws directly on the work of the sociologist Alvin Gouldner (1957), who sought to understand how academic professionals with strong ties to the discipline in which they were trained, but also potentially strong ties to the institution that serves as their employer, negotiate these twin pulls on the loyalty of American academics.

23. It should be emphasized that these data apply only to the public sector in the United States. In the US private sector, academic salaries tend to be higher overall (see chapter 7), especially at the full professor level—most likely yielding higher senior-to-junior salary ratios where the private sector is included in the US data.

24. Caveat: these 2007 data preceded the global economic tightening that affected higher academic work and careers in many, if not most, instances.

25. It should be noted that influence over the establishment of new academic programs, which nearly always involves a major commitment of institutional resources, must be distinguished from general, ongoing superintendence of the curriculum.

REFERENCES

Altbach, Philip G., Liz Reisberg, Maria Yudkevich, Gregory Androushcak, and Ivan F. Pacheco. 2012. *Paying the Professoriate.* New York: Routledge.

Ben-David, Joseph. 1977. *Centers of Learning: Britain,, France, Germany, United States.* New York: McGraw-Hill.

Caplow, Theodore, and Reece J. McGee. 1958. *The Academic Marketplace.* New York: Basic Books.

Clark, Burton R. 1983. The Higher Education System: Academic Organization in Cross-National Perspective. Berkeley, CA: University of California Press.

Clark, Burton R. 1987. *The Academic Life: Small Worlds, Different Worlds.* Princeton, NJ: Carnegie Foundation for the Advancement of Teaching.

Cowley, W.H. 1980. *Presidents, Professors and Trustees.* Edited by Donald T. Williams. San Francisco: Jossey-Bass.

Cummings, William K., and I. Amano. 1977. "The Changing Role of the Japanese Professor." *Higher Education*, 6 (May): 209–34

Duryea, Edwin. 1973. "Evolution of University Organization." In *The University As an Organization*, edited by James A. Perkins, 15–37. New York: McGraw-Hill.

European Commission. 2013. *Study on Mobility Patterns and Career Paths of EU Researchers.* Brussels: European Commission, Research Directorate.

Finkelstein, Martin J. 2012. "American Faculty and Their Institutions: A Multi-National Comparison." In *The NEA 2012 Almanac of Higher Education*, edited by the National Education Association, 63–78. Washington, DC: NEA Higher Education Research Center.

Finkelstein, Martin J., and William K. Cummings. 2012. "American Faculty and Their Institutions: The Global View." *Change: The Magazine of Higher Learning* 44 (May–June): 48–59.

Finkelstein, Martin J., Ming Ju, and William K. Cummings. 2010. "The United States of America: Perspectives on Faculty Governance, 1992–2007." In *Changing Governance and Management in Higher Education*, edited by William Locke, William Cummings, and Donald Fisher, 199–222. Dordrecht, NL: Springer.

Gouldner, Alvin W. 1957. "Cosmopolitan and Local: Towards an Analysis of Latent Social Roles I." *Administrative Science Quarterly* 2 (December): 281–306.

Hentschke, Guilbert, Vicente Lechuga, William Tierney, and Marc Tucker. 2010. *For-Profit Colleges and Universities: Their Markets, Regulation, Performance, and Place in Higher Education.* Sterling, VA: Stylus Publishing.

Johnstone, D. Bruce. 2003. "The International Comparative Study of Higher Education: Lessons from the Contemplation of How Others Might See Us." *Forum for the Future of Higher Education.* Washington, DC: EDUCAUSE.

Kehm, Barbara. 2014. "Entering Academia: Realities for New Faculty in German Higher Education." In *The Future of the Academic Profession: Young Faculty in International Perspective*, edited by Philip G. Altbach, Maria Yudkevich, and Laura Rumbley, 111–39. Albany, NY: SUNY Press.

Musselin, Christine. 2010. *The Market for Academics.* New York: Routledge.

Schuster, Jack H., and Martin J. Finkelstein. 2006. *The American Faculty: The Restructuring of Academic Work and Careers.* Baltimore, MD: Johns Hopkins University Press.

PART V / Prospects for the Academic Profession

The previous four parts encompassing their eleven chapters have sought to provide a framework for understanding the contemporary academic life in these challenging times. Especially in chapters 3 through 11 we have tried to infuse our overview and argument with current relevant data. That is, we have attempted to establish probative evidence—beyond the commonplace rhetoric—upon which we have based our thesis that the "faculty factor" remains, prescriptively, pivotal in importance while becoming, descriptively, less potent in exerting influence on the academic core functions of higher education.

Now in part 5 we turn, first, in chapter 12, to outline what we see to be the principal lessons learned and conclusions reached about higher education and its faculty that characterize this third paradigm. Beyond fleshing out the distinctive characteristics of this new model, we establish the wide-reaching implications for American higher education, for academic work and careers, and for the national interest—especially in terms of the stakes for global leadership in higher learning.

Finally, we turn in chapter 13 to suggesting policy interventions at institutional, system, and national and federal levels that we believe will make a positive difference in how we "do" higher education in the United States. While there have been innumerable published litanies during the past decade or several of higher education's woes and inadequacies (as alluded to in chapter 1), we seek in this final chapter to close on a more upbeat note by suggesting several strategies that can at least partially remedy the deficiencies.

12

American Academic Life Restructured

The starting point for this summary of the condition and outlook for the academic profession—and why it matters—is the authors' recognition that the depth and breadth of recent changes for faculty members has been pervasive, is continuing to occur at a velocity arguably unprecedented, and will have far-reaching effects. American higher education has entered a new era, paradigm 3 in our terminology, replete with intriguing possibilities as well as threats to basic values. The evidence of this extensive transformation is grounded in the data we have garnered from many sources.[1] It is not hyperbolic, we submit, to suggest that the essence of postsecondary education and, more specifically, of the faculty charged with implementing its missions is undergoing an immense metamorphosis.

We have identified in prior chapters numerous vectors of change that have contributed, over relatively few years, to the massive reconfiguration of who the faculty are, the nature of their work effort, and the trajectory of their careers. These chapters have identified and elaborated on the characteristics of the emerging "new" faculty.

Among the most important recent changes to the faculty and their work and careers are

- a redistributed affiliation by type of institution
- a redistributed affiliation by academic field and curriculum emphasis
- the expanded extent of specialization in faculty work roles
- a more diverse faculty
- more-diverse pathways into the faculty
- increasingly nonlinear progression, once "on board," during faculty members' academic careers

- a more complex pattern of exiting from the faculty
- a more constrained extent of faculty participation in academic decision making, often a function of increased managerialism by (largely) nonacademic authorities based on extra-academic considerations

Each of these aspects has been addressed heretofore, and each—among still other characteristics not listed above—impacts the academic profession in truly significant ways.

Consider, for example, the dynamic and often contentious issue of interpreting changes in faculty demographics. During recent decades, the record establishes that the faculty have become more diverse in crucial respects, including gender and race/ethnicity (as documented especially in chapter 3). We conclude that demonstrable progress has occurred, constituting a somewhat closer resemblance to the demographics of the larger American society. Once more, that process has been uneven across institutional categories, academic fields, and appointment types. We maintain that much remains to be done.

But none of these elements is as portentous as the continuing redistribution of types of academic appointments. Put another way, the faculty, in the opening decades of the twenty-first century, has been sweepingly redefined, principally by the revolutionary expansion in the number and proportion of non-"regular" faculty members. Here we speak to two major clusters of faculty: the full-time but off-tenure-track academics and the part-time faculty members, commonly described as "adjuncts," employed (usually exclusively for teaching) on a course-by-course basis. While many current faculty members perform traditional roles, the clear majority (by headcount) do not. The roles for this growing majority are more specialized, beyond just academic subfield expertise, than was once the case. The consequences for the profession and for post-secondary education more generally are pervasive—a rich tangle of positives and negatives.

We turn now to addressing the overarching areas of inquiry—the research questions—that we raised in chapter 1.

The Condition of the American Faculty

What is the current condition of the American faculty, including faculty demographics, their work patterns, and the nature of their academic careers, and to what extent have those dimensions of academic life changed in recent years?

There can be little question that the well-being and status of today's college and university faculty members (factoring in the swarms of less-than-full-time faculty) have grown weaker in recent years as measured by crucial criteria. The usual caveat obtains: generalizations must be subjected to the reality, as posited in chapter 1, that higher education, upon even superficial examination, devolves into numerous components, broken out most palpably by institution types and, too, by academic field and, further (it is increasingly clear), by the differentiation of academic appointment types. Notwithstanding that very large qualifier, some general observations are evident, even indisputable. Several of the most important developments follow.

Extent and Type of Academic Engagement: The Radical Redistribution of Academic Appointments

The first indicator of marked change is the continuing diminution of "regular" traditional faculty positions (that is, the terms of their academic appointments) in contrast to "nonregular" appointments. Thus the long-identified process by which regular, on-tenure-track appointments are being traded off for the increased flexibility and presumed significant cost savings associated with various types of so-called contingent (term-limited) appointments continues to accelerate (as described in the most recent available data, reported particularly in chapters 3 and 4). Here, without doubt, the academic labor market exerts a potent influence. The wide array of off-track appointments, ranging from full-time faculty holding nontenurable appointments to part-time positions (often, as noted, referred to as adjuncts), reflects both a heavily employer favorable marketplace (wherein the supply of would-be faculty far exceeds the demand for them, making allowances for significant variations by field). This circumstance gives rise to a growing number of academic job seekers who are obliged to settle for part-time teaching as an initial means of latching on until a full-time appointment materializes.

There are many other part-timers whose circumstances and motivations place them in a different situation. Thus a considerable subset of faculty members are not seeking full-time teaching positions. Some of them already hold such an appointment elsewhere and may be seeking to supplement current academic (or other) employment. Others, prototypically fully employed professionals, may pursue academic work on a part-time basis for more personal (not to exclude economic) satisfactions. (These varied pathways are described in chapter 4.)

This redistribution, the consequence of multiple factors, has profound effects, as mentioned, on who the faculty are, what constitutes their on-the-job priorities, and the very nature of their careers. So pervasive is this reconfiguration as to lead us to reexamine a long-standing, foundational premise about the professoriate. We start with the insight encapsulated decades ago by Burton R. Clark, namely, the inadequacy—really, the basic error—of attempts to generalize about higher education as a whole. As is obvious, the reality is much more akin to the "small worlds, different worlds" metaphor that Clark (1987) employed to describe academe and its faculty practitioners. By this phrase he disavowed the existence of "the academy" as a singular entity. Such a hypothetical entity had little practical meaning, for academic life "on the ground" was powerfully differentiated by institutional type (meaning institutional mission beyond basic public or independent status) and by academic field. Thus to oversimplify, the professional life (job priorities and rewards) of, say, a philosopher at a nonresidential community college is vastly different from that of, say, a plant geneticist at a research university. Thus in other words, the work-related activity inside each of those two cells, created by institutional type and field, when juxtaposed, is patently different (however difficult it is to measure in a nuanced fashion).

It is striking just how rapidly the preponderance of a regular full-time faculty has given way to droves of part-time instructors and researchers. This continuing revolution encapsulates the concomitant expansion in the number and size of postsecondary institutions, many of them relatively new entities that operate entirely, or nearly so, online—and which, so far as we can ascertain, characteristically employ very few, if any, full-time faculty members.[2] This process adds thousands of persons to the ranks of the part-time faculty, but this observation tends to obscure the fact that numerous traditional four-year colleges and universities have undergone remarkable—to many, unsettling—realignments in their academic workforces (as established in chapter 3). To gauge the consequences of this extensive faculty makeover, which is still gaining momentum, presents a very large challenge.

Reconceptualizing the Worlds of Academic Life

Clark's trenchant phrase, "small worlds, different worlds," as noted, underscored the hazard of attempts to generalize about how higher education functions. His message was that higher education could best be understood by realizing that two uber-phenomena pervasively shape and differentiate academic life, namely, institutional type and academic field. Thus he observed, academic activity is manifested in innumerable "cells" which, considered together, form a two-by-two matrix created by the intersection of institutional type and academic field of knowledge. That is to say, to provide another illustration, what comprises the professorial work of an academic practicing, for example, biochemistry (or some sub-sub-specialty thereof) at a research university in reality is very different—even dramatically different—from academic life as practiced in another matrix cell that represents the intersection of, for instance, political science (or philosophy or nursing) within a community college setting. These sharply contrasting realities help to illustrate that this recognition of the near-infinite varieties of how academic work is carried out is fundamental to understanding who the faculty are and what they do (both descriptively and prescriptively). This realization is a crucial—perhaps the most important—lens through which to view the rich complexities of academic life.

However, our exploration of how contemporary faculty perform their work and how careers have morphed in recent years has led us to conclude that Clark's two principal portals through which to portray academic life is today less compelling, less dispositive, than was the case when he wrote *The Academic Life* three decades ago (1987).

Why is this so? It is because, in our estimation, a third dimension of academic life has risen to prominence so swiftly and has exerted so much influence on academic activity "on the ground" as to justify that it, too, must be considered as an additional *unavoidable* portal through which to observe the postsecondary enterprise, namely, the type of academic appointment.

The redistribution of academic appointments, touched on earlier in this chapter and explored in more detail in prior chapters, is by no means a new phenomenon. The growing presence of part-time and of full-time non-tenure-track academic positions has been observed, and their complex implications have been discussed, for some decades. Indeed, the redistribution of academic appointments and its widespread significance is a central theme of *The American Faculty* (2006).[3] That volume underscored the leap in full-time, off-track appointments in the late 1980s and the ensuing second order rise in part-time appointments in the 1990s. In the years since, the presence of nontenurable and non-tenure-track appointments has become more prominent as more and more postsecondary institutions increasingly resort to such appointments, as we have attempted to describe especially in chapters 3 and 7 of the current volume. This development has reshaped the basic ecology of higher education

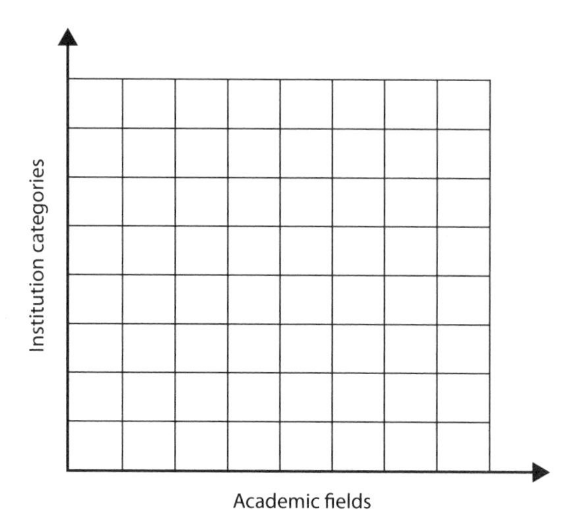

Figure 12.1 Academic "worlds," traditional representation depicted via two-dimension matrix: Academic field and institution type. *Source:* Produced by authors.

in terms of how institutions seek to accomplish their respective missions and, in narrowing the focal point to the faculty itself, depicting the very nature of faculty members' work and the trajectory of their careers. In visual terms, as a way of suggesting how profoundly the world of academic work has been affected, we propose that the more parsimonious two-dimensional matrix envisioned by Clark (see figure 12.1) be superseded by a three-dimensional cube-like representation (see figure 12.2). Simplistic as this visual exercise certainly is, the intended effect is to demonstrate the much more complicated realities of contemporary academic life.

Accelerated Specialization among Faculty

The faculty role has become more specialized in two quite different but highly consequential ways in this paradigm 3 era. The first derives from subject matter and the proliferation of areas of highly specialized knowledge. The second form of specialization revolves around a given faculty member's on-the-job responsibilities.

Content Specialization

Knowledge ever broadens and deepens. (One can question whether the same can be said of wisdom, but that more philosophical issue is better left to others to

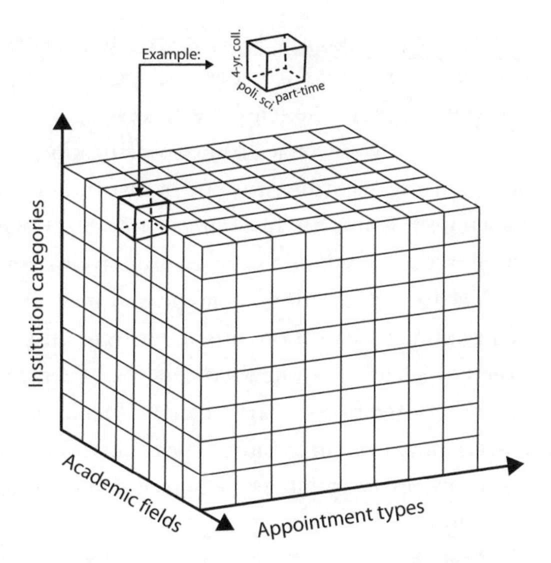

Figure 12.2 Academic "worlds," contemporary representation via three-dimension cube: Academic field, institution type, and appointment category. *Source:* Produced by authors.

---

debate.) In all areas constituting postsecondary curricula, whole new fields arise (commonly cutting across historic disciplinary boundaries). And in all fields, emerging and long-standing alike, differentiated subfields and sub-subfields are spawned. A scattering of examples were suggested in chapter 2 as manifested in the proliferation of subfield-specialized professional associations and corresponding more narrowly focused academic periodicals. Thus for both teaching and research purposes, faculty members shoulder the parallel but intersecting and reinforcing tasks of advancing knowledge in ever more specialized subfields.

Role Specialization

The phenomenon of faculty specialization is reflected, too, in the increasing proportion of faculty members whose institutional roles are more narrowly channeled. This trend—commonly referred to as "unbundling"—has yielded a crisper division of labor, particularly in the larger proportions of faculty members employed exclusively to teach. And so it is that many contingent faculty members are teachers—first, foremost, and very often exclusively. Situated in juxtaposition, more and more faculty members are focused primarily on research and scholarly production. Often this academic activity is entirely free from formalized teaching, leaving aside the kind of teaching that occurs in mentoring others—commonly via research associate or postdoc responsibilities—that are prominent and crucial in the scholarly process.

To be sure, both general forms of academic specialization—subject matter and work role—vary greatly according to type of institution. Accordingly, in those institutions whose mission has little or nothing to do with generating original scholarship and are predominantly or exclusively "teaching institutions," role migration (the unbundling phenomenon) may be negligible; the contemporary faculty at such institutions are, in terms of mission and on-the-job priorities, largely unchanged from what they had been in earlier times (notwithstanding the proliferation of part-timers).[4] The impact of intensified specialization is much more evident at those types of institutions that have the advancement of scholarship as an integral—indeed, paramount—component of institutional mission.

The reasons fueling this move toward accentuated specialization in roles are multiple. The prevalence of market conditions lies at the base. As colleges and universities are drawn, irresistibly it appears, to hiring off-track contingent faculty, we sense that the core faculty themselves are in part complicit in this trend. That is to say, it seems quite common that numbers of tenured full-time faculty members at research-oriented institutions are amenable to the prospect of passing on their responsibilities for teaching undergraduates, particularly those "lower division" undergraduates (meaning those in their first or second years), if part-time or off-track full-time teaching specialists can be deployed in their stead.

In sum, the two distinct forms of specialization have had powerful effects on the components of faculty work. Concurrently, the province of specialization is inextricably interwoven with the deepening of expertise, both in terms of subject content and role responsibilities. A corollary of these prominent trends is that the all-purpose academic generalist is a vanishing species, increasingly an anachronism. The net effect of this seismic shift is still being explored.

New Pathways: Entering, Progressing Through, and Exiting Academic Careers

Part 2 (chapters 4–6) explored faculty career paths, in three more-or-less distinct phases: pathways into, progression during, and exit from academic careers. Chapter 4 documented the much more varied routes, compared with earlier decades, for entrance into academic work and careers, particularly as increasing proportions of women, of non-PhD holders, and larger numbers of professionals initially employed outside academe following receipt of their highest degree now transition into academic careers. Entry often entails a series of transitions from one status to another before achieving traction.

Chapter 5 emphasized the kinds of faculty mobility that occur during the unfolding of academic careers, underscoring the more fluid nature of those careers once embarked upon. This relative fluidity stands in contrast to the greater stability and attachment, meaning more mutual loyalty between institutions of higher education and their faculty members, that more often characterized faculty-institution relationships in years past. Thus career progression, formerly much more linear—that is, unidirectional on a single "ladder"—has given way in many instances to academic careers that are more discursive, reflecting the wider array of appointment types and work roles. While there is still some modicum of "regularity" on the tenure track, the timing of career milestones (for instance, attaining full professorship) has been extended, especially for those who change jobs.

Then chapter 6 described the strikingly varied avenues for exiting academic careers, multiple patterns today that diverge from the more predominant, limited "flip-a-switch," "in-or-out" modes in past years. The pathways for exiting an academic career, much more often than in yesteryear, involve a sequence of role transitions, a much more varied range of ways to separate. One key net effect of multiplying these options for "regular" faculty to depart is to lengthen the pathway out, thereby contributing, as one consequence, to the clogged entry pipeline phenomenon.

In all, the relative stability and predictability of ingress and egress—and what happens in between—have been giving way to a grander variety of patterns characterizing the evolution of careers for increasingly numerous members of faculty. Fluidity now prevails; lockstep has been supplanted.

Compensation

And what about faculty members' compensation? We have substantiated that "real" faculty salaries for full-time faculty have not changed very much, when adjusted for inflation, over recent decades. As the data in chapter 9 show, the word "flat" could be used to describe the movement of full-time faculty salaries. But such an overall characterization, however applicable in the main, fails to provide a nuanced account of at least five important issues.

First, it essentially ignores the situation that obtains for the significant—and increasing—*majority* of all faculty members, namely, part-time faculty. Reliable numbers describing compensation for part-time (adjunct) faculty are very hard to come by. What is available has been reported in chapter 9. One inescapable conclusion is that payment to part-timers (predominantly, payment per course taught), while varying (of course) by institution, is modest. For those faculty members dependent on income as part-time instructors, it is challenging to earn enough, even if teaching three or four courses per academic term, to constitute a respectable income, a living wage. More starkly, there appear to be many instances in which scrambling part-timers are unable to exceed submarginal—even poverty—income levels, as described in chapter 9.

A second shortcoming of the broad characterization of faculty income is that this overall picture fails to capture the accelerating dispersion by academic field. Thus considerable and expanding disparities reflect responsiveness to omnipresent market forces that propel compensation upward in some fields (most notably, some professions and the fields of science, technology, engineering, and mathematics) while bypassing any hint of progress in other fields (the humanities and social sciences, except for economics). So upon closer scrutiny, "flat" or "stuck," as a generalization, ignores substantial intrafaculty variation and movement in terms of compensation.

Third, these data gloss over how academic salaries compare with those of other professionals whose education preparation for their respective occupations is roughly comparable to that of faculty members in terms of postbaccalaureate study. Here, as observed in chapter 9, if only in passing, compensation data from the US Bureau of Labor Statistics suggest that income trends in some other professions, namely law and medicine, have been uneven at best, with increasing numbers of doctors and lawyers becoming corporate, nonequity employees and thereby not participating in the kinds of professional practice arrangements much more typical in earlier decades. That phenomenon may have accounted in the past for wider disparities.

A fourth prism through which to view the compensation of academics is the international perspective. As seen in chapters 10 and 11, various comparative measures tend to confirm that the compensation of US faculty members, though hardly robust, is nevertheless more substantial than faculty counterparts almost everywhere else. But method-related caveats are especially in order because the pitfalls, particularly efforts to compare compensation, including benefits, across national borders, are formidable.

Fifth is the sprawling area of benefits, which constitutes a significant component of faculty compensation—roughly one-third. This elusive facet, complex and volatile, is touched on in chapters 6 and 8. In general, it appears that the monetary value of benefits has been accounting for larger proportions of faculty compensation packages and, at least for full-time faculty, constituted a not-negligible economic safety net. But, like salaries themselves, benefits have not, on the whole, made a substantial positive difference over time, in the economic well-being of American academics.

In sum, the realignments in the components of faculty work and the trajectories of faculty careers have changed markedly over the past several decades. The effect has been to transform what it means to be a faculty member. Consider, by way of summary, the following: On the one hand, the overall mission and priorities of individual institutions have not altered appreciably. (This assessment leaves aside several developments that complicate the overall pictures, for example, the explosive growth of for-profit institutions that, with few if any exceptions, engage in teaching but not in research activities and which, apparently, employ few persons functioning as full-time faculty members.) A further phenomenon entails individual institutions striving to broaden their respective missions ("mission creep"), thereby blurring the earlier delineations between, say, associate-granting and baccalaureate-granting institutions, or, for another example, between public and independent four-year campuses limited to undergraduate students, including instances wherein such institutions add master's programs.

On the other hand, the distribution of types of work-related activity undertaken by individual faculty members appears to have changed significantly for large portions of the faculty. This development reflects the broad and deep trend of role specialization whereby a larger proportion of faculty members engage exclusively in teaching (albeit via more dispersed modes of delivery). This shift in individuals' work priorities constitutes, over recent decades, a need to reckon anew just what faculty members do on the job. Proportionately, ever fewer faculty members are called upon to cover the traditional (if largely idealized) tripartite components of faculty responsibilities: teaching, research and scholarly publication, and service (in its various guises). Put another way, what constitutes being a faculty member—pivoting around what academic work consists of and how academic careers are lived (from entrance through exit)—is continuing to transform powerfully in the paradigm 3 model of current higher education, as characterized in chapter 1. In all, the role of the faculty has been repurposed, redirected in more narrow channels.

Diminishing Faculty Influence

To what extent do the contemporary American faculty exert influence over higher education, and how has that degree of influence—the "faculty factor"—changed in recent years?

The bottom line: faculty influence over academic matters has been diminishing. The faculty as a major stakeholder in higher education, by a virtual consensus of opinion, has lost considerable ground in being able to exert influence over academic matters. Succinctly put, the faculty's influence has shrunk.[5] This shrinkage is especially noticeable in, say, framing the curriculum and delineating academic programs (deletions, merges, and additions) as well as institutional planning and budgeting. And while the loss of faculty influence may not be so stark in personnel decisions (e.g., hiring and promotion), nonetheless, the managerial decisions that determine curriculum and program priorities in effect undermine faculty influence even in the academic personnel realm (sometimes described as the last domain of potent faculty influence).

Thus, if there was, in the not so distant past, a golden age, at least according to some observers (Jencks and Riesman 1968, among others), wherein faculty had realized a level of professionalization and, relatively speaking, exerted ample influence over institutional academic matters, that era has long dissipated. And, more to the present point, that decline appears to be gathering momentum, as described at greater length in a discussion of shared governance presented in chapter 8. Put in other terms, the faculty's stewardship over the academic heart of the enterprise—their autonomy, albeit always relative—has been compromised by a combination of exogenous forces (again, refer to chapter 1), as well as pressures within higher education that are reprioritizing the entire enterprise to a more student-centric orientation.

This is not to suggest that student centricity is undesirable—not at all. Student learning lies at the core of institutional mission (though, as noted repeatedly, the weight of that priority ranges from near-exclusive and preeminent to being "merely" competitive with faculty scholarly activity, depending on institutional type). Some aspects of student centricity in a competitive marketplace for enrollments can be seen in "student life": fetching residence halls and recreation centers (some with iconic climbing walls), and the like. But if a reinvigoration and elevation of student learning are to be achieved, the risk of concomitant *de*preciation of the faculty's pivotal role in student learning must enter the equation with adequate weight. That is to say, if the faculty factor is relegated to peripheral importance, then the long-term deleterious effects on student learning and on higher education more broadly and deeply—and, indeed, on the national interest—are thereby compromised. Put another way, student learning is directly dependent on the quality and commitment of the faculty, that is, "student centricity" in the fullest sense requires also affording due recognition to the faculty's proper prerogative.

In all, the perennial efforts by faculty for a larger say in shared governance has been a notably steeper uphill struggle in more recent years. Viewed through another lens, the challenge of arriving at a proper, effective balance, at multipurposed institutions of higher education, is formidable and urgent: enhancing the teaching-learning process, that is, honoring the student-centric component of faculty work while still enabling the faculty to engage meaningfully in the processes of discovery and scholarship and shaping the institution's academic core. If such a balance can be struck, despite perennially inadequate resources, then academia's daunting responsibilities will come much closer to realization.

The Implications of Changes Under Way

What are the implications of these changes, and anticipated further changes, for academic work and careers and for higher education in general?

As we have noted throughout this volume, the rapid change in the characteristics of academic work and careers is a product of many forces. Some of these developments—many, in fact—are not at all unique to institutions of higher education but are products of the constantly evolving larger society in which the higher education sector is embedded. Thus the higher education enterprise is swept up by, and profoundly reconfigured by, realities that simultaneously afford exciting new opportunities (for example, technological breakthroughs) and impose challenging constraints (for instance, the inadequacy of resources to satisfy the unquenchable appetite for "more").

Our characterization of the features of academic work and careers in preceding pages has emphasized how those characteristics have recently changed—dramatically in some crucial respects. This, in turn, leads naturally to a cluster of questions about what the foreseeable future likely holds for postsecondary education and its faculty.

While that future is invariably elusive, our basic premise is that even the proximate future is less knowable than it ever has been. In chapter 1, we identified some of the powerful forces that are reshaping almost every facet of society—indisputably affecting the postsecondary sector in innumerable ways. It follows that efforts to gauge the future are riven with large unknowables. (And yes, we recognize that, at least in the last century or so, efforts to project the future have become less predictable, ever murkier.) These cautionary observations aside, we judge that the outlook for the mission of postsecondary education and for the sanctity of its academic professionals is at best shaky.

We are also keenly aware that the college and university enterprise is among the most resilient sectors in the sprawling organizational landscape; these institutions have been extant for nearly a millennium and are not likely to disappear. We refer the reader again to the concise historical encapsulation presented in chapter 2, in which the tenacity and adaptability of the sector, despite enduring harsh criticism, are plainly evident. Will higher education continue to transform? Beyond any doubt. That has been a constant feature. But transform to a degree barely recognizable through contemporary lenses? Quite likely so, for both good and for ill. In the longer term, prognosticating what postsecondary education may look like beyond the next two decades is a more challenging undertaking, one that we do not explore in depth in these pages. For many years thoughtful observers have suggested that foreseeable technological advances will render existing physical campuses all the more inefficient—wasteful anachronisms; campuses as we have known them, some critics foresee, are destined to disappear. For instance, the management guru Peter Drucker wrote, alarmingly, "Thirty years from now the big university campuses will be relics. Universities won't survive. It's as large a change as when we first got the printed book. . . . The college won't survive as a residential institution. Today's buildings are hopelessly unsuited and totally unneeded" (Lenzer and Johnson 1997, 127) Two recent publications continue that drumbeat: Kevin Carey's (2015) *The End of College: Creating the Future of Learning and the University of Everywhere* and Michael Kirst and Mitchell Stevens (2015) *Remaking College: The Changing Ecology of Higher Education.*

The plausible scenarios for the proximate future include a highly polarized system (even more polarized than is currently the case) that is markedly undemocratic, more stratified. At one end of a long, uneven continuum of possibilities lies a small, privileged, largely residential, richly resourced elite sector, producing, in the main, high-quality results, that is, demonstrably high student value-added outcomes. Another aspect of this scenario is the unprecedented accessibility for students, made feasible by student financial aid to compensate for the challenge to students to pay, at least in part, for the soaring sticker costs of attending. This relatively elite sector spans a relatively small number of baccalaureate-granting residential liberal arts colleges (perhaps 75 to 125) and top-tier research universities that are very selective in postsecondary admissions as well as in graduate and professional degree programs.[6] Depending on where the inevitably porous lines are drawn, this more elite, more secure sector may encompass one hundred (more-or-less) institutions or even, say more than two hundred, but surely not many more than that, in our estimation.

This small subset of affluent, highly selective institutions is juxtaposed, at the other end of the continuum, with a much more extensive, and more openly accessible but more seriously undernourished sector. These institutions tend, on the whole, to be relatively "low touch" (that is, high to very-high student to faculty, instructor, and facilitator ratios), wholly (or predominantly) nonresidential, much more dependent on an impressive array of learning delivery systems but, on the whole, financially strapped at the margin or sometimes even badly broken. At this more problematic end of the continuum, the priorities in the curriculum, with few exceptions, will continue to be overwhelmingly pragmatic: career oriented, with, in most instances, a bare nod, at best, to traditional liberal arts curricular content.

Thus we foresee higher learning in this paradigm 3 era being conducted in the proximate future, given current potent and unrelenting pressures, in a wide variety of settings using widely varying instructional methods. This resculpted future will surely feature a stunning spectrum of models, stoked by technological capabilities well beyond existing methods for operations, especially in the modes of delivering and assessing subject matter content. We are heartened by movement toward a higher education that most likely will be more accessible and more focused on student outcomes.

In all, there will be many reasons to celebrate the improved means for facilitating the teaching-learning processes as well as to be deeply concerned about the veritable certainty of polarized features of the system that disproportionately favor a small number—perhaps several hundred in all—of relatively elite institutions and their faculty and students, those so-called islands of excellence.

Some of the changes in academic life, although traceable to the cascade of environing societal developments, are products of *intracampus* decisions. These are adaptations, some of them strategic and others tactical choices, that seek the most propitious way to adapt to the volatile mix of opportunities and constraints. It is these wide-ranging intracampus policy decisions that more directly affect the faculty factor. Consider, for example, a host of campus decisions to be made: How best to deploy an instructional staff to respond most effectively to the mix of teaching requirements (taking into account, for instance, the highly variable students' ability levels and the extent of their academic preparation) and the near-endless choices among subject matter possibilities? What tactical adaptations need to be made to the unrelenting pressures to expand access, improve degree completion rates, and, of course, to link students more effectively to the needs of employers for work-ready "products"? And what priority to assign to instructional staff regarding their availability to students for guidance and mentoring? Also, and more fundamental, what are realistic expectations of faculty themselves to participate meaningfully in the range of shared governance activities at various institutional levels?

These and other mixes of institutional missions require adjustments, small and large, in staffing and thereby make necessary a reassessment of the potency or impotency of the faculty factor. In other words, to what extent does this ever-evolving mélange of demands on the faculty serve to siphon its ability to shape those activities that define the academic heart of the university?

The principal effects for academic work and careers in recent years, and as best we can project in the foreseeable future, can be summarized as follows. With a larger proportion of faculty members holding off-track appointments, there are, by definition, proportionately fewer faculty holding full-time, on-track appointments. The work itself has been reapportioned and decidedly more specialized. Growing numbers and proportions of faculty members are employed solely within the teaching realm of academic activity. With fewer faculty members among all instructional faculty constituting the core of the faculty, that remnant, smaller proportion of faculty is thereby eligible—or suitable, one could say—for meaningful participation in campus governance. And so, in effect, shared governance has reverted to an earlier era, in part owing to the avalanche of part-time faculty, when a relative handful of faculty members constituted the faculty voice while other academic staff were relegated to the proverbial governance sidelines.

A Global Perspective

How does the condition of the US academic profession compare with its counterparts in other advanced economies?

Part 4 of this volume, "American Academics in Global Perspective," provided a wider prism through which to view American higher education and its faculty: relentless movement toward globalization and the press of economic-political factors, among others, as exerting immense force in realigning the newly global realities of higher education. Thus the accelerating exchange of learners and instructional staff across national boundaries render those boundaries less tangible, less meaningful. One consequence is that the freer flow of bodies—figuratively as well as physically—will contribute to increased competition for that talent. These developments need to be understood in the larger context of the extent to which access-enhancing technology increasingly will make less useful actual physical human exchanges. Among the many lessons drawn from those pages (see chapters 10 and 11) is that, relative to the American experience, the faculty at universities in other developed countries tend to exert more influence over academic affairs than do their US counterparts.

From a global perspective, a remarkable, unsettling irony is becoming apparent. Since the middle of the twentieth century, by almost all accounts, American higher education has arrived at a position of premier global leadership. The sheer numbers (and variety) of institutions of higher education, the huge numbers (and, again, variety) of students, at associate, baccalaureate and postbaccalaureate levels (having relatively ready access to higher education), and the very large number of faculty engaged primarily in teaching and research has dwarfed that of any other national system of postsecondary education. The resources channeled to higher education in the US—governmental (federal, state, local) and private or independent—overwhelmed comparable investments of resources in any other nation. The proportion of "the best universities worldwide," by every account, was dominated by leading US universities, drawn from both independent and public sectors. Even universities not widely regarded as being on anyone's list of the very top tier of American universities (but nevertheless very solid universities) often expended more funds on research activities than all but a few institutions of higher education worldwide. (For illustrative purposes, some that come to mind—albeit an arbitrary selection—that reflect this phenomenon might include, say, Washington State University, San Diego State University, the University of Georgia, State University of New York at Albany, Georgetown University, Case Western Reserve University, and Syracuse University.) One observation is that the radically decentralized US "system" triggered intense competition, which, in turn, led to numerous pinnacles of excellence and also produced scores of universities generally not thought to be among the very top tier but which nevertheless are extraordinarily productive by measures of scholarly output viewed in international perspective.

The Scramble for Competitive Advantage

Some observers may take issue with this assertion of US higher education predominance since World War II. Others will underscore, correctly, that in many countries, research activities are often funneled through research institutes or agencies unaffiliated with (or only loosely connected to) universities, thereby making direct comparisons of national higher education systems inherently flawed. Nonetheless, the American model (or models) commanded much respect and envy globally.

And so it is not surprising that one interpretation of the shake-up of higher education, spanning Western and Eastern Europe, China and India, is the emulation of some basic characteristics of the American decentralized approach. This has led, particularly in the last decade or two, to national governments abandoning strategies of allocating funding on a more even basis among its universities and, instead, deploying financial support much less evenly so as to identify a relatively small proportion of universities targeted to become centers of excellence. (Examples of such reformulated national strategies are evident in, for example, China, Japan, France, the United Kingdom, and Spain, to highlight several such national systems.)

Thus the accelerating exchange of learners and instructional staff across national boundaries renders those boundaries less meaningful. One consequence is that the freer international flow of bodies will contribute to increased competition for those teacher-scholars. These developments need to be understood in the larger context of the extent to which access-enhancing technology increasingly will make less useful actual physical exchanges.

In all, the large divide that once separated the US system (more accurately, perhaps, the US nonsystem) of higher education from all the others is diminishing. American world leadership in this highly consequential domain is becoming less clear, more susceptible to challenge.

Conclusion

We have sought throughout this volume to scrutinize the faculty factor over recent decades, particularly during the currently evolving paradigm 3 era, and we have attempted to peer into the proximate and intermediate future. Put in other words, we have tried to describe the trajectory of the faculty condition and its influence in shaping the academic estate and its priorities. Toward that end we have striven to ground our analyses and conclusions on the best available data. We have described an era in extraordinarily rapid transformation—as everyone is keenly aware—and within that vibrant setting, the role of the faculty (their work and careers) has undergone, and is continuing to undergo, jolting change.

Virtually everything about the faculty itself has been in a mode of accelerating transition in the past decade in particular. This transformation is redefining just who the faculty are, in terms of gender, nationality, and race/ethnicity. Furthermore, this far-reaching transition incorporates how the faculty entered into the academic life, progressed throughout their careers, and exited from those careers. The previous chapters have additionally described ways in which the faculty factor—the extent of the faculty's influence—has shrunk perceptibly in recent years, relegating faculty in many situations to more peripheral roles. Buffeted by unrelenting marketplace pressures, political pressures, and the harsh realities of constrained resources, the faculty factor has thus diminished.

The gist of this examination of the academic profession has been the authors' argument that the academic staff of American colleges and universities are in a precarious position. They are in a relatively fluid, unstable situation, their condition heavily influenced by the relentless forces of the marketplace. That is, compared with other national systems of higher education, the US system—and its faculty—arguably are the most vulnerable to the exertions of marketplace demands. Thus as Burton Clark (1983, 136–81) observed some years ago, relative to other higher education systems among developed countries, the influence of market forces upon US higher education, compared with the strength of either state (government) authority or the academic oligarchy itself, was already distinctively high. Today, the condition of the American academic profession is, more so than its counterparts, even more subject to the volatile shifts in market conditions. We have found no reason to question the exceptional influence of that marketplace factor in the United States and the polyglot mix of trade-offs that it brings. We have contended also, along with Sheila Slaughter and Gary Rhoades (2004), among others, that this influence has intensified perceptibly in recent years, having provided a basis for what we have dubbed paradigm 2—the precursor to the now prevailing paradigm 3.

We observed in chapter 1 and in subsequent chapters that several megaforces have been reshaping society at an unprecedented rate. Among the forces we cited earlier, the rapid succession of technological revolutions inevitably will further massively transform how higher education is conducted, and, particularly, who the faculty are (especially their types of appointments) and what they do—at any point during their careers and, cumulatively, throughout their careers. Some of these sweeping changes wrought by new technologies are readily observable—in ways simultaneously exciting, bursting with huge promise, and, too, riddled with trade-offs that should give serious pause. And here we speak only of the technological breakthroughs already palpable; the kinds of future revolutions hidden from present view surely will have spectacular effects on every facet of society including, of course, higher learning. But for now we focus on the proximate future, leaving to others the more speculative adventure of suggesting what might lie deeper into the future, including the formidable advances in neuroscience that portend wondrous implications for pedagogy that will reshape the teaching-learning realm.

But not all of the adjustments necessitated by the new era have been adverse for the faculty and for their institutions' missions. In the authors' view, some of the recalibrations have been positive. Opportunities have surfaced that have enabled some changes for the better. To draw attention to these opportunities for improvement, the concluding chapter, in response to our final line of inquiry, advances some ideas that the authors propose. Their adoption would, we think, serve to slow down the further draining of the faculty's—and higher education's—influence and would enable the higher education enterprise to better realize its vital missions.

And so: What are some of the most appropriate interventions that should be undertaken by higher education leadership, including faculty leaders, and by public policymakers? We turn to the concluding chapter.

NOTES

1. The authors have sought to ground their analyses and conclusions on the best, most reliable data. Comprehensive data about faculty demographics, work, and careers are especially sparse since the discontinuation after 2004 of the (theretofore) periodic administration of the National Survey of Postsecondary Faculty. Given the need to marshal relevant evidence, the authors on many occasions consulted, when authorized, restricted data files and generated original interpolations of existing publicly accessible data bases.

2. It appears that some staff are tabulated by their employer institutions as "full-time faculty" although most (even all) of the employee's responsibilities are administrative in nature.

3. See Schuster and Finkelstein (2006), especially chapter 7, "The Revolution in Academic Appointments: A Closer Look," 191–233.

4. The spread among types of institutions of research activity and expectations is noted in chapter 7.

5. Several recent tracts have hammered home the point of shrinking faculty influence, as cited in chapter 1.

6. For the thesis of "islands" of excellence, see Steven Brint (2007).

REFERENCES

Brint, Steven. 2007. "Can Public Universities Compete?" In *The Future of American Public Research Universities*, edited by Roger L. Geiger, Carol L. Colbeck, Christian K. Anderson, and Roger L. Williams, 91–118. Rotterdam, NL: Sense Publishers.

Carey, Kevin. 2015. *The End of College: Creating the Future of Learning and the University Everywhere*. New York: Riverhead Books.

Clark, Burton R. 1983. *The Higher Education System: Academic Organization in Cross-National Perspective*. Berkeley, CA: University of California Press.

Clark, Burton R. 1987. *The Academic Life: Small Worlds, Different Worlds*. Princeton, NJ: Carnegie Corporation for the Advancement of Teaching.

Jencks, Christopher, and David Riesman. 1968. *The Academic Revolution*. Garden City, NY: Doubleday.

Kirst, Michael W., and Mitchell L. Stevens, eds. 2015. *Remaking College: The Changing Ecology of Higher Education*. Stanford, CA: Stanford University Press.

Lenzer, Robert, and Stephen S. Johnson. 1997. "Seeing Things As They Really Are." *Forbes*, March 10, 1997, 122–28.

Schuster, Jack H., and Martin J. Finkelstein. 2006. *The American Faculty: The Restructuring of Academic Work and Careers*. Baltimore, MD: Johns Hopkins University Press.

Slaughter, Sheila, and Gary Rhoades. 2004. *Academic Capitalism and the New Economy: Markets, State, and Higher Education*. Baltimore, MD: Johns Hopkins University Press.

13

Where from Here? Interventions to Reinvigorate the Faculty Factor

We turn now to the last of our five lines of inquiry:

> *What are the most appropriate interventions that should be undertaken by higher education leadership (within both higher education institutions and their national organizations), by the faculty itself, and by public policymakers?*

In the preceding chapters we have sought to scrutinize the faculty factor over recent decades, especially during the decade following the 2007–08 Great Recession, and we have attempted to peer into the proximate and intermediate future. Put in other words, we have sought to describe the trajectory of the faculty condition and the faculty's ability to influence the academic environment and its priorities, more specifically, the faculty's influence over academic decisions and policy making. We have described an era in higher education characterized by extraordinarily rapid transformation—as everyone is keenly aware—and within that setting we have highlighted the role of the faculty undergoing jolting change. Throughout our examination we have sought to ground our analyses and conclusions in the best available data.

This concluding chapter constitutes our effort to suggest several key policy interventions that strike us as being relevant to today's higher education complexities and vulnerabilities. These challenges to higher education, we have argued, disproportionately threaten effective, balanced participation by faculty members in the pursuit of enhancing higher learning. We do not, in this chapter, attempt to address the full range of challenges confronting higher education itself. Instead, we have focused on a select number of issues that bear directly on the struggle to maintain and restore a robust faculty in the prevailing environment and in so doing, we submit, to more effectively serve the interest of student-learners.

We take up, in order, the federal role in higher education, focusing on the challenge to revitalize the Pell Grant program; the compelling need for more frequent collection and analysis of systematic information on the faculty of American colleges and universities; the challenge to address growing imbalances in the redistribution of types of academic appointments; the tenure dilemma, by reconsidering a key aspect of tenure practice; and the need to restore balance in regional and professional accreditation.

The Vital Federal Role: The Pell Grant Challenge

The role of the federal government in shaping American higher education is as contentious and varied as the larger tensions embedded within federalism itself, both as a source of and as an adjudicator of issues replete with very high stakes, reflecting omnipresent struggles between centrist and decentralized national impulses. This history and the underlying political dynamics have been ably recounted in numerous scholarly treatments, sometimes spreading across all of education but in many instances focusing on postsecondary education.

This is not the place to expound on that many-faceted narrative but rather to leap forward to the present day in which the vital federal role is being played out in all three branches of government. It is perhaps propitious that as this study of the faculty is nearing a conclusion, the current embodiment of the pathbreaking Higher Education Act of 1965 is being scrutinized for a periodic reauthorization—just about exactly half a century since its initial enactment.

We do not herein propose specific levels of funding for particular programs. Rather, a principle that we advocate for higher education and for the national interest is that students enrolled in institutions of higher education be supported more fully to better assure access to postsecondary education. One excellent place to start would be appropriations aimed at restoring the "purchasing power" for students of the venerable, need-linked Pell Grant Program (initially, the Basic Educational Opportunity Grants program), dating from 1972. As is widely known, the value of these portable grants has deteriorated significantly as a function of year-to-year inflation, in recent years slipping well below previous levels, in total awards and maximum awards, in constant dollars. More perniciously, the Pell grant cap in effect limits these grants to an ever-declining percentage of rapidly escalating costs to students to attend colleges and universities; this policy, while economy minded, seriously dilutes Pell's impact.

Thus among higher education's numerous needs for federal subsidy (including research funds), closing (or movement toward closing) that yawning Pell subsidy gap would constitute a superb beginning and would serve to restore the federal commitment to surmount financial obstacles to student access to higher education.

The Harmful Faculty Data Gap

One vitally needed policy intervention entails the restoration of the capacity to collect, and then to analyze, data pertaining to the instructional workforce, that is, the faculty. The capacity to dissect and comprehend basic information and trend lines encompassing perhaps 1.7 million full- and part-time academic employees has been allowed to degenerate in recent years. Specifically, the heretofore periodically administered US Department of Education's National Study of Postsecondary Faculty (NSOPF) was discontinued after 2003. After 2003, funding for the NSOPF ceased (NSOPF data collected previously had been published three times: 1988, 1993, and 1999 and the final data set in 2004.)[1] Thus the most reliable potential source for obtaining data directly from the American faculty has, in effect, gone missing for well over a decade. This lapse is especially crucial in that the 2003 NSOPF data predates the more recent torrent of changes throughout postsecondary education triggered in part by economic constraints, shifting political priorities, further technological advances not fully operational a decade ago, and the steep rise of proprietary higher education.

The current NSOPF vacuum should be put in perspective, for a number of other periodic reports issued by government and nongovernment sources provide essential information. For example, the National Science Foundation collects key data annually from recipients of doctoral degrees, focused primarily on PhDs earned in the so-called STEM fields (science—including the social sciences–technology, engineering, and mathematics). Many of these PhD recipients go on to seek academic careers. Also, the US Department of Labor's Bureau of Labor Statistics generates a wealth of data each year; while not comprehensive, some perspective is nonetheless provided on the economic condition of the faculty.

Among the most important nongovernmental sources of periodic data is the American Association of University Professors' annual study of faculty compensation; these data appear each year in a special issue of *Academe* (the organization's bimonthly periodical), which often, in addition to tracking academic compensation institution-by-institution, elucidates one selected dimension of faculty compensation.[2]

Basic demographic data describing the faculty and instructional workforce has continued (for now) via the annual US Department of Education's Integrated Postsecondary Education Data System (IPEDS). However, the scope of these data, derived from the every-other-year IPEDS Fall Staff Survey, has been severely narrowed in recent years, thereby limiting those surveys' utility. Additional useful faculty data, spanning several decades, are reported in the UCLA Higher Education Research Institute's triennial faculty survey, published as The American College Teacher: National Norms for the [given year] HERI Faculty Survey.

However, each of these sources has its own focus, and none is as comprehensive as the former NSOPF.[3] Accordingly, there exists a compelling need to fund anew an NSOPF survey, or something akin to it, to yield multidimensional data about faculty. Such data are all the more essential to understand the rapid—even dramatic—changes in many aspects of faculty realities in this third-paradigm era. These include, for example, demographics, aspects of faculty work, the types and distribution of academic appointments, and faculty career pathways. Such data also would enable analysts (scholars and others) and public policymakers to be much better informed, especially providing vital trend-line information, beyond the basic descriptive information routinely available through IPEDS.

In short, data about the faculty urgently need to be expanded substantially toward the goals of better understanding contemporary postsecondary education and thereby better informing higher education's policy decisions and broader public policy processes.

Seeking Norms for Academic Appointments Categories

Of the many dimensions in which the academic profession has been transformed in recent years, the most consequential, arguably, has been the large expansion of part-time (adjunct) faculty (and, as well, the sharp increase in full-time, off-tenure-track appointments). The sheer numbers of part-timers and their expanded proportion of the entire faculty has been referred to in chapters 1, 3, and 12. This phenomenon, probed in our 2006 volume, is examined also in chapters 4, 5, 7, 8, and, with a focus on compensation, chapter 9 of this current volume. We recognize the indispensable role part-timers play and acknowledge that many of them, not aspiring to full-time appointments, prefer that focused role.

The overall impact of this profusion of part-timers, particularly when viewed alongside the parallel expansion of off-tenure-track full-time appointments, has been to transform what it means to be a faculty member, especially in terms of the nature of academic work.

We are aware of the numerous variables, both from within academe and forged by larger societal forces beyond the campus, that for years have been propelling this far-reaching faculty metamorphosis—and the circumstances that have been fueling this reconfiguration. We recognize, on the plus side of the balance sheet, the considerable, even dramatic, cost savings associated with increasing utilization of and reliance on adjunct faculty. But, as we have argued, we grow increasingly concerned and perplexed by the intangible downsides of those tangible out-of-pocket savings.

We urge that a number of measures be undertaken to address this powerfully transformative phenomenon. These we divide into two sets of recommendations.

First among these is the expansion of basic fact finding and making those facts more transparent to students, parents, and the larger higher education community. Some important data are already collected by the National Center for Education Statistics and made available through the College Navigator function on the US Department of Education website. Such data include for each of the nation's postsecondary campuses basic information about faculty: student-faculty ratio, the number of full-time faculty, the ratio of the number of course sections taught by part-time instructors to the number of course sections taught by full-time faculty, the mean and median years of employment for part-time instructors, and the number of graduate assistants with primarily instructional responsibilities. These data, however, do not report internal variation by academic field, a key variable delineating organizational structure of colleges and universities. Instructional staffing patterns even on the same campus often vary widely by academic unit and discipline. Nor do they report precisely what the various categories of appointees actually do, in terms of number of courses taught or the numbers of students advised or supervised at various degree levels. The goal, at a minimum, would require institutions of higher education to more precisely tabulate the types of academic appointments distributed across the different academic units on their campus, as well as some indicators of the distribution of workload across appointment types; this will make it possible for a more nuanced picture to emerge and to enable identifying trend lines that can be more accurately ascertained and comprehended.

Such an endeavor is predicated on arriving at workable definitions of the many types of academic appointments. We recognize that the number of such categories has increased significantly at the more complex research universities and that categorizing these appointment types is a prerequisite for meaningful compilations and for generating even more useful breakouts. These elaborations would include academic field and the demographics of faculty members (gender, race/ethnicity, age groupings, and so forth) and length of service, to name several basic descriptors. Such an expanded database should also distinguish between full-time faculty members who carry a full-time teaching or research load (according to individual institutional norms) and those whose job components include significant responsibilities outside the classroom, say one-half or more in academic administration (e.g., as department chair) or in other pursuits (e.g., student affairs administration or institutional research).

If the first interrelated set of academic appointment-related recommendations is to more accurately measure the phenomenon, the second series is to stimulate dissemination of the enriched data and their use, thereby prompting action. We urge that the academy seek to establish and publicize norms for the proportion of faculty members that are full-time or essentially full-time. We do not intend that limits should be set (that would not be plausible or appropriate) but rather that guidelines should be established. And we recognize that different norms should obtain for different institutional types and perhaps as well for different academic subunits with different missions.

Perhaps a starting point in this inherently complicated and controversial process would be to review the guidelines set forth by the American Association of Universities to establish an advisory panel, drawing on participation by several leading national higher education associations—perhaps the American Council on Education and/or the Association of American Colleges and Universities. Such a panel should also include representation from one or more national faculty organizations or accrediting bodies. That advisory panel would be charged with the dual tasks of recommending the criteria for how full-time faculty members should be counted and upper limits for the proportion of less-than-full-time faculty for associate-, baccalaureate-, master's-, and doctoral-level institutions.

We do not recommend establishing limits as such; that, as noted, would be totally unworkable and, indeed, undesirable. But in the absence of language designed to discourage the further conversion of faculty into a largely part-time workforce, we fear that current trends will build unabated.

Our hope is that some useful norms, albeit roughly drawn, will begin to emerge from which institutions that are extreme outliers can be identified. This move toward transparency will enable prospective students to take that factor into account, enabling them to make a more informed decision. Some college choosers will be attracted, and some discouraged, by this otherwise invisible (really, unattainable) information; in any event, the student qua consumer can make a decision that includes, in the authors' opinion, information about an institution's instructional staff that speaks tellingly to that institution's culture, values, and modus operandi.

Confronting the Tenure Dilemma

In chapter 8 we explored key dimensions of the rationale, history, and contemporary practice of conferring and respecting the principles of tenure. As stated earlier, we wholeheartedly embrace the concept of tenure and the concomitant requirement for due process as preeminent safeguards for protecting academic freedom, without which institutions of higher education would be severely compromised.[4] But, we argued, the protective armor of tenure, where tenure exists, can be abused. In practice tenure can be treated, in effect, as lifelong security of employment, regardless of a faculty member's performance, enabling some proportion of faculty members to coast, to slide by under the radar, to circumvent standards of performance in those activities vital to a given campus's mission.[5] This shield protecting tenure also, too often, we believe, operates also at a psychological level. This is perhaps especially so in the absence of meaningful, periodic posttenure reviews; such conditions of minimal accountability, including merely superficial faculty performance reviews, serve, as a practical matter, to hold harmless marginally effective faculty members. How often do such distortions occur whereby tenure is perceived as an impenetrable buffer to protect unacceptably low performance? There is no way to measure this, but the incontrovertible answer is, sometimes.

We propose a bold, inherently controversial policy that may prove to be useful in this new era, namely, that tenure per se be discontinued at age seventy. All aspects of anti–age-discrimination legal protections would, of course, continue to apply, unaffected. And, too, the principles of academic freedom would continue in force—unaffected, undiluted. But tenure itself, post age seventy, would vanish. Is the age seventy arbitrary? Well, yes; one might propose instead a cutoff of, say, sixty-eight or seventy-two. But any specified age would be arbitrary.

What would such an age cap on tenure (not on employment or academic freedom) accomplish? What are the trade-offs?

We think that such a limitation on tenure's reach would strike an important blow to the all-too-common criticism that once tenured, tenured forevermore—in effect, a perception of lifetime employment security. Too often, we think, tenure is deemed to be an unbreachable, ironclad shield despite whatever defects may be evident. It comes down to this, as suggested earlier: the effect of such a change would be mainly psychological, to discourage faculty and their institutions from reacting to tenure as if it were a guarantee of protected employment in all but egregious misbehavior or extreme malperformance.

Will there be legal challenges, on the grounds of violations of the federal Age Discrimination in Employment Act (ADEA)? And corresponding state policies? Undoubtedly. But employment linked to age is not threatened by this proposal. This change in practice that we advocate does not compromise the fundamental mandate forbidding age-discrimination policy nor the principles that drive the ADEA.

In sum, tenure has long been a contentious issue in higher education, often misunderstood and surely underappreciated by its critics. We now see an opportunity to revitalize or reimagine tenure for this new age. How then to best preserve tenure's inviolate core, its indispensable function without risking grievous damage to institutions of higher education? And, for that matter, to society itself? How, that is to say, can that crucial value of protecting academic freedom be balanced with the compelling need to unclog the academic pipeline and, concurrently, to boost productivity and effectiveness among low-performing faculty? We think that in this new third-paradigm era a bold opportunity does exist.

We foresee three principal interlocking strategies. The first, as suggested, consists of implementing a radical age-related capping of tenure itself. A second facet entails an intensification of long-standing commonplace higher education practice—namely, serious posttenure review. Third is deploying a reinvigorated set of policies that provide positive incentives for transitioning into retirement.

First, then, is to prescribe an age, albeit arbitrary and controversial, by which tenure would automatically cease. Such decoupling of age from tenure would not and should not directly affect one's current employment. At a subliminal level, however, an age-related cessation of tenure would affect whatever sense of entitlement that a tenure holder might have to the effect that his or her position is entirely secure as a practical matter. This redefinition of tenure, patterned after the ADEA exemption (1986–93), would serve to remove that protective layer after, say, age seventy (to invoke the ADEA once-upon-a-time age cap—though, as noted, the cap could be set at sixty-five or sixty-eight or seventy-two or whatever). A faculty member who is still performing adequately (by institutional norms by whatever means of assessment) would still be secure and not subject to dismissal because of having exceeded whatever age has been established as the upper limit for holding tenure. Such a seemingly drastic alteration does not portend sharp declines in older faculty. As a practical matter, the effect is more likely to be psychological—consciousness raising–which, in turn, will (or should) lead to more self-examination.

Will such an age cap on tenure itself be challenged in courts of law? Yes, undoubtedly. But we are unaware of any case precedent that militates against, much less forbids, instituting such an age cap on one aspect of employment, such as we envision. And, in our judgment, such a cap on tenure does not violate any provision of the Age Discrimination in Employment Act.

Can this modification lead to employer abuses? Yes, of course. Will there be uncertainties—for employer and employee alike—within that expanding gray area where older faculty are slowing down but still managing? Certainly and inevitably. Nevertheless, might proposed built-in age limitations related to tenure per se be dismissed by courts attuned to the intentions of the ADEA? Well, yes, that possibility exists. Although legislation (comparable to the aforementioned 1986 exemption for faculty) can potentially be enacted, might courts disallow such potential exceptions made for faculty members? Again, yes, although exemptions from the protections of the ADEA are provided in special cases.[6]

The thrust of this age-conscious strategy is to link conceptually to the second factor, namely, the widespread practice of post-tenure peer review. Critics of post-tenure review may point to the alleged infrequencies and superficialities of what some see as a toothless, mere pro forma activity (Neal 2008). On the other hand, rigorously, routinely, and fairly performed post-tenure review sends clearer (if blunter) messages to tenure holders found to be coasting or underperforming (Clotfelter 2002). And, yes, we are mindful that meaningful post-tenure reviews are costly, both to the reviewee and to reviewers, in terms of valuable time absorbed by such a process. The corollary is that a well-functioning system of performance reviews *can* have a positive effect. It is likely that such a system, if implemented evenly, will encourage some proportion of faculty members—whom colleagues may deem to be contributing inadequately and who may see their own contribution as having become more marginal—to opt to retire sooner than might otherwise be the case.

A third component of a strategic approach to diminish the potentially adverse effects of a faculty member invoking tenure as a justification for staying on too long can be found in positive intervening policies: providing incentives to make more attractive phased retirement. Such institutional strategies should yield win-win career exits. (Some observers may be dubious about the cost-benefit effects of institutional incentive-laden retirement strategies, apprehensive that such measures may thereby prompt disproportionately the abler, more productive among their retirement-eligible faculty members to opt for phasing out. There is no reliable measure of such a pattern, but in the absence of systematic evidence, beyond anecdotal accounts, an institution of higher education seems likely, on balance, to benefit. Examples of long-standing phased retirement options abound. Elsewhere in this volume the issue is examined in more detail (see especially chapter 6).

In sum, the net effects of such approaches to "the tenure dilemma" are likely to be modest but, under prevailing staffing conditions, could well be nonetheless significant. Tenure would remain intact, more clearly focused on the priority for which it was intended—the protection of academic freedom. However, coupled with prospective messages derived from rigorous (but fair) performance reviews and a meaningful array of incentives that commonly are woven into phased retirement plans, the effects would quite likely be salutary.

Evaluating Tenured Professors

The award of tenure status to faculty members raises a cluster of issues pertaining to post-tenure review, especially poignant in an era in which the demand for accountability is intense. These issues include, most fundamentally, the extent (that is, the degree of comprehensiveness) to which a faculty member's performance should be evaluated, and, too, the timing of such reviews (the spacing of intervals). A range of issues regarding tenure and post-tenure review were identified and described in chapter 8. We now propose several principles to guide the implementation of these periodic assessments.

The first is to acknowledge the compelling need for formal, periodic reviews to be conducted principally by faculty peers; this should establish the basis for recommendations to academic administrators.

Second, these reviews should be consequential, that is, they should be a factor in determining compensation and, where appropriate, promotion decisions. Moreover, when findings of significant deficiencies are shown to persist, the process might, in extreme instances, lead to termination.

Correspondingly, a third criterion is to create a procedure that is sufficiently deep and broad to determine the adequacy of a faculty member's performance. And the process must correspond to the role expectations that apply to the faculty member being reviewed. This entails meeting the challenge of prescribing just what evidence should be required to evaluate each of the pertinent areas of faculty activity (instruction, scholarship, and service, as deemed to be relevant).

A fourth criterion is to recognize the cost in time—the unavoidable burden—required of reviewers and the person being reviewed. This necessitates a reasonable schedule for reviews such that neither too much nor too little time elapses between reviews. We take no position on how long that that interval—striking that ideal balance—should be beyond observing that such reviews are commonly scheduled at five- to seven-year intervals.

Fifth is the mandate that the description of the process and evaluative criteria should be laid out plainly.

Sixth—or perhaps this should be first—is that the overarching purpose of post-tenure reviews should be constructive, that is, helpful developmentally to the faculty member. While such reviews should serve dual purposes (both summative and formative, as noted in chapter 8), the basic thrust should be to enable the faculty members to realize their greater potential. This positive emphasis should not minimize the usefulness of identifying those faculty members who are found to be merely coasting along, who are minimally effective in meeting their responsibilities.

Finally, whether such periodic reviews should be augmented by more frequent, if far less formal, assessments—such as, for instance, a department chair's annual review—falls within the purview of individual campuses (or systems of institutions), but, in the main, we advocate more feedback rather than less.

Accreditation: The Need for Rebalancing

The historical record establishes that accreditation was conceived as a pivotal means by which academia initiated and enforced standards for quality assurance. Described succinctly, accreditation is "the primary means of assuring and improving academic quality in U.S. higher education" (Eaton 2015). The central dynamic was, and continues to be, that the process is fundamentally a matter of *self*-policing, featuring criteria developed from beyond an individual, self-contained campus. And this principle applies across all types of degree-granting institutions and, crucially, cuts across public and private sectors. This dynamic, both in theory and practice, was intended to empower the academic sector to determine what constituted acceptable quality (and would articulate just what those criteria would be) and, correspondingly, would diffuse the influence directly exerted by interests external to the academy, principally by governmental (political) policymakers.[7]

Over the past several decades, however, the purposes, processes, and uses of accreditation in higher education, ever dynamic, have tilted significantly. The overall effect has been a mix of positives and negatives (as viewed by the authors), but consonant with the book's overall thesis, the changes in accreditation—and quality assessment measures more generally—that have been implemented have served to diminish the faculty's influence over the academic core of postsecondary education. Thus as we see it, the faculty factor has thereby been diluted. This troubling change is evident both in the regional accreditation of institutions of higher education (as conducted by the seven regional associations) and the numerous organizations that accredit professional "specialized" programs. Here is not the place to explore the numerous and complex aspects of accreditation beyond several observations.[8]

First, in the past decade the criteria for meeting acceptable standards of quality continues to shift, veering further away from a predominant emphasis on "inputs" (for example, faculty qualifications, library holdings, financial resources, and so on) toward a process that is almost exclusively focused on "outcome" metrics (such as retention and degree completion percentages, movement of graduates into jobs, etc.). This notable transformation continues, but in our view has swung so far toward complying with performance and output criteria promulgated by government entities and, too, regional accreditors—virtually disregarding the proportion of full-time faculty—as to seriously compromise at least two traditional core values in accreditation: the importance of peer review and institutional and program autonomy.

Second, in this dynamic tug-of-war among contenders for influence, the faculty factor has been—and continues to be—adversely affected. With the increasing emphasis on accreditors' role as "gatekeeper" for establishing minimum standards for an institution (or specialized program) to qualify to receive federal student financial assistance, the faculty's role has been diminished. That is to say, in the very complex and nuanced task of assessing and assuring academic quality, the role of academic practitioners themselves—of faculty experts—in the accreditation process has increasingly been relegated to the sidelines.

We urge that in the ongoing process of recalibrating how gatekeeping and quality assurance are to be determined, some rebalancing is called for. Regional and specialized accreditors should be more sensitive to, and show more support for, the vital role of faculty expertise in determining what constitutes acceptable quality in higher education. At this writing, that responsibility should most certainly extend to amending the statutory provisions and the corresponding implementing regulations that are related to the reauthorization of the Higher Education Act.

Conclusion

The above recommendations are limited in number and do not purport to address many vexing aspects of contemporary higher education. While controversial, these recommendations are intended to prompt further exploration and debate over the most effective ways to address several portentous, complex challenges to the academic profession—and thereby strengthen the faculty factor.

NOTES

1. In each instance, including the 2004 report, the faculty survey itself had been conducted the previous fall. Thus the 2004 NSOPF report was based on fall 2003 survey reports. It is worth noting that all five NSOPF reports also included a survey of institutions of higher education.

2. Examples include periodic emphases on persisting inequities in the compensation for women and non-tenure-track faculty; the growth and number of, and compensation for, campus administrators (Curtis and Thornton 2014); and the cost of benefits (Barnshaw and Dunietz 2015).

3. Other data sources exist describing the faculty, a number of which are drawn on in chapter 3. (See, in particular, appendix A for more details.)

4. Among the numerous sources used to examine current tenure policies and practices are American Association of University Professors (2015); Baldwin and Chronister (2001); Breneman (1997); Chait (2002); Finkin (1996); Hammond and Morgan (1991); Hofstadter and Metzger (1955); Metzger (1973); Tierney and Bensimon (1996); Trower (2012); Wilson (2010); and Zemsky (2008).

5. Relevant here is the Collaborative on Academic Careers in Higher Education's finding, reported in chapter 8, about some faculty members' dissatisfaction with some senior faculty members' "intellectual vitality."

6. Although we emphatically are not advocating the reinstituting of a mandatory retirement age for faculty members (such as had been made legally allowable during the 1986–93 period), it should be noted that there are numerous permissible exceptions to the 1986 amendments to the Age Discrimination in Employment Act that have been established in federal, state, and local policies. These exemptions apply, with varying specifications, to such employee classifications as air traffic controllers, federal law enforcement officers, national park rangers, airline pilots, and local police and firefighters.

7. One such prominent example is the so-called Spellings Report, which exclaimed that "a transformation of accreditation" is required (see US Department of Education 2006, 15, 25). This report is a product of the Commission on the Future of Higher Education appointed by U.S. Secretary of Education Margaret Spellings.

8. For a more extensive exploration of accreditation in higher education, see Gaston (2013). See also Eaton and Neal (2015).

REFERENCES

American Association of University Professors (AAUP). 2015. *Policy Documents and Reports.* Washington, DC: AAUP.

Baldwin, Roger G., and Jay L. Chronister. 2001. *Teaching without Tenure: Policies and Practices for a New Era.* Baltimore, MD: Johns Hopkins University Press.

Barnshaw, John and Samuel Dunietz. 2015. "Busting the Myths: The Annual Report on the Economic Status of the Profession 2014–15." *Academe* 101 (March-April): 4–19.

Breneman, David W. 1997. *Alternatives to Tenure for the Next Generation of Academics: New Pathways; Faculty Career and Employment for the 21st Century.* Working Paper Series, Inquiry 14. April. Washington, DC: American Association for Higher Education.

Chait, Richard P., ed. 2002. *The Questions of Tenure.* Cambridge, MA: Harvard University Press.

Clotfelter, Charles T. 2002. "Can Faculty Be Induced to Relinquish Tenure?" In *The Questions of Tenure,* edited by Richard P. Chait, 221–45. Cambridge, MA: Harvard University Press.

Curtis, John and Saranna Thornton. 2014. "Losing Focus: The Annual Report on the Economic Status of the Profession, 2013–14." *Academe* 100 (March-April): 4–17.

Eaton, Judith S. 2015. "Accreditation: What It Does and What It Should Do." *Change* 47 (January–February): 24–26.

Eaton, Judith S., and Anne Neal. 2015. "Accreditation's Future." *Change* 47 (January–February): 20–27.

Finkin, Matthew W., ed. 1996. *The Case for Tenure.* Ithaca, NY: Cornell University Press.

Gaston, Paul L. 2013. *Higher Education Accreditation: How It's Changing, Why It Must.* Sterling, VA: Stylus Publishing.

Hammond, P. Brett, and Harriet P. Morgan, eds. 1991. *Ending Mandatory Retirement in Higher Education.* Committee on Mandatory Retirement in Higher Education, Commission on Behavioral and Social Sciences and Education, National Research Council. Washington, DC: National Academy Press.

Hofstadter, Richard, and Walter P. Metzger. 1955. *The Development of Academic Freedom.* New York: Columbia University Press.

Metzger, Walter P. 1973. "Academic Tenure in America: A Historical Essay." In *Faculty Tenure: A Report and Recommendations by the Commission on Academic Tenure in Higher Education*, 93–159. San Francisco, CA: Jossey-Bass.

Neal, Anne D. 2008. "Reviewing Post-Tenure Review." *Academe* 94 (September–October): 27–30.

Tierney, William G., and Estela Mara Bensimon. 1996. *Promotion and Tenure: Community and Socialization in Academe.* Albany, NY: State University of New York Press.

Trower, Cathy A. 2012. *Success on the Tenure Track: Five Keys to Faculty Job Satisfaction.* Baltimore, MD: Johns Hopkins University Press.

US Department of Education. 2006. *A Test of Leadership: Charting the Future of US Higher Education.* Washington, DC.

Wilson, Robin. 2010. "Tenure, RIP: What the Vanishing Status Means for the Future of Education." *Chronicle of Higher Education*, http://Chronicle.com/article/Tenure-RIP/66114/.

Zemsky, Robert. 2008. "Tenure Wild Cards." *Academe* 94 (September–October): 19–21.

Afterword

Walter P. Metzger some four decades ago traced the gradual evolution of academic workers. He described the Age of the Master, the Age of the Employee, and the Age of the Professional (Metzger 1973). Yes, these are gross generalizations, but they serve to capture the basic transitions from (semi)autonomous "master" to a less influential, more ordinary "employee" but then ascending to coveted "professional" status: the faculty had acquired greater deference in academic matters, greater influence in shaping institutional priorities and values, more recognition and appreciation as experts.

But we have argued in these pages that a new era of harsher realities is upon us. The faculty, thrust into this new era, are being profoundly reshaped in terms of who they are and what they do. The "faculty factor" as an influence in its varied higher education settings is under threat. The broad, multidimensional transformation of the academy and its instructional staff, apparent especially during this past decade—perhaps most striking since the tightening of economic strictures circa 2008 and the unrelentingly firmer grip of marketplace pressures—situates academic men and women on the cusp of a lamentable regression. Thus in Metzger's terminology, the faculty in many respects is being relegated back to an earlier era, reverting to a pre-"professional" status of "employee."

The central thrust of this book has been to convey our deep apprehension that the faculty's influence to shape higher education's academic contents and priorities is being siphoned off at a disconcerting rate. This perceptible retreat defies precise measurement, though we have attempted to marshal relevant evidence. At risk is the capacity of the academic profession to attract the best potential faculty members and to be able to retain them.

Viewed in global perspective, there is further cause for alarm. Yes, the American distinctive array of two- and four-year postsecondary institutions, for all its flaws, is still the envy of the world. The unique achievements of mass access and unmatched scholarly productivity—embodying dual dedication to both quantity and quality—have inspired worldwide emulation. Yet American leadership in higher learning is now being challenged, a function of simultaneous declining support for its repositioned and more narrowly repurposed faculty *and* the demonstrable increased attention other developed countries have been paying to their respective higher education systems and to their faculties. This latter resurgence is occurring, ironically it seems, as American education and its core resource, the faculty, are being subjected to heightened stresses.

In all, the societal veneer once protecting the still vaunted American higher education system and its remarkable faculty is fragile and, to us, frighteningly vulnerable. If that veneer is further pierced, the consequences for intellectual life and for the institutions that struggle to nourish their faculty will be severely costly. The stakes, not just for the academic profession, but more consequentially for the larger society, are enormous.

REFERENCE

Metzger, Walter P. 1973. "Academic Tenure in America: A Historical Essay." In *Faculty Tenure: A Report and Recommendations by the Commission on Academic Tenure in Higher Education*, 93–159. San Francisco, CA: Jossey-Bass.

Appendix A

DATA SOURCES: AN OVERVIEW AND STATUS REPORT

In 2006, we judged that "the scope and volume of reliable national data [on the American academic profession] is unprecedented . . . and exceeds national databases on faculty anyplace else in the world" (Schuster and Finkelstein 2006, 392).

Ten years later, that characterization no longer holds. On one hand, the federal government in the United States has abandoned its responsibility for all but the most cursory periodic data collection on the instructional staffs of colleges and universities[1] (see chapter 13); on the other hand, some two dozen nations, including the major European economies, as well as the European Commission, China, Japan, and South Korea in East Asia, and Argentine, Brazil, and Latin America are now investing in periodic data collection of their academic workforces, including a 2007–08 twenty-nation Changing Academic Profession Survey (CAP), and a twenty-nation follow-up in 2015–16 (see chapter 12).

So, as we approached our update of *The American Faculty*, and especially our goal of assessing the impact of the Great Recession of 2008 on academic work and careers, we found ourselves almost immediately up against a wall: beyond the last National Center for Education Statistics (NCES) National Study of Postsecondary Faculty (NSOPF) in 2004 (data collected in fall 2003), there were simply no publicly available, comprehensive national snapshots of the American professoriate beyond some basic census counts of the numbers of instructional faculty and their distribution by gender, race, and rank as provided by the NCES's biennial Fall Staff Survey conducted for the past half century as a component of the Integrated Postsecondary Education Data System (IPEDS). Rather, we confronted a landscape of proprietary, usually special purpose, data sources on specific topics, most of which offered idiosyncratic definitions of similarly named focal variables and national surveys of related populations, for example, PhD natural and social scientists, some portion of whom served on the instructional staff of colleges and universities, ad hoc professional association, special-interest-group data collection and reports, and so on.

While we initially devoted our energies to the search for fugitive data sources that might be of help—and spent not a little time cursing the darkness—we eventually settled on a two-pronged strategy. The first piece of our strategy was to thoroughly mine the last comprehensive, national data collection initiative—the 2004 National Study of Postsecondary Faculty (NSOPF:04)—and extend it, insofar as possible, with the basic census data provided by the biennial NCES's Fall Staff Survey. Indeed, the Fall Staff Survey provided the basic infrastructure for chapter 3. Data from the NSOPF:04 was not included in our earlier volume since the restricted data file did not become available until after submission of our earlier manuscript. So, whatever its limitations,[2] the NSOPF:04 restricted data file offered an opportunity to bring relatively "new," if ten years old, data into the mix. Moreover, perhaps in part as a function of its abbreviated format or the decision by the NCES to abandon the NSOPF and redirect its data collection and dissemination energies, the NSOPF:04 had been relatively underutilized as the source of published data analyses related to the American faculty. In some sense, then, we felt we could make a contribution to the national conversation by bringing analyses of the 2004 NSOPF onto the center stage from which it had largely been absent. The NCES's Human Resource Component (formerly the Fall Staff Survey) data could provide limited updates on a few basic demographic features.

With the NSOPF:04—as bolstered by IPEDS–as a solid, credible, if dated, foundational source, we adopted as the second prong of our strategy one of triangulation at multiple levels. First, having identified various special purpose data sources, we sought to test their findings for the first years of the twenty-first century against the NSOPF and IPEDS foundations for convergence or consistency. Second, we sought a second-order triangulation among multiple sources to test whether any findings from more recent, but limited, sources were internally consistent and constituted either a departure from or continuity with the earlier NSOPF-IPEDS foundation.

In what follows, we provide a basic overview of each of our fifteen principal data sources. Before leaving the reader to inspect the individual source descriptions, some general comments may be useful.

Foundational Sources: SDR and HERI

Beyond the 2004 National Study of Postsecondary Faculty and the biennial IPEDS Human Resources Component, we employed two other foundational sources: the National Science Foundation's Survey of Doctorate Recipients (SDR) and UCLA's Higher Education Research Institute's biennial faculty surveys (HERI). The SDR is a national survey conducted every two to three years by the National Science Foundation of PhDs in the physical, life, and social sciences and engineering. What is unique to the SDR is its sampling frame. Half of the sample is drawn from all individuals who received PhDs in the focal fields over the previous three years (since the last administration of the SDR). The other half of the sample is drawn from individuals who responded to the immediately previous administration of the SDR. While each administration cycle represents a snapshot of new and continuing PhDs, the sampling strategy makes possible the identification of PhDs in the restricted biennial data files who have responded to two or more successive administrations of the SDR. After securing licenses for the SDR restricted data files for the nine surveys since 1993 (the first year of the survey in its current format), we were able to construct a "quasi-longitudinal" sample of PhDs who responded to a minimum of two and a maximum of nine surveys. This quasi-longitudinal sample, of course, shrunk in size as we added more surveys: numbers were robust for those PhDs with two data points and considerably smaller for those with nine—potentially introducing a bias toward those who were most willing to respond.

Insofar as we were seeking to identify difference in the career experiences of PhDs who received their degrees and entered the labor market in different historical eras, we identified a cohort of respondents to the 1993 survey who responded to two or more subsequent surveys; and then a second cohort of respondents to the 2003 survey who responded to two or more subsequent surveys. Each such cohort was further disaggregated by career stage: new entrants were defined as those who earned their PhD in the previous three years and were responding to their first SDR administration; early-career PhDs were defined as those who had received their PhD four to eight years earlier, mid-career as those who had earned their PhD nine to fifteen years earlier, and senior were defined as those who had earned their PhDs more than fifteen years earlier. For the new entrants, the subject of chapter 4, we created a third cohort of those responding to the 2010 survey for the first time and then again in 2013—the last year for which data was available at the time of publication, allowing us to examine three cohorts of new entrants entering the PhD labor market in 1993, 2003, and in 2010 (after the Great Recession of 2008) over the first three to five years of their career. In chapters 4 and 5, we examined the experience of two cohorts of early-, mid- and senior-career PhDs in faculty positions at three points in time, about a ten-year chunk of their careers. In chapter 6, we examined the nature and timing of retirement decisions among three cohorts of senior faculty.

In each instance—whether examining a cohort at two or three points in time—cases were weighted longitudinally by the case weight assigned in the last survey year, a practice that has become the norm for those who have sought to develop "quasi-longitudinal" data files from SDR data (Connolly, Lee, and Savoy 2015).[3]

The HERI Faculty Survey

The HERI has conducted a biennial faculty survey since 1989. The survey, however, is conducted as a proprietary venture to provide information to institutions that subscribe to the Higher Education Research Institute's Cooperative Institutional Research Program (CIRP) project. As such, it is administered to a convenience sample of more than 1,000 member institutions and covers only those faculty engaged in undergraduate instruction and only those areas that are of broad interest to the membership.[4] While the HERI survey has maintained some continuity in content covered and even in the wording of some items, nonetheless there have been subtle changes as membership and broader national policy priorities change, making it difficult to assemble trend data over time. Moreover, given its proprietary nature, the data files themselves are not publicly available, and the major sources of analysis are drawn from the published reports of individual surveys on the HERI website. Effectively, that limits analysis to those control variables used to construct tables in the public reports: institutional type (defined by sector and degree level), gender, and faculty rank. The HERI survey has a relative paucity of data on career variables and job history but provides robust data on a number of attitudinal variables, including job stresses and satisfaction, perceptions of governance and campus decision making, and several basic dimensions of workload, including how faculty spend their time between different aspects related to teaching, research, and service. We build upon trends in these HERI surveys in chapter 7, on work trends and sources of stress and satisfaction, and in chapter 8, on attitudes toward governance.

Other Special Purpose Data Sets

Beyond the NSOPF:04, the SDR, and HERI, we have relied on a motley assemblage of special-purpose data files. These include studies of the international aspects of faculty and their work, studies of faculty compensation, studies of graduate students and new faculty, studies of contingent faculty, and studies of faculty governance. The major international data sources include the baseline 1992 Carnegie Foundation for the Advancement of Teaching International Survey of the Academic Profession (Altbach 1996); its fifteen-year follow-up, the Changing Academic Profession Survey of 2007–08; and two more recent comparative studies of faculty compensation (Altbach et al. 2011) and newly entering faculty (Yudkevich et al. 2015). Insofar as the Changing Academic Profession survey of 2007–08 provides the substantive foundation for chapter 10 and 11—and has not been widely disseminated in the United States—a separate appendix D is devoted to a detailed discussion of its sample and methods.

Data sources on faculty compensation are discussed in some detail in appendix G of *The American Faculty*. To the major sources identified there—the NSOPF, the American Association of University Professors (AAUP) Annual Survey, the College and University Professional Association for Human Resources (CUPA), and Oklahoma State Faculty Salary surveys—we have added the US Department of Labor, Bureau of Labor Statistics biennial Occupational and Employment Statistics (OES) Survey, which, by utilizing the Standard Occupational Classification system (SOC) and the North American Industry Classification System (NAICS), provides data on salaries for a comprehensive array of job classifications in most fields and industry sectors covered by the US workforce. Furthermore, the OES survey covers, and reports on, all full-time and part-time wage and salary workers in nonfarm industries. The survey does not cover the self-employed, owners and partners in unincorporated firms, household workers, or unpaid family workers.

The 2010 Standard Occupational Classification system is used by federal agencies to classify workers into job categories for the purpose of data collection and reporting. All workers are classified into one of 840 detailed occupations according to their occupational definition. Detailed occupations in the SOC with similar job duties, and in some cases skills, education, or training, are grouped together. To facilitate classification, detailed occupations are combined to form twenty-three major groups, identified by the first two digits of the job code. These groups are then further divided into ninety-seven minor groups, identified by the third digit of the job code. Finally, occupations are divided again into broad occupations, identified through the fourth and fifth digit, and then detailed occupations, identified by the sixth digit of the individual's job code.

For example, a chemistry postsecondary teacher is classified with an SOC code of 25-1052. The first two digits, 2 and 5, indicate the position is located within the Education, Training, and Library occupations group. The third digit, 1, indicates that the individual is a postsecondary teacher (as opposed to, for example, an elementary school teacher, which is coded 25-2021, with the 2 indicating a preschool, primary, secondary, and special education teacher), the 05 indicating a physical sciences occupation group (as opposed to a 08 code, representing an education and library sciences occupation group), and the 2 representing chemistry (as opposed to a physics postsecondary teacher, which is coded 25-1054).

While the SOC allows us to identify specific occupational groups, the inclusion of NAICS codes used by the OES allows one to target specific segments of a given industry. For some background, the NAICS is a two- through six-digit hierarchical classification system, offering five levels of detail. Each digit in the code is part of a series of progressively narrower categories, and the more digits in the code signify greater classification detail. The first two digits designate the economic sector, the third digit designates the subsector, the fourth digit designates the industry group, the fifth digit designates the NAICS industry, and the sixth digit designates the national industry. The five-digit NAICS code is the level at which there is comparability in code and definitions for most of the NAICS sectors across the three countries participating in NAICS (the United States, Canada, and Mexico). A complete and valid NAICS code contains six digits. This coding structure allows one to identify specific occupations (through the SOC) but also to isolate those individuals who work in specific industries. For example, one can utilize NAICS codes to identify postsecondary chemistry teachers who work in four-year educational institutions (NAICS code 611310 for Colleges, Universities, and Professional schools) and exclude postsecondary chemistry teachers who work in two-year institutions (NAICS code 611210).

Data sources on "new" faculty include the Collaborative on Academic Careers in Higher Education (COACHE) project. This includes a series of Tenure Track Faculty Job Satisfaction surveys conducted between 2006 and 2011 at the more than 200 consortium member institutions, focusing on faculty perceptions of the path to tenure, including sources of stress and satisfaction.

Data sources on contingent, primarily part-time, faculty include the Coalition on the Academic Workforce (CAW) survey of some 30,000 part-time and non-tenure-track faculty in 2010. The CAW survey results are organized into five data files: an institution file (including all courses and faculty organized by institutional ID); a file organized by individual respondent; a file organized by course; a fourth file including full-time non-tenure-track faculty and researchers; and a fifth file with data on demographics and benefits.

Data sources on faculty governance include, in addition to the HERI Faculty Survey and the Changing Academic Profession Survey, the Survey of Faculty Senate Leaders undertaken at the Center for the Study of Higher Education at Ohio University in 2007–08 as well as an electronic file of faculty union contracts assembled by the National Center for the Study of Collective Bargaining in Higher Education and the Professions at Hunter College, City University of New York.

National Center for Education Statistics, US Department of Education

The National Center for Education Statistics currently conducts thirteen surveys to obtain data related to postsecondary education, including data on institutions and students. The two surveys related to postsecondary faculty are the Integrated Postsecondary Education Data System and the National Study of Postsecondary Faculty.

Integrated Postsecondary Education Data System

The Integrated Postsecondary Education Data System was established as the single, comprehensive system of postsecondary education data collection program for the NCES and consists of a system of surveys to collect data from all primary postsecondary education institutions. The IPEDS survey is designed around a series of interrelated surveys to collect institutional-level data related to enrollments, program completions, graduation rates, faculty and staff, finances, institutional prices, and student financial aid.

The IPEDS survey obtains data from institutions in the fifty states, the District of Columbia, and outlying areas that participate in Title IV of the federal Higher Education Act of 1965, student financial aid programs. For 2013–14, IPEDS collected data from approximately 7,477 postsecondary institutions. For IPEDS purposes, postsecondary institutions are classified as those institutions whose primary purpose is to provide instruction to students beyond the high school level. Academic, vocational, and continuing education programs are included, while avocational or adult basic education programs are excluded.

The postsecondary institutions are grouped into nine categories structured as a three-by-three matrix: three variables for control (public, private nonprofit, and private for-profit) and three for institutional type (institutions offering baccalaureate or higher degrees, two-year colleges, and institutions offering a less-than-two-year programs, often for an occupation certified).

The survey ordinarily collects data annually for full-time instructional faculty at degree-granting institutions that award associate, bachelor's, master's, doctoral, or first professional degrees. Data collected regarding salaries and fringe benefits are available by rank, gender, tenure status, and length of contract. The survey consists of nine interrelated survey components that are collected over three collection periods (fall, winter, and spring) each year. The fall collection components include institutional characteristics, completions, and twelve-month enrollments. The winter collection components include student financial aid, graduation rates, and 200% graduation rates. The spring collection components include fall enrollment, finance, and human resources. All components of IPEDS are mandatory, and as a result, IPEDS response rates for each component are nearly 100%.

The 2013–14 IPEDS survey used a web-based data collection method. The system automatically calculated totals, averages, and percentages and compared the responses with the 2012–13 submission for the same institution to ensure the data were consistent. If data were missing following the edit checks, or if an institution had not responded to a survey component, analysts calculated imputations to ensure a complete database was available for analysis. The IPEDS survey applies a single imputation method for both unit and item nonresponse based on the returns from responding institutions.

Additional information about IPEDS can be obtained from the National Center for Education Statistics website at http://nces.ed.gov/ipeds.

National Study of Postsecondary Faculty

The National Study of Postsecondary Faculty was designed for education researcher, planners, and policymakers to address the need for data on faculty and instructors or those who directly affect the quality of postsecondary institutions. The NSOPF collects data regarding who faculty are, what they do, and whether, how, and why they are changing.

Four cycles of the NSOPF were completed, including 1987–88, 1992–93, 1998–99, and 2003–04 data points. The institutional and faculty sample sizes of the four cycles compare as follows:

	1987–88	1992–93	1998–99	2003–04
Sample size				
Institutions	480	974	960	1,080
Chairpersons	3,000+	—	—	—
Faculty	11,000	31,354	18,000	35,630
Response rate				
Institutions	88	94	93	91
Chairpersons	80	—	—	—
Faculty subsample	76	84	83	76

NSOPF Survey Design

As described by the NCES, the NSOPF uses a two-stage stratified, clustered probability design, stratifying the 3,380 institutions in the universe on the basis of the highest degree conferred and the amount of federal research dollars they received.

Institutional sample and survey instrument The institution universe for NSOPF is defined by the following criteria: Title IV participating, degree-granting institutions;

public and private not-for-profit institutions; institutions that confer associate's, bachelor's, or advanced degrees; and institutions that are located in the United States. The survey excludes for-profit institutions.

The 2003–04 cycle (NSOPF:04) included a sample of 1,080 public and private not-for-profit degree-granting postsecondary institutions and a sample of 35,000 faculty and instructional staff. The weighted response rates for the two surveys were 86% and 76%, respectively.

Faculty Member Sample and Survey Instrument

All four cycles of NSOPF gathered information regarding the backgrounds, responsibilities, workloads, salaries, benefits, attitudes, and future plans of both full- and part-time faculty. Those designated as faculty, whether or not their responsibilities included instruction, plus nonfaculty personnel with instructional responsibilities were included across all cycles. Administrators and researchers who held faculty positions, even if they did not teach, were also included in the samples. Teaching assistants, however, were not included in the samples.

In addition to asking sampled individuals to report on their individual salary and benefits, the faculty member survey asked for demographic and social characteristics of the faculty and their academic and professional background; employment history and current employment status, including rank and tenure; workload; field of instruction; publications; job satisfaction and attitudes; and career and retirement plans. Moreover, information was gathered from institutional and department-level respondents (department-level data collected in 1988 only) on such issues as faculty composition, turnover, recruitment, retention, and tenure policies.

Additional information about the NSOPF can be obtained from the National Center for Education Statistics website at http://nces.ed.gov/surveys/nsopf.

To access NSOPF public-use data, the NCES developed the Data Analysis System (DAS). The system can generate and print tables drawn from the NSOPF survey items, including frequency counts, percentages, means, and correlation coefficients. In addition to the public-use data files, researchers deemed qualified by the Department of Education may obtain restricted-access data files that detail analytical options. More information about the DAS, and related files, can be obtained from the DAS website at http://nces.ed.gov/das.

A note on reconciling data from IPEDS and NSOPF is warranted. A challenge to interpreting faculty compensation data arises from the differences between IPEDS and the NSOPF data. Different results are to be expected because the data sources are so different: for IPEDS purposes, the data are institution-wide salary data, derived from "official" institutional payrolls, but for NSOPF purposes, data are provided by the individual faculty members, who may not have at hand their precise salary information at the time of responding to the questionnaire. More problematic is that the sampling frame for faculty members can be an issue; in any event, the NSOPF response rates, although impressively high compared with those of other surveys, are consistently lower than IPEDS institutional response rates.

American Association of University Professors

The American Association of University Professors, founded in 1915, is a nonprofit professional organization with a membership in 2014 of approximately 47,000, with over 500 local campus chapters and 39 state organizations. The AAUP represents faculty, librarians, and academic professionals at four-year and two-year accredited public and private colleges and universities.

Each fall, the AAUP conducts a widely used survey of institutions of higher education regarding faculty salaries and benefits. The results of the *Annual Report on the Economic Status of the Profession* are published in the March–April issue of *Academe*, the AAUP magazine. Salary data from the 2013–14 report, *Losing Focus: The Annual Report on the Economic Status of the Profession*, is based on responses from 1,159 institutions.

AAUP Survey Definitions

Instructional Faculty

The instructional faculty comprises those members of the staff who are employed on a full-time basis and whose major regular assignment is instruction, including those with released time for research. Faculty members on sabbatical leave are counted at their regular salaries even though they may be receiving a reduced salary while on leave. Replacements for those on leave with pay are not counted; replacements for those on leave without pay are counted. All faculty members who have contracts for the full academic year are included, regardless of whether their status is considered "permanent." Faculty who teach only part of the year, or part-time, are excluded. Faculty in preclinical or clinical medicine, instructional faculty members who are in military organizations, administrative officers, and teaching assistants are also excluded.

Salary

Salary data from the AAUP represent the contracted salary for the standard nine-month academic calendar. Salaries for eleven- or twelve-month contacts are prorated. This figure excludes summer teaching, stipends, extra load, or other forms of remuneration.

Major Fringe Benefits

These include benefits for which payments are made by the institution (or via a public agency for some public institutions) on behalf of an individual faculty member. They include Social Security, retirement contributions, medical and dental insurance, group life insurance, disability income protection, unemployment compensation, and worker's compensation. Also included are tuition waivers or remissions for faculty or dependents, and benefits, either in kind of with cash alternatives, such as moving expenses, housing, or cafeteria plans with cash options.

The faculty salary data is grouped into five institutional categories:

Category I	Doctoral
Category IIA	Master's
Category IIB	Baccalaureate
Category III	Associate's with academic ranks
Category IV	Associate's without academic ranks

The AAUP provides data on average salary and average compensation broken out for all ranks combined as well as by each rank and gender. The AAUP also calculates faculty salaries in two ways: for all faculty and for "continuing" faculty, that is, those faculty members who were employed by the institution both in the current and the preceding year. Year-to-year percentage changes, calculated in these two ways, provide different lenses: the former method, by substituting ordinarily lower-paid new faculty for ordinarily higher-paid continuing faculty, shows how the faculty as a whole did from one year to the next, whereas the calculation that is limited to continuing faculty members indicates how the ongoing instructional staff has fared from one year to the next.

The 2013–14 *Annual Report on the Economic Status of the Profession* is available from the AAUP website at http://www.aaup.org/reports-publications/2013-14salarysurvey.

National Science Foundation

The National Science Foundation currently conducts fourteen surveys to obtain data related to the education of scientists and engineers; research and development funding and expenditures; science and engineering research facilities; and the science and engineering workforce. The two surveys related to postsecondary faculty are the Survey of Doctorate Recipients and Survey of Earned Doctorates.

Survey of Doctorate Recipients

The National Science Foundation's Survey of Doctorate Recipients, repeated every two to three years, is a panel survey designed to provide demographic and career history information about individuals who earned a research doctoral degree in a science, technology, engineering, or mathematics (STEM) field from a US academic institution. The SDR provides the broadest swath of data on doctoral recipients in the natural and social science fields at the point of degree receipt and over multiple subsequent administrations.

The SDR follows a sample of individuals with STEM doctorates throughout their careers from the year of their degree award until age seventy-six. The panel is refreshed each survey cycle with a sample of new STEM doctoral degree earners. Results of the survey are used to make decisions related to the educational and occupational achievements and career movement of the nation's doctoral scientists and engineers.

The SDR uses a trimodal data collection approach composed of self-administered questionnaire by mail, self-administered online survey, and computer-assisted telephone interview. The SDR is based on a complex sampling design and uses sampling weights that are attached to each respondent's record to produce accurate population estimates. The final analysis weights were calculated to account for differential sampling rates, adjust for unknown location or unknown eligibility, adjust for nonresponse, and align estimates with post-stratification control totals. Although the SDR is subject to sampling error, estimates based on the total sample have relatively small sampling errors. Estimates of sampling errors associated with the SDR are included in the methodology report for each survey.

The response unit of the SDR is at the individual level and includes an approximate population size of 840,000 and an approximate sample size of 47,000. The survey initially began in 1973, and the most recent year of available data is 2013.

Additional information about SDR can be obtained from the National Science Foundation website at http://nsf.gov/statistics/srvydoctoratework.

Higher Education Research Institute

The Higher Education Research Institute at UCLA seeks to inform education policy, encourage institutional improvement, and foster institutional understanding and improvement by providing longitudinal research designed to allow better understanding of the relationship between higher education, college students, and faculty. The survey related to postsecondary faculty is the HERI Faculty Survey.

HERI Faculty Survey

The Higher Education Research Institute's Faculty Survey provides institutions a comprehensive, research-based picture of key aspects of the faculty experience. The HERI Faculty Survey, issued on a triennial basis to faculty at two- and four-year institutions, is designed to provide institutions with actionable information related to pedagogical practices, faculty goals and expectations for students, research and service activities, sources of stress and satisfaction, and the connection between learning in the classroom and practices in the local and global community.

The HERI Faculty Survey is a web-based survey that includes a core survey instrument used by all institutions, with optional modules available. Each institution selects its own sample and has the ability to customize the survey for its administration. The HERI Faculty Survey is designed to be used with all faculty, including full- or part-time, graduate faculty, or administrators with teaching responsibilities.

Optional modules of the survey include brief sets of related items that may be of interest based on an institution's mission, goals, and needs. For example, the STEM Module examines practices and expectations in STEM disciplines, focusing on the use of active learning techniques and faculty values related to STEM majors. Other optional modules include the Campus Climate Module, Academic Advising Module, and Spirituality Module.

Participation in the HERI Faculty Survey entitles institutions to unique institutional reports, including selecting peer comparison groups; an institutional profile; findings broken out by gender, full-time, part-time, and graduate faculty separately; and a data file of within-institution faculty responses.

Results from the HERI Faculty Survey are used in strategic planning, faculty recruitment and retention, faculty development activities, assessment and accreditation, and discussions relating pedagogy to student learning experiences.

Additional information about the Faculty Survey can be obtained from the Higher Education Research Institute website at http://heri.ucla.edu/facoverview.php.

College and University Professional Association for Human Resources

The College and University Professional Association for Human Resources provides leadership on higher education workplace issues in the United States and abroad. Specifically, CUPA serves higher education by providing the knowledge, resources, advocacy, and connections to achieve organizational and workforce excellence. Membership in CUPA includes more than 18,000 human resources professionals and campus leaders at over 1,900 member organizations. Institutions range from 91% of all US doctoral institutions, 77% of all master's institutions, 57% of all bachelor's institutions, and 600 community colleges and specialized institutions.

Faculty in Higher Education Salary Survey

The Faculty in Higher Education Salary Survey, conducted by CUPA on an annual basis, provides comprehensive and current salary data for faculty. The survey is designed to help administrators manage their human resource costs by providing a broad range of salary data to evaluate current faculty salary and compensation budgets. The survey is conducted separately at both four-year and two-year institutions.

The 2014 survey includes salary data by discipline and rank for 234,075 full-time faculty at 792 four-year institutions nationwide, including 178,717 tenured and tenure-track faculty, 51,149 non-tenure-track teaching faculty, and 4,209 non-tenure-track research faculty. Salary data for full-time tenured and tenure-track faculty are collected by discipline for the ranks of professor, associate professor, assistant professor, new assistant professor, and instructor. Data for assistant professors also include the salaries of the new assistant professors. The same ranks are used for non-tenure-track faculty; however, data are not collected separately for new assistant professors, and the instructor category is expanded to include lecturers.

The Faculty in Higher Education Salary Survey is conducted entirely online, using SurveyOnline (SOL), CUPA's web-based data collection and reporting system. Results for the survey can be accessed via a published survey report or by using DataOnDemand (DOD) to conduct advanced analyses.

Additional information about the Faculty in Higher Education Salary Survey can be obtained from the College and University Professional Association for Human Resources website at http://cupahr.org/surveys/fhe4.aspx.

Collaborative on Academic Careers in Higher Education at the Harvard Graduate School of Education

Founded in 2002, the Collaborative on Academic Careers in Higher Education is a research initiative seeking best practices, rooted in sound data, related to the recruitment and management of faculty talent and their own leadership. COACHE is supported by the Ford Foundation and Atlantic Philanthropies and is based at the Harvard Graduate School of Education and is supported by its members.

COACHE is a full-service partner for improving the workplace as academic leaders at over 200 colleges, universities, and systems have strengthened their capacity to identify drivers of faculty success and to implement informed changes. Enrollment in COACHE is open to all four-year colleges and universities with tenure-system faculty.

COACHE Faculty Job Satisfaction Survey

The COACHE Faculty Job Satisfaction Survey seeks to provide actionable and pivotal data that are of immediate use to academic policymakers. COACHE survey instruments are targeted to measure the tenure-stream faculty population's levels of engagement in the teaching, research, and service enterprise at their institutions and to determine how supported and satisfied they are with the terms and conditions of their employment.

The Faculty Job Satisfaction Survey is intended to help participating chief academic officers answer three primary sets of questions:

- How do faculty of different career stages experience academic work life at my institution? How do their experiences compare with those of faculty at peer institutions?
- Do their experiences differ by rank, gender, or race/ethnicity?
- What policies or practices are associated with high levels of faculty satisfaction and vitality?

The primary survey themes include nature of the work (overall, research, teaching, and service); resources and support; interdisciplinary work; collaboration; mentoring; tenure and promotion; institutional governance and leadership; engagement; work and personal life balance; climate, culture, and collegiality; appreciation and recognition; recruitment and retention; and global satisfaction.

Additional information about the Faculty Job Satisfaction Survey can be obtained from the Collaborative on Academic Careers in Higher Education website at http://isites.harvard.edu/icb/icb.do?keyword=coache&pageid=icb.page307142.

Coalition on the Academic Workforce

Founded in 1997, the Coalition on the Academic Workforce comprises twenty-six higher education associations, disciplinary associations, and faculty organizations committed to addressing issues related to deteriorating faculty working conditions and their effect on college and university students in the United States.

The coalition seeks to collect and distribute information related to faculty members in full- and part-time off-tenure-track positions, including the implications for students, parents, faculty members, and institutions. With an emphasis on part-time, adjunct, and similar faculty appointments, CAW's purpose is to explore the extent and consequences, both short- and long-term, of changes in the faculty across disciplines and its relationship with society and the public good. Moreover, CAW intends to promote conditions by which all faculty members can strengthen their teaching and scholarship, better serve their students, and advance their professional careers.

Survey of Contingent Faculty Members and Instructors

Initiated in fall 2010, CAW developed a survey designed to address the lack of data on contingent faculty members and their working conditions, specifically examining the courses these faculty members taught that term, where they were teaching these courses, and for what pay and compensation. The survey yielded approximately 30,000 responses, the majority coming from about 20,000 individuals who identified themselves as working in a contingent position at one or more higher education institutions during the fall 2010 term.

While the majority of responses came from faculty members in contingent roles, the survey was open to any faculty member or instructor. Numbering more than 700,000, the part-time population of faculty members represents more than 70% of the contingent academic workforce and almost half the entire higher education faculty in the United States. Faculty members in part-time positions were the largest group of respondents in the CAW survey, providing 10,331 of the 19,850 responses from contingent faculty members. The responses to the survey provided a rich story of the work patterns, remuneration, and employment conditions for the fastest-growing and presently largest part of the academic workforce.

Additional information about the Survey of Contingent Faculty Members can be obtained from the Coalition on the Academic Workforce website at http://www.academicworkforce.org.

Changing Academic Profession Survey of 2007–08

The Changing Academic Profession Survey, a follow-up to a similar survey first conducted by The Carnegie Foundation for the Advancement of Teaching in the early 1990s, is the largest international comparative study and included participation from twenty countries. Participating countries were Argentina, Australia, Brazil, Canada, China and Hong Kong, Finland, France, Germany, India, Japan, South Korea, Malaysia, Mexico, Norway, Portugal, Russia, South America, The Netherlands, United Kingdom, and the United States.

The survey sought to address the following central questions:

- To what extent is the nature of academic work changing?
- What are the external and internal drivers of these changes?
- To what extent do changes differ across countries, disciplines, and types of higher education institutions?
- How do the academic professions respond to changes in their external and internal environment?
- What are the consequences for the attractiveness of an academic career?
- What are the consequences for the capacity of academics to contribute to the further development of knowledge societies and the attainment of national goals?

The survey was designed to examine the nature and extent of the changes experienced by the academic profession, including the reasoning and consequences of these changes. The survey relied on a six-stage model of change and attempted to make comparisons on these matters among different national higher education systems, institutional types, disciplines, and generations of academics.

Each participating country research team obtained a nationally representative sample of its academic profession. To ensure international comparisons, all countries conformed to the highest standards of sampling and data collection. The study used a self-administered survey instrument that maintained a high level of standardization, specifically related to question order, question wording, response options, reference periods, and layout and format design.

Data collection was completed by the end of 2008 and followed by data entry and cleaning by each country team. The international data set was made available in late 2009.

Additional information about the Changing Academic Profession survey is contained in appendix D below and can be obtained from the LH Martin Institute website at http://www.lhmartininstitute.edu.au/research-and-projects/research/20-the-changing-academic-profession.

Carnegie 1992 International Survey of the Academic Profession

A precursor to the Changing Academic Profession Survey, the International Survey of the Academic Profession, was administered by the Carnegie Foundation for the Advancement of Teaching in 1992. Fourteen countries participated: Korea, Hong Kong, Japan, Australia, Brazil, Chile, Mexico, United States, England, Germany, Netherlands, Russia, Sweden, and Israel. The largest of its kind, the survey included an extensive questionnaire covering seventy-two topics and received 19,472 responses.

In the United States, a two-stage sampling procedure was used to identify a representative sample. Within the United States, twelve top-tier universities and twenty-eight others were initially selected, and a one-on-five random sample within this group yielded 3,528 responses, or a 46% return. Across the fourteen participating countries, response rates were generally between 33 and 50%, with the exception of Russia, at 14%.

The questionnaire included facets related to personal and career data, professional activity (hours and conditions of work, teaching, research, students, access, and governance), and international perception.

Additional information about the 1992 International Survey of the Academic Profession can be obtained from the Carnegie Foundation for the Advancement of Teaching's website at http://www.carnegiefoundation.org.

Oklahoma State University Faculty Salary Survey by Discipline

Since 1974, the Office of Planning, Budget, and Institutional Research at Oklahoma State University has conducted its Faculty Salary Survey by Discipline. Participating institutions include members of the Association of Public and Land-Grant Universities (APLU) that award doctoral degrees in at least five disciplines; primarily the flagship public institutions in each state. The university attempts to include institutions from every state so that a national sample of average public faculty salaries by discipline can be generated.

Of the 147 qualified institutions invited to participate, data from 114 institutions was included in the final 2013–14 report. Institutions are asked to provide data on average, high, and low salaries of faculty. The 2013–14 survey includes two significant changes, including reporting by both Carnegie classification and geographic location and a breakdown by tenure status as reported by institutions. Due to the recent addition of tenure status, not at all institutions supplied this information for 2013–14, but the university expects an increased number of institutions will provide this data in the future.

Salary information is presented annually for all participating institutions and grouped by the 2010 Carnegie Classifications, including Very High Research Activity (VHR), High Research Activity (HR), and Doctoral/Research Activity (DR). To help identify the relationship between average faculty salaries and the salaries of health professionals, the data are provided in three sections: section A, major fields grouped into discipline categories; section B, major fields but excluding health professions; and section C, health professions only. Results from the survey are intended to assist higher education administrators and government officials with salary budget decisions.

Additional information about the Oklahoma State University Faculty Salary Survey by Discipline can be obtained from the Oklahoma State University website at http://irim.okstate.edu/FSS.

Bureau of Labor Statistics Occupational Employment Statistics Survey

The Bureau of Labor Statistics' Occupational Employment Statistics (OES) program produces employment and wage estimates annually for over 800 occupations, which are identified through the Standard Occupational Classification system. The SOC system is used by federal statistical agencies to classify workers into occupational categories for the purpose of collecting, calculating, or disseminating data. All workers are classified into one of 840 detailed occupations according to their occupational definition. To facilitate classification, detailed occupations are combined to form 461 broad occupations, 97 minor groups, and 23 major groups. Detailed occupations in the SOC with similar job duties, and in some cases skills, education, or training, are grouped together. Additional information about the Standard Occupational Classification system can be obtained from http://www.bls.gov/soc/home.htm.

The employment and wage estimates are available for the nation as a whole, for individual states, and for metropolitan and nonmetropolitan areas; national occupational estimates for specific industries are also available. To inform these estimates, the OES program conducts a semi-annual mail survey designed to produce estimates of employment and wages for specific occupations. It is important to note that the OES survey covers all full-time and part-time wage and salary workers in nonfarm industries. The survey does not cover the self-employed, owners and partners in unincorporated firms, household workers, or unpaid family workers.

Methodologically, the Bureau of Labor Statistics produces the survey materials and selects the establishments to be surveyed. The sampling frame (the list from which establishments to be surveyed are selected) is derived from the list of establishments maintained by state workforce agencies for unemployment insurance purposes. Establishments to be surveyed are selected in order to obtain data from every metropolitan and nonmetropolitan area in every state, across all surveyed industries, and from establishments of varying sizes. The workforce agencies mail the survey materials to the selected establishments and make follow-up calls to request data from nonrespondents or to clarify data. Using these procedures, the OES program surveys approximately 200,000 establishments per panel (every six months), taking three years to fully collect the sample of 1.2 million establishments. To reduce respondent burden, the collection is on a three-year survey cycle that ensures that establishments are surveyed at most once every three years.

By utilizing the data captured through these survey administrations, the Bureau of Labor Statistics produces occupational employment and wage estimates for over 450 industry classifications at the national level. These industry classifications correspond to the sector, three-, four-, and selected five- and six-digit NAICS industrial groups.

The NAICS is a two- through six-digit hierarchical classification system, offering five levels of detail. Each digit in the code is part of a series of progressively narrower categories, and the more digits in the code signify greater classification detail.

The first two digits designate the economic sector, the third digit designates the subsector, the fourth digit designates the industry group, the fifth digit designates the NAICS industry, and the sixth digit designates the national industry. The five-digit NAICS code is the level at which there is comparability in code and definitions for most of the NAICS sectors across the three countries participating in NAICS (the United States, Canada, and Mexico). The six-digit level allows for the United States, Canada, and Mexico each to have country-specific detail. A complete and valid NAICS code contains six digits. Additional information on NAICS, the specific codes used for each industry, and its history, can be obtained at http://www.census.gov/eos/www/naics/index.html.

The OES program is the only comprehensive source of regularly produced occupational employment and wage rate information for the US economy, as well as states, the District of Columbia, Guam, Puerto Rico, the US Virgin Islands, and all metropolitan and nonmetropolitan areas in each State.

Occupational Employment Statistics data are used by several government programs, such as the Bureau of Labor Statistics' Employment Projections program, the Employment and Training Administration, and the Employment Standards Administration. Furthermore, OES data are used to establish the fixed employment weights for the Employment Cost Index and in the calculation of occupational rates for the Survey of Occupational Injuries and Illnesses.

Also, employment and wage data for detailed science, engineering, mathematical, and other occupations are provided to the National Science Foundation, along with the complete staffing patterns for all industries. Finally, employment and wage data are used by academic and government researchers to study labor markets and wage and employment trends.

Additional information about the OES program can be obtained from the US Department of Labor's Bureau of Labor Statistics website at http://www.bls.gov/oes.

TIAA-CREF and the TIAA-CREF Institute

TIAA-CREF is a national financial services organization with $613 billion in total assets under management as of June 2014. It is the leading provider of retirement services in the academic, research, medical, and cultural fields. The TIAA-CREF Institute seeks to advance the manner in which individuals and institutions plan for financial security and organizational effectiveness. The TIAA-CREF Institute conducts in-depth research, provides access to a network of thought leaders, and enables those it serves to anticipate trends, plan future strategies, and maximize opportunities for future success.

Retirement Confidence Survey

In response to concern by public sector workers regarding retirement security, the TIAA-CREF Institute and the Center for State and Local Government Excellence completed the most recent Retirement Confidence Survey of the State and Local Government Workforce in 2014. The report's findings are based on a telephone survey of 1,263 government employees, including teachers, police, and firefighters, who described their retirement planning and saving experiences and their confidence in their ability to draw income in retirement. Of those surveyed in 2014, 507 were K–12 teachers, 102 were firefighters, 153 were policy officers, and 501 were in other occupations. Responses were weighted to be representative of the aggregate public sector workforce.

Additional information about the TIAA-CREF Retirement Confidence Survey can be obtained from the TIAA-CREF Institute's website at https://www.tiaa-crefinstitute.org/public/institute/research.

National Center for the Study of Collective Bargaining in Higher Education and the Professions

The National Center for the Study of Collective Bargaining in Higher Education is housed and supported by the City University of New York–Hunter College and its five hundred institutional and individual members. The center provides a clearinghouse and forum for scholarly research and ideas concerning labor relations, collective bargaining, and labor law issues related to higher education. It has published directories of faculty contracts, bibliographies on collective bargaining topics, and scholarly journals and newsletters since its inception in 1972.

The Directory of US Faculty Contracts and Bargaining Agents in Institutions of Higher Education is a compilation of statistical analyses of full- and part-time faculty and graduate student employee collective bargaining agreements throughout the United States. The most recent edition of the directory was published in 2012 and encompasses 368,473 faculty members across 639 separate bargaining units and distributed across 519 institutions or systems of higher education on 1,174 campuses. This represents a 14% increase compared with the total published in the 2006 directory.

Additional information about the Directory of US Faculty Contracts and Bargaining Agents in Institutions of Higher Education can be obtained from the National Center for the Study of Collective Bargaining in Higher Education and the Professions' website at http://www.hunter.cuny.edu/ncscbhep/.

NOTES

1. In 2008, the National Center for Education Statistics abandoned plans to continue its twice a decade National Study of Postsecondary Faculty, first initiated in 1988, and has since limited its national data collection to a few basic demographics in the Integrated Postsecondary Education Data System (IPEDS), including numbers of full and part-time faculty, their distribution by gender and race/ethnicity, and their salaries collected biennially.

2. The NSOPF:04 Faculty Questionnaire underwent significant shortening from the 1999 version, especially in areas of career history.

3. The NSF is actively engaged at the present in exploring the development of longitudinal weighting procedures. Connolly, Mark R., You-Geon Lee, and Julia N. Savoy (2015) constructed a weighted data file using the Survey of Doctorate Recipients in their "*Faculty Hiring and Tenure by Sex and Race: New Evidence from a National Survey*" presentation

at the Annual Meeting of the American Educational Research Association in Chicago, IL.

4. Since 2006–07, HERI has begun to include two-year community college faculty

REFERENCES

Altbach, Philip G., ed. 1996. *The International Academic Profession: Portraits of Fourteen Countries.* Princeton, NJ: Carnegie Foundation for the Advancement of Teaching.

Altbach, Philip G. and Jamil Salmi. 2011. *The Road to Academic Excellence: The Making of World Class Research Universities.* Washington, DC: The World Bank.

Connolly, Mark R., You-Geon Lee, and Julia N. Savoy. 2015. "Faculty Hiring and Tenure by Sex and Race: New Evidence from a National Survey." Paper presented at the Annual Meeting of the American Educational Research Association, Chicago, IL, April 16–20.

Schuster, Jack and Martin Finkelstein. 2006. *The American Faculty: The Restructuring of Academic Work and Careers.* Baltimore, MD: Johns Hopkins University Press.

Yudkevich, Maria, Philip G. Altbach, and Laura Rumbley, eds. 2015. *Young Faculty in the Twenty-First Century: International Perspectives.* Albany, NY: State University of New York Press.

Appendix B

PhD PRODUCTION AND DISTRIBUTION TRENDS

By way of background, our modal story of new PhDs taking up academic careers begins with some basic context about supply: trends in doctoral education and degree attainment. As can be seen from table B.1, the United States produced 52,749 doctorates in 2013,[1] of which 39,000 (74%) were in the STEM fields[2] (including psychology and the social sciences, *N*=8,400, or just over one-fifth—21.5%—of the STEM total) and 13,800 (26%) in non-STEM fields. While they represent an overall 33% increase over 1993 (39,505) and over 2003 (40,766), the non-STEM fields grew by only 3.6%, with the exception of the humanities fields, where the number of doctorates increased by the group average (33%) while the STEM fields increased by about 27.3%.[3] So, in some sense, doctoral degree production has grown modestly over the past two decades, distributed among those fields where the best jobs are—with the exception of the humanities. Its differential growth in disciplinary mix has reflected the richer opportunities in the STEM fields and conversely the more limited opportunities in the non-STEM fields, including education.

Changing Demographics

Irrespective of the overall numbers, what about the composition of the PhD supply pool? Three basic highlights are clear from the National Science Foundation's annual Survey of Earned Doctorates. First, the proportion of women has increased from 38.5% in 1993 to 46% in 2013. The presence of women increased in both the STEM and non-STEM fields, although the increase in the STEM fields was smaller and women still constitute a minority of STEM doctorates (about 25%). Second, the number of doctorates awarded to temporary visa holders grew by more than 50% between 1993–2013, with the lion's share of increase over the past decade. Third, doctoral recipients are getting older: the median age of PhD recipients in 2010 reached thirty-three (compared with thirty-two a decade earlier), and this despite a decline since 1985 of more than a year in the average time to degree from entry into graduate school to degree award.[4] Moreover, that figure conceals enormous variation by field: in physics the median age was twenty-nine, while in the humanities, several of the social sciences and education, it was closer to thirty-eight. That means that PhD

Table B.1 Number of PhD awarded by gender, race, citizenship, and academic fields, 1993, 2003, 2013

	1993	2003	% change (1993–2003)	2013	% change (2003–13)	% change (1993–2013)
All fields						
Gender	39,505	40,766	3.2	52,749	29.4	33.5
Male	24,384	22,257	−8.7	28,353	27.4	16.3
Female	15,121	18,509	22.4	24,396	31.8	61.3
Race or ethnicity	28,722	28,172	−1.9	33,942	20.5	18.2
Asian	2,005	2,033	1.4	2,888	42.1	44.0
URM	2,372	3,658	54.2	5,270	44.1	122.2
White	24,040	21,162	−12.0	24,739	16.9	2.9
Citizenship	39,800	40,766	2.4	52,760	29.4	32.6
U.S. citizen or permanent resident	28,722	28,172	−1.9	33,942	20.5	18.2
Temporary visa holder	9,964	10,595	6.3	15,678	48.0	57.3
Unknown citizenship	1,114	1,999	79.4	3,140	57.1	181.9
Life sciences	7,416	8,508	14.7	12,302	44.6	65.9
Male	4,312	4,398	2.0	5,495	24.9	27.4
Female	3,104	4,110	32.4	6,807	65.6	119.3
Physical sciences	6,358	5,831	−8.3	9,287	59.3	46.1
Male	5,034	4,286	−14.9	6,589	53.7	30.9
Female	1,324	1,545	16.7	2,698	74.6	103.8
Social sciences	6,725	7,004	4.1	8,400	19.9	24.9
Male	3,378	3,117	−7.7	3,419	9.7	1.2
Female	3,347	3,887	16.1	4,981	28.1	48.8
Engineering	5,619	5,280	−6.0	8,961	69.7	59.5
Male	5,097	4,368	−14.3	6,910	58.2	35.6
Female	522	912	74.7	2,051	124.9	292.9
Education	6,669	6,651	−0.3	4,944	−25.7	−25.9
Male	2,748	2,256	−17.9	1,575	−30.2	−42.7
Female	3,921	4,395	12.1	3,369	−23.3	−14.1
Humanities	4,244	5,192	22.3	5,661	9.0	33.4
Male	2,235	2,565	14.8	2,760	7.6	23.5
Female	2,009	2,627	30.8	2,901	10.4	44.4
Other						
Male	1,580	1,267	−19.8	1,605	26.7	1.6
Female	894	1,033	15.5	1,589	53.8	77.7

Source: NSF/NIH/USED/USDA/NEH/NASA, Survey of Earned Doctorates (1993, 2003, 2013).

recipients are embarking on an academic career later in their thirties than one or two decades ago, and among them, some are a bit earlier while others are much later.

This later finding becomes particularly significant when we add one other fact to the demographic portrait: women PhDs are more likely to be married than they were one to two decades earlier (Schuster and Finkelstein 2006). Taken together with the increase in median age at PhD receipt and the fact that women actually take on average one-half to one year longer to earn their degree than men, we see that the increasing pool of PhD women is arriving at the entry portal to an academic career married and near the upper limit of child-bearing age. This spawns a heightened "family" consciousness among newly entering academic women and a rising concern about work-family balance issues.

These sorts of concerns are reinforced more generally by the emerging character of the millennial generation—those born after 1980 and coming to academic age now in the second decade of the twenty-first century. In 1969 the American faculty was dominated by members of the World War II generation, and the newest recruits were members of the baby boom generation. It is the baby boom generation that are now at the end of their careers, being replaced at once by Generation Xers and members of the millennial generation (Howe and Strauss 2000). This is a generation focused more self-consciously on family and work-life balance issues, a generation focused on teamwork and service in the name of the greater good. They pose a distinct challenge to the traditional norms of "blurring" lines between work and personal life and the valorization of professional autonomy above all else (see Howe and Strauss 2000). Anecdotal evidence suggests that they are less willing to sacrifice everything on the altar of work. Moreover, there are behavioral data that suggest that women and minority faculty are leaving academic jobs at a higher rate than white men, although the actual magnitude of that rate is not clear (Trower 2002, cited by Gappa et al. 2007; Leslie 2007; see also chapters 4 and 5 supra).

Intellectual Quality

A generation ago, Bowen and Schuster (1986) first sounded the alarm about the risk posed to the future American academic profession of the "best and brightest" young Americans forsaking academic careers for the more rewarding career prospects of business, medicine, and law. To that end, they examined the careers of intellectual elites, including Rhodes and Marshall Scholarship winners, members of academic honor societies, such as Phi Beta Kappa, and the graduates of America's most elite private colleges as revealed in surveys of the Consortium for Finance of Higher Education. While the evidence was mixed, and while there was no doubt that academic careers were being less frequently chosen by college students than they had been during the 1960s, nonetheless a survey of the chairs of the leading university departments in eight disciplines showed that the quality of "new hires" continued to be impressive, and indeed there had been no perceived decline in the intellectual quality of such new entrants. More recently, Schuster and Finkelstein (2006) resurveyed leading graduate departments at US research universities and reported no perceived

Table B.2 Employment sector of doctoral recipients with definite employment commitments, 1990–2010

Sector and year of commitment	Total	Life sciences*	Physical sciences*	Social sciences*	Engineering	Education	Humanities
				Number			
All US employment commitments							
1990	15,239	1,325	1,780	2,935	1,872	4,020	1,922
1995	15,303	1,456	1,666	2,736	1,890	3,913	2,178
2000	17,246	1,949	2,033	3,116	2,335	3,907	2,575
2005	15,658	1,713	1,785	2,731	2,129	3,550	2,399
2010	14,429	1,763	1,849	2,644	2,025	2,794	1,984
				Percentage			
Academe							
1990	51.5	48.5	38.7	50.3	26.3	46.4	83.2
1995	52.4	51.4	41.8	53.4	19.1	48.3	82.8
2000	48.6	46.0	33.7	51.6	14.8	47.9	79.3
2005	54.3	53.2	40.6	61.7	18.5	50.2	83.0
2010	52.6	49.0	35.9	59.9	16.9	53.4	81.7
Government							
1990	8.8	16.3	8.3	12.8	11.9	7.2	2.2
1995	8.1	14.1	8.6	12.5	10.9	6.0	1.8
2000	7.4	13.6	5.8	11.5	9.0	4.6	2.0
2005	6.9	12.7	6.6	10.1	9.3	4.1	2.3
2010	8.9	14.5	9.8	13.9	12.8	3.5	2.3

Industry and business*							
1990	21.9	26.4	50.6	18.4	59.1	6.2	4.7
1995	21.7	24.5	45.3	16.4	66.1	6.0	5.1
2000	26.1	28.9	54.7	17.7	72.9	5.7	6.5
2005	22.8	25.3	48.7	14.4	68.7	4.1	4.2
2010	23.2	24.6	48.1	13.7	64.4	4.5	4.9
Not-for-profit organization							
1990	6.7	7.3	1.6	13.3	2.2	5.7	5.7
1995	6.3	7.3	2.2	11.5	2.2	5.1	5.8
2000	5.9	6.9	2.0	11.5	1.8	4.6	6.0
2005	5.3	7.1	2.5	8.8	2.3	4.3	6.2
2010	5.2	8.4	2.7	7.2	3.2	4.4	4.9
Other or unknown*							
1990	11.1	1.5	0.8	5.2	0.5	34.5	4.1
1995	11.4	2.7	2.1	6.2	1.6	34.6	4.5
2000	12.0	4.6	2.8	7.8	1.5	37.2	6.1
2005	10.7	1.8	1.6	5.0	1.2	37.3	4.3
2010	10.1	3.5	3.5	5.3	2.7	34.1	6.2

Source: NSF/NIH/USED/USDA/NEH/NASA, 2010 Survey of Earned Doctorates.

*Life sciences includes agricultural sciences/natural resources, biological/biomedical sciences, and health sciences. Physical sciences includes mathematics and information sciences. Social sciences includes psychology.

decline in the quality of either current doctoral students or recent hires. Moreover, they found that after a serious decline in the 1980s, a slightly growing, and stable, percentage of US college freshman were aspiring to careers as college teachers (albeit still less than 3%). They concluded that while the evidence was not dispositive, there was no compelling basis for estimating that the quality of the academic profession was deteriorating in the near or medium term. And in light of both the continued infusion of foreign talent to American graduate education chronicled in chapter 3 (typically the global "best and brightest") and the increasing number of women with doctorates, the prospects for maintaining the intellectual quality of the new academic generation shows no signs of decline, and perhaps even suggests the potential to be strengthened.

Moving from PhD Receipt to the Job Market: Historical Trends

In the halcyon days of the 1960s and 1970s, prospective academics were often plucked out of graduate school by the age of thirty, while still completing their doctoral dissertations for full-time, tenure-track positions with excellent career prospects. That is no longer the case. Table B.2 shows the employment sector of doctoral-degree recipients with definite employment commitments between 1990–2010.[5] A glance at the table suggests at least two clear trends. First, in the aggregate, there is remarkable durability in immediate postgraduate employment plans of doctorates over the past twenty years: about half typically enter academe in some capacity, about one-fifth to one-quarter enter industry and less than a tenth enter government or the nonprofit sector. Second, there is enormous variation in employment sector by academic field: at one end of the spectrum, nearly four-fifths of humanities doctorates enter academe (closely followed by social science doctorates, at three-fifths), while at the other end, less than one-fifth of engineering doctorates do so (closely followed by physical science doctorates at one-third). It is important to note that while half of new PhDs move into academe upon degree receipt, the move is not necessarily into career-ladder faculty positions. In 2010, for example, among 13,000 science and engineering doctoral recipients with definite plans, 48.8% were planning postdoctoral study, 18.7% academic employment, 13.7% other (elementary or secondary education, government, nonprofit), 13.1% industry, and 5.3% work abroad. Most of the academic sector employment reported, at least initially, is either in postdoctoral fellowship positions or in other nonregular positions, including part-time and fixed-contract full-time instructional or research positions as well as administrative positions (see chapter 4).

NOTES

1. This N=52,749 refers to the number of academic PhD degrees in the disciplines and generally excludes professional doctorates, for example, MD, JD, DDS, DBA, PysD, which constitute approximately an additional 100,000 annually.

2. STEM is the acronym coined by the National Science Foundation in the United States to refer to science-, technology-, engineering-, and mathematics-related disciplines.

3. The number of non-STEM doctorates actually declined from 15,400 to 14,900, but that was accounted for largely by the decline in education doctorates (EdD), which

are no longer counted as research PhD for National Science Foundation purposes. Even after the EdD reclassification, education remained the largest non-science-and-engineering field, reporting 5,294 doctorates awarded in 2010. Over the past decade, doctoral degrees in non-science-and-engineering fields (other than education) increased 7.5%. The number of doctorates awarded in health sciences showed substantial growth (32.7%) over this period, as did the number of doctorates in other non-science-and-engineering fields (27.9%).

4. While now averaging 7.7 years, there is considerable variation by field, ranging from 6.7 years in the physical sciences to 12.5 years in education, closely followed by 9.3 years in the humanities. Given that individuals typically enter graduate study two years after receipt of the baccalaureate degree, and that the baccalaureate degree is typically earned in the early twenties, doctoral recipients are on average in their early thirties at degree receipt, younger in the physical sciences and engineering and significantly older in education and the humanities.

5. It should be noted that only about one-third of doctoral recipients annually typically have definite employment commitments on which to report at the time of degree award, so this may not reflect a representative sample.

REFERENCES

Bowen, Howard R., and Jack H. Schuster. 1986. *American Professors: A National Resource Imperiled.* New York: Oxford University Press.

Howe, Neil, and William Strauss. 2000. *Millennials Rising: The Next Great Generation.* New York: Vintage Books.

Leslie, David W. 2007. "The Re-Shaping of America's Academic Workforce." *TIAA-CREF Research Dialogue* 87 (March): 3–23.

Schuster, Jack H., and Martin J. Finkelstein. 2006. *The American Faculty: The Restructuring of Academic Work and Careers.* Baltimore, MD: Johns Hopkins University Press.

Appendix C

RACE AND ETHNICITY CLASSIFICATIONS: AN UPDATE

In *The American Faculty*, we identified challenges that evolving sensibilities and historical realities pose for analysis and discussion of trends in race and ethnicity. Approaches to classification had changed several times during the thirty-five years covered in the earlier volume, including changes in terms applied to identify racial/ethnic groups and analytical distinctions drawn between race qua race and ethnicity (usually in terms of geographic or cultural origin). Moreover, beyond differences in categorization and terminology applied to individual subgroups, there are issues of small *N*s that frequently require that researchers aggregate racial/ethnic subgroups into uber categories, such as underrepresented racial minorities, for analysis.

In this volume, our tabulations of race/ethnicity align with the categories for collecting and reporting data to the federal government. Before 1997, the US Department of Education's National Center for Education Statistics (NCES) used the following definition of race/ethnicity in its Integrated Postsecondary Education Data System (IPEDS): "Race/ethnicity (old definition) Categories used to describe groups to which individuals belong, identify with, or belong in the eyes of the community. The categories do not denote scientific definitions of anthropological origins. A person may be counted in only one group. The groups used to categorize U.S. citizens, resident aliens, and other eligible noncitizens are as follows: Black, non-Hispanic, American Indian/Alaska Native, Asian/Pacific Islander, Hispanic, White, non-Hispanic" (National Center for Education Statistics 2015).

In 1997, the Office of Management and Budget announced final guidance on the collection and reporting of race/ethnicity categories in the Federal Register (see *Final Guidance on Maintaining, Collecting, and Reporting Racial and Ethnic Data to the U.S. Department of Education*), and revisions to the standards on its website (Office of Management and Budget 1997). The updated definition for race/ethnicity in the IPEDS Glossary is:

> Race/ethnicity: Categories developed in 1997 by the Office of Management and Budget (OMB) that are used to describe groups to which individuals belong, identify with, or belong in the eyes of the community. The categories do not

denote scientific definitions of anthropological origins. The designations are used to categorize U.S. citizens, resident aliens, and other eligible non-citizens. Individuals are asked to first designate ethnicity as: Hispanic or Latino, or Not Hispanic or Latino. Second, individuals are asked to indicate all races that apply among the following:

- American Indian or Alaska Native
- Asian
- Black or African American
- Native Hawaiian or Other Pacific Islander
- White (National Center for Education Statistics 2015).

The specific definitions for the new race and ethnicity categories are:

- Hispanic or Latino—a person of Cuban, Mexican, Puerto Rican, South or Central American, or other Spanish culture or origin, regardless of race; or
- Not Hispanic or Latino

Second, individuals are asked to indicate one or more races that apply among the following:

- American Indian or Alaska Native—a person having origins in any of the original peoples of North and South America (including Central America) who maintains cultural identification through tribal affiliation or community attachment.
- Asian—a person having origins in any of the original peoples of Far East, Southeast Asia, or the Indian Subcontinent, including, for example, Cambodia, China, India, Japan, Korea, Malaysia, Pakistan, the Philippine Islands, Thailand, and Vietnam.
- Black or African American—a person having origins in any of the black racial groups of Africa.
- Native Hawaiian or Other Pacific Islander—a person having origins in any of the original peoples of Hawaii, Guam, Samoa, or other Pacific Islands,
- White—a person having origins in any of the original peoples of Europe, the Middle East, or North Africa.
- Nonresident alien—a person who is not a citizen or national of the United States and who is in this country on a visa or temporary basis and does not have the right to remain indefinitely.

Note: Nonresident aliens are to be reported separately in the places provided, rather than in any of the racial/ethnicity categories described above (National Center for Education Statistics 2015).

In this volume, we have identified five racial categories as follows: White, non-Hispanic; African American or Black; Latino, nonwhite; Native American; Asian and Pacific Islander. For analytical purposes, we have aggregated the three categories of

Black or African American, Latino nonwhite, and Native American into the aggregated category of Underrepresented Racial Minorities (URM), following the convention employed by the National Science Foundation in its annual publication, *Science and Engineering Indicators*. The URM category is then juxtaposed with White and Asian/Pacific Islander as the three-fold classification for most of our analyses in chapter 3. In other chapters, the numbers have been insufficient, for the most part, to allow us to conduct analyses by race,—even with aggregated, uber categories. It should be noted that the 1997 OMB *Revisions to the Standards for Classification of Federal Data on Race and Ethnicity* directed that the Asian or Pacific Islander category be separated into two categories: Asian and Native Hawaiian or Other Pacific Islander (Office of Management and Budget, 1997). We have aggregated Pacific Islanders into the Asian category, however, for at least two reasons: it is not always possible to separate out Pacific Islanders from the combined Asian/Pacific Islander category as it appears in some instruments; and the numbers are too small to affect either the Asian or the URM category.

The major innovation in our treatment of race/ethnicity, however, has been in distinguishing between race/ethnicity, on the one hand, and nativity, on the other. Specifically, the concept of URM assumes that members of a give racial or ethnic group are native born and, as such, have been socially and economically disadvantaged over a lifetime by their race/ethnicity in the US context. However, the number of foreign-born scholars, as we noted in chapter 3, has been growing considerably, and they have tended to be classified based on their race/ethnicity with native-born citizens. As our colleague Daryl Smith has noted (Smith et al. 2012), when we disaggregate the recently arrived, foreign born from those who were born and educated in the United States, the numbers of URMs changes dramatically. Most of these racially diverse, foreign-born and foreign-educated faculty members appear in institutional records as nonresident aliens. Nonresident aliens are defined as foreign-born, non-US citizens who have not qualified for a green card. Foreign nationals who have received a green card are classified as resident aliens.

REFERENCES

National Center for Education Statistics (NCES). 2015. "IPEDS 2015–16 Survey Materials: Glossary." https://surveys.nces.ed.gov/ipeds/Downloads/Forms/IPEDSGlossary.pdf, Washington, DC: National Center for Education Statistics.

Office of Management and Budget. 1997. "Revisions to the Standards for the Classification of Federal Data on Race and Ethnicity." https://www.whitehouse.gov/omb/fedreg_1997standards. *Federal Register Notice*, October 30, 1997, Washington, DC: Office of Management and Budget.

Smith, Daryl G., Esau Tovar, and Hugo Garcia. 2012. "Where Are They? A Multilens Examination of the Distribution of Full-Time Faculty by Institutional Type, Race/Ethnicity, Gender, and Citizenship." *New Directions for Institutional Research* 155 (Fall): 5–26.

Appendix D

CHANGING ACADEMIC PROFESSIONS SURVEY, 2007–08:

METHODOLOGY

This appendix describes the framework underlying the Changing Academic Profession Survey of 2007–08 (CAP), the sampling and data collection procedures as well as the nature of the survey instrument. While it provides a general conceptual and methodological backdrop for the entire international initiative involving nineteen individual national studies, we focus here on the methodological details of the on-line US survey.

Conceptual Framework: A General Systems Model

The 2007–08 CAP survey sought to examine the nature and extent of the changes experienced by the academic profession in recent years, drawing in part on comparisons of current developments with those documented in the first International Survey of the Academic Profession conducted in 1991–92. The project proposed a six-stage model for the investigation of change in the academic profession that draws substantially on general systems theory (see Bess and Dee 2008; Astin 1985). We differentiated the larger environment of higher education institutions into drivers (macro social and economic trends, e.g., globalization of the world economy, that were broadly reshaping national economies, workforce requirements, and higher education research and training objectives) and conditions to describe the concrete structures, including institutional mission differentiation, stakeholder identification, and financing mechanisms, that became the proximate environment for institutions of higher education. We conceptualized the throughput as including beliefs of both internal and external stakeholders about institutional goals, priorities, and appropriate instrumentalities and roles and practices, that is, the division of academic labor, the perceived interrelationships among the basic components of teaching, research, and service, and perceptions about the structure and trajectory of academic careers. Finally, in our model, we distinguished between *outputs*, by which we meant the proximate products of teaching, research, and service at the individual and institutional levels, and *outcomes*, by which we meant the macro consequences for the larger system.

Research Questions Addressed

Within the context of this model of change, the CAP study addressed six research questions.

1. To what extent is the nature of academic work and the trajectory of academic careers changing?
2. What are the external and internal drivers of these changes?
3. To what extent do changes differ between countries and types of higher education institution?
4. How have the academic professions responded—attitudinally and behaviorally—to changes in their external and internal environment?
5. What are the consequences of the changes and faculty responses to them for the attractiveness of an academic career?
6. What are the consequences for the capacity of academics—and their universities—to contribute to the further development of knowledge societies and the attainment of national goals?

Participating Countries

The following nineteen countries participated by conducting national surveys during 2007–08 with a common sampling frame and instrument: Argentina, Australia, Brazil, Canada, China, Hong Kong,[1] Finland, Germany, Italy, Japan, Malaysia, Mexico, Netherlands, Norway, Portugal, South Africa, South Korea, the United Kingdom, and the United States.

Sample Design of the US Survey

The universe of four-year colleges and universities in the United States was stratified by two characteristics: size and degree level and control. A total of eighty institutions were selected from among four strata (defined by large graduate, public; large graduate, private; small undergraduate, public; small undergraduate, private) and their faculty lists secured. Having determined the proportion of academic staff in the population in each of the four institutional strata so defined, a random sample of faculty was selected within each institutional stratum so as to approximate their proportions in the population. This approach yielded a total sample of 5,772 faculty at eighty four-year colleges and universities across the United States.

Following completion of the survey of four-year institutions to correspond with other national samples, a second sample of two-year community college faculty was drawn with the goal of replicating the survey with this supplemental sample. The sampling method for the US two-year colleges was a random sample of all regionally accredited (public and private) community colleges (*N*=1,685) stratified by the five accreditation regions (Northeast, Southeast, Midwest, Southwest, and West). The faculty sent surveys were selected by systematic random sample of the full-time faculty as listed on the website for the community college. This approach yielded a total sample of 1,000 faculty at two-year colleges across the United States.

Development of the Survey Instrument

Several sets of considerations underlay the design of the survey instrument. In terms of item content, the design sought to include a critical mass of questions related to each of the CAP project's three major themes: relevance, internationalization, and managerialism. The items on managerialism, which included perceptions of the power and influence in campus decision making (governance) of various internal and external constituencies, institutional policies and practices on budgeting, evaluation of academic personnel, their teaching and research, and faculty self-perceptions of their own power and influence in their institutions and local academic units, were consolidated in one of six sections of the survey. Items related to faculty internationalization, on the other hand, were distributed over what became separate sections on faculty teaching and research activities, respectively, as well as on a career history and mobility and on their demographic background (including citizenship and education background). Similarly, items related to the relevance theme were distributed over the separate sections on faculty teaching and research activities as well as over their career history.

A second set of considerations derived from considerations of the modes available for assessing change over time on a wide variety of dimensions of academic work and careers. We identified at least three approaches to assessing change: questions that directly inquired about changes or the degree of change since the respondent's initial entry into full-time academic work; questions posed in 2007–08 that replicated word for word those asked in the earlier 1992 Carnegie International surveys, which would allow for direct comparisons between years; and disaggregating responses to 2007 survey items by career age (stage) to allow for generational comparisons.[2] In the first case, we planned to cross-tabulate perceptions of change with respondent career age (stage), allowing us to align level of perceived change with years of experience in the profession (effectively partialing out any "experience" effect). In the case of repeated earlier questions, we sought in particular to include verbatim a number of items directly from the 1991–92 First International Survey of the Academic Profession conducted by Philip Altbach and Ernest Boyer under the auspices of the Carnegie Foundation for the Advancement of Teaching. This would allow for comparisons across countries on the very same items (Altbach 1996). Finally, based on the earlier work of Finkelstein, Seal, and Schuster (1998), we sought to apply what had proved to be an illuminating lens of generational analysis to the assessment and interpretation of change.

A third set of considerations stemmed directly from the comparative focus of the project. In order to draw comparisons across national systems, we needed to pose questions that allowed for the development of common metrics and equivalencies across national systems. That required us to pose questions in a form or format that would be answerable across very different contexts and systems. Thus, for example, we allowed each national team to specify its own national systems for academic rank, and based on these national designations we later were able to group positions in terms of senior rank versus junior rank. A final set of considerations concerned survey length. Previous experience with national surveys had suggested that an instrument requiring any more than thirty to forty minutes for completion would seriously depress response rates. We strove therefore to limit the length of the instrument, cutting out questions that were deemed nonessential. A copy of the final US instrument is available in Cummings and Finkelstein's *Scholars in the Changing American Academy* (2011).

The nineteen CAP countries agreed to a core set of items that defined a common instrument employed by all nineteen national teams. Individual countries were allowed, however, to supplement the common instrument with questions deemed especially critical or relevant to their individual system. The United States, Canada, and Mexico teams, in light of the recent NAFTA and GATT treaties, sought to include a number of questions focused specifically on academic collaboration across these internal North American boundaries.

Data Collection

The U.S. team contracted with the Research Services Division of the Statistical Package for the Social Sciences (SPSS) to program and host the on-line American English version of the CAP survey. The survey link with an individually coded identifier was e-mailed to all 5,772 faculty on October 3, 2007. A total of five reminders were sent out electronically between October 15 and December 7, 2007. In March 2008, a paper version of the survey was mailed to approximately 1,000 of the nonrespondents in an effort to capture additional responses from those who were unwilling to respond to an on-line survey.

Response Rate

Ultimately, a total of 1,146 responses were received from faculty at seventy-eight four-year institutions for an effective response rate of 21.4 percent. Table D.1 provides a comparison of our respondents to the entire sample. It suggests that our respondents mirror the basic distribution of the sample between research universities and other four-year institutions. Among other four-year institutions, however, faculty at doctorate-granting universities tend to be overrepresented among respondents (32.2% vs. 17.6% in the sample) and faculty at baccalaureate colleges tend to be underrepresented among respondents (3.5% vs. 10.4% in the faculty sample). Faculty at public institutions are slightly overrepresented among respondents (67.1%) compared with the sample (62.4%) and faculty in the private sector slightly underrepresented among respondents (32.9%) compared with the faculty sample (37.6%). Based on these findings, the data file was weighted to ensure that respondents represented the distribution of US faculty across institutional types. Of the 1,000 surveys that were distributed to two-year institutions, 252 faculty responded from seventy-five two-year institutions.

Table D.1 US four-year faculty sample and respondents by institutional type

	Institutional sample			Faculty sample		Respondents	
Institution type	Total	Public	Private	*N*	%	Total	%
Research universities	29	21	8	2,718	47.1	499	46.0
Other four-year	51	26	25	3,054	52.9	585	54.0
Doctor granting	11	6	5	1,014	17.6	349	32.2
Master offering	28	17	11	1,440	24.9	260	24.0
Baccalaureate	12	3	9	600	10.4	38	3.5
All	80	47	33	5,772	100.0	1,084	100.0

Source: 2009 CAP US data file.

Recent work by Groves (2007) and Groves and Peytcheva (2008) has reinforced the notion that visibly low response rates do not necessarily indicate sample bias. Indeed, they recently proposed a number of strategies to test for sample bias in studies with relatively low response rates. Two of their proposed strategies were particularly appropriate for this study. They include comparing basic frequencies of demographic and career variables as well as bivariate measures of association between the focal study and more robust, large sample studies in the literature; and comparing frequency and cross-tabulations between the weighted and unweighted files of the focal study in order to determine the magnitude and significance of the differences between the two data files. To the extent that differences are minimal, the inferences, they argue, can be made that sample bias is not affecting the findings.

For the first set of comparisons, we examined the following variable values in our focal study in both unweighted and weighted data files and compared their values with the population estimates obtained from the National Study of Postsecondary Faculty, 2004: gender (% female), institutional type (% research university), academic rank (% associate and full professors), type of appointment (% tenured or tenure eligible), and academic field (% natural sciences and engineering). As reported in table D.2, we found the following:

Table D.2 US Faculty sample estimates and NSOPF:04 population parameters (percentage)

	CAP (weighted)	CAP (unweighted)	NSOPF 2004
Gender: female	37.8	41.9	37.4
Institutional type: res + PhD	67.0	74.0	65.1
Discipline: natural science + engineering	28.2	23.0	29.9
Appointment type: tenure track	72.0	82.9	75.6
Rank: full + associate	55.0	64.9	54.5

Source: 2009 CAP US data file; NSOPF:04.

The results above suggest that the weighted sample of respondents for this study approximates the parameters of the national faculty population as estimated by the National Study of Postsecondary Faculty 2004 (US Department of Education 2006) with respect to gender, academic field, type of appointment, academic rank and institutional type. We conclude that in our US survey, our relatively low response rate of 21.4 percent was not associated with significant sample bias.

Data Coding and Analysis

Coding

An international codebook was created for the core survey by a team of research associates at the INCHER at Kassel University in Germany. Requirements for international comparability of the various national data files, including the US dataset, required a number of coding modifications to accommodate differences in terminology across national systems. Thus, for example, differences in how various national systems operationalize academic ranks required that we collapse academic rank categories in the US data file to senior (associate and full professor) and junior (assistant professor and other). Similarly, despite the rather high level of institutional differentiation in the US system by international standards,[3] the institutional type variables were tri-chotomized as university—specifically including Research I and II universities and PhD Granting I and II universities in the traditional Carnegie scheme (Carnegie Council 1994)—other four-year institutions, and two-year institutions.[4]

Data Analysis

Basic frequencies were computed on all items from the weighted data file. Beyond these basic frequencies, cross-tabulations of focal variables in any given analysis were computed against some key control variables, including institutional type (coded as indicated above), academic field, gender, type of appointment (tenured or tenure track versus limited term). Beyond such basic descriptive statistics, several of the analyses reported in this volume, notably those in chapters 10 and 11, include the use of regression analysis. The details of those analyses are described in the individual chapters.

Missing Data

The on-line survey was "programmed" by SPSS personnel to require that respondents answer all questions on a given screen before they were allowed to proceed to the next screen. Moreover, built into the programming were minimum and maximum allowable values for various individual items as well as consistency checks between items so that, for example, respondents entering an "out-of-range" value were so advised and asked to recheck their response once before accepting the value entered. Or, as another example, respondents could not enter a year of their first academic appointment that preceded their year of birth. When such inconsistencies were identified, respondents were alerted and asked to change one or another of their responses. While this programming approach, together with the substantial length of the survey, irritated some respondents, and ipso facto depressed response rates,[5] it yielded two immeasurable benefits in term of data quality: there were virtually no missing data among respondents who completed at least four of the six sections in the survey instrument (the threshold we employed for including respondents in the dataset); and there were no anomalous values to individual items that required that such responses be recoded as "no answer."

Summary

While the 2007–08 Changing Academic Profession Survey represents in some sense a fifteen-year follow-up to the original 1991–92 Carnegie Foundation for the Advancement of Teaching's Survey of the International Academic Profession, and involved many of the same investigators among participating nations, nonetheless it is distinguishable in terms both of its distinctive focus on change and its foundation in a theoretical conception of change and in the exploration of three a prior defined substantive dimensions of change: relevance, internationalization, and managerialism.

All nineteen nations employed a similar two-stage sampling frame, agreed to a minimal sample size, a substantial set of common questions asked in the same way, in the same time frame, and with the same basic response categories, differing only in language. Given wide variation in Internet access, funding levels, the majority of nations employed a paper and pencil survey and used mail or in-person distribution and collection. The United States was one of three nations (Canada and South Korea being the others) to employ an on-line survey. The survey was programmed and hosted by SPSS Research Services and elicited about 1,100 responses from an effective sample of about 5,000 four-year faculty and an additional 250 responses from about 1,000 two-year faculty.[6] While the response rate of 21.4 percent appeared at first blush to be small, it was in line with the norms of what social scientists report as the typical response rate to on-line in contradistinction to paper-and-pencil surveys. Moreover, a subsequent analysis comparing respondents with population allowed us to weight respondents to approximate very closely some major population parameters. While many of the analyses are descriptive and employ simple cross-tabulations, several types of multivariate regression analyses have been undertaken to allow for some well-founded inferences to the larger population of American academics.

NOTES

1. In the 1992 survey, Hong Kong, still under British rule, was treated as a separate country from mainland China. In 2007, even though Hong Kong had reverted a decade earlier to Chinese control, separate surveys were conducted in Hong Kong and mainland China to allow for 1992–2007 comparisons.

2. Such differences may, of course, reflect differences between historical generations in their values and perceptions quite beyond any differences in actual descriptive conditions.

3. Reflected historically in the nine-step classification of the Carnegie Foundation for the Advancement of Teaching and the myriad missions of institutions carrying the label of university in the United States as compared with the much clearer and more singular meaning of the term *university* in most other national systems.

4. We subsequently added a third category for all two-year institutions granting the associates degree or less.

5. We received e-mails from sixty-odd respondents indicating that they were unhappy with those constraints and chose to abandon the survey rather than complete it under such conditions. Based on those e-mails, we estimate that the irritation factor as a depressor of response rate was modest.

6. By effective sample, we simply mean the number of surveys that were actually delivered to faculty university inboxes (and not spammed), and the proportion of those that were returned.

REFERENCES

Altbach, Philip G., ed. 1996. *The International Academic Profession: Portraits of Fourteen Countries.* Princeton, NJ: Carnegie Foundation for the Advancement of Teaching.

Astin, Alexander. 1985. *Achieving Academic Excellence.* San Francisco, CA: Jossey-Bass.

Bess, James L., and Jay R. Dee. 2008. *Understanding College and University Organization: Theories for Effective Policy and Practice.* Vols. 1 and 2. Sterling, VA: Stylus Publishing.

Carnegie Council for Policy Studies. 1994. *A Classification of Institutions of Higher Education.* New York: McGraw-Hill.

Cummings, William K., and Martin J. Finkelstein. 2011. *Scholars in the Changing American Academy: New Roles and New Rules.* Dordrecht, NL: Springer.

Finkelstein, Martin, Robert K. Seal, and Jack H. Schuster. 1998. *The New Academic Generation: A Profession in Transformation.* Baltimore, MD: Johns Hopkins University Press.

Groves, Robert M. 2006. "Non-Response Rates and Non-Response Bias in Household Surveys." *Public Opinion Quarterly* 70, no. 5: 646–75.

Groves, Robert M., and Emilia Peytcheva. 2008. "The Impact of Non-Response Rates on Non-Response Bias: A Meta-Analysis." *Public Opinion Quarterly* 72 (Summer): 167–89.

US Department of Education. 2006. *2004 National Study of Postsecondary Faculty: Methodology Report.* NCES 2006179. Washington, DC: National Center for Education Statistics.

Appendix E

APPENDIX TABLES

[Tables begin next page]

Table A-4.1 Characteristics of PhD recipients entering into part-time appointments, by academic field, 2003 ($N=9{,}585$) (percentage)

	Business ($N=449$)	Education ($N=1{,}685$)	Engineering ($N=328$)	Fine arts ($N=94$)	Health sciences ($N=353$)	Humanities ($N=1{,}774$)	Natural sciences ($N=2{,}035$)	Social sciences ($N=2067$)	All other programs ($N=800$)
Institution type[a]									
Research	33.6	13.9	24.7	35.1	28.0	26.3	14.4	8.6	0.0
Doctoral	6.2	8.0	0.0	0.0	20.1	14.7	12.2	16.2	7.0
Comprehensive	60.1	43.1	75.0	64.9	0.0	25.0	37.9	28.3	22.4
Liberal arts	0.0	8.0	0.0	0.0	0.0	15.3	9.9	4.9	4.5
Two-year	0.0	27.0	0.0	0.0	51.6	9.9	24.1	31.8	63.0
Tenure status									
Tenured	0.0	0.0	0.0	0.0	0.0	0.0	0.0	0.0	0.0
On tenure track but not tenured	0.0	2.1	0.0	0.0	23.2	0.0	0.0	0.0	0.0
Not on tenure track	80.6	87.6	100.0	100.0	76.5	99.8	100.0	98.9	93.3
Not tenured or no tenure system	19.4	10.3	0.0	0.0	0.0	0.2	0.0	1.1	6.6
Gender									
Female	16.7	72.2	24.7	100.0	51.3	42.7	40.8	42.4	34.9
Male	83.3	27.8	75.0	0.0	48.4	57.3	59.2	57.6	65.1
Age									
< 35	0.0	8.4	0.0	0.0	51.3	42.2	23.1	23.9	25.3
35–44	0.0	28.2	76.2	100.0	0.0	29.8	37.3	38.8	52.9
45–54	63.3	30.8	0.0	0.0	20.1	19.3	20.5	26.4	21.9
55–64	36.7	29.5	23.8	0.0	28.3	8.6	12.2	6.1	0.0
65–70	0.0	3.1	0.0	0.0	0.0	0.0	0.0	4.6	0.0
71 or above	0.0	0.0	0.0	0.0	0.0	0.0	6.8	0.0	0.0

Retirement status									
Not retired	52.6	80.8	100.0	100.0	100.0	97.4	79.0	87.4	100.0
Retired	47.4	19.2	0.0	0.0	0.0	2.6	21.0	12.6	0.0
Previous job outside postsecondary education since highest degree									
No	39.9	34.2	51.2	35.1	51.3	59.5	52.6	24.8	26.6
Yes	60.1	65.8	48.8	64.9	48.4	40.5	47.4	75.2	73.3
Previous employment, sector									
No job immediately prior	16.7	2.3	0.0	0.0	0.0	12.1	8.8	15.2	12.8
4- or 2-year postsecondary institution	25.6	6.5	0.0	35.1	23.2	25.8	30.3	24.1	8.5
Other education institution	0.0	53.2	15.5	0.0	0.0	14.4	19.6	10.2	0.0
Government or military organization	0.0	5.7	0.0	0.0	20.1	5.3	0.0	0.8	16.9
Foundation or nonprofit organization	0.0	12.2	0.0	64.9	0.0	25.0	0.0	17.0	8.5
For-profit business or industry	57.7	16.3	75.0	0.0	28.3	10.9	27.2	8.3	40.3
Other	0.0	3.7	9.1	0.0	28.0	6.5	14.1	24.5	13.1
Part-time employment is primary employment									
No	35.9	63.7	76.2	64.9	100.0	44.0	45.1	80.1	82.9
Yes	64.1	36.2	23.8	35.1	0.0	56.0	54.8	19.9	17.1
Part-time, but full-time preferred									
No	77.1	66.9	66.8	64.9	71.7	35.6	39.4	52.4	71.8
Yes	22.9	33.1	32.9	35.1	28.3	64.4	60.5	47.6	28.3

(continued)

Table A-4.1 (continued)

	Business ($N=449$)	Education ($N=1{,}685$)	Engineering ($N=328$)	Fine arts ($N=94$)	Health sciences ($N=353$)	Humanities ($N=1{,}774$)	Natural sciences ($N=2{,}035$)	Social sciences ($N=2067$)	All other programs ($N=800$)
Concurrent employment (fall 2003)									
No	47.4	20.6	0.0	35.1	0.0	61.8	50.2	27.8	0.1
Yes, nonpostsecondary education instruction	41.0	67.5	100.0	64.9	76.5	28.0	43.9	58.8	88.3
Yes, postsecondary education instruction	6.2	8.2	0.0	0.0	23.2	6.9	5.9	7.3	10.8
Other current jobs, full-time employment									
Not full-time other job	70.4	51.8	32.9	35.1	0.0	72.0	66.9	48.8	34.8
Full-time other job	29.6	48.2	66.8	64.9	100.0	28.0	33.1	51.2	65.1
Other current jobs, number in postsecondary instruction									
Zero	88.4	88.1	100.0	100.0	76.5	89.9	94.1	86.6	88.4
One or more	11.6	11.9	0.0	0.0	23.2	10.1	5.9	13.4	11.6

Source: NSOPF:04. (Refer to appendix A for key.)

Note: Rounding accounts for percentages not totaling 100.

[a]Institutions classified as Specialized Institution in NSOPF:04 are not included.

Table A-7.1 Hours per week spent on scheduled teaching, by institutional type and gender, 1989–1990 to 2013–2014

		All			Male			Female		
	Year	< 9 hrs.	9–12 hrs.	> 12 hrs.	< 9 hrs.	9–12 hrs.	> 12 hrs.	< 9 hrs.	9–12 hrs.	> 12 hrs.
All baccalaureate institutions	1989–90	41.1	36.9	22.1	42.9	36.6	20.4	35.6	37.6	26.7
	1992–93	36.5	39.9	23.5	38.6	39.2	22.2	31.3	41.7	27.1
	1995–96	42.9	36.9	20.2	45.3	36.0	18.8	37.3	39.0	23.6
	1998–99	44.3	37.1	18.5	46.0	36.7	17.4	41.0	37.9	21.1
	2001–02	43.5	38.3	18.2	45.3	37.1	17.5	39.9	40.4	19.6
	2004–05	43.8	36.9	19.4	45.2	36.2	18.7	41.4	38.1	20.6
	2007–08	45.2	35.1	19.6	47.1	35.0	17.9	42.6	35.4	22.1
	2010–11	56.2	28.6	15.0	57.9	28.3	13.9	53.9	29.1	16.9
	2013–14	55.1	30.2	14.8	56.4	29.6	14.1	53.2	30.9	15.8
Public universities	1989–90	60.5	27.1	12.3	62.6	26.1	11.3	53.0	30.6	16.4
	1992–93	56.8	29.1	14.1	59.9	27.2	12.8	46.6	35.0	18.6
	1995–96	66.6	22.1	11.3	68.8	21.3	9.8	60.2	24.6	15.2
	1998–99	66.4	23.1	10.6	68.0	22.4	9.7	62.3	24.8	12.8
	2001–02	62.0	26.0	12.1	63.9	24.4	11.7	57.5	29.8	12.7
	2004–05	64.4	22.9	12.7	66.3	21.8	12.0	60.6	25.3	14.0
	2007–08	62.7	24.7	12.6	66.5	23.7	9.8	55.6	26.6	17.7
	2010–11	66.9	22.1	10.9	67.1	22.7	10.2	66.7	21.1	12.2
	2013–14	72.8	18.2	9.0	73.1	18.0	8.9	72.3	18.5	9.2
Private universities	1989–90	72.2	21.9	5.8	73.2	21.4	5.4	68.4	24.0	7.5
	1992–93	56.1	34.5	9.5	57.2	34.2	8.6	52.7	35.3	11.8
	1995–96	69.1	24.0	7.0	71.7	22.1	6.2	61.1	29.6	9.4
	1998–99	66.7	26.3	6.9	69.0	24.6	6.5	61.1	30.7	8.3
	2001–02	65.6	25.3	9.0	67.7	23.9	8.4	60.6	28.7	10.7
	2004–05	64.1	27.0	8.9	65.3	26.6	8.1	61.3	28.0	10.8
	2007–08	62.5	27.2	10.4	63.2	27.3	9.6	61.1	26.8	11.9
	2010–11	75.9	16.5	7.6	79.5	14.0	6.3	69.6	20.8	9.6
	2013–14	69.5	21.9	8.5	71.8	20.5	7.7	65.7	24.3	10.1

(continued)

Table A-7.1 (continued)

	Year	All			Male			Female		
		< 9 hrs.	9–12 hrs.	> 12 hrs.	< 9 hrs.	9–12 hrs.	> 12 hrs.	< 9 hrs.	9–12 hrs.	> 12 hrs.
Public 4-year colleges	1989–90	24.8	45.0	30.1	25.0	46.1	28.8	24.1	42.3	33.6
	1992–93	19.3	48.9	31.7	19.2	49.9	30.9	19.5	46.7	33.9
	1995–96	22.1	50.0	27.8	22.9	50.6	26.4	20.8	48.7	30.7
	1998–99	27.6	49.0	23.3	27.6	50.1	22.4	27.8	47.2	25.1
	2001–02	29.0	49.2	21.9	29.3	49.7	21.1	28.6	48.2	23.1
	2004–05	26.7	48.2	25.0	26.3	48.9	24.8	27.6	47.1	25.2
	2007–08	31.5	43.9	24.6	31.0	45.9	23.1	32.4	41.1	26.5
	2010–11	30.1	44.8	25.2	29.0	48.0	23.0	31.4	40.9	27.5
	2013–14	32.4	44.9	22.6	31.1	45.9	23.0	33.9	43.8	22.2
All private 4-year colleges	1989–90	20.4	46.9	32.7	19.4	48.6	31.9	22.7	43.1	34.3
	1992–93	23.0	44.7	32.3	22.4	45.0	32.6	23.9	44.1	31.9
	1995–96	23.6	46.7	29.6	22.7	47.4	29.9	25.6	45.3	29.1
	1998–99	25.5	45.5	29.8	24.0	47.3	28.7	28.2	42.4	29.5
	2001–02	26.3	47.0	26.6	24.9	47.6	27.3	28.3	46.1	25.4
	2004–05	27.2	46.3	26.5	25.1	47.5	27.3	30.0	44.5	25.5
	2007–08	30.8	42.0	27.3	29.1	42.4	28.4	33.0	41.4	25.6
	2010–11	39.0	39.0	22.0	38.6	38.9	22.6	39.6	39.3	21.1
	2013–14	39.5	40.2	20.2	38.3	42.3	19.4	40.9	37.8	21.2

Sources: HERI:89; HERI:92; HERI:95; HERI:98; HERI:01; HERI:04; HERI:07; HERI:10; HERI:13. (Refer to appendix A for key.)

Table A-7.2 Hours per week spent on preparing for teaching, by institutional type and gender, 1989–1990 to 2013–2014 (percentage)

		All			Male			Female		
	Year	< 9 hrs.	9–12 hrs.	> 12 hrs.	< 9 hrs.	9–12 hrs.	> 12 hrs.	< 9 hrs.	9–12 hrs.	> 12 hrs.
All baccalaureate institutions	1989–90	31.7	25.0	43.3	33.1	25.3	41.7	27.4	24.2	48.3
	1992–93	30.5	25.7	43.8	32.2	26.2	41.6	26.1	24.5	49.3
	1995–96	30.5	25.2	44.2	32.0	25.3	42.7	27.0	25.0	48.0
	1998–99	31.6	25.9	42.4	34.0	26.5	39.5	27.0	24.9	48.2
	2001–02	34.2	25.1	40.8	37.1	25.2	37.7	28.7	25.0	46.3
	2004–05	35.5	24.8	39.8	43.8	24.8	36.8	30.0	24.8	45.1
	2007–08	34.5	24.5	41.1	37.3	25.3	37.4	30.1	23.4	46.5
	2010–11	40.8	22.4	36.7	44.6	23.5	32.0	35.6	20.7	43.7
	2013–14	43.5	22.1	34.4	47.0	22.2	30.8	38.8	21.9	39.2
Public universities	1989–90	36.9	25.9	37.2	38.8	25.5	35.6	29.7	27.3	42.9
	1992–93	35.7	27.7	36.5	38.5	27.8	33.8	27.2	27.6	45.3
	1995–96	37.2	27.1	35.7	38.3	27.5	34.3	33.9	26.0	40.0
	1998–99	37.1	26.8	36.1	39.2	27.2	33.4	31.6	25.8	42.7
	2001–02	40.5	25.9	33.6	43.6	25.6	30.8	33.1	26.7	40.1
	2004–05	44.3	25.2	30.4	48.4	24.3	27.5	35.8	27.2	37.1
	2007–08	40.4	25.3	34.2	44.0	25.7	30.2	33.9	24.7	41.5
	2010–11	44.6	22.6	32.7	47.9	23.5	28.6	39.5	21.3	39.3
	2013–14	52.0	22.5	25.5	55.1	22.0	22.9	47.1	23.2	29.6
Private universities	1989–90	37.6	26.3	36.0	39.8	27.7	32.5	29.4	20.6	50.2
	1992–93	31.1	25.9	42.8	33.3	26.9	40.0	24.6	23.0	52.5
	1995–96	35.1	25.9	39.0	37.4	25.8	36.8	28.5	26.2	45.4
	1998–99	36.8	27.6	35.6	39.4	28.5	32.1	29.9	25.4	45.3
	2001–02	39.9	25.7	34.3	42.4	26.8	30.8	33.8	22.9	43.3
	2004–05	42.0	25.4	32.6	44.3	25.9	29.8	36.9	24.4	38.7
	2007–08	41.0	25.3	33.8	44.3	25.4	30.3	34.7	25.0	40.4
	2010–11	51.2	20.4	28.4	54.3	21.6	24.2	45.8	18.4	35.7
	2013–14	51.5	19.5	29.1	54.5	17.9	27.7	46.4	22.2	31.5

(continued)

Table A-7.2 (continued)

	Year	All			Male			Female		
		< 9 hrs.	9–12 hrs.	> 12 hrs.	< 9 hrs.	9–12 hrs.	> 12 hrs.	< 9 hrs.	9–12 hrs.	> 12 hrs.
Public 4-year colleges	1989–90	29.8	24.9	45.2	30.3	25.3	44.5	28.5	23.9	47.5
	1992–93	28.4	25.0	46.5	28.9	25.4	45.6	27.4	24.1	48.4
	1995–96	26.3	24.7	48.8	27.4	24.3	48.1	23.9	25.5	50.5
	1998–99	29.3	26.1	44.6	31.2	26.2	42.5	25.6	25.8	48.4
	2001–02	30.2	25.7	44.2	32.8	25.5	41.6	25.4	26.0	48.5
	2004–05	29.2	24.7	46.1	31.0	25.2	43.7	26.6	23.8	49.6
	2007–08	31.4	24.0	44.4	32.6	25.7	41.7	30.1	21.7	48.2
	2010–11	30.7	24.4	44.9	34.6	25.9	39.6	26.0	22.7	51.4
	2013–14	34.1	22.1	43.8	37.4	22.9	39.7	30.4	21.1	48.4
All private 4-year colleges	1989–90	23.7	23.0	53.1	24.1	23.2	52.7	23.0	22.7	54.3
	1992–93	25.4	23.7	50.8	26.2	24.4	49.4	23.8	22.4	53.6
	1995–96	24.4	22.8	52.8	25.2	22.8	52.0	22.9	22.9	54.2
	1998–99	25.1	23.6	51.3	26.5	24.3	49.3	22.8	22.5	54.6
	2001–02	28.3	23.0	48.7	29.6	23.1	47.4	26.2	22.9	50.9
	2004–05	28.1	24.1	47.9	29.5	24.4	46.0	25.6	23.6	50.8
	2007–08	27.0	23.8	49.3	29.0	24.1	46.9	24.3	23.4	52.4
	2010–11	32.8	21.5	45.6	35.2	23.4	41.4	30.0	19.2	50.7
	2013–14	34.1	23.2	42.7	35.5	25.2	39.4	32.4	20.9	46.7

Sources: HERI:89; HERI:92; HERI:95; HERI:98; HERI:01; HERI:04; HERI:07; HERI:10; HERI:13. (Refer to appendix A for key.)

Table A-7.3 Hours per week spent on advising and counseling students, by institutional type and gender, 1989–1990 to 2013–2014 (percentage)

		All		Male		Female	
	Year	≤4 hrs.	> 4 hrs.	≤4 hrs.	> 4 hrs.	≤4 hrs.	> 4 hrs.
All baccalaureate institutions	1989–90	58.4	41.6	60.0	40.1	54.0	46.0
	1992–93	58.0	41.9	60.0	40.0	53.2	46.9
	1995–96	60.2	39.8	62.1	37.8	55.7	44.3
	1998–99	61.1	38.8	63.1	36.9	57.0	43.1
	2001–02	64.4	35.5	67.0	32.9	59.5	40.5
	2004–05	66.2	33.8	68.4	31.8	62.3	37.8
	2007–08	59.7	40.5	62.7	37.3	54.9	45.2
	2010–11	61.1	38.9	62.1	38.0	59.7	40.2
	2013–14	61.3	38.6	63.3	36.7	58.6	41.2
Public universities	1989–90	62.5	37.4	64.1	35.8	56.7	43.2
	1992–93	62.9	37.3	63.4	36.6	61.3	38.7
	1995–96	61.5	38.5	62.5	37.6	58.6	41.4
	1998–99	62.7	37.3	64.1	35.8	59.2	40.9
	2001–02	66.1	33.8	67.8	32.2	62.2	37.8
	2004–05	67.4	32.7	68.1	31.9	66.1	33.8
	2007–08	62.1	37.9	64.0	35.9	58.8	41.2
	2010–11	64.1	35.8	64.1	36.0	64.1	35.8
	2013–14	63.5	36.6	63.4	36.8	63.6	36.3
Private universities	1989–90	63.8	36.2	63.4	36.5	65.4	34.7
	1992–93	54.3	45.7	56.6	43.3	47.2	52.7
	1995–96	63.1	37.0	64.9	35.1	57.6	42.4
	1998–99	61.3	38.6	62.5	37.4	58.1	41.9
	2001–02	66.3	33.7	68.8	31.3	60.1	39.9
	2004–05	69.1	30.9	71.2	28.8	64.4	35.7
	2007–08	61.9	38.2	63.3	36.8	58.9	41.1
	2010–11	61.0	39.0	59.5	40.6	63.6	36.3
	2013–14	58.3	41.7	59.2	40.8	56.9	43.1

(continued)

Table A-7.3 (continued)

	Year	All		Male		Female	
		≤4 hrs.	> 4 hrs.	≤4 hrs.	> 4 hrs.	≤4 hrs.	> 4 hrs.
Public 4-year colleges	1989–90	55.1	44.7	56.4	43.5	51.7	48.4
	1992–93	54.8	45.2	56.8	43.1	50.2	49.9
	1995–96	58.9	41.1	60.8	39.2	54.7	45.3
	1998–99	60.8	39.1	63.2	36.7	56.4	43.5
	2001–02	63.3	36.6	66.2	33.8	58.5	41.6
	2004–05	64.4	35.6	67.2	32.7	59.9	40.1
	2007–08	57.6	42.4	61.9	38.1	52.0	48.1
	2010–11	56.6	43.4	60.1	39.8	52.5	47.6
	2013–14	60.2	39.8	63.4	36.5	56.5	43.5
All private 4-year colleges	1989–90	54.5	45.6	56.4	43.5	50.2	49.9
	1992–93	57.8	42.2	61.1	38.8	51.1	48.7
	1995–96	58.8	41.2	61.9	38.0	52.9	47.3
	1998–99	59.3	40.9	61.9	38.1	55.1	45.0
	2001–02	62.6	37.5	65.6	34.4	57.8	42.2
	2004–05	65.1	34.8	68.5	31.4	60.3	39.7
	2007–08	57.7	42.3	61.7	38.3	52.6	47.4
	2010–11	58.8	41.1	61.6	38.3	55.4	44.7
	2013–14	61.3	38.8	66.4	33.6	55.2	44.7

Sources: HERI:89; HERI:92; HERI:95; HERI:98; HERI:01; HERI:04; HERI:07; HERI:10; HERI:13. (Refer to appendix A for key.)

Table A-7.4 Hours per week spent on research and scholarly writing, by institutional type and gender, 1989–1990 to 2013–2014 (percentage)

		All			Male			Female		
	Year	None	1–4 hrs.	> 4 hrs.	None	1–4 hrs.	> 4 hrs.	None	1–4 hrs.	> 4 hrs.
All baccalaureate institutions	1989–90	11.9	26.9	61.2	9.9	24.7	65.4	17.8	33.5	48.6
	1992–93	14.9	32.0	53.0	13.2	29.9	56.9	19.5	37.5	43.1
	1995–96	15.6	30.6	53.7	13.6	28.6	57.8	20.6	35.5	43.9
	1998–99	15.1	31.0	53.9	13.0	28.6	58.4	19.6	35.9	44.6
	2001–02	14.5	32.4	53.1	12.7	29.6	57.8	18.0	38.0	44.0
	2004–05	16.0	32.5	51.5	13.9	29.9	56.2	19.7	36.7	43.6
	2007–08	15.5	32.3	52.1	13.2	29.3	57.4	19.1	36.9	44.0
	2010–11	13.1	30.3	56.7	10.3	27.7	62.0	17.1	34.2	48.6
	2013–14	16.7	32.8	50.4	13.9	30.8	55.3	20.6	35.7	43.6
Public universities	1989–90	5.4	17.7	77.0	4.3	15.9	79.8	9.5	24.7	65.9
	1992–93	7.8	22.0	70.2	6.5	19.7	73.7	12.1	29.5	58.5
	1995–96	7.6	19.8	72.5	6.3	17.4	76.4	11.7	26.9	61.6
	1998–99	8.0	21.0	71.1	6.5	19.3	74.1	11.6	25.2	63.2
	2001–02	8.5	23.3	68.2	7.2	20.5	72.3	11.7	29.9	58.4
	2004–05	10.4	23.2	66.4	8.3	21.4	70.2	14.7	26.9	58.5
	2007–08	13.0	23.9	63.1	10.9	21.1	68.0	16.9	28.8	54.4
	2010–11	12.2	25.4	62.3	9.2	23.6	67.2	17.1	28.4	54.6
	2013–14	12.9	24.4	62.7	10.8	22.8	66.4	16.4	26.9	56.8
Private universities	1989–90	3.8	14.2	81.8	3.0	13.5	83.5	7.1	17.1	75.8
	1992–93	7.6	25.0	67.4	6.5	23.7	69.9	11.3	29.2	59.4
	1995–96	8.3	19.6	72.2	6.1	18.2	75.6	14.7	23.8	61.4
	1998–99	6.8	22.3	70.8	5.7	19.6	74.7	9.6	29.1	61.3
	2001–02	8.0	22.7	69.3	6.9	19.2	73.8	10.7	31.4	57.9
	2004–05	9.9	23.9	66.0	9.2	21.4	69.2	11.3	29.6	59.2
	2007–08	11.3	24.2	64.6	8.9	22.4	68.8	15.9	27.7	56.4
	2010–11	7.3	16.3	76.5	4.7	14.2	81.2	11.7	20.1	68.2
	2013–14	10.8	24.0	65.3	8.5	22.1	69.5	14.9	27.4	57.7

(continued)

Table A-7.4 (continued)

		All			Male			Female		
	Year	None	1–4 hrs.	> 4 hrs.	None	1–4 hrs.	> 4 hrs.	None	1–4 hrs.	> 4 hrs.
Public 4-year colleges	1989–90	13.5	33.3	53.2	11.6	31.3	56.9	18.4	38.5	43.2
	1992–93	19.1	38.6	42.3	17.6	36.9	45.3	22.7	42.4	35.0
	1995–96	18.8	39.1	42.0	17.6	38.0	44.4	21.3	41.7	37.0
	1998–99	16.6	37.2	46.1	14.7	34.6	50.8	20.2	42.1	37.8
	2001–02	15.8	37.0	47.3	14.0	35.2	50.9	18.8	40.2	41.2
	2004–05	17.0	38.6	44.5	15.3	35.8	48.9	19.6	42.9	37.5
	2007–08	15.4	37.6	46.9	13.3	34.5	52.2	18.3	41.7	40.0
	2010–11	15.3	42.3	42.4	13.2	40.2	46.7	17.9	44.9	37.2
	2013–14	18.7	44.8	36.6	15.2	44.4	40.3	22.6	45.3	32.1
All private 4-year colleges	1989–90	23.6	38.1	38.4	21.1	36.6	42.2	29.2	41.4	29.4
	1992–93	23.2	40.8	35.9	21.6	39.9	38.4	26.4	42.6	31.1
	1995–96	26.8	40.4	32.9	24.5	39.9	35.5	31.1	41.2	27.7
	1998–99	27.5	40.7	31.9	25.1	40.2	34.6	31.3	41.6	27.2
	2001–02	24.4	43.7	32.0	23.1	42.2	34.7	26.5	46.1	27.4
	2004–05	25.5	41.2	33.3	23.5	40.3	36.3	28.4	42.4	29.3
	2007–08	21.1	40.9	38.0	19.2	38.9	41.9	23.8	43.5	32.7
	2010–11	18.4	42.9	38.6	16.6	40.6	42.8	20.7	45.7	33.6
	2013–14	24.9	40.4	34.7	22.8	38.9	38.3	27.3	42.1	30.6

Sources: HERI:89; HERI:92; HERI:95; HERI:98; HERI:01; HERI:04; HERI:07; HERI:10; HERI:13. (Refer to appendix A for key.)

Table A-7.5 Hours per week spent on committee work and meetings, by institutional type and gender, 1989–1990 to 2013–2014 (percentage)

	Year	All		Male		Female	
		≤4 hrs	>4 hrs	≤4 hrs	>4 hrs	≤4 hrs	>4 hrs
All baccalaureate institutions	1989–90	71.2	28.8	72.0	28.0	68.7	31.3
	1992–93	74.7	25.3	75.9	24.2	71.2	28.7
	1995–96	71.4	28.5	72.9	27.1	67.9	32.2
	1998–99	70.5	29.5	72.5	27.5	66.6	33.5
	2001–02	72.0	27.9	73.4	26.5	69.5	30.4
	2004–05	77.7	22.3	75.3	24.7	71.0	29.0
	2007–08	62.2	37.7	64.2	35.8	59.3	40.8
	2010–11	65.6	34.4	67.1	32.9	63.3	36.7
	2013–14	62.9	37.1	65.3	34.8	59.6	40.4
Public universities	1989–90	68.4	31.6	69.0	31.1	66.0	34.0
	1992–93	73.4	26.5	74.7	25.3	69.7	30.4
	1995–96	65.2	31.0	69.9	30.1	66.3	33.7
	1998–99	67.7	32.2	68.5	31.5	65.8	34.3
	2001–02	71.4	28.6	72.5	27.5	68.7	31.3
	2004–05	77.5	22.4	73.2	26.7	71.0	28.9
	2007–08	61.0	39.0	61.3	38.8	60.3	39.8
	2010–11	64.8	35.2	65.5	34.4	63.5	36.4
	2013–14	61.9	38.2	62.7	37.4	60.6	39.3
Private universities	1989–90	76.4	23.6	75.7	24.2	78.7	21.3
	1992–93	75.1	24.8	75.7	24.2	73.3	26.6
	1995–96	73.7	26.3	75.0	25.0	69.8	30.2
	1998–99	74.1	25.9	75.3	24.7	70.8	29.1
	2001–02	72.3	27.6	73.1	26.9	70.6	29.4
	2004–05	78.4	21.6	77.1	22.9	71.3	28.7
	2007–08	65.5	34.5	67.0	32.9	62.5	37.4
	2010–11	68.5	31.5	70.6	29.4	65.1	34.8
	2013–14	64.5	35.6	65.8	34.2	62.2	37.6
Public 4-year colleges	1989–90	69.1	31.0	70.7	29.2	64.6	35.4
	1992–93	75.6	24.3	76.6	24.3	73.3	26.6
	1995–96	70.3	29.5	72.4	27.5	65.9	34.2
	1998–99	68.4	31.5	71.6	28.3	62.7	37.2
	2001–02	69.9	29.9	71.6	28.4	67.2	32.9
	2004–05	79.0	20.9	72.7	27.2	68.5	31.5
	2007–08	58.5	41.5	61.6	38.5	54.2	45.8
	2010–11	61.8	38.3	63.2	36.7	60.0	40.0
	2013–14	58.9	41.1	63.4	36.5	53.7	46.3

(continued)

Table A-7.5 (continued)

	Year	All		Male		Female	
		≤4 hrs	> 4 hrs	≤4 hrs	> 4 hrs	≤4 hrs	> 4 hrs
All private 4-year colleges	1989–90	75.6	24.4	76.6	23.4	73.2	26.8
	1992–93	74.6	26.3	77.3	22.7	69.1	31.0
	1995–96	75.2	24.8	77.4	22.6	71.3	28.6
	1998–99	75.3	24.7	78.2	21.7	70.7	29.3
	2001–02	75.4	24.5	77.2	22.7	72.8	27.2
	2004–05	76.1	24.1	80.7	19.4	74.0	26.0
	2007–08	66.9	33.1	69.8	30.2	63.0	37.1
	2010–11	68.3	31.7	71.0	28.9	65.0	35.0
	2013–14	67.7	32.1	71.8	28.3	63.2	36.8

Sources: HERI:89; HERI:92; HERI:95; HERI:98; HERI:01; HERI:04; HERI:07; HERI:10; HERI:13. (Refer to appendix A for key.)

Table A-7.6 Hours per week spent on community and public service, by institutional type and gender, 1989–1990 to 2013–2014 (percentage)

		All			Male			Female		
	Year	None	1–4 hrs.	> 4 hrs.	None	1–4 hrs.	> 4 hrs.	None	1–4 hrs.	> 4 hrs.
All baccalaureate institutions	1992–93	32.2	54.2	13.7	33.8	52.5	13.7	28.3	58.2	13.5
	1995–96	33.4	55.6	11.0	34.9	53.8	11.2	29.8	59.5	10.6
	1998–99	32.8	54.3	12.8	34.1	52.6	13.2	30.2	57.6	12.1
	2001–02	34.1	53.1	12.9	35.6	51.3	13.1	31.2	56.3	12.4
	2004–05	38.8	50.1	11.0	40.5	48.1	11.4	35.0	54.1	10.8
	2007–08	37.3	49.1	13.7	40.0	47.0	12.9	33.1	52.3	14.7
	2010–11	46.6	43.7	9.7	49.1	41.0	10.0	42.9	47.6	9.4
	2013–14	42.8	44.2	13.0	43.0	43.6	13.4	42.4	45.1	12.4
Public universities	1992–93	36.3	51.2	12.5	37.5	50.4	12.3	32.3	54.0	13.7
	1995–96	36.5	53.3	10.2	37.5	52.4	10.0	33.6	55.8	10.7
	1998–99	35.5	52.7	11.8	36.5	51.7	11.7	33.2	55.2	11.6
	2001–02	36.6	51.9	11.4	37.1	51.3	11.5	35.4	53.3	11.3
	2004–05	42.4	48.0	9.5	38.2	49.9	11.8	37.9	52.7	9.3
	2007–08	39.9	47.1	13.1	42.9	45.1	11.9	34.3	50.7	15.1
	2010–11	49.9	41.0	9.1	52.1	39.0	8.8	46.2	44.2	9.6
	2013–14	47.9	39.9	12.3	47.8	39.1	13.2	48.0	41.2	10.8
Private universities	1992–93	37.8	48.8	13.5	38.7	46.8	14.5	34.9	54.9	10.2
	1995–96	45.8	45.9	8.3	46.5	45.0	8.4	43.6	48.5	8.0
	1998–99	44.0	44.1	11.9	43.3	43.6	13.1	45.7	45.4	8.9
	2001–02	39.8	46.9	13.3	41.3	45.1	13.6	36.4	51.3	12.4
	2004–05	45.2	44.2	10.6	44.6	45.8	9.7	42.0	47.6	10.5
	2007–08	40.8	41.9	17.2	43.1	39.2	17.7	36.4	47.2	16.4
	2010–11	55.1	37.8	7.2	56.2	36.0	7.9	53.1	40.9	6.0
	2013–14	44.5	41.3	14.2	43.4	41.2	15.4	46.3	41.5	12.2

(continued)

Table A-7.6 (continued)

	Year	All			Male			Female		
		None	1–4 hrs.	> 4 hrs.	None	1–4 hrs.	> 4 hrs.	None	1–4 hrs.	> 4 hrs.
Public 4-year colleges	1992–93	26.6	58.1	15.3	28.4	56.2	15.3	22.5	62.4	15.1
	1995–96	27.5	59.9	12.6	29.5	57.8	12.7	23.4	64.4	12.2
	1998–99	27.5	58.4	14.1	29.5	56.4	14.0	24.1	62.1	13.9
	2001–02	30.4	55.8	13.7	32.5	53.9	13.5	26.9	58.9	14.2
	2004–05	33.6	53.7	12.7	46.7	42.6	10.8	30.0	57.4	12.7
	2007–08	34.4	51.9	13.6	37.0	50.5	12.5	30.9	53.8	15.4
	2010–11	36.2	51.3	12.5	38.9	47.7	13.4	32.9	55.7	11.3
	2013–14	35.5	50.5	14.0	34.6	52.8	12.6	36.6	47.9	15.5
All private 4-year colleges	1992–93	32.3	55.0	12.7	33.5	53.5	13.1	29.9	58.0	12.1
	1995–96	30.7	57.7	11.5	31.8	55.8	12.5	28.8	61.3	9.8
	1998–99	30.9	56.0	13.1	31.9	54.1	13.9	29.3	59.0	11.6
	2001–02	32.6	54.1	13.4	33.9	51.7	14.4	30.6	57.9	11.4
	2004–05	37.5	51.1	11.4	36.0	51.2	12.7	35.4	54.0	10.6
	2007–08	35.5	51.9	12.7	37.5	50.1	12.2	33.0	54.2	12.8
	2010–11	41.5	47.7	11.0	43.7	44.9	11.5	38.8	51.1	10.1
	2013–14	40.8	46.6	12.6	42.6	44.2	13.2	38.7	49.4	11.8

Sources: HERI:89; HERI:92; HERI:95; HERI:98; HERI:01; HERI:04; HERI:07; HERI:10; HERI:13. (Refer to appendix A for key.)

Table A-10.1 Logistic regression results for "collaboration with international colleagues in research," full-time faculty in the United States, 2007–2008

	Beta	Std. Err	Exp(B)	Sig.
Male	−0.150	0.198	0.861	
US citizen at birth	−0.083	0.290	0.921	
Years since first faculty appointment	0.029	0.011	1.029	**
Years since first faculty appointment (squared)	−0.002	0.001	0.998	**
Years abroad post baccalaureate (1 or 2 years)	1.036	0.272	2.817	***
Years abroad post baccalaureate (3+ years)	0.860	0.272	2.364	**
Discipline: artistic	−0.393	0.317	0.675	
Discipline: enterprising	0.442	0.385	1.555	
Discipline: investigative	0.878	0.282	2.405	**
Institution type: research or PhD university	0.081	0.299	1.084	
Tenure status: tenured or tenure eligible	0.696	0.244	2.005	**
Faculty drive campus international initiatives	0.678	0.239	1.970	**
Administration has supportive attitude toward research	0.091	0.253	1.096	
There is increased pressure to raise external research funds	0.277	0.307	1.319	
Institution considers research quality in making personnel decisions	0.123	0.275	1.131	
Primarily teach undergraduates	−0.056	0.201	0.945	
Orientation primarily to teaching	−1.008	0.214	0.365	***
Primary research is "basic"	0.265	0.232	1.304	
Primary research is "applied/ practically-oriented"	−0.185	0.285	0.831	
Primary research is "commercially-oriented/ for technology transfer"	0.656	0.224	1.928	**
Primary research is "socially-oriented for the betterment of society"	−0.006	0.228	0.994	
Primary research is based in one discipline	0.179	0.212	1.195	
Primary Research is multidisciplinary	0.659	0.298	1.933	*
High involvement in research	1.054	0.211	2.871	***

Source: CAP:07. With kind permission from Springer Science+Media Business: Martin J. Finkelstein, Elaine Walker, and Rong Chen, "The American Faculty in an Age of Globalization: Predictors of Internationalization of Research Content and Professional Networks." *Higher Education* 66 (3): 325–40. Copyright © Springer Science+Business Media Dordrecht 2013.

* $p<.05$, ** $p<.01$, *** $p<.001$

Table A-10.2 Logistic regression results for "research is international in scope," full-time faculty in the United States, 2007–2008

	Beta	Std. Err.	Exp(B)	Sig.
Male	0.098	0.198	1.103	
US citizen at birth	−0.028	0.326	0.972	
Years since first faculty appointment	0.025	0.009	1.025	**
Years since first faculty appointment (squared)	0.000	0.001	1.000	
Years abroad post baccalaureate (1 or 2 years)	0.962	0.281	2.618	**
Years abroad post baccalaureate (3+years)	1.000	0.398	2.717	*
Discipline: artistic	0.361	0.314	1.434	
Discipline: enterprising	−0.039	0.359	0.961	
Discipline: investigative	0.008	0.240	1.008	
Institutional type: research or PhD university	0.126	0.246	1.134	
Tenure status: tenured or tenure eligible	−0.193	0.253	0.824	
Faculty drive campus international initiatives	0.370	0.202	1.448	
Administration has supportive attitude towards research	−0.030	0.249	0.970	
There is increased pressure to raise external research funds	0.171	0.439	1.186	
Institution considers research quality in making personnel decisions	−0.729	0.279	0.483	*
Primarily teach undergraduates	0.374	0.211	1.454	
Orientation primarily to teaching	−0.685	0.214	0.504	**
Primary research is "basic"	0.478	0.242	1.613	*
Primary research is "applied/ practically-oriented"	−0.437	0.256	0.646	
Primary research is "commercially-oriented/ for technology transfer"	0.715	0.255	2.045	**
Primary research is "socially-oriented for the betterment of society"	0.721	0.230	2.057	**
Primary research is based in one discipline	0.401	0.212	1.493	
Primary Research is multidisciplinary	0.851	0.290	2.341	**
High involvement in research	0.607	0.205	1.835	**

Source: CAP:07. With kind permission from Springer Science+Media Business: Martin J. Finkelstein, Elaine Walker, and Rong Chen, "The American Faculty in an Age of Globalization: Predictors of Internationalization of Research Content and Professional Networks." *Higher Education* 66 (3): 325–40. Copyright © Springer Science+Business Media Dordrecht 2013.

$^{*}p<.05$, $^{**}p<.01$, $^{***}p<.001$

Table A-10.3 Variables in final logistic regression model for overall level of faculty internationalization of full-time faculty in the United States, 2007–2008

		Beta	Std. err.	Exp (B)	Sig.
Country characteristics	Country size	–0.722	0.046	0.486	***
	Asian region	–0.769	0.080	0.463	***
	Primarily English	–1.046	0.071	0.351	***
	Mature conomy	0.018	0.071	1.018	
Organizational characteristics	Faculty driven international initiatives	0.432	0.062	1.540	***
	University	0.434	0.072	1.543	***
Professional characteristics	Hard sciences	0.818	0.062	2.267	***
	Primary research is applied/practical	0.128	0.027	1.137	***
	Paper presented at a scholarly conference	0.046	0.005	1.047	***
	Articles published in an academic book or journal	0.040	0.004	1.041	***
	Research report/monograph written for a funded project	0.032	0.010	1.033	**
	Teaching undergraduate programs	–0.005	0.001	0.995	***
	Primary research is multi-disciplinary	–0.132	0.025	0.877	***
	Junior rank	–0.238	0.072	0.788	**
	Primarily teaching	–0.752	0.065	0.471	***
	Years since 2007 for first appointment	0.007	0.005	1.007	
	Primary research is commerce or technology	0.030	0.025	1.030	
Personal characteristics	Gender = male	0.167	0.065	1.182	*
	Time in other countries (outside the country of your first degree and current employment)	0.144	0.013	1.155	***
	Age group	–0.126	0.025	0.881	***
	Country of first degree same as current country	–0.789	0.136	0.454	***
	Country birth same as current country	0.079	0.136	1.082	

Source: CAP:07. With kind permission from Springer Science+Media Business: Martin J. Finkelstein and Wendiann Sethi, "Patterns of Faculty Internationalization: A Predictive Model." In *The Internationalization of the Academy: Changes, Realities, and, Prospects*, ed. Futao Huang, Martin J. Finkelstein, and Michele Rostan, pp. 237–57. Copyright © Springer Science+Business Media Dordrecht 2014.

* $p<.05$, ** $p<.01$, *** $p<.001$

Index

Note: Page numbers in *italics* indicate figures and tables.